Prepare for the Great Tribulation and the Era of Peace

Complete Volumes Index
Volumes 1 - 50

by John Leary

Queenship

PUBLISHING COMPANY
P.O. Box 220 • Goleta, CA 93116
(800) 647-9882 • (805) 692-0043 • Fax: (805) 967-5133
www.queenship.org

Dedication

To the Most Holy Trinity

God

The Father, Son and Holy Spirit

The Source of

All

Life, Love and Wisdom

Cover art by Josyp Terelya

© 2008 Queenship Publishing - All Rights Reserved.

Library of Congress Number # 95-73237

Published by

Queenship Publishing
P.O. Box 220
Goleta, CA 93116
(800) 647-9882 • (805) 692-0043 • Fax: (805) 967-5133
www.queenship.org

Printed in the United States of America

ISBN: 978-1-57918-365-4

Table of Contents
for
Stories by Carol Leary & Illustrations

Remember to Pray First 13

St. Michael, Josyp Terelya Illustration 27

St. Patrick's Invitation to Ireland 41

Angel, Josyp Terelya Illustration 55

St. Therese's Rose 69

St. Anthony Saves Our Luggage 83

Angel, Josyp Terelya Illustration 97

St. Anthony, Finder of Lost Objects 111

The Luminous Cross 125

Our Lady in Venezuela Saved Our Lives 139

Blessed Trinity, Josyp Terelya Illustration 153

St. Michael the Archangel 167

Jesus Icon, Josyp Terelya Illustration 181

David John Leary's Intercessions 194

Baby Jesus, Josyp Terelya Illustration 209

The Foot of Jesus on TV 222

From the Publisher

Queenship is pleased to offer a complete Index by topic of messages found in the books, Prepare for the Great Tribulation and the Era of Peace, Volume I through L.

You will find this a valuable resource in finding messages by topic and will be amazed to see the numerous messages on certain subjects.

We have included in the book a few of the beautiful and inspirational illustrations that Josyp Terelya has so graciously contributed over the years. Also, there are a few experiences written by Carol Leary on some of the mini-miracles they have experienced during their mission for the Lord.

We pray that you will find this Index to be a benefit to you in looking for particular messages given to John over the years.   May God continue to enlighten you on your journey closer to our Lord through the messages received by John Leary.

Reflections from Carol Leary

Many times we have to look back to understand the big picture as to how the Lord is guiding our lives. When John and I met, we were both praying to meet the right person. We met at the St. Thomas More Club for young singles. On the first night we sensed this was God's Will for us. We were married a year later on the feast day of St. Thomas. I might add that Jesus is not without a sense of humor. I said, "You know that I am giving up a trip to Europe with my girlfriend to marry you, so I hope we do some traveling in our life together." Little did I know.

We lived an ordinary family life raising our three daughters and staying active in our parish and community, especially Right to Life. At forty years old, we had our only son, David John. He lived only four days. It wasn't until a few years ago that he told John that the Lord took him because he would have been too young to leave to do this mission for Him. After he died in January of 1983, John took up the computers. I think it was to take his mind off of his death. Unfortunately, this turned into the addiction that Jesus asked him to stop when He came to John in Medjugorje in April of 1993. David usually gives a message around January 11, and frequently is offering to intercede for the family. In fact, there have been some miracles worked through his intercession. One lady at 46 was trying to become pregnant. After praying she became pregnant two weeks later and delivered a beautiful son exactly nine months to the day of the anniversary of David's death. David said that Jesus listens to His little ones. This is a reminder to all of us to ask the intercession of our family members in heaven.

In 1972, we started our prayer group as a Fatima cell. We met in our home every week for 22 years. After the messages began, we moved to our parish to accommodate the increased numbers. We have been there for 14 years and have dedicated it to the Eternal Father. When you see seven messages given at the prayer group, John is writing throughout the three mysteries of the rosary.

When we went to Medjugorje in April 1993, I noticed that John was spending several hours a day in the Adoration Chapel instead of being with the group. He really didn't tell me anything that was happening to him until we were going home. He probably was reluctant to admit that Jesus wanted him off the computer. When we returned home and he quit cold turkey, I knew it was the grace of God. The events unfolded as he has just told you.

As a family, we believed him because he was always a very honest person and mentally sound. He had gone to daily Mass since he was 17 and never sought out attention. In fact, to ever speak publically was the last thing that he would have chosen to do. We believed and accepted God's Will, but had no idea what was going to happen next or what any of it meant. Everything

unfolded so naturally and gradually. Even though some of the messages are difficult, Jesus has always given us a balance with His promise of help, protection and love. We have always been at peace with it. Some may think that the messages are doom and gloom, but we see them as filled with hope. Jesus promises not to leave us orphans.

This mission has had a tremendous impact on our lives. Previously, we prayed and tried to be faithful, but split our time between God's time and ours. Today, we see our relationship with Jesus as a total life experience. He permeates every aspect of it. We try to focus each minute of the day on Him and the mission. In Scripture, Jesus would often speak in parables by using the simple things of daily life. In the messages, He will utilize some little event or situation to become a teachable moment for us. He KNOWS EVERY DETAIL of our lives, be it our thoughts or actions. He reminds us that He even knows the number of the hairs on our heads. Many times people will ask for prayers for a special intention. In His infinite wisdom, He will often answer in a universal way so many can benefit from it.

I could write another volume on the beautiful stories, adventures and experiences that we have had in our travels throughout the United States and the world. One of our greatest joys has been to meet so many faithful people and have the opportunity to share in the Lord's love and works. The greatest joy, of course, is to see a conversion of heart. This sharing of our faith in our life's journeys binds us together in the Mystical Body of Christ.

I must admit to one deep concern. It is knowing that to whom much is given, much is expected. I am always asking myself, what more can and should I be doing to bring souls to Jesus and prepare them for the tribulation? This is an awesome responsibility which we both take very seriously.

Recently, Jesus has asked us to ask Him to multiply our prayers when we pray as the scales of prayer and sin are way out of balance. We would appreciate it if you could remember a prayer for us to be faithful and strong in this mission as we remember all of you who read the books each day. May the Lord bless all of you.

Acknowledgments

It is in a spirit of deep gratitude that I would like to acknowledge first the Holy Trinity: Father, (Jesus), and the Holy Spirit; the Blessed Virgin Mary and the many saints and angels who have made this book possible.

My wife, Carol, has been an invaluable partner. Her complete support of faith and prayers has allowed us to work as a team. This was especially true in the many hours of indexing and proofing of the manuscript. All of our family have been a source of care and support.

I am greatly indebted to Josyp Terelya for his very gracious offer to provide the art work for this publication. He has spent three months of work and prayer to provide us with a selection of many original pictures. He wanted very much to enhance the visions and messages with these beautiful and provocative works. You will experience some of them throughout these volumes.

A very special thank you goes to my spiritual director, Fr. Leo J. Klem, C.S.B. No matter what hour I called him, he was always there with his confident wisdom, guidance and discernment. His love, humility, deep faith and trust are a true inspiration.

Equal gratitude also goes to our new spiritual advisor, Father Donald McCarthy, C.S.B.

My appreciation also goes to Father John V. Rosse, my good pastor who is retiring from Holy Name of Jesus Church. He has been open, loving and supportive from the very beginning.

There are many friends and relatives whose interest, love and prayerful support have been a real gift from God. Our own Wednesday, Monday and First Saturday prayer groups deserve a special thank you for their loyalty and faithfulness.

Finally, I would like to thank Bob and Claire Schaefer of Queenship Publishing for providing the opportunity to bring this message of preparation, love and warnings to you, the people of God.

John Leary, Jr.

Volume Numbers & Dates

Volume I: July, 1993 through June, 1994.

Volume II: July, 1994 through June, 1995.

Volume III: July, 1995 through July 10, 1996.

Volume IV: July 11, 1996 through September 30, 1996.

Volume V: October 1, 1996 through December 31, 1996.

Volume VI: January 1, 1997 through March 31, 1997.

Volume VII: April 1, 1997 through June 30, 1997.

Volume VIII: July 1, 1997 through September 30, 1997.

Volume IX: October 1, 1997 through December 31, 1997.

Volume X: January 1, 1998 through March 31, 1998.

Volume XI: April 1, 1998 through June 30, 1998.

Volume XII: July 1, 1998 through September 30, 1998.

Volume XIII: October 1, 1998 through December 31, 1998.

Volume XIV: January 1, 1999 through March 31, 1999.

Volume XV: April 1, 1999 through June 13, 1999.

Volume XVI: July 1, 1999 through September 30, 1999.

Volume XVII: October 1, 1999 through December 31, 1999.

Volume XVIII: January 1, 2000 through March 31, 2000.

Volume XIX: April 1, 2000 through June 30, 2000.

Volume XX: July 1, 2000 through September 30, 2000.

Volume XXI: October 1, 2000 through December 31, 2000.

Volume XXII: January 1, 2001 through March 31, 2001

Volume XXIII April 1, 2001 through June 30, 2001

Volume XXIV July 1, 2001 through Sept 30, 2001

Volume XXV October 1, 2001 through December 31, 2001

Volume XXVI January, 2002 through March 31, 2002

Volume XXVII April 1, 2002 through June 30, 2002

Volume XXVIII July 1, 2002 through September 30, 2002

Volume XXIX October 1, 2002 through December 31, 2002

Volume XXX January 1, 2003 through March 31, 2003

Volume XXXI April 1, 2003 through June 30, 2003.

Volume XXXII July 1, 2003 through September 30, 2003

Volume XXXIII October 1, 2003 through December 31, 2003

Volume XXXIV January 1, 2004 through March 31, 2004

Volume XXXV April 1, 2004 through June 30, 2004

Volume XXXVI July 1, 2004 through September 30, 2004

Volume XXXVII October 1, 2004 through December 31, 2004

Volume XXXVIII January 1, 2005 through March 31, 2005

Volume XXXIX April 1, 2005 through June 30, 2005.

Volume XXXX July 1, 2005 through September 30, 2005

Volume XLI October 1, 2005 through December 31, 2005

Volume XLII January 1, 2006 through March 31, 2006

Volume XLIII April 1, 2006 through June 30, 2006

Volume XLIV July 1, 2006 through September 30, 2006

Volume XLV October 1, 2006 through December 31, 2006

Volume XLVI January 1, 2007 through March 31, 2007

Volume XLVII April 1, 2006 through June 30, 2007

Volume XLVIII July 1, 2007 through September 30, 2007

Volume XLIX October 1, 2007 through December 31, 2007

Volume L January 1, 2008 through March 31, 2008

Complete Index Volumes 1 - 50

10 Commandments based in love (Jesus)   10/12/06 Vol. 45
13 days comment on movie (Jesus)   1/26/01 Vol. 22
1996 calendar NATO (Jesus)   5/31/95 Vol. 2
1998 increase in evil events (Jesus)   12/30/97 Vol. 9
2008 message to be year like no other (Jesus)   1/3/08 Vol. 50
3 days darkness by Great Chastisement (Jesus)   5/24/06 Vol. 43
3 days darkness punishment for evil ones (Jesus)   12/2/05 Vol. 41
3 days of darkness Armageddon   9/22/93 Vol. 1
3 days of darkness at end of tribulation (Jesus)   9/14/07 Vol. 48
3 days of darkness by comet (Jesus)   7/18/01 Vol. 24
3 days of darkness candles, fire (Jesus)   1/30/97 Vol. 6
3 days of darkness cross on forehead (Jesus)   8/28/94 Vol. 2
3 days of darkness day of victory (Jesus)   4/17/01 Vol. 23
3 days of darkness earth out of orbit (Jesus)   12/7/94 Vol. 2
3 days of darkness Egyptians (Jesus)   10/15/94 Vol. 2
3 days of darkness faithful shielded (Jesus)   4/1/07 Vol. 47
3 days of darkness have blessed candles (Jesus)   11/6/05 Vol. 41
3 days of darkness mark of the beast   9/13/93 Vol. 1
3 days of darkness purification (Jesus)   1/21/97 Vol. 6
3 days of darkness renew the earth (Jesus)   5/2/01 Vol. 23
3 days of darkness renewed earth (Jesus)   3/24/96 Vol. 3
3 days of darkness tribulation (Jesus)   7/29/94 Vol. 2
3 days of darkness triumph (Jesus)   5/11/94 Vol. 1
3 days of darkness victory over evil (Jesus)   12/21/01 Vol. 25
3 days of darkness victory over evil (Jesus)   12/22/00 Vol. 21
3 days of darkness victory over evil (Jesus)   12/28/00 Vol. 21
3 days of darkness volcanic activity, comet (Jesus)   11/5/97 Vol. 9
3 rosaries fasting (Mary)   12/5/96 Vol. 5
3 rosaries prayer warriors (Jesus)   7/4/94 Vol. 2
30th wed anniversary freedom (Jesus)   7/3/95 Vol. 3
4 angels of Apocalypse marking the faithful (Jesus)   10/27/97 Vol. 9
4 horseman of Apoc seals broken,battle begin (Jesus)   10/20/97 Vol. 9
4 horses prepare   9/21/93 Vol. 1
5000 relics of saints martyrs (Jesus)   11/12/95 Vol. 3
666, Antichrist 1998, Hale-Bopp sign (Jesus)   11/2/98 Vol. 13
7 levels of Heaven perfection (Jesus)   8/26/94 Vol. 2
7 Sorrows of Our Lady (Jesus)   9/15/06 Vol. 44
7-25-01 reference demon attacks increase (Jesus)   9/16/01 Vol. 24
9/11 stock market rich profited (Jesus)   10/3/07 Vol. 49
9-11 unanswered questions (Jesus)   10/14/06 Vol. 45
911 Report inside job or not (Jesus)   8/20/07 Vol. 48
abomination to create life unnaturally (Jesus)   8/9/01 Vol. 24
abomination of desolation image of beast on altars (Jesus)   7/7/02 Vol. 28
abomination of desolation in tribulation (God the Father)   8/7/99 Vol. 16
abomination of desolation offering worship to beast (Jesus)   4/5/00 Vol. 19
abomination of desolation worship of beast (Jesus)   7/13/01 Vol. 24
abomination of desolation worship of Satan on altars (Jesus)   9/8/03 Vol. 32

aborted babies denied a long life (Jesus)   6/5/03 Vol. 31
aborted babies martyrs for Jesus (Jesus)   12/28/00 Vol. 21
aborted babies martyrs in heaven (Jesus)   1/23/04 Vol. 34
aborted fetal stem cells should be condemned (Jesus)   7/15/04 Vol. 36
abortion & euthanasia (Jesus)   1/31/01 Vol. 22
abortion 30 pieces of silver (Jesus)   8/17/00 Vol. 20
abortion a gridlock is "no" vote (Jesus)   12/13/00 Vol. 21
abortion a very serious sin (Jesus)   7/11/99 Vol. 16
abortion abuse (St. Therese)   10/12/93 Vol. 1
abortion accept all life (Jesus)   12/18/97 Vol. 9
abortion affair, no children (Our Lady)   11/10/07 Vol. 49
abortion against fifth Commandment (Jesus)   12/28/00 Vol. 21
abortion always a mortal sins (Jesus)   12/5/05 Vol. 41
abortion America facing punishment (Jesus)   9/15/05 Vol. 40
abortion America will be no more (Jesus)   1/20/03 Vol. 30
abortion America, repent (Mary)   2/26/97 Vol. 6
abortion American Indians (Jesus)   6/21/94 Vol. 1
abortion and major storms (Jesus)   1/24/03 Vol. 30
abortion and sins of the flesh (Jesus)   1/22/02 Vol. 26
abortion and sins of the flesh (Jesus)   2/11/99 Vol. 14
abortion angels reporting to God Mark   11/3/98 Vol. 13
abortion angels watching over (Jesus)   1/23/97 Vol. 6
abortion answer at judgment (Jesus)   5/31/01 Vol. 23
abortion as form of birth control (Jesus)   12/20/01 Vol. 25
abortion assisted suicide (Jesus)   6/12/96 Vol. 3
abortion avoid conception first (Jesus)   11/22/04 Vol. 37
abortion babies are sacrificed (Jesus)   7/5/01 Vol. 24
abortion babies who did not see birth (Jesus)   12/13/02 Vol. 29
abortion baby's right to live (Jesus)   3/24/00 Vol. 18
abortion baptize babies (Jesus)   3/16/97 Vol. 6
abortion bleeding statues,stigmata for (Jesus)   4/7/98 Vol. 11
abortion blood like rivers (Jesus)   1/28/02 Vol. 26
abortion blood money, wrath (Jesus)   1/22/03 Vol. 30
abortion blood money,US ceases (Jesus)   10/26/96 Vol. 5
abortion blood payment for America (Jesus)   12/28/05 Vol. 41
abortion bringing nation to ruin (Jesus)   1/20/02 Vol. 26
abortion can overturn by prayer,faith (Jesus)   8/22/06 Vol. 44
abortion catastrophy   9/18/93 Vol. 1
abortion causing fewer children (Jesus)   1/26/08 Vol. 50
abortion causing reduced population (Jesus)   1/23/06 Vol. 42
abortion chastisements for sin (Jesus)   5/23/02 Vol. 27
abortion chastisements of USA (Jesus)   8/28/96 Vol. 4
abortion children (Jesus)   12/28/94 Vol. 2
abortion chromosomes on cross (Jesus)   5/29/96 Vol. 3
abortion clinic bombers (Jesus)   1/16/97 Vol. 6
abortion confession (Jesus)   7/22/94 Vol. 2
abortion continue to fight (Jesus)   1/31/08 Vol. 50

abortion culture of death (Jesus)	10/3/02 Vol. 29	abortion no good reason for Our Lady	11/10/07 Vol. 49
abortion death warrant for all (Jesus)	3/30/00 Vol. 18	abortion not man's right to kill (Jesus)	12/2/98 Vol. 13
abortion destroying society (Jesus)	7/24/03 Vol. 32	abortion obtuse spirit (Jesus)	11/9/95 Vol. 3
abortion destruction if not stopped (Jesus)	9/5/02 Vol. 28	abortion offense of mother,doctor (Jesus)	11/7/99 Vol. 17
abortion disunity (Jesus)	5/22/95 Vol. 2	abortion only vote prolife (Jesus)	1/22/04 Vol. 34
abortion do not listen to the devil (Jesus)	12/18/97 Vol. 9	abortion our worst defilement (Jesus)	1/4/01 Vol. 22
abortion doctors,mothers to pay (Jesus)	12/28/98 Vol. 13	abortion pray and fight, genocide (Jesus)	3/4/97 Vol. 6
abortion don't vote for pro-abortion people (Jesus)	1/22/04 Vol. 34	abortion pray for leaders to change (Jesus)	12/25/00 Vol. 21
abortion double standard (Jesus)	1/22/04 Vol. 34	abortion pray the rosary to stop (Mary)	2/11/97 Vol. 6
abortion effect on mothers (Jesus)	5/10/97 Vol. 7	abortion prayers mitigate wrath (Jesus)	5/14/05 Vol. 39
abortion endangered species (Jesus)	5/29/96 Vol. 3	abortion President (Jesus)	4/8/94 Vol. 1
abortion evangelize value of life (Jesus)	8/28/96 Vol. 4	abortion protest for Commandments (Jesus)	4/12/02 Vol. 27
abortion fight evil in society (Jesus)	5/8/97 Vol. 7	abortion punishment in weather (Jesus)	1/17/01 Vol. 22
abortion fight with prayers/actions (Mary)	8/7/96 Vol. 4	abortion refusal to fight, sin of omission (Mary)	12/12/07 Vol. 49
abortion for body parts & stem cells (Jesus)	12/12/00 Vol. 21	abortion remove financial gain (Jesus)	3/22/07 Vol. 46
abortion for convenience & luxury (Jesus)	1/22/98 Vol. 10	abortion repent & seek forgiveness (Mary)	12/18/97 Vol. 9
abortion for own pleasures (Jesus)	7/8/01 Vol. 24	abortion rescind laws (Jesus)	1/18/01 Vol. 22
abortion frustrating God's plan (Jesus)	10/17/96 Vol. 5	abortion responsibility for laws (Jesus)	12/28/99 Vol. 17
abortion gift to gods of materialism (Jesus)	12/12/01 Vol. 25	abortion responsible for inaction (Mary)	9/8/96 Vol. 4
abortion given deaf ear (Jesus)	6/16/01 Vol. 23	abortion rivers of blood (Jesus)	1/21/03 Vol. 30
abortion greed,prayer can stop (Mary)	1/9/97 Vol. 6	abortion rosaries to stop abortion (Mary)	12/12/96 Vol. 5
abortion heaven calls for justice (Jesus)	12/28/00 Vol. 21	abortion roses of prayers (St. Therese)	12/12/96 Vol. 5
abortion help unwed mothers (Jesus)	11/16/07 Vol. 49	abortion sanctity of life (Jesus)	8/21/96 Vol. 4
abortion holocaust like the Jews (Jesus)	9/1/97 Vol. 8	abortion set in place by court (Jesus)	1/11/01 Vol. 22
Abortion hypocracy of wars and (Jesus)	1/15/04 Vol. 34	abortion sins of flesh,against God (Jesus)	11/21/00 Vol. 21
abortion issue in Supreme Court (Jesus)	7/14/05 Vol. 40	abortion sins of the flesh (Jesus)	8/28/97 Vol. 8
abortion Jesus present in unborn (Mary)	9/19/96 Vol. 4	abortion small window of opportunity (Jesus)	12/27/00 Vol. 21
abortion Jesus,Mary crying over (Jesus)	8/22/06 Vol. 44	abortion sold like Jesus (Jesus)	3/13/98 Vol. 10
abortion judge (Mary)	1/26/94 Vol. 1	abortion St. Therese (Jesus)	8/30/95 Vol. 3
abortion judgment of America on (Jesus)	8/22/06 Vol. 44	abortion stand for life (Jesus)	7/1/04 Vol. 36
abortion justice of nation (Jesus)	9/13/00 Vol. 20	abortion stop daily holocaust (Jesus)	4/7/98 Vol. 11
abortion justice on USA (Mary)	5/12/96 Vol. 3	abortion stop or see His justice (Jesus)	10/9/97 Vol. 9
abortion kill Jesus in the unborn (Jesus)	6/25/97 Vol. 7	abortion stopped for any reason (Jesus)	11/20/05 Vol. 41
abortion killing of civilians (Jesus)	11/7/01 Vol. 25	abortion stops God's plan for life (Jesus)	10/16/02 Vol. 29
abortion leaders must change laws (Jesus)	11/4/00 Vol. 21	abortion take moral stand (Jesus)	8/24/00 Vol. 20
abortion makes blood money (Jesus)	9/19/06 Vol. 44	abortion thirty pieces of silver (Mary)	3/5/98 Vol. 10
abortion martyrs,cosmetic use (Jesus)	1/21/99 Vol. 14	abortion thwarts God's plan (Jesus)	6/24/01 Vol. 23
abortion material reasons (Jesus)	3/20/97 Vol. 6	abortion thwarts God's plan (Jesus)	8/31/96 Vol. 4
abortion modern halocaust (Jesus)	5/31/01 Vol. 23	abortion to suffer persecution for (Jesus)	4/7/98 Vol. 11
abortion more disasters if no change (Jesus)	11/3/05 Vol. 41	abortion US will pay for (Jesus)	8/5/99 Vol. 16
abortion mortal sin (Jesus)	8/7/01 Vol. 24	abortion USA (Jesus)	1/22/94 Vol. 1
abortion most offensive sin to God (Jesus)	9/13/07 Vol. 48	abortion value of life (Jesus)	1/23/97 Vol. 6
abortion most offensive sin to God (Jesus)	2/15/00 Vol. 18	abortion violence kept secret (Jesus)	8/29/97 Vol. 8
abortion mother's guilt (Jesus)	12/5/97 Vol. 9	abortion virtual reality Father	5/11/94 Vol. 1
abortion nations will fall (Mary)	12/12/97 Vol. 9	abortion vote candidates favoring life (Jesus)	11/2/00 Vol. 21
abortion never rightfully advocated (Jesus)	8/12/99 Vol. 16	abortion we will pay for our sins (Jesus)	5/31/01 Vol. 23
abortion new executioners (Jesus)	2/6/98 Vol. 10	abortion weather,disease are testings (Jesus)	3/13/98 Vol. 10

abortion weighs against US (Jesus) 1/22/98 Vol. 10
abortion weighs heavy on nation (Jesus) 7/11/99 Vol. 16
abortion will bring justice for (Jesus) 1/8/99 Vol. 14
abortion work to change laws (Jesus) 1/22/08 Vol. 50
abortion work to stop (Jesus) 10/4/01 Vol. 25
abortion worst of crimes (Jesus) 12/30/96 Vol. 5
abortion wrath of God (Jesus) 8/12/96 Vol. 4
abortion & euthanasia defenseless life needs help (Jesus) 1/22/07 Vol. 46
abortion & euthanasia life is most precious gift (Jesus) 5/18/99 Vol. 15
abortion & euthanasia money promoting both (Jesus) 4/28/99 Vol. 15
abortion & euthanasia pray to stop (Jesus) 1/27/99 Vol. 14
abortion & euthanasia protect life (Jesus) 11/22/01 Vol. 25
abortion & euthanasia respect life (Jesus) 5/29/02 Vol. 27
abortion & killing is the worst sin (Jesus) 4/12/05 Vol. 39
abortion & sins of flesh mock God's laws (Jesus) 7/3/03 Vol. 32
abortion & war stop killing to have peace (Jesus) 11/7/02 Vol. 29
abortion & war stop the killing (Jesus) 4/3/07 Vol. 47
abortion & wars break society restrictions (Jesus) 2/24/08 Vol. 50
abortion & wars stop the killing (Jesus) 12/17/05 Vol. 41
abortion acceptance does not make it right (Jesus) 9/2/99 Vol. 16
abortion anniversary proper burial for infants (Jesus) 1/22/05 Vol. 38
abortion clinic closed across from image (Mary) 2/28/98 Vol. 10
abortion descriptions hard to avoid loss of life (Jesus) 1/22/05 Vol. 38
abortion doctors should fear spiritual death (Jesus) 11/10/98 Vol. 13
abortion fight struggle to stop killing babies (Jesus) 6/22/00 Vol. 19
abortion groups undermined by clinic bombs (Jesus) 9/15/98 Vol. 12
Abortion in America crossroads to change (Jesus) 3/22/99 Vol. 14
abortion in America punishment in weather (Jesus) 1/15/07 Vol. 46
abortion innocents from sexual sins (Jesus) 12/28/07 Vol. 49
abortion laws flawed in reasoning (Jesus) 2/10/01 Vol. 22
abortion laws need removal or ruin coming (Jesus) 11/27/00 Vol. 21
abortion laws opportunity for change (Jesus) 2/6/01 Vol. 22
abortion laws pro-life candidates can change (Jesus) 10/14/04 Vol. 37
abortion laws repent and change (Jesus) 5/26/01 Vol. 23
abortion mentality coming, medical profession (Jesus) 8/5/98 Vol. 12
abortion mothers not condemned for killing (Jesus) 9/17/01 Vol. 24
abortion of babies America's downfall (Jesus) 8/5/02 Vol. 28
abortion of humans revealed by technology (Jesus) 8/6/02 Vol. 28
abortion of innocent unborn double standard of justice (Jesus) 8/1/02 Vol. 28
abortion punishment America will pay (Jesus) 1/26/05 Vol. 38
abortion reality acceptance of taking life in womb (Jesus) 10/29/03 Vol. 33
abortion reasons avoid convenience,blood money (Jesus) 5/19/04 Vol. 35
abortion sins brought America destruction (Jesus) 9/18/01 Vol. 24
abortion tombstones deaths not acknowledged (Jesus) 7/20/00 Vol. 20
abortion, euthanasia accepted with no shame (Jesus) 12/4/98 Vol. 13
abortion, partial birth law has little meaning (Jesus) 12/30/03 Vol. 33
abortion, sexual sins speak out against (Jesus) 8/29/03 Vol. 32

abortion, sexual sins stand up against (Jesus) 9/15/07 Vol. 48
abortion, sins of flesh bringing down America (Jesus) 4/7/05 Vol. 39
abortion, wars masons profit from killing (Jesus) 11/25/02 Vol. 29
abortion,candidates for vote against (Jesus) 10/3/00 Vol. 21
abortion,Holy Innocents who decides who will die (Jesus) 6/29/00 Vol. 19
abortion,pornography speak out against (Jesus) 11/15/05 Vol. 41
abortion,sexual sins speak out against (Jesus) 3/14/07 Vol. 46
abortionists trying to close hospitals (Jesus) 1/22/02 Vol. 26
abortions a consequence of sin (Jesus) 3/3/05 Vol. 38
abortions acknowledge deaths of humans (Jesus) 12/28/04 Vol. 37
abortions and deviant lifestyles (Jesus) 10/12/03 Vol. 33
abortions and sexual sins (Jesus) 9/9/00 Vol. 20
abortions and sins of the flesh (Jesus) 12/11/01 Vol. 25
abortions and sins of the flesh (Jesus) 1/7/01 Vol. 22
abortions angels attest to crimes (Jesus) 1/21/99 Vol. 14
abortions are a national sin (Jesus) 7/19/05 Vol. 40
abortions as human sacrifices (Jesus) 2/12/02 Vol. 26
abortions atrocities in the womb (Jesus) 3/29/99 Vol. 14
abortions babies martyred (Jesus) 9/20/02 Vol. 28
abortions blackened Christmas tree (Jesus) 12/28/02 Vol. 29
abortions bodies not shown (Jesus) 3/29/99 Vol. 14
abortions bringing wrath on America (Jesus) 1/16/03 Vol. 30
abortions calling down wrath of God (Jesus) 6/20/02 Vol. 27
abortions causing our testing (Jesus) 10/10/01 Vol. 25
abortions change your way America (Jesus) 12/30/97 Vol. 9
abortions country judged (Jesus) 2/17/97 Vol. 6
abortions cry out for justice (Jesus) 7/10/01 Vol. 24
abortions culture of death (Jesus) 7/7/03 Vol. 32
abortions destroy society from within (Jesus) 10/30/01 Vol. 25
abortions disasters & storms (Jesus) 1/6/97 Vol. 6
abortions enemies to consume US (Jesus) 10/10/02 Vol. 29
abortions fight or condone it (Jesus) 9/20/02 Vol. 28
abortions fight the battle Holy Spirit 1/23/97 Vol. 6
abortions genocide & holocaust (Jesus) 11/7/96 Vol. 5
abortions guardian angels of souls (Mary) 12/9/96 Vol. 5
abortions hypocritical to believe in (Jesus) 5/4/04 Vol. 35
abortions justice will fall (Mary) 9/26/96 Vol. 4
abortions killing continues with no sorrow (Jesus) 11/11/04 Vol. 37
abortions life's value priceless (Jesus) 11/25/99 Vol. 17
abortions moral decline (Jesus) 3/13/03 Vol. 30
abortions most offend Jesus (Jesus) 8/15/04 Vol. 36
abortions nations to pay for (Jesus) 7/5/02 Vol. 28
abortions natural disasters (Jesus) 1/20/03 Vol. 30
abortions need to fight or face destruction (Jesus) 10/22/03 Vol. 33
abortions new life potential thwarted (Jesus) 6/30/00 Vol. 19
abortions offered to gods of money (Jesus) 9/21/00 Vol. 20
abortions offering to gods of materialism (Jesus) 12/12/02 Vol. 29

abortions on going holocaust (Jesus) — 4/26/99 Vol. 15

abortions Our Lady of Guadalupe (Mary) — 12/12/96 Vol. 5

abortions partial-birth debate (Jesus) — 6/5/03 Vol. 31

abortions pray & fight for life (Jesus) — 2/17/97 Vol. 6

abortions pray and educate (Jesus) — 1/4/01 Vol. 22

abortions pray to stop (Mary) — 12/12/06 Vol. 45

abortions pray to stop (Jesus) — 8/29/98 Vol. 12

abortions protest in love (Jesus) — 4/2/02 Vol. 27

abortions purpose for each life (Jesus) — 8/21/00 Vol. 20

abortions rose a symbol of life (Jesus) — 2/6/99 Vol. 14

abortions see them as own children (Jesus) — 12/28/00 Vol. 21

abortions senseless killings in NYCity (Jesus) — 9/25/01 Vol. 24

abortions sin against the Spirit (Jesus) — 10/26/96 Vol. 5

abortions sins against life (Jesus) — 11/28/01 Vol. 25

abortions sins of the flesh (Jesus) — 5/3/97 Vol. 7

abortions speak out against (Jesus) — 2/4/05 Vol. 38

abortions stop or US will be destroyed (Jesus) — 8/26/04 Vol. 36

abortions stop with prayer and deeds (Jesus) — 5/19/98 Vol. 11

abortions the worst abuse David — 1/11/01 Vol. 22

abortions thirty pieces of silver (Jesus) — 2/12/01 Vol. 22

abortions to cause our takeover (Jesus) — 7/19/05 Vol. 40

abortions used for facial creams (Jesus) — 8/10/01 Vol. 24

abortions warnings fall on deaf ears (Jesus) — 9/23/99 Vol. 16

abortions weather,Nineveh (Jesus) — 4/10/97 Vol. 7

abortions & euthanasia today's pagan society (Jesus) — 1/30/06 Vol. 42

abortions & sins justice & wrath (Jesus) — 3/14/03 Vol. 30

abortions & wars how long tolerated? (Jesus) — 11/13/05 Vol. 41

abortions & wars offend God the most (Jesus) — 1/23/07 Vol. 46

abortions and sins in Russia are worse (Jesus) — 10/17/01 Vol. 25

abortions in America human garbage discarded (Jesus) — 6/28/02 Vol. 27

abortions in America to bring US to its knees (Jesus) — 1/22/05 Vol. 38

abortion's loss life never to be loved (Jesus) — 4/13/99 Vol. 15

abortions, martyrs Franciscan robes, body gone (Jesus) — 12/25/02 Vol. 29

abortions, small families desires for material things (Jesus) — 5/7/07 Vol. 47

abortions, stop by action in Congress (Jesus) — 11/15/04 Vol. 37

abortions, stop change Supreme Court (Jesus) — 11/3/04 Vol. 37

abortions, stop obey Fifth Commandment (Jesus) — 12/18/06 Vol. 45

abortions,arms,drugs blood money (Jesus) — 3/27/99 Vol. 14

abortions,doctors in defying oath,taking money (Jesus) — 10/13/00 Vol. 21

Abraham had faith tested (Jesus) — 10/14/01 Vol. 25

Abraham trusted in the impossible (Jesus) — 6/25/05 Vol. 39

abuse of food,abortions America to be tested for (Jesus) — 5/8/00 Vol. 19

abuses of children mental & physical (Jesus) — 5/3/05 Vol. 39

abuses of nature we will pay dearly (Jesus) — 12/27/98 Vol. 13

acceptance of Jesus gives love in actions (Jesus) — 11/10/03 Vol. 33

accomplishments done for God's glory (Jesus) — 8/14/96 Vol. 4

accountability for those of more faith (Jesus) — 10/14/03 Vol. 33

accountant gifts (Jesus) — 8/25/94 Vol. 2

Act of Contrition at bed time,analyze sins daily (Jesus) — 8/2/04 Vol. 36

Act of Contrition at night in case of death (Jesus) — 12/3/07 Vol. 49

Act of Contrition for forgiveness (Jesus) — 2/15/03 Vol. 30

Act of contrition pray each night (Jesus) — 5/28/02 Vol. 27

Act of God West/sin (Jesus) — 1/17/94 Vol. 1

act of mercy to others take away distractions (Jesus) — 2/13/06 Vol. 42

actions determine your judgment (Jesus) — 6/23/99 Vol. 15

actions heavenly reason/earthly purpose (Jesus) — 10/23/03 Vol. 33

actions tell your real faith (Jesus) — 6/18/07 Vol. 47

actions & fruits needed at judgment (Jesus) — 2/25/01 Vol. 22

actions & motives reflect on in Lent (Jesus) — 3/27/06 Vol. 42

actions in life choose heaven or hell (Jesus) — 6/5/06 Vol. 43

actions of life from mind & heart (Jesus) — 7/11/06 Vol. 44

actions on display witness to good example (Jesus) — 11/8/99 Vol. 17

actions, daily witness of love of Jesus (Jesus) — 10/21/03 Vol. 33

actions,personal on display for everyone (Jesus) — 6/22/00 Vol. 19

activities we race too much (Jesus) — 2/14/98 Vol. 10

acts of mercy intention of the heart (Jesus) — 1/18/95 Vol. 2

Adam first man of creation (Jesus) — 10/4/97 Vol. 9

Adam live as in New Era (Jesus) — 1/10/98 Vol. 10

Adam share in paradise (Jesus) — 9/26/97 Vol. 8

Adam & Eve ate forbidden fruit (Mary) — 2/13/99 Vol. 14

Adam & Eve cannot hide sins (Jesus) — 2/14/03 Vol. 30

Adam & Eve death if they ate the fruit (Jesus) — 11/21/00 Vol. 21

Adam & Eve devil attacked pride of (Jesus) — 2/9/08 Vol. 50

Adam & Eve hid from God as we do (Jesus) — 2/25/99 Vol. 14

Adam & Eve one flesh in sin (Jesus) — 2/8/07 Vol. 46

Adam & Eve tempted by Satan (Jesus) — 2/20/99 Vol. 14

Adam & Eve Tree of life (Jesus) — 3/30/03 Vol. 30

Adam & Eve, new in Jesus & Mary (Mary) — 12/8/05 Vol. 41

Adam & Eve, New Jesus & Mary (Jesus) — 5/31/06 Vol. 43

Adam and Eve banished from garden (Jesus) — 1/31/98 Vol. 10

Adam and Eve cast from Garden of Eden (Jesus) — 7/16/98 Vol. 12

Adam brought death Jesus brings life (Jesus) — 4/10/03 Vol. 31

Adam vs. Jesus sin and its redemption (Jesus) — 12/13/98 Vol. 13

Adam vs. Jesus sin vs. Light (Jesus) — 11/29/03 Vol. 33

Adam, new Jesus unblemished Lamb (Jesus) — 2/2/05 Vol. 38

Adam's sin born to die (Jesus) — 1/11/98 Vol. 10

Adam's sin closed gates of heaven (Jesus) — 11/29/01 Vol. 25

Adam's sin under shroud of sin & death (Jesus) — 4/8/98 Vol. 11

Adams, John funeral message (Jesus) — 7/22/05 Vol. 40

addiction to sin (Jesus) — 10/23/02 Vol. 29

addiction demons alcohol,drugs,computers (Jesus) — 8/30/05 Vol. 40

addictions abuse of body, demons of control (Jesus) — 10/3/04 Vol. 37

addictions avoid, be good example (Jesus) — 10/10/05 Vol. 41

addictions detours from heaven (Jesus) — 7/12/03 Vol. 32

addictions drugs, alcohol, and eating (Jesus)   4/28/05 Vol. 39

addictions drugs,alcohol,cigarettes (Jesus)   12/20/96 Vol. 5

addictions gambling,drugs,alcohol (Jesus)   6/8/97 Vol. 7

addictions have demons attached to them (Jesus)   2/14/08 Vol. 50

addictions how to deal with (Jesus)   11/3/06 Vol. 45

addictions make prisoners of people (Jesus)   12/19/02 Vol. 29

addictions need deliverance prayers (Jesus)   10/30/05 Vol. 41

addictions need prayer and help (Jesus)   3/1/07 Vol. 46

addictions need prayers and help (Jesus)   2/13/04 Vol. 34

addictions sins against own body (Jesus)   6/1/06 Vol. 43

addictions stop to save money (Jesus)   11/10/05 Vol. 41

addictions TV, money, sports, etc. (Jesus)   10/12/03 Vol. 33

addictions & bad habits control your life (Jesus)   3/7/06 Vol. 42

addictions & evil fight with prayer & fasting (Jesus)   6/15/05 Vol. 39

addictions & occult invite demons in (Jesus)   10/13/06 Vol. 45

addicts drain on society (Jesus)   6/23/03 Vol. 31

addict's free will what needs to change (Jesus)   10/3/04 Vol. 37

adoption answer to abortion (Our Lady)   11/10/07 Vol. 49

Adoration 10 minute quiet contemplation (Jesus)   8/2/07 Vol. 48

adoration Antichrist   9/23/93 Vol. 1

adoration ask for graces (Jesus)   10/10/97 Vol. 9

Adoration blessing for parish (Jesus)   1/31/03 Vol. 30

Adoration brings graces to parish (Jesus)   11/9/02 Vol. 29

Adoration brings many blessings (Jesus)   7/4/01 Vol. 24

Adoration calms our souls (Jesus)   10/28/02 Vol. 29

Adoration chandelier as light (Jesus)   1/8/03 Vol. 30

adoration crosses   9/12/93 Vol. 1

Adoration drink in graces (Jesus)   10/12/02 Vol. 29

adoration encourage priests for (Jesus)   2/15/99 Vol. 14

Adoration encouraged by pope (Jesus)   2/19/05 Vol. 38

Adoration encourages vocations (Jesus)   10/25/02 Vol. 29

Adoration encourages vocations (Jesus)   8/10/06 Vol. 44

adoration expresses our love (Jesus)   5/21/01 Vol. 23

Adoration give thanks to God (Jesus)   12/4/04 Vol. 37

Adoration gives honor & glory to God (Jesus)   2/8/07 Vol. 46

adoration gives us rest (Jesus)   9/30/97 Vol. 8

Adoration gracs for people & parish (Jesus)   6/16/05 Vol. 39

Adoration helps fight temptations (Jesus)   9/21/02 Vol. 28

Adoration inspires vocations (Jesus)   2/5/04 Vol. 34

Adoration Jesus invites visits to (Jesus)   7/10/07 Vol. 48

Adoration Jesus shares love,graces (Jesus)   8/6/99 Vol. 16

adoration love and peace (Jesus)   2/2/96 Vol. 3

Adoration love God & neighbor (Jesus)   1/12/03 Vol. 30

Adoration love of Jesus in Host (Jesus)   5/29/05 Vol. 39

Adoration Magi & gentiles (Jesus)   1/5/03 Vol. 30

Adoration make up for others (Jesus)   10/16/03 Vol. 33

Adoration Mary takes rosary to Jesus (Jesus)   1/8/03 Vol. 30

Adoration needed to help priests,vocations (Jesus)   3/14/02 Vol. 26

adoration needs promoting (Jesus)   2/28/00 Vol. 18

adoration on earth and heaven (Jesus)   1/7/99 Vol. 14

adoration proper to kneel (Jesus)   5/31/96 Vol. 3

Adoration quiet time as prayer (Jesus)   3/16/06 Vol. 42

adoration share abundant graces (Jesus)   3/7/99 Vol. 14

Adoration sign of power (Jesus)   6/24/04 Vol. 35

adoration source of blessings (Jesus)   6/7/01 Vol. 23

Adoration take opportunity to visit (Jesus)   6/10/04 Vol. 35

Adoration three Magi came afar (Jesus)   1/4/03 Vol. 30

Adoration training for heaven (Jesus)   9/19/07 Vol. 48

Adoration where Church is thriving (Jesus)   4/19/05 Vol. 39

adoration will receive blessings (Jesus)   2/10/99 Vol. 14

Adoration witness of faith (Jesus)   9/18/97 Vol. 8

Adoration & Communion taste of heaven (Jesus)   5/1/03 Vol. 31

Adoration & Confession shine mercy & love (Jesus)   8/9/03 Vol. 32

Adoration & prayer do early before sleep (Jesus)   4/3/03 Vol. 31

Adoration needed for atonement of sin (Jesus)   1/27/05 Vol. 38

Adoration needed graces given for visits (Jesus)   3/13/04 Vol. 34

adoration of Bl Sacra. promote in Churches (Jesus)   6/28/98 Vol. 11

Adoration of Bl Sacra. more graces to diocese (Jesus)   4/18/02 Vol. 27

Adoration of Bl Sacra. special blessings for (Jesus)   6/26/02 Vol. 27

Adoration of Eucharist little jewels of My love (Jesus)   7/12/96 Vol. 4

Adoration of Host golden rays of flames (Jesus)   1/20/07 Vol. 46

Adoration of Host is Real Presence (Jesus)   11/15/05 Vol. 41

Adoration of Jesus done out of love,not obligation (Jesus)   10/9/04 Vol. 37

Adoration of Jesus needs encouragement (Jesus)   10/21/00 Vol. 21

Adoration of Jesus needs promoting (Jesus)   2/10/00 Vol. 18

adoration of Jesus source of blessings (Jesus)   2/17/00 Vol. 18

Adoration of Jesus wellspring of love (Jesus)   1/30/99 Vol. 14

Adoration places opportunity to love God (Jesus)   1/5/06 Vol. 42

Adoration places remove world's clutter (Jesus)   1/6/06 Vol. 42

adoration places to be protected in tribulation (Jesus)   7/13/05 Vol. 40

Adoration time more useful than watching TV (Jesus)   3/12/02 Vol. 26

Adoration time reward in heaven (Jesus)   11/3/06 Vol. 45

Adoration visits sign of love for Jesus (Jesus)   9/6/07 Vol. 48

adoration,perpetual struggle to maintain,protect (Jesus)   7/16/00 Vol. 20

Adoration,tabernacle place of Jesus our king (Jesus)   6/3/00 Vol. 19

adorers get special graces (Jesus)   9/27/02 Vol. 28

Adorers given extra graces (Jesus)   9/12/03 Vol. 32

adorers given special graces (Jesus)   7/18/05 Vol. 40

Adorers have special protection (Jesus)   8/19/06 Vol. 44

adorers special followers (Jesus)   7/22/03 Vol. 32

adorers of Bl Sacra. get heavenly blessings (Jesus)   1/23/03 Vol. 30

Adorers of Eucharist receive graces for all (Jesus)   3/28/05 Vol. 38

adorers of Jesus receive blessings,thanks (Jesus)   4/21/99 Vol. 15

Adorers who listen Jesus speaks to hearts (Jesus)   11/15/05 Vol. 41

Adorers,prayer warriors fighting all evil (Jesus)   8/24/06 Vol. 44

adult children, old parents need care (Jesus)   7/4/04 Vol. 36

adultery destroys marriages (Jesus)   2/1/08 Vol. 50

Advent blessing of salvation (Jesus)   11/15/01 Vol. 25

Advent chance to purify soul (Jesus)   12/1/07 Vol. 49

Advent cross (Jesus)   12/3/95 Vol. 3

Advent Infant of Prague,king (Jesus)   11/30/97 Vol. 9

Advent peace & repenting of sin (Jesus)   12/2/02 Vol. 29

Advent preparation time (Mary)   12/5/96 Vol. 5

Advent preparations (Jesus)   12/1/03 Vol. 33

Advent prepare souls for Christmas (Jesus)   12/12/00 Vol. 21

Advent spiritual preparation (Jesus)   12/10/94 Vol. 2

Advent time for prayer & shopping (Jesus)   12/11/03 Vol. 33

Advent time of prayer & fasting (Jesus)   11/27/00 Vol. 21

Advent time to share love (Jesus)   11/29/98 Vol. 13

Advent beginning vision of judgment (Jesus)   11/27/05 Vol. 41

Advent cheer to touch cold hearts (Jesus)   12/8/02 Vol. 29

Advent model found in St. John (Jesus)   12/13/04 Vol. 37

Advent preparation Nativity Scene (Jesus)   11/26/07 Vol. 49

Advent readings relate to end times (Jesus)   12/20/07 Vol. 49

Advent season symbols:light,gifts,star (Jesus)   11/24/97 Vol. 9

Advent time mankind in darkness of sin (Jesus)   11/28/03 Vol. 33

Advent wreath good tradition (Jesus)   12/5/96 Vol. 5

adversity test of faith (Jesus)   8/3/00 Vol. 20

adversity tribulation (Jesus)   2/23/95 Vol. 2

advice be friendly,good example (Jesus)   12/23/97 Vol. 9

affluence fast from things you like (Jesus)   11/23/96 Vol. 5

affluence, immorality problems for leading holy life (Jesus) 11/9/03 Vol. 33

affluence,complacency test efforts for souls (Jesus)   6/11/03 Vol. 31

affluence,spoiled by squandering God's blessings (Jesus) 11/16/04 Vol. 37

affluent & lukewarm wake up,morals are bad (Jesus)   5/5/99 Vol. 15

Afghanistan deplete troops and money (Jesus)   1/24/02 Vol. 26

Afghanistan do not seek vengence on (Jesus)   12/20/01 Vol. 25

Afghanistan do not widen war (Jesus)   12/5/01 Vol. 25

Afghanistan feed the poor (Jesus)   11/15/01 Vol. 25

Afghanistan have exit strategy (Jesus)   10/31/01 Vol. 25

Afghanistan UN troops (Jesus)   1/16/02 Vol. 26

Afghanistan war to drag on,tie down troops (Jesus)   3/21/02 Vol. 26

Afghanistan & Israel food shortages (Jesus)   4/11/02 Vol. 27

Afghanistan war war for September 11th (Jesus)   3/8/04 Vol. 34

Afghanistan war footing danger of more countries at war (Jesus)
  11/3/01 Vol. 25

Africa all peoples   8/29/93 Vol. 1

African bombing foretelling of terrorists action (Jesus)   8/6/98 Vol. 12

Africa's poverty calls for charity (Jesus)   7/8/06 Vol. 44

agape love higher than erotic love (Jesus)   11/11/99 Vol. 17

agape love spiritual love of God (Jesus)   5/28/04 Vol. 35

age of apostasy affecting priests (Jesus)   2/4/00 Vol. 18

Agnes Vernacotola funeral message (Agnes)   2/8/02 Vol. 26

Agony in Garden pray one hour   8/25/93 Vol. 1

Agony in the Garden call on Father's help (Jesus)   12/1/99 Vol. 17

agricultural crops becoming more important (Jesus)   5/24/06 Vol. 43

AIDS & ebola created by man (Jesus)   3/21/01 Vol. 22

AIDS & Ebola man-made origins (Jesus)   7/20/05 Vol. 40

AIDS, SARS, ebola pestilences of end times (Jesus)   12/18/03 Vol. 33

AIDS,ebola,West Nile man-made diseases (Jesus)   9/19/02 Vol. 28

air ducts filter, used to spread disease (Jesus)   11/5/05 Vol. 41

air pollution reduce emissions (Jesus)   5/19/05 Vol. 39

air pollution ways to avoid (Jesus)   6/5/07 Vol. 47

air technology did not require Concorde (Jesus)   11/25/03 Vol. 33

aircraft carrier on way to Iran (Jesus)   5/11/06 Vol. 43

airplane travel accidents are deadly (Jesus)   5/4/06 Vol. 43

airplane travel to demand smart cards (Jesus)   9/7/06 Vol. 44

airport threat missiles in hands of terrorists (Jesus)   3/25/02 Vol. 26

airs of deception be humble, modest (Jesus)   12/21/99 Vol. 17

Al Rappl death of (Jesus)   9/28/06 Vol. 44

alcohol monstrance (Jesus)   8/16/95 Vol. 3

alcohol & drugs to escape problems (Jesus)   6/25/01 Vol. 23

alcohol & drugs to escape trials of life (Jesus)   6/11/01 Vol. 23

alcohol abuse ruins lives,help with God (Jesus)   9/6/03 Vol. 32

alcohol,drugs,eating control appetites (Jesus)   6/1/06 Vol. 43

alcoholics addictions cause sickness (Jesus)   12/19/02 Vol. 29

alcoholics need help, can be healed (Jesus)   8/22/03 Vol. 32

alcoholism & drinking effects on, need help (Jesus)   7/28/03 Vol. 32

alcoholism & drugs abuse of the body (Jesus)   2/13/04 Vol. 34

Alice N. Mass heaven (Jesus)   10/18/95 Vol. 3

alien gods jealous (Jesus)   8/19/95 Vol. 3

All Saints' Day Communion of Saints (Jesus)   11/1/05 Vol. 41

All Saints' Day follow will with love (Jesus)   11/1/96 Vol. 5

All Saints' Day need perfection to enter heaven (Jesus) 10/30/03 Vol. 33

All Saints' Day suffer now,not Purgatory (Jesus)   11/1/97 Vol. 9

All Souls' Day pray for relatives (Jesus)   11/1/07 Vol. 49

almsgiving give dearly not just a mite (Jesus)   3/16/00 Vol. 18

almsgiving give freely to charities (Jesus)   2/26/06 Vol. 42

almsgiving give of substance,not token (Jesus)   3/25/03 Vol. 30

almsgiving Lenten penance (Jesus)   3/9/06 Vol. 42

almsgiving means of sharing God's gifts (Jesus)   3/8/02 Vol. 26

almsgiving rewarded in heaven (Jesus)   1/8/05 Vol. 38

Alpah & Omega beginning & end of creation (Jesus)   4/6/04 Vol. 35

Alpha & Omega awesome power of God (Jesus)   12/23/96 Vol. 5

Alpha & Omega before Abraham, 'I AM' (Jesus)   4/4/98 Vol. 11

Alpha & Omega home now and in heaven (Jesus)   7/18/98 Vol. 12

Alpha & Omega Jesus as Son of God (Jesus)   1/3/02 Vol. 26

alpha & omega paradise in Era of Peace (Jesus)   2/23/99 Vol. 14

alpha and omega beginning and the end (Jesus)   6/14/98 Vol. 11
alpha and omega eternal now (Jesus)   10/1/99 Vol. 17
altar red light for home prayer vigil (Jesus)   7/12/01 Vol. 24
altars made for God, not man (Jesus)   3/19/07 Vol. 46
altars in homes special place of prayer (Jesus)   1/22/99 Vol. 14
altars stripped of crucifix, statues (Jesus)   10/28/04 Vol. 37
alternate fuels ethanol, wind, hydrogen (Jesus)   2/23/06 Vol. 42
alternate fuels held back by oil (Jesus)   2/2/06 Vol. 42
alternate fuels needed to avoid oil (Jesus)   1/10/06 Vol. 42
alternative fuels are needed in America (Jesus)   2/17/06 Vol. 42
alternative fuels for cold winter (Jesus)   9/1/06 Vol. 44
aluminum foil thwarts chip microwaves (Jesus)   7/24/07 Vol. 48
Alverus' funeral message of hope (Jesus)   10/5/07 Vol. 49
amateur astronomers to warn of comet (Jesus)   8/24/99 Vol. 16
America a listing of our sins (Jesus)   10/30/99 Vol. 17
America a mission land (Jesus)   8/3/06 Vol. 44
America abortion most offensive sin (Jesus)   9/19/06 Vol. 44
America abortion,finances-one world (Jesus)   11/12/98 Vol. 13
America actions to determine fate (Jesus)   8/28/04 Vol. 36
America Antichrist, persecution (Jesus)   10/7/97 Vol. 9
America army in ruin (Jesus)   7/4/99 Vol. 16
America arrogant for power (Jesus)   4/4/03 Vol. 31
America as broken people (Jesus)   5/25/02 Vol. 27
America as in Babylonian Exile (Jesus)   6/30/06 Vol. 43
America as runaway train to disaster (Jesus)   2/9/03 Vol. 30
America as Sodom & Gomorrah (Jesus)   10/10/01 Vol. 25
America awake from sins (Jesus)   9/10/98 Vol. 12
America bankruptcy for sins (Jesus)   2/24/04 Vol. 34
America becoming a mission land (Jesus)   7/9/98 Vol. 12
America becoming too arrogant (Jesus)   3/18/03 Vol. 30
America been greatly blessed (Jesus)   12/3/99 Vol. 17
America being brought to our knees (Jesus)   9/16/04 Vol. 36
America being led into oblivion (Jesus)   4/19/05 Vol. 39
America beset by sin and wars (Jesus)   9/1/03 Vol. 32
America black casket (Jesus)   11/20/94 Vol. 2
America blessed with food,resources (Jesus)   6/5/02 Vol. 27
America blessings withdrawn (Jesus)   10/13/99 Vol. 17
America blueprint for demise (Jesus)   2/11/03 Vol. 30
America brought down in wars & debts (Jesus)   7/25/03 Vol. 32
America brought own chastisements (Jesus)   1/2/02 Vol. 26
America brought to her knees (Jesus)   5/12/04 Vol. 35
America brought to its knees (Jesus)   7/2/03 Vol. 32
America brought to knees (Jesus)   9/5/02 Vol. 28
America brought to knees by disasters (Jesus)   6/8/04 Vol. 35
America brought to our knees (Jesus)   5/8/02 Vol. 27
America cannot afford rebuilding countries (Jesus)   9/4/03 Vol. 32
America cannot force governments (Jesus)   1/26/06 Vol. 42

America cannot police the world (Jesus)   2/13/03 Vol. 30
America chastised for sins (Jesus)   6/15/04 Vol. 35
America chastised like Jerusalem (Jesus)   6/25/04 Vol. 35
America chastisements (Jesus)   7/4/02 Vol. 28
America choice of God or money (Jesus)   8/25/03 Vol. 32
America cities to face destruction (Jesus)   6/26/03 Vol. 31
America comforts to decrease (Jesus)   6/25/07 Vol. 47
America condemned as in Noah's day (Jesus)   7/24/03 Vol. 32
America controlled by bankers,masons (Jesus)   12/21/03 Vol. 33
America convert or lose blessings (Jesus)   1/4/01 Vol. 22
America crumbled to the ground (Jesus)   9/28/00 Vol. 20
America cup of wrath filling (Jesus)   2/14/07 Vol. 46
America days are numbered (Jesus)   2/1/07 Vol. 46
America days of freedom numbered (Jesus)   2/8/07 Vol. 46
America dead corpse, chose fate (Jesus)   3/27/03 Vol. 30
America death culture brings to ruin (Jesus)   1/16/03 Vol. 30
America debtor nation (Jesus)   10/31/02 Vol. 29
America decadent society cause ruin (Jesus)   9/30/98 Vol. 12
America decay in society (Jesus)   10/3/97 Vol. 9
America decaying from within (Jesus)   5/7/02 Vol. 27
America decline as Roman Empire (Jesus)   10/10/02 Vol. 29
America decline for removing God (Jesus)   7/3/03 Vol. 32
America declining in influence (Jesus)   1/6/04 Vol. 34
America demanding God's justice (Jesus)   8/19/02 Vol. 28
America demise for abortions (Jesus)   9/21/00 Vol. 20
America demons among people (Jesus)   4/24/05 Vol. 39
America destroyed by traitors (Jesus)   7/31/03 Vol. 32
America destroyed by wars & debts (Jesus)   7/24/03 Vol. 32
America destroying self by decadence (Jesus)   11/25/01 Vol. 25
America destruction for unrepentance (Jesus)   4/6/03 Vol. 31
America destruction sought (Jesus)   12/18/01 Vol. 25
America disasters for our sins (Jesus)   4/22/04 Vol. 35
America do not bully other nations (Jesus)   12/24/04 Vol. 37
America do not engage in war (Jesus)   10/4/01 Vol. 25
America do not expand war (Jesus)   11/13/01 Vol. 25
America does not see its sins (Jesus)   6/20/02 Vol. 27
America easy target for destruction (Jesus)   9/22/03 Vol. 32
America economic,military downfall (Jesus)   12/6/00 Vol. 21
America economy declining (Jesus)   1/14/04 Vol. 34
America exporting its wealth (Jesus)   3/3/06 Vol. 42
America faces defeat for decadence (Jesus)   9/22/03 Vol. 32
America falling as Roman Empire did (Jesus)   3/12/05 Vol. 38
America falling from weight of sin (Jesus)   2/12/04 Vol. 34
America falling into ruin (Jesus)   7/11/01 Vol. 24
America falling into ruin (Jesus)   5/22/01 Vol. 23
America fist of God striking (Jesus)   2/21/05 Vol. 38
America forces stretched too thin (Jesus)   6/12/04 Vol. 35

America forcing will on others (Jesus)	3/1/03 Vol. 30	America needs spiritual renewal (Jesus)	7/31/06 Vol. 44
America forcing will on others (Jesus)	2/20/03 Vol. 30	America needs to repent of sins (Jesus)	11/15/01 Vol. 25
America forcing will on others (Jesus)	3/20/03 Vol. 30	America needs to repent of sins (Jesus)	11/4/04 Vol. 37
America gambled for short war, lost (Jesus)	3/31/03 Vol. 30	America needs to repent of sins (Jesus)	9/14/06 Vol. 44
America going into bankruptcy from wars (Jesus)	6/15/06 Vol. 43	America needs to repent or fall (Jesus)	8/19/04 Vol. 36
America greed, sins of flesh (Mary)	12/9/96 Vol. 5	America new attacks cause ID (Jesus)	9/10/02 Vol. 28
America greenhouse gases (Jesus)	6/4/02 Vol. 27	America no change, cease to exist (Jesus)	11/23/00 Vol. 21
America has immoral laws as abortion (Jesus)	9/20/04 Vol. 36	America no gain in Iraq war (Jesus)	3/23/05 Vol. 38
America has pride in wealth (Jesus)	1/2/08 Vol. 50	America not enough prayer to save (Jesus)	2/21/05 Vol. 38
America has spiritual cold feet (Jesus)	12/20/01 Vol. 25	America on trial for abortions (Jesus)	1/8/99 Vol. 14
America has superficial faith (Jesus)	7/14/03 Vol. 32	America only dirt on grave left (Jesus)	7/31/03 Vol. 32
America heading for ruin (Jesus)	2/2/03 Vol. 30	America out of control (Jesus)	4/14/03 Vol. 31
America hide to avoid capture (Jesus)	11/23/98 Vol. 13	America persecution (Jesus)	7/25/94 Vol. 2
America house built on sand (Jesus)	11/21/94 Vol. 2	America plan to destroy by wars (Jesus)	2/21/03 Vol. 30
America humbled in weapon destruction (Jesus)	7/19/05 Vol. 40	America police state & wars (Jesus)	5/20/03 Vol. 31
America immorality calling for justice (Jesus)	4/14/05 Vol. 39	America possessions & weather (Jesus)	4/9/96 Vol. 3
America in constant wars (Jesus)	7/3/03 Vol. 32	America pray for conversion of (Jesus)	9/4/03 Vol. 32
America in darkness of sin (Jesus)	9/3/98 Vol. 12	America pray or fall (Jesus)	8/23/98 Vol. 12
America in decline (Jesus)	2/5/04 Vol. 34	America prison camps abound (Jesus)	12/26/06 Vol. 45
America in moral decay (Jesus)	2/20/03 Vol. 30	America punished for defying laws (Jesus)	8/8/03 Vol. 32
America in moral decay (Jesus)	6/11/05 Vol. 39	America punishment for sins (Jesus)	8/30/06 Vol. 44
America irreverence for God (Jesus)	11/28/07 Vol. 49	America rejects God, seals fate (Jesus)	3/20/03 Vol. 30
America is a mission land (Jesus)	10/19/05 Vol. 41	America religious persecution in (Jesus)	5/1/98 Vol. 11
America is not repenting (Jesus)	5/18/99 Vol. 15	America repent & change lifestyle (Jesus)	7/2/04 Vol. 36
America judged by abortions (Jesus)	8/22/06 Vol. 44	America repent before too late (Jesus)	7/31/03 Vol. 32
America judgment for sins (Father)	1/24/97 Vol. 6	America repent now or brought to knees (Jesus)	1/22/03 Vol. 30
America justice for sins (Jesus)	8/17/00 Vol. 20	America repent now or justice to fall (Jesus)	12/2/03 Vol. 33
America justice, overflowing cup (Jesus)	5/15/01 Vol. 23	America repent or be captured (Jesus)	1/22/02 Vol. 26
America leaders leading to ruin (Jesus)	10/19/99 Vol. 17	America repent or be on knees (Jesus)	2/24/03 Vol. 30
America like harlot Israel (Jesus)	7/12/01 Vol. 24	America repent or crumble (Jesus)	3/14/03 Vol. 30
America like Sodom & Gomorrah (Jesus)	10/6/01 Vol. 25	America repent or face God's justice (Jesus)	2/13/08 Vol. 50
America like Sodom and Gomorrah (Jesus)	3/26/03 Vol. 30	America repent or have chastisements (Jesus)	12/6/01 Vol. 25
America like stench of sewer (Jesus)	5/29/02 Vol. 27	America revolt coming for survival (Jesus)	2/28/04 Vol. 34
America loosing freedoms (Jesus)	4/7/03 Vol. 31	America ripe for takeover (Jesus)	3/27/03 Vol. 30
America lost sense of sin (Jesus)	3/26/03 Vol. 30	America ripe for takeover (Jesus)	1/20/03 Vol. 30
America lower standard of living (Jesus)	9/24/06 Vol. 44	America ruined by decadence (Jesus)	6/14/99 Vol. 15
America many unknowns (Jesus)	9/25/02 Vol. 28	America runaway train to war (Jesus)	3/13/03 Vol. 30
America marching to its own funeral (Jesus)	9/3/98 Vol. 12	America seek forgiveness of sins (Jesus)	12/11/01 Vol. 25
America military crumbling (Jesus)	1/1/02 Vol. 26	America severe chastisements (Jesus)	6/23/04 Vol. 35
America moral decadence (Jesus)	4/7/98 Vol. 11	America shouldering cost of war (Jesus)	3/27/03 Vol. 30
America moral decay in loss of religion (Jesus)	11/13/04 Vol. 37	America signed our fate (Jesus)	4/25/03 Vol. 31
America moral decay on trial (Jesus)	1/21/99 Vol. 14	America sins are scarlet (Jesus)	6/25/03 Vol. 31
America mourns 9-11-01 (Jesus)	9/11/02 Vol. 28	America sins calling on God's wrath (Jesus)	9/7/04 Vol. 36
America needs religious renewal (Jesus)	2/19/01 Vol. 22	America sins cause our struggling (Jesus)	8/28/03 Vol. 32
America needs repentance for its sins (Jesus)	2/25/02 Vol. 26	America sins destroy within (Jesus)	2/1/07 Vol. 46
America needs repentance,or destruction (Jesus)	10/30/06 Vol. 45	America spiritual bodies emaciated (Jesus)	2/12/04 Vol. 34
America needs spiritual renewal (Jesus)	2/8/07 Vol. 46	America spiritual renewal needed (Jesus)	1/4/07 Vol. 46

America spoiled by freedoms,rich (Jesus) 6/16/99 Vol. 15
America spoiled in possessions (Jesus) 1/12/99 Vol. 14
America state of decline (Jesus) 5/22/03 Vol. 31
America stop aggressive wars (Jesus) 4/21/03 Vol. 31
America stop bullying nations (Jesus) 4/11/03 Vol. 31
America storms and fires (Jesus) 10/3/02 Vol. 29
America stripped by poor jobs (Jesus) 6/25/98 Vol. 11
America stripped of freedom soon (Jesus) 1/3/02 Vol. 26
America struggling for jobs,education (Jesus) 9/16/04 Vol. 36
America swift justice for abortions (Jesus) 12/30/04 Vol. 37
America takeover by foreign troops (Jesus) 3/27/03 Vol. 30
America terror excuse for takeover (Jesus) 8/14/06 Vol. 44
America terrorist attacks (Jesus) 3/20/03 Vol. 30
America tested for abortions (Jesus) 6/30/98 Vol. 11
America time is running out (Jesus) 6/25/98 Vol. 11
America to be stripped of possessions (Jesus) 12/6/00 Vol. 21
America to be tested by fire (Jesus) 2/25/02 Vol. 26
America to build up Afghanistan (Jesus) 12/20/01 Vol. 25
America to come down in ruin (Jesus) 10/17/99 Vol. 17
America to destroy itself in wars (Jesus) 7/31/02 Vol. 28
America to fall like Israel (Jesus) 6/20/02 Vol. 27
America to have massive disasters (Jesus) 3/5/07 Vol. 46
America to lose blessings (Jesus) 6/16/01 Vol. 23
America to lose possessions,freedoms (Jesus) 4/18/00 Vol. 19
America to lose world status (Jesus) 9/27/98 Vol. 12
America to suffer as rest of world (Jesus) 8/28/03 Vol. 32
America to suffer for our sins (Jesus) 5/3/99 Vol. 15
America to suffer from chastisements (Jesus) 7/18/02 Vol. 28
America to suffer more disasters (Jesus) 3/29/06 Vol. 42
America trusts in weapons, not God (Jesus) 3/27/03 Vol. 30
America turned back on God by sins (Jesus) 2/7/04 Vol. 34
America use more diplomacy (Jesus) 4/14/05 Vol. 39
America uses 1/4 of world's fuels (Jesus) 9/6/07 Vol. 48
America volcanoes out West (Jesus) 3/5/07 Vol. 46
America wake up (Jesus) 1/30/01 Vol. 22
America wake up (Jesus) 9/15/00 Vol. 20
America wake up and repent (Jesus) 1/26/08 Vol. 50
America wake up from sins (Jesus) 1/12/05 Vol. 38
America wake up from spiritual blindness (Jesus) 11/28/01 Vol. 25
America wake up,days are numbered (Jesus) 7/4/98 Vol. 12
America war hard to finish (Jesus) 3/9/03 Vol. 30
America war to cause our oblivion (Jesus) 9/26/02 Vol. 28
America wars & debts to cause demise (Jesus) 10/2/03 Vol. 33
America wars to cause downfall (Jesus) 10/29/02 Vol. 29
America weakened by wars (Jesus) 3/15/03 Vol. 30
America wealth drained like blood (Jesus) 3/27/03 Vol. 30
America what will history say? (Jesus) 5/2/03 Vol. 31

America whirlwind of events (Jesus) 10/1/02 Vol. 29
America will be a captive nation (Jesus) 4/21/99 Vol. 15
America will be bankrupted, destroyed (Jesus) 7/26/06 Vol. 44
America will be brought to knees (Jesus) 1/15/99 Vol. 14
America will be ruined without God (Jesus) 8/28/98 Vol. 12
America will be sorry for war (Jesus) 10/30/02 Vol. 29
America will collapse for its decay (Jesus) 2/25/98 Vol. 10
America will fall (Jesus) 12/6/01 Vol. 25
America will fall soon in ruin (Jesus) 8/17/98 Vol. 12
America window of opportunity (Jesus) 5/7/01 Vol. 23
America with moral decay (Jesus) 4/19/01 Vol. 23
America without God, will fail (Jesus) 7/9/98 Vol. 12
America worse than Sodom/Gomorrah (Jesus) 7/4/03 Vol. 32
America worships idols of money,things (Jesus) 7/7/04 Vol. 36
America can repent like Nineveh (Jesus) 2/6/08 Vol. 50
America crumbling from within (Jesus) 11/27/07 Vol. 49
America crushed if wars, sins are not stopped (Jesus) 9/5/04 Vol. 36
America destroyed without repentance (Jesus) 7/4/02 Vol. 28
America drained in money & military (Jesus) 2/11/05 Vol. 38
America facing storms terrorism,recession,disasters (Jesus) 11/6/01 Vol. 25
America falling justice for abortions (Jesus) 11/26/97 Vol. 9
America falls like tower of Babel (Jesus) 3/20/03 Vol. 30
America humbled God allowed enemy attack (Jesus) 9/18/01 Vol. 24
America in flames cities destroyed as Jerusalem (Jesus) 7/27/01 Vol. 24
America in sin needs repentance (Jesus) 10/9/07 Vol. 49
America in war faces our own grave (Jesus) 8/27/02 Vol. 28
America invincible fall like Rome (Jesus) 3/20/03 Vol. 30
America like Israel about to be forced into exile (Jesus) 4/2/00 Vol. 19
America mourns large scale of terrorism (Jesus) 9/12/01 Vol. 24
America must repent or face downfall (Jesus) 4/26/06 Vol. 43
Am. near bankruptcy due to debts, reckless spending (Jesus) 9/9/04 Vol. 36
America needs a spiritual renewal (Jesus) 5/1/06 Vol. 43
America needs care mourning,healing process (Jesus) 9/13/01 Vol. 24
America needs forgiveness to calm storms of sin (Jesus) 11/6/01 Vol. 25
Am. needs repentance or destruction may follow (Jesus) 10/8/07 Vol. 49
Am. needs repentance or will face chastisements (Jesus) 11/16/04 Vol. 37
Am. needs to repent as woman caught in adultery (Jesus) 9/16/04 Vol. 36
Am. needs to repent storm speeded up, hitting land (Jesus) 8/14/04 Vol. 36
America neutralized needed for world conquest (Jesus) 11/6/01 Vol. 25
America on stage war in Iraq a test (Jesus) 12/17/98 Vol. 13
America on trial murdering millions unborn (Jesus) 2/12/01 Vol. 22
America persecuted to wake us up (Jesus) 8/1/01 Vol. 24
America plundered to lose freedoms & things (Jesus) 4/2/00 Vol. 19
America repent or more disasters to come (Jesus) 10/5/05 Vol. 41
America scarred by millions of abortions (Jesus) 10/29/03 Vol. 33
America spoiled help each other (Jesus) 9/18/03 Vol. 32
America stripped for senseless killings (Jesus) 9/25/01 Vol. 24

America struck by fire modern city in flames (Jesus)   7/28/01 Vol. 24

America suffers wrath for abortions (Jesus)   1/22/04 Vol. 34

America supports war as an arms dealer (Jesus)   11/6/04 Vol. 37

America takeover failed to listen to prophets (Jesus)   8/10/00 Vol. 20

America tested by disasters, wars, terrorism (Jesus)   5/12/04 Vol. 35

America tested by storms for sins (Jesus)   9/22/05 Vol. 40

America tested by terrorists & disasters (Jesus)   3/30/06 Vol. 42

America to its knees by decline in morals (Jesus)   8/10/04 Vol. 36

America to our knees by disasters, wars, terrorism (Jesus) 7/26/04 Vol. 36

America to suffer for abortions,adultery, etc. (Jesus)   8/3/05 Vol. 40

America, bad laws abortion, homosexual laws (Jesus)   6/26/03 Vol. 31

America, decline of from gay marriage, live ins (Jesus)   12/27/02 Vol. 29

America, fall in ruin from abortion,sins of flesh (Jesus)   10/23/98 Vol. 13

America, Middle earthquake, more damage (Jesus)   3/30/06 Vol. 42

America, possible riots over exported jobs (Jesus)   12/13/05 Vol. 41

America, pray needs spiritual improvement (Jesus)   11/28/05 Vol. 41

America, repent lesson from Nineveh (Jesus)   3/7/01 Vol. 22

America, repent suffering high fuel prices (Jesus)   9/9/05 Vol. 40

America, sins of calling down wrath of God (Jesus)   11/26/03 Vol. 33

America,mission land mission churches in CA (Jesus)   7/1/05 Vol. 40

American car jobs exported for profit (Jesus)   1/17/08 Vol. 50

American change in standard of living (Jesus)   9/1/05 Vol. 40

American cities calling for justice (Jesus)   6/30/03 Vol. 31

American decadence morals are deteriorating (Jesus)   3/21/02 Vol. 26

American decadence results from unrepentant sin (Jesus) 11/8/01 Vol. 25

American destruction signs on the wall (Jesus)   9/27/01 Vol. 24

American disasters increase after June '06 (Jesus)   5/23/06 Vol. 43

Am. economy on fire from debts,wars,disasters (Jesus)   3/25/04 Vol. 34

American employers deaf to slavery (Jesus)   12/18/07 Vol. 49

American energy dependent on gas & oil (Jesus)   9/1/05 Vol. 40

American Exile sex sins,wars,abortions (Jesus)   3/18/06 Vol. 42

American factories losing to competition (Jesus)   6/22/06 Vol. 43

American finances Federal Reserve rescue attempt (Jesus) 3/17/08 Vol. 50

American freedoms at stake over war (Jesus)   2/17/07 Vol. 46

American government to be changed by turmoil (Jesus)   1/3/08 Vol. 50

American immorality cause of chastisements (Jesus)   2/2/05 Vol. 38

American Indians being exploited (Jesus)   11/4/04 Vol. 37

American Indians injustices (Jesus)   6/4/98 Vol. 11

American jobs sold to foreigners (Jesus)   1/17/08 Vol. 50

American jobs down losing to competition (Jesus)   3/3/06 Vol. 42

American laws defying God's laws (Jesus)   12/28/02 Vol. 29

American laws need grounding in God (Jesus)   11/2/04 Vol. 37

American leadership running adrift (Jesus)   2/17/06 Vol. 42

American morals choice to improve or die (Jesus)   1/24/06 Vol. 42

American morals declining divorce, living together (Jesus) 8/5/07 Vol. 48

American pride will not lose face (Jesus)   2/24/03 Vol. 30

American sins as Sodom & Gomorrah (Jesus)   3/22/02 Vol. 26

American takeover by foreign troops (Jesus)   4/20/07 Vol. 47

American takeover through wars and debts (Jesus)   11/7/02 Vol. 29

American wealth riches are from God (Jesus)   11/17/98 Vol. 13

American wealth should be shared with poor (Jesus)   7/6/05 Vol. 40

American work force low wage threat (Jesus)   8/30/07 Vol. 48

American workers cheated by employers (Jesus)   11/1/07 Vol. 49

American workers suffering most in recovery (Jesus)   11/11/03 Vol. 33

American workers under siege by employers (Jesus)   12/8/05 Vol. 41

Americans brainwashed with lies (Jesus)   3/24/03 Vol. 30

Americans consume too much fuels (Jesus)   11/25/07 Vol. 49

Americans imprisoned over freedoms (Jesus)   11/30/02 Vol. 29

Americans knocked out of complacency (Jesus)   9/17/03 Vol. 32

Americans live like royalty (Jesus)   6/5/02 Vol. 27

Americans living in a fog of sin (Jesus)   6/13/03 Vol. 31

America's oil dependency (Jesus)   2/17/06 Vol. 42

America's affluence cause some to expect free help (Jesus) 12/26/03 Vol. 33

America's bad laws will bring us to our knees (Jesus)   12/28/04 Vol. 37

America's blessings dissipating by abortions (Jesus)   9/20/04 Vol. 36

America's collapse wars, debts, deficits (Jesus)   1/2/07 Vol. 46

America's courts unjust judges (Jesus)   12/29/05 Vol. 41

America's cup of sin overflowing, call for justice (Jesus) 1/23/07 Vol. 46

Am's death culture disasters,terrrorism,takeover (Jesus) 12/31/04 Vol. 37

America's decadence losing its blessings (Jesus)   4/18/02 Vol. 27

America's decision choice over life or destruction (Jesus) 11/1/04 Vol. 37

America's demise destroy economy, military (Jesus)   5/28/05 Vol. 39

America's demise from constant wars (Jesus)   12/21/02 Vol. 29

America's destruction as destruction of Jerusalem (Jesus) 10/12/00 Vol. 21

America's destruction by deficits,wars,disasters (Jesus)   5/1/06 Vol. 43

America's disasters punishment for sin (Jesus)   10/23/07 Vol. 49

America's epitaph with every abortion (Jesus)   9/20/02 Vol. 28

America's fuel needs becoming a weakspot (Jesus)   10/14/04 Vol. 37

America's government needs moral foundation (Jesus)   2/13/01 Vol. 22

America's grave decay from within (Jesus)   12/27/05 Vol. 41

America's judgment needs repentance (Jesus)   9/27/05 Vol. 40

America's military tested by Iraq (Jesus)   3/20/03 Vol. 30

America's military weak for takeover (Jesus)   9/11/02 Vol. 28

America's military weakened for takeover (Jesus)   2/26/03 Vol. 30

America's morals causing chastisements (Jesus)   12/30/04 Vol. 37

America's path to destruction (Jesus)   11/25/05 Vol. 41

America's pride and idol worship punished (Jesus)   7/31/06 Vol. 44

America's problems from immoral society (Jesus)   4/26/06 Vol. 43

America's ruin immorality & extended wars (Jesus)   1/30/02 Vol. 26

America's satellites vulnerable to lasers (Jesus)   2/21/06 Vol. 42

America's sins anchor holding us back (Jesus)   2/13/01 Vol. 22

America's sins are sealing our fate (Jesus)   2/18/04 Vol. 34

America's sins bring ruin in seeming affluence (Jesus)   1/14/04 Vol. 34

America's sins lack of repentance (Jesus)   6/1/06 Vol. 43

America's sins lack of repentance (Jesus)	6/20/06 Vol. 43
America's sins path to destruction (Jesus)	2/21/05 Vol. 38
America's sins to be our downfall (Jesus)	3/29/00 Vol. 18
America's sins to meet God's swift justice (Jesus)	12/26/05 Vol. 41
America's sovereignty threatened by one worlders (Jesus)	5/25/07 Vol. 47
America's wars destroy homes & lives (Jesus)	2/13/03 Vol. 30
America's weather vulnerable to storms (Jesus)	3/14/06 Vol. 42
anchor in faith unwavering in resolve (Jesus)	9/18/99 Vol. 16
angel from Heaven Catherine (Mark)	9/3/95 Vol. 3
angel help by prayer no fear of demons (Jesus)	12/31/06 Vol. 45
angel of refuges will protect from evil ones (Jesus)	5/5/00 Vol. 19
angel power to assist in tribulation (Jesus)	1/18/00 Vol. 18
angel power to fight demons (Jesus)	9/2/03 Vol. 32
angel protection call on Jesus for (Jesus)	9/5/06 Vol. 44
Angela's funeral love of Mary (Jesus)	7/20/06 Vol. 44
angels adoration vigil (Jesus)	3/6/95 Vol. 2
angels allow us not to be seen (Jesus)	1/15/04 Vol. 34
angels angel of destruction (Jesus)	8/18/96 Vol. 4
angels announce miraculous births (Jesus)	12/19/05 Vol. 41
angels battle and judgment (Jesus)	4/27/96 Vol. 3
angels battle of good and evil (Jesus)	4/20/96 Vol. 3
angels battle of good and evil (Jesus)	6/14/95 Vol. 2
angels block finding us,Exodus (Jesus)	10/29/96 Vol. 5
angels blowing the trumpets (Jesus)	9/25/97 Vol. 8
angels book of life (Jesus)	12/14/94 Vol. 2
angels book of life,mark forehead (Jesus)	12/26/96 Vol. 5
angels call on for help (Jesus)	6/1/05 Vol. 39
angels call on for protection (Jesus)	2/27/03 Vol. 30
angels call on them for help (St. Michael)	7/20/97 Vol. 8
angels call on them in need (Mary)	7/5/97 Vol. 8
angels can bring fury on earth (Jesus)	11/17/05 Vol. 41
angels chain demons, evil people (Jesus)	7/15/97 Vol. 8
angels clear caves & tunnels (Jesus)	7/27/06 Vol. 44
angels constantly praise God (Mark,angel)	6/28/01 Vol. 23
angels difficult to help in serious sin (St. Michael)	2/26/98 Vol. 10
angels for protection (Jesus)	9/21/06 Vol. 44
angels gather evil and faithful (Jesus)	10/27/97 Vol. 9
angels give Bread of Angels (Jesus)	9/30/96 Vol. 4
angels gleaming bright light (St. Michael)	9/29/03 Vol. 32
angels guardian angel (Mark)	7/8/94 Vol. 2
angels guide souls to heaven (Jesus)	3/30/97 Vol. 6
angels harvest (Jesus)	11/16/94 Vol. 2
angels lead to best place (Jesus)	8/11/01 Vol. 24
angels lead to refuge (Jesus)	1/12/04 Vol. 34
angels lead to refuge or cave (Jesus)	6/18/99 Vol. 15
angels lead to refuges (Jesus)	10/19/01 Vol. 25
angels lead to refuges (Jesus)	8/24/00 Vol. 20
angels lead to refuges (Jesus)	9/7/00 Vol. 20
angels lead to refuges,share love (Jesus)	7/24/97 Vol. 8
angels lead to safe havens (Jesus)	2/13/98 Vol. 10
angels lead to safe havens (Jesus)	1/20/99 Vol. 14
angels lead to safety (Jesus)	7/2/99 Vol. 16
angels lead us (Jesus)	5/14/96 Vol. 3
angels lead us in battle (Jesus)	2/18/99 Vol. 14
angels lead us to safe havens (Jesus)	10/18/99 Vol. 17
angels lead us to safe havens (Jesus)	5/29/99 Vol. 15
angels lead us to the refuges (Jesus)	10/7/06 Vol. 45
angels lead with physical sign (Jesus)	1/27/01 Vol. 22
angels lead you for protection (Jesus)	2/5/98 Vol. 10
angels light the caves (Jesus)	6/11/96 Vol. 3
angels make only one choice (St. Michael)	9/29/05 Vol. 40
Angels mark foreheads,book life (Jesus)	3/13/97 Vol. 6
angels marking cross on foreheads (Jesus)	7/3/98 Vol. 12
angels marking crosses on foreheads (Jesus)	8/16/06 Vol. 44
angels messengers & guides (Jesus)	1/9/97 Vol. 6
angels more powerful protection (Jesus)	11/11/97 Vol. 9
angels need spiritual guard up (St. Michael)	9/29/98 Vol. 12
angels personal (Mark)	5/24/94 Vol. 1
angels praise God in every tabernacle (Jesus)	4/26/03 Vol. 31
angels praise of Infant Jesus (Jesus)	1/1/06 Vol. 42
angels pray to them for help (Jesus)	10/16/97 Vol. 9
angels prepare 1st & 2nd coming (Jesus)	12/10/97 Vol. 9
angels prepare for the evil age (Jesus)	11/12/96 Vol. 5
angels prepare for tribulation (God the Father)	5/20/99 Vol. 15
angels present at prayer groups (Jesus)	1/27/00 Vol. 18
angels present at tabernacles (Jesus)	1/27/00 Vol. 18
angels protect children in trial (Jesus)	1/21/99 Vol. 14
angels protect each refuge (Jesus)	5/11/02 Vol. 27
Angels protect little ones (Jesus)	1/23/97 Vol. 6
angels protect refuges (Jesus)	9/20/00 Vol. 20
angels protect us (Jesus)	7/21/98 Vol. 12
angels protect us in our work (Jesus)	3/15/98 Vol. 10
angels protected & provided for (Jesus)	7/8/99 Vol. 16
angels protection at refuges (Jesus)	6/5/01 Vol. 23
angels protection from Antichrist (Jesus)	9/15/97 Vol. 8
angels protection in tribulation (Jesus)	10/26/97 Vol. 9
angels protection of remnant (Jesus)	7/15/02 Vol. 28
angels ready for battle (Jesus)	10/5/06 Vol. 45
angels return (Jesus)	5/30/95 Vol. 2
Angels safe havens (Jesus)	8/25/96 Vol. 4
angels serve and adore God (Jesus)	3/20/98 Vol. 10
angels shield us from evil ones (Jesus)	2/22/07 Vol. 46
angels slay evil ones at refuges (Jesus)	6/2/04 Vol. 35
angels sound trumpets last days (Jesus)	8/9/97 Vol. 8

angels strength in end days (Mary) — 1/1/98 Vol. 10

angels strengthen & protect (Jesus) — 3/3/97 Vol. 6

angels test America with storms (Jesus) — 9/22/05 Vol. 40

angels time (Jesus) — 12/1/93 Vol. 1

angels to bring Holy Communion (Jesus) — 12/16/00 Vol. 21

angels to bring Hosts (Jesus) — 1/3/08 Vol. 50

angels to lead and protect (Jesus) — 7/1/03 Vol. 32

angels to protect messengers (Jesus) — 10/5/01 Vol. 25

angels tribulation (Jesus) — 2/13/95 Vol. 2

angels visible at safe havens (Jesus) — 1/14/99 Vol. 14

angels wheat — 10/30/93 Vol. 1

angels will assist us (Jesus) — 5/21/99 Vol. 15

angels will protect our souls (Mark) — 6/17/99 Vol. 15

angels with red cloud of God's wrath (Jesus) — 4/9/98 Vol. 11

angels & manna feed Hosts, healing, water (Jesus) — 7/26/00 Vol. 20

angels & saints one with God (Jesus) — 5/8/03 Vol. 31

angels for protection Holy Family and refuges (Jesus) — 12/31/06 Vol. 45

angels in church around the Blessed Sacrament (Jesus) — 2/23/08 Vol. 50

angels in last battle great chastisement (Jesus) — 3/18/99 Vol. 14

angels marked souls to be saved (Jesus) — 3/12/99 Vol. 14

angels of Apocalypse famine,pestilence,plagues (Jesus) — 11/3/96 Vol. 5

angels of Revelation blowing trumpets (Jesus) — 12/31/00 Vol. 21

angels over Bethlehem celebration of Redeemer (Jesus) — 12/24/02 Vol. 29

angels preparing to battle Antichrist (Jesus) — 9/16/99 Vol. 16

angels ready for lamp stands,trumpets (St. Michael) — 9/29/99 Vol. 16

angels to give Communion at refuges (Jesus) — 6/17/02 Vol. 27

angels to lead us safe places in tribulation (Mark) — 4/24/97 Vol. 7

angels,guardian examples,guides to salvation (Jesus) — 10/2/00 Vol. 21

angels,tribulation with scrolls and trumpets (Jesus) — 8/21/99 Vol. 16

anger be slow to act (Jesus) — 10/4/03 Vol. 33

anger do not over react (Jesus) — 6/18/01 Vol. 23

anger put aside to love neighbor (Jesus) — 10/28/98 Vol. 13

anger & despair should not consume us (Jesus) — 2/15/00 Vol. 18

anger & hate need to be managed, stop killing (Jesus) — 8/26/04 Vol. 36

anger management patience in difficulties, problems (Jesus) — 9/27/04 Vol. 36

anger with God do not rebel (Jesus) — 2/26/04 Vol. 34

anger, impatience curb devil's attacks (Jesus) — 3/8/04 Vol. 34

anger, righteous do not condemn others (Jesus) — 7/28/03 Vol. 32

anger, sins of avoid them (Jesus) — 11/10/06 Vol. 45

anger,greed abide without love in heart (Jesus) — 3/16/00 Vol. 18

Angie funeral message (Jesus) — 4/2/07 Vol. 47

angry response curb with slow reaction (Jesus) — 9/10/01 Vol. 24

animals in harmony on new earth (Jesus) — 9/16/96 Vol. 4

animals no fear in Era of Peace (Jesus) — 6/11/98 Vol. 11

animals part of balance of nature (Jesus) — 8/7/07 Vol. 48

animals vs. man compete for land use (Jesus) — 8/7/07 Vol. 48

Anitchrist one worlders' support (Jesus) — 11/20/06 Vol. 45

annihilation of nations pray to stop (Mary) — 2/19/98 Vol. 10

anniversary personal (Mary) — 7/3/96 Vol. 3

Anniversary blessing 38th wedding anniversary (Jesus) — 7/3/03 Vol. 32

anniversary of messages testing souls (Jesus) — 7/21/94 Vol. 2

anniversary, 40th prayer life avoids divorce (Jesus) — 7/3/05 Vol. 40

annoyances pray for Jesus' mercy (Jesus) — 3/8/03 Vol. 30

annulments in unusual cases (Jesus) — 8/18/06 Vol. 44

Annunciation God's favor (Mary) — 3/18/98 Vol. 10

Annunciation important time for Mary (Mary) — 3/31/08 Vol. 50

Annunciation joined hearts,flesh with Mary (Jesus) — 3/25/04 Vol. 34

Annunciation Messiah for mankind (Jesus) — 12/20/06 Vol. 45

Annunciation relation to Jesus and mission (Jesus) — 4/4/05 Vol. 39

Annunciation second coming (Mary) — 12/20/93 Vol. 1

Annunciation suffered embarrassment (Jesus) — 3/25/03 Vol. 30

answer prayers (Jesus) — 5/9/95 Vol. 2

anti-abortion laws thwarted by liberal courts (Jesus) — 12/1/05 Vol. 41

antibiotics failing new drugs fail vs. disease (Jesus) — 4/27/99 Vol. 15

Antichrist about to assume power (Jesus) — 7/28/98 Vol. 12

Antichrist abuse with chips (Jesus) — 2/15/04 Vol. 34

Antichrist after Warning (Jesus) — 7/9/03 Vol. 32

Antichrist agents of the UN (Jesus) — 7/26/97 Vol. 8

Antichrist allowed hour of control (Jesus) — 11/18/05 Vol. 41

Antichrist an Arab leader (Jesus) — 8/8/06 Vol. 44

Antichrist an Arab, brief reign (Jesus) — 8/25/04 Vol. 36

Antichrist and mark of the beast (Jesus) — 8/4/99 Vol. 16

Antichrist and New World Order (Jesus) — 4/19/01 Vol. 23

Antichrist and one world people (Jesus) — 2/6/98 Vol. 10

Antichrist and second beast chained (Jesus) — 6/11/06 Vol. 43

Antichrist annointed by priests in Egypt (Jesus) — 8/23/07 Vol. 48

Antichrist answer unrest in world (Jesus) — 1/30/03 Vol. 30

Antichrist appeared as an Arab (Jesus) — 3/10/04 Vol. 34

Antichrist appears as Moslem leader (Jesus) — 5/10/01 Vol. 23

Antichrist appears signs & wonders (Jesus) — 11/18/97 Vol. 9

Antichrist Arab & religious leader (Jesus) — 10/5/01 Vol. 25

Antichrist arises from Egypt (Jesus) — 12/28/00 Vol. 21

Antichrist arises from world war (Jesus) — 7/12/06 Vol. 44

Antichrist as an Arab (Jesus) — 7/2/01 Vol. 24

Antichrist as man of peace, tyrant (Jesus) — 8/29/06 Vol. 44

Antichrist as world ruler (Jesus) — 2/1/07 Vol. 46

Antichrist assumes power,bankers (Jesus) — 5/20/99 Vol. 15

Antichrist at height of power defeated (Jesus) — 6/3/04 Vol. 35

Antichrist authority over nations (Jesus) — 12/12/96 Vol. 5

Antichrist avoid any information,pictures (Jesus) — 8/30/04 Vol. 36

Antichrist avoid facing,chips in hand (Jesus) — 11/3/00 Vol. 21

Antichrist avoid his evil gaze (Jesus) — 11/13/03 Vol. 33

Antichrist avoid his signs & wonders (Jesus) — 4/16/98 Vol. 11

Antichrist avoid looking at eyes (Jesus) — 12/23/05 Vol. 41

Remember to Pray First

We were with Mary's Pilgrims again in Italy. This time we were at the Vatican on Dec. 9, 2000 as they were completing the visits for the Holy Year. There were tens of thousands of people in front of St. Peter's Basilica waiting to go through the Holy Doors. Since we had only a few hours before boarding the ship, our tour director was asking if we could go in the exit side. I was taking pictures and when I turned around, everyone in the group was gone. I thought our group got permission and they may have gone in. It turns out that I was the only one to get in. The original plan for anyone lost was to meet at the Obelisk in the center of the square. So I went there with confidence and prayed the rosary. After an hour and it was getting dark at 5:30 p.m., I was getting a bit nervous. I went to the Swiss guard station and they did not understand English, so they were not much help.

Since the group went shopping instead of going into St. Peter's, they changed the meeting place for anyone who got lost to go to the shopping area. John did not know that I was missing until I did not show up on the bus. After John visited three police stations and tried to call for me, he remembered that he had not prayed to find me. Just as he finished his prayer, I walked out of the crowd between the pillars of an arch. I have to say that I was about to stop at the restroom, but something just pushed me to go forward. Now how do we get to St. Paul's Outside the Walls to meet the group? All the taxis were full and we were about out of time before the ship was about to leave. At that moment, we saw the spiritual director of Colette Coulombe walking toward us. He is from Canada and was studying in Rome. He called one of his seminarians over to drive us and we again made it by the hand of God. Jesus reminded us that we need to <u>always pray</u> first so He can make things go smoother.

Message Reference: December 9, 2000 (volume 21)

Antichrist avoid worshiping (Jesus)	5/10/05 Vol. 39	Antichrist charisma & demonic power (Jesus)	1/5/02 Vol. 26
Antichrist backed by the rich (Jesus)	2/3/06 Vol. 42	Antichrist charisma,deceiver (Jesus)	2/22/99 Vol. 14
Antichrist bankers and UN control (Jesus)	6/28/01 Vol. 23	Antichrist chip to buy and sell (Jesus)	8/24/97 Vol. 8
Antichrist battle for souls (Jesus)	5/15/97 Vol. 7	Antichrist chip,mark of the beast (Jesus)	5/11/96 Vol. 3
Antichrist battle of good and evil (Holy Spirit)	10/16/96 Vol. 5	Antichrist choice of good or evil (Jesus)	10/16/01 Vol. 25
Antichrist brief reign (Jesus)	10/31/07 Vol. 49	Antichrist churches closed,burned (Jesus)	1/11/98 Vol. 10
Antichrist brief reign is soon (Jesus)	3/12/05 Vol. 38	Antichrist claims man of peace (Jesus)	8/2/03 Vol. 32
Antichrist brief reign of evil (Jesus)	1/20/99 Vol. 14	Antichrist cold blue light in the sky (Jesus)	11/21/96 Vol. 5
Antichrist brings religious persecution (Jesus)	5/27/04 Vol. 35	Antichrist cold with no love (Jesus)	4/20/98 Vol. 11
Antichrist call for protection from (Jesus)	5/27/97 Vol. 7	Antichrist come to power by one worlders (Jesus)	2/11/03 Vol. 30
Antichrist chaos (Jesus)	1/29/96 Vol. 3	Antichrist come to power in Europe (Jesus)	1/4/04 Vol. 34
Antichrist chaos causing takeover (Jesus)	8/6/98 Vol. 12	Antichrist comes to power after Warning (Jesus)	4/20/05 Vol. 39
Antichrist chaos in cities over food (Jesus)	9/1/96 Vol. 4	Antichrist comes to power in tribulation (Jesus)	8/24/06 Vol. 44

Antichrist comet sign of being on earth (Jesus) — 9/3/04 Vol. 36
Antichrist comet,sign in the sky (Jesus) — 5/14/96 Vol. 3
Antichrist contrived shortages (Jesus) — 3/16/96 Vol. 3
Antichrist control by chips in the body (Jesus) — 11/22/00 Vol. 21
Antichrist control food,jobs,money (Jesus) — 1/21/99 Vol. 14
Antichrist control in chips, weather (Jesus) — 3/15/01 Vol. 22
Antichrist control is short (Jesus) — 2/16/07 Vol. 46
Antichrist control mind (Jesus) — 7/24/97 Vol. 8
Antichrist control minds by TV (Jesus) — 4/19/02 Vol. 27
Antichrist control of all nations (Jesus) — 6/9/05 Vol. 39
Antichrist control of communications (Jesus) — 11/14/96 Vol. 5
Antichrist control of food and jobs (Jesus) — 1/9/97 Vol. 6
Antichrist control of food,jobs,money (Jesus) — 7/7/98 Vol. 12
Antichrist control of media (Jesus) — 11/10/97 Vol. 9
Antichrist control of TV (Jesus) — 6/9/99 Vol. 15
Antichrist control of UN troops (Jesus) — 8/8/97 Vol. 8
Antichrist control people to worship him (Jesus) — 4/15/01 Vol. 23
Antichrist control through chips (Jesus) — 9/26/02 Vol. 28
Antichrist control through devices (Jesus) — 7/29/97 Vol. 8
Antichrist control with electronics (Jesus) — 5/23/98 Vol. 11
Antichrist control world by chips (Jesus) — 5/2/02 Vol. 27
Antichrist controlling government (Jesus) — 3/12/96 Vol. 3
Antichrist controls those with chip (Jesus) — 6/8/98 Vol. 11
Antichrist convert before tribulation (Jesus) — 5/21/95 Vol. 2
Antichrist declaration amidst chaos (Jesus) — 2/10/98 Vol. 10
Antichrist Declaration is near (Jesus) — 5/10/97 Vol. 7
Antichrist declaration not far off (Jesus) — 8/7/97 Vol. 8
Antichrist declaration triggered (Jesus) — 2/19/98 Vol. 10
Antichrist declared then victory near (Jesus) — 6/4/02 Vol. 27
Antichrist defeated at height of power (Jesus) — 4/26/01 Vol. 23
Antichrist defeated by angels (Jesus) — 5/10/03 Vol. 31
Antichrist defeated when conquers world (Jesus) — 3/20/03 Vol. 30
Antichrist defeated when in power (Jesus) — 3/15/05 Vol. 38
Antichrist demon incarnated body (Jesus) — 7/27/94 Vol. 2
Antichrist demonic powers & control (Jesus) — 2/3/03 Vol. 30
Antichrist destroyed by comet (Jesus) — 3/5/05 Vol. 38
Antichrist devil crushed (Jesus) — 12/12/94 Vol. 2
Antichrist do not be deceived by miracles (Jesus) — 10/9/03 Vol. 33
Antichrist do not believe illusions (Jesus) — 3/19/98 Vol. 10
Antichrist do not believe lies,illusions (Jesus) — 6/14/98 Vol. 11
Antichrist do not follow him (Jesus) — 5/28/98 Vol. 11
Antichrist do not follow him (Jesus) — 2/28/98 Vol. 10
Antichrist do not give in to (Jesus) — 6/18/01 Vol. 23
Antichrist do not keep his literature (Jesus) — 10/15/97 Vol. 9
Antichrist do not look at (Jesus) — 5/30/02 Vol. 27
Antichrist do not look at eyes (Jesus) — 11/4/05 Vol. 41
Antichrist do not look on him (Jesus) — 11/20/97 Vol. 9

Antichrist do not take chip in body (Jesus) — 7/21/05 Vol. 40
Antichrist do not take chips (Jesus) — 5/30/01 Vol. 23
Antichrist do not watch on TV (Jesus) — 2/10/00 Vol. 18
Antichrist do not watch on TV (Jesus) — 10/27/99 Vol. 17
Antichrist do not watch TV screen (Jesus) — 3/20/02 Vol. 26
Antichrist does not want evil exposed (Jesus) — 11/17/98 Vol. 13
Antichrist don't watch TV,literature (Jesus) — 12/26/97 Vol. 9
Antichrist double cross of leaders (Jesus) — 7/9/07 Vol. 48
Antichrist dramatic events come (God the Father) — 8/7/99 Vol. 16
Antichrist draws people to stadiums (Jesus) — 2/12/06 Vol. 42
Antichrist electric devices (Jesus) — 11/2/94 Vol. 2
Antichrist electronic devices, mark (Jesus) — 2/27/96 Vol. 3
Antichrist electronics in cars (Jesus) — 3/18/97 Vol. 6
Antichrist embraced by New Age (Jesus) — 7/7/02 Vol. 28
Antichrist empire destroyed (Jesus) — 9/7/00 Vol. 20
Antichrist empty promises (Jesus) — 2/1/98 Vol. 10
Antichrist events speeded up (Jesus) — 4/21/95 Vol. 2
Antichrist everything in place for (Jesus) — 11/23/99 Vol. 17
Antichrist evil control over Europe (Jesus) — 10/10/02 Vol. 29
Antichrist evil vanquished (Jesus) — 7/1/03 Vol. 32
Antichrist faithful outlawed (Jesus) — 1/5/98 Vol. 10
Antichrist false peace & illusions (Jesus) — 10/22/96 Vol. 5
Antichrist famine,plagues,sky signs (Jesus) — 12/23/96 Vol. 5
Antichrist father of lies (Jesus) — 9/8/03 Vol. 32
Antichrist father of lies & illusions (Jesus) — 10/24/96 Vol. 5
Antichrist follow to save money (Jesus) — 6/20/02 Vol. 27
Antichrist food/jobs/hiding (Jesus) — 5/4/96 Vol. 3
Antichrist forced labor (Jesus) — 9/26/02 Vol. 28
Antichrist general crisis,financial (Jesus) — 9/21/97 Vol. 8
Antichrist given base of control (Jesus) — 8/24/98 Vol. 12
Antichrist government controls (Jesus) — 3/11/97 Vol. 6
Antichrist ground work laid for (Jesus) — 1/26/04 Vol. 34
Antichrist guard your souls (Jesus) — 12/27/96 Vol. 5
Antichrist guardian angel (Jesus) — 7/1/95 Vol. 3
Antichrist has Clinton replaced (Jesus) — 10/23/99 Vol. 17
Antichrist has taste for killing (Jesus) — 9/10/98 Vol. 12
Antichrist head crushed (Jesus) — 10/31/94 Vol. 2
Antichrist head of European Union (Jesus) — 3/11/06 Vol. 42
Antichrist help aura (David) — 6/7/95 Vol. 2
Antichrist hide from imposter (Jesus) — 5/1/97 Vol. 7
Antichrist hiding, signs (Jesus) — 2/20/97 Vol. 6
Antichrist hiding,control TV & radio (Jesus) — 10/30/96 Vol. 5
Antichrist hiding,sacramentals (Jesus) — 4/24/96 Vol. 3
Antichrist high priest (Jesus) — 10/22/94 Vol. 2
Antichrist his mark to buy and sell (Jesus) — 7/25/06 Vol. 44
Antichrist his power sends to caves (Jesus) — 4/24/97 Vol. 7
Antichrist his powers and plans (Jesus) — 9/13/96 Vol. 4

Antichrist Holy Lands (Jesus) 11/9/94 Vol. 2
Antichrist hypnotic eyes (Jesus) 6/10/02 Vol. 27
Antichrist hypnotize 10/14/93 Vol. 1
Antichrist illusions & false signs (Jesus) 4/3/97 Vol. 7
Antichrist illusions & tricks (Jesus) 4/26/01 Vol. 23
Antichrist illusions in the sky (Jesus) 2/20/97 Vol. 6
Antichrist illusions, TV, control (Jesus) 3/31/98 Vol. 10
Antichrist image of beast on altar (Jesus) 2/3/99 Vol. 14
Antichrist in stadiums for control (Jesus) 10/9/06 Vol. 45
Antichrist in turban, to control UN (Jesus) 10/26/00 Vol. 21
Antichrist inspired by Satan (Jesus) 7/17/01 Vol. 24
Antichrist internet web,buying & selling (Jesus) 8/24/01 Vol. 24
Antichrist Jesus' victory over him (Jesus) 4/21/03 Vol. 31
Antichrist Jesus will triumph over fast (Jesus) 5/14/98 Vol. 11
Antichrist justice falling on his reign (Jesus) 3/5/98 Vol. 10
Antichrist kills for fame & power (Jesus) 7/1/99 Vol. 16
Antichrist lasers and illusions (Jesus) 6/19/97 Vol. 7
Antichrist leader of one world religion (Jesus) 6/19/05 Vol. 39
AntiChrist leaders eliminated (Jesus) 7/22/96 Vol. 4
Antichrist leads New World Order (Jesus) 6/10/00 Vol. 19
Antichrist lives on the earth (Jesus) 12/8/05 Vol. 41
Antichrist man of peace, charisma (Jesus) 2/18/00 Vol. 18
Antichrist manna, angels, refuge (Jesus) 7/9/97 Vol. 8
Antichrist mark of the beast (Jesus) 10/16/94 Vol. 2
Antichrist mark of the beast (Jesus) 12/28/97 Vol. 9
Antichrist mark of the beast (Jesus) 11/12/93 Vol. 1
Antichrist mark of the beast (Jesus) 2/21/97 Vol. 6
Antichrist mark of the beast (Jesus) 3/11/99 Vol. 14
Antichrist messages fulfilled (Jesus) 6/2/97 Vol. 7
Antichrist messengers speaking stops (Jesus) 4/2/98 Vol. 11
Antichrist mind control (Jesus) 1/9/97 Vol. 6
Antichrist mind control, attractions (Jesus) 7/30/98 Vol. 12
Antichrist misleads by lies,miracles (Jesus) 5/14/99 Vol. 15
Antichrist never take mark of beast (Jesus) 12/9/97 Vol. 9
Antichrist no pictures or literature of (Jesus) 6/9/99 Vol. 15
Antichrist omens in the sky (Jesus) 1/3/97 Vol. 6
Antichrist one world coup (Jesus) 1/30/97 Vol. 6
Antichrist one world order (Jesus) 8/7/94 Vol. 2
Antichrist one world order (Jesus) 7/19/94 Vol. 2
Antichrist one world order (Jesus) 12/7/94 Vol. 2
Antichrist one world people (Jesus) 9/12/00 Vol. 20
Antichrist one world people with (Jesus) 10/23/97 Vol. 9
Antichrist one world religion for control (Jesus) 7/13/00 Vol. 20
Antichrist panic & chaos, takeover (Jesus) 10/27/97 Vol. 9
Antichrist perfoms illusions by satellite (Jesus) 7/27/98 Vol. 12
Antichrist perform great signs (Jesus) 10/23/97 Vol. 9
Antichrist persecuted for faith (Jesus) 1/16/97 Vol. 6

Antichrist power in his eyes (Jesus) 6/21/01 Vol. 23
Antichrist power in pictures & books (Jesus) 6/19/97 Vol. 7
Antichrist power of persuasion (Jesus) 4/2/98 Vol. 11
Antichrist power through his eyes (Jesus) 8/11/03 Vol. 32
Antichrist powers beyond human (Jesus) 11/27/96 Vol. 5
Antichrist powers of suggestion (Jesus) 4/8/97 Vol. 7
Antichrist pray for protection (Jesus) 3/29/96 Vol. 3
Antichrist pray to avoid (Jesus) 5/9/97 Vol. 7
Antichrist preparations to take over (Jesus) 11/14/96 Vol. 5
Antichrist promises problems solved (Jesus) 7/19/01 Vol. 24
Antichrist promises to save us (Jesus) 3/4/99 Vol. 14
Antichrist protection 10/22/93 Vol. 1
Antichrist put in power by central bankers (Jesus) 7/12/07 Vol. 48
Antichrist raised up from Egypt (Jesus) 12/28/98 Vol. 13
Antichrist ready to assume power (Jesus) 5/14/99 Vol. 15
Antichrist refuse chips (Jesus) 3/31/98 Vol. 10
Antichrist refuse enticements (Jesus) 2/12/99 Vol. 14
Antichrist refuse his food, jobs (Jesus) 1/20/00 Vol. 18
Antichrist refuse his jobs and chips (Jesus) 11/28/00 Vol. 21
Antichrist refuse his jobs,chips,worship (Jesus) 10/31/03 Vol. 33
Antichrist refuse to look at his eyes (Jesus) 6/9/05 Vol. 39
Antichrist refuse to watch on TV (Jesus) 4/6/00 Vol. 19
Antichrist reign ended (Jesus) 4/1/07 Vol. 47
Antichrist reign will be short (Jesus) 12/5/99 Vol. 17
Antichrist reign will not be long (Jesus) 11/16/05 Vol. 41
Antichrist rise to power coming (Jesus) 9/22/99 Vol. 16
Antichrist rule in financial collapse (Jesus) 3/5/98 Vol. 10
Antichrist satellites and chips (Jesus) 5/15/97 Vol. 7
Antichrist scorpions (Jesus) 9/19/94 Vol. 2
Antichrist secret armies,hiding (Jesus) 10/31/96 Vol. 5
Antichrist see as father of lies (Jesus) 7/24/97 Vol. 8
Antichrist seek souls by chips (Jesus) 3/1/01 Vol. 22
Antichrist send fire down from sky (Jesus) 5/31/02 Vol. 27
Antichrist short reign of evil (Jesus) 4/13/03 Vol. 31
Antichrist sign in the heavens (Jesus) 12/16/96 Vol. 5
Antichrist sign of in the heavens (Jesus) 11/15/96 Vol. 5
Antichrist signs of his time coming (Jesus) 6/9/03 Vol. 31
Antichrist smart cards & chips (Jesus) 8/15/00 Vol. 20
Antichrist smite as he comes to power (Jesus) 4/16/98 Vol. 11
Antichrist smited as power gained (Jesus) 3/8/99 Vol. 14
Antichrist society crumbles (Jesus) 12/28/97 Vol. 9
Antichrist soon to come to power (Jesus) 2/7/04 Vol. 34
Antichrist soon to declare himself (Jesus) 10/27/97 Vol. 9
Antichrist souls (Jesus) 6/17/94 Vol. 1
Antichrist spiritual weapons (Jesus) 1/19/96 Vol. 3
Antichrist spiritual weapons,angels (Jesus) 1/26/97 Vol. 6
Antichrist spying on our habits (Jesus) 6/24/97 Vol. 7

Antichrist stadium events,defeat (Jesus)	10/23/97 Vol. 9	Antichrist to lead the world (Jesus)	2/15/07 Vol. 46
Antichrist stage set by famine, war (Jesus)	7/17/98 Vol. 12	Antichrist to persecute religions (Jesus)	10/19/01 Vol. 25
Antichrist stand up & do not deny faith (Jesus)	3/31/04 Vol. 34	Antichrist to remove religion,priests (Jesus)	10/19/98 Vol. 13
Antichrist superhuman powers (Jesus)	5/5/98 Vol. 11	Antichrist to remove religious freedom (Jesus)	2/14/02 Vol. 26
Antichrist superhuman powers (Jesus)	7/11/98 Vol. 12	Antichrist to solve problems (Jesus)	6/10/98 Vol. 11
Antichrist superhuman powers,stopped (Jesus)	9/17/98 Vol. 12	Antichrist to solve world's problems (Jesus)	7/18/02 Vol. 28
Antichrist support of media,illusions (Jesus)	12/11/97 Vol. 9	Antichrist to torment non-believers (Jesus)	12/14/06 Vol. 45
Antichrist supported by one world people (Jesus)	11/17/05 Vol. 41	Antichrist to use large stadiums (Jesus)	2/15/07 Vol. 46
Antichrist take nothing from him (Jesus)	8/28/01 Vol. 24	Antichrist to use sports stadiums (Jesus)	11/2/06 Vol. 45
Antichrist take over all governments (Jesus)	7/24/99 Vol. 16	Antichrist to use technology for control (Jesus)	1/13/06 Vol. 42
Antichrist take over of country (Jesus)	12/5/96 Vol. 5	Antichrist trade groups (Jesus)	5/6/97 Vol. 7
Antichrist take power in European Union (Jesus)	8/23/07 Vol. 48	Antichrist tribulation (Jesus)	5/19/95 Vol. 2
Antichrist takeover by one worlders (Jesus)	7/31/01 Vol. 24	Antichrist triumph (Jesus)	7/18/94 Vol. 2
Antichrist takeover by world unions (Jesus)	5/5/07 Vol. 47	Antichrist triumph (Jesus)	7/17/94 Vol. 2
Antichrist takeover in chaos (Jesus)	10/6/99 Vol. 17	Antichrist UN helps takeover (Jesus)	9/11/03 Vol. 32
Antichrist takeover in Europe (Jesus)	11/30/01 Vol. 25	Antichrist UN troops, helicopters (Jesus)	1/20/97 Vol. 6
Antichrist takeover prepared (Jesus)	5/10/01 Vol. 23	Antichrist UN/mark beast/hiding (Jesus)	12/29/95 Vol. 3
Antichrist takeover soon after Warning (Jesus)	10/6/03 Vol. 33	Antichrist unnatural powers (Jesus)	12/4/95 Vol. 3
Antichrist takeover when US falls (Jesus)	12/17/01 Vol. 25	Antichrist unprecedented evil (Jesus)	7/16/03 Vol. 32
Antichrist technology in place for (Jesus)	1/25/98 Vol. 10	Antichrist unrest, hiding & angels (Jesus)	12/19/96 Vol. 5
Antichrist terrorism/peacemaker (Jesus)	5/25/96 Vol. 3	Antichrist use war or martial law (Jesus)	1/4/99 Vol. 14
Antichrist test of the end times (Jesus)	9/19/96 Vol. 4	Antichrist uses illusions, magic (Jesus)	6/10/99 Vol. 15
Antichrist test signs in the sky (Jesus)	1/30/98 Vol. 10	Antichrist vanquished at heigh of power (Jesus)	5/29/01 Vol. 23
Antichrist test the spirit (Jesus)	4/20/98 Vol. 11	Antichrist war (Jesus)	3/1/94 Vol. 1
Antichrist time is near (Jesus)	5/13/03 Vol. 31	Antichrist watch England (Jesus)	11/7/97 Vol. 9
Antichrist time of tribulation (Jesus)	12/16/04 Vol. 37	Antichrist web of evil (Jesus)	5/2/96 Vol. 3
Antichrist to appear as man of peace (Jesus)	11/30/00 Vol. 21	Antichrist will attempt to destroy Church (Jesus)	5/2/05 Vol. 39
Antichrist to assume power in Europe (Jesus)	1/20/03 Vol. 30	Antichrist will be Arab leader (Jesus)	4/4/02 Vol. 27
Antichrist to assume seat of power (Jesus)	11/20/06 Vol. 45	Antichrist will be defeated quickly (Jesus)	4/9/05 Vol. 39
Antichrist to be allowed his hour (Jesus)	4/22/05 Vol. 39	Antichrist will be overcome,Era of Peace (Jesus)	10/11/04 Vol. 37
Antichrist to be chained in hell (Jesus)	7/7/04 Vol. 36	Antichrist will claim to be Christ (Jesus)	11/21/00 Vol. 21
Antichrist to close churches (Jesus)	4/21/05 Vol. 39	Antichrist will claim to be Jesus (Jesus)	8/14/03 Vol. 32
Antichrist to come in power in chaos (Jesus)	7/26/98 Vol. 12	Antichrist will control minds (Jesus)	5/2/01 Vol. 23
Antichrist to come in time of chaos (Jesus)	11/8/01 Vol. 25	Antichrist will control the police (Jesus)	5/5/05 Vol. 39
Antichrist to come out of Egypt (Jesus)	10/3/01 Vol. 25	Antichrist will double cross leaders (Jesus)	1/18/01 Vol. 22
Antichrist to control all unions (Jesus)	12/1/07 Vol. 49	Antichrist will doublecross leaders (Jesus)	5/7/99 Vol. 15
Antichrist to control food & jobs (Jesus)	8/12/99 Vol. 16	Antichrist will exploit leaders (Jesus)	11/6/97 Vol. 9
Antichrist to control food, money, jobs (Jesus)	12/1/98 Vol. 13	Antichrist will force to worship him (Jesus)	5/29/01 Vol. 23
Antichrist to control international unions (Jesus)	2/7/08 Vol. 50	Antichrist will have demonic powers (Jesus)	2/2/02 Vol. 26
Antichrist to control money (Jesus)	4/25/01 Vol. 23	Antichrist will have shrines to him (Mary)	7/14/02 Vol. 28
Antichrist to control the world (Jesus)	12/6/01 Vol. 25	Antichrist will kill one world people (Jesus)	5/28/98 Vol. 11
Antichrist to control world food,jobs (Jesus)	11/2/98 Vol. 13	Antichrist will kill traitors (Jesus)	7/3/99 Vol. 16
Antichrist to declare himself (Jesus)	8/17/06 Vol. 44	Antichrist will replace world leaders (Jesus)	4/20/99 Vol. 15
Antichrist to declare himself (Jesus)	9/15/97 Vol. 8	Antichrist will rule earth as tyrant (Jesus)	4/7/98 Vol. 11
Antichrist to declare himself (Jesus)	12/17/97 Vol. 9	Antichrist will use churches (Jesus)	12/3/00 Vol. 21
Antichrist to destroy churches (Jesus)	9/22/00 Vol. 20	Antichrist will use TV for control (Jesus)	7/2/01 Vol. 24
Antichrist to hypnotise people (Jesus)	5/25/02 Vol. 27	Antichrist worse than Saddam (Jesus)	3/27/03 Vol. 30

Antichrist worship & suffering (Jesus) 9/11/96 Vol. 4

Antichrist worship his image (Jesus) 6/4/98 Vol. 11

Antichrist & chips refuse both,trust in God (Jesus) 10/19/00 Vol. 21

Antichrist & evil only a short duration (Jesus) 2/28/04 Vol. 34

Antichrist & Satan Jesus' victory over them (Jesus) 7/22/05 Vol. 40

Antichrist as Arab avoid influence,pictures (Jesus) 7/13/00 Vol. 20

Antichrist as tyrant to remove all that is holy (Jesus) 12/10/98 Vol. 13

Antichrist at hand temple built in Jerusalem (Jesus) 12/16/99 Vol. 17

Antichrist blessing Egyptian occult gods (Jesus) 4/26/07 Vol. 47

Antichrist coming Era of Peace soon (Jesus) 12/30/04 Vol. 37

Antichrist coming flee cities from capture (Jesus) 12/5/97 Vol. 9

Antichrist coming from financial collapse (Jesus) 9/29/99 Vol. 16

Antichrist coming preparations for his time (Jesus) 8/3/00 Vol. 20

Antichrist coming prepare soul while time (Jesus) 3/30/05 Vol. 38

Antichrist control through Y2K compliance (Jesus) 9/4/99 Vol. 16

Antichrist declaration accepted by EU (Jesus) 6/9/05 Vol. 39

Antichrist declaration on world people sponsor (Jesus) 4/26/07 Vol. 47

Antichrist declaration rejoice in Jesus' victory (Jesus) 6/21/07 Vol. 47

Antichrist declaration rid electrical devices (Jesus) 11/29/97 Vol. 9

Antichrist declaration seek refuges then (Jesus) 10/12/07 Vol. 49

Antichrist evil brings 3 days of darkness (Jesus) 6/30/07 Vol. 47

Antichrist illusions lights,lasers,holograms (Jesus) 12/1/97 Vol. 9

Anti. in end times tradition of Church in St. John (Jesus) 12/31/03 Vol. 33

Antichrist in stadiums avoid eyes on TV, pictures (Jesus) 1/15/05 Vol. 38

Antichrist in stadiums for worshiping him (Jesus) 9/8/06 Vol. 44

Anti. in stadiums mind control to worship him (Jesus) 8/29/04 Vol. 36

Antichrist or God death vs. life (Jesus) 7/8/05 Vol. 40

Antichrist power base spiritual & material (Jesus) 7/5/00 Vol. 20

Antichrist preparation prayer life,sacramentals (Jesus) 11/13/98 Vol. 13

Antichrist reign by chaos & crash (Jesus) 8/20/01 Vol. 24

Antichrist reign demonic powers, persecution (Jesus) 3/29/04 Vol. 34

Antichrist reign Jesus to allow start (Jesus) 8/2/00 Vol. 20

Antichrist rule all seemed lost (Jesus) 10/26/02 Vol. 29

Antichrist takeover food & financial problems (Jesus) 4/27/00 Vol. 19

Antichrist takeover puppet governments at table (Jesus) 9/28/01 Vol. 24

Antichrist time evil never seen (Jesus) 4/24/07 Vol. 47

Antichrist vs sainthood hell vs heaven (Jesus) 4/7/01 Vol. 23

Antichrist worship encouraged by Antipope (Jesus) 3/15/99 Vol. 14

Antichrist worship refuse chip in hand,forehead (Jesus) 10/13/98 Vol. 13

Antichrist, eyes of avoid, remove TV,monitors (Jesus) 10/12/07 Vol. 49

Antichrist, Moslem Europe base of operations (Jesus) 3/6/01 Vol. 22

Antichrist, Satan to be cast into hell (Jesus) 12/25/06 Vol. 45

Antichrist's coming saved by only God's help (Jesus) 12/28/98 Vol. 13

Antichrist's coming sign of Jesus' coming (Jesus) 11/29/07 Vol. 49

Antichrist's Declaration seek hiding,detention cent (Jesus) 4/29/97 Vol. 7

Antichrist's eyes could control minds (Jesus) 4/29/05 Vol. 39

Antichrist's lies no justice til Jesus comes (Jesus) 12/27/99 Vol. 17

Antichrist's mark attraction to keep money (Jesus) 12/17/99 Vol. 17

Antichrist's mark refuse his food,jobs,etc. (Jesus) 4/5/00 Vol. 19

Antichrist's reign have sacramentals,protection (Jesus) 10/7/06 Vol. 45

Antichrist's reign is short, keep hope (Jesus) 2/4/08 Vol. 50

Antichrist's reign to be brief (Jesus) 8/24/99 Vol. 16

antiques entrance for demon attacks (Jesus) 5/28/07 Vol. 47

anxieties Scripture (Jesus) 1/13/94 Vol. 1

anxieties trust in God for our needs (Jesus) 7/29/04 Vol. 36

apathy lazy in good times (Jesus) 9/8/98 Vol. 12

apathy renewal of faith (Jesus) 3/9/96 Vol. 3

apathy from no testing pleasures threaten faith (Jesus) 7/4/00 Vol. 20

apathy to sin sends souls to hell (Jesus) 3/1/03 Vol. 30

Apocalypse black horseman (Jesus) 6/17/99 Vol. 15

Apocalypse four horsemen (Jesus) 2/23/97 Vol. 6

Apocalypse horses red-war,black-death (Jesus) 7/18/02 Vol. 28

apostasy abortion (Jesus) 12/13/95 Vol. 3

apostasy age comes to a close (God the Father) 1/7/99 Vol. 14

apostasy apostles 9/13/93 Vol. 1

apostasy as tribulation approaches (Jesus) 2/13/98 Vol. 10

apostasy before Antichrist (Jesus) 10/13/97 Vol. 9

apostasy churches (Jesus) 7/6/95 Vol. 3

apostasy churches (Jesus) 3/21/94 Vol. 1

apostasy evangelize now (Jesus) 3/8/97 Vol. 6

apostasy fewer people at church (Jesus) 1/24/02 Vol. 26

apostasy irreverence,theologians (Jesus) 3/7/97 Vol. 6

apostasy lost sense of sin (Jesus) 2/3/99 Vol. 14

Apostasy messengers, signs of (Jesus) 5/1/97 Vol. 7

apostasy needs heaven's intervention (Jesus) 6/19/02 Vol. 27

apostasy New Age,disobedience (Jesus) 12/23/97 Vol. 9

apostasy pray for strength in (Jesus) 7/26/02 Vol. 28

apostasy prophets, messengers sent (Jesus) 6/28/01 Vol. 23

apostasy religious persecution (Jesus) 4/5/95 Vol. 2

apostasy sign of end times (Jesus) 7/6/01 Vol. 24

Apostasy signs of rejection (Jesus) 5/7/97 Vol. 7

apostasy stay faithful to John Paul II (Jesus) 11/6/97 Vol. 9

apostasy stay true to God's Word (Jesus) 9/26/97 Vol. 8

apostasy time to evangelize (Jesus) 10/13/01 Vol. 25

apostasy in clergy causing financial problems (Jesus) 8/24/02 Vol. 28

Apostasy increasing Antichrist seeks worship (Jesus) 4/17/97 Vol. 7

apostasy time before the judgment (Jesus) 11/23/99 Vol. 17

apostasy, age of lazy & weak in faith (Jesus) 1/30/01 Vol. 22

apostasy, age of rich have no need of God (Jesus) 10/31/98 Vol. 13

apostle messengers (Jesus) 11/30/94 Vol. 2

apostles fearful on stormy sea (Jesus) 6/28/05 Vol. 39

apostles fishers of men (Jesus) 8/24/01 Vol. 24

apostles follow faith & tradition (Jesus) 11/13/97 Vol. 9

apostles formed & spread Church (Jesus) 5/7/02 Vol. 27

apostles helped by the Holy Spirit (Jesus) 5/7/05 Vol. 39

apostles salvation (Jesus) 4/17/95 Vol. 2

apostles sent two by two (Jesus) 7/7/99 Vol. 16

apostles strengthened by Holy Spirit (Jesus) 5/24/01 Vol. 23

apostles strengthened by Holy Spirit (Jesus) 6/29/98 Vol. 11

apostles as fisherman called from simple lives (Jesus) 5/13/00 Vol. 19

apostles' hope needed against evil (Jesus) 6/15/00 Vol. 19

apostles, new urgency to coming Antichrist (St. John) 11/1/98 Vol. 13

Apostolate Holy Family holy ground,sacramentals (Mary) 11/9/96 Vol. 5

apostolic calling evangelize (Jesus) 3/4/95 Vol. 2

apostolic calling to save souls (Jesus) 12/27/07 Vol. 49

apparition messages require miracles for authority (Jesus) 12/12/03 Vol. 33

apparition places refuges in tribulation time (Jesus) 8/15/07 Vol. 48

apparition site golden glow of love (Mary) 7/31/97 Vol. 8

Apparition sites hiding places from Antichrist (Mary) 8/6/98 Vol. 12

apparition sites many souls converted (Mary) 11/20/98 Vol. 13

apparition sites refuges (Jesus) 8/15/03 Vol. 32

apparitions affirm truths (Jesus) 12/8/03 Vol. 33

apparitions light beams of messages (Jesus) 12/15/06 Vol. 45

apparitions signs of Second Coming (Mary) 12/19/96 Vol. 5

apparitions soon ending (Mary) 9/25/97 Vol. 8

apparitions & locutions to prepare for coming evil (Jesus) 5/3/07 Vol. 47

apparitions to children innocence, openness to Word (Jesus) 7/14/04 Vol. 36

appearance of soul in and out (Jesus) 6/24/04 Vol. 35

appearance personal & spiritual (Jesus) 1/23/97 Vol. 6

appearance physically & spiritually (Jesus) 4/23/01 Vol. 23

appearance signs in the sky (Jesus) 6/11/94 Vol. 1

appearance of soul how you will be judged (Jesus) 10/14/98 Vol. 13

appearances look inward not outward (Jesus) 11/1/97 Vol. 9

appearances of soul and body (Jesus) 1/6/04 Vol. 34

appearances outward and inward (Jesus) 4/25/02 Vol. 27

appearances physical & spiritual (Jesus) 9/17/02 Vol. 28

April as digit 4 month spectacular event (Jesus) 9/28/99 Vol. 16

Arab governments fruitless to change (Jesus) 3/28/07 Vol. 46

Arab lands control of land is focus (Jesus) 3/11/02 Vol. 26

Arab militants want to destroy US economy (Jesus) 1/20/06 Vol. 42

Arab Nations exploited by Antichrist (Jesus) 6/10/00 Vol. 19

Arab nations still a threat to war (Jesus) 6/23/99 Vol. 15

Arab nukes threaten war & oil (Jesus) 1/19/06 Vol. 42

Arabs Armageddon (Father) 1/26/94 Vol. 1

Arabs end times (Jesus) 5/23/94 Vol. 1

Arabs false prophet (Jesus) 6/29/96 Vol. 3

Arabs hate Christians (Jesus) 8/2/03 Vol. 32

Arabs leading a holy war (Jesus) 3/27/98 Vol. 10

Arabs some work with dark side (Jesus) 11/13/97 Vol. 9

Arabs & Antichrist defeated again by prayer (Jesus) 4/4/02 Vol. 27

Arabs domination to increase in world (Jesus) 3/10/04 Vol. 34

Arabs, militant want constant war (Jesus) 1/19/06 Vol. 42

archangel devils (St. Michael) 9/29/94 Vol. 2

archangels battle the demons for us (St. Michael) 9/29/04 Vol. 36

Archangels call on to fight demons (Jesus) 9/29/06 Vol. 44

archangels Divine Will 9/29/93 Vol. 1

Archangels power & gratitude (Jesus) 9/29/97 Vol. 8

Archangels School is blessed (Mary) 6/20/01 Vol. 23

architects of churches give glory to themselves (Jesus) 4/17/07 Vol. 47

Argentina collapsed by one worlders (Jesus) 12/20/01 Vol. 25

ark covenant (Jesus) 3/27/95 Vol. 2

Ark of Covenant in Blessed Mother (Jesus) 9/8/04 Vol. 36

Ark of New Covenant found in Mary (Mary) 7/25/05 Vol. 40

Ark of the covenant gave Presence of God (Jesus) 8/2/01 Vol. 24

Ark of the Covenant laws unchangeable (Jesus) 6/26/04 Vol. 35

Ark of the Covenant Mary prepared from birth (Mary) 3/31/08 Vol. 50

Ark of the Covenant materialism (Jesus) 7/1/94 Vol. 2

Ark of the Covenant promise of 10 Commandments (Jesus) 8/11/05 Vol. 40

Ark of the Covenant promise of eternal life (Jesus) 5/24/03 Vol. 31

Ark of the Covenant we carry Holy Communion (Jesus) 7/10/04 Vol. 36

Ark of the Covenant we will carry Host like (Jesus) 4/27/98 Vol. 11

Ark of the Covenant,new renewed in Real Presence (Jesus) 5/5/00 Vol. 19

Arkansas tornadoes Clinton's abortion decrees (Jesus) 1/25/99 Vol. 14

Armageddon battle in Israel (Jesus) 11/30/98 Vol. 13

Armageddon birds pick carcasses (Jesus) 2/9/98 Vol. 10

Armageddon building up soon (Jesus) 6/8/02 Vol. 27

Armageddon forces building for battle (Jesus) 5/11/04 Vol. 35

Armageddon is being prepared (Jesus) 12/6/01 Vol. 25

Armageddon MidEast (Jesus) 5/13/94 Vol. 1

Armageddon mother of all battles (Jesus) 2/19/98 Vol. 10

Armageddon pray for peace in Mideast (Jesus) 11/13/97 Vol. 9

Armageddon prepare for battle of (Jesus) 6/3/04 Vol. 35

Armageddon purification (Jesus) 10/8/95 Vol. 3

Armageddon running in reckless abandon (Jesus) 1/27/98 Vol. 10

Armageddon sides lining up (Jesus) 4/1/02 Vol. 27

Armageddon taking shape daily (Jesus) 2/4/02 Vol. 26

Armageddon victory (Jesus) 11/24/95 Vol. 3

Armageddon victory over evil (Jesus) 9/22/97 Vol. 8

Armageddon, battle of good & bad angels (Jesus) 5/13/07 Vol. 47

Armageddon, Battle of if war expands (Jesus) 3/17/03 Vol. 30

armaments better to trust in God (Jesus) 6/28/01 Vol. 23

armaments trust in God instead (Jesus) 7/31/96 Vol. 4

armaments will not save us (Jesus) 7/17/97 Vol. 8

Armed Forces being destroyed,diluted (Jesus) 4/25/00 Vol. 19

Armegeddon last battle (Jesus) 5/10/01 Vol. 23

armor of grace to protect your soul (Jesus) 11/6/99 Vol. 17

arms neighbor (Jesus) 12/9/94 Vol. 2

Arms and guns do not take up (Jesus) 4/20/98 Vol. 11

arms dealers profit from wars (Jesus)   1/1/05 Vol. 38

arms makers supporters of wars (Jesus)   12/17/04 Vol. 37

arms sales perpetuate wars (Jesus)   8/3/07 Vol. 48

arms sellers double standard Russia, US (Jesus)   12/12/02 Vol. 29

arms selling on both sides for profit (Jesus)   11/2/00 Vol. 21

arms vs. control put trust in God (Jesus)   2/18/01 Vol. 22

Army trucks, new no answer to Iraq war (Jesus)   7/18/07 Vol. 48

arson new form of terror (Jesus)   12/5/06 Vol. 45

art of Early Christians signs of faith (Jesus)   7/18/06 Vol. 44

art work insults Mary,Christians (Jesus)   9/30/99 Vol. 16

artificial conception serious sin, violates law (Mark)   11/3/98 Vol. 13

Artist, Grand God's creation (Jesus)   12/26/02 Vol. 29

artists given talents by God (Jesus)   7/1/04 Vol. 36

artists talents give glory to God (Jesus)   4/22/04 Vol. 35

Arunas diamond heart (Arunas)   8/24/07 Vol. 48

Ascension Eucharist (Jesus)   5/12/94 Vol. 1

Ascension evangelize all nations (Jesus)   5/13/99 Vol. 15

Ascension evangelize with Holy Spirit (Jesus)   5/8/97 Vol. 7

Ascension faithful rise like Jesus (Jesus)   5/29/03 Vol. 31

Ascension gifts of Pentecost (Holy Spirit)   5/21/95 Vol. 2

Ascension Holy Spirit (Jesus)   5/16/96 Vol. 3

Ascension Holy Spirit sent (Jesus)   5/21/98 Vol. 11

Ascension preparation for Holy Spirit (Jesus)   5/5/05 Vol. 39

Ascension presence of Holy Spirit (Jesus)   5/8/97 Vol. 7

Ascension so Holy Spirit can come (Jesus)   5/24/01 Vol. 23

Ascension of Jesus hope for Jesus' return (Jesus)   4/27/06 Vol. 43

Ascension Thursday Groom left His apostles (Jesus)   5/20/04 Vol. 35

Ash Wednesday ashes to humble oneself (Jesus)   3/1/06 Vol. 42

Ash Wednesday Lenten resolutions (Jesus)   2/17/99 Vol. 14

ashes sign of repentance (Jesus)   2/6/08 Vol. 50

assassination for the uncooperative (Jesus)   6/21/01 Vol. 23

assassination of head of state (Jesus)   10/30/01 Vol. 25

assassination of head of state (Jesus)   4/27/05 Vol. 39

assassination of head of state (Jesus)   9/2/04 Vol. 36

Assumption Blessed Mother as model (Jesus)   8/15/00 Vol. 20

Assumption feast of (Jesus)   8/15/03 Vol. 32

Assumption give our 'yes' (Mary)   8/15/97 Vol. 8

Assumption Mary crowned as Queen (Jesus)   8/14/01 Vol. 24

Assumption Mary's mission & ours (Mary)   8/15/96 Vol. 4

Assumption mediatrix (Mary)   8/14/95 Vol. 3

Assumption sharing her resurrection (Mary)   8/15/98 Vol. 12

Assumption Church funds for repairs (Jesus)   1/7/08 Vol. 50

Assumption of Mary Queen of heaven (Jesus)   8/15/02 Vol. 28

asteroids omens in sky (Jesus)   8/15/02 Vol. 28

asteroids refuge (Jesus)   1/20/95 Vol. 2

asteroids & comets Great Chastisement coming (Jesus)   7/25/02 Vol. 28

asteroids of justice abortion (Jesus)   1/18/95 Vol. 2

astrology avoid fortune telling (Jesus)   5/19/05 Vol. 39

astrology do not be influenced (Jesus)   1/2/98 Vol. 10

astrology do not follow (Jesus)   8/26/97 Vol. 8

astrology and occult used by masons (Jesus)   4/23/98 Vol. 11

astronauts Shuttle disaster (Jesus)   2/5/03 Vol. 30

atheists trying to remove 'God' (Jesus)   11/26/03 Vol. 33

atheists worship themselves (God the Father)   8/20/03 Vol. 32

athletes not gods flawed and only human (Jesus)   5/25/00 Vol. 19

ATOMIC dark for 10 seconds   8/13/93 Vol. 1

atomic give up greed or have war (Jesus)   12/30/94 Vol. 2

atomic attack could bring WWIII (Jesus)   1/25/05 Vol. 38

atomic bomb new life   9/7/93 Vol. 1

atomic bomb protected from at refuges (Jesus)   9/20/00 Vol. 20

atomic weapons desire to be superpowers (Jesus)   1/17/00 Vol. 18

attack on cities nations jealous of wealth (Jesus)   9/13/01 Vol. 24

attacks on trips personal message (Jesus)   4/17/02 Vol. 27

attention daily (Jesus)   4/1/95 Vol. 2

attentiveness at Mass can you remember the Gospel? (Jesus)   11/6/03 Vol. 33

attics, hiding at interim refuges (Jesus)   6/19/07 Vol. 47

attraction for God rest,peace for soul (Jesus)   12/29/06 Vol. 45

attributes of God a mystery (Jesus)   10/22/99 Vol. 17

Audrey Santos preciousness of life (Mary)   1/15/98 Vol. 10

Audrey Santos suffering servant (Jesus)   1/14/98 Vol. 10

Auriesville martyrs (St.Issac Jogue)   10/19/94 Vol. 2

Australia rosaries for protection (Mary)   7/17/97 Vol. 8

authority challenged by truth (Jesus)   3/4/00 Vol. 18

authority threats to (Jesus)   4/12/02 Vol. 27

authority of God challenged Moses, Jesus (Jesus)   8/2/05 Vol. 40

authority of God Ten Commandments (God the Father)   8/20/03 Vol. 32

authority of Jesus call on for protection (Jesus)   1/13/04 Vol. 34

authority of Jesus threat to pharisees (Jesus)   1/30/00 Vol. 18

avarice do not desire money for itself (Jesus)   8/18/98 Vol. 12

avarice love money for its own sake (Jesus)   11/26/01 Vol. 25

avoid gossip show love instead (Jesus)   11/22/99 Vol. 17

awards & possessions refuse to seek possessions (Jesus)   11/5/98 Vol. 13

awards, attraction of for earthly gain (Jesus)   6/7/03 Vol. 31

awesome God in nature and Spirit (Jesus)   11/4/99 Vol. 17

babe of Christmas brings peace and love (Jesus)   12/7/98 Vol. 13

babe of Christmas make room in hearts (Jesus)   12/21/99 Vol. 17

Babel, new towers of discoveries & inventions (Jesus)   1/27/00 Vol. 18

babies and budding flowers (Jesus)   9/5/02 Vol. 28

Babylon & America parallel destruction (Jesus)   11/28/07 Vol. 49

Babylonian Captivity example to America (Jesus)   6/25/98 Vol. 11

backbone of faith to speak out (Jesus)   1/17/05 Vol. 38

backpack items sacramentals, needs (Jesus)   2/1/06 Vol. 42

backpacks have ready soon (Jesus)   5/1/02 Vol. 27

backpacks to refuges sacramentals, camping gear (Jesus)   5/21/07 Vol. 47

Backus, Sarah Baptism of granddaughter (Jesus)	11/30/02 Vol. 29
bacteria in rainfall from chem trails (Jesus)	3/3/08 Vol. 50
bad habits avoid occasions of sin (Jesus)	6/17/04 Vol. 35
bad habits change by grace and prayer (Jesus)	8/27/98 Vol. 12
bad habits drugs, alcohol, profiteers (Jesus)	12/22/03 Vol. 33
bad habits root out (Jesus)	2/20/07 Vol. 46
bad habits, earthly desires stop to gain heaven (Jesus)	1/17/07 Vol. 46
badgered into war by Satan's plans (Jesus)	9/14/01 Vol. 24
baggage, excess rid consumers of time (Jesus)	11/16/99 Vol. 17
balance of nature abused by man (Jesus)	8/1/02 Vol. 28
balance of nature abused by man (Jesus)	5/15/03 Vol. 31
balance of nature being abused (Jesus)	2/15/07 Vol. 46
balance of nature being destroyed by man (Jesus)	1/25/06 Vol. 42
balance of nature cannot improve on perfection (Jesus)	4/24/03 Vol. 31
balance of nature chastisements in weather (Jesus)	8/21/01 Vol. 24
balance of nature disrupted by cloning (Jesus)	3/27/03 Vol. 30
balance of nature endangered by diseases (Jesus)	3/24/08 Vol. 50
balance of nature God's perfection (Jesus)	8/30/03 Vol. 32
balance of nature is abused (Jesus)	1/28/02 Vol. 26
balance of nature is being destroyed (Jesus)	3/8/05 Vol. 38
balance of nature is being upset (Jesus)	7/6/01 Vol. 24
balance of nature must be respected (Jesus)	4/25/05 Vol. 39
balance of nature needs preserving (Jesus)	2/2/08 Vol. 50
balance of nature protect as God wills (Jesus)	7/10/06 Vol. 44
balance of nature protect the environment (Jesus)	5/24/01 Vol. 23
balance of nature protect the environment (Jesus)	2/16/08 Vol. 50
balance of nature renew resources (Jesus)	9/24/02 Vol. 28
balance of nature resources depleted (Jesus)	5/29/03 Vol. 31
balance of nature respect, do not distort (Jesus)	4/20/04 Vol. 35
balance of nature solve problems naturally (Jesus)	4/25/02 Vol. 27
balance of nature teaches man's place (Jesus)	9/4/06 Vol. 44
balance of nature threatened by man (Jesus)	3/7/07 Vol. 46
balance of nature to be restored (Jesus)	4/9/02 Vol. 27
balance of nature upset by man's violence (Jesus)	8/5/00 Vol. 20
balance of nature upset materialism (Jesus)	10/27/95 Vol. 3
Balkan unrest Albanians stirring trouble (Jesus)	3/29/01 Vol. 22
ball of fire chastisement	8/23/93 Vol. 1
Bangladesh need donations (Jesus)	11/29/07 Vol. 49
Bangladesh flooding thousands dead, homeless (Jesus)	11/20/07 Vol. 49
bank markdowns predator loans (Jesus)	11/15/07 Vol. 49
bankers ten regions (Jesus)	6/1/01 Vol. 23
bankers bad debts bailed out with taxes (Jesus)	10/8/98 Vol. 13
bankers, central control through debts,arms (Jesus)	11/6/00 Vol. 21
bankers, central manipulate events (Jesus)	2/13/02 Vol. 26
bankers, central privacy needed to cover deeds (Jesus)	3/16/02 Vol. 26
bankers, corporations running US government (Jesus)	5/10/07 Vol. 47
bankrupt churches from pedophile suits (Jesus)	4/19/05 Vol. 39
bankruptcies increasing (Jesus)	1/14/04 Vol. 34
bankruptcy moral & financial (Jesus)	10/2/03 Vol. 33
bankruptcy threatens America (Jesus)	3/2/06 Vol. 42
bankruptcy of US plan of one worlders (Jesus)	11/8/07 Vol. 49
banquet table in heaven (Jesus)	1/5/01 Vol. 22
banquet table preview of Transfiguration (Jesus)	9/23/99 Vol. 16
banquet table reward in heaven (Jesus)	2/19/06 Vol. 42
Baptism begin journey to Calvary (Jesus)	1/10/99 Vol. 14
Baptism Christian initiation (Jesus)	6/24/98 Vol. 11
Baptism cleansed of original sin (Jesus)	7/13/03 Vol. 32
Baptism cleanses your sins (Jesus)	3/24/98 Vol. 10
Baptism cleansing waters (Jesus)	1/2/02 Vol. 26
Baptism cure for Original Sin (Jesus)	2/22/01 Vol. 22
Baptism grace for Original Sin (Jesus)	1/7/99 Vol. 14
baptism (Holy Spirit)	9/1/93 Vol. 1
Baptism indwelling (Holy Spirit)	1/9/95 Vol. 2
Baptism initiation, Original Sin (Jesus)	5/24/00 Vol. 19
Baptism light (Jesus)	10/9/94 Vol. 2
Baptism living water of Jesus (Jesus)	12/28/99 Vol. 17
Baptism of Justin David (Jesus)	5/26/02 Vol. 27
Baptism our call to ministry (Jesus)	1/11/98 Vol. 10
baptism penance (Jesus)	7/9/94 Vol. 2
Baptism prove faith by living it (Jesus)	1/13/02 Vol. 26
Baptism reconciliation (Jesus)	1/27/96 Vol. 3
Baptism renew vows (Jesus)	5/21/98 Vol. 11
Baptism renew vows & evangelize (Jesus)	7/14/05 Vol. 40
Baptism renewed life as in spring (Jesus)	3/23/01 Vol. 22
Baptism renounce devil & world (Jesus)	1/8/00 Vol. 18
Baptism responsibility for children (Mary)	11/21/96 Vol. 5
Baptism salvation (Father)	1/8/96 Vol. 3
Baptism saved from sins (Jesus)	1/13/97 Vol. 6
baptism soul glows (Jesus)	9/18/97 Vol. 8
Baptism takes away original sin (Jesus)	1/8/05 Vol. 38
Baptism the living water (Jesus)	3/28/98 Vol. 10
Baptism Trinity (Holy Spirit)	1/3/95 Vol. 2
Baptism washes away Original Sin (Jesus)	7/28/98 Vol. 12
Baptism washes original sin (Jesus)	4/1/04 Vol. 35
Baptism & Confession Advent penitential season (Jesus)	12/16/02 Vol. 29
Baptism & Confession cleanse sin at birth to death (Jesus)	3/30/04 Vol. 34
Baptism & Confession cleanse sins (Jesus)	11/1/05 Vol. 41
Baptism & Confirmation cleanse sins (Jesus)	4/3/07 Vol. 47
Baptism & Confirmation free you from sins (Jesus)	2/2/05 Vol. 38
Baptism & Confirmation water and light (Jesus)	3/2/04 Vol. 34
Baptism & death new life situations (Jesus)	11/25/06 Vol. 45
Baptism at death new life in the Spirit (Jesus)	8/23/05 Vol. 40
Baptism of Holy Spirit love (Holy Spirit)	5/1/96 Vol. 3
Baptism of infants cleanse original sin (Jesus)	7/26/01 Vol. 24

Baptism of Jesus manifestation of Trinity (Jesus) 1/13/08 Vol. 50

Baptism of Jesus start of public ministry (Jesus) 1/11/04 Vol. 34

Baptism waters tower of grace in water (Jesus) 8/13/00 Vol. 20

Baptism, Confession born again (Jesus) 4/5/05 Vol. 39

Baptism, Confession contract of fidelity with God (Jesus) 1/12/06 Vol. 42

Baptism, Confession free soul of sin (Jesus) 3/20/07 Vol. 46

Baptism, Confirmation needed for spiritual health (Jesus) 10/15/04 Vol. 37

Baptism,Confirmation to evangelize souls (Jesus) 6/5/03 Vol. 31

Baptismal vows should be renewed (Jesus) 9/12/99 Vol. 16

baptized faithful need personal commitment (Jesus) 1/25/06 Vol. 42

barriers overcome by seeking Jesus' help (Jesus) 3/1/01 Vol. 22

Basil Oleksyn funeral Mass (Jesus) 9/15/04 Vol. 36

battle evil (Jesus) 10/3/94 Vol. 2

battle victory (St. Michael) 10/15/95 Vol. 3

battle Antichrist not to fear,use God's help (Jesus) 2/24/00 Vol. 18

battle for heaven follow God's Will,suffering (Jesus) 11/2/01 Vol. 25

battle for souls God vs. Satan (Jesus) 12/5/06 Vol. 45

battle for souls love vs. hate (Jesus) 5/7/02 Vol. 27

Battle of Armageddon all out war thwarted (Jesus) 11/17/05 Vol. 41

Battle of Armageddon angels lead to victory (Jesus) 3/8/99 Vol. 14

Battle of Armageddon angels to fight for you (Jesus) 3/18/99 Vol. 14

Battle of Armageddon between armies of world (Jesus) 4/13/00 Vol. 19

battle of Armageddon defeats Satan, Antichrist (Jesus) 5/20/99 Vol. 15

Battle of Armageddon dissent in military (Jesus) 9/22/06 Vol. 44

Battle of Armageddon eclipses (Jesus) 9/27/96 Vol. 4

Battle of Armageddon good vs. evil (Jesus) 2/1/99 Vol. 14

Battle of Armageddon involves many nations (Jesus) 6/5/97 Vol. 7

Battle of Armageddon pray for peace (Jesus) 8/7/97 Vol. 8

Battle of Armageddon separate good and evil (Jesus) 8/14/97 Vol. 8

Battle of Armageddon St. Michael and angels (Jesus) 4/7/96 Vol. 3

Battle of Armageddon triumph over armies (Jesus) 11/23/99 Vol. 17

Battle of Armageddon wars leading to (Jesus) 7/1/99 Vol. 16

Battle of Armegeddon at time of Antichrist (Jesus) 1/18/07 Vol. 46

battle of good & evil angels, era of peace (Jesus) 10/10/97 Vol. 9

battle of good & evil Antichrist,bankers,1 world (Jesus) 7/16/97 Vol. 8

battle of good & evil arm spiritually (Jesus) 9/6/03 Vol. 32

battle of good & evil attacks on family (Jesus) 8/24/03 Vol. 32

battle of good & evil be alert every hour (Jesus) 9/29/03 Vol. 32

battle of good & evil between good and bad angels (Jesus) 7/10/04 Vol. 36

battle of good & evil coming to a head (Jesus) 10/9/01 Vol. 25

battle of good & evil coming to a head (Jesus) 4/17/05 Vol. 39

battle of good & evil control of people (Jesus) 3/3/00 Vol. 18

battle of good & evil devil never sleeps (Jesus) 6/6/02 Vol. 27

battle of good & evil evidenced in holidays (Jesus) 10/3/03 Vol. 33

battle of good & evil exist at same time (Jesus) 7/21/02 Vol. 28

battle of good & evil fight for soul until death (Jesus) 7/3/00 Vol. 20

battle of good & evil flames all around us (Jesus) 4/22/05 Vol. 39

battle of good & evil for souls (Jesus) 6/7/06 Vol. 43

battle of good & evil fought each day (Jesus) 1/14/06 Vol. 42

battle of good & evil God vs. possessions, idols (Mary) 7/14/02 Vol. 28

Battle of good & evil gossiping & judging (Jesus) 6/23/03 Vol. 31

Battle of good & evil guardian angels (Mary) 4/7/97 Vol. 7

battle of good & evil in age of apostasy (Jesus) 10/21/01 Vol. 25

battle of good & evil in end times (Jesus) 7/26/03 Vol. 32

battle of good & evil is desperate (Jesus) 8/4/06 Vol. 44

battle of good & evil love will conquer all (Jesus) 8/9/01 Vol. 24

battle of good & evil need help of the Holy Spirit (Jesus) 6/4/06 Vol. 43

battle of good & evil powerful to destroy (Jesus) 8/19/03 Vol. 32

battle of good & evil preach the gospel (Jesus) 4/11/99 Vol. 15

Battle of good & evil principalities & powers (Jesus) 1/10/03 Vol. 30

battle of good & evil reflected in weather (Jesus) 9/15/00 Vol. 20

battle of good & evil save souls (Jesus) 9/4/96 Vol. 4

battle of good & evil seek God's & angels help (Jesus) 9/18/97 Vol. 8

battle of good & evil take narrow road to heaven (Jesus) 6/18/05 Vol. 39

battle of good & evil to save souls (Jesus) 11/25/00 Vol. 21

battle of good & evil today as with Moses (Jesus) 6/3/04 Vol. 35

battle of good & evil with love and good example (Jesus) 4/29/04 Vol. 35

battle of good and evil arm with sacramentals (Jesus) 12/21/97 Vol. 9

battle of good and evil armor of faith and trust (Jesus) 2/8/98 Vol. 10

battle of good and evil challenged to live one's faith (Jesus) 7/17/98 Vol. 12

battle of good and evil fight to save souls (Jesus) 7/20/98 Vol. 12

battle of good, evil good angels vs. demons (St. Michael) 9/29/99 Vol. 16

battle of good,evil going on in Church (Jesus) 5/9/00 Vol. 19

battle weapons Scripture, rosary (Jesus) 2/1/00 Vol. 18

battle,good & evil use weapons against evil (Jesus) 12/22/05 Vol. 41

beacon of faith share faith & love (Jesus) 2/6/05 Vol. 38

beacon of Host faithful will not get lost (Jesus) 12/20/99 Vol. 17

beacons of Light bring souls to God (Jesus) 2/18/01 Vol. 22

beacons of light to share faith with others (Jesus) 1/19/05 Vol. 38

beast man of peace, then tyrant (Jesus) 7/9/07 Vol. 48

BEAST stores all info on everyone (Jesus) 6/9/05 Vol. 39

beasts of evil to attack the Church (Jesus) 2/5/00 Vol. 18

beasts of Revelation lead to Antichrist (Jesus) 11/28/03 Vol. 33

beasts of Revelation time coming near (Jesus) 5/5/07 Vol. 47

beatific vision ecstasy in joy with God (Jesus) 3/29/01 Vol. 22

beatific vision faithful to behold (Jesus) 11/22/00 Vol. 21

beatific vision infinite love and peace (Jesus) 8/31/98 Vol. 12

beatific vision praise with angels,saints (Jesus) 7/22/99 Vol. 16

beatific vision reward of constant ecstasy (Jesus) 1/10/01 Vol. 22

beatific vision spiritually whole in heaven (Jesus) 6/5/99 Vol. 15

Beatitudes commandments (Jesus) 1/28/96 Vol. 3

beatitudes God vs. idols (Jesus) 2/3/02 Vol. 26

Beatitudes seek heavenly treasures (Jesus) 6/10/02 Vol. 27

Beatitudes lived in love of God & neighbor (Jesus) 1/31/99 Vol. 14

beauty physical & spiritual (Jesus) 4/23/03 Vol. 31

beauty soul (Mary) 9/26/94 Vol. 2

beauty tidy souls (Jesus) 8/21/95 Vol. 3

beauty of Real Presence most precious gift (Jesus) 3/9/00 Vol. 18

bee population threat from mites,insecticides (Jesus) 2/29/08 Vol. 50

beer mug,sanctuary light drink & drugs are new god (Jesus) 4/27/97 Vol. 7

behavior be examples of faith (Jesus) 3/10/99 Vol. 14

behavior give good example (Jesus) 9/11/97 Vol. 8

behavior, good better than gift giving (Jesus) 12/3/02 Vol. 29

beheaded torture in tribulation (Jesus) 6/18/99 Vol. 15

beheading by Guillotine martyrdom in tribulation (Jesus) 5/24/00 Vol. 19

belief in God true at all times (Jesus) 3/28/01 Vol. 22

belief in Jesus foolishness to worldly (Jesus) 1/20/07 Vol. 46

belief in Jesus with empty tomb (Jesus) 3/26/05 Vol. 38

believe without seeing blessed in faith (Jesus) 5/5/00 Vol. 19

believers, true will be few in number (Jesus) 3/8/06 Vol. 42

Bello Wedding uniting hearts (Jesus) 8/22/98 Vol. 12

Bello, Ernie & Susan wedding (Jesus) 9/17/05 Vol. 40

Benedictine crosses & holy water for protection (Jesus) 7/12/01 Vol. 24

Benedictine crosses demon protection (Jesus) 11/30/06 Vol. 45

Benedictine Crosses for protection from demons (Jesus) 9/14/02 Vol. 28

Benedictine crosses for protection from evil (Jesus) 1/6/01 Vol. 22

Benedictine Crosses protection from demons (Jesus) 3/12/05 Vol. 38

Benediction should be done often (Jesus) 2/28/00 Vol. 18

Betania blessings (Mary) 2/4/95 Vol. 2

Betania faith remnant (Mary) 5/19/95 Vol. 2

Betania graces (Mary) 2/19/94 Vol. 1

Betania graces for trial (Mary) 2/7/96 Vol. 3

Betania graces of pilgrimages (Jesus) 9/21/06 Vol. 44

Betania Holy Spirit dove (Mary) 2/12/96 Vol. 3

Betania Lent (Mary) 3/5/94 Vol. 1

Betania messages for family (Jesus) 12/20/07 Vol. 49

Betania miraculous flakes (Mary) 1/10/96 Vol. 3

Betania mission (Mary) 2/27/94 Vol. 1

Betania mission (Mary) 2/26/94 Vol. 1

Betania pilgrimage (Mary) 1/11/96 Vol. 3

Betania pilgrimage (Mary) 1/28/94 Vol. 1

Betania pilgrims (Mary) 2/20/94 Vol. 1

Betania pilgrims (Mary) 2/20/94 Vol. 1

Betania prepare (Jesus) 2/28/94 Vol. 1

Betania share blessings, healings (Jesus) 12/14/06 Vol. 45

Betania share graces (Jesus) 8/23/07 Vol. 48

Betania wear Benedictine crosses (Jesus) 11/29/07 Vol. 49

Betania IV affirmed by Jesus & Mary (Jesus) 2/22/08 Vol. 50

Betania IV blessing of Shrine (Jesus) 2/23/08 Vol. 50

Betania message trumpets of Jesus' coming (Jesus) 5/30/07 Vol. 47

Betania pilgrim welcome from Blessed Mother (Mary) 12/7/07 Vol. 49

Betania pilgrimage charitable opportunities (Jesus) 12/6/06 Vol. 45

Betania retreat houses preparation for refuges (Jesus) 12/20/07 Vol. 49

Betania Shrine harvest masters (Jesus) 2/5/95 Vol. 2

Betania Shrine materialism (Mary) 2/11/95 Vol. 2

Betania Shrine Mystical Body (Mary) 2/6/95 Vol. 2

Betania Shrine rewarded by Blessed Mother Our Lady 8/14/07 Vol. 48

Be. Shrine pilgrimage suffer discomforts for graces (Jesus) 11/30/06 Vol. 45

Betania Shrine trip when to travel there (Jesus) 2/22/08 Vol. 50

Betania statue alive blue butterfly of Mary (Mary) 12/8/06 Vol. 45

Betania trip communists gaining control (Jesus) 8/9/07 Vol. 48

Betania trip threat by Chavez (Jesus) 6/26/07 Vol. 47

Betania water refuge, consecrated ground (Jesus) 12/6/06 Vol. 45

Bethlehem birth in a cave, manger (Jesus) 12/7/98 Vol. 13

Bethlehem free will (Jesus) 12/15/95 Vol. 3

Bethlehem judged (Jesus) 12/5/93 Vol. 1

Bethlehem Messiah to come from (Jesus) 12/17/03 Vol. 33

Bethlehem Nativity Church safe (Jesus) 5/11/02 Vol. 27

Bethlehem salvation (Jesus) 12/10/95 Vol. 3

Bethlehem start to Calvary (Jesus) 10/30/98 Vol. 13

Bethlehem Star place of Jesus' birth (Jesus) 11/28/07 Vol. 49

betrothal consecration (Mary) 12/20/95 Vol. 3

Betty Leary funeral message (Betty Leary) 7/24/04 Vol. 36

Betty Leary's death experience (Jesus) 7/22/04 Vol. 36

Bianchini Family blessings of hospitality (Jesus) 12/6/06 Vol. 45

Bible blueprint of events (Jesus) 9/11/98 Vol. 12

Bible cannot hold all Jesus did (Jesus) 1/29/04 Vol. 34

Bible comes alive in Holy Lands (Jesus) 6/26/00 Vol. 19

Bible Gospels (Jesus) 8/13/94 Vol. 2

Bible living last book, Revelation (Jesus) 7/28/98 Vol. 12

Bible read daily (Jesus) 1/1/98 Vol. 10

Bible read to assure salvation (Jesus) 11/3/99 Vol. 17

Bible scripture fulfilled (Jesus) 5/13/97 Vol. 7

Bible with misinterpretations (Jesus) 6/4/04 Vol. 35

Bible availability thankful for printed copies (Jesus) 5/18/00 Vol. 19

Bible prophecy all fulfilled in Jesus (Jesus) 1/3/02 Vol. 26

Bible reading defend faith through Word (Jesus) 6/8/00 Vol. 19

Bible study helps growth in faith (Jesus) 2/17/05 Vol. 38

Bible study to understand parables (Jesus) 9/17/05 Vol. 40

bible study needed pass on to children (Jesus) 10/1/98 Vol. 13

Bible to be banned Antichrist desires his worship (Jesus) 11/3/00 Vol. 21

Bible translations change meaning of texts (Jesus) 7/24/02 Vol. 28

Bible, crucifix protection from evil (Jesus) 7/8/04 Vol. 36

Bible, spiritual books meditate on serving, loving God (Jesus) 9/8/04 Vol. 36

Bible, The read and study (Jesus) 6/2/98 Vol. 11

Bible,daily reading meditation,road to perfection (Jesus) 7/28/00 Vol. 20

Bibles words changed (Jesus) 1/3/99 Vol. 14

Bible's location in special prominent place (Jesus) 6/28/00 Vol. 19

Bible's Word will last forever (Jesus)	11/20/06 Vol. 45	birth control be open to laws of life (Jesus)	10/18/02 Vol. 29
bibles, rosaries needed in tribulation (Jesus)	7/25/00 Vol. 20	birth control Corpus Christi (Jesus)	6/18/95 Vol. 2
Bibles,catechisms guard against changes (Jesus)	10/17/98 Vol. 13	birth control grave sin (Jesus)	7/30/03 Vol. 32
Biblical history repeats itself (Jesus)	6/18/98 Vol. 11	birth control mortal sin (Jesus)	7/11/01 Vol. 24
Biblical proportion events of end times (Jesus)	11/26/02 Vol. 29	birth control mortal sin in stopping conception (Jesus)	5/19/04 Vol. 35
bicycle means to travel to refuge (Jesus)	5/21/05 Vol. 39	birth control mortal sin, violates God (Mark)	11/3/98 Vol. 13
bicycle need for fuel shortages (Jesus)	5/28/06 Vol. 43	birth control natural family planning (Jesus)	9/23/03 Vol. 32
bicycles best to travel at night (Jesus)	9/19/02 Vol. 28	birth control precursor for abortion (Jesus)	12/28/07 Vol. 49
bicycles gas shortages, tracking (Jesus)	8/4/97 Vol. 8	birth control vasectomies,mortal sins (Jesus)	8/10/01 Vol. 24
bicycles have ready (Jesus)	10/20/06 Vol. 45	birth control methods lead to abortion (Jesus)	1/22/07 Vol. 46
bicycles may be only travel (Jesus)	1/28/99 Vol. 14	birth control, abortion life is precious (Jesus)	6/17/02 Vol. 27
bicycles & helmets for hiding (Jesus)	7/30/01 Vol. 24	birth of Jesus fetal membrane around cross (Jesus)	10/7/00 Vol. 21
bicycles & helmets have ready (Jesus)	10/27/06 Vol. 45	birth rates down abortion, small families (Jesus)	1/4/07 Vol. 46
bicycles needed for going to refuge (Jesus)	11/21/07 Vol. 49	birth, death celebrated in heaven (Jesus)	12/30/03 Vol. 33
bicycles, on foot when gas runs out (Jesus)	6/27/04 Vol. 35	birthday mother (Mary)	8/5/94 Vol. 2
big bang theories evolution is unproven (Jesus)	10/6/05 Vol. 41	birthday prayer request (Mary)	9/8/94 Vol. 2
big picture needed for spiritual direction (Jesus)	12/30/06 Vol. 45	Birthdays & conception of Jesus & Mary (Jesus)	12/8/04 Vol. 37
bikes needed to reach refuges (Jesus)	3/12/06 Vol. 42	births in lifetime natural,born again, born in spirit (Jesus)	7/23/04 Vol. 36
bikes for refuges when no fuel is there (Jesus)	5/19/06 Vol. 43	Bishop Hickey's funeral witness of faith (Jesus)	10/11/99 Vol. 17
bikes needed for going to refuges (Jesus)	12/13/04 Vol. 37	Bishop Roman 50th anniversary as priest (Our Lady)	10/13/07 Vol. 49
bikes needed for travel to refuges (Jesus)	11/24/04 Vol. 37	Bishop Sheen role models (Jesus)	6/19/95 Vol. 2
bikes to refuges fuel short,chip license (Jesus)	8/13/02 Vol. 28	bishops church (Jesus)	11/17/93 Vol. 1
Bill of Rights being usurped (Jesus)	2/1/07 Vol. 46	bishops discernment (Jesus)	4/4/95 Vol. 2
Bin Laden cannot be found in caves (Jesus)	11/15/01 Vol. 25	bishops errors, authority, obedience (Jesus)	9/28/98 Vol. 12
Bin Laden tapes spread hate (Jesus)	12/13/01 Vol. 25	Bishops evangelize (Jesus)	4/28/96 Vol. 3
bind sins to foot of cross (Jesus)	2/9/05 Vol. 38	bishops financial problems (Jesus)	7/17/02 Vol. 28
binoculars evil spies (Jesus)	10/26/93 Vol. 1	bishops guardian of truth vs. heresies (Jesus)	6/2/00 Vol. 19
biological and chemical weapons (Jesus)	1/30/03 Vol. 30	bishops must follow the pope (Jesus)	6/2/00 Vol. 19
biological terrorism planned for large numbers (Jesus)	11/5/03 Vol. 33	bishops need prayers to stop pride (Jesus)	8/19/98 Vol. 12
biological warfare be prepared for (Jesus)	11/5/05 Vol. 41	bishops need your prayers (Jesus)	12/29/01 Vol. 25
biological weapons abuse of viruses,mind control (Jesus)	3/15/01 Vol. 22	bishops not standing up for morals (Jesus)	8/18/04 Vol. 36
biological weapons designed to reduce population (Jesus)	11/1/00 Vol. 21	bishops penance (Jesus)	11/7/93 Vol. 1
biological weapons of one world people (Jesus)	9/19/02 Vol. 28	bishops pope (Jesus)	11/30/93 Vol. 1
biological weapons when Saddam desperate (Jesus)	10/16/02 Vol. 29	bishops pope (Jesus)	9/28/94 Vol. 2
biological,chemical arms millions at risk (Jesus)	11/22/02 Vol. 29	bishops pray for (Jesus)	7/23/06 Vol. 44
bird flu drugs not effective (Jesus)	5/12/06 Vol. 43	bishops pray for them (Jesus)	1/25/97 Vol. 6
bird flu from man-made causes (Jesus)	1/12/06 Vol. 42	bishops priests (Jesus)	4/28/94 Vol. 1
bird flu pray for protection from (Jesus)	10/13/05 Vol. 41	Bishops under more scrutiny (Jesus)	2/25/99 Vol. 14
bird flu pray to stop (Jesus)	11/3/05 Vol. 41	bishops & cardinals in revolt (Jesus)	1/31/97 Vol. 6
bird's nest in hair vanity (Jesus)	12/22/95 Vol. 3	bishops & priests need prayers (Jesus)	5/11/04 Vol. 35
birds of the air the Father provides (Jesus)	7/31/01 Vol. 24	bishops & priests need prayers (Jesus)	8/18/04 Vol. 36
birth new earth (Jesus)	9/12/94 Vol. 2	Bishops and Cardinals have heavy responsibility (Jesus)	9/6/98 Vol. 12
birth of body & soul (Jesus)	7/23/04 Vol. 36	bishops and priests pray for them (Jesus)	3/17/98 Vol. 10
birth & death as part of life (Jesus)	7/13/06 Vol. 44	bishops under attack from lawsuits and terrorism (Jesus)	3/19/02 Vol. 26
birth & death death is birth to new life (Jesus)	11/21/02 Vol. 29	bishops, erring do not follow errors,justice (Jesus)	8/19/98 Vol. 12
birth control and sexual sins (Jesus)	3/18/03 Vol. 30	bishops, priests needed for sacraments (Jesus)	4/13/99 Vol. 15
birth control avoid sins with devices (Jesus)	11/22/04 Vol. 37	Bl. Sister Faustina honor and trust Jesus (Bl Faustina)	2/15/97 Vol. 6

black and red flag Antichrist (Jesus) — 1/4/95 Vol. 2

black book of your life's events (Jesus) — 8/26/05 Vol. 40

black cross on wall Mass in the home (Jesus) — 1/5/95 Vol. 2

black helicopters attack on religious (Jesus) — 6/21/07 Vol. 47

black helicopters chip of the beast (Jesus) — 8/23/94 Vol. 2

black helicopters control of crowds (Jesus) — 2/3/97 Vol. 6

black helicopters one world take over (Jesus) — 12/27/96 Vol. 5

black man prejudice — 8/17/93 Vol. 1

black market created by mandatory chips (Jesus) — 8/8/02 Vol. 28

black masses abuse of Hosts (Jesus) — 7/26/02 Vol. 28

black masses channeling,exorcism (Jesus) — 11/1/96 Vol. 5

black masses demons (Jesus) — 1/29/96 Vol. 3

black masses desecrate Hosts (Jesus) — 7/30/06 Vol. 44

black masses desecration of hosts (Jesus) — 9/7/96 Vol. 4

black masses Eucharist desecrated in (Jesus) — 12/3/00 Vol. 21

black masses Hosts are desecrated (Jesus) — 9/1/04 Vol. 36

black masses in Churches (Jesus) — 3/23/97 Vol. 6

black masses in churches (Jesus) — 1/12/01 Vol. 22

black masses vocations (Jesus) — 12/27/95 Vol. 3

black masses with animal sacrifices (Jesus) — 7/12/01 Vol. 24

black monstrance mocking of Adoration (Jesus) — 9/8/03 Vol. 32

black UN helicopters mapping your address (Jesus) — 7/24/07 Vol. 48

black,pale green horses of Revelation, signs of death (Jesus) 8/9/07 Vol. 48

blackout one world people testing (Jesus) — 9/6/97 Vol. 8

blackouts appreciate little things (Jesus) — 8/14/03 Vol. 32

blackouts Canada and U.S. (Jesus) — 1/25/98 Vol. 10

blackouts & fuel conserve resources (Jesus) — 9/4/03 Vol. 32

blasphemers put down eucharistic miracle (Jesus) — 4/5/98 Vol. 11

blasphemy to serve alien gods (Jesus) — 6/21/01 Vol. 23

bleeding Hosts Eucharistic miracles (Jesus) — 3/16/99 Vol. 14

bleeding hosts miracles to believe (Jesus) — 4/18/98 Vol. 11

bleeding hosts raise our faith (Jesus) — 1/15/98 Vol. 10

blessed candles light in darkness (Jesus) — 9/14/07 Vol. 48

blessed candles masses,3 days darkness (Jesus) — 4/15/99 Vol. 15

blessed homes protection from demons (Jesus) — 3/27/06 Vol. 42

Blessed Mother 7 sorrows of (Jesus) — 9/15/06 Vol. 44

Blessed Mother acknowledgement (Mary) — 5/23/96 Vol. 3

Blessed Mother announcing 2nd Coming (Jesus) — 10/10/99 Vol. 17

Blessed Mother Ark of the New Covenant (Mary) — 7/25/05 Vol. 40

Blessed Mother as intercessor & model (Jesus) — 6/23/06 Vol. 43

Blessed Mother at Lourdes (Mary) — 2/11/08 Vol. 50

Blessed Mother birth and lineage (Jesus) — 9/8/04 Vol. 36

Blessed Mother birth free of sin (Mary) — 9/8/97 Vol. 8

Blessed Mother birth, greatest moment (Jesus) — 12/24/00 Vol. 21

Blessed Mother brings you to Jesus (Mary) — 9/19/96 Vol. 4

Blessed Mother calls us to Confession (Jesus) — 8/22/00 Vol. 20

Blessed Mother cannot hold Son's arm back (Jesus) — 8/22/06 Vol. 44

Blessed Mother carry out old messages (Blessed Mother) — 9/6/07 Vol. 48

Blessed Mother celebrate feast days (Jesus) — 12/9/04 Vol. 37

Blessed Mother crushes head of Satan (Jesus) — 7/16/04 Vol. 36

Blessed Mother doing more in heaven also (Our Lady) — 8/14/07 Vol. 48

Blessed Mother example of perfection (Jesus) — 7/20/02 Vol. 28

Blessed Mother gives signs of end times (Jesus) — 6/6/06 Vol. 43

Blessed Mother held Son's arm back (Mary) — 6/19/97 Vol. 7

Blessed Mother help at death (Jesus) — 5/17/01 Vol. 23

Blessed Mother holy intercession (Jesus) — 10/11/03 Vol. 33

Blessed Mother in rosary & scapular (Jesus) — 3/17/05 Vol. 38

Blessed Mother in suffering with Jesus (Jesus) — 2/2/07 Vol. 46

Blessed Mother intercessor for prayer (Jesus) — 7/10/04 Vol. 36

Blessed Mother leads to Jesus (Jesus) — 3/25/03 Vol. 30

Blessed Mother lived in Divine Will (Jesus) — 5/31/03 Vol. 31

Blessed Mother lived in Divine Will (Jesus) — 9/8/00 Vol. 20

Blessed Mother many refuse to honor (Jesus) — 10/3/01 Vol. 25

Blessed Mother mother of all (Jesus) — 8/5/04 Vol. 36

Blessed Mother mother to all (Jesus) — 5/6/04 Vol. 35

Blessed Mother New Ark of the Covenant (Jesus) — 5/24/03 Vol. 31

Blessed Mother One in His Light (Jesus) — 8/15/06 Vol. 44

Blessed Mother pray for sinners (Jesus) — 9/18/06 Vol. 44

Blessed Mother pray rosaries (Jesus) — 12/6/01 Vol. 25

Blessed Mother prayer intercessor (Jesus) — 9/12/05 Vol. 40

Blessed Mother prepare for tribulation (Jesus) — 8/18/00 Vol. 20

Blessed Mother prepare triumph (Jesus) — 8/15/00 Vol. 20

Blessed Mother protects children (Jesus) — 2/8/07 Vol. 46

Blessed Mother responsibility to raise Jesus (Jesus) — 12/31/00 Vol. 21

Blessed Mother role in Incarnation of Jesus (Jesus) — 8/30/04 Vol. 36

Blessed Mother role in salvation (Jesus) — 2/8/07 Vol. 46

Blessed Mother scapular and rosary (Mary) — 9/29/96 Vol. 4

Blessed Mother servant and mother to all (Jesus) — 10/25/05 Vol. 41

Blessed Mother servant of God (Jesus) — 12/29/05 Vol. 41

Blessed Mother sinless at Jesus' conception (Jesus) — 3/26/01 Vol. 22

Blessed Mother takes all petitions to Jesus (Jesus) — 4/2/02 Vol. 27

Blessed Mother thanks prayer group (Mary) — 4/30/05 Vol. 39

Blessed Mother the new Eve (Jesus) — 8/5/06 Vol. 44

Blessed Mother umbilical cord to faithful (Jesus) — 6/28/03 Vol. 31

Blessed Mother union of Divine Will (Jesus) — 8/15/03 Vol. 32

Blessed Mother Virgin sign in Isaiah (Jesus) — 3/25/06 Vol. 42

Blessed Mother watches over us (Jesus) — 3/1/07 Vol. 46

Blessed Mother devotees helped at judgment (Jesus) — 7/20/06 Vol. 44

Blessed Mother Mary mediatrix of grace (Jesus) — 4/29/01 Vol. 23

Blessed Mother Mary messages ending (Mary) — 2/5/98 Vol. 10

Blessed Mother Mary protector & intercessor (Jesus) — 8/14/01 Vol. 24

Blessed Mother Proclamation announcement by pope (Jesus) 10/3/04 Vol. 37

Bl. Mother refuges protection for faithful remnant (Jesus) 8/28/01 Vol. 24

Blessed Mother, St. Joseph exemplar parents (Jesus) — 5/18/07 Vol. 47

Blessed Mother's day mother of mankind at cross (Mary) 5/14/00 Vol. 19
Blessed Mother's faith for Cana miracle (Jesus) 1/14/01 Vol. 22
Blessed Mother's intercession has better hearing (Jesus) 7/16/04 Vol. 36
Blessed Mother's role in bringing Jesus into world (Jesus) 12/4/04 Vol. 37
Blessed Sacrament adoration-reward in heaven (Jesus) 3/6/98 Vol. 10
Blessed Sacrament always preserved (Jesus) 6/17/02 Vol. 27
Blessed Sacrament angels always around (Jesus) 4/17/07 Vol. 47
Blessed Sacrament attack on Real Presence (Jesus) 5/14/02 Vol. 27
Blessed Sacrament attacked and removed (Jesus) 7/26/02 Vol. 28
Blessed Sacrament attacked by demons,masons (Jesus) 5/19/04 Vol. 35
Blessed Sacrament attacked by Satan (Jesus) 7/25/07 Vol. 48
Blessed Sacrament attacks by deceivers (Jesus) 7/7/07 Vol. 48
Blessed Sacrament being hidden (Jesus) 9/8/03 Vol. 32
Blessed Sacrament being stripped from churches (Jesus) 10/22/02 Vol. 29
Blessed Sacrament blessings (Jesus) 5/13/95 Vol. 2
Blessed Sacrament Blood over lintel (Jesus) 7/20/01 Vol. 24
Blessed Sacrament build up spiritual stamina (Jesus) 2/25/97 Vol. 6
Blessed Sacrament communicates God's love (Jesus) 2/25/05 Vol. 38
Blessed Sacrament confession (Jesus) 3/6/96 Vol. 3
Blessed Sacrament Divine Will (Jesus) 9/28/96 Vol. 4
Blessed Sacrament do not hide in back rooms (Jesus) 4/27/03 Vol. 31
Blessed Sacrament emanates golden light (Jesus) 6/20/02 Vol. 27
Blessed Sacrament encourage exposition (Jesus) 7/30/97 Vol. 8
Blessed Sacrament encourage exposition (Jesus) 2/4/99 Vol. 14
Blessed Sacrament gift of Jesus to us (Jesus) 3/15/08 Vol. 50
Blessed Sacrament give honor and reverence (Jesus) 7/23/98 Vol. 12
Blessed Sacrament give proper respect (Jesus) 3/13/98 Vol. 10
Blessed Sacrament give proper respect (Jesus) 7/9/98 Vol. 12
Blessed Sacrament give respect (Jesus) 8/18/97 Vol. 8
Blessed Sacrament give respect to (Jesus) 7/20/03 Vol. 32
Blessed Sacrament give reverence to (Jesus) 4/26/03 Vol. 31
Blessed Sacrament give reverence to (Jesus) 6/10/05 Vol. 39
Blessed Sacrament give thanks (Jesus) 12/21/97 Vol. 9
Blessed Sacrament give thanks & praise (Jesus) 1/18/98 Vol. 10
Blessed Sacrament gives rest & peace (Jesus) 1/3/01 Vol. 22
Blessed Sacrament gives strength for trials (Jesus) 6/21/02 Vol. 27
Blessed Sacrament greatest treasure in Jesus (Jesus) 4/3/06 Vol. 43
Blessed Sacrament help from Jesus (Jesus) 4/12/07 Vol. 47
Blessed Sacrament in a shopping mall (Jesus) 11/10/01 Vol. 25
Blessed Sacrament in back rooms (Jesus) 8/23/03 Vol. 32
Blessed Sacrament in public processions (Jesus) 4/22/04 Vol. 35
Blessed Sacrament in tribulation (Jesus) 1/15/96 Vol. 3
Blessed Sacrament inspires messages (Jesus) 10/13/01 Vol. 25
Blessed Sacrament is holy ground (Jesus) 6/4/04 Vol. 35
Blessed Sacrament is Light of grace (Jesus) 6/14/01 Vol. 23
Blessed Sacrament Jesus is with us always (Jesus) 5/24/01 Vol. 23
Blessed Sacrament Jesus' very presence among us (Jesus) 2/26/02 Vol. 26

Blessed Sacrament jewel of Real Presence (Jesus) 10/21/99 Vol. 17
Blessed Sacrament keep in main church (Jesus) 4/1/06 Vol. 43
Blessed Sacrament keep reverence (Jesus) 5/1/03 Vol. 31
Blessed Sacrament less reverence (Jesus) 7/4/96 Vol. 3
Blessed Sacrament light of faith (Jesus) 7/26/96 Vol. 4
Blessed Sacrament Light of Jesus overcomes sin (Jesus) 10/16/00 Vol. 21
Blessed Sacrament light of the world (Jesus) 9/16/96 Vol. 4
Blessed Sacrament listen,discern God's plan (Jesus) 10/9/04 Vol. 37
Blessed Sacrament Living Water of soul (Jesus) 4/28/01 Vol. 23
Blessed Sacrament love (Jesus) 4/19/94 Vol. 1
Blessed Sacrament makes Church holy & heals (Jesus) 7/14/06 Vol. 44
Blessed Sacrament makes churches holy (Jesus) 8/8/02 Vol. 28
Blessed Sacrament makes churches holy (Jesus) 5/8/01 Vol. 23
Blessed Sacrament makes churches holy (Jesus) 7/21/04 Vol. 36
Blessed Sacrament makes churches holy (Jesus) 7/18/05 Vol. 40
Blessed Sacrament most precious gift of God (Jesus) 11/17/05 Vol. 41
Blessed Sacrament most treasured gift (Jesus) 12/6/97 Vol. 9
Blessed Sacrament move (Jesus) 10/17/95 Vol. 3
Blessed Sacrament need to visit often (Jesus) 7/24/06 Vol. 44
Blessed Sacrament New Covenant (Jesus) 11/12/06 Vol. 45
Blessed Sacrament new Holy of Holies (Jesus) 9/25/07 Vol. 48
Blessed Sacrament one on one love of God (Jesus) 6/26/02 Vol. 27
Blessed Sacrament pillars defend reverence for (Jesus) 11/15/04 Vol. 37
Blessed Sacrament pouring out of love (Jesus) 1/23/97 Vol. 6
Blessed Sacrament power & glory (Jesus) 9/21/02 Vol. 28
Blessed Sacrament power of Corpus Christi refuge (Jesus) 8/9/05 Vol. 40
Blessed Sacrament power of the Eucharist (Jesus) 11/16/96 Vol. 5
Blessed Sacrament praise,worship as angels (Jesus) 4/27/06 Vol. 43
Blessed Sacrament prayer and reverence (Jesus) 7/12/02 Vol. 28
Blessed Sacrament Presence most important (Jesus) 6/8/06 Vol. 43
Blessed Sacrament presence of Trinity (Jesus) 4/13/06 Vol. 43
Blessed Sacrament Presence of Trinity (Jesus) 6/6/04 Vol. 35
Blessed Sacrament present through tribulation (Jesus) 1/19/06 Vol. 42
Blessed Sacrament preserve,Keep visible (Jesus) 4/19/01 Vol. 23
Blessed Sacrament protect from black masses (Jesus) 8/10/02 Vol. 28
Blessed Sacrament protect from desecration (Jesus) 7/30/06 Vol. 44
Blessed Sacrament protect from desecration (Jesus) 4/22/01 Vol. 23
Blessed Sacrament protect in secrecy in future (Jesus) 6/28/98 Vol. 11
Blessed Sacrament protection from vandals (Jesus) 5/4/06 Vol. 43
Blessed Sacrament radiance & power (Jesus) 10/4/97 Vol. 9
Blessed Sacrament radiates heat of love (Jesus) 2/12/03 Vol. 30
Blessed Sacrament real presence (Jesus) 2/27/98 Vol. 10
Blessed Sacrament Real Presence of Jesus (Jesus) 9/6/01 Vol. 24
Blessed Sacrament Real Presence of Jesus (Jesus) 11/3/06 Vol. 45
Blessed Sacrament receive worthily (Jesus) 6/26/04 Vol. 35
Blessed Sacrament remnant (Jesus) 4/24/94 Vol. 1
Blessed Sacrament respect as holy ground (Jesus) 2/4/99 Vol. 14

Blessed Sacrament rest for your soul (Jesus)   3/14/99 Vol. 14
Blessed Sacrament reverence for Real Presence (Jesus)   7/27/03 Vol. 32
Blessed Sacrament reverence kneeling, no shoes (Jesus)   10/16/03 Vol. 33
Blessed Sacrament reverence needed (Jesus)   12/15/05 Vol. 41
Blessed Sacrament reverence needed (Jesus)   1/19/08 Vol. 50
Blessed Sacrament reverence needed (Jesus)   10/27/07 Vol. 49
Blessed Sacrament reverence, gift of love (Jesus)   7/11/97 Vol. 8
Bl Sacra. reverence,Moses with sandles (God the Father)   7/15/00 Vol. 20
Blessed Sacrament reverence,thanksgiving (Jesus)   7/4/97 Vol. 8
Blessed Sacrament sacred minimized (Jesus)   3/22/03 Vol. 30
Blessed Sacrament sacrilege (Jesus)   5/30/95 Vol. 2
Blessed Sacrament small taste of heaven (Jesus)   10/26/98 Vol. 13
Blessed Sacrament source of peace and love (Jesus)   4/28/02 Vol. 27
Blessed Sacrament special gift of Jesus (Jesus)   12/15/00 Vol. 21
Blessed Sacrament strength where praised (Jesus)   6/6/00 Vol. 19
Blessed Sacrament strengthens your spirit (Mary)   2/21/97 Vol. 6
Blessed Sacrament tabernacle of Real Presence (Jesus)   10/26/98 Vol. 13
Blessed Sacrament take time for Him (Jesus)   1/20/97 Vol. 6
Blessed Sacrament target of demons to remove (Jesus)   7/30/05 Vol. 40
Blessed Sacrament taste of heaven (Jesus)   12/11/04 Vol. 37
Blessed Sacrament the gift of adoration (Jesus)   5/12/97 Vol. 7
Blessed Sacrament time (Jesus)   6/7/94 Vol. 1
Blessed Sacrament to be adored (Jesus)   11/16/00 Vol. 21
Blessed Sacrament to be vandalized more (Jesus)   9/1/04 Vol. 36
Blessed Sacrament trying to remove (Jesus)   10/20/02 Vol. 29
Blessed Sacrament under attack (Jesus)   1/25/03 Vol. 30
Blessed Sacrament underground in tribulation (Jesus)   6/9/96 Vol. 3
Blessed Sacrament visit for Lent (Jesus)   3/1/07 Vol. 46
Blessed Sacrament will (Jesus)   5/7/94 Vol. 1
Blessed Sacrament witness to messages (Jesus)   7/21/96 Vol. 4
Blessed Sacrament witness to the gospel (Jesus)   4/12/96 Vol. 3
Blessed Sacrament Adoration graces for people (Jesus)   8/30/07 Vol. 48
Blessed Sacra. adored priesthood flourishes there (Jesus)   6/14/02 Vol. 27
Blessed Sacra. attacked to remove Real Presence (Jesus)   8/14/02 Vol. 28
Blessed Sacra. attacks on Adoration & tabernacles (Jesus)   2/4/05 Vol. 38
Blessed Sacrament visits spiritual nourishment (Jesus)   3/13/04 Vol. 34
Blessed Sacrament visits take time in schedule for (Jesus)   8/9/98 Vol. 12
blessed sacramentals protection from demons (Jesus)   7/25/01 Vol. 24
blessed sacramentals protection from demons (Jesus)   3/27/06 Vol. 42
blessed sacramentals protection from demons (Jesus)   2/24/06 Vol. 42
blessed sacramentals protection from demons (Jesus)   2/9/06 Vol. 42
blessed sacramentals protection from demons (Jesus)   1/5/06 Vol. 42
blessed sacramentals protection from demons (Jesus)   11/13/07 Vol. 49
blessed sacramentals protection from evil (Jesus)   1/27/00 Vol. 18
Blessed Seelos in vision laughing (Jesus)   6/23/04 Vol. 35
Blessed Trinity all present in tabernacle (Jesus)   7/6/00 Vol. 20
Blessed Trinity are inseparable (Jesus)   4/13/06 Vol. 43

Blessed Trinity at Baptism of Jesus (Jesus)   1/8/07 Vol. 46
Blessed Trinity call on for needs, graces (Jesus)   5/16/06 Vol. 43
Blessed Trinity hard to comprehend (Jesus)   5/5/07 Vol. 47
Blessed Trinity honored in Hosts (Jesus)   5/26/06 Vol. 43
Blessed Trinity inseparable (Jesus)   8/9/06 Vol. 44
Blessed Trinity intimacy of Holy Communion (Jesus)   5/8/05 Vol. 39
Blessed Trinity present at Jesus' birth (Jesus)   7/18/05 Vol. 40
Blessed Trinity present at Transfiguration (Jesus)   8/6/07 Vol. 48
Blessed Trinity present everywhere (Jesus)   9/7/07 Vol. 48
Blessed Trinity Scripture of Jesus' Baptism (Jesus)   1/3/06 Vol. 42
Blessed Trinity should be seen in each person (Jesus)   3/10/02 Vol. 26
Blessed Trinity unity of Three Persons (Jesus)   5/9/07 Vol. 47
Blessed Trinity in Host all seen at once (Jesus)   6/25/00 Vol. 19
Blessed Virgin birthday mother prepared for all time (Jesus) 9/8/01 Vol. 24
Blessed Virgin Mary birthday as Ark of Covenant (Jesus)   9/8/05 Vol. 40
Blessed Virgin Mary intercessor for our sins (Jesus)   9/12/06 Vol. 44
Blessed Virgin Mary mantle of protection (Jesus)   2/6/08 Vol. 50
blessing curse (Jesus)   8/6/95 Vol. 3
blessing personal message (Jesus)   5/10/96 Vol. 3
blessing poured out as the sun shines on us (Jesus)   10/5/00 Vol. 21
blessings gifts of the Holy Spirit (Jesus)   6/7/95 Vol. 2
blessings give thanks,honor,glory (Jesus)   7/3/97 Vol. 8
blessings given and taken away (Jesus)   11/26/98 Vol. 13
blessings money (Jesus)   4/5/94 Vol. 1
blessings pride (Jesus)   8/18/95 Vol. 3
blessings trials for rejecting (Jesus)   2/25/96 Vol. 3
blessings from God not man's accomplishments (Jesus)   7/13/00 Vol. 20
blessings, abundant responsibility to share with poor (Jesus) 3/8/02 Vol. 26
Blood & grace needed for spiritual survival (Jesus)   3/31/02 Vol. 26
blood and pie votes for abortion,affairs (Jesus)   10/11/00 Vol. 21
blood money abortions,arms,drugs (Jesus)   3/27/99 Vol. 14
blood money forsaking mission (Jesus)   2/11/99 Vol. 14
blood money rich profit from wars, abortions (Jesus)   12/22/03 Vol. 33
Blood of Jesus gives entrance to heaven (Jesus)   4/6/06 Vol. 43
Blood of Jesus ransom for souls (Jesus)   3/24/07 Vol. 46
Blood of Lamb washes away sin (Jesus)   9/21/06 Vol. 44
Blood of Lamb worthy sacrifice to Father (Jesus)   4/6/06 Vol. 43
blood on hands from abortions (Jesus)   6/5/03 Vol. 31
Blood Sacrifice atonement for all sins (Jesus)   9/23/05 Vol. 40
blood sacrifice links Passover & Crucifixion (Jesus)   3/28/02 Vol. 26
Blood Sacrifice of Jesus redeemed all (Jesus)   9/14/05 Vol. 40
Blood sacrifice price of man's sins (Jesus)   4/8/07 Vol. 47
Blood sacrifice of Jesus redemption of all mankind (Jesus) 11/12/04 Vol. 37
Blood to last drop given up for sinners (Jesus)   2/14/00 Vol. 18
blue ball of Mary protection through rosary (Jesus)   7/26/01 Vol. 24
blue butterfly sign of Our Lady's presence (Our Lady)   8/15/07 Vol. 48
blue clouds in NYC anesthetized people (Jesus)   7/12/05 Vol. 40

St. Michael the Archangel, Defend us in the Battle.

blue turban Arabs (Jesus) — 11/5/94 Vol. 2

blueprint for life in Scriptures (Jesus) — 12/16/99 Vol. 17

blueprints for life following God's plan (Jesus) — 9/4/99 Vol. 16

blur of events cover end time signs (Jesus) — 11/29/02 Vol. 29

boast in God not yourself (Jesus) — 2/12/05 Vol. 38

boast in the Lord not of fame & fortune (Jesus) — 7/10/00 Vol. 20

boasting avoid wealth, possessions (Jesus) — 5/22/06 Vol. 43

boasting only in Jesus' name (Jesus) — 1/17/04 Vol. 34

boat leap of faith (Jesus) — 7/27/94 Vol. 2

boat of St. Peter Church through the ages (Jesus) — 5/12/05 Vol. 39

Bob Leary funeral message (Bob Leary) — 8/16/06 Vol. 44

bodies die souls live forever (Jesus) — 2/19/04 Vol. 34

bodily abuse avoid alcohol,drugs,sexual sins (Jesus) — 12/19/03 Vol. 33

bodily appearance keep natural beauty (Mary) — 8/7/97 Vol. 8

bodily restraints require faith & grace (Jesus) — 1/17/07 Vol. 46

body receives earthly gifts (Jesus) — 4/15/07 Vol. 47

Body & Blood of Christ gives eternal life (Jesus) — 4/30/04 Vol. 35

Body & Blood of Jesus belief in Real Presence (Jesus) — 5/6/06 Vol. 43

Body & Blood of Jesus Real Presence (Jesus) — 5/1/04 Vol. 35

body & soul desires & weaknesses (Jesus) — 7/1/04 Vol. 36

body & soul in struggle (Jesus) — 6/25/01 Vol. 23

body & soul with free will (Jesus) — 11/16/01 Vol. 25

body and soul conscience (Jesus) — 11/10/95 Vol. 3

body to dust soul lives on forever (Jesus) — 12/26/01 Vol. 25

body vs. soul battle during life (Jesus) — 2/3/00 Vol. 18

body vs. soul struggle for perfection (Jesus) — 2/1/05 Vol. 38

Body&Blood of Jesus Real Presence of God (Jesus)   10/26/00 Vol. 21
body, out of near death, Warning (Jesus)   11/24/07 Vol. 49
body, prison of because of mortality,sin (Jesus)   11/25/02 Vol. 29
Body,Blood of Jesus must eat to have life (Jesus)   7/30/00 Vol. 20
body's cravings not satisfied with things (Jesus)   12/9/03 Vol. 33
body's death white beam of soul leaves (Jesus)   6/7/07 Vol. 47
Boe, Marian's funeral comments on her life (Jesus)   5/27/05 Vol. 39
bomb,nuclear neutron bomb,biological war (Jesus)   9/17/98 Vol. 12
bombs, electronic effect chips & brains (Jesus)   3/5/03 Vol. 30
bombs, radiation microwave machines (Jesus)   8/29/03 Vol. 32
bombs, roadside jam or detonate (Jesus)   6/14/07 Vol. 47
bondage martydom   10/19/93 Vol. 1
bonds of sin break old habits (Jesus)   4/10/00 Vol. 19
bonds of sin broken by ransom of Jesus (Jesus)   8/6/00 Vol. 20
bonds of sin need releasing (Jesus)   3/2/06 Vol. 42
Bonsignore, Adele funeral (Jesus)   6/5/04 Vol. 35
book grace & evangelize (Jesus)   4/24/96 Vol. 3
book messages (Jesus)   12/28/95 Vol. 3
book messages (St. Therese)   12/29/95 Vol. 3
book messages & preparation (Jesus)   5/1/96 Vol. 3
book personal advice (St. Therese)   3/22/96 Vol. 3
book suffering (Jesus)   1/17/96 Vol. 3
book of life cross on forehead (Holy Spirit)   5/1/96 Vol. 3
Book of Life demons   10/18/93 Vol. 1
Book of Life faithful crossed on forehead (Jesus)   8/21/02 Vol. 28
book of life heaven on earth (Jesus)   8/4/95 Vol. 3
book of life judgment (Jesus)   3/18/95 Vol. 2
Book of Life names of souls for heaven (Jesus)   8/26/05 Vol. 40
book of life record of faithful (Jesus)   3/23/00 Vol. 18
Book of Life record of life kept (Jesus)   4/25/01 Vol. 23
Book of Life separated for heaven (Jesus)   6/3/04 Vol. 35
Book of Life spiritual choices (Jesus)   5/15/01 Vol. 23
book of life the beast   8/24/93 Vol. 1
Book of Revelation prepare for end times (Jesus)   5/13/07 Vol. 47
bookcover description messages (Jesus)   12/8/95 Vol. 3
books help to evangelize (St. Therese)   3/20/96 Vol. 3
books & messages effect on people (Jesus)   1/28/97 Vol. 6
books censored by one world people (Jesus)   11/18/99 Vol. 17
books of evil focus on man and nature (Jesus)   6/9/97 Vol. 7
border requirements chips will be needed to cross (Jesus) 10/1/98 Vol. 13
borders more scanning, persecution (Jesus)   2/27/04 Vol. 34
born again by water and Holy Spirit (Jesus)   4/19/04 Vol. 35
born again in Spirit of Christmas (Jesus)   12/14/03 Vol. 33
born again make personal commitment (Jesus)   7/23/04 Vol. 36
born again of water & the Spirit (Jesus)   4/16/07 Vol. 47
born with nothing die with nothing (Jesus)   9/5/99 Vol. 16
Bosnia contrition (Jesus)   11/29/95 Vol. 3

Bosnia peace (Jesus)   3/9/94 Vol. 1
Bosnia war (St. Blaise)   2/3/94 Vol. 1
Bosnia war (Jesus)   2/6/94 Vol. 1
bracelets to honor Mary (Jesus)   8/15/05 Vol. 40
brain marvel of use in man (Jesus)   11/18/02 Vol. 29
brainwashing protected by angels (Jesus)   11/21/01 Vol. 25
bread multiplied miraculously (Jesus)   2/24/00 Vol. 18
bread & wine become heavenly harvest (Jesus)   8/5/01 Vol. 24
bread & wine changed to Body & Blood (Jesus)   3/28/02 Vol. 26
bread & wine Consecration of Mass (Jesus)   8/31/05 Vol. 40
bread & wine into Jesus' Body & Blood (Jesus)   9/28/01 Vol. 24
bread breaking manna (Jesus)   7/31/94 Vol. 2
bread from heaven reverence (Jesus)   7/26/95 Vol. 3
Bread multiplied Exodus,loaves & fish (Jesus)   12/1/04 Vol. 37
Bread of life Body & Blood for eternal life (Jesus)   12/1/04 Vol. 37
Bread of Life Body & Blood of Jesus (Jesus)   9/10/03 Vol. 32
Bread of Life by Real Presence in Host (Jesus)   4/22/99 Vol. 15
Bread of Life enlightens soul (Jesus)   4/14/01 Vol. 23
Bread of Life gives us eternal life (Jesus)   6/22/03 Vol. 31
Bread of Life grace for daily trials (Jesus)   5/7/97 Vol. 7
Bread of life in Blessed Sacrament (Jesus)   2/27/01 Vol. 22
Bread of Life in Jesus (Jesus)   7/14/05 Vol. 40
Bread of Life in Mass & Last Supper (Jesus)   7/25/01 Vol. 24
Bread of Life manna & Eucharist (Jesus)   7/23/03 Vol. 32
Bread of Life never go hungry (Jesus)   8/1/99 Vol. 16
Bread of Life receive worthily (Jesus)   5/17/03 Vol. 31
bread of life sacrilege (Jesus)   8/7/94 Vol. 2
Bread of Life share gift of love (Jesus)   4/18/02 Vol. 27
Bread of Life source of life (Jesus)   8/19/00 Vol. 20
Bread of Life unconditional love (Jesus)   1/7/03 Vol. 30
bread, unleavened from Jewish Passover (Jesus)   3/24/07 Vol. 46
breaking of bread Real Presence in Host (Jesus)   1/30/07 Vol. 46
breaking of bread recognized Jesus by (Jesus)   4/19/06 Vol. 43
breaking of bread repeated at Holy Communion (Jesus)   3/30/05 Vol. 38
breaking of bread share in Eucharist (Jesus)   5/3/07 Vol. 47
breathing to lungs as grace to soul (Jesus)   5/23/02 Vol. 27
bridge over evil span the dark abyss (Jesus)   1/27/00 Vol. 18
bridge security safety concern (Jesus)   10/18/07 Vol. 49
bridges challenged by nature (Jesus)   12/4/97 Vol. 9
bridges new terrorist target (Jesus)   10/10/07 Vol. 49
bridges in life strengthened by faith in God (Jesus)   7/27/00 Vol. 20
bridges of friendship peacemakers to stop wars (Jesus)   3/17/01 Vol. 22
bridges of love to God & neighbor (Jesus)   3/31/06 Vol. 42
bridges, tunnels vulnerable to storms (Jesus)   9/22/05 Vol. 40
broad road vs. narrow road (Jesus)   8/18/05 Vol. 40
broken heart of Jesus (Jesus)   10/3/01 Vol. 25
broken relationships Jesus, the great healer (Jesus)   5/11/00 Vol. 19

broken relationships urgency to repair (Jesus) — 3/28/00 Vol. 18

brokenness share Jesus' suffering (Jesus) — 3/9/07 Vol. 46

brokenness in Church life up the lukewarm (Jesus) — 2/21/08 Vol. 50

bronze serpent healing through Moses (Jesus) — 5/4/00 Vol. 19

bronze serpent prefigures Jesus on cross (Jesus) — 3/11/08 Vol. 50

bronze serpent preview of Jesus on cross (Jesus) — 4/4/06 Vol. 43

brown scapular Mary's mantle of protection (Jesus) — 9/18/06 Vol. 44

brown scapular St. Simon Stock given (Jesus) — 7/16/07 Vol. 48

Buchheit funeral wedding banquet in heaven (Jesus) — 3/18/04 Vol. 34

Bucky Sotile at daughter's wedding (Bucky) — 5/20/06 Vol. 43

budgets choose to help people or war (Jesus) — 1/26/06 Vol. 42

Buffalo storm be prepared (Jesus) — 10/19/06 Vol. 45

Buffalo storm take notice to prepare (Jesus) — 10/21/06 Vol. 45

building up Jesus' Church in the people (Jesus) — 10/27/07 Vol. 49

Buonemani, Ray funeral Mass (Jesus) — 3/10/08 Vol. 50

burden of life Jesus will help (Jesus) — 11/22/06 Vol. 45

burden of man's sins carried on cross of Jesus (Jesus) — 7/6/00 Vol. 20

burden of sin lifted by Confession (Jesus) — 7/22/00 Vol. 20

burdened evangelize (Jesus) — 7/17/94 Vol. 2

burdens & trials call on Jesus for help (Jesus) — 7/21/05 Vol. 40

Burke,Tom message for family,friends (Tom Burke) — 7/16/98 Vol. 12

burning bush God is not mocked (God the Father) — 3/19/95 Vol. 2

burning bush love of God the Father (Jesus) — 8/23/99 Vol. 16

burning bush sign of eternal love (God the Father) — 3/22/98 Vol. 10

burning bush ten commandments (Father) — 8/19/93 Vol. 1

burning church lifetime (Jesus) — 10/14/95 Vol. 3

Bush converted life (Jesus) — 2/19/01 Vol. 22

Bush & leaders stand for life (Jesus) — 1/22/01 Vol. 22

Bush elected to change abortion laws (Jesus) — 12/13/00 Vol. 21

Bush, President influenced by one worlders (Jesus) — 7/26/03 Vol. 32

Bush, president lawmakers uphold principles (Jesus) — 1/18/01 Vol. 22

Bush, president pushed into war (Jesus) — 2/9/03 Vol. 30

Bush, President unsettling nations (Jesus) — 9/25/02 Vol. 28

Bush, President why does he want war? (Jesus) — 9/20/02 Vol. 28

Bush,president siding with one worlders (Jesus) — 5/7/01 Vol. 23

Bush-State of Union war, abortion issues (Jesus) — 2/2/05 Vol. 38

business illegally financed (Jesus) — 7/1/99 Vol. 16

business sexual ads to sell goods (Jesus) — 10/15/02 Vol. 29

business leaders steal people's money, kill (Jesus) — 9/19/98 Vol. 12

business tycoons slave wages, no benefits (Jesus) — 1/24/08 Vol. 50

businesses controlled by 1 world people (Jesus) — 12/21/00 Vol. 21

busy life slow down for Jesus (Jesus) — 5/27/06 Vol. 43

busy lives require time for God (Jesus) — 11/15/99 Vol. 17

butterfly new spiritual life (Jesus) — 9/28/07 Vol. 48

butterfly stages of life (Jesus) — 3/31/99 Vol. 14

butterfly symbol of conversion (Jesus) — 7/14/06 Vol. 44

butterfly web of confusion (Jesus) — 7/16/94 Vol. 2

Cabrini creation (Jesus) — 7/17/95 Vol. 3

Cabrini Mother — 8/12/93 Vol. 1

Cabrini top grotto springs (Mother Cabrini) — 7/1/94 Vol. 2

Cabrini,Mother inspired great works (Jesus) — 11/13/01 Vol. 25

cadavers preserved in plastic (Jesus) — 7/2/06 Vol. 44

Cain & Abel first killing (Jesus) — 2/12/07 Vol. 46

California earthquake & bridges (Jesus) — 7/23/06 Vol. 44

California ready for big earthquake (Jesus) — 3/30/06 Vol. 42

California stripped of possessions (Jesus) — 1/4/01 Vol. 22

California coastline changed by earthquakes (Jesus) — 7/26/05 Vol. 40

California disasters snow,rain,quakes,mud slides (Jesus) — 12/30/03 Vol. 33

California earthquake to change coastline (Jesus) — 11/7/05 Vol. 41

California fires arson, millions of dollars lost (Jesus) — 10/25/07 Vol. 49

California fires chastisement for sins (Jesus) — 10/30/03 Vol. 33

California fires natural disasters test (Jesus) — 10/22/07 Vol. 49

California fires near 'R' movie actors (Jesus) — 9/30/05 Vol. 40

California fires next event to storms (Jesus) — 9/29/05 Vol. 40

California fires punishment for stars (Jesus) — 1/25/07 Vol. 46

California fires worst disaster since Katrina (Jesus) — 10/23/07 Vol. 49

California's bad movies to face God's wrath (Jesus) — 12/14/05 Vol. 41

call to holiness Lenten call to save souls (Jesus) — 3/27/00 Vol. 18

calling of Jesus to follow Him (Jesus) — 1/22/06 Vol. 42

callings, vocations religious,lay,messengers (Jesus) — 1/27/08 Vol. 50

calls, movement everyone monitored (Jesus) — 8/8/07 Vol. 48

calm the seas when boarding cruise ship (Jesus) — 12/6/99 Vol. 17

Calvary captivity of sins (Jesus) — 8/23/96 Vol. 4

Calvary desert of Lent to (Jesus) — 3/16/98 Vol. 10

Calvary represents life's trials (Jesus) — 3/22/05 Vol. 38

Calvary suffer crosses,martyrdom (Jesus) — 1/15/97 Vol. 6

Calvary suffer with Jesus (Jesus) — 7/14/99 Vol. 16

Calvary walk needed for wedding feast (Jesus) — 12/16/98 Vol. 13

Calvary,personal suffering for forgiveness of sin (Jesus) — 8/7/00 Vol. 20

Calvary's cross take up our own cross (Jesus) — 8/27/99 Vol. 16

cameras,security smart cards,chips in hand (Jesus) — 4/23/99 Vol. 15

Cana wedding feast (Jesus) — 5/2/02 Vol. 27

Cana Wedding Blessed Mother's care (Jesus) — 1/7/06 Vol. 42

Canada punishment in ice storm (Jesus) — 1/15/98 Vol. 10

Canadian government to fall to Antichrist (Jesus) — 6/25/99 Vol. 15

cancer caused by chemical pollutants (Jesus) — 4/7/05 Vol. 39

cancer & diseases result of man's progress (Jesus) — 2/6/06 Vol. 42

cancer, AIDS created for money (Jesus) — 2/3/01 Vol. 22

cancers hybrids & gene studies (Jesus) — 8/2/01 Vol. 24

cancers & viruses to reduce population (Jesus) — 9/21/00 Vol. 20

candle meaning acknowledges Real Presence (Jesus) — 2/21/02 Vol. 26

candles in life Easter & Baptism (Jesus) — 2/2/06 Vol. 42

candles, intention prayers for intentions (Jesus) — 9/28/05 Vol. 40

Canticle of Zachary morning prayer (Jesus) — 5/31/07 Vol. 47

capital punishment discouraged by pope (Jesus)   1/28/99 Vol. 14

capital punishment opposed by pope, Church (Jesus)   6/22/00 Vol. 19

captives forever worship Jesus (Jesus)   4/24/97 Vol. 7

captivity of body drugs, passions, riches (Jesus)   9/5/03 Vol. 32

captivity to sin released in Confession (Jesus)   11/3/01 Vol. 25

car breakdown opportunity to help others (Jesus)   5/8/07 Vol. 47

car engine like soul fuel vs grace, lifeblood (Jesus)   4/4/01 Vol. 23

car headlights out similar to mortal sin (Jesus)   4/10/99 Vol. 15

car makers, oil companies reason for high gas cost (Jesus)   5/11/07 Vol. 47

Cardinal Stepinac man of faith in Croatia (Jesus)   7/10/02 Vol. 28

care givers pray for their strength (Jesus)   6/17/04 Vol. 35

care givers suffer with Jesus (Jesus)   1/30/01 Vol. 22

caregivers receive many blessings (Jesus)   10/19/99 Vol. 17

Carmelite Monastery place of protection (Mary)   9/6/97 Vol. 8

Carmelites basis of order (St. Therese)   5/28/97 Vol. 7

carnival carnal pleasures desired (Jesus)   5/8/06 Vol. 43

carry your cross Jesus helps as Simon (Jesus)   2/14/00 Vol. 18

carry your cross without complaining (Jesus)   5/14/03 Vol. 31

carrying cross uphill struggle in life (Jesus)   2/15/01 Vol. 22

carrying crosses Jesus' help as Simon's (Jesus)   5/16/00 Vol. 19

cars fuel to be scarce (Jesus)   7/2/98 Vol. 12

cars search for alternate fuels (Jesus)   3/31/05 Vol. 38

cars tracked by satellites (Jesus)   5/12/97 Vol. 7

cars use older vehicles for hiding (Jesus)   7/23/98 Vol. 12

cars detected triumph (Jesus)   4/30/95 Vol. 2

cars, need for necessary transportation (Jesus)   6/17/03 Vol. 31

cars,trucks vulnerable to gas shortages (Jesus)   11/2/00 Vol. 21

cartoons bad for children (Jesus)   12/11/98 Vol. 13

cartoons have evil agenda (Jesus)   2/2/03 Vol. 30

cartoons mislead children (Jesus)   5/15/97 Vol. 7

cartoons twist children's minds (Jesus)   8/16/03 Vol. 32

cartoons of Muhammad stirring Muslim protests (Jesus)   2/9/06 Vol. 42

cartoons on TV guide children from control (Jesus)   11/28/02 Vol. 29

cartoons, violent have children avoid (Jesus)   10/30/03 Vol. 33

cashless society diseases (Jesus)   5/25/94 Vol. 1

cashless society mandatory chips in body (Jesus)   5/3/07 Vol. 47

Casilda funeral message (Casilda)   5/13/97 Vol. 7

Casini Space probe technology at risk (Jesus)   10/14/97 Vol. 9

casinos & sins brought our destruction (Jesus)   10/5/05 Vol. 41

casinos, gambling causing more addictions (Jesus)   1/22/06 Vol. 42

casket death (Jesus)   8/2/94 Vol. 2

castle tower interior home (Jesus)   8/27/94 Vol. 2

casualties,$50 billion hard questions to answer (Jesus)   8/27/02 Vol. 28

cataclysmic event trust in God's help (Jesus)   12/22/98 Vol. 13

catacombs hide for protection (Jesus)   6/30/01 Vol. 23

catacombs hiding from persecutors (Jesus)   6/30/99 Vol. 15

Catacombs martyrs for Jesus' Name (Jesus)   7/20/96 Vol. 4

catacombs Masses underground (Jesus)   10/26/05 Vol. 41

catacombs place of hiding (Jesus)   4/29/98 Vol. 11

catacombs seclusion before triumph (Jesus)   10/14/96 Vol. 5

cataract healing with fish gall (Jesus)   6/8/07 Vol. 47

catastrophic events endure for sins (Jesus)   10/28/99 Vol. 17

Catechism for proper interpretation (Jesus)   5/27/02 Vol. 27

catechism know faith (Jesus)   5/6/96 Vol. 3

catechumens prepared for Baptism (Jesus)   3/1/99 Vol. 14

Catherine intercessor (Kateri T.)   10/23/94 Vol. 2

Catherine namesakes (Kateri Tekakwitha)   4/3/96 Vol. 3

Catherine personal (Kateri)   7/14/94 Vol. 2

Catholic Church attacked by Satan (Jesus)   9/18/07 Vol. 48

Catholic Church established by Jesus (Jesus)   5/1/07 Vol. 47

Catholic persecution to be more violent (Jesus)   11/7/07 Vol. 49

Catholic Schools are breaking down, closed (Jesus)   10/28/04 Vol. 37

Catholic schools being closed for lack of faith (Jesus)   11/13/04 Vol. 37

Catholic schools give support to (Jesus)   10/5/06 Vol. 45

Catholic schools,churches being closed (Jesus)   5/9/05 Vol. 39

Catholic teaching apostasy (Jesus)   11/23/95 Vol. 3

Catholic traditions real presence in Host (Jesus)   3/12/99 Vol. 14

Catholics persecuted & prejudiced (Jesus)   9/9/02 Vol. 28

Cat., fallen away need invitation & encouragement (Jesus)   2/27/02 Vol. 26

cave hiding (Jesus)   5/21/94 Vol. 1

cave Jesus was born in a (Jesus)   12/28/00 Vol. 21

cave made under shrine by angels (Jesus)   8/19/06 Vol. 44

cave protection from persecution (Jesus)   10/17/03 Vol. 33

cave protection with angels (Jesus)   2/3/97 Vol. 6

cave simple but gives protection (Jesus)   12/27/01 Vol. 25

cave stable (Jesus)   11/28/94 Vol. 2

cave vision of light (Jesus)   10/21/94 Vol. 2

cave / mail trial through the phone (Jesus)   8/2/95 Vol. 3

cave for hiding survival (Jesus)   9/12/95 Vol. 3

cave inserts plastic,metal in ground (Jesus)   6/22/07 Vol. 47

cave refuges led by angels to (Jesus)   8/7/02 Vol. 28

caves angels lead in hiding (Jesus)   10/6/96 Vol. 5

caves Antichrist (Jesus)   6/21/96 Vol. 3

caves as home to Taliban (Jesus)   11/15/01 Vol. 25

caves as refuge & protection (Jesus)   5/9/01 Vol. 23

caves as refuges of protection (Jesus)   10/22/05 Vol. 41

caves best protection (Jesus)   1/27/98 Vol. 10

caves carved out by angels (Jesus)   7/31/07 Vol. 48

caves carved out in mountains (Jesus)   8/6/98 Vol. 12

caves dug by us or angels (Jesus)   6/16/98 Vol. 11

caves for hiding (Jesus)   10/7/99 Vol. 17

caves for Mass in persecution (Jesus)   8/24/04 Vol. 36

caves for protection (Jesus)   1/8/04 Vol. 34

caves for protection (Jesus)   6/10/05 Vol. 39

caves for protection (Jesus)   3/4/05 Vol. 38

caves for protection as saints (Jesus)   1/28/03 Vol. 30

caves for protection now, past (Jesus)   10/27/06 Vol. 45

caves for protection, dress warm (Jesus)   4/9/05 Vol. 39

caves for refuges (Jesus)   11/21/07 Vol. 49

caves healing water in grotto (Jesus)   7/21/98 Vol. 12

caves help of the angels (Jesus)   12/20/97 Vol. 9

caves Jesus' birth & hiding (Jesus)   12/27/04 Vol. 37

caves light provided inside (Jesus)   4/20/05 Vol. 39

caves manna (Jesus)   10/17/94 Vol. 2

caves mark of the beast (Jesus)   6/10/96 Vol. 3

caves miraculous protection (Jesus)   1/21/99 Vol. 14

caves need food, warm clothes (Jesus)   1/6/08 Vol. 50

caves place of hiding (Jesus)   9/23/00 Vol. 20

caves places of protection (Jesus)   5/17/00 Vol. 19

caves places of protection in (Jesus)   8/17/06 Vol. 44

caves precedence in Bible (Jesus)   7/10/97 Vol. 8

caves prepared for needs (Jesus)   9/7/00 Vol. 20

caves protect in nuclear war (Jesus)   2/19/98 Vol. 10

caves protected from comet (Jesus)   12/4/99 Vol. 17

caves protected in tribulation (Jesus)   2/19/99 Vol. 14

caves protection & purgatory (Jesus)   6/7/01 Vol. 23

caves protection and shelter (Jesus)   10/16/97 Vol. 9

caves protection from Antichrist (Jesus)   4/24/01 Vol. 23

caves protection from evil men (Jesus)   11/4/96 Vol. 5

caves protection in persecution (Jesus)   8/25/97 Vol. 8

caves protection in tribulation (Mary)   1/16/98 Vol. 10

caves protection in war (Jesus)   7/27/06 Vol. 44

caves provide protection (Jesus)   4/29/98 Vol. 11

caves refuge in tribulation (Jesus)   2/24/00 Vol. 18

caves refuges for protection (Jesus)   1/15/04 Vol. 34

caves renewed earth (Jesus)   5/6/95 Vol. 2

caves safe havens (Jesus)   6/1/94 Vol. 1

caves scorned message (Jesus)   8/10/96 Vol. 4

caves with miraculous light,water (Jesus)   5/4/05 Vol. 39

caves with water, light, air (Jesus)   6/18/02 Vol. 27

caves & catacombs for protection (Jesus)   4/30/04 Vol. 35

caves & grottos in Jesus' life (Jesus)   8/15/03 Vol. 32

caves & refuges protected & perfected (Jesus)   11/21/01 Vol. 25

caves and healing healing waters (Jesus)   8/14/98 Vol. 12

caves as refuges for protection in tribulation (Jesus)   1/31/05 Vol. 38

caves carved by angels to provide protection (Jesus)   10/22/98 Vol. 13

caves carved by God mark of the beast (Jesus)   2/28/95 Vol. 2

caves for hiding extra exit for air, escape (Jesus)   6/9/07 Vol. 47

caves for protection during tribulation (Jesus)   10/13/00 Vol. 21

caves for refuges vent for air,water springs (Jesus)   1/28/08 Vol. 50

caves in Bethlehem & Egypt for Jesus (Jesus)   11/21/07 Vol. 49

caves of protection like in Bethlehem,Egypt (Jesus)   12/22/99 Vol. 17

caves prepared carved by angels (Jesus)   9/28/99 Vol. 16

caves protected angels protect from harm (Jesus)   9/16/98 Vol. 12

caves, ground homes bomb shelters (Jesus)   8/25/05 Vol. 40

caves, hiding in for saints & prophets (Jesus)   12/25/06 Vol. 45

Cecilia funeral (Jesus)   3/23/06 Vol. 42

Cecilia resting in better place (Jesus)   3/15/06 Vol. 42

celebration hope (Jesus)   4/19/95 Vol. 2

celebrations share joys & sorrows (Jesus)   10/10/96 Vol. 5

cell phones for tracking (Jesus)   1/15/04 Vol. 34

cell towers easily disrupted by God (Jesus)   11/9/00 Vol. 21

cell towers new towers of Babel (Jesus)   2/15/04 Vol. 34

cell towers transmit data for smart cards (Jesus)   5/31/04 Vol. 35

cell towers,fiber optics control communications (Jesus)   8/22/02 Vol. 28

cellular phone towers with satellites,avoid TV (Jesus)   10/13/98 Vol. 13

center of our lives in Jesus, not world (Jesus)   7/13/04 Vol. 36

central bankers caused inflated currency (Jesus)   9/24/07 Vol. 48

central bankers collect interest on debt (Jesus)   5/29/03 Vol. 31

central bankers control finances (Jesus)   8/24/06 Vol. 44

central bankers control flow of money (Jesus)   6/7/04 Vol. 35

central bankers control food prices (Jesus)   7/3/03 Vol. 32

central bankers control markets,debts (Jesus)   4/18/00 Vol. 19

central bankers desire secrecy for work (Jesus)   6/8/01 Vol. 23

central bankers finance dictators (Jesus)   2/11/03 Vol. 30

central bankers financial power (Jesus)   5/28/04 Vol. 35

central bankers hold the loans (Jesus)   3/19/05 Vol. 38

central bankers make money on wars (Jesus)   7/3/03 Vol. 32

central bankers plans to control us (Jesus)   10/3/07 Vol. 49

central bankers profit from national debts (Jesus)   4/5/01 Vol. 23

central bankers profit from wars (Jesus)   2/21/03 Vol. 30

central bankers promote constant wars (Jesus)   4/19/07 Vol. 47

central bankers selling us out in debts & wars (Jesus)   7/3/03 Vol. 32

central bankers want takover (Jesus)   7/8/05 Vol. 40

central bankers with international companies (Jesus)   2/18/07 Vol. 46

central bankers vs voters on Iraq War (Jesus)   11/8/07 Vol. 49

chair empty Holy (Father)   9/6/93 Vol. 1

chances and risks use your own talents (Jesus)   10/4/96 Vol. 5

change tradition (Jesus)   10/27/94 Vol. 2

change & conversion needed to gain heaven (Jesus)   8/25/05 Vol. 40

change life turn over a new leaf (Jesus)   5/16/04 Vol. 35

change of heart needed for conversion (Jesus)   3/21/00 Vol. 18

change our ways call of the Gospel (Jesus)   3/30/00 Vol. 18

changeless faith better to be true than false (Jesus)   6/4/00 Vol. 19

changes in Church clergy to mislead people (Jesus)   12/14/98 Vol. 13

changing your life difficult to live out (Jesus)   1/30/00 Vol. 18

chaos prepare in spirit,body (Jesus)   3/3/99 Vol. 14

chaos weather,satellites (Jesus)   10/6/99 Vol. 17

chaos vs order which are you adding to? (Jesus)   3/24/04 Vol. 34
chaplet of Divine Mercy Divine Will (Jesus)   9/26/96 Vol. 4
Chaplet of Divine Mercy Divine Will (Bl.Sr. Faustina)   12/12/96 Vol. 5
Chaplet of Divine Mercy Stations of Cross (Jesus)   4/10/97 Vol. 7
charitable help go beyond donations,heart (Jesus)   7/12/07 Vol. 48
charities food shelves,relief,poor (Jesus)   9/6/01 Vol. 24
charities to help those in need (Jesus)   11/29/01 Vol. 25
charity do not be selfish (Jesus)   9/30/07 Vol. 48
charity feed the hungry (Jesus)   6/1/07 Vol. 47
charity give cheerfully (Jesus)   12/6/03 Vol. 33
charity give in secret (Jesus)   7/15/07 Vol. 48
charity give of substance (Jesus)   3/3/98 Vol. 10
charity in sharing faith to save souls (Jesus)   10/14/06 Vol. 45
charity out of love in heart (Jesus)   9/16/03 Vol. 32
charity rich in heavenly treasures (Jesus)   6/2/02 Vol. 27
charity share life's burdens (Jesus)   11/16/00 Vol. 21
charity share talents & treasure (Jesus)   11/21/01 Vol. 25
charity sharing, not greedy or selfish (Jesus)   7/27/04 Vol. 36
charity should not expect to be returned (Jesus)   8/16/04 Vol. 36
charity St. E. Seton (St. E. Seton)   1/4/95 Vol. 2
charity to poor and needy (Mother Seton)   3/20/96 Vol. 3
charity & giving 10% of income, standard (Jesus)   9/13/07 Vol. 48
charity & prayers for the starving (Jesus)   5/12/07 Vol. 47
charity donations more heavenly treasures (Jesus)   3/10/00 Vol. 18
charity donations more than token amounts (Jesus)   9/18/05 Vol. 40
charity for victims rewarded in heaven (Jesus)   1/5/06 Vol. 42
charity in giving heavenly treasure if given alive (Jesus) 10/30/00 Vol. 21
charity needed for poor & homeless (Jesus)   9/15/05 Vol. 40
charity needed giving money, time to poor (Jesus)   3/5/01 Vol. 22
charity needed in natural disasters (Jesus)   1/16/07 Vol. 46
charity needed many selfish with money (Jesus)   9/2/01 Vol. 24
charity needed share with others (Jesus)   5/16/06 Vol. 43
charity needed with time & money (Jesus)   9/29/01 Vol. 24
charity to neighbor sharing in Mystical Body (Jesus)   4/14/99 Vol. 15
charity to poor can share surplus (Jesus)   2/26/06 Vol. 42
charity to poor cannot return help (Jesus)   6/19/03 Vol. 31
charity to poor give away now (Jesus)   1/6/03 Vol. 30
charity, true selfless love (Jesus)   1/28/07 Vol. 46
Charley, Hurricane trials of (Jesus)   8/14/04 Vol. 36
chastisement World War (Jesus)   2/9/94 Vol. 1
chastisement comet not stopped by missiles (Jesus)   11/9/00 Vol. 21
Chastisement, Great by fire (Jesus)   4/1/07 Vol. 47
Chastisement, Great will not be stopped (Jesus)   6/14/02 Vol. 27
Chastisement,Great prepare,not far off (Jesus)   4/10/97 Vol. 7
chastisements abortion & sins of flesh (Jesus)   10/30/97 Vol. 9
chastisements connected to sins (Jesus)   10/12/05 Vol. 41
chastisements droughts & floods (Jesus)   8/30/96 Vol. 4

chastisements droughts and floods (Jesus)   10/24/96 Vol. 5
chastisements fire and water (Jesus)   7/10/96 Vol. 3
chastisements for apathy in killings (Jesus)   9/12/04 Vol. 36
chastisements for our sins (Jesus)   6/11/02 Vol. 27
chastisements for sins of nations, cities (Jesus)   9/30/05 Vol. 40
chastisements God will not be mocked (Jesus)   8/8/99 Vol. 16
chastisements in areas of great sin (Jesus)   1/10/05 Vol. 38
chastisements in areas of greater sin (Jesus)   11/7/96 Vol. 5
chastisements in areas of sin (Jesus)   3/10/05 Vol. 38
chastisements in weather,diseases,outages (Jesus)   12/4/03 Vol. 33
chastisements lessened with repentance (Jesus)   6/19/97 Vol. 7
chastisements of end times (Jesus)   8/7/03 Vol. 32
chastisements plagues,famines,disease (Jesus)   6/15/96 Vol. 3
chastisements rain sign of cleansing (Jesus)   1/9/98 Vol. 10
chastisements sin (Jesus)   1/24/96 Vol. 3
chastisements sufferings for sins (Jesus)   6/8/03 Vol. 31
chastisements weather,disasters,bugs (Jesus)   3/1/99 Vol. 14
chastisements weather,fires,floods (Jesus)   1/14/97 Vol. 6
chastisements will bring mankind to their knees (Jesus)   3/20/02 Vol. 26
chastisements for sin Jesus can calm the storm (Jesus)   10/22/98 Vol. 13
chastisements lessened if killing is stopped (Jesus)   7/15/04 Vol. 36
chastisements vs. sin lose possessions,God's Will (Jesus)   7/30/98 Vol. 12
chastity even if outcast (Jesus)   8/17/01 Vol. 24
chastity permissive society (Jesus)   11/18/96 Vol. 5
chastity teach to children (Jesus)   7/5/06 Vol. 44
cheating to make money (Jesus)   2/15/06 Vol. 42
cheating on taxes stealing from the public (Jesus)   6/7/03 Vol. 31
Chechnya terrorists in Russia (Jesus)   9/2/04 Vol. 36
chem trail & pulse cause of epidemic diseases (Jesus)   3/1/06 Vol. 42
chem trails cause of pandemic virus (Jesus)   3/2/08 Vol. 50
chem trails cause of viruses & flu (Jesus)   3/3/08 Vol. 50
chem trails pandemic diseases (Jesus)   3/24/08 Vol. 50
chem trails to spread diseases (Jesus)   2/18/08 Vol. 50
chemical,bioweapons inhumanity of weapons (Jesus)   1/6/00 Vol. 18
chemtrails by government & one worlders (Jesus)   12/5/03 Vol. 33
chemtrails by military planes (Jesus)   6/9/06 Vol. 43
chemtrails described and effects of (Jesus)   12/5/03 Vol. 33
chemtrails upset balance of nature (Jesus)   6/12/06 Vol. 43
Chernobyl messages (Jesus)   5/18/94 Vol. 1
Chernobyl nuclear plant problem (Jesus)   4/10/96 Vol. 3
Chicago refuge Queen of Heaven Cemetery (Mary)   8/28/05 Vol. 40
Chicago refuge vision of protecting angel (Jesus)   11/10/02 Vol. 29
child abuse children need our protection (Jesus)   7/5/02 Vol. 28
child like faith needed for heaven (Jesus)   2/22/06 Vol. 42
child like faith needed to enter heaven (Jesus)   8/29/01 Vol. 24
child predators on internet (Jesus)   10/24/07 Vol. 49
child-like to enter heaven (Jesus)   8/13/02 Vol. 28

childlike faith to carry out God's plan (Jesus) 3/1/00 Vol. 18

child-like faith innocent in spirit (Mary) 8/15/99 Vol. 16

child-like faith needs trust, hope in Jesus (Jesus) 12/24/98 Vol. 13

child-like faith not of the world (Jesus) 1/29/00 Vol. 18

child-like faith to be molded by God (Jesus) 7/14/04 Vol. 36

child-like trust in God needed (Jesus) 2/12/05 Vol. 38

child-like trust needed in work for perfection (Jesus) 6/13/02 Vol. 27

children abortion (Jesus) 11/16/93 Vol. 1

children abortion and abuses (Jesus) 1/17/96 Vol. 3

children abuse (Jesus) 3/26/95 Vol. 2

children abused & aborted (Jesus) 2/8/07 Vol. 46

children are gifts of God (Jesus) 12/18/97 Vol. 9

children be as little as (Jesus) 1/12/04 Vol. 34

children be examples of faith for (Jesus) 7/8/98 Vol. 12

children be good role models (Jesus) 10/26/97 Vol. 9

children be like them in faith (Jesus) 5/19/01 Vol. 23

children beware day care providers (Jesus) 12/30/96 Vol. 5

children Bosnia (Jesus) 2/16/94 Vol. 1

children bring up in love (Jesus) 6/1/05 Vol. 39

children Christian (Mary) 9/11/94 Vol. 2

children come as a child, trust (Jesus) 5/24/97 Vol. 7

children come to God in simple faith (Jesus) 6/26/05 Vol. 39

children come to Jesus as (Jesus) 6/18/04 Vol. 35

children consider spiritual welfare (Jesus) 5/6/04 Vol. 35

children control TV for (Jesus) 8/11/06 Vol. 44

children corruption of innocence (Jesus) 12/26/96 Vol. 5

children day care and abuses (Jesus) 8/7/97 Vol. 8

children do not abuse (Jesus) 5/22/01 Vol. 23

children do not give up on them (Jesus) 9/5/97 Vol. 8

children do not watch cartoons (Jesus) 2/2/03 Vol. 30

children encourage Confession (Jesus) 7/11/03 Vol. 32

children example (Jesus) 6/10/95 Vol. 2

children example (St. Anne) 7/26/95 Vol. 3

children example of faith (Jesus) 8/21/96 Vol. 4

children gifts of the Spirit (Jesus) 3/20/94 Vol. 1

children give faith & example of love to (Jesus) 4/26/04 Vol. 35

children give faith to (Jesus) 9/25/03 Vol. 32

children give good example (Jesus) 5/20/99 Vol. 15

children give love & tenderness (Jesus) 9/13/06 Vol. 44

children give religious education (Jesus) 8/15/06 Vol. 44

children give responsible care (Jesus) 4/23/98 Vol. 11

children grandchildren (Jesus) 7/14/95 Vol. 3

children great responsibility for faith (Jesus) 3/8/98 Vol. 10

children grieved by their parents (Jesus) 1/31/06 Vol. 42

children have faith like (Jesus) 4/13/05 Vol. 39

children help orphans (Jesus) 8/12/04 Vol. 36

children help poor and abused (Jesus) 9/3/00 Vol. 20

children help the desperate ones (Jesus) 7/22/04 Vol. 36

children infant (Jesus) 12/25/94 Vol. 2

children influence of TV (Jesus) 8/9/96 Vol. 4

children influenced by TV (Jesus) 5/18/99 Vol. 15

children innocence corrupted (Jesus) 5/22/03 Vol. 31

children invite to sacraments (Jesus) 1/13/99 Vol. 14

children Jesus loves (Jesus) 10/4/01 Vol. 25

children love (Jesus) 11/11/95 Vol. 3

children media TV (Jesus) 4/24/95 Vol. 2

children moral formation of (Jesus) 3/26/98 Vol. 10

children need a good example (Jesus) 10/15/05 Vol. 41

children need faith example for heaven (Jesus) 7/28/05 Vol. 40

children need faith,good prayer life (Jesus) 5/22/04 Vol. 35

children need good prayer lives (Jesus) 6/11/03 Vol. 31

children need good role models (Jesus) 4/3/03 Vol. 31

children need good spiritual habits young (Jesus) 2/23/02 Vol. 26

children need mom at home (Jesus) 5/6/04 Vol. 35

children need parental guidance (Jesus) 8/27/05 Vol. 40

children need parental protection (Jesus) 3/12/06 Vol. 42

children need physical protection (Jesus) 8/13/02 Vol. 28

children need spiritual direction (Jesus) 4/22/03 Vol. 31

children need spiritual help (Jesus) 11/13/07 Vol. 49

children no vacation from prayers (Jesus) 6/17/04 Vol. 35

children nurture in faith (Jesus) 4/21/05 Vol. 39

children parental responsibility (Jesus) 5/12/96 Vol. 3

children parents care for souls (Jesus) 11/29/96 Vol. 5

children parents need to teach faith (Jesus) 11/4/04 Vol. 37

children parent's responsibility (Jesus) 5/3/05 Vol. 39

children parent's responsibility (Jesus) 8/7/97 Vol. 8

children parents responsible for faith (Jesus) 8/9/01 Vol. 24

children parents responsible for faith (Jesus) 2/5/02 Vol. 26

children parents responsible for TV (Jesus) 8/16/03 Vol. 32

children parent's spiritual responsibility (Jesus) 5/9/04 Vol. 35

children parents,grandparents help (Jesus) 7/17/97 Vol. 8

children pass faith on to (Jesus) 8/10/02 Vol. 28

children pass faith on to (Jesus) 8/3/99 Vol. 16

children pass on faith (Jesus) 12/30/97 Vol. 9

children pass on faith to (Jesus) 7/25/03 Vol. 32

children pass on faith to (Jesus) 6/16/01 Vol. 23

children peace (Jesus) 12/18/93 Vol. 1

children plan for life (Jesus) 9/5/02 Vol. 28

children protect & care for (Jesus) 7/1/04 Vol. 36

children protect and help (Jesus) 6/22/98 Vol. 11

children protect and teach (Jesus) 10/17/02 Vol. 29

children protect from abuse (Jesus) 9/13/02 Vol. 28

children protect from abuse (Jesus) 7/24/03 Vol. 32

children protect from abuse (Jesus) 3/3/05 Vol. 38

children protect from bad movies (Jesus) 9/18/02 Vol. 28
children protect from bad TV (Jesus) 6/10/04 Vol. 35
children protect physically & spiritually (Jesus) 2/14/02 Vol. 26
children protect physically,spiritually (Jesus) 6/15/04 Vol. 35
children provide good environment (Jesus) 12/3/03 Vol. 33
children religious education (Jesus) 11/15/97 Vol. 9
children responsibilities (Jesus) 2/19/96 Vol. 3
children responsibility for (Jesus) 5/19/98 Vol. 11
children responsibility of parents (Jesus) 10/10/96 Vol. 5
children responsibility of parents (Jesus) 1/13/99 Vol. 14
children responsibility of teaching faith (Jesus) 6/18/03 Vol. 31
children responsibility to teach faith (Jesus) 1/23/04 Vol. 34
children rosary (Mary) 11/24/93 Vol. 1
children share Christmas gifts (Jesus) 12/4/03 Vol. 33
children share joy of faith with (Jesus) 10/17/05 Vol. 41
children spiritual education (Mary) 9/3/97 Vol. 8
children spiritual guardians (Jesus) 10/2/97 Vol. 9
children tabernacle (Holy Spirit) 10/17/93 Vol. 1
children take to Mass & Adoration (St. Therese) 3/3/98 Vol. 10
children take to Mass and Adoration (Jesus) 5/3/98 Vol. 11
children take to Mass, trust (Jesus) 7/14/97 Vol. 8
children take to sacraments (Jesus) 5/28/98 Vol. 11
children teach and defend (Jesus) 7/18/99 Vol. 16
children teach and love (Jesus) 1/10/96 Vol. 3
children teach by example (Jesus) 7/10/96 Vol. 3
children teach Christmas meaning (Jesus) 12/24/97 Vol. 9
children teach faith (Jesus) 8/11/97 Vol. 8
children teach faith & prayer to (Jesus) 4/25/04 Vol. 35
children teach faith properly (Jesus) 10/10/02 Vol. 29
children teach faith to (Jesus) 11/18/01 Vol. 25
children teach faith to (Jesus) 1/21/99 Vol. 14
children teach faith, be like little (Jesus) 4/7/05 Vol. 39
children teach faith,pray for (Jesus) 10/26/99 Vol. 17
children teach faith,take to Mass (Mary) 4/10/97 Vol. 7
children teach love and faith in God (Jesus) 9/5/03 Vol. 32
children teach love of God,neighbor (Jesus) 7/14/05 Vol. 40
children teach Real Presence (Jesus) 2/25/05 Vol. 38
children teach the faith (Jesus) 2/21/98 Vol. 10
children teach the faith (Jesus) 7/11/98 Vol. 12
children teach the faith (Jesus) 9/22/96 Vol. 4
children teach the faith to (Jesus) 7/15/99 Vol. 16
children teach them faith (Jesus) 1/14/99 Vol. 14
children teach them faith,prayers (Jesus) 12/2/96 Vol. 5
children teach traditions (Jesus) 4/2/04 Vol. 35
children teachers (Mary) 2/2/94 Vol. 1
children thank mothers for life (Mary) 5/9/99 Vol. 15
children their beauty is fleeting (Jesus) 5/6/04 Vol. 35

children trial (Holy Spirit) 8/31/95 Vol. 3
children US wakeup (Jesus) 11/4/94 Vol. 2
children victims of day care mentality (Jesus) 9/3/98 Vol. 12
children violence,abuse,abortion (Jesus) 8/10/96 Vol. 4
children & parents gifts desired (Jesus) 12/30/02 Vol. 29
children & weapons terrorism in the schools (Jesus) 5/4/99 Vol. 15
children abuse abortion, killing (Jesus) 11/29/07 Vol. 49
children abused more valuable than pets (Jesus) 7/19/07 Vol. 48
children abused parental responsibility (Mary) 5/3/02 Vol. 27
children corrupted by pornography & TV (Jesus) 4/24/97 Vol. 7
ch. during tribulation tribulation,purgatory on earth (Jesus) 10/9/98 Vol. 13
children in killings used to change gun laws (Jesus) 6/28/00 Vol. 19
children killed from tidal waves (Jesus) 12/30/04 Vol. 37
children killed Pharaoh,Herod,abortions (Jesus) 12/28/06 Vol. 45
children need Jesus to know Real Presence (Jesus) 3/2/00 Vol. 18
children need love make time for attention (Jesus) 4/22/99 Vol. 15
children of God give burdens to Jesus (Jesus) 8/16/03 Vol. 32
children revelations gifts to everyone (Jesus) 7/26/07 Vol. 48
children safety in schools (Jesus) 8/23/07 Vol. 48
children to visit Jesus encourage adoration (Jesus) 8/9/98 Vol. 12
children trained in need of sacraments (Jesus) 8/31/99 Vol. 16
children under 7 safe in tribulation (Jesus) 12/3/98 Vol. 13
children, abortions pass faith on to them (Jesus) 10/2/98 Vol. 13
children, games avoid violence, occult (Jesus) 12/18/06 Vol. 45
children, grandchildren need spiritual nourishment (Jesus) 11/30/06 Vol. 45
children, grandchildren present for sacraments (Jesus) 5/18/06 Vol. 43
children, problems need protection from hell (Jesus) 3/11/04 Vol. 34
children,innocence of needed in love of God (Jesus) 4/12/99 Vol. 15
children,teaching of teach only the truth (Jesus) 11/28/02 Vol. 29
children's cartoons bad influence,wasted time (Jesus) 4/6/00 Vol. 19
children's gifts share with the poor (Jesus) 11/23/07 Vol. 49
children's needs love & concern, not penalties (Jesus) 3/6/08 Vol. 50
China awakened after Warning (Jesus) 10/26/01 Vol. 25
China competitor for oil & goods (Jesus) 11/18/04 Vol. 37
China consecrate to destroy evil (Jesus) 10/27/01 Vol. 25
China dominant in manufacturing (Jesus) 12/9/02 Vol. 29
China dragon of Apocalypse (Jesus) 4/26/01 Vol. 23
China extending its power (Jesus) 9/27/98 Vol. 12
China influenced by evil (Jesus) 7/8/97 Vol. 8
China laughing at us (Jesus) 4/15/02 Vol. 27
China mistake to invest in (Jesus) 1/19/06 Vol. 42
China pollution out of control (Jesus) 4/15/02 Vol. 27
China pray for consecration (Jesus) 10/23/01 Vol. 25
China pray for pope to consecrate (Jesus) 10/20/01 Vol. 25
China pray for the oppressed (Jesus) 10/21/01 Vol. 25
China secrets give away to (Jesus) 8/30/00 Vol. 20
China troops for the UN (Jesus) 9/1/00 Vol. 20

China & Russia given our secrets (Jesus) — 10/19/99 Vol. 17
China & Russia more superstitious (Jesus) — 10/31/01 Vol. 25
China & Taiwan pray against war there (Jesus) — 10/27/05 Vol. 41
China plane incident surveillance danger (Jesus) — 4/5/01 Vol. 23
China recalls no country origin label (Jesus) — 10/11/07 Vol. 49
China trade exploiting the West (Jesus) — 6/22/06 Vol. 43
China trade used against us (Jesus) — 2/4/02 Vol. 26
China, job loss to Cuban style takeover (Jesus) — 12/22/05 Vol. 41
Chinese war (Jesus) — 9/14/94 Vol. 2
Chinese communists US financing war-making (Jesus) — 8/26/99 Vol. 16
chip in hand being promoted in ads (Jesus) — 1/14/00 Vol. 18
chip in the hand controlled,not removable (Jesus) — 2/11/00 Vol. 18
chip undetected could mean prison (Jesus) — 1/17/08 Vol. 50
chips avoid in body, mark of beast (Jesus) — 8/8/04 Vol. 36
chips can cause mind control (Jesus) — 6/16/06 Vol. 43
chips can cause voices (Jesus) — 10/3/06 Vol. 45
chips can control our minds (Jesus) — 1/16/08 Vol. 50
chips coming in passports, licenses (Jesus) — 4/21/05 Vol. 39
chips contain retina & finger info (Jesus) — 7/28/04 Vol. 36
chips control as in death camps WWII (Jesus) — 5/5/05 Vol. 39
chips control of minds (Jesus) — 5/17/03 Vol. 31
chips destroyed in Chastisement (Jesus) — 6/9/05 Vol. 39
chips do not take in the hand (Jesus) — 4/15/01 Vol. 23
chips for Antichrist's control (Jesus) — 7/25/06 Vol. 44
chips for buying and selling (Jesus) — 5/23/98 Vol. 11
chips for control of mind & body (Jesus) — 9/21/06 Vol. 44
chips for control only (Jesus) — 2/1/07 Vol. 46
chips for daily necessities (Jesus) — 8/28/03 Vol. 32
chips in forehead can control mind (Jesus) — 5/2/02 Vol. 27
chips in passports & licenses (Jesus) — 11/3/05 Vol. 41
chips in passports, licenses (Jesus) — 1/16/08 Vol. 50
chips in wrist watches (Jesus) — 5/5/01 Vol. 23
chips made mandatory (Jesus) — 2/7/08 Vol. 50
chips mandatory use (Jesus) — 8/7/06 Vol. 44
chips outlaws if refused (Jesus) — 8/30/06 Vol. 44
chips power in hands of a few (Jesus) — 6/22/04 Vol. 35
chips pray for strength to refuse (Jesus) — 9/20/06 Vol. 44
chips refuse even under death (Jesus) — 10/17/06 Vol. 45
chips refuse in body under threats (Jesus) — 8/29/06 Vol. 44
chips refuse in the body (Jesus) — 10/9/06 Vol. 45
chips refuse to take in body (Jesus) — 8/24/06 Vol. 44
chips revealed in Warning (Jesus) — 10/6/03 Vol. 33
chips soon control buying & selling (Jesus) — 1/5/04 Vol. 34
chips store food to avoid (Jesus) — 12/17/03 Vol. 33
chips to begin martial law (Jesus) — 7/12/05 Vol. 40
chips to control buying & selling (Jesus) — 9/26/02 Vol. 28
chips to control buying & selling (Jesus) — 10/4/03 Vol. 33

chips to control minds (Jesus) — 2/22/03 Vol. 30
chips to control minds, souls (Jesus) — 8/28/01 Vol. 24
chips to control you (Jesus) — 10/7/06 Vol. 45
chips to make us slaves (Jesus) — 1/2/08 Vol. 50
chips various stages (Jesus) — 5/10/02 Vol. 27
chips will be outlaws without them (Jesus) — 5/25/02 Vol. 27
chips wrap in aluminum foil (Jesus) — 1/29/08 Vol. 50
chips & computers do not be slaves to (Jesus) — 9/18/03 Vol. 32
chips & databases readied for everyone (Jesus) — 3/6/03 Vol. 30
chips & prices to force people under control (Jesus) — 8/29/01 Vol. 24
chips & smart cards avoid controlling you (Jesus) — 8/11/03 Vol. 32
chips & smart cards refuse to take (Jesus) — 1/16/02 Vol. 26
chips & smart cards test of our comforts (Jesus) — 6/19/05 Vol. 39
chips are flawed vulnerable to radiation,surges (Jesus) — 10/12/98 Vol. 13
chips control shopping,bills,services (Jesus) — 11/25/03 Vol. 33
chips control wealth control of Antichrist (Jesus) — 8/20/02 Vol. 28
chips forced to buy and sell (Jesus) — 7/3/03 Vol. 32
chips implanted those going along with leaders (Jesus) — 8/11/04 Vol. 36
chips in body avoid control of mind (Jesus) — 11/9/07 Vol. 49
chips in body avoid taking (Jesus) — 5/21/05 Vol. 39
chips in body call to refuges (Jesus) — 3/23/06 Vol. 42
chips in body control with voices (Jesus) — 2/18/07 Vol. 46
chips in body control you as robots (Jesus) — 5/24/06 Vol. 43
chips in body danger to children (Jesus) — 6/4/03 Vol. 31
chips in body do not take, better to starve (Jesus) — 8/12/04 Vol. 36
chips in body downfall of technology (Jesus) — 4/4/01 Vol. 23
chips in body make people into robots (Jesus) — 1/24/08 Vol. 50
chips in body mandatory,leave for refuges (Jesus) — 8/8/07 Vol. 48
chips in body mind control voices (Jesus) — 8/31/06 Vol. 44
chips in body no need for mind control (Jesus) — 9/7/06 Vol. 44
chips in body or bankrupt people (Jesus) — 5/28/04 Vol. 35
chips in body refuse even to death (Jesus) — 9/8/06 Vol. 44
chips in body refuse even to death (Jesus) — 11/29/06 Vol. 45
chips in body refuse for any reason (Jesus) — 7/15/04 Vol. 36
chips in body refuse mark of the beast (Jesus) — 12/23/05 Vol. 41
chips in body refuse to take (Jesus) — 12/31/05 Vol. 41
chips in body refuse to take (Jesus) — 11/21/00 Vol. 21
chips in body refuse, store food, refuges (Jesus) — 11/19/03 Vol. 33
chips in body time for going to refuge (Jesus) — 2/10/05 Vol. 38
chips in body time for refuges (Jesus) — 5/28/06 Vol. 43
chips in body to be mandated later (Jesus) — 2/1/06 Vol. 42
chips in body to be mandatory (Jesus) — 5/21/05 Vol. 39
chips in body to control your mind (Jesus) — 1/6/06 Vol. 42
chips in body to control your mind (Jesus) — 4/23/07 Vol. 47
chips in body mandatory time to go to refuges (Jesus) — 8/8/05 Vol. 40
chips in body, avoid suffer here than in hell (Jesus) — 8/14/04 Vol. 36
chips in food monitored supply (Jesus) — 8/8/02 Vol. 28

Christian duties love God & neighbor (Jesus) — 1/16/08 Vol. 50

Christian faith lived good deeds, sharing (Jesus) — 9/1/99 Vol. 16

Christian fellowship reach out to everyone (Jesus) — 2/21/00 Vol. 18

Christian life contrary to desires of body (Jesus) — 8/11/00 Vol. 20

Christian life hard without justice (Jesus) — 3/24/00 Vol. 18

Christian Life help people, good example (Jesus) — 9/9/07 Vol. 48

Christian life needs to be lived out (Jesus) — 2/24/01 Vol. 22

Christian life no fear, trust in God (Jesus) — 11/8/04 Vol. 37

Christian life not a popularity contest (Jesus) — 7/28/01 Vol. 24

Christian life one of faith and hope (Jesus) — 5/29/99 Vol. 15

Christian life seen by your actions (Jesus) — 1/25/05 Vol. 38

Christian life time, prayer and money (Jesus) — 7/7/96 Vol. 3

Christian living spiritual dimension in duties (Jesus) — 9/20/01 Vol. 24

Christian martyrdom is returning (Jesus) — 10/28/04 Vol. 37

Christian martyrs from masons, Moslems (Jesus) — 7/26/00 Vol. 20

Christian persecution to get worse (Jesus) — 12/15/04 Vol. 37

Christian principles live in daily actions (Jesus) — 5/22/06 Vol. 43

Christian responsibility finances,work in Church (Jesus) — 8/18/05 Vol. 40

Christian responsibility to children and elderly (Jesus) — 9/4/97 Vol. 8

Christian vs pagan civilization choices (Jesus) — 1/26/06 Vol. 42

Christian witness by your good example (Jesus) — 2/5/05 Vol. 38

Christian, good taught by miracles,parables (Jesus) — 12/6/02 Vol. 29

Christian, loving put aside riches (Jesus) — 12/22/02 Vol. 29

Christianity demands of (Jesus) — 4/10/02 Vol. 27

Christianity masons want to destroy (Jesus) — 6/23/02 Vol. 27

Christianity persecuted from militant Arabs, finances (Jesus) — 3/19/02 Vol. 26

Christians action not spectators (Jesus) — 2/17/03 Vol. 30

Christians follow narrow road (Jesus) — 2/19/04 Vol. 34

Christians martyred for sport by Antichrist (Jesus) — 7/6/00 Vol. 20

Christians outcasts like lepers (Jesus) — 1/18/01 Vol. 22

Christians persecuted world wide (Jesus) — 12/20/07 Vol. 49

Christians speak out more (Jesus) — 10/26/06 Vol. 45

Christians stand up against atheists (Jesus) — 12/1/05 Vol. 41

Christians tolerance for each other (Jesus) — 10/1/06 Vol. 45

Christians in catacombs hiding from persecution (Jesus) — 5/25/00 Vol. 19

Christians killed coming in tribulation (Jesus) — 10/17/07 Vol. 49

Christians killed in public display, returns (Jesus) — 3/25/04 Vol. 34

Christians of today need original fervor (Jesus) — 4/22/06 Vol. 43

Christians persecuted by one world religion (Jesus) — 10/28/03 Vol. 33

Christians persecuted for belief in Jesus (Jesus) — 12/16/99 Vol. 17

Christians persecuted in killings worldwide (Jesus) — 6/21/00 Vol. 19

Christians persecuted speaking on religious subjects (Jesus) — 12/18/03 Vol. 33

Christina Confirmation spiritual milestone (Jesus) — 5/22/07 Vol. 47

Christina Gallagher House of Prayer (Jesus) — 8/18/06 Vol. 44

Christmas angels (Jesus) — 12/24/95 Vol. 3

Christmas angels (Jesus) — 12/20/95 Vol. 3

Christmas atheists trying to remove (Jesus) — 12/10/02 Vol. 29

Christmas celebrate true meaning of (Jesus) — 12/18/00 Vol. 21

Christmas charity, true meaning (Jesus) — 11/30/96 Vol. 5

Christmas children,real meaning (Jesus) — 12/1/96 Vol. 5

Christmas display crip, give praise (Jesus) — 12/9/99 Vol. 17

Christmas family celebration (Jesus) — 12/14/00 Vol. 2

Christmas gifts love is more important (Jesus) — 11/10/05 Vol. 41

Christmas give Jesus best gifts (Jesus) — 12/13/01 Vol. 25

Christmas inconveniences of first (Jesus) — 12/24/00 Vol. 21

Christmas is too commercialized (Jesus) — 11/23/05 Vol. 41

Christmas Jesus taken out of (Jesus) — 12/12/00 Vol. 21

Christmas joy (Jesus) — 12/24/94 Vol. 2

Christmas keep Nativity scenes public (Jesus) — 12/19/01 Vol. 25

Christmas Light of love (Jesus) — 12/6/97 Vol. 9

Christmas love (Jesus) — 12/18/93 Vol. 1

Christmas money worshiped before Jesus (Jesus) — 11/27/04 Vol. 37

Christmas no room at the inn (Jesus) — 12/18/96 Vol. 5

Christmas plan of salvation (Jesus) — 12/18/00 Vol. 21

Christmas prepare hearts properly (Jesus) — 11/6/97 Vol. 9

Christmas prepare spiritually for (Jesus) — 12/8/01 Vol. 25

Christmas present with a clean soul (Jesus) — 12/10/99 Vol. 17

Christmas read Scriptural account (Jesus) — 11/29/01 Vol. 25

Christmas real sign in crib (Jesus) — 12/24/97 Vol. 9

Christmas received in Eucharist (Jesus) — 12/23/04 Vol. 37

Christmas rejoice in this season (Jesus) — 12/9/97 Vol. 9

Christmas salvation of sins (Jesus) — 12/25/96 Vol. 5

Christmas share love and good will (Jesus) — 12/26/96 Vol. 5

Christmas shrouded in gifts than Jesus (Jesus) — 11/11/02 Vol. 29

Christmas sign of Kingdom of God (Jesus) — 12/6/99 Vol. 17

Christmas sing for joy (Jesus) — 12/16/01 Vol. 25

Christmas spiritual over commercial (Jesus) — 11/2/05 Vol. 41

Christmas what love is all about (Jesus) — 12/23/98 Vol. 13

Chris. at Eucharist Real Presence sought by soul (Jesus) — 12/23/03 Vol. 33

Christmas Carols heavenly prayers (Jesus) — 12/14/00 Vol. 21

Christmas celebrations atheists trying to stop (Jesus) — 12/4/03 Vol. 33

Christmas charity to orphans in gifts (Jesus) — 12/26/06 Vol. 45

Christmas cheer help others out of love (Jesus) — 12/15/05 Vol. 41

Christmas crib bring gift of self (Jesus) — 11/29/01 Vol. 25

Christmas displays express freedom of religion (Jesus) — 11/21/02 Vol. 29

Christmas everyday in Holy Communion (Jesus) — 12/21/98 Vol. 13

Christmas gift clean soul from Confession (Jesus) — 12/18/99 Vol. 17

Christmas gifts do not spoil children (Jesus) — 12/4/03 Vol. 33

Christmas gifts exploited by shopkeepers (Jesus) — 12/1/05 Vol. 41

Christmas gifts fighting vs. joy (Jesus) — 11/23/07 Vol. 49

Christmas gifts hearts & souls for Jesus (Jesus) — 12/2/02 Vol. 29

Christmas holiness understood by most people (Jesus) — 12/24/03 Vol. 33

Christmas joy share time & money (Jesus) — 12/20/07 Vol. 49

Christmas Light increases,winter solstice (Jesus) — 12/21/05 Vol. 41

Christmas love must be shared (Jesus)　　12/20/07 Vol. 49

Christmas Mass come to Mass on Sunday (Jesus)　　12/18/98 Vol. 13

Christmas message mankind's salvation (Jesus)　　11/26/07 Vol. 49

Christmas Nativity leave up all year (Jesus)　　1/2/03 Vol. 30

Christmas peace share love of God, man (Jesus)　　12/22/05 Vol. 41

Christmas preparations ready for trials (Jesus)　　12/1/05 Vol. 41

Christmas Season ray of sunlight (Jesus)　　12/2/05 Vol. 41

Christmas season tested by events (Jesus)　　10/16/02 Vol. 29

Christmas singing share love with God, neighbor (Jesus)　　12/25/07 Vol. 49

Christmas spirit nurture all year long (Jesus)　　12/24/00 Vol. 21

Christmas spirit spiritual gifts to Jesus (Jesus)　　12/14/04 Vol. 37

Christmas time to heal family rifts (Jesus)　　12/26/99 Vol. 17

Christmas toys for the poor (Jesus)　　11/20/03 Vol. 33

Christmas, success of number of hearts at peace (Jesus)　　12/3/02 Vol. 29

Christmas, taste of every day in Host (Jesus)　　12/23/06 Vol. 45

Christmas,Easter bombs insult to feasts of Jesus (Jesus)　　3/23/99 Vol. 14

Church a great celebration in (Jesus)　　5/14/98 Vol. 11

Church baptism (Jesus)　　6/7/94 Vol. 1

Church built by daily crosses (Jesus)　　6/24/04 Vol. 35

Church conversion (Jesus)　　2/14/94 Vol. 1

Church demons trying to destroy it (Jesus)　　4/18/03 Vol. 31

Church destroy from within (Jesus)　　6/16/99 Vol. 15

Church divided, East & West (Jesus)　　9/18/97 Vol. 8

Church division (Jesus)　　5/20/95 Vol. 2

Church division, remnant underground (Jesus)　　4/21/05 Vol. 39

Church doctrines upheld (Jesus)　　12/19/96 Vol. 5

church end of time　　9/30/93 Vol. 1

Church faithfulness to rosary (Jesus)　　1/8/99 Vol. 14

church family (Jesus)　　10/2/94 Vol. 2

church first pope (St. Peter)　　12/31/93 Vol. 1

Church follow teaching of (Jesus)　　4/30/97 Vol. 7

Church gates of hell not to prevail against (Jesus)　　6/22/04 Vol. 35

Church gates of hell will not prevail (Jesus)　　6/24/02 Vol. 27

Church gates of hell will not prevail over (Jesus)　　6/4/04 Vol. 35

Church great changes in (Jesus)　　6/3/04 Vol. 35

Church great division coming (Jesus)　　6/23/04 Vol. 35

Church groom (Jesus)　　9/3/94 Vol. 2

Church in confusion (Jesus)　　4/25/04 Vol. 35

Church keep tradition,commands (Jesus)　　12/27/97 Vol. 9

Church keys of Peter & Pope (Jesus)　　2/22/96 Vol. 3

Church never destroyed by evil (Jesus)　　1/3/08 Vol. 50

Church papal successor (Jesus)　　4/3/95 Vol. 2

Church persecuted as catacombs (Jesus)　　1/17/01 Vol. 22

Church physical & mystical body (Jesus)　　11/11/01 Vol. 25

church physical care (Jesus)　　11/9/07 Vol. 49

Church prevails over the gates of hell (Jesus)　　2/8/04 Vol. 34

Church protect teachings of (Jesus)　　11/9/01 Vol. 25

Church protected from gates of hell (Jesus)　　6/29/98 Vol. 11

Church protected in persecution (Jesus)　　1/15/02 Vol. 26

Church Satan's influence on (Jesus)　　4/23/02 Vol. 27

Church scandals (Jesus)　　1/30/03 Vol. 30

Church split in turmoil (Jesus)　　6/13/96 Vol. 3

church tabernacle (Jesus)　　11/9/94 Vol. 2

Church termites of evil in (Jesus)　　2/14/03 Vol. 30

Church test (Jesus)　　7/24/95 Vol. 3

church threat of schism (Jesus)　　10/3/03 Vol. 33

Church three signs of schism (Jesus)　　8/20/04 Vol. 36

Church to prevail against gates of hell (Jesus)　　4/12/04 Vol. 35

Church unite East & West (Jesus)　　12/15/96 Vol. 5

church wakeup (Jesus)　　1/31/94 Vol. 1

Church will survive split (Jesus)　　7/2/97 Vol. 8

Church & priests attacked by demons (Jesus)　　10/20/02 Vol. 29

church & state better to obey God than man (Jesus)　　8/1/02 Vol. 28

church & state separation taking God out of public (Jesus)　　11/19/04 Vol. 37

church affiliation evidence against faithful (Jesus)　　4/26/07 Vol. 47

church and state diabolical separation (Jesus)　　7/4/02 Vol. 28

church and state distorted view of separation (Jesus)　　7/4/98 Vol. 12

Church and State separation abused (Jesus)　　4/7/98 Vol. 11

church attendance decreasing (Jesus)　　8/1/01 Vol. 24

church break-ins vandals & thieves (Jesus)　　11/12/07 Vol. 49

Church buildings keep statues and crosses (Jesus)　　7/22/98 Vol. 12

church closings low attendance, few priests (Jesus)　　9/29/05 Vol. 40

church closings priest, laity problems (Jesus)　　5/1/06 Vol. 43

church conflict between building up, destroying (Jesus)　　7/17/04 Vol. 36

Church corruption homosexual, financial (Jesus)　　12/27/05 Vol. 41

church decline lost faith causes ruin (Jesus)　　2/21/02 Vol. 26

church destructions from hate of man (Jesus)　　2/23/06 Vol. 42

Church division schismatic and faithful remnant (Jesus)　　11/18/05 Vol. 41

church events as part of life (Jesus)　　5/11/01 Vol. 23

Church hierarchy need support, & prayers (Jesus)　　8/18/05 Vol. 40

church inspiration by man or God (Jesus)　　11/9/99 Vol. 17

Church Laws six enumerated (Jesus)　　8/9/04 Vol. 36

Church lists used by Antichrist for mark (Jesus)　　11/14/98 Vol. 13

Church needs building through Gospel converts (Jesus)　　5/2/99 Vol. 15

Church not destroyed promise of Jesus (Jesus)　　4/3/99 Vol. 15

Church protected gates of hell will not prevail (Jesus)　　6/2/06 Vol. 43

Church renovations keep statues,crucifixes (Jesus)　　1/10/99 Vol. 14

church repairs needed not closing or stripping (Jesus)　　8/25/05 Vol. 40

Church scandal cleansed (Jesus)　　4/13/02 Vol. 27

Church scandals prayer is the answer (Jesus)　　6/14/02 Vol. 27

church stripping makes way for New Age (Jesus)　　2/23/06 Vol. 42

Church structure changing from priest shortage (Jesus)　　4/19/05 Vol. 39

Church support tithing desired by God (Jesus)　　9/2/01 Vol. 24

church theft theft of Hosts, black masses (Jesus)　　11/12/07 Vol. 49

Church traditions help the faithful (Jesus) 2/5/06 Vol. 42

Church unity false teachings (Jesus) 4/24/95 Vol. 2

Church year begins excitement for Advent (Jesus) 11/30/03 Vol. 33

Church Year, new sin less, pray more (Jesus) 12/21/06 Vol. 45

Church, attacks on vandalism,sexual offenses (Jesus) 2/17/02 Vol. 26

Church, build up call of Jesus (Jesus) 9/21/07 Vol. 48

Church, support of financial,teaching,food for poor (Jesus) 10/20/04 Vol. 37

church,state separation twisted logic for atheism (Jesus) 5/18/00 Vol. 19

churches afraid to speak out (Jesus) 10/17/97 Vol. 9

churches banished (Jesus) 2/4/94 Vol. 1

churches being closed (Jesus) 1/3/08 Vol. 50

churches being stripped (Jesus) 5/1/03 Vol. 31

churches being stripped (Jesus) 6/23/05 Vol. 39

churches being stripped (Jesus) 4/19/01 Vol. 23

churches being stripped for New Age (Jesus) 7/6/04 Vol. 36

churches being undermined (Jesus) 10/8/03 Vol. 33

churches boarded up,underground (Jesus) 4/12/96 Vol. 3

Churches burned and desecrated (Jesus) 6/7/99 Vol. 15

Churches burned down (Jesus) 2/3/99 Vol. 14

churches burned, go underground (Jesus) 7/24/97 Vol. 8

Churches closed & persecuted (Jesus) 9/1/97 Vol. 8

Churches closed & underground (Jesus) 1/23/97 Vol. 6

churches closed and changed (Jesus) 11/24/01 Vol. 25

churches closed, underground Masses (Jesus) 6/17/02 Vol. 27

churches could become bankrupt (Jesus) 4/7/02 Vol. 27

churches declining, & faith lost (Jesus) 10/2/03 Vol. 33

churches degraded by modernism (Jesus) 7/19/06 Vol. 44

Churches destroyed (Jesus) 5/14/98 Vol. 11

churches destroyed by New Age (Jesus) 4/19/01 Vol. 23

churches destroyed by renovations (Jesus) 2/14/04 Vol. 34

churches destroyed in tribulation (Jesus) 2/12/04 Vol. 34

churches do not strip (Jesus) 8/7/01 Vol. 24

churches do not strip them empty (Jesus) 1/24/02 Vol. 26

churches focus on God not man (Jesus) 4/19/01 Vol. 23

churches full when we are suffering (Jesus) 7/18/99 Vol. 16

churches glorify man and not God (Jesus) 9/18/02 Vol. 28

churches holy by Real Presence (Jesus) 1/15/02 Vol. 26

churches hypocrisy (Jesus) 6/4/96 Vol. 3

churches keep holy & reverent (Jesus) 6/16/05 Vol. 39

churches keep sacred & reverent (Jesus) 2/6/02 Vol. 26

churches keep traditions (Jesus) 1/31/08 Vol. 50

Churches Mass in secret (Jesus) 11/23/96 Vol. 5

churches moving to the left (Jesus) 6/24/05 Vol. 39

churches need to preserve traditions (Jesus) 8/21/06 Vol. 44

churches New Age promoted in (Jesus) 8/24/06 Vol. 44

Churches new buildings are colder (Jesus) 7/27/98 Vol. 12

Churches persecuted (Jesus) 6/1/98 Vol. 11

churches planned destruction (Jesus) 9/7/03 Vol. 32

churches preserve beauty,reverence (Jesus) 10/2/02 Vol. 29

Churches priority of money vs. souls (Jesus) 2/11/99 Vol. 14

churches run as business vs worship place (Jesus) 3/7/02 Vol. 26

churches should uplift the spirit (Jesus) 8/2/99 Vol. 16

churches some fall to evil one (Jesus) 9/27/02 Vol. 28

Churches strip statues, kneelers (Jesus) 6/8/98 Vol. 11

churches stripped (Jesus) 6/2/01 Vol. 23

churches stripped (Jesus) 9/27/02 Vol. 28

churches stripped by modernism (Jesus) 6/10/05 Vol. 39

churches stripped for New Age (Jesus) 9/24/03 Vol. 32

churches stripped of holiness (Jesus) 10/7/05 Vol. 41

churches stripped of statues & crucifixes (Jesus) 9/4/03 Vol. 32

churches support financially (Jesus) 11/9/05 Vol. 41

churches tax exemption removal threat (Jesus) 1/19/06 Vol. 42

churches tax status pressure (Jesus) 7/23/01 Vol. 24

churches to be destroyed in tribulation (Jesus) 11/30/03 Vol. 33

churches to be set on fire (Jesus) 6/22/02 Vol. 27

churches treasure now, before lost (Jesus) 10/2/03 Vol. 33

churches under attack by evil ones (Jesus) 7/26/06 Vol. 44

Churches underground,museums (Jesus) 3/23/97 Vol. 6

churches will be destroyed (Jesus) 11/7/07 Vol. 49

churches with image of the beast (Jesus) 8/22/01 Vol. 24

Churches worship will deteriorate (Jesus) 5/7/98 Vol. 11

churches & schools are under attack (Jesus) 11/19/04 Vol. 37

churches & schools closed by money,priest shortage (Jesus) 5/18/05 Vol. 39

churches being sold to pay priests' lawsuits (Jesus) 11/9/06 Vol. 45

churches burned fire of hell involved (Jesus) 5/19/05 Vol. 39

churches burned scheme of 1 world people (Jesus) 12/28/97 Vol. 9

Churches closed from religious persecution (Jesus) 8/4/98 Vol. 12

churches closed lawsuits and taxes (Jesus) 4/29/02 Vol. 27

churches closed meet in homes (Jesus) 10/12/02 Vol. 29

Churches closed museums,worship beast (Jesus) 1/23/99 Vol. 14

churches closed protect the Hosts (Jesus) 12/30/99 Vol. 17

churches closing lack of priests, weak faith (Jesus) 10/23/03 Vol. 33

churches closing pray for more priests (Jesus) 12/8/05 Vol. 41

churches desecrated museums or burned (Jesus) 11/25/97 Vol. 9

churches full when suffering losses (Jesus) 10/6/01 Vol. 25

Churches of God now are churches of man (Jesus) 1/23/99 Vol. 14

churches stripped because of Satanic influence (Jesus) 7/28/05 Vol. 40

churches stripped holiness lost (Jesus) 5/17/03 Vol. 31

churches stripped house of prayer,not for thieves (Jesus) 6/11/04 Vol. 35

churches stripped Jesus, saints present (Jesus) 4/1/06 Vol. 43

churches stripped of beauty (Jesus) 3/16/07 Vol. 46

churches stripped of holy objects (Jesus) 5/18/05 Vol. 39

churches stripped reverence removed (Jesus) 7/4/02 Vol. 28

churches stripped statues,icons,crucifixes (Jesus) 10/28/99 Vol. 17

churches stripped to make way for New Age (Jesus)   7/20/02 Vol. 28
churches, closed source of grace lost (Jesus)   11/9/05 Vol. 41
churches, hollow missing reverence,sense sacred (Jesus)   2/21/02 Vol. 26
churches, older better than new ones (Jesus)   2/28/06 Vol. 42
churches, poor need money for heating (Jesus)   11/29/07 Vol. 49
churches, stripped need restoration (Jesus)   10/5/07 Vol. 49
churches, underground from persecution (Jesus)   4/29/02 Vol. 27
Church's new year spiritual preparations (Jesus)   12/1/03 Vol. 33
CIA & FBI do one worlders bidding (Jesus)   8/8/07 Vol. 48
circle of life found in seasons (Jesus)   9/30/97 Vol. 8
circling saucer warning   10/25/93 Vol. 1
Circumcision in the Temple (Jesus)   2/2/07 Vol. 46
cities blessing or curse (Jesus)   2/6/96 Vol. 3
cities flee from, evil (Jesus)   1/6/97 Vol. 6
cities protection underground (Jesus)   3/4/05 Vol. 38
cities violence (Jesus)   3/12/95 Vol. 2
cities of America face wrath of God (Jesus)   6/26/03 Vol. 31
cities underground built by government (Jesus)   8/27/04 Vol. 36
cities will be in ruin stripped of possessions (Jesus)   11/23/99 Vol. 17
city crime Antichrist (Jesus)   9/2/95 Vol. 3
City of God heaven   10/12/93 Vol. 1
civilization America headed for demise (Jesus)   5/24/02 Vol. 27
civilization could see destruction of (Jesus)   1/2/02 Vol. 26
civilization US a wasteful society (Jesus)   10/3/02 Vol. 29
civilizations collapse from evil within (Jesus)   10/30/01 Vol. 25
civilizations collapsed from within (Jesus)   9/4/96 Vol. 4
civilizations destroyed by unnatural (Jesus)   8/2/01 Vol. 24
civilizations destroyed themselves (Jesus)   3/4/99 Vol. 14
civilizations destroyed by pride,lack of forgiveness (Jesus)   4/10/01 Vol. 23
civilizations,immoral were destroyed (Jesus)   12/30/03 Vol. 33
claim graces from Jesus for the soul (Jesus)   12/31/99 Vol. 17
class struggle through job losses (Jesus)   7/26/98 Vol. 12
clay of potter cannot form itself (Jesus)   9/19/01 Vol. 24
clay, be like for Jesus to mold us (Jesus)   4/27/06 Vol. 43
clean robes Advent (Jesus)   12/11/94 Vol. 2
clean souls by organizing spiritual life (Jesus)   3/8/02 Vol. 26
cleansing body and soul (Jesus)   5/28/02 Vol. 27
cleansing of sins Baptism & Confession (Jesus)   12/1/02 Vol. 29
cleansing of sins Confession needed by many (Jesus)   9/13/01 Vol. 24
cleansing of sins in Confession (Jesus)   3/29/99 Vol. 14
cleansing of souls needed in Confession (Jesus)   7/18/04 Vol. 36
Clearwater miracle removal of religious images (Jesus)   3/4/04 Vol. 34
Clearwater, Florida miraculous image (Mary)   2/28/98 Vol. 10
clergy held to a higher code (Jesus)   9/21/06 Vol. 44
clergy need prayers, identity (Jesus)   11/20/97 Vol. 9
clergy not feeding the flock (Jesus)   12/23/97 Vol. 9
clergy pray for them (Jesus)   9/6/98 Vol. 12

clergy pray for to be strong (Mary)   6/4/05 Vol. 39
clergy wolves in lambs clothing (Jesus)   9/16/06 Vol. 44
Clinton abortion stand will humble (Jesus)   10/17/96 Vol. 5
Clinton adocates killing children (Jesus)   12/28/98 Vol. 13
Clinton all sinners need repentance (Jesus)   9/11/98 Vol. 12
Clinton banking system (Jesus)   5/31/95 Vol. 2
Clinton cause of country to suffer (Jesus)   10/17/96 Vol. 5
Clinton detective (Jesus)   12/7/94 Vol. 2
Clinton disasters from abortion stand (Jesus)   8/14/98 Vol. 12
Clinton humiliated for abortion stand (Jesus)   9/10/98 Vol. 12
Clinton immoral presidency (Jesus)   2/19/01 Vol. 22
Clinton inauguaral address (Jesus)   1/16/97 Vol. 6
Clinton lying, sins (Jesus)   1/8/99 Vol. 14
Clinton removal of opposition (Jesus)   1/9/97 Vol. 6
Clinton smoted (Jesus)   11/9/94 Vol. 2
Clinton spouses need to be faithful (Jesus)   9/12/98 Vol. 12
Clinton treacherous president (Jesus)   8/30/00 Vol. 20
Clinton USA (Jesus)   11/17/93 Vol. 1
Clinton will answer to God (Jesus)   1/23/98 Vol. 10
Clinton & abortion Arkansas tornadoes (Jesus)   1/25/99 Vol. 14
Clinton & leaders used as puppets (Jesus)   11/6/97 Vol. 9
Clinton chastized trail of immorality & death (Jesus)   10/11/00 Vol. 21
Clinton, like people fix your own souls first (Jesus)   12/10/98 Vol. 13
Clinton, president drug connection (Jesus)   3/13/96 Vol. 3
Clinton, President struggle for power (Jesus)   10/23/99 Vol. 17
clock repentance   9/1/93 Vol. 1
clock watch with me   8/26/93 Vol. 1
clocks should not run your life (Jesus)   2/18/05 Vol. 38
cloning doomed to failure (Jesus)   3/10/01 Vol. 22
cloning morals getting worse (Jesus)   1/18/03 Vol. 30
cloning sins against nature (Jesus)   8/2/01 Vol. 24
cloning to help bring Warning (Jesus)   1/1/03 Vol. 30
cloning & DNA abuses of science (Jesus)   1/23/03 Vol. 30
cloning experiments question of human cloning (Jesus)   3/29/01 Vol. 22
cloning, fetal stem cells will not be successful (Jesus)   4/25/05 Vol. 39
cloning, manipulating DNA against God's plan (Jesus)   8/31/04 Vol. 36
cloning,artificial babies mortal sins (Jesus)   7/8/01 Vol. 24
clon.,DNA manipulation Jesus will not let succeed (Jesus)   11/21/01 Vol. 25
closed heart to God's love (Jesus)   3/24/00 Vol. 18
clothed in the sun red host (Mary)   8/15/93 Vol. 1
clutter physical and spiritual (Jesus)   4/24/03 Vol. 31
clutter and junk clean house & soul (Jesus)   1/27/02 Vol. 26
CO2 & pollutants can be limited (Jesus)   5/2/07 Vol. 47
coal important to factories (Jesus)   1/4/06 Vol. 42
coal & energy sources being used up (Jesus)   10/13/05 Vol. 41
coal mine safety compromised for profits (Jesus)   8/11/07 Vol. 48
coal mines safety vs. profit (Jesus)   2/2/06 Vol. 42

St. Patrick's Invitation to Ireland

St. Patrick came once and said it would be nice if we could visit the old sod sometime in Ireland, as this was John's paternal heritage. Several months later we were invited to go to Ireland. Unfortunately, our first experiences in Dublin left much to be desired. The taxi driver tried to cheat us out of our change, and anyone that we asked for directions brushed us off. Finally, as we got off of the bus, I approached the driver who must have been taking his break. He pulled out his newspaper and ignored our request for directions. Now a bit disgruntled, I said to St. Patrick: You invited us to come to Ireland and now that we are here, nobody has been very cooperative in helping us. We got off the bus. The sidewalk was deserted and the shops were all closed as it was dusk. Just then as we were wondering what to do, a tiny old lady approached us from nowhere and she was wearing wire glasses low on her nose and very sweet. She said: "My dear, may I help you?" I said, yes, that we would like to know how to get to this street for this special program. She gave us directions and as I turned to thank her, she was gone as quickly as she appeared. I guess St. Patrick was tired of my complaining.

Messages: March 17, 1994 (volume 1) and June 12, 1996 (volume 3)

coastal city inundated with water (Jesus)	1/2/02 Vol. 26	colorless roses abortions (Jesus)	1/11/95 Vol. 2
coastlines, avoid live in high places (Jesus)	12/15/06 Vol. 45	Co-Mediatrix in Blessed Mother's Yes (Jesus)	8/22/07 Vol. 48
cobra vs. red rose death not a pro-life position (Jesus)	9/15/98 Vol. 12	comet 3 days of darkness (Jesus)	4/13/03 Vol. 31
coins with image of the beast (Jesus)	3/2/99 Vol. 14	comet angels deflect missiles (Jesus)	9/22/00 Vol. 20
cold weather (Jesus)	12/11/95 Vol. 3	comet Antichrist (Jesus)	12/5/95 Vol. 3
cold & snow help those in need (Jesus)	2/8/07 Vol. 46	comet begins days of darkness (Jesus)	4/11/97 Vol. 7
cold & snow return to North in US (Jesus)	1/16/07 Vol. 46	comet brings Triumph over evil (Jesus)	9/15/03 Vol. 32
cold air,spiritual weapons Antichrist (Jesus)	12/7/95 Vol. 3	comet cannot destroy it (Jesus)	5/31/01 Vol. 23
cold heart need to empty self (Jesus)	1/13/00 Vol. 18	comet cataclysm of conversion (Jesus)	8/21/97 Vol. 8
cold hearts blocks Christian love (Jesus)	3/6/08 Vol. 50	comet causes 3 days of darkness (Jesus)	12/21/01 Vol. 25
cold hearts demons	10/23/93 Vol. 1	comet chastisement (Jesus)	3/24/96 Vol. 3
cold hearts gift giving (Jesus)	12/13/94 Vol. 2	comet defeat of Antichrist (Jesus)	6/4/98 Vol. 11
cold hearts lack of God's love (Jesus)	2/17/01 Vol. 22	comet destroys Antichrist's power (Jesus)	8/4/01 Vol. 24
cold hearts need warmth of God's love (Jesus)	1/21/05 Vol. 38	comet effect on earth at Warning (Jesus)	10/8/99 Vol. 17
cold hearts persevere in prayer (Jesus)	1/18/02 Vol. 26	comet fire	8/21/93 Vol. 1
cold weather causes hardships (Jesus)	1/22/00 Vol. 18	comet headed for earth (Jesus)	5/13/02 Vol. 27
cold winter in unusual areas (Jesus)	9/30/99 Vol. 16	comet hits in Atlantic Ocean (Jesus)	12/22/00 Vol. 21
Cole ship incident vulnerability to terrorists (Jesus)	10/12/00 Vol. 21	comet information blacked out (Jesus)	9/4/00 Vol. 20
college killings life is precious (Jesus)	4/19/07 Vol. 47	comet judgment (Jesus)	7/22/94 Vol. 2
color in creation brilliant in sun (Jesus)	10/16/07 Vol. 49	comet judgment (Jesus)	5/17/94 Vol. 1
colored money track buying & selling (Jesus)	5/13/04 Vol. 35	comet Jupiter (Jesus)	7/15/94 Vol. 2

comet justice visible,cleanse evil (Jesus) — 4/15/97 Vol. 7
comet low oxygen levels (Jesus) — 9/17/94 Vol. 2
comet materialism (Jesus) — 5/28/94 Vol. 1
comet messages (Jesus) — 11/15/95 Vol. 3
comet of chastisement (Jesus) — 6/2/04 Vol. 35
comet of chastisement (Jesus) — 5/2/01 Vol. 23
comet of chastisement (Jesus) — 9/7/00 Vol. 20
comet of chastisement (Jesus) — 12/4/99 Vol. 17
comet of chastisement near (Jesus) — 4/17/01 Vol. 23
comet of the triumph (Jesus) — 2/1/99 Vol. 14
comet of Warning (Jesus) — 9/4/00 Vol. 20
comet on day of Warning (Jesus) — 3/18/05 Vol. 38
comet on track for earth (Jesus) — 8/10/97 Vol. 8
comet polar shift/out of orbit (Jesus) — 7/23/96 Vol. 4
comet purification (Jesus) — 8/8/94 Vol. 2
comet purification (Jesus) — 9/2/95 Vol. 3
comet safe in caves from (Jesus) — 4/24/01 Vol. 23
comet sign of the Warning (Jesus) — 6/6/01 Vol. 23
comet soon to be visible (Jesus) — 1/14/99 Vol. 14
comet supernatural intervention (Jesus) — 11/19/00 Vol. 21
comet tidal waves — 9/24/93 Vol. 1
comet tidal waves/many die (Jesus) — 8/17/96 Vol. 4
comet to cleanse earth (Jesus) — 11/19/01 Vol. 25
comet to conquer evil, renew earth (Jesus) — 7/25/06 Vol. 44
comet to defeat the Antichrist (Jesus) — 2/15/04 Vol. 34
comet to destroy all evil (Jesus) — 8/29/03 Vol. 32
comet to destroy Antichrist's reign (Jesus) — 3/5/05 Vol. 38
comet to vanquish evil (Jesus) — 11/8/01 Vol. 25
comet will deliver triumph (Jesus) — 5/14/98 Vol. 11
comet coming means of Jesus' triumph (Jesus) — 8/24/99 Vol. 16
comet coming to remove evil people (Jesus) — 12/15/98 Vol. 13
comet experiments could alter course to earth (Jesus) — 1/20/05 Vol. 38
comet of chastisement already on its way (Jesus) — 6/22/05 Vol. 39
comet of chastisement already on its way to earth (Jesus) — 8/21/98 Vol. 12
comet of chastisement end to electronic control (Jesus) — 10/1/98 Vol. 13
comet of chastisement fire on evil people (Jesus) — 9/20/01 Vol. 24
comet of chastisement kept from public,secret (Jesus) — 8/8/00 Vol. 20
Comet of Chastisement protected by angels (Jesus) — 12/28/05 Vol. 41
comet of chastisement sign of judgment (Jesus) — 11/23/99 Vol. 17
comet of chastisement tidal wave in Atlantic Ocean (Jesus) — 10/5/00 Vol. 21
comet of chastisement to cleanse earth of all evil (Jesus) — 7/6/00 Vol. 20
comet of chastisement to consume lost sinners (Jesus) — 5/3/99 Vol. 15
comet of chastisement triumph over Antichrist (Jesus) — 9/28/99 Vol. 16
comet of chastisement triumph over evil (Jesus) — 12/13/98 Vol. 13
comet of chastisement triumph over evil (Jesus) — 5/6/99 Vol. 15
comet of chastisement will not be destroyed (Jesus) — 2/20/01 Vol. 22
comet of chastisement will not be stopped (Jesus) — 3/29/01 Vol. 22

comet of destruction evil as in Noah's day (Jesus) — 8/19/99 Vol. 16
comet of destruction justice for our apostasy (Jesus) — 3/21/00 Vol. 18
Comet of Warning to be comet of chastisement (Jesus) — 1/26/07 Vol. 46
Comet of Warning view behind in space (Jesus) — 6/7/07 Vol. 47
comet probe for future destruction (Jesus) — 12/28/05 Vol. 41
comets & asteroids collisions on earth (Jesus) — 3/14/98 Vol. 10
comets & asteroids flying into planets (Jesus) — 6/14/02 Vol. 27
comets & asteroids media ignore collision (Jesus) — 10/16/06 Vol. 45
comets and asteroids signs in the sky (Jesus) — 6/5/04 Vol. 35
comfort Betania Dominic's Angel — 11/4/95 Vol. 3
comfort in Jesus as parents at home (Jesus) — 11/26/07 Vol. 49
comfort relatives in good times & bad times (Jesus) — 2/22/01 Vol. 22
comfort the suffering do not add to their pain (Jesus) — 3/16/00 Vol. 18
comfort threatened forgiveness,taking insults (Jesus) — 6/29/99 Vol. 15
comfort zone move out for charity (Jesus) — 3/15/01 Vol. 22
comfort zones reach out of (Jesus) — 4/23/04 Vol. 35
comforts & pleasures can lull you into spiritual sleep (Jesus) — 3/31/04 Vol. 34
comforts & pleasures mislead us from God (Jesus) — 11/12/05 Vol. 41
comforts & possessions does not give God's peace (Jesus) — 8/10/06 Vol. 44
comforts are temporary lost due to sins (Jesus) — 1/8/00 Vol. 18
comforts stripped to get our attention (Jesus) — 9/12/04 Vol. 36
comforts,earthly distract your purpose here (Jesus) — 2/19/00 Vol. 18
coming of Jesus curtain about to go up (Jesus) — 6/24/07 Vol. 47
Coming of Jesus in your lifetime (Jesus) — 3/16/06 Vol. 42
coming of Jesus told by modern prophets (Jesus) — 5/14/07 Vol. 47
Commandment, First worship only God not things (Jesus) — 8/1/04 Vol. 36
Commandments do not follow the crowd (Jesus) — 6/12/01 Vol. 23
Commandments follow to be saved (Jesus) — 5/4/03 Vol. 31
commandments follow traditions (Jesus) — 12/15/97 Vol. 9
Commandments fulfilled by Jesus (Jesus) — 2/27/08 Vol. 50
Commandments fulfilled in love of Jesus (Jesus) — 12/21/03 Vol. 33
Commandments love God & neighbor (Jesus) — 4/17/04 Vol. 35
Commandments love God & neighbor (Jesus) — 10/23/05 Vol. 41
Commandments love God & neighbor (Jesus) — 6/2/05 Vol. 39
Commandments love of God & neighbor (Jesus) — 8/27/07 Vol. 48
Commandments no peace without love (Jesus) — 3/25/99 Vol. 14
Commandments removal from public (Jesus) — 10/17/96 Vol. 5
Commandments revere God,respect neighbor (Jesus) — 3/29/00 Vol. 18
commandments seek forgiveness (Jesus) — 9/21/97 Vol. 8
Commandments the greatest is love (Jesus) — 6/3/04 Vol. 35
Commandments to form right conscience (Jesus) — 4/25/04 Vol. 35
Commandments unchangeable in any age (Jesus) — 11/20/02 Vol. 29
Commandments vine and the branches (Jesus) — 6/2/96 Vol. 3
Commandments wages of sin is death (Jesus) — 10/23/97 Vol. 9
Commandments walk to perfection (Jesus) — 4/29/01 Vol. 23
Commandments forgot in lustful pleasures (Jesus) — 4/3/01 Vol. 23
Commandments of love truth will set you free (Jesus) — 5/1/05 Vol. 39

Commandments, Great Love God, Love neighbor (Jesus) 8/19/05 Vol. 40
Commandments, obey not sexual sins,wars,killings (Jesus) 11/25/03 Vol. 33
Commandments,consecration to gain heaven (Jesus) 10/2/03 Vol. 33
Commandments,signs way to come to heaven (Jesus) 5/11/00 Vol. 19
Commands,changeless not meant to be popular (Jesus) 5/22/00 Vol. 19
commercial airplanes threat from missile attack (Jesus) 10/19/07 Vol. 49
commercial, military planes provide chem trails (Jesus) 7/5/07 Vol. 48
commercialism true Christmas meaning (Jesus) 11/14/96 Vol. 5
commitment choice (Jesus) 4/15/94 Vol. 1
commitment will (Jesus) 3/29/94 Vol. 1
commitment in faith consecrate everything to God (Jesus) 9/8/01 Vol. 24
commitment needed God's personal relationship (Jesus) 1/25/00 Vol. 18
commitment to God for eternal life in heaven (Jesus) 5/8/07 Vol. 47
commitment varies daily, Sunday, holidays (Jesus) 12/6/05 Vol. 41
commitment, full share everything with God (Jesus) 11/11/00 Vol. 21
commitment, total call from Jesus (Jesus) 12/11/07 Vol. 49
commodities, scarce control by one world people (Jesus) 3/7/00 Vol. 18
commodity,manipulation to control population (Jesus) 10/6/00 Vol. 21
communal living share talents at refuge (Jesus) 1/30/08 Vol. 50
communcations stop if Antichrist influenced (Jesus) 8/30/04 Vol. 36
communicate but not with force (Jesus) 5/15/05 Vol. 39
communicate to get along (Jesus) 1/10/02 Vol. 26
communication being spied on (Jesus) 2/1/07 Vol. 46
communication Echelon System (Jesus) 9/22/06 Vol. 44
communication in marriage, prayers (Jesus) 6/2/99 Vol. 15
communication physical and spiritual (Jesus) 7/8/04 Vol. 36
communication priorities of time (Jesus) 5/28/96 Vol. 3
communication spiritual and physical (Jesus) 6/19/02 Vol. 27
communication to God & neighbor (Jesus) 2/9/99 Vol. 14
communication with love (Jesus) 10/29/06 Vol. 45
communication to God vertically & horizontally (Jesus) 9/29/01 Vol. 24
communication to God we need grace & love (Jesus) 8/30/01 Vol. 24
communication,new be aware others listening (Jesus) 4/17/97 Vol. 7
communications abuses of privacy (Jesus) 6/10/03 Vol. 31
communications being listened by others (Jesus) 5/3/04 Vol. 35
communications careful of eavesdropping (Jesus) 7/30/96 Vol. 4
communications for spying (Jesus) 2/18/04 Vol. 34
communications heard by one worlders (Jesus) 11/13/02 Vol. 29
communications intercepted (Jesus) 1/10/02 Vol. 26
communications monitored by government (Jesus) 2/9/06 Vol. 42
communications phone, TV, Internet (Jesus) 9/13/96 Vol. 4
communications prayer time needed (Jesus) 9/10/04 Vol. 36
communications used for spying (Jesus) 1/15/04 Vol. 34
communications wire-tapping & TV (Jesus) 1/16/97 Vol. 6
communications garbled new tower of Babel (Jesus) 8/24/00 Vol. 20
communications open through constant prayer (Jesus) 8/29/99 Vol. 16
Communion for spiritual strength (Jesus) 5/30/97 Vol. 7

Communion is a taste of heaven (Jesus) 10/30/05 Vol. 41
Communion love (Jesus) 8/2/95 Vol. 3
Communion manna (Jesus) 7/24/94 Vol. 2
Communion of Saints faith enriched by (Jesus) 10/24/98 Vol. 13
Communion of Saints imitate their lives (Jesus) 11/1/99 Vol. 17
Communion of Saints in Mystical Body (Jesus) 8/17/07 Vol. 48
Communion of Saints join on resurrection (Jesus) 5/21/00 Vol. 19
Communion of Saints on earth,heaven,purgatory (Jesus) 11/1/05 Vol. 41
Communion of Saints pray to be in (Jesus) 6/13/01 Vol. 23
Communion thanksgiving for gifts of God (Jesus) 10/14/07 Vol. 49
Communism Antichrist environment (Jesus) 3/15/96 Vol. 3
Communism atomic war (Jesus) 4/10/96 Vol. 3
communism control of world (Jesus) 12/19/96 Vol. 5
communism controlled by monied people (Jesus) 8/28/98 Vol. 12
communism is not dead (Jesus) 9/27/98 Vol. 12
communism not dead, Europe (Jesus) 5/29/97 Vol. 7
communism not dead, UN (Jesus) 5/1/97 Vol. 7
communism persecution (Jesus) 5/24/94 Vol. 1
communism Russia (Jesus) 10/21/95 Vol. 3
communism Russia and China (Jesus) 6/19/96 Vol. 3
communism sponsored by 1 world people (Jesus) 9/3/98 Vol. 12
communism returns in new faces as China (Jesus) 12/9/02 Vol. 29
Communist China luring money for war-making (Jesus) 10/19/98 Vol. 13
Communist China US dependent on imports (Jesus) 5/26/07 Vol. 47
communists conversion pray for (Our Lady) 10/13/07 Vol. 49
compassion rejection (Jesus) 12/2/93 Vol. 1
compassion volunteer our services (Jesus) 5/17/01 Vol. 23
compassion needed for those being killed (Jesus) 10/7/07 Vol. 49
complacency spirit affecting clergy & laity (Jesus) 8/9/02 Vol. 28
complaining be joyful and not cranky (Jesus) 10/28/06 Vol. 45
complaining put on a happy face (Jesus) 5/26/99 Vol. 15
complaining & swearing love others instead (Jesus) 6/26/02 Vol. 27
complaints of trials avoid to gain perfection (Jesus) 2/26/05 Vol. 38
compromise & love needed in good marriage (Jesus) 10/31/06 Vol. 45
computer vulnerable to viruses (Jesus) 8/2/01 Vol. 24
computer addictions in children (Jesus) 10/24/07 Vol. 49
computer addictions limit kids time on computer (Jesus) 7/21/07 Vol. 48
computer failures as year progresses (Jesus) 12/10/99 Vol. 17
computer failures potential martial law (Jesus) 8/18/99 Vol. 16
computer failures return to simple life (Jesus) 6/10/99 Vol. 15
computer problems could cause power failure (Jesus) 9/9/99 Vol. 16
computer problems do not believe media (Jesus) 10/22/99 Vol. 17
computer problems vulnerable to attack (Jesus) 10/19/99 Vol. 17
computer problems worse by government lies (Jesus) 8/26/99 Vol. 16
computer systems to be replaced (Jesus) 10/27/99 Vol. 17
computer technology being exported (Jesus) 2/17/05 Vol. 38
computer technology helped by evil ones (Jesus) 8/11/03 Vol. 32

computer viruses to steal identities (Jesus)	1/14/05 Vol. 38
computers abused as a little god (Jesus)	11/13/97 Vol. 9
computers Antichrist (Jesus)	4/10/95 Vol. 2
computers Internet (Jesus)	10/26/94 Vol. 2
computers puffed up in technology (Jesus)	6/1/99 Vol. 15
computers to stop working (Jesus)	6/17/99 Vol. 15
computers too dependent on (Jesus)	1/4/99 Vol. 14
computers vulnerable to meltdown (Jesus)	11/29/98 Vol. 13
concentration camps for resisters (Jesus)	2/1/07 Vol. 46
concentration camps for those not taking mark (Jesus)	10/24/99 Vol. 17
concentration camps to house millions (Jesus)	6/24/04 Vol. 35
conception artificial abuses are sins (Jesus)	8/10/01 Vol. 24
conception soul gets spirit of life (Jesus)	9/5/98 Vol. 12
conception problems pray for infertile couples (Jesus)	7/12/07 Vol. 48
conception, sins against contraception,artificial (Jesus)	5/13/06 Vol. 43
condemnation comes from God only (Jesus)	9/27/05 Vol. 40
conference workers for Father's honor (God the Father)	4/17/99 Vol. 15
Conference(2003) Rochester on Mercy Sunday (Jesus)	4/11/02 Vol. 27
Conferences longer Confession lines (Jesus)	11/16/06 Vol. 45
confess your sins no excuse to neglect (Jesus)	3/19/00 Vol. 18
confessing of sins important soul cleaning (Jesus)	3/5/06 Vol. 42
Confession a haven for sinners (Jesus)	5/31/99 Vol. 15
Confession a spiritual lifesaver (Jesus)	5/6/05 Vol. 39
Confession absolution as a waterfall (Jesus)	1/13/02 Vol. 26
Confession accept we are sinners (Jesus)	7/9/99 Vol. 16
Confession act of humility (Jesus)	8/29/04 Vol. 36
Confession adds light to the soul (Jesus)	10/13/06 Vol. 45
Confession admit we are sinners (Jesus)	4/9/03 Vol. 31
confession admit you are sinners (Jesus)	8/30/96 Vol. 4
Confession all are sinners (Jesus)	1/13/03 Vol. 30
Confession allows soul preparation (Jesus)	6/21/02 Vol. 27
Confession always be prepared (Jesus)	6/12/04 Vol. 35
Confession always be prepared (Jesus)	10/26/99 Vol. 17
Confession always be prepared (Jesus)	6/4/99 Vol. 15
Confession an oasis of grace (Jesus)	8/10/03 Vol. 32
Confession and daily consecration (Jesus)	9/20/03 Vol. 32
Confession as newly baptized (Jesus)	7/5/03 Vol. 32
Confession as spiritual life preservers (Jesus)	4/8/05 Vol. 39
Confession ask for forgiveness (Jesus)	2/21/99 Vol. 14
confession at least monthly (Jesus)	3/5/97 Vol. 6
Confession at least montly (Jesus)	3/1/07 Vol. 46
Confession avoid occasions of sin (Jesus)	6/18/04 Vol. 35
confession be prepared to die (Jesus)	1/30/97 Vol. 6
Confession be prepared to die (Jesus)	3/9/98 Vol. 10
Confession beauty of pure souls (Jesus)	5/8/03 Vol. 31
Confession best source of healing (Jesus)	3/15/05 Vol. 38
Confession binding & loosing (Jesus)	4/1/04 Vol. 35
Confession binding and loosing (Jesus)	4/30/02 Vol. 27
Confession breaks bonds of sin (Jesus)	9/9/02 Vol. 28
Confession bring children to (Jesus)	5/24/01 Vol. 23
Confession brings closer to perfection (Jesus)	5/27/99 Vol. 15
Confession call to repent (Jesus)	9/28/02 Vol. 28
Confession can break sinful habits (Jesus)	1/19/07 Vol. 46
Confession can heal darkness of sin (Jesus)	2/8/06 Vol. 42
Confession clean as at Baptism (Jesus)	7/2/02 Vol. 28
Confession cleans away all sins (Jesus)	9/6/07 Vol. 48
Confession cleans out trash of sins (Jesus)	5/20/04 Vol. 35
Confession cleanse inside as outside (Jesus)	8/26/04 Vol. 36
Confession cleanses our sins (Jesus)	6/13/99 Vol. 15
Confession cleanses sin (Jesus)	7/28/98 Vol. 12
Confession cleanses sins (Jesus)	10/13/06 Vol. 45
Confession confess sins (Jesus)	6/14/98 Vol. 11
Confession contemplate sins (Jesus)	8/11/98 Vol. 12
Confession contrite hearts (Jesus)	6/14/04 Vol. 35
Confession contrition and forgiveness (Jesus)	2/15/98 Vol. 10
confession conversion & forgiveness (Jesus)	1/25/97 Vol. 6
Confession do not be fearful of (Jesus)	9/23/06 Vol. 44
Confession do not ignore cleansing of sin (Jesus)	8/25/03 Vol. 32
Confession encourage children (Jesus)	7/11/03 Vol. 32
Confession encourage family members (Jesus)	3/22/07 Vol. 46
Confession encouraged by Padre Pio (Jesus)	5/8/03 Vol. 31
Confession examination of conscience (Jesus)	10/26/00 Vol. 21
Confession faith for trial (Jesus)	8/22/00 Vol. 20
Confession filth of sin cleansed from souls (Jesus)	8/24/04 Vol. 36
Confession firm purpose not to repeat (Jesus)	1/19/08 Vol. 50
Confession for grace in temptation (Jesus)	2/5/04 Vol. 34
Confession for inner beauty (Jesus)	7/11/05 Vol. 40
Confession for pure soul (Jesus)	7/30/03 Vol. 32
Confession for pure wedding garment (Jesus)	10/9/05 Vol. 41
Confession for spiritual life (Jesus)	5/7/01 Vol. 23
confession forgiveness (Jesus)	6/8/94 Vol. 1
Confession forgiveness of sins (Jesus)	6/3/05 Vol. 39
Confession free from bondage of sin (Jesus)	7/21/03 Vol. 32
Confession free from bondage of sin (Jesus)	1/16/04 Vol. 34
Confession gives grace & advice (Jesus)	8/1/06 Vol. 44
Confession gives life to dead souls (Jesus)	10/9/99 Vol. 17
Confession go frequently (Jesus)	1/23/01 Vol. 22
Confession grace cleanses souls (Jesus)	2/15/03 Vol. 30
Confession grace for pure souls (Jesus)	10/14/05 Vol. 41
Confession grace for temptations (Jesus)	6/28/04 Vol. 35
Confession grace gives light to soul (Jesus)	9/9/03 Vol. 32
Confession grace is lifeblood of soul (Jesus)	5/3/01 Vol. 23
Confession grace to gain strength (Jesus)	10/29/05 Vol. 41
Confession grace to overcome weakness (Jesus)	4/8/05 Vol. 39

Confession greatest Healer in Jesus (Jesus)	5/23/02 Vol. 27	Confession prepare for death,warning (Jesus)	3/24/99 Vol. 14
Confession greatest weapon against Satan (Jesus)	4/9/05 Vol. 39	Confession prepare for judgment (Jesus)	8/31/00 Vol. 20
Confession have contrite hearts (Jesus)	3/1/99 Vol. 14	confession priest (Jesus)	1/14/94 Vol. 1
Confession healing repentant sinners (Jesus)	3/23/07 Vol. 46	Confession Prodigal Son (Jesus)	9/16/07 Vol. 48
Confession heals sins, humble (Jesus)	10/28/07 Vol. 49	Confession proper wedding garment (Jesus)	10/10/99 Vol. 17
Confession humbles pride (Jesus)	6/5/05 Vol. 39	Confession public declaration of sins (Jesus)	9/19/02 Vol. 28
Confession inspiration on St. Pio's life (Jesus)	9/18/04 Vol. 36	Confession purifies soul, restores grace (Jesus)	6/26/04 Vol. 35
Confession is a haven for the sinner (Jesus)	3/14/02 Vol. 26	Confession purify souls for heaven (Jesus)	1/7/08 Vol. 50
Confession Jesus best guest (Jesus)	5/15/03 Vol. 31	Confession puts out fire of hell (Jesus)	7/8/03 Vol. 32
Confession Jesus died for our sins (Jesus)	2/21/04 Vol. 34	Confession reasons for, monthly needed (Jesus)	7/13/07 Vol. 48
Confession Jesus present in priest (Jesus)	9/11/04 Vol. 36	Confession rejoicing over soul saved (Jesus)	12/24/97 Vol. 9
Confession Jesus waiting to forgive (Jesus)	7/7/05 Vol. 40	Confession release in freedom from bondage (Jesus)	8/2/07 Vol. 48
Confession judgment and sin (Jesus)	5/5/96 Vol. 3	Confession removes stain of sin (Jesus)	4/30/05 Vol. 39
Confession keep soul tidy (Jesus)	8/21/03 Vol. 32	Confession renew grace,spiritual life (Jesus)	8/30/01 Vol. 24
Confession keeps soul pure (Jesus)	7/1/06 Vol. 44	Confession renew soul's grace (Jesus)	8/17/01 Vol. 24
Confession life raft from sins (Jesus)	4/15/99 Vol. 15	Confession renewal of Baptism (Jesus)	7/26/07 Vol. 48
Confession lifeblood of the soul (Jesus)	2/27/99 Vol. 14	confession renewal of grace (Jesus)	1/23/97 Vol. 6
Confession lifts us up from sin (Jesus)	3/10/06 Vol. 42	Confession renews beauty of soul (Jesus)	8/30/98 Vol. 12
Confession light of our soul (Jesus)	3/30/98 Vol. 10	Confession renews grace in soul (Jesus)	4/3/05 Vol. 39
Confession lost sense of sin (Jesus)	11/17/01 Vol. 25	Confession renews life of soul (Jesus)	9/9/03 Vol. 32
Confession lost sense of sin (Jesus)	2/5/04 Vol. 34	Confession renews our soul (Jesus)	8/17/03 Vol. 32
Confession lost sense of sin (Jesus)	8/3/06 Vol. 44	Confession renews soul (Jesus)	2/22/07 Vol. 46
Confession maintains grace in soul (Jesus)	12/4/03 Vol. 33	Confession renews strength (Jesus)	5/16/02 Vol. 27
Confession makes us new creations (Jesus)	2/14/99 Vol. 14	confession reparation for sins (Jesus)	6/27/96 Vol. 3
Confession making peace with God (Jesus)	2/26/05 Vol. 38	Confession repent (Jesus)	5/20/98 Vol. 11
Confession mercy awaits all (Jesus)	3/23/05 Vol. 38	confession repent and convert (Mary)	6/21/97 Vol. 7
Confession mercy for sins (Jesus)	5/19/03 Vol. 31	Confession repent of sins (Jesus)	3/22/05 Vol. 38
confession mortal sin (Jesus)	12/11/93 Vol. 1	Confession repent while still time (Jesus)	2/13/03 Vol. 30
Confession necessary for salvation (Jesus)	1/15/98 Vol. 10	Confession repent with contrite hearts (Jesus)	10/23/04 Vol. 37
Confession necessary for soul (Jesus)	4/22/03 Vol. 31	Confession replenish grace to soul (Jesus)	6/21/01 Vol. 23
Confession need for repentance (Jesus)	8/1/02 Vol. 28	Confession restore graces (Jesus)	9/10/00 Vol. 20
Confession need to be purified (Jesus)	12/15/05 Vol. 41	Confession restore life in Spirit (Jesus)	10/28/99 Vol. 17
Confession need to come to Jesus (Jesus)	12/18/05 Vol. 41	Confession restore soul's beauty (Jesus)	9/19/00 Vol. 20
Confession needed for pure souls (Jesus)	3/2/06 Vol. 42	Confession restore to grace (Jesus)	1/8/98 Vol. 10
Confession needed for sins of abortion (Jesus)	12/28/00 Vol. 21	Confession restored to graces (Jesus)	8/12/99 Vol. 16
Confession needed for venial sins (Jesus)	6/12/03 Vol. 31	Confession restores bond of love (Jesus)	6/4/98 Vol. 11
Confession needed preparation for Eucharist (Jesus)	11/15/03 Vol. 33	Confession restores grace (Jesus)	9/21/06 Vol. 44
Confession needed to restore life to soul (Jesus)	5/10/00 Vol. 19	Confession restores grace to soul (Jesus)	11/28/01 Vol. 25
Confession new lease on life (Jesus)	8/21/00 Vol. 20	Confession restores grace to soul (Jesus)	7/8/04 Vol. 36
Confession oasis of grace (Jesus)	8/16/01 Vol. 24	Confession restores our souls (Jesus)	4/15/04 Vol. 35
Confession oasis of grace (Jesus)	2/14/02 Vol. 26	Confession restores soul to grace (Jesus)	5/27/02 Vol. 27
Confession oasis of grace for soul (Jesus)	6/23/00 Vol. 19	Confession restores spiritual power (Jesus)	2/17/05 Vol. 38
Confession our amnesty from sin (Jesus)	2/14/03 Vol. 30	Confession return like prodigal son (Jesus)	7/12/01 Vol. 24
Confession our best fire insurance (Jesus)	5/3/01 Vol. 23	Confession return to path of love (Jesus)	6/23/01 Vol. 23
confession peace (Mary)	8/15/94 Vol. 2	Confession sacrilege (St.JohnVianny)	8/4/95 Vol. 3
Confession physical,spiritual cleansing (Jesus)	10/18/05 Vol. 41	Confession saves souls from sinking (Jesus)	8/7/05 Vol. 40
Confession preparation for heaven (Jesus)	11/1/06 Vol. 45	Confession Savior (Mary)	12/21/95 Vol. 3

Congress assert more authority (Jesus)	2/1/07 Vol. 46	consecration give all to Jesus (Jesus)	3/19/05 Vol. 38
Congress controlled by one worlders (Jesus)	2/16/07 Vol. 46	consecration give all totally (Jesus)	8/2/06 Vol. 44
Congress needs to assert itself (Jesus)	3/8/06 Vol. 42	consecration give total commitment (Jesus)	2/7/02 Vol. 26
Congress not assertive in laws,wars (Jesus)	7/26/03 Vol. 32	consecration give totally in (Jesus)	3/15/07 Vol. 46
Congress take authority on Iraq War (Jesus)	7/30/07 Vol. 48	consecration gives us treasures in heaven (Jesus)	7/29/03 Vol. 32
Congress' powers usurped by courts,executive (Jesus)	9/28/06 Vol. 44	Consecration graces/electrical cord (Mary)	5/19/96 Vol. 3
Congress, New with mandate (Jesus)	11/8/06 Vol. 45	consecration invite Jesus in your life (Jesus)	4/27/06 Vol. 43
conjunction Antichrist	10/26/93 Vol. 1	Consecration Lenten devotions (Mary)	2/28/96 Vol. 3
conscience Confession (Jesus)	10/29/95 Vol. 3	Consecration miracle of daily Mass (Jesus)	7/6/98 Vol. 12
conscience form proper one (Jesus)	3/6/07 Vol. 46	consecration of everything to God (Jesus)	8/23/04 Vol. 36
conscience sin in evil age (Jesus)	5/20/96 Vol. 3	consecration of whole life (Jesus)	9/3/02 Vol. 28
conscience sins (Jesus)	2/5/94 Vol. 1	Consecration only by priests (Jesus)	6/10/06 Vol. 43
conscience formation on Church and laws (Jesus)	5/15/98 Vol. 11	consecration pray daily (Jesus)	6/8/02 Vol. 27
conscience, form right know right from wrong (Jesus)	12/1/05 Vol. 41	consecration prayer (Mary)	3/22/94 Vol. 1
conscience, formed know right from wrong (Jesus)	2/26/05 Vol. 38	consecration preparation & perfection (Mary)	3/20/96 Vol. 3
conscience, proper know right from wrong (Jesus)	4/12/06 Vol. 43	Consecration Real Body & Blood (Jesus)	2/26/04 Vol. 34
conscience, right needed to know sins (Jesus)	3/13/99 Vol. 14	Consecration Real Presence (Jesus)	3/26/97 Vol. 6
consciences form properly (Jesus)	7/21/03 Vol. 32	consecration renew each day (Jesus)	12/6/01 Vol. 25
consciences proper formation of (Jesus)	6/18/96 Vol. 3	consecration reparation (Mary)	3/6/96 Vol. 3
consecrate Holy Places	9/7/93 Vol. 1	Consecration Resurrection (St. Therese)	3/22/95 Vol. 2
consecrate life each day (Jesus)	10/8/02 Vol. 29	Consecration rosaries (Mary)	3/25/95 Vol. 2
consecrate everything to Jesus (Jesus)	11/30/07 Vol. 49	consecration Sacred & Immaculate hearts (Jesus)	5/8/00 Vol. 19
consecrate homes protection, Belgium (Jesus)	7/10/97 Vol. 8	consecration total commitment to God (Jesus)	11/30/04 Vol. 37
consecrate life of prayer and deeds (Jesus)	8/24/00 Vol. 20	consecration triumph (Mary)	12/5/94 Vol. 2
Consecration August 15,preparation (Mary)	7/5/97 Vol. 8	Consecration turn life over to God (Jesus)	1/14/03 Vol. 30
consecration conversion (Mary)	3/25/96 Vol. 3	consecration way to keep holy (Jesus)	3/31/07 Vol. 46
consecration daily (Jesus)	1/5/03 Vol. 30	consecration whole life given up to God (Jesus)	8/12/01 Vol. 24
consecration daily strength (Jesus)	5/17/97 Vol. 7	Consecration words changed or omitted (Jesus)	1/20/04 Vol. 34
consecration detach from earthly things (Jesus)	8/28/05 Vol. 40	consecration needed for God to mold us (Jesus)	9/19/01 Vol. 24
consecration detachment from earthly things (Jesus)	11/23/03 Vol. 33	con. of everything give back to God what is His (Jesus)	3/13/02 Vol. 26
consecration die to self (Jesus)	4/23/01 Vol. 23	consecration of world Jubilee Year event (Jesus)	10/5/00 Vol. 21
consecration do daily (Jesus)	1/4/02 Vol. 26	consecration prayer makes work holy (Jesus)	7/29/05 Vol. 40
consecration do daily (Jesus)	4/23/03 Vol. 31	Consecration prayers invalid if changed (Jesus)	9/7/03 Vol. 32
consecration do daily (Jesus)	2/7/08 Vol. 50	consecration prayers reminder to pray (Mary)	11/11/96 Vol. 5
consecration do daily for vocation (Jesus)	10/3/07 Vol. 49	consecration to Jesus each day for direction (Jesus)	4/20/02 Vol. 27
consecration do each day (Jesus)	10/14/01 Vol. 25	consecration to Jesus give up sins & bad habits (Jesus)	12/3/02 Vol. 29
Consecration do not change words of (Jesus)	4/19/01 Vol. 23	consecration to Jesus needed for evangelizing (Jesus)	9/12/99 Vol. 16
consecration dying to self (Jesus)	2/17/04 Vol. 34	consecration to Mary 33 days before feast (Jesus)	8/11/05 Vol. 40
consecration each day (Jesus)	6/18/02 Vol. 27	consecration, daily offer trials & hurts to Jesus (Jesus)	9/5/07 Vol. 48
consecration emptying of self (Jesus)	4/19/06 Vol. 43	consecration, daily will make life less burdensome (Jesus)	8/3/04 Vol. 36
consecration evangelize, two hearts (Mary)	7/13/97 Vol. 8	consecration, detachment needed for heaven (Jesus)	3/30/04 Vol. 34
consecration faithful to daily (Jesus)	9/28/02 Vol. 28	consecration, total count costs (Jesus)	9/19/05 Vol. 40
consecration focus on heavenly things (Jesus)	2/8/05 Vol. 38	consecration, total needed to gain heaven (Jesus)	8/5/05 Vol. 40
consecration for China's conversion (Jesus)	10/20/01 Vol. 25	consequences of sin loss of soul's life (Jesus)	2/13/01 Vol. 22
consecration for daily help (Jesus)	8/20/03 Vol. 32	conservation & efficiency to use less fuel (Jesus)	6/5/07 Vol. 47
consecration for perfection (Jesus)	10/23/06 Vol. 45	conservation of gas to lessen fuel demands (Jesus)	8/11/05 Vol. 40
consecration Fr. Shamon (Mary)	3/25/94 Vol. 1	conservation, efficiency can reduce gas demand (Jesus)	5/11/07 Vol. 47

consolation Ed A. (Jesus)   11/18/95 Vol. 3
constitutional government crumble, take over (Jesus)   11/21/96 Vol. 5
Constitutional rights struck down (Jesus)   12/22/96 Vol. 5
consumer spending could lead to massive debts (Jesus)   11/14/02 Vol. 29
consumerism and technology (Jesus)   6/17/02 Vol. 27
contemplation Blessed Sacrament (Jesus)   5/11/95 Vol. 2
contemplation blessings (Jesus)   6/3/95 Vol. 2
contemplative life prayer of faith (Jesus)   7/17/07 Vol. 48
contemplative life to save souls (St. Therese)   1/16/99 Vol. 14
contemplative prayer avoid distractions (Jesus)   8/10/06 Vol. 44
contemplative prayer better than watching TV (Jesus)   12/5/07 Vol. 49
contemplative prayer mitigates natural disasters (Jesus)   5/27/05 Vol. 39
contraception leave open to conception (Jesus)   12/22/05 Vol. 41
contraception masturbation,prostitution (Jesus)   5/18/96 Vol. 3
contraception sterilization (Jesus)   3/9/97 Vol. 6
contraception vasectomies (Jesus)   9/21/97 Vol. 8
contrails cause of allergies & flu (Jesus)   6/13/02 Vol. 27
contrails causing diseases (Jesus)   10/17/02 Vol. 29
contrails viruses & diseases (Jesus)   2/25/03 Vol. 30
contrails viruses spread by (chemtrails) (Jesus)   2/22/03 Vol. 30
contributions lost from dead unborn (Jesus)   6/5/03 Vol. 31
contrite heart finds rest in Jesus (Jesus)   4/19/99 Vol. 15
contrition for sin needed in Confession (Jesus)   8/3/02 Vol. 28
control by things avoid focus on Jesus (Jesus)   2/9/06 Vol. 42
control over mind avoid these things (Jesus)   4/21/06 Vol. 43
conventional war very brief (Jesus)   10/10/07 Vol. 49
conventional warfare wars are quick (Jesus)   9/3/07 Vol. 48
conversations used against us (Jesus)   9/22/06 Vol. 44
conversion an oasis of grace to soul (Jesus)   2/6/01 Vol. 22
conversion ask for grace (Jesus)   2/20/03 Vol. 30
conversion before Second Coming (Jesus)   3/9/97 Vol. 6
conversion burning in soul (Jesus)   2/24/04 Vol. 34
conversion change life (Jesus)   3/14/97 Vol. 6
conversion changing world (Jesus)   9/24/96 Vol. 4
conversion comes freely from heart (Jesus)   2/7/06 Vol. 42
conversion confession of sins (Jesus)   11/5/96 Vol. 5
conversion do not delay (Jesus)   9/2/02 Vol. 28
conversion do not waste time (Jesus)   8/21/03 Vol. 32
conversion fight the good fight (St. Therese)   1/9/98 Vol. 10
conversion follow Divine Will (Jesus)   5/18/03 Vol. 31
conversion free time (Jesus)   4/16/95 Vol. 2
conversion from earthly desires (Jesus)   9/21/05 Vol. 40
conversion from hearts of stone (Jesus)   6/24/96 Vol. 3
conversion harder with technology (Jesus)   11/14/02 Vol. 29
conversion live Ten Commandments (Mary)   7/26/99 Vol. 16
conversion need open hearts (Jesus)   11/24/00 Vol. 21
conversion need prayer, encouraging (Jesus)   10/25/04 Vol. 37

conversion now is acceptable time (Jesus)   5/19/97 Vol. 7
conversion now is acceptable time (Jesus)   11/14/99 Vol. 17
conversion open hearts (Jesus)   9/10/00 Vol. 20
conversion or be taken over (Jesus)   6/25/98 Vol. 11
conversion personal, missionary (Jesus)   12/3/96 Vol. 5
conversion pray for poor souls here (Jesus)   8/27/96 Vol. 4
conversion prepare,discern message (Jesus)   5/2/97 Vol. 7
conversion Resurrection (Jesus)   4/27/95 Vol. 2
conversion save souls (Mary)   10/17/96 Vol. 5
conversion save souls (St. Therese)   8/14/96 Vol. 4
conversion seek forgiveness of sins (Jesus)   3/1/04 Vol. 34
conversion speak the truth (Jesus)   9/28/97 Vol. 8
conversion spiritual healing,short time (Jesus)   11/17/97 Vol. 9
conversion spiritual project (Jesus)   3/13/96 Vol. 3
conversion stiff necked people (Jesus)   8/30/96 Vol. 4
conversion time is short (Jesus)   8/13/96 Vol. 4
conversion time is short (Jesus)   12/3/00 Vol. 21
conversion time of judgment (Jesus)   1/6/97 Vol. 6
conversion to complete our mission (Jesus)   6/13/06 Vol. 43
conversion unconditional love (Jesus)   5/4/97 Vol. 7
conversion by love witness God's love (Jesus)   3/13/01 Vol. 22
conversion experience love of God & neighbor (Jesus)   4/18/02 Vol. 27
conversion experience more purpose in life (Jesus)   7/20/00 Vol. 20
conversion from sins needed to love God (Jesus)   9/10/05 Vol. 40
conversion graces opportunity for salvation (Jesus)   2/21/01 Vol. 22
conversion in heart open door of heart to Jesus (Jesus)   3/16/04 Vol. 34
conversion needed must have progress (Jesus)   2/5/01 Vol. 22
conversion needed stiff-necked people (Jesus)   8/2/96 Vol. 4
conversion of relatives do not give up (Jesus)   3/13/03 Vol. 30
conversion of sinners mission for all faithful (Jesus)   6/1/00 Vol. 19
conversion of sinners pray for (Jesus)   9/20/07 Vol. 48
conversion of sinners require foundation in faith (Jesus)   4/10/00 Vol. 19
conversion of sinners spiritual responsibility (Jesus)   11/10/07 Vol. 49
conversion of souls can come anytime (Jesus)   8/17/05 Vol. 40
con. requirement personal commitment to Jesus (Jesus)   1/25/05 Vol. 38
conversion steps sinner,sorry,forgiveness (Jesus)   2/16/02 Vol. 26
conversion time short evangelize lost souls (Jesus)   8/19/99 Vol. 16
conversion to God most important event (Jesus)   12/19/04 Vol. 37
conversion, early can yield more fruit (Jesus)   8/17/05 Vol. 40
con.,urgency for modern Sodom & Gomorrah (Jesus)   11/22/02 Vol. 29
conversions are heavenly riches (Jesus)   1/24/01 Vol. 22
conversions cause rejoicing in heaven (Jesus)   8/9/00 Vol. 20
conversions come through prayers (Jesus)   2/1/05 Vol. 38
conversions keep reaching out for souls (Jesus)   11/23/98 Vol. 13
conversions like leaven in bread (Jesus)   11/9/06 Vol. 45
conversions likened to healthy wheat (Jesus)   5/15/02 Vol. 27
conversions pray for daily (Jesus)   1/25/02 Vol. 26

conversions pray for, teach faith (Jesus)   8/24/05 Vol. 40

conversions pray,pray,pray for (Mary)   6/10/04 Vol. 35

conversions in faith first call in evangelism (Jesus)   3/8/02 Vol. 26

Conyers pray for peace (Mary)   10/16/97 Vol. 9

Conyers safe havens (Jesus)   7/7/95 Vol. 3

Co-redemptrix with Jesus (Blessed Mother)   2/14/05 Vol. 38

corn crop used for ethanol (Jesus)   5/24/07 Vol. 47

cornerstone faith and trust (Jesus)   6/3/96 Vol. 3

cornerstone Jesus is the (Jesus)   10/21/99 Vol. 17

cornerstone in Jesus Church protected (Jesus)   8/30/01 Vol. 24

cornerstone of Church found in Jesus (Jesus)   1/12/00 Vol. 18

cornerstone of Church is Jesus (Jesus)   7/21/04 Vol. 36

cornerstone of Church Jesus gave keys to St. Peter (Jesus) 10/4/98 Vol. 13

cornerstone of Church not fringe religion of Jews (Jesus) 4/17/00 Vol. 19

cornerstone rejected by scribes & pharisees (Jesus)   4/15/99 Vol. 15

cornerstone, Jesus He is only Savior (Jesus)   4/13/07 Vol. 47

Coromoto Shrine pride (Mary)   2/7/95 Vol. 2

Coromoto Shrine rosary (Mary)   2/22/94 Vol. 1

Coromoto, Our Lady of shrines to Mary (Jesus)   12/28/06 Vol. 45

corporal acts of mercy hunger and disasters (Jesus)   1/2/97 Vol. 6

corporal works avoid sins of omission (Jesus)   11/19/02 Vol. 29

corporal works of mercy action, not words (Jesus)   3/10/03 Vol. 30

corporal works of mercy be a servant for the rest (Jesus) 9/18/06 Vol. 44

corporal works of mercy build up heavenly graces (Jesus) 1/11/01 Vol. 22

corporal works of mercy good example to others (Jesus) 7/31/98 Vol. 12

corporal works of mercy help at judgment (Jesus)   1/8/02 Vol. 26

corporal works of mercy prove your love for God (Jesus) 2/20/98 Vol. 10

corporal works of mercy rewarded 100 fold (Jesus)   9/27/00 Vol. 20

corporal works of mercy to sick and dying (Jesus)   7/16/99 Vol. 16

corporal works of mercy visit sick,imprisoned,elderly (Jesus) 3/8/01 Vol. 22

corporate cutbacks help jobless (Jesus)   1/22/98 Vol. 10

corporate leaders abuse American workers (Jesus)   12/18/07 Vol. 49

corporations employers abuse workers (Jesus)   7/24/97 Vol. 8

corpus removed from cross (Jesus)   4/23/06 Vol. 43

Corpus Christi celebrate Real Presence (Jesus)   6/17/01 Vol. 23

Corpus Christi feast of love (Jesus)   6/2/02 Vol. 27

Corpus Christi graces & food for soul (Jesus)   6/13/04 Vol. 35

Corpus Christi honoring Real Presence (Jesus)   6/18/06 Vol. 43

Corpus Christi miracles of Eucharist (Jesus)   6/1/97 Vol. 7

Corpus Christi Adoration place of refuge, protection (Jesus) 8/9/05 Vol. 40

corpus on cross true meaning of Crucifixion (Jesus)   8/7/00 Vol. 20

corruption in business & government (Jesus)   10/2/03 Vol. 33

corruption in government needs changing (Jesus)   2/6/01 Vol. 22

cost of discipleship unconditional love (Jesus)   9/8/01 Vol. 24

cost of faith in Jesus renounce our possessions (Jesus) 11/4/99 Vol. 17

costs counted for gaining heaven (Jesus)   12/9/04 Vol. 37

couch potato prayers   12/29/93 Vol. 1

countries & cities repent of sin (Jesus)   7/18/06 Vol. 44

country gifts (Mother Cabrini)   12/22/93 Vol. 1

coup of USA world leaders (Jesus)   12/22/96 Vol. 5

courage speak out against evil (Jesus)   7/21/02 Vol. 28

courage in faith against all persecution (Jesus)   12/24/03 Vol. 33

courage in faith even to die as martyr for faith (Jesus) 3/24/02 Vol. 26

court martyrdom (Jesus)   12/2/95 Vol. 3

court system used to support abortion (Jesus)   10/22/03 Vol. 33

court system abuses will see God's justice (Jesus)   3/10/08 Vol. 50

courts abuses of evidence,witness (Jesus)   8/13/98 Vol. 12

courts legislating immorality (Jesus)   2/28/06 Vol. 42

covenant ark of, first & second (Mary)   12/22/96 Vol. 5

covenant commandments (Jesus)   3/24/94 Vol. 1

covenant fulfill prophecies (Jesus)   1/27/97 Vol. 6

Covenant irreverence (Jesus)   11/30/95 Vol. 3

Covenant love and mercy (Jesus)   3/2/96 Vol. 3

covenant second coming (Jesus)   3/6/94 Vol. 1

Covenant of Jesus promise of salvation for all (Jesus) 8/11/05 Vol. 40

covenants defeat of evil,God's promise (Jesus)   10/19/00 Vol. 21

covenants fulfilled in Scripture (God the Father)   3/21/02 Vol. 26

covenants in Old, New Testaments (Jesus)   3/4/07 Vol. 46

Covenants of Old & New Testament (Jesus)   7/24/99 Vol. 16

covenants & promises made on mountains (Jesus)   3/21/07 Vol. 46

covenants in Bible rainbow,Redeemer (Jesus)   2/15/01 Vol. 22

cover scene cross & black night (Jesus)   11/5/95 Vol. 3

craftsmen old ways, better made (Jesus)   3/26/01 Vol. 22

crash of stocks & banks one world caused panic (Jesus) 11/30/97 Vol. 9

created us out of unconditional love (Jesus)   12/3/01 Vol. 25

creation appreciate every day (Jesus)   5/8/03 Vol. 31

creation appreciate gift of (Jesus)   7/6/03 Vol. 32

creation appreciate harmony of (Jesus)   4/24/03 Vol. 31

creation at risk from pollution (Jesus)   9/16/05 Vol. 40

creation awesomeness of God (Jesus)   7/27/99 Vol. 16

creation balance of nature (Jesus)   12/14/97 Vol. 9

creation beauty and gift of (Jesus)   10/11/97 Vol. 9

creation beauty and order of (Jesus)   10/28/05 Vol. 41

creation beauty is gift of love (Jesus)   5/6/02 Vol. 27

creation beauty of (Jesus)   6/2/04 Vol. 35

creation beauty of body and soul (Jesus)   7/26/96 Vol. 4

creation better than hybrids (Jesus)   3/26/08 Vol. 50

creation by God, not man (Jesus)   2/15/07 Vol. 46

creation by the Master Builder (Jesus)   2/2/98 Vol. 10

creation complete & perfect (Jesus)   10/22/99 Vol. 17

creation confrontation with (Jesus)   6/15/98 Vol. 11

creation created good (Jesus)   2/21/99 Vol. 14

creation darkened by sin (Jesus)   8/17/00 Vol. 20

creation do not abuse (Jesus)   8/15/01 Vol. 24

creation everything has goodness (Jesus) — 11/14/01 Vol. 25

creation existence (Father) — 12/2/95 Vol. 3

creation exists by God's Will (Jesus) — 7/9/99 Vol. 16

creation food, crops, life (Jesus) — 5/15/96 Vol. 3

creation for praise & glory of God (Jesus) — 2/12/04 Vol. 34

creation gift of life (Jesus) — 2/10/97 Vol. 6

creation gifts of God (Jesus) — 2/7/05 Vol. 38

creation give praise and glory to God (Jesus) — 7/16/98 Vol. 12

creation gives praise to God (Jesus) — 7/1/04 Vol. 36

creation glory of kingship (Jesus) — 11/26/01 Vol. 25

Creation God is First Cause (Jesus) — 10/6/05 Vol. 41

creation God is in control of (Jesus) — 4/20/01 Vol. 23

creation God made everything perfectly (Jesus) — 7/15/04 Vol. 36

creation God's artistry of perfection (Jesus) — 7/2/99 Vol. 16

Creation God's gift to us (Jesus) — 4/22/04 Vol. 35

creation harmony (Jesus) — 7/25/95 Vol. 3

creation harmony, love needed (Jesus) — 9/10/07 Vol. 48

creation has Divine signature (Jesus) — 9/25/99 Vol. 16

creation hope offered in harmony (Jesus) — 4/2/95 Vol. 2

creation immortal souls (Jesus) — 4/9/96 Vol. 3

creation in God's perfection (Jesus) — 4/25/05 Vol. 39

creation is good, but abused (Jesus) — 7/13/98 Vol. 12

creation love reflected in seasons (Jesus) — 4/2/04 Vol. 35

creation man's place (Jesus) — 2/10/03 Vol. 30

creation nature (St. Francis) — 10/4/95 Vol. 3

creation of body & soul (Jesus) — 11/16/01 Vol. 25

creation order of (Jesus) — 7/29/02 Vol. 28

creation perfection ruined (Jesus) — 9/9/03 Vol. 32

creation praise only the Creator (Jesus) — 1/30/04 Vol. 34

creation protect, do not abuse (Jesus) — 8/31/06 Vol. 44

creation reason for angels praise (Jesus) — 12/4/98 Vol. 13

creation reflection of His love (Jesus) — 4/17/98 Vol. 11

creation reflects beauty & order (Jesus) — 7/24/05 Vol. 40

creation rejoice in power and love (Jesus) — 4/13/98 Vol. 11

creation restored from abuses (Jesus) — 2/6/07 Vol. 46

creation sacredness of life (Jesus) — 5/27/98 Vol. 11

creation see how heavens obey (Jesus) — 3/5/03 Vol. 30

creation seek a higher authority (Jesus) — 7/6/97 Vol. 8

creation sign of Diving in everything (Jesus) — 5/19/05 Vol. 39

creation stop abuse of gifts & talents (Jesus) — 8/17/04 Vol. 36

creation subject to God over Satan (Jesus) — 12/2/02 Vol. 29

creation thank God for all (Jesus) — 3/17/05 Vol. 38

creation vocations (Jesus) — 6/15/94 Vol. 1

creation vs. Darwin's unproven theory (Jesus) — 4/17/05 Vol. 39

creation vs. evolution (Jesus) — 9/20/96 Vol. 4

creation will (God the Father) — 1/5/94 Vol. 1

creation worship God, not earth (Jesus) — 5/7/98 Vol. 11

creation by God everything created by God (Jesus) — 8/19/05 Vol. 40

creation by God in Genesis (Jesus) — 2/5/07 Vol. 46

creation in Genesis explicit & ordered (Jesus) — 7/14/05 Vol. 40

creation of God will never be made better (Jesus) — 3/10/01 Vol. 22

creation of man is unique with soul (Jesus) — 11/10/05 Vol. 41

creation of universe by God, not theories (Jesus) — 1/15/06 Vol. 42

creation threat hybrids, cloning (Jesus) — 8/1/07 Vol. 48

creation vs. man man a speck of sand (Jesus) — 11/23/99 Vol. 17

creation, all of gives glory to God (Jesus) — 3/11/01 Vol. 22

creation, love in seen in beauty in nature (Jesus) — 5/1/04 Vol. 35

creation,understanding needs a large perspective (Jesus) — 3/12/01 Vol. 22

creations bow to God's Will (Jesus) — 4/11/03 Vol. 31

creation's beauty do not destroy it (Jesus) — 6/12/97 Vol. 7

creation's beauty in flowers (Jesus) — 6/5/03 Vol. 31

creation's beauty in flowers, sunrises, man (Jesus) — 5/13/04 Vol. 35

creation's beauty praise,thanks to Creator (Jesus) — 2/25/01 Vol. 22

creation's beauty seen on vacation (Jesus) — 9/4/06 Vol. 44

Creator creation circles around (Jesus) — 12/24/02 Vol. 29

Creator give glory and thanks (Jesus) — 4/6/04 Vol. 35

Creator greater than creatures (Jesus) — 4/8/04 Vol. 35

Creator worship God, not things (Jesus) — 2/12/08 Vol. 50

Creator of man deserves honor & respect (Jesus) — 3/26/00 Vol. 18

creator source of life other gods are evil (Jesus) — 9/7/99 Vol. 16

Creator vs. Satan battle of good & evil for souls (Jesus) — 10/12/00 Vol. 21

Creator's call to follow His plan (Jesus) — 3/24/06 Vol. 42

Creator's love more valuable than things (Jesus) — 12/30/99 Vol. 17

creatures Divine Will (Mary) — 12/22/94 Vol. 2

creatures free will (Father) — 12/30/93 Vol. 1

creatures of God to know, love and serve God (Jesus) — 5/7/98 Vol. 11

crematoriums for opposing new world order (Jesus) — 3/10/05 Vol. 38

crematoriums,gassing in tribulation all over (Jesus) — 7/26/00 Vol. 20

crib scene display publicly (Jesus) — 12/22/98 Vol. 13

crimes murder,drugs,stealing (Jesus) — 1/16/03 Vol. 30

critical charity (St. Therese) — 7/7/95 Vol. 3

criticism do not judge (Jesus) — 7/12/04 Vol. 36

criticism in Warning experience (Jesus) — 6/12/02 Vol. 27

criticism look to self first (Jesus) — 12/23/97 Vol. 9

criticism not to be feared (Jesus) — 9/15/99 Vol. 16

criticism & forgiveness do not be rude in speech (Jesus) — 6/21/00 Vol. 19

criticism accepted to give Gospel message (Jesus) — 2/9/00 Vol. 18

criticism and gossip replace with joy and love (Jesus) — 9/2/98 Vol. 12

criticism of others correct imperfections first (Jesus) — 3/13/01 Vol. 22

criticism of people take out of our lives (Jesus) — 2/18/00 Vol. 18

criticism, accept without anger,resentment (Jesus) — 3/4/06 Vol. 42

criticism, avoid love & assist people (Jesus) — 3/4/06 Vol. 42

criticism, avoid no judgments by man (Jesus) — 8/4/02 Vol. 28

criticism,judgments get spiritual house in order (Jesus) — 10/2/01 Vol. 25

criticizing abuse of tongue (Jesus) — 1/26/01 Vol. 22
criticizing do not be hypocrites (Jesus) — 10/25/99 Vol. 17
Croatia blessed for faithfulness (Jesus) — 7/13/02 Vol. 28
Croatian refuge Mary Bistrica Shrine (Jesus) — 7/12/02 Vol. 28
crocodiles teeth demon attack on souls (Jesus) — 4/26/07 Vol. 47
crop conditions worsening food shortages (Jesus) — 4/4/00 Vol. 19
crop destruction new warfare threat (Jesus) — 12/15/02 Vol. 29
crop prices suffer for not feeding poor (Jesus) — 10/3/96 Vol. 5
crop shortages from rain & hurricanes (Jesus) — 11/11/04 Vol. 37
crops blessings (Jesus) — 6/5/95 Vol. 2
crops damaged by drought & bugs (Jesus) — 8/15/02 Vol. 28
crops, freedoms in danger natural disasters, terrorism (Jesus) — 6/27/02 Vol. 27
crops, fresh water plentiful in U.S. (Jesus) — 11/2/06 Vol. 45
cross body — 11/9/93 Vol. 1
cross body (Jesus) — 11/27/93 Vol. 1
cross bronze serpent (Jesus) — 10/16/94 Vol. 2
cross carry cross like Jesus (Jesus) — 6/21/03 Vol. 31
cross comfort zone (Jesus) — 3/28/95 Vol. 2
Cross Confession (Jesus) — 7/11/94 Vol. 2
cross freedom from sins (Jesus) — 9/19/96 Vol. 4
cross heaven (Jesus) — 7/19/94 Vol. 2
Cross heaven (Jesus) — 3/31/94 Vol. 1
cross horizontal, vertical dimensions (Jesus) — 6/7/07 Vol. 47
cross is a symbol of life (Jesus) — 4/8/98 Vol. 11
cross life's decisions (Jesus) — 9/6/96 Vol. 4
cross Mass gone — 8/27/93 Vol. 1
cross Mass/BlessedSacrament (Jesus) — 1/19/94 Vol. 1
cross meditate on Passion (Jesus) — 3/13/97 Vol. 6
cross punishment — 9/14/93 Vol. 1
cross purify self by suffering (Jesus) — 9/10/96 Vol. 4
Cross share sufferings with Jesus (Jesus) — 12/14/07 Vol. 49
cross suffer (Jesus) — 4/30/94 Vol. 1
Cross Triumph of the (Jesus) — 4/9/04 Vol. 35
cross will (Jesus) — 12/14/93 Vol. 1
cross will (Mary) — 8/15/95 Vol. 3
cross of Calvary everyone has to carry one (Jesus) — 5/2/99 Vol. 15
cross of Jesus example to carry our cross (Jesus) — 1/31/05 Vol. 38
Cross of Jesus like cross of man (Jesus) — 3/26/06 Vol. 42
cross of Jesus shared by faithful (Jesus) — 12/6/05 Vol. 41
Cross of Jesus trials of Venezuela (Jesus) — 12/10/06 Vol. 45
cross of life all carry it to Calvary (Jesus) — 4/5/99 Vol. 15
cross of life carry it with Jesus (Jesus) — 4/2/06 Vol. 43
cross on forehead written in Book of Life (Jesus) — 8/21/02 Vol. 28
cross with corpus promise of eternal life (Jesus) — 9/6/06 Vol. 44
cross with corpus we also will suffer (Jesus) — 12/9/96 Vol. 5
Cross, daily imitation of Jesus (Jesus) — 5/2/06 Vol. 43
Cross, daily must be suffered (Jesus) — 4/24/99 Vol. 15

cross, daily road to Calvary wins heaven (Jesus) — 9/14/98 Vol. 12
cross, shadow of responsibilities for holy life (Jesus) — 9/17/07 Vol. 48
cross, take up follow Jesus in life (Jesus) — 1/1/00 Vol. 18
cross, take up refuse,suffer twice the grief (Jesus) — 2/23/01 Vol. 22
Cross, true relic strong for healing (Jesus) — 7/28/05 Vol. 40
cross, wood of haven for Jesus' help (Jesus) — 5/2/00 Vol. 19
cross, wood of share in suffering of Jesus (Jesus) — 8/26/07 Vol. 48
cross,gold consecrate yourself to God (Jesus) — 5/19/00 Vol. 19
cross,hollow empty tomb,victory over devil (Jesus) — 9/14/01 Vol. 24
cross,specially made fits individual capabilities (Jesus) — 7/13/00 Vol. 20
cross,struggle in life love of God,our shelter (Jesus) — 6/12/00 Vol. 19
crosses carry as Jesus did (Jesus) — 7/7/01 Vol. 24
crosses carry them (Jesus) — 7/6/96 Vol. 3
crosses carry with Jesus (Jesus) — 5/30/98 Vol. 11
crosses carry without grumbling (Jesus) — 2/2/04 Vol. 34
crosses (Catherine) — 9/18/93 Vol. 1
crosses Divine Will in peace & love (Jesus) — 8/5/96 Vol. 4
crosses each carry our own (Jesus) — 2/19/04 Vol. 34
crosses each one fits their cross (Jesus) — 4/10/98 Vol. 11
crosses follow these few years (Jesus) — 8/23/96 Vol. 4
crosses help in carrying them (Jesus) — 6/5/05 Vol. 39
crosses hope & trust, will (Jesus) — 12/13/96 Vol. 5
crosses Immaculate Conception (Jesus) — 12/8/93 Vol. 1
crosses martyrs — 8/14/93 Vol. 1
crosses of life (Jesus) — 3/16/05 Vol. 38
crosses offer up, do not complain (Jesus) — 8/1/01 Vol. 24
crosses on altar a sign of love (Jesus) — 6/16/05 Vol. 39
crosses pain (Jesus) — 11/23/94 Vol. 2
crosses pick up again (Jesus) — 2/16/04 Vol. 34
crosses pick up daily (Jesus) — 1/31/04 Vol. 34
crosses priorities (Jesus) — 9/20/94 Vol. 2
crosses rose from tomb, not cross (Jesus) — 10/18/99 Vol. 17
crosses sorrow (Jesus) — 1/16/95 Vol. 2
crosses strip your possessions (Mary) — 10/13/96 Vol. 5
crosses suffering (Jesus) — 8/14/94 Vol. 2
crosses sufferings joined (Jesus) — 3/23/97 Vol. 6
crosses take up as Jesus (Jesus) — 2/22/07 Vol. 46
crosses take up daily (Jesus) — 3/20/97 Vol. 6
crosses to have corpuses (Jesus) — 1/17/99 Vol. 14
crosses trials (Jesus) — 9/14/94 Vol. 2
crosses walk in footsteps of Jesus (Jesus) — 12/17/03 Vol. 33
crosses carried all must suffer for survival (Jesus) — 10/15/00 Vol. 21
crosses in life accept like Jesus (Jesus) — 1/2/05 Vol. 38
crosses in life carry to Calvary (Jesus) — 3/16/07 Vol. 46
crosses in life take up daily (Jesus) — 2/7/08 Vol. 50
crosses on foreheads sign of protection (Jesus) — 8/16/06 Vol. 44
crosses, daily keep good prayer life (Jesus) — 8/12/03 Vol. 32

crosses, daily share suffering of Jesus (Jesus) — 11/6/04 Vol. 37

crosses, daily treasures in heaven (Jesus) — 8/11/03 Vol. 32

crosses, luminous healing during tribulation (Jesus) — 11/1/01 Vol. 25

crosses, luminous places of healing (Jesus) — 9/14/02 Vol. 28

crosses, white luminous heal all diseases (Jesus) — 5/11/02 Vol. 27

crossroads for America abortion,Serbian war (Jesus) — 3/22/99 Vol. 14

crossroads in life chance for change from sin (Jesus) — 5/15/04 Vol. 35

crowd & Antichrist do not follow (Jesus) — 12/7/05 Vol. 41

crowd, following the can lead to sin (Jesus) — 12/10/05 Vol. 41

crown of salvation claim your Savior,repent (Jesus) — 12/13/99 Vol. 17

crown of thorns Betania blessing (Jesus) — 2/10/96 Vol. 3

crown of thorns mocked Jesus' kingship (Jesus) — 4/6/06 Vol. 43

crown of thorns mocked Jesus' kingship (Jesus) — 5/4/00 Vol. 19

crown of thorns suffering for bad thoughts (Jesus) — 10/14/99 Vol. 17

crown of thorns to cleanse thoughts (Jesus) — 5/21/98 Vol. 11

crucible of life test by living purgatory (Jesus) — 1/5/00 Vol. 18

crucified love (Jesus) — 12/1/93 Vol. 1

crucifix be proud to wear it (Jesus) — 10/19/97 Vol. 9

crucifix conquered sin & death (Jesus) — 5/29/01 Vol. 23

crucifix help priest (Jesus) — 10/4/07 Vol. 49

crucifix helps remember love of Jesus (Jesus) — 6/20/02 Vol. 27

crucifix love (Jesus) — 11/12/95 Vol. 3

crucifix miracle of one discarded (Jesus) — 2/16/04 Vol. 34

crucifix more meaning with corpus (Jesus) — 2/21/02 Vol. 26

crucifix protection from evil spirits (Jesus) — 3/12/98 Vol. 10

crucifix real feeling of Jesus' love (Jesus) — 4/23/06 Vol. 43

crucifix reverence (Jesus) — 7/31/95 Vol. 3

crucifix scapular (Jesus) — 1/24/95 Vol. 2

crucifix should be prominent on altars (Jesus) — 4/25/04 Vol. 35

crucifix sign of God's love (Jesus) — 11/8/07 Vol. 49

crucifix sign of His death (Jesus) — 1/19/99 Vol. 14

crucifix sign of our redemption (Jesus) — 5/6/99 Vol. 15

crucifix to share suffering (Jesus) — 9/14/00 Vol. 20

crucifix why Jesus came to earth (Jesus) — 12/2/07 Vol. 49

crucifix honored in churches, homes (Jesus) — 11/18/99 Vol. 17

crucifix on altar after 40 yrs of none (Jesus) — 10/20/07 Vol. 49

crucifix on altar answer to novena (Jesus) — 11/8/07 Vol. 49

crucifix on altar continue prayers for (Jesus) — 9/6/07 Vol. 48

Crucifix on altar feel suffering Christ (Jesus) — 5/6/07 Vol. 47

crucifix on altar focus on all year long (Jesus) — 3/16/08 Vol. 50

crucifix on altar focus on Jesus' death (Jesus) — 8/28/07 Vol. 48

crucifix on altar for love of Jesus (Jesus) — 7/19/06 Vol. 44

crucifix on altar Holy Name 40th anniv. (Jesus) — 10/29/07 Vol. 49

crucifix on altar portrays pain & suffering (Jesus) — 8/21/02 Vol. 28

crucifix on altar remember Jesus' death (Jesus) — 4/8/99 Vol. 15

Crucifix on altar remember Jesus' redemption (Jesus) — 9/23/05 Vol. 40

crucifix on altar share sufferings with Jesus (Jesus) — 4/12/07 Vol. 47

crucifix on altar shows Jesus' suffering (Jesus) — 1/18/05 Vol. 38

crucifix on altar take up cross of life (Jesus) — 8/2/07 Vol. 48

crucifix on altar to remember Jesus' sacrifice (Jesus) — 7/24/07 Vol. 48

crucifix, altar remember Jesus' sacrifice (Jesus) — 7/28/05 Vol. 40

crucifix, given make a stand for (Jesus) — 9/13/07 Vol. 48

crucifix, holy pictures in every room of home (Jesus) — 2/17/05 Vol. 38

crucifix, power in miraculous crosses (Jesus) — 5/31/07 Vol. 47

crucifix, small new stand made (Jesus) — 11/15/07 Vol. 49

cru.,Blessed Sacrament attacked by demons,masons (Jesus) 5/19/04 Vol. 35

crucifixes being removed (Jesus) — 8/8/06 Vol. 44

crucifixes display as remembrance (Jesus) — 1/22/98 Vol. 10

crucifixes gift of love (Jesus) — 6/6/98 Vol. 11

crucifixes needed on every altar (Jesus) — 2/26/04 Vol. 34

crucifixes remember Jesus to children (Jesus) — 3/8/02 Vol. 26

crucifixes removed from churches (Jesus) — 1/4/01 Vol. 22

crucifixes sacrifice of love (Jesus) — 3/20/03 Vol. 30

crucifixes show depth of love (Jesus) — 4/2/04 Vol. 35

crucifixes show Divine sacrifice (Jesus) — 2/20/98 Vol. 10

crucifixes sign of suffering (Jesus) — 5/28/98 Vol. 11

crucifixes St.Benedict,exorcism (Jesus) — 4/28/96 Vol. 3

crucifixes test the spirits (Jesus) — 8/21/97 Vol. 8

crucifixes to convert by Jesus' love (Padre Pio) — 8/7/01 Vol. 24

crucifixes to protect from evil (Jesus) — 8/17/01 Vol. 24

crucifixes to remember His love (Jesus) — 9/14/02 Vol. 28

crucifixes want corpus to see suffering (Jesus) — 8/3/04 Vol. 36

crucifixes we become like (Jesus) — 4/28/02 Vol. 27

crucifixes with corpus (Jesus) — 1/31/04 Vol. 34

crucifixes with suffering corpuses (Jesus) — 2/21/96 Vol. 3

crucifixes & statues being removed from churches (Jesus) 5/12/02 Vol. 27

crucifixes & statues helps inspire people (Jesus) — 1/19/03 Vol. 30

crucifixes with corpus need in churches, homes (Jesus) — 5/1/99 Vol. 15

crucifixes, large to be on altars (Jesus) — 1/9/08 Vol. 50

crucifixes, pictures in homes as example (Jesus) — 3/3/04 Vol. 34

crucifixion and cruelty today (Jesus) — 3/1/07 Vol. 46

Crucifixion healing in Jesus' Blood (Jesus) — 2/26/04 Vol. 34

crucifixion opened gates to heaven (Jesus) — 8/13/99 Vol. 16

crucifixion Trinity feels pain (Jesus) — 4/5/04 Vol. 35

crucifixion of Jesus victory over sin & death (Jesus) — 8/1/02 Vol. 28

crucifixion on cross large falls to forgive everyone (Jesus) 3/27/02 Vol. 26

cryogenics never brings immortality (Jesus) — 1/21/99 Vol. 14

Cuba Pope brought love (Jesus) — 1/23/98 Vol. 10

culture of death abortion & killings (Jesus) — 7/27/02 Vol. 28

culture of death by one world people (Jesus) — 4/23/03 Vol. 31

culture of death hide abortion in language (Jesus) — 1/26/05 Vol. 38

culture of death keep life precious (Jesus) — 2/6/04 Vol. 34

culture of death reverse for blessings (Jesus) — 9/26/02 Vol. 28

culture of death stop evil laws (Jesus) — 5/6/02 Vol. 27

culture of death stops plan for life (Jesus)	5/22/02 Vol. 27	daily Mass people special faithful (Jesus)	5/8/98 Vol. 11
culture of death under influence of (Jesus)	12/14/01 Vol. 25	daily Mass people special graces & protection (Jesus)	9/16/06 Vol. 44
culture of death violence & abortions (Jesus)	7/7/03 Vol. 32	daily Mass, Adoration special in Jesus' heart (Jesus)	8/10/02 Vol. 28
culture of death vs. sanctity of life (Jesus)	1/24/04 Vol. 34	daily offering Confession (St. Therese)	10/16/95 Vol. 3
culture of death wars, abortions, killing (Jesus)	1/21/03 Vol. 30	daily offering correct your motives (Jesus)	5/1/95 Vol. 2
culture of death vs. life vote against killing (Jesus)	11/2/06 Vol. 45	daily plan directed by God (Jesus)	6/15/02 Vol. 27
cup of justice need God's mercy (Jesus)	1/13/00 Vol. 18	daily prayer fights temptations (Jesus)	3/16/06 Vol. 42
cup of wrath overflowing (Jesus)	1/27/01 Vol. 22	daily prayer hell (Jesus)	9/17/94 Vol. 2
curiosity Adam and Eve (Jesus)	9/1/95 Vol. 3	daily prayer make time each day (Jesus)	7/31/05 Vol. 40
curiosity can lead you into sin (Jesus)	10/25/04 Vol. 37	daily prayer priorities of life (Jesus)	8/20/03 Vol. 32
curiosity keep focus on Jesus (Jesus)	10/16/97 Vol. 9	daily prayer & sacraments best defense against sin (Jesus)	6/30/05 Vol. 39
curiosity obsession for information (Jesus)	3/6/08 Vol. 50	daily prayer hour to keep awake spiritually (Jesus)	5/19/00 Vol. 19
curiosity of earthly things (Jesus)	3/26/99 Vol. 14	daily prayer needed not just desperate prayers (Jesus)	5/10/07 Vol. 47
curiosity of sin do not be drawn into (Jesus)	7/5/04 Vol. 36	daily prayers needed to Jesus & Mary (Jesus)	9/12/05 Vol. 40
currencies unified in Americas (Jesus)	4/26/01 Vol. 23	daily rosary prayer (St. Theresa)	2/17/95 Vol. 2
cur., interest rates controlled by central bankers (Jesus)	5/28/04 Vol. 35	daily strength from Jesus (Jesus)	2/16/00 Vol. 18
currencies,new to drain savings (Jesus)	4/4/02 Vol. 27	daily trials need grace to endure (Jesus)	12/29/05 Vol. 41
currents of life body vs. the soul (Jesus)	11/27/99 Vol. 17	daily trials seek His grace (Jesus)	6/12/98 Vol. 11
cycle of life Baptism,Marriage,death (Jesus)	2/2/01 Vol. 22	daily troubles worse outside of America (Jesus)	3/5/01 Vol. 22
cycle of life in cycle of seasons (Jesus)	11/3/05 Vol. 41	damage destruction	8/4/93 Vol. 1
cycle of life learn from past mistakes (Jesus)	3/25/01 Vol. 22	Daniel and Susanna (Jesus)	3/14/05 Vol. 38
cycle of life life is very short (Jesus)	4/4/98 Vol. 11	Daniel writing on the wall (Jesus)	11/29/95 Vol. 3
cycle of life on loan from God (Jesus)	5/17/01 Vol. 23	dark ages of spiritual life (Jesus)	8/25/01 Vol. 24
cycle of life reminder in four seasons (Jesus)	11/11/02 Vol. 29	dark night of soul saints suffered (Jesus)	9/5/07 Vol. 48
cycle of life short on earth (Jesus)	8/30/02 Vol. 28	dark night of the soul when blessings are few (Jesus)	7/23/99 Vol. 16
cycle of life & death share God's love (Jesus)	10/26/06 Vol. 45	dark shadow demons (Jesus)	10/23/93 Vol. 1
cylindrical tube warning (Jesus)	2/13/95 Vol. 2	dark side power source of inventions (Jesus)	4/4/01 Vol. 23
Dad Leary calls us to join him (Jesus)	8/3/01 Vol. 24	dark valley Antichrist (Jesus)	12/2/94 Vol. 2
Dad's farewell from the grave (Dad)	2/8/01 Vol. 22	darkness black cloud	7/23/93 Vol. 1
daily cares frustration (Mary)	9/8/95 Vol. 3	darkness difficult to find way (Jesus)	2/11/01 Vol. 22
daily cross always with us (Jesus)	10/9/07 Vol. 49	darkness in purgatory & hell (Jesus)	3/7/07 Vol. 46
daily cross consecration needed to take up (Jesus)	10/19/03 Vol. 33	darkness over earth at Warning (Jesus)	11/26/00 Vol. 21
daily cross desire God's Will (Jesus)	9/14/99 Vol. 16	darkness sin (Jesus)	12/15/93 Vol. 1
daily cross honor to suffer Christ (Jesus)	11/24/97 Vol. 9	darkness in sky during the day (Jesus)	6/20/05 Vol. 39
daily cross suffer daily toward perfection (Jesus)	11/16/98 Vol. 13	darkness of evil shies from Jesus' Light (Jesus)	11/28/05 Vol. 41
daily cross suffer Purgatory on earth (Jesus)	11/15/97 Vol. 9	darkness of sin dispelled by Jesus (Jesus)	12/24/06 Vol. 45
daily cross way to eternal life (Jesus)	10/31/98 Vol. 13	darkness of sin enlightened by Jesus' coming (Jesus)	12/10/02 Vol. 29
daily cross in jobs duty to save souls (Jesus)	10/22/98 Vol. 13	darkness removed by Blood of Jesus (Jesus)	12/13/98 Vol. 13
daily cross,pick up to follow Jesus (Jesus)	2/26/05 Vol. 38	Darwin Theory not proven (Jesus)	1/26/04 Vol. 34
daily crosses follow Light of Jesus (Jesus)	12/8/05 Vol. 41	dates crown (Jesus)	2/19/95 Vol. 2
daily crosses, carry to suffer with Jesus (Jesus)	9/23/04 Vol. 36	dates do not worry about (Jesus)	12/30/97 Vol. 9
daily job not to dictate your life (Jesus)	11/1/98 Vol. 13	dates live for today (Jesus)	7/6/99 Vol. 16
daily life ups & downs of (Jesus)	2/26/04 Vol. 34	dates not important,faith is (Jesus)	11/28/97 Vol. 9
daily lives cheerful (Jesus)	5/1/94 Vol. 1	dates time directed by the Father (Jesus)	5/24/98 Vol. 11
daily Mass encourage all to attend (Jesus)	5/13/05 Vol. 39	David 20th anniversary of death (David)	1/11/03 Vol. 30
daily Mass greatest gift (Jesus)	9/9/98 Vol. 12	David anniversary of death (David's angel)	1/11/95 Vol. 2
daily Mass miracle,grace every day (Jesus)	5/5/00 Vol. 19	David asks prayers against abortion (David)	1/11/01 Vol. 22

David his picture in prayer room (David) 1/11/07 Vol. 46

David my son, died for my mission (David) 1/11/04 Vol. 34

David my son's message (David) 1/12/06 Vol. 42

David pray for intercession (David) 1/8/98 Vol. 10

David protection of family (David) 1/7/99 Vol. 14

David & Goliath victory with Jesus (Jesus) 1/21/04 Vol. 34

David, King adultery with Bathsheba (Jesus) 2/1/08 Vol. 50

David, my son abortion, appreciate life (Jesus) 1/6/00 Vol. 18

David, my son anniversary of death message (David) 1/10/08 Vol. 50

David, my son intercessor for petitions (David) 5/31/07 Vol. 47

David, my son personal message (David) 1/11/05 Vol. 38

David, our son happy for new lives (David) 1/10/02 Vol. 26

David's(son) welcome greeting from dead relatives (David) 2/8/01 Vol. 22

Davinci Code avoid blasphemous movie (Jesus) 5/25/06 Vol. 43

Davinci Code heresy of man (Jesus) 5/19/06 Vol. 43

day of purification man cannot prevent (Jesus) 12/28/98 Vol. 13

dead do not all go to heaven (Jesus) 11/1/03 Vol. 33

dead man's bones holy men & women need (Jesus) 6/26/97 Vol. 7

dead souls need Light of forgiveness (Jesus) 12/24/06 Vol. 45

dead stones can praise Him (Jesus) 9/23/96 Vol. 4

dead, mourning the live in present, not the past (Jesus) 12/11/03 Vol. 33

Dean's funeral taken to heaven (Jesus) 1/20/99 Vol. 14

Dean's memorial Mass respect life (Jesus) 2/6/99 Vol. 14

death a part of life (Jesus) 5/17/01 Vol. 23

death acceptance of (Jesus) 5/17/01 Vol. 23

death all appointed to die (Jesus) 9/15/00 Vol. 20

death all are appointed to die (Jesus) 9/25/99 Vol. 16

death always be prepared for (Jesus) 2/19/04 Vol. 34

death always be prepared for (Jesus) 5/17/99 Vol. 15

death and resurrection (Jesus) 9/9/03 Vol. 32

death anxiety of the unknown (Jesus) 3/28/99 Vol. 14

death as dark curtain drawn on life (Jesus) 3/23/02 Vol. 26

death be always on guard (Jesus) 4/30/98 Vol. 11

death be prepared for (Jesus) 8/27/03 Vol. 32

death be ready to face judgment (Jesus) 11/13/04 Vol. 37

death beginning for your soul (Jesus) 7/19/99 Vol. 16

death Confession (Jesus) 10/29/94 Vol. 2

death consequences of Adam's sin (Jesus) 3/24/01 Vol. 22

death consequences of sin (Jesus) 7/8/04 Vol. 36

death crown (Jesus) 11/30/95 Vol. 3

death cycles of life (Jesus) 11/4/96 Vol. 5

death do not fear (Jesus) 8/3/01 Vol. 24

death do not worry about pain (Jesus) 7/22/97 Vol. 8

death doorway to next life (Jesus) 6/5/97 Vol. 7

death dust (Jesus) 11/22/94 Vol. 2

death experience of (Jesus) 8/19/03 Vol. 32

death experience of soul at (Jesus) 12/10/01 Vol. 25

death family needs comforting (Jesus) 11/19/04 Vol. 37

death fear of (Jesus) 10/25/06 Vol. 45

death few go directly to heaven (Jesus) 9/12/03 Vol. 32

death gift of life returned (Jesus) 1/11/02 Vol. 26

death good deeds and holiness (Jesus) 6/8/96 Vol. 3

death graduation to heaven (Jesus) 1/3/99 Vol. 14

death greeted by relatives at (Jesus) 7/22/04 Vol. 36

death has lost its sting (Jesus) 4/24/00 Vol. 19

death has no hold on Jesus (Jesus) 6/27/99 Vol. 15

death have no fear of (Jesus) 5/8/01 Vol. 23

death have no fear with pure soul (Jesus) 7/2/02 Vol. 28

death heaven (Jesus) 12/9/95 Vol. 3

death heaven,purgatory or hell (Jesus) 7/25/02 Vol. 28

death hell (Jesus) 9/25/95 Vol. 3

death hell (Jesus) 5/1/95 Vol. 2

death immortality of soul (Jesus) 2/18/98 Vol. 10

death influence (Jesus) 1/13/95 Vol. 2

death is part of life (Jesus) 1/20/99 Vol. 14

death Jesus overcame (Jesus) 9/9/03 Vol. 32

death judgment, purgatory (Jesus) 5/15/97 Vol. 7

death late to improve holiness (Jesus) 11/27/06 Vol. 45

death life (Jesus) 6/3/94 Vol. 1

death life beginning in spirit world (Jesus) 11/3/03 Vol. 33

death love God & neighbor (Jesus) 2/18/97 Vol. 6

death many not ready for (Jesus) 8/2/06 Vol. 44

death new earth (Jesus) 12/13/94 Vol. 2

death not to be feared (Jesus) 5/23/06 Vol. 43

death particular judgment (Jesus) 9/28/00 Vol. 20

death places of judgment (Jesus) 1/30/96 Vol. 3

death plan for eternity (Jesus) 11/11/97 Vol. 9

death prayer (Jesus) 1/7/96 Vol. 3

death prayer (Jesus) 4/11/95 Vol. 2

death preparation (Jesus) 11/14/94 Vol. 2

death preparation (Jesus) 2/19/95 Vol. 2

death prepare (Jesus) 10/11/95 Vol. 3

death prepare (Jesus) 10/28/95 Vol. 3

death prepare for by good life (Jesus) 2/1/02 Vol. 26

death prepare for heaven (Jesus) 11/28/01 Vol. 25

death prepare life for (Jesus) 7/21/06 Vol. 44

death prepare with Confession (Jesus) 2/23/98 Vol. 10

death prepared (Jesus) 12/15/95 Vol. 3

death purgatory and love (Jesus) 2/26/96 Vol. 3

death purification (Jesus) 6/8/94 Vol. 1

death purpose to live for God (Jesus) 1/11/00 Vol. 18

death race against time (Jesus) 12/29/97 Vol. 9

death see preciousness of life (Jesus) 2/6/99 Vol. 14

death separates body & soul (Jesus) 7/12/06 Vol. 44

death souls drawn to Light (Jesus)	7/8/02 Vol. 28	death transition to life in Spirit (Jesus)	4/8/98 Vol. 11
death spiritual & physical (Jesus)	5/18/02 Vol. 27	death transition to next life (Jesus)	6/6/02 Vol. 27
death stay near bodies (Jesus)	2/8/01 Vol. 22	death transition to next life (Jesus)	11/23/07 Vol. 49
death store up heavenly treasures (Jesus)	10/22/01 Vol. 25	death transition to next life (Jesus)	1/5/99 Vol. 14
death time (Jesus)	11/5/94 Vol. 2	death transition to spiritual world (Jesus)	11/5/04 Vol. 37
death training (Jesus)	10/4/94 Vol. 2	death treat each day as your last (Jesus)	10/24/00 Vol. 21
death transition (Jesus)	1/11/94 Vol. 1	death wake-up call (Jesus)	9/30/02 Vol. 28
death transition to life in heaven (Jesus)	11/14/02 Vol. 29	death what happens at that time (Jesus)	5/27/97 Vol. 7

death wisp of light leaves body (Jesus) — 6/4/01 Vol. 23

death & dying difficult at any age (Jesus) — 8/26/04 Vol. 36

death & judgment Jesus will protect us (Jesus) — 7/20/01 Vol. 24

death & judgment meditate on life's choices (Jesus) — 11/19/98 Vol. 13

death & mortality choose heaven (Jesus) — 5/15/02 Vol. 27

death & resurrection choose to follow Christ (Jesus) — 11/15/98 Vol. 13

death & tomorrow cause fears (Jesus) — 10/29/07 Vol. 49

death a certainty bodies are mortal (Jesus) — 7/26/01 Vol. 24

death and life accounting at judgment (Jesus) — 3/21/99 Vol. 14

death and life soul animates body (Jesus) — 5/26/01 Vol. 23

death any time repent of sins (Jesus) — 3/18/01 Vol. 22

death by killing most serious sin (Jesus) — 6/26/97 Vol. 7

death coming wars, terrorism,disasters (Jesus) — 11/5/02 Vol. 29

death culture abortions, euthanasia (Jesus) — 8/5/07 Vol. 48

death culture change to love of God,neighbor (Jesus) — 8/28/04 Vol. 36

death culture consumed by justice (Jesus) — 6/25/97 Vol. 7

death culture God will intervene (Jesus) — 1/26/01 Vol. 22

death culture media promotes (Jesus) — 10/6/06 Vol. 45

death culture promotes destruction (Jesus) — 4/1/02 Vol. 27

death culture readied for tribulation (Jesus) — 2/12/98 Vol. 10

death culture seeking rights to kill (Jesus) — 4/22/99 Vol. 15

death culture stand up against evil society (Mary) — 12/12/07 Vol. 49

death culture stop now (Jesus) — 2/5/08 Vol. 50

death culture supported by one worlders (Jesus) — 3/3/08 Vol. 50

death culture to bring society to ruin (Jesus) — 7/15/04 Vol. 36

death culture TWA 800 flight (Jesus) — 8/26/96 Vol. 4

death culture violence & abortion (Jesus) — 7/5/99 Vol. 16

death culture vs. people for life (Jesus) — 11/2/04 Vol. 37

death culture wars, abortions, euthanasia (Jesus) — 5/4/04 Vol. 35

death feeling eclipse confirmation of deaths (Jesus) — 12/4/02 Vol. 29

death mentality in war and abortion (Jesus) — 8/29/98 Vol. 12

death of a child need acceptance of God's Will (Jesus) — 1/31/06 Vol. 42

death of America from wages of sin (Jesus) — 9/2/99 Vol. 16

death of body soul's experience on death (Jesus) — 4/27/00 Vol. 19

death of Jesus foretold in Scripture (Jesus) — 1/14/01 Vol. 22

death of Jesus payment for mankind's sin (Jesus) — 4/14/00 Vol. 19

death of Jesus share with dying people (Jesus) — 3/25/05 Vol. 38

death of young child John Paul Lyon (Jesus) — 2/4/06 Vol. 42

death of young people life fragile,vulnerable (Jesus) — 12/29/99 Vol. 17

death on cross center of faith in Jesus (Jesus) — 2/24/00 Vol. 18

death penalty all killing is wrong (Jesus) — 6/11/01 Vol. 23

death penalty criticized by pope (Jesus) — 1/28/99 Vol. 14

death penalty only God is judge (Jesus) — 9/4/03 Vol. 32

death penalty only God to judge (Jesus) — 6/14/01 Vol. 23

death preparations give up earthly for heavenly (Jesus) — 10/25/00 Vol. 21

death risk for faith foolish in eyes of the world (Jesus) — 8/14/00 Vol. 20

death stages metamorphosis (Jesus) — 11/9/01 Vol. 25

death to new life resurrection of the body (Jesus) — 3/31/99 Vol. 14

death to sin Let My People Go (Jesus) — 4/9/06 Vol. 43

death toll high from tidal waves (Jesus) — 12/30/04 Vol. 37

death transition adjustment by relatives (Jesus) — 4/4/00 Vol. 19

death transition life's preparation (Jesus) — 5/30/06 Vol. 43

death, fear of judgment time (Jesus) — 11/2/07 Vol. 49

death, fear of unknown is cause of fear (Jesus) — 5/29/00 Vol. 19

death, no fear of who are faithful to God (Jesus) — 10/23/04 Vol. 37

death, pictures review of a person's life (Jesus) — 11/26/04 Vol. 37

death, preparation for love Jesus, others (Jesus) — 5/23/06 Vol. 43

death, prep. for needed to face God in judgment (Jesus) — 11/8/04 Vol. 37

death, prepare for before your judgment (Jesus) — 3/25/05 Vol. 38

death, prepare for especially in older years (Jesus) — 3/19/04 Vol. 34

death, ready for? be in sanctifying grace (Jesus) — 10/28/00 Vol. 21

death, sudden not prepared for (Jesus) — 8/13/06 Vol. 44

death,preparation for will be as thief in night (Jesus) — 11/4/99 Vol. 17

death,preparations for can die any day (Jesus) — 5/29/00 Vol. 19

death,short life do not love worldly things (Jesus) — 8/21/98 Vol. 12

deaths more souls called now (Jesus) — 5/10/01 Vol. 23

death's door transition to next life (Jesus) — 6/5/03 Vol. 31

deaths this year wars, disasters (Jesus) — 1/1/03 Vol. 30

deaths, births remembered at Thanksgiving (Jesus) — 11/16/06 Vol. 45

debts control people, governments (Jesus) — 12/21/03 Vol. 33

debts increasing causing worse finances (Jesus) — 1/27/05 Vol. 38

decadence of America could destroy our civilization (Jesus) — 11/8/01 Vol. 25

decaying stars cause baffling radiation (Jesus) — 9/23/99 Vol. 16

deceased loved ones remember to pray for (Jesus) — 11/10/07 Vol. 49

deceased relatives pray for them (Jesus) — 6/4/01 Vol. 23

dec., messages from from heaven, upper purgatory (Jesus) — 5/28/07 Vol. 47

decisions accept our responsibility (Jesus) — 2/7/98 Vol. 10

decisions how to discern (Jesus) — 9/23/06 Vol. 44

decisions opportunities (Jesus) — 5/10/95 Vol. 2

decisions & priorities centered around eternal life (Jesus) — 8/13/00 Vol. 20

decisions for God all against evil options (Jesus) — 10/3/98 Vol. 13

decisions in life base on Divine Will (Jesus) — 1/29/98 Vol. 10

decisions in life for or against God (Jesus) — 1/13/00 Vol. 18

decisions in life trust in Jesus (Jesus) — 2/3/08 Vol. 50

decisions of life led by love (Jesus) — 12/19/97 Vol. 9

Declaration Independence blessings can be lost (Jesus) — 3/25/99 Vol. 14

Decla.,Independenc freedom of religion to atheism (Jesus) — 6/27/00 Vol. 19

Decrees & edicts power can force idol worship (Jesus) — 3/31/04 Vol. 34

deeds & prayer mark good Lenten activity (Jesus) — 2/28/02 Vol. 26

deeds for show avoid selfish motives (Jesus) — 2/23/00 Vol. 18

deeds, good better for God's glory, not ours (Jesus) — 8/21/04 Vol. 36

deer knives needed preparation (Jesus) — 9/2/04 Vol. 36

deer meat provided at refuges (Jesus) — 9/2/04 Vol. 36

deer meat provided at refuges (Jesus) — 3/7/05 Vol. 38

defense budgets strive for peace (Jesus) 5/3/01 Vol. 23

defense complex greed for money (Jesus) 8/2/01 Vol. 24

defense in Jesus not worldly riches (Jesus) 2/17/00 Vol. 18

Defense Industrial complex run wars (Jesus) 2/5/08 Vol. 50

defense industry terrorism to make weapons (Jesus) 8/30/01 Vol. 24

defense of terrorism pray, avoid targets (Jesus) 7/7/05 Vol. 40

defense spending help people,do not kill them (Jesus) 4/7/05 Vol. 39

Deficit of payments problems in trade (Jesus) 11/24/06 Vol. 45

deficits caused by war costs (Jesus) 11/17/07 Vol. 49

deficits & disasters can cause martial law (Jesus) 1/19/06 Vol. 42

deficits & wars goal of central bankers (Jesus) 5/28/04 Vol. 35

deficits & wars need to be stopped (Jesus) 2/11/05 Vol. 38

deficits,trade,budget need correcting (Jesus) 11/17/04 Vol. 37

Delaney, Bill funeral message (Bill Delaney) 12/10/01 Vol. 25

deliverance & exorcism pray in groups (Jesus) 10/8/05 Vol. 41

deliverance prayers for exorcisms (Jesus) 8/30/05 Vol. 40

deliverance prayers releases demons (Jesus) 5/16/05 Vol. 39

deliverers Jesus and Moses (Jesus) 6/24/01 Vol. 23

democracy in Iraq not forceable on Arab countries (Jesus) 5/11/04 Vol. 35

Democratic Congress new leadership (Jesus) 11/16/06 Vol. 45

demon attack drugs,adult shops,prostitutes (Jesus) 1/28/08 Vol. 50

demon attack now,worse in tribulation (Jesus) 9/10/01 Vol. 24

demon attacks attempt to stop mission (Jesus) 6/21/07 Vol. 47

demon attacks battle of good & evil (Jesus) 7/25/01 Vol. 24

demon image in sky evil time of Antichrist (Jesus) 9/17/98 Vol. 12

demon lies temptations for sins (Jesus) 5/23/00 Vol. 19

demon of death holocaust coming again (Jesus) 8/9/07 Vol. 48

demon possession how demons are invited (Jesus) 1/11/06 Vol. 42

demon possession Ouija boards, potions (Jesus) 8/30/05 Vol. 40

demon possession sign in super-human strength (Jesus) 1/30/06 Vol. 42

demon possession witchcraft,potions,Quija boards (Jesus) 5/16/05 Vol. 39

demon protection sacraments, sacramentals (Jesus) 8/1/07 Vol. 48

demon protections holy water, sacramentals (Jesus) 1/11/06 Vol. 42

demon removal requires prayer & fasting (Jesus) 2/20/06 Vol. 42

demon temptations use pride, waste time (Jesus) 2/13/06 Vol. 42

demon visions realism of their existence (Jesus) 12/27/99 Vol. 17

demonic attacks on faithful, call on Jesus (Jesus) 6/9/05 Vol. 39

demonic influence music,ready for Antichrist (Jesus) 2/17/01 Vol. 22

demonic possession protect with sacramentals (Jesus) 1/18/01 Vol. 22

demons Antichrist 11/5/93 Vol. 1

demons Antichrist (Jesus) 1/15/95 Vol. 2

demons attached to addictions (Jesus) 2/14/08 Vol. 50

demons attack us every day (Jesus) 11/24/06 Vol. 45

demons bell 9/28/93 Vol. 1

demons blot out the sun (Jesus) 10/29/93 Vol. 1

demons call on Jesus for help (Jesus) 12/7/01 Vol. 25

demons cannot enter refuges (Jesus) 5/17/06 Vol. 43

demons come from volcanoes (Jesus) 3/12/98 Vol. 10

demons command to foot of cross (Jesus) 10/8/05 Vol. 41

demons do not be afraid of (Jesus) 1/30/01 Vol. 22

demons drag souls to hell (Jesus) 2/27/03 Vol. 30

demons era of peace 9/9/93 Vol. 1

demons evangelize (Jesus) 11/27/95 Vol. 3

demons fight against with rosary (Jesus) 8/8/06 Vol. 44

demons holy water (Jesus) 11/25/94 Vol. 2

demons Jesus has power over (Jesus) 2/4/08 Vol. 50

demons Jesus' power is greater (Jesus) 6/6/06 Vol. 43

demons know time is short (Jesus) 6/20/02 Vol. 27

demons like ravenous wolves (Jesus) 11/10/99 Vol. 17

demons martyrs (Jesus) 12/10/93 Vol. 1

demons rid by prayer & fasting (Jesus) 6/1/05 Vol. 39

demons roaming the earth (Jesus) 8/17/94 Vol. 2

demons spiritual weapons (St. Michael) 6/1/96 Vol. 3

demons stirring up wars in MidEast (Jesus) 6/2/07 Vol. 47

demons triumph (Jesus) 11/12/94 Vol. 2

demons unleashed through volcanoes (Jesus) 4/22/05 Vol. 39

demons violate soul bodies in hell (Jesus) 9/28/06 Vol. 44

demons warning (Jesus) 2/25/95 Vol. 2

demons warnings 7/29/93 Vol. 1

demons ways they attack us (Jesus) 7/23/02 Vol. 28

demons attacking Eucharist to remove God (Jesus) 1/29/07 Vol. 46

demons in tribulation faith in Jesus' help (Jesus) 1/5/07 Vol. 46

demons invited in by occult & drugs (Jesus) 10/13/06 Vol. 45

demons of control in addictions (Jesus) 10/3/04 Vol. 37

demons out of hell in tribulation (Jesus) 3/1/00 Vol. 18

demon's presence cold and dark (Jesus) 5/15/06 Vol. 43

demons released from volcano, end times (Jesus) 2/29/08 Vol. 50

demons vs angels battle of good and evil (Jesus) 12/4/97 Vol. 9

demons, end times coming out of volcanoes (Jesus) 5/23/07 Vol. 47

demons, masons attacking crucifix,Eucharist (Jesus) 5/19/04 Vol. 35

demons, witchcraft how to fight against (Jesus) 4/18/07 Vol. 47

denial of self hard to give up our agenda (Jesus) 3/27/01 Vol. 22

denial of self needed to gain heaven (Jesus) 8/18/05 Vol. 40

denominations in church causes:pride & interpretation (Jesus) 6/7/00 Vol. 19

deny self follow God's Will (Jesus) 3/25/07 Vol. 46

deny self give burdens to Jesus (Jesus) 8/10/00 Vol. 20

depair not in sins accept being a sinner (Jesus) 3/20/00 Vol. 18

depend on God not earthly possessions (Jesus) 9/15/99 Vol. 16

depend on God not wealth (Jesus) 8/18/03 Vol. 32

depend on God not your wealth (Jesus) 3/10/01 Vol. 22

dependence on God for everything (Jesus) 7/23/03 Vol. 32

dependence on God for everything (Jesus) 3/8/07 Vol. 46

dependence on God, not man (Jesus) 2/24/07 Vol. 46

dependence on God for all that man has in life (Jesus) 11/12/00 Vol. 21

dependence on God full commitment (Jesus)   11/1/07 Vol. 49

dependence on God necessary during tribulation (Jesus)   11/27/02 Vol. 29

dependence on God need for worship (Jesus)   10/6/07 Vol. 49

dependence on God to forgive sins (Jesus)   4/9/07 Vol. 47

dependence on God true for everyone (Jesus)   10/26/07 Vol. 49

dependence on God your own efforts are futile (Jesus)   6/12/97 Vol. 7

deposit of faith in traditions and writings (Jesus)   7/18/06 Vol. 44

deposit of faith Vatican theologians preserve (Jesus)   4/7/04 Vol. 35

depression from war (Jesus)   2/6/03 Vol. 30

depression & anxiety lift up hearts to heaven (Jesus)   2/20/04 Vol. 34

depression,economic history repeats itself (Jesus)   9/3/98 Vol. 12

depression,world like roller coaster (Jesus)   8/20/01 Vol. 24

descendants can treasure gift of faith (Jesus)   11/29/99 Vol. 17

desecration of dead bodies (Jesus)   7/2/06 Vol. 44

desecration of statues and icons (Jesus)   7/23/98 Vol. 12

desert prepare, 'dry' time (Jesus)   2/16/97 Vol. 6

desert purification of soul (Jesus)   7/17/07 Vol. 48

desires vs. loving spiritual difference (Jesus)   3/22/04 Vol. 34

despair seek God's help (Jesus)   1/17/02 Vol. 26

despair of the poor dispel with love (Jesus)   4/14/99 Vol. 15

despair, avoid from failures, help in Confession (Jesus)   2/17/02 Vol. 26

despair,avoid in life trust in promise of Jesus (Jesus)   3/7/00 Vol. 18

destination of life directed by God's plan (Jesus)   9/12/99 Vol. 16

destination,spiritual change now,cannot later (Jesus)   9/7/01 Vol. 24

destruction bridges,earthquakes (Jesus)   12/6/01 Vol. 25

destruction humbled by powers (Jesus)   7/3/97 Vol. 8

destruction massive event (Jesus)   10/4/06 Vol. 45

destruction by nature punishment for abortions (Jesus)   11/7/99 Vol. 17

destruction of churches stripped altars (Jesus)   11/9/06 Vol. 45

destruction of cities migrate from water damage (Jesus)   8/11/05 Vol. 40

destruction worsening disasters,diseases,terrorism (Jesus)   6/25/03 Vol. 31

detach from luxuries preparation for tribulation (Jesus)   5/9/00 Vol. 19

detach from things to find eternal life (Jesus)   2/28/00 Vol. 18

detach yourself from earthly things (Jesus)   2/16/06 Vol. 42

detachment cannot worship earthly things (Jesus)   11/8/03 Vol. 33

detachment from materialism needed (Jesus)   5/5/05 Vol. 39

detachment of comforts,pleasures for heaven (Jesus)   12/29/04 Vol. 37

detachment roam without a house (Jesus)   4/11/95 Vol. 2

detachment from things no gods in possessions (Jesus)   1/28/00 Vol. 18

detachment needed from earthly things (Jesus)   11/12/03 Vol. 33

detachment of things denial of self (Jesus)   11/25/06 Vol. 45

detachment of wealth money cannot get you heaven (Jesus)   11/11/00 Vol. 21

details, increased sign of coming tribulation (Jesus)   9/4/07 Vol. 48

detention camps built by military (Jesus)   6/5/01 Vol. 23

detention camps faithful persecuted (Jesus)   2/1/01 Vol. 22

detention camps for those who refuse mark (Jesus)   1/27/01 Vol. 22

detention camps growing in size,number (Jesus)   3/1/00 Vol. 18

detention center for Arabs, to retaliate (Jesus)   8/25/04 Vol. 36

detention center in Cuba (Jesus)   5/2/02 Vol. 27

detention center martial law is close (Jesus)   2/10/05 Vol. 38

detention center martyrs for faith (Jesus)   4/8/06 Vol. 43

detention center martyrs for refusing mark (Jesus)   7/6/00 Vol. 20

detention centers all over America (Jesus)   11/30/02 Vol. 29

detention centers Antichrist (Jesus)   3/30/97 Vol. 6

detention centers AntiChrist (Jesus)   8/11/96 Vol. 4

detention centers Antichrist control (Jesus)   1/16/97 Vol. 6

detention centers at old military bases (Jesus)   11/9/05 Vol. 41

detention centers bicycles vs. trucks (Jesus)   5/22/97 Vol. 7

detention centers colors for treatment (Jesus)   2/20/97 Vol. 6

detention centers crematoriums for bodies (Jesus)   4/15/05 Vol. 39

detention centers death camps,creamations (Jesus)   9/20/98 Vol. 12

detention centers decadence (Jesus)   10/26/94 Vol. 2

detention centers diseases,hiding,refuges (Jesus)   11/30/96 Vol. 5

detention centers enemies,New World Order (Jesus)   1/7/99 Vol. 14

detention centers evil men controlling people (Jesus)   4/29/99 Vol. 15

detention centers for not taking chip in body (Jesus)   8/14/06 Vol. 44

detention centers for not taking chips (Jesus)   7/7/06 Vol. 44

detention centers for not taking mark (Jesus)   7/8/03 Vol. 32

detention centers for refusing mark of the beast (Jesus)   12/8/98 Vol. 13

detention centers for religious and patriots (Jesus)   8/14/04 Vol. 36

detention centers for those not chipped (Jesus)   6/9/05 Vol. 39

detention centers for those refusing chips (Jesus)   1/16/02 Vol. 26

detention centers for those refusing chips (Jesus)   8/20/05 Vol. 40

detention centers for those refusing chips (Jesus)   4/14/05 Vol. 39

detention centers for those refusing chips (Jesus)   4/19/01 Vol. 23

detention centers for those refusing mark (Jesus)   4/7/99 Vol. 15

detention centers for those who do not leave (Jesus)   10/4/03 Vol. 33

detention centers for torturing, killing faithful (Jesus)   9/1/04 Vol. 36

detention centers forced labor & martyrs (Jesus)   7/17/01 Vol. 24

detention centers green serpent (Jesus)   10/19/94 Vol. 2

detention centers hiding & martyrdom (Jesus)   10/14/96 Vol. 5

detention centers hiding,Antichrist (Jesus)   11/17/96 Vol. 5

detention centers in our country (Jesus)   12/9/99 Vol. 17

detention centers in parklands (Jesus)   6/21/01 Vol. 23

detention centers in parklands (Jesus)   8/24/06 Vol. 44

detention centers in US parks (Jesus)   7/18/02 Vol. 28

detention centers martryed or protected (Jesus)   10/29/96 Vol. 5

detention centers martyrs, tortured, slaves (Jesus)   4/30/97 Vol. 7

detention centers messages (Jesus/Mary)   9/13/95 Vol. 3

detention centers more than just for terrorists (Jesus)   12/27/01 Vol. 25

detention centers National parks, U.N. (Jesus)   7/10/97 Vol. 8

detention centers need to go to the refuges (Jesus)   5/5/05 Vol. 39

detention centers New World Order (Jesus)   3/6/03 Vol. 30

detention centers on U.S. parklands (Jesus)   10/7/03 Vol. 33

detention centers persecution in America (Jesus) 4/12/98 Vol. 11

detention centers persecution/relig/political (Jesus) 8/21/96 Vol. 4

detention centers prisoners, martyred (Jesus) 6/3/97 Vol. 7

detention centers prisoners,martyrdom (Jesus) 4/26/96 Vol. 3

detention centers ready for prisoners (Jesus) 3/29/07 Vol. 46

detention centers religious,patriots sought for (Jesus) 7/19/07 Vol. 48

detention centers some faithful captured (Jesus) 9/1/97 Vol. 8

detention centers spies (Jesus) 11/21/95 Vol. 3

detention centers take prisoners to (Jesus) 2/5/98 Vol. 10

detention centers those who stay home (Jesus) 10/15/03 Vol. 33

detention centers tortured & martyred (Jesus) 9/12/96 Vol. 4

detention centers trains carry captured to (Jesus) 2/19/05 Vol. 38

detention centers troop captures to come (Jesus) 9/3/05 Vol. 40

detention centers troops cut back (Jesus) 11/13/97 Vol. 9

detention centers trucks carrying prisoners (Jesus) 12/4/97 Vol. 9

detention centers UN,one world people (Jesus) 9/15/97 Vol. 8

detention centers using trailer trucks (Jesus) 4/1/00 Vol. 19

detention centers you are future prisoners (Jesus) 10/22/98 Vol. 13

detention centers in US new world order prisons (Jesus) 5/10/06 Vol. 43

detention centers of UN New World Order police (Jesus) 7/17/96 Vol. 4

detention death camps for religious & patriots (Jesus) 4/23/07 Vol. 47

detention death camps persecution in tribulation (Jesus) 5/16/07 Vol. 47

detention trucks dark windows,for prisoners (Jesus) 5/3/00 Vol. 19

detours from God wealth, pleasure (Jesus) 7/13/04 Vol. 36

device in car hiding (Jesus) 6/14/95 Vol. 2

devil attacks of evil (Jesus) 7/17/02 Vol. 28

devil avoid snares as in the desert (Jesus) 4/9/05 Vol. 39

devil be on guard against (Jesus) 11/11/97 Vol. 9

devil behind wars for greed (Jesus) 5/30/07 Vol. 47

devil chained shortly (Jesus) 6/20/97 Vol. 7

devil creature of God (Jesus) 7/30/01 Vol. 24

devil distraction (Jesus) 7/9/94 Vol. 2

devil do not give him credit (Jesus) 2/7/98 Vol. 10

devil he and hell do exist (Jesus) 12/29/96 Vol. 5

devil humility (Jesus) 10/23/95 Vol. 3

devil liar & tempter (Jesus) 2/9/08 Vol. 50

devil lurking to place snares (Jesus) 6/28/04 Vol. 35

devil permanent sign 8/24/93 Vol. 1

devil tries to stop evangelization (Jesus) 5/27/03 Vol. 31

devil trying to destroy faith (Jesus) 6/10/06 Vol. 43

devil wants people to sell souls (Jesus) 8/17/01 Vol. 24

devil & hell really exist as danger to soul (Jesus) 3/7/02 Vol. 26

devil as Prince of Darkness evil as yet to be seen (Jesus) 1/10/04 Vol. 34

devil as wolf constant temptations (Jesus) 3/26/08 Vol. 50

devil attacks earthly weaknesses (Jesus) 9/12/07 Vol. 48

devil tests us with worldly desires (Jesus) 1/15/05 Vol. 38

devil vs. God struggle for souls (Jesus) 11/8/07 Vol. 49

devil worship dealing principalities,powers (Jesus) 8/13/98 Vol. 12

devil,renounce or fall into hell (Jesus) 3/27/00 Vol. 18

devil's attacks daily battle in decisions (Jesus) 5/14/04 Vol. 35

devil's attacks know your weaknesses (Jesus) 3/8/04 Vol. 34

devil's attacks with venom of sin (Jesus) 4/3/04 Vol. 35

devils not seen need to be on guard (Jesus) 3/2/06 Vol. 42

devil's temptations fasting,prayer distractions (Jesus) 8/1/00 Vol. 20

devil's territory occasions of sin (Jesus) 5/15/06 Vol. 43

devil's ways his temptations (Jesus) 8/1/07 Vol. 48

devotions chaplet,stations,adoration (Jesus) 3/20/98 Vol. 10

devotions to help spiritual life (Jesus) 1/24/04 Vol. 34

diamond facets mirror facets of life (Jesus) 8/28/02 Vol. 28

diamond souls need cutting, polishing (Jesus) 5/21/06 Vol. 43

diasters, financial problems chastisement for sins (Jesus) 3/5/04 Vol. 34

Dick Mauer witness of faith (Jesus) 1/5/06 Vol. 42

dictators disregard for life's value (Jesus) 3/30/99 Vol. 14

dictators funded by one worlders (Jesus) 9/5/06 Vol. 44

dictators in many countries (Jesus) 2/8/07 Vol. 46

dictators to create wars (Jesus) 3/7/03 Vol. 30

die for faith instead of taking mark (Jesus) 12/13/99 Vol. 17

diet, proper to avoid bad diseases (Jesus) 6/8/07 Vol. 47

difficulties in anger call on Jesus' help (Jesus) 12/31/98 Vol. 13

difficulties in life avoid,minimize,take head on (Jesus) 3/12/01 Vol. 22

difficulties in life do not get angry with God (Jesus) 2/26/04 Vol. 34

difficulties, response to offer up, no anger (Jesus) 4/21/06 Vol. 43

digital angel watch as smart card (Jesus) 6/28/01 Vol. 23

dinner time for family to share (Jesus) 10/27/05 Vol. 41

direction unity (Jesus) 12/13/93 Vol. 1

direction of Jesus Good Shepherd to heaven (Jesus) 10/26/00 Vol. 21

dirty bombs plots and threats (Jesus) 6/11/02 Vol. 27

dirty rags in body effect of sin on soul (Jesus) 6/2/00 Vol. 19

disabilities in old age corporal works of mercy in help (Jesus)
8/26/04 Vol. 36

disabled need our help (Jesus) 11/14/07 Vol. 49

disappointments nothing vs. major disasters (Jesus) 12/10/03 Vol. 33

DISASTER newspaper 7/21/93 Vol. 1

disaster areas may wish to move from (Jesus) 11/7/05 Vol. 41

disaster increase unless change in lives (Jesus) 10/24/05 Vol. 41

disaster victims help with donations (Jesus) 1/6/05 Vol. 38

disasters affecting economy (Jesus) 6/14/07 Vol. 47

disasters another planned (Jesus) 2/1/07 Vol. 46

disasters are a chance to share (Jesus) 2/1/02 Vol. 26

disasters are a result of sin (Jesus) 8/19/04 Vol. 36

disasters bring man to his knees (Jesus) 12/29/05 Vol. 41

disasters bring people together (Jesus) 7/1/04 Vol. 36

disasters chastisement for sins (Jesus) 12/2/00 Vol. 21

disasters donate and pray for victims (Jesus) 10/20/05 Vol. 41

disasters expect more (Jesus) — 1/10/08 Vol. 50

disasters for sexual sins (Jesus) — 6/8/04 Vol. 35

disasters help and pray for new start (Jesus) — 10/20/05 Vol. 41

disasters help each other (Jesus) — 2/12/98 Vol. 10

disasters in areas of sin (Jesus) — 10/18/05 Vol. 41

disasters in places of great sin (Jesus) — 12/26/05 Vol. 41

disasters insurance companies (Jesus) — 2/2/96 Vol. 3

disasters linked to sin (Jesus) — 3/4/06 Vol. 42

disasters mirror image of souls (Jesus) — 8/31/01 Vol. 24

disasters more frequent (Jesus) — 9/4/96 Vol. 4

disasters natural & man-made (Jesus) — 10/1/03 Vol. 33

disasters of trains and planes (Jesus) — 4/25/02 Vol. 27

disasters one after the other (Jesus) — 1/27/01 Vol. 22

disasters physical and spiritual (Jesus) — 4/24/03 Vol. 31

disasters pray for protection (Jesus) — 10/19/06 Vol. 45

disasters relation to sin not seen (Jesus) — 9/4/04 Vol. 36

disasters stripped of comforts (Jesus) — 2/12/98 Vol. 10

disasters testing America (Jesus) — 11/15/01 Vol. 25

disasters to bring us repentance (Jesus) — 10/6/01 Vol. 25

disasters to get our attention (Jesus) — 3/10/98 Vol. 10

disasters to increase after June,'06 (Jesus) — 6/29/06 Vol. 43

disasters to worsen if no repentance (Jesus) — 10/4/05 Vol. 41

disasters tsunami on East coast (Jesus) — 2/18/08 Vol. 50

disasters war, famine, pestilence (Jesus) — 2/5/98 Vol. 10

disasters will bring us to our knees (Jesus) — 2/4/02 Vol. 26

disasters & fires occur in areas of sin (Jesus) — 1/31/02 Vol. 26

dis. & hurricanes wake up to leave comfort zones (Jesus) — 9/13/04 Vol. 36

disasters & storms cleanse pride,need for things (Jesus) — 3/22/01 Vol. 22

disasters and war bring hate & destruction (Jesus) — 10/6/05 Vol. 41

disaster's cause natural order,punishment (Jesus) — 1/4/05 Vol. 38

disasters continuous chastisements for sins (Jesus) — 8/19/99 Vol. 16

disasters for 2004 natural & man-made (Jesus) — 12/30/03 Vol. 33

disasters in weather difficult to grow crops (Jesus) — 2/3/00 Vol. 18

disasters in weather violence mirrored in sins (Jesus) — 6/15/00 Vol. 19

disasters increasing for our sins (Jesus) — 4/12/05 Vol. 39

disasters to continue increase in expenses coming (Jesus) — 12/16/05 Vol. 41

disasters to worsen will affect crops (Jesus) — 7/2/04 Vol. 36

disasters, money crisis testing Americans (Jesus) — 3/19/08 Vol. 50

disasters, natural chastisements for sins (Jesus) — 1/20/05 Vol. 38

disasters, natural for defying Commandments (Jesus) — 9/26/02 Vol. 28

disasters, natural punishment for sins (Jesus) — 7/24/03 Vol. 32

disasters, wars result of unrepentance (Jesus) — 10/9/07 Vol. 49

discern messengers by fruits of work (Jesus) — 1/19/03 Vol. 30

discernment flames (Jesus) — 11/20/95 Vol. 3

discernment found in Jesus (Jesus) — 2/10/06 Vol. 42

discernment of false prophets (Jesus) — 8/30/03 Vol. 32

discernment pray to Holy Spirit (Jesus) — 12/31/96 Vol. 5

discernment to know the truth (Jesus) — 5/3/05 Vol. 39

discernment & help pray to the Holy Spirit (Jesus) — 6/21/02 Vol. 27

discernment needed avoid being misled by evil (Jesus) — 11/15/98 Vol. 13

disciple,active living Gospel message of love (Jesus) — 10/19/00 Vol. 21

disciples ambassador (St. Andrew) — 11/30/93 Vol. 1

disciples die to self, money (Jesus) — 12/13/96 Vol. 5

disciples example (Jesus) — 8/28/95 Vol. 3

disciples foolish to world (Jesus) — 8/9/01 Vol. 24

disciples hard to accept eating Body (Jesus) — 5/4/02 Vol. 27

disciples heaven (Jesus) — 5/7/94 Vol. 1

disciples making God's team in heaven (Jesus) — 8/28/04 Vol. 36

disciples strive for perfection (Jesus) — 6/22/97 Vol. 7

disciples suffer persecution (Jesus) — 5/12/98 Vol. 11

disciples yes/no (Jesus) — 2/18/94 Vol. 1

discipleship be active, not passive (Jesus) — 12/20/01 Vol. 25

discipleship faith in action (Jesus) — 2/17/03 Vol. 30

discipleship practice what you preach (Jesus) — 8/7/97 Vol. 8

discipleship trust & follow Will of God (Jesus) — 8/16/01 Vol. 24

discouragement call on God's help (Jesus) — 6/7/01 Vol. 23

discoveries, inventions give glory to God (Jesus) — 12/1/05 Vol. 41

discrimination against poor,color,faiths (Jesus) — 10/29/05 Vol. 41

discrimination be open minded (Jesus) — 2/26/03 Vol. 30

disease weapon for population control (Jesus) — 8/12/98 Vol. 12

disease & earthquakes caused by man's technology (Jesus) — 11/5/02 Vol. 29

disease & pestilence result from tidal waves (Jesus) — 12/30/04 Vol. 37

disease from water due to lack of needed minerals (Jesus) — 3/15/02 Vol. 26

disease outbreaks for control (Jesus) — 7/19/01 Vol. 24

diseases by man and nature (Jesus) — 3/12/98 Vol. 10

diseases caused by dabbling in cells (Jesus) — 6/15/98 Vol. 11

diseases created by one world people (Jesus) — 6/7/01 Vol. 23

diseases cured at safe havens,caves (Jesus) — 3/27/98 Vol. 10

diseases from disasters and weather (Jesus) — 3/26/98 Vol. 10

diseases help the poor (Jesus) — 8/7/03 Vol. 32

diseases in tribulation (Jesus) — 9/19/96 Vol. 4

diseases made by man (Jesus) — 11/8/05 Vol. 41

diseases manipulated by man (Jesus) — 5/7/01 Vol. 23

diseases man-made (Jesus) — 9/4/03 Vol. 32

diseases man-made (Jesus) — 4/12/03 Vol. 31

diseases man-made (Jesus) — 9/9/03 Vol. 32

diseases one world people tactics (Jesus) — 12/25/03 Vol. 33

diseases resist antibiotics (Jesus) — 1/31/03 Vol. 30

diseases transmitted by weapons (Jesus) — 10/31/05 Vol. 41

diseases & disasters natural and man-made (Jesus) — 4/17/04 Vol. 35

diseases & epidemics germ warfare (Jesus) — 9/16/97 Vol. 8

diseases & epidemics signs of the end times (Jesus) — 5/25/01 Vol. 23

diseases & epidemics to reduce population (Jesus) — 7/19/01 Vol. 24

diseases & pestilence of suspicious origin (Jesus) — 4/14/98 Vol. 11

diseases & viruses as chastisements (Jesus) 12/2/03 Vol. 33

diseases and plagues cured at caves and refuges (Jesus) 5/4/98 Vol. 11

diseases created SARS,AIDS,ebola,West Nile (Jesus) 5/15/03 Vol. 31

diseases healed at refuges (Jesus) 4/3/01 Vol. 23

diseases in water help poor countries (Jesus) 10/13/05 Vol. 41

diseases, AIDS man-made for control (Jesus) 2/21/03 Vol. 30

diseases, terminal prepare for death (Jesus) 1/11/02 Vol. 26

diseases,man-made causing AIDS,cancer (Jesus) 11/6/02 Vol. 29

diseases,man-made luminous crosses (Jesus) 6/4/03 Vol. 31

diseases,man-made population control (Jesus) 6/18/03 Vol. 31

diseases,new and old new warfare on cities (Jesus) 9/17/98 Vol. 12

disorder in nature caused by man (Jesus) 12/5/05 Vol. 41

distractions discern priorities (Jesus) 4/17/96 Vol. 3

distractions gadgets (Jesus) 7/18/95 Vol. 3

distractions gone tomorrow, do not worry (Jesus) 11/17/05 Vol. 41

distractions keep forcus on Jesus (Jesus) 6/10/06 Vol. 43

distractions of the world (Jesus) 7/16/03 Vol. 32

distractions pray to clear mind (Jesus) 2/24/98 Vol. 10

distractions pray to go away (Jesus) 1/2/08 Vol. 50

distractions spiritual reading (Jesus) 1/1/98 Vol. 10

distractions strip clutter of life (Jesus) 7/23/99 Vol. 16

distractions & desires avoid, take narrow road (Jesus) 5/8/03 Vol. 31

distractions & detours lead away from God (Jesus) 1/11/06 Vol. 42

distractions in prayer shopping & entertainment (Jesus) 4/26/07 Vol. 47

distractions of world removed by prayer (Jesus) 7/5/07 Vol. 48

distractions to prayer use Lenten devotions (Jesus) 3/16/00 Vol. 18

distractions, worldly blind us to God's love (Jesus) 9/10/04 Vol. 36

disturbances demands (personal) (St. Therese) 6/4/96 Vol. 3

Divinci Code brings doubts to truths (Jesus) 7/6/06 Vol. 44

Divine Child & infancy honor all year (Jesus) 1/6/05 Vol. 38

Divine intervention need Jesus to be saved (Jesus) 10/25/03 Vol. 33

Divine Mercy 3:00 hour for prayers (Jesus) 5/16/04 Vol. 35

Divine Mercy available to all sinners (Jesus) 4/18/04 Vol. 35

Divine Mercy meaning of (Jesus) 5/3/03 Vol. 31

Divine Mercy receive Communion pure (Jesus) 4/16/98 Vol. 11

Divine Mercy warning (Jesus) 4/10/94 Vol. 1

Divine Mercy Chaplet 3 a.m. & 3 p.m. (Jesus) 8/7/03 Vol. 32

Divine Mercy Chaplet at 3:00 p.m. (Jesus) 3/23/05 Vol. 38

Divine Mercy Chaplet grace and mercy (Jesus) 9/30/00 Vol. 20

Divine Mercy Chaplet honors 3:00 hour (Jesus) 4/6/06 Vol. 43

Divine Mercy Chaplet passion of Jesus (Bl Faustina) 2/15/97 Vol. 6

Divine Mercy Chaplet remnant (Jesus) 3/4/94 Vol. 1

Divine Mercy Conference call to evangelize (Jesus) 8/9/03 Vol. 32

Divine Mercy Conference healing of sins (Jesus) 4/11/02 Vol. 27

Divine Mercy Novena remission of reparation for sin (Jesus) 3/31/05 Vol. 38

Divine Mercy Novena reparation for sins (Jesus) 4/15/04 Vol. 35

Divine Mercy Novena reparation for sins (Jesus) 4/12/07 Vol. 47

Divine Mercy prayers for forgotten living souls (Jesus) 3/30/08 Vol. 50

Divine Mercy Sunday a blessing of mercy (Jesus) 4/22/01 Vol. 23

Divine Mercy Sunday open hearts to convert (Jesus) 4/27/03 Vol. 31

Divine Mercy Sunday warning (Jesus) 4/14/96 Vol. 3

Divine obedience needed to follow God's Will (Jesus) 3/28/05 Vol. 38

Divine presence Blessed Sacrament (Jesus) 10/17/95 Vol. 3

Divine Sacrifice atoned for all sin (Jesus) 4/21/00 Vol. 19

Divine Sacrifice paid for man's sins (Jesus) 7/3/06 Vol. 44

Divine Will adversities (Mary) 6/11/94 Vol. 1

Divine Will angel (Mark) 8/5/95 Vol. 3

Divine Will assured of salvation (Jesus) 4/19/98 Vol. 11

Divine Will be good examples (Jesus) 5/10/99 Vol. 15

Divine Will be humble and repent (Jesus) 7/15/98 Vol. 12

Divine Will Blessed Mother lived in (Jesus) 4/8/02 Vol. 27

Divine Will carry cross of life (Jesus) 4/27/98 Vol. 11

Divine Will carrying our crosses (Jesus) 4/10/98 Vol. 11

Divine Will complete surrender (Jesus) 8/13/03 Vol. 32

Divine Will conform your will to Mine (Jesus) 7/25/98 Vol. 12

Divine Will consecration, our 'yes' (Jesus) 1/11/01 Vol. 22

Divine Will daily marching orders (Jesus) 5/21/02 Vol. 27

Divine Will depend on God only (Jesus) 1/14/03 Vol. 30

Divine Will die to self (Jesus) 6/18/98 Vol. 11

Divine Will die to self (Jesus) 5/30/98 Vol. 11

Divine Will die to self (Jesus) 11/2/97 Vol. 9

Divine Will do not want to give up to (Jesus) 3/26/98 Vol. 10

Divine Will follow and live in (Jesus) 10/15/01 Vol. 25

Divine Will follow God's request (Jesus) 9/8/00 Vol. 20

Divine Will follow in everything (Jesus) 9/23/96 Vol. 4

Divine Will follow instead of our will (Jesus) 7/13/04 Vol. 36

Divine Will follow our mission (Jesus) 3/18/05 Vol. 38

Divine Will follow to do mission (Jesus) 5/2/05 Vol. 39

Divine Will gain crown (Jesus) 1/3/98 Vol. 10

Divine Will give our will over to (Mary) 8/26/97 Vol. 8

Divine Will give up pride,selfishness (Jesus) 5/19/99 Vol. 15

Divine Will home in heaven (Jesus) 1/1/97 Vol. 6

Divine Will in Era of Peace (Jesus) 12/4/99 Vol. 17

Divine Will in perfecting our actions (Jesus) 2/11/99 Vol. 14

Divine Will involve Jesus in every action (Jesus) 5/23/00 Vol. 19

Divine Will keep focused on (Jesus) 12/4/00 Vol. 21

Divine Will keep focused on Jesus (Jesus) 1/7/98 Vol. 10

Divine Will kingdom of heaven open (Jesus) 9/4/97 Vol. 8

Divine Will leads to heaven (Jesus) 8/8/01 Vol. 24

Divine Will leads to perfection (Jesus) 1/24/03 Vol. 30

Divine Will let Jesus mold us to (Jesus) 8/29/98 Vol. 12

Divine Will live as Blessed Mother (Jesus) 3/25/03 Vol. 30

Divine Will live close to (Mary) 3/25/98 Vol. 10

Divine Will live His Will every moment (Jesus) 11/10/96 Vol. 5

Divine Will live in for perfection (Jesus) | 10/14/05 Vol. 41
Divine Will live in for perfection (Jesus) | 10/14/05 Vol. 41
Divine Will love God and neighbor (Mary) | 10/7/97 Vol. 9
Divine Will models in Jesus & Mary (Jesus) | 12/9/02 Vol. 29
Divine Will new earth (Jesus) | 1/31/95 Vol. 2
Divine Will obedient as Jesus to Father (Jesus) | 4/28/04 Vol. 35
Divine Will our goal for heaven (Jesus) | 9/3/98 Vol. 12
Divine Will part of living Jesus (Jesus) | 6/22/97 Vol. 7
Divine Will perfection of the soul (Jesus) | 5/17/98 Vol. 11
Divine Will prayer (Jesus) | 6/29/94 Vol. 1
Divine Will reject ways of the world (Jesus) | 12/16/00 Vol. 21
Divine Will saints found salvation in (Jesus) | 12/27/97 Vol. 9
Divine Will submit,narrow gate (Jesus) | 10/31/96 Vol. 5
Divine Will suffering (Jesus) | 2/25/97 Vol. 6
Divine Will takes faith, commitment (Jesus) | 6/8/01 Vol. 23
Divine Will thy Will be done (Jesus) | 6/19/03 Vol. 31
Divine Will to fulfill our mission (Jesus) | 4/30/05 Vol. 39
Divine Will to gain heaven only (Jesus) | 5/16/03 Vol. 31
Divine Will total obedience (Jesus) | 5/18/03 Vol. 31
Divine Will united to our will (Jesus) | 3/19/05 Vol. 38
Divine Will vs. our will (Jesus) | 3/1/03 Vol. 30
Divine Will walk in the Light (Jesus) | 6/22/01 Vol. 23
Divine Will Warning prepares for (Jesus) | 10/4/02 Vol. 29
Divine Will way to live in (Jesus) | 1/7/08 Vol. 50
Divine Will word and example (Jesus) | 1/24/96 Vol. 3
Divine Will,laws will gain you heaven (Jesus) | 7/8/01 Vol. 24
Divine Will,live in higher place in heaven (Jesus) | 12/14/00 Vol. 21
Divinity of Jesus Incarnation a mystery (Jesus) | 4/13/00 Vol. 19
Divinity of Jesus proclaimed in John's Gospel (Jesus) | 3/29/07 Vol. 46
Divinity of Jesus still doubted by many (Jesus) | 8/25/02 Vol. 28
Divinity of Jesus unbelievers to be judged (Jesus) | 6/7/00 Vol. 19
Div., humanity of Son depth of God, depth of love (Jesus) | 12/31/02 Vol. 29
division among religions caused by Satan (Jesus) | 11/22/98 Vol. 13
division in Church coming in end days (Jesus) | 5/9/07 Vol. 47
division in Church modernism vs. faithful (Jesus) | 11/17/98 Vol. 13
division in Church schismatic vs remnant (Jesus) | 5/24/07 Vol. 47
division in the Church sign of coming Antichrist (Jesus) | 5/11/05 Vol. 39
division of USA world powers vs God's powers (Jesus) | 11/8/00 Vol. 21
divisions need for healing (Jesus) | 3/31/05 Vol. 38
divisions in religion by Satan (Jesus) | 8/9/07 Vol. 48
divorce needs forgiveness (Jesus) | 6/30/04 Vol. 35
divorce scourge of society (Jesus) | 12/29/96 Vol. 5
divorce separations (Jesus) | 8/27/97 Vol. 8
divorce ways to save marriage (Jesus) | 10/8/06 Vol. 45
divorce & annulments not accepted norm by God (Jesus) | 8/13/04 Vol. 36
divorce & separation spouses need full commitment (Jesus) | 11/10/02 Vol. 29
divorce in marriage meant to be for life (Jesus) | 8/12/05 Vol. 40

divorce needs stopping add love of God to family (Jesus) | 10/10/98 Vol. 13
divorce, avoid avoid adultery (Jesus) | 7/9/05 Vol. 40
divorce, marital problems job stress, infidelity (Jesus) | 5/4/04 Vol. 35
divorces lack of responsibility (Jesus) | 2/25/00 Vol. 18
DNA abuse of science (Jesus) | 5/29/02 Vol. 27
DNA beauty of creation (Jesus) | 6/27/07 Vol. 47
DNA bodies changed (Jesus) | 3/17/97 Vol. 6
DNA do not manipulate (Jesus) | 3/9/05 Vol. 38
DNA effects of manipulation (Jesus) | 5/4/01 Vol. 23
DNA manipulation has problems (Jesus) | 7/6/01 Vol. 24
DNA manipulation of (Jesus) | 3/21/05 Vol. 38
DNA moral decisions in experiments (Jesus) | 7/18/02 Vol. 28
DNA testing for control (Jesus) | 10/9/02 Vol. 29
DNA & cloning abuses of God's perfection (Jesus) | 2/5/07 Vol. 46
DNA & gene research not better than God's perfection (Jesus)
| 7/15/04 Vol. 36
DNA abuse balance of nature disrupted (Jesus) | 3/27/03 Vol. 30
DNA and computers abuse of knowledge (Jesus) | 8/24/00 Vol. 20
DNA knowledge affecting hybrids,genes,cloning (Jesus) | 3/6/02 Vol. 26
DNA manipulated man exploiting for profit (Jesus) | 4/27/99 Vol. 15
DNA manipulation abominations to God (Jesus) | 11/20/05 Vol. 41
DNA manipulation cannot improve on perfection (Jesus) | 7/24/05 Vol. 40
DNA manipulation causes diseases (Jesus) | 4/7/05 Vol. 39
DNA manipulation do not research (Jesus) | 8/2/01 Vol. 24
DNA manipulation endangering balance of nature (Jesus) | 12/19/07 Vol. 49
DNA manipulation hybrids and cloning abuses (Jesus) | 6/27/07 Vol. 47
DNA manipulation leads to disaster (Jesus) | 1/1/03 Vol. 30
DNA manipulation unnatural (Jesus) | 8/23/01 Vol. 24
DNA manipulation violates balance of nature (Jesus) | 9/10/07 Vol. 48
DNA of plants,animals man trying to improve on God (Jesus)
| 10/31/03 Vol. 33
DNA research seek God's perfection (Jesus) | 3/9/05 Vol. 38
DNA research,cloning offends God (Jesus) | 8/17/04 Vol. 36
DNA ribbon creation (God the Father) | 2/26/95 Vol. 2
DNA, hybrids changing nature (Jesus) | 9/16/05 Vol. 40
DNA, hybrids examples of man's destruction (Jesus) | 11/18/03 Vol. 33
doctors doing abortions need prayers,conversion (Jesus) | 10/13/00 Vol. 21
doghouse lack of communication (Jesus) | 8/5/00 Vol. 20
dogs as demons prayer, sacramental protection (Jesus) | 12/18/03 Vol. 33
Dominic C. Betania (Mary) | 8/8/95 Vol. 3
donations give to reputable groups (Jesus) | 1/10/05 Vol. 38
donations, prayers for Bangladesh people (Jesus) | 11/20/07 Vol. 49
doom & gloom a real message of hope (Jesus) | 9/26/97 Vol. 8
doom & gloom wake-up call (Jesus) | 9/29/97 Vol. 8
doom and gloom spiritual preparation (Jesus) | 5/22/97 Vol. 7
door open soul (Jesus) | 10/22/94 Vol. 2
door of your heart hospitality to Jesus (Jesus) | 4/19/99 Vol. 15

door to hearts replace pride with Jesus (Jesus) — 8/8/98 Vol. 12

doorway to Heaven judgment (Jesus) — 9/19/94 Vol. 2

doorway to heaven miraculous pictures (Jesus) — 1/19/98 Vol. 10

doorway to Heaven My Will (Jesus) — 11/15/93 Vol. 1

doorways to heaven pictures are sign of victory (Jesus) — 12/16/00 Vol. 21

Dorothy Geyssens funeral, pillar of church (Jesus) — 1/4/07 Vol. 46

dove passion — 8/9/93 Vol. 1

downsizings Wall Street control (Jesus) — 2/1/01 Vol. 22

Dozule Cross at Guadeloupe refuge (Jesus) — 8/21/06 Vol. 44

Dozule Cross represents Christ's cross (Jesus) — 5/14/05 Vol. 39

draft for viable military (Jesus) — 8/3/06 Vol. 44

draft for army to allow more wars (Jesus) — 5/18/04 Vol. 35

dress wear respectable clothes (Jesus) — 6/27/98 Vol. 11

dress women should be modest (Jesus) — 5/30/02 Vol. 27

dress at Mass should be respectful (Jesus) — 6/8/99 Vol. 15

dress modestly especially in church (Jesus) — 8/2/03 Vol. 32

dress properly for coming to Mass (Jesus) — 10/31/04 Vol. 37

dress properly causes sin (Jesus) — 7/31/97 Vol. 8

dressing immodestly in occasions of sin (Jesus) — 7/28/06 Vol. 44

drinking & carousing dulls senses for sin (Jesus) — 2/4/04 Vol. 34

drinking & lust sinful addictions, confess (Jesus) — 7/9/05 Vol. 40

drinking & sex avoid in youth trips (Jesus) — 3/22/07 Vol. 46

drinking water store in case of poisoning (Jesus) — 9/10/99 Vol. 16

driver's license to require chips,biometrics (Jesus) — 1/6/06 Vol. 42

driver's licenses to require chips (Jesus) — 2/1/06 Vol. 42

driver's licenses with chips to come (Jesus) — 1/15/08 Vol. 50

driving controlled by chips (Jesus) — 8/24/06 Vol. 44

driving annoyances slow life down, be patience (Jesus) — 8/19/98 Vol. 12

driving trials chance to improve peace (Jesus) — 3/2/06 Vol. 42

driving your car demands your patience (Jesus) — 7/17/99 Vol. 16

drought serious problem (Jesus) — 9/26/02 Vol. 28

droughts cause people to move (Jesus) — 6/10/04 Vol. 35

droughts heat and lack of rain (Jesus) — 6/12/02 Vol. 27

droughts in MidEast & Africa (Jesus) — 5/24/05 Vol. 39

droughts in population shifts (Jesus) — 5/29/03 Vol. 31

droughts squandered fresh water (Jesus) — 10/3/02 Vol. 29

droughts to cause food shortages (Jesus) — 7/5/03 Vol. 32

droughts & famine to increase with time (Jesus) — 5/16/07 Vol. 47

droughts & fires in Europe & America (Jesus) — 8/25/05 Vol. 40

droughts & floods change in rains (Jesus) — 5/15/07 Vol. 47

droughts & floods chastisements (Jesus) — 8/30/96 Vol. 4

droughts & floods to worsen (Jesus) — 10/19/07 Vol. 49

drug addictions death to body & soul (Jesus) — 8/16/01 Vol. 24

drug companies charge too much (Jesus) — 8/23/01 Vol. 24

drug companies make money on diseases (Jesus) — 11/8/05 Vol. 41

drug companies manipulations for money (Jesus) — 1/16/06 Vol. 42

drug companies profitting from bird flu (Jesus) — 5/12/06 Vol. 43

drug effects cause liver & kidney problems (Jesus) — 1/16/06 Vol. 42

drug money for black government projects (Jesus) — 6/26/01 Vol. 23

drug problem being allowed to continue (Jesus) — 8/26/99 Vol. 16

drug smuggling helped by governments (Jesus) — 3/22/07 Vol. 46

drugs corruption in government (Jesus) — 3/11/99 Vol. 14

drugs ties in government (Jesus) — 7/5/99 Vol. 16

drugs tool for destruction (Jesus) — 6/26/01 Vol. 23

drugs & alcohol and sexual sins (Jesus) — 3/26/03 Vol. 30

drugs & alcohol avoid evil places (Jesus) — 7/5/03 Vol. 32

drugs & alcohol controlled by Satan (Jesus) — 6/23/03 Vol. 31

drugs & alcohol invoke Most Precious Blood (Jesus) — 7/20/01 Vol. 24

drugs & alcoholism weakness and sin (Jesus) — 2/24/96 Vol. 3

drugs & opium destroy lives (Jesus) — 4/11/02 Vol. 27

drugs and alcohol ruined lives (Jesus) — 6/29/98 Vol. 11

drugs, alcohol addictions (Jesus) — 2/9/03 Vol. 30

drugs, illegal lead to addictions (Jesus) — 1/31/07 Vol. 46

drugs, legal to cure bad eating (Jesus) — 1/31/07 Vol. 46

drugs, medical side effects worse than cure (Jesus) — 10/12/04 Vol. 37

drugs,smoking,sex in excess (Jesus) — 10/23/02 Vol. 29

drunkenness hard to forgive (Jesus) — 9/11/05 Vol. 40

dry & green time of tribulation (Jesus) — 8/10/07 Vol. 48

dry bones to life sign of Resurrection (Jesus) — 2/19/08 Vol. 50

dry martyr dying to self in consecration (Jesus) — 7/25/00 Vol. 20

dry martyrdom faithful may die for Jesus (St. Therese) — 9/30/99 Vol. 16

DVD talk needs prayer and action (Jesus) — 12/27/07 Vol. 49

DVD talks make available (Jesus) — 9/13/07 Vol. 48

DVD's of talk move quickly on it (Jesus) — 1/10/08 Vol. 50

dwelling in heaven resting place prepared (Jesus) — 3/22/01 Vol. 22

dwellings multiplied at refuges (Jesus) — 2/22/07 Vol. 46

dying pray for the (Jesus) — 5/17/01 Vol. 23

dying protection needed pray for protection from Satan (Jesus) — 7/20/04 Vol. 36

eagle freedoms lost in USA (Jesus) — 7/2/94 Vol. 2

Early Christian martyrs vindicated in Rome's collapse (Jesus) — 12/1/04 Vol. 37

Early Church beginnings in Acts of the Apostles (Jesus) — 3/27/08 Vol. 50

Early Fathers protection from heresies (Jesus) — 6/27/07 Vol. 47

earth purified and renewed (Jesus) — 10/29/02 Vol. 29

earth day praise God for creation (Jesus) — 4/22/04 Vol. 35

earth faster on axes time speeded up (Jesus) — 9/2/06 Vol. 44

earth purified like in Noah's day (Jesus) — 4/12/03 Vol. 31

earth renewed that man despoiled (Jesus) — 11/12/05 Vol. 41

earthly attractions cause detours from heaven (Jesus) — 2/27/02 Vol. 26

earthly comforts distract your purpose here (Jesus) — 2/19/00 Vol. 18

earthly death better than spiritual death (Jesus) — 9/20/99 Vol. 16

earthly desires cleansed to enter heaven (Jesus) — 9/28/04 Vol. 36

earthly desires detach to gain heaven (Jesus) — 4/30/06 Vol. 43

earthly desires empty self for heaven (Jesus) — 3/14/06 Vol. 42
earthly desires give up for heaven (Jesus) — 12/31/05 Vol. 41
earthly desires let go to be free (Jesus) — 3/29/06 Vol. 42
earthly desires must be purged for heaven (Jesus) — 7/9/04 Vol. 36
earthly desires need cleansing for heaven (Jesus) — 12/11/04 Vol. 37
earthly desires need healing for heaven (Jesus) — 11/11/07 Vol. 49
earthly desires need purification before death (Jesus) — 3/19/04 Vol. 34
earthly desires not real peace (Jesus) — 10/18/06 Vol. 45
earthly desires purge now than later (Jesus) — 5/2/07 Vol. 47
earthly desires strip to have heavenly desires (Jesus) — 10/2/04 Vol. 37
earthly distractions dulls spiritual awareness (Jesus) — 9/9/07 Vol. 48
earthly distractions leaving no time for God (Jesus) — 6/13/03 Vol. 31
earthly home surpassed in heaven (Jesus) — 6/30/02 Vol. 27
earthly life more than just entertainment (Jesus) — 5/16/00 Vol. 19
earthly life vs heaven great hope in peace of heaven (Jesus) — 3/25/04 Vol. 34
earthly life vs. eternal life time is precious (Jesus) — 12/9/98 Vol. 13
earthly pleasures enticements of the devil (Jesus) — 9/12/05 Vol. 40
earthly pleasures moderation ok,abuse in sin (Jesus) — 3/9/02 Vol. 26
earthly things avoid control & worship of (Jesus) — 5/5/06 Vol. 43
earthly things can be gods to control you (Jesus) — 11/17/03 Vol. 33
earthly things do not be controlled by (Jesus) — 6/13/07 Vol. 47
earthly things need to be detached (Jesus) — 9/6/06 Vol. 44
earthly things never satisfy the soul (Jesus) — 4/6/01 Vol. 23
earthly things should not control you (Jesus) — 10/22/07 Vol. 49
earthly things will not make you happy (Jesus) — 3/23/04 Vol. 34
earthly things will pass away (Jesus) — 8/28/07 Vol. 48
earthly thoughts empty without Jesus (Jesus) — 4/26/06 Vol. 43
earthly troubles should not disturb our peace (Jesus) — 2/15/00 Vol. 18
earthly vs. spiritual life schism cause of division (Jesus) — 10/23/98 Vol. 13
earthquake at city on coastline (Jesus) — 4/5/06 Vol. 43
earthquake California, large (Jesus) — 5/3/97 Vol. 7
earthquake chastisement (Jesus) — 1/16/95 Vol. 2
earthquake in California near (Jesus) — 9/6/97 Vol. 8
earthquake in modern city (Jesus) — 11/30/04 Vol. 37
earthquake large boom warning (Jesus) — 7/5/06 Vol. 44
earthquake most of California under water (Jesus) — 11/7/05 Vol. 41
earthquake occur in places of sin (Jesus) — 3/1/95 Vol. 2
earthquake red plague,rivers to blood (Jesus) — 12/31/96 Vol. 5
earthquake sign of end times (Jesus) — 12/29/04 Vol. 37
earthquake 9.0 for sexual sins (Jesus) — 10/24/05 Vol. 41
earthquake activity higher with more deaths (Jesus) — 3/29/05 Vol. 38
earthquake disaster punishment for sin (Jesus) — 5/8/06 Vol. 43
earthquake on Calvary death conquered (Jesus) — 1/1/00 Vol. 18
earthquake zones move away from (Jesus) — 11/16/06 Vol. 45
earthquake, large cause ridge on land,coast (Jesus) — 1/18/06 Vol. 42
earthquake, large sign of end times (Jesus) — 12/26/04 Vol. 37
earthquake,center US houses not ready (Jesus) — 5/29/06 Vol. 43

earthquake,West Coast worsened by water (Jesus) — 2/2/06 Vol. 42
earthquakes & future volcanic eruptions (Jesus) — 1/15/04 Vol. 34
earthquakes and volcanoes (Jesus) — 6/29/04 Vol. 35
earthquakes California, middle USA (Jesus) — 10/12/05 Vol. 41
earthquakes chastisement for sin (Jesus) — 7/26/04 Vol. 36
earthquakes evidence of end times (Jesus) — 1/6/00 Vol. 18
earthquakes for sins in California (Jesus) — 11/12/01 Vol. 25
earthquakes in areas of sin (Jesus) — 4/11/02 Vol. 27
earthquakes in Indonesia (Jesus) — 6/1/06 Vol. 43
earthquakes increase & intensity (Jesus) — 8/31/96 Vol. 4
earthquakes increase as sign of times (Jesus) — 6/26/05 Vol. 39
earthquakes increased by solar wind (Jesus) — 5/16/98 Vol. 11
earthquakes more frequent & severe (Jesus) — 1/2/03 Vol. 30
earthquakes more frequent and intense (Jesus) — 6/29/01 Vol. 23
earthquakes more severe to come (Jesus) — 5/23/02 Vol. 27
earthquakes move from area of (Jesus) — 7/23/06 Vol. 44
earthquakes on the increase (Jesus) — 5/10/01 Vol. 23
earthquakes shake out complacency (Jesus) — 5/26/96 Vol. 3
earthquakes sign (Jesus) — 1/17/96 Vol. 3
earthquakes sign of coming eruptions (Jesus) — 3/20/04 Vol. 34
earthquakes sign of end times (Jesus) — 9/21/00 Vol. 20
earthquakes sign of the times (Jesus) — 1/29/01 Vol. 22
earthquakes sign of times (Jesus) — 9/12/02 Vol. 28
earthquakes to change face of earth (Jesus) — 6/24/99 Vol. 15
earthquakes to damage skyscrapers (Jesus) — 12/10/98 Vol. 13
earthquakes tribulation (Jesus) — 5/26/94 Vol. 1
earthquakes trust in angels in safe havens (Jesus) — 8/12/98 Vol. 12
earthquakes volcanoes and famine (Jesus) — 5/1/97 Vol. 7
earthquakes will spread even to US (Jesus) — 9/9/99 Vol. 16
earthquakes & volcanoes about to cause great events (Jesus) — 8/9/04 Vol. 36
earthq. & volcanoes increase in as sign of tribulation (Jesus) — 7/29/04 Vol. 36
earthquakes & volcanoes reflect man's violence (Jesus) — 7/19/06 Vol. 44
earthquakes & volcanoes signs of end times (Jesus) — 4/14/05 Vol. 39
earthquakes continuing with major deaths to come (Jesus) — 3/30/05 Vol. 38
earthquakes in West greater than in Turkey (Jesus) — 8/19/99 Vol. 16
earthquakes, volcanoes sign of end times (Jesus) — 11/11/04 Vol. 37
earthquakes,severe means to test affluent (Jesus) — 11/17/99 Vol. 17
earthquakes,volcanoes by microwaves (Jesus) — 3/21/05 Vol. 38
earthquakes,volcanoes signs of the end times (Jesus) — 9/7/97 Vol. 8
earthquakes,volcanoes will reshape the land (Jesus) — 8/21/97 Vol. 8
earth's conditions need preserving (Jesus) — 6/16/03 Vol. 31
East coast tsunami (Jesus) — 2/18/08 Vol. 50
Easter is a freedom to love (Jesus) — 4/15/01 Vol. 23
Easter Lenten preparation (St. Joseph) — 3/20/96 Vol. 3
Easter life (Jesus) — 4/3/94 Vol. 1
Easter remember true meaning (Jesus) — 3/17/05 Vol. 38
Easter victory over death (Jesus) — 3/30/97 Vol. 6

Easter Candle Alpha & Omega of life (Jesus) — 4/27/06 Vol. 43

Easter Candle at birth & death (Jesus) — 4/12/05 Vol. 39

Easter celebration triumph of Jesus (Jesus) — 4/3/99 Vol. 15

Easter Conference title given (Jesus) — 12/4/03 Vol. 33

Easter duty Confession for (Jesus) — 3/1/07 Vol. 46

Easter Duty Confession in Lent,Easter (Jesus) — 3/23/07 Vol. 46

Easter duty go to Confession (Jesus) — 3/4/98 Vol. 10

Easter duty purify inside to match outside (Jesus) — 3/21/02 Vol. 26

Easter new life from Confession,devotions (Jesus) — 3/29/99 Vol. 14

Easter people gift of faith from evangelist (Jesus) — 4/16/97 Vol. 7

Easter Resurrection reflected in nature (Jesus) — 4/16/02 Vol. 27

Easter Season cannot praise God enough (Jesus) — 4/29/07 Vol. 47

Easter Season gift of new life (Jesus) — 4/17/01 Vol. 23

Easter Season of Light & new life (Jesus) — 4/23/05 Vol. 39

Easter Sunday gates of heaven opened (Jesus) — 4/12/98 Vol. 11

Easter Sunday new celebration of Jesus (Jesus) — 4/30/06 Vol. 43

Eastern mysticism attention away from God (Jesus) — 9/7/99 Vol. 16

Eastern Rite more reverence than Catholics (Jesus) — 1/14/05 Vol. 38

Eastern Rite churches have kept traditions (Jesus) — 9/9/04 Vol. 36

Eastern Rite Churches pray for unity (Jesus) — 5/16/98 Vol. 11

eavesdropping on conversations (Jesus) — 6/5/01 Vol. 23

ebola deadlier weapons desired (Jesus) — 11/1/00 Vol. 21

eclipse a whirlwind of events (Jesus) — 2/19/98 Vol. 10

eclipse Antichrist (Jesus) — 10/14/94 Vol. 2

eclipse omen of evil (Jesus) — 8/12/99 Vol. 16

eclipse sign in the heavens (Jesus) — 2/20/97 Vol. 6

eclipse sign of dramatic events (Jesus) — 1/29/98 Vol. 10

eclipse sign of events (Mary) — 10/9/97 Vol. 9

eclipse sign of evil (Jesus) — 8/5/99 Vol. 16

eclipse signs & omens of war (Jesus) — 9/26/96 Vol. 4

eclipse warning (Jesus) — 12/3/94 Vol. 2

eclipse warning (Jesus) — 4/9/95 Vol. 2

eclipse of sun sign of evil (Jesus) — 12/26/00 Vol. 21

eclipses and asteroids omens of things to come (Jesus) — 3/12/98 Vol. 10

economic changes jobs controlled (Jesus) — 5/3/98 Vol. 11

economic decline shadows US moral decline (Jesus) — 7/25/02 Vol. 28

economic depression stability (Jesus) — 2/5/99 Vol. 14

economic downturn and food shortages (Jesus) — 1/18/01 Vol. 22

economies ready to collapse (Jesus) — 9/3/98 Vol. 12

economies chaotic signs for Antichrist (Jesus) — 8/31/98 Vol. 12

economy affected by disasters (Jesus) — 6/12/02 Vol. 27

economy affected by war (Jesus) — 10/1/02 Vol. 29

economy and fuel supplies (Jesus) — 11/3/05 Vol. 41

economy and ID chips (Jesus) — 10/16/02 Vol. 29

economy bankruptcies,markets to fall (Jesus) — 3/19/98 Vol. 10

economy brought down by war (Jesus) — 1/16/03 Vol. 30

economy brought to knees (Jesus) — 6/6/02 Vol. 27

economy bubble of debt, severe problems (Jesus) — 1/14/04 Vol. 34

economy deficits self-defeating (Jesus) — 5/29/03 Vol. 31

economy downturn (Jesus) — 1/30/03 Vol. 30

economy effected by a war (Jesus) — 12/6/01 Vol. 25

economy factories (Jesus) — 7/4/95 Vol. 3

economy food and jobs (Jesus) — 2/3/96 Vol. 3

economy inevitable collapse (Jesus) — 10/2/03 Vol. 33

economy is suffering for sins (Jesus) — 9/4/03 Vol. 32

economy jobs exported (Jesus) — 9/26/02 Vol. 28

economy problems persist (Jesus) — 1/16/02 Vol. 26

economy recession to deepen (Jesus) — 2/7/08 Vol. 50

economy rich demand more profits (Jesus) — 1/29/98 Vol. 10

economy standard of living declining (Jesus) — 7/18/02 Vol. 28

economy stock market brought low (Jesus) — 1/14/99 Vol. 14

economy strained by hurricane (Jesus) — 10/5/05 Vol. 41

economy taxes & stock market (Jesus) — 1/30/03 Vol. 30

economy teetering on disaster (Jesus) — 6/28/01 Vol. 23

economy to continue problems (Jesus) — 12/11/01 Vol. 25

economy turns down (Jesus) — 9/26/00 Vol. 20

economy war destroys markets (Jesus) — 10/7/02 Vol. 29

economy worsened by war (Jesus) — 10/31/02 Vol. 29

economy & jobs struggle because of sins (Jesus) — 7/5/04 Vol. 36

economy & jobs unrepentent sins (Jesus) — 1/8/04 Vol. 34

economy of America into bankruptcy & default (Jesus) — 1/4/04 Vol. 34

economy of America suffers from fuel problems (Jesus) — 5/27/04 Vol. 35

ecosystem is finite on earth (Jesus) — 3/7/07 Vol. 46

ecumenism in one world religion (Jesus) — 4/13/00 Vol. 19

ecumenism,false follows one world religion (Jesus) — 7/27/00 Vol. 20

ecumenism,false see in New Age movement (Jesus) — 6/4/00 Vol. 19

Ed Leary, my father Jocelyn linked (Jesus) — 2/4/08 Vol. 50

Ed Leary's funeral thanks to helpers (Dad) — 2/8/01 Vol. 22

educate children in faith (Jesus) — 9/6/02 Vol. 28

Education children (Mary) — 2/20/94 Vol. 1

education children (Mary) — 2/20/94 Vol. 1

education of young people in faith (Jesus) — 8/1/01 Vol. 24

education parents' responsibility (Jesus) — 10/2/97 Vol. 9

education proud (Jesus) — 12/3/94 Vol. 2

education secular,religious classes (Jesus) — 10/30/97 Vol. 9

education costs need to be cut (Jesus) — 9/14/06 Vol. 44

education, Catholic watered down (Jesus) — 10/22/02 Vol. 29

Egypt Antichrist (Jesus) — 4/8/95 Vol. 2

Egypt evil raised up from (Jesus) — 5/14/98 Vol. 11

Egypt evil reborn (Mary) — 12/4/97 Vol. 9

Egypt flight to avoid Herod (Jesus) — 12/28/00 Vol. 21

Egypt old gods worshipped (Jesus) — 12/5/96 Vol. 5

Egypt temple (Jesus) — 12/29/94 Vol. 2

Egypt use of evil for good (Jesus) — 7/11/97 Vol. 8

Egypt old gods return knowledge (Jesus)   9/20/95 Vol. 3
Egyptian gods resurface in New Age (Jesus)   1/6/00 Vol. 18
Egyptians pride brought down (Jesus)   12/6/00 Vol. 21
Eight nation meeting secrecy of meetings (Jesus)   6/25/02 Vol. 27
Eight Nations modern day lions (Jesus)   6/26/97 Vol. 7
El Nino causing more storms (Jesus)   1/2/03 Vol. 30
El Nino storm chastisements (Jesus)   9/25/97 Vol. 8
El Nino weather machines (Jesus)   1/15/03 Vol. 30
elderly help and cheer up (Jesus)   2/14/08 Vol. 50
elderly need your assistance (Jesus)   3/27/08 Vol. 50
elderly people in sickness and death (Jesus)   4/14/04 Vol. 35
Elect follow Jesus' way of life (Jesus)   2/16/06 Vol. 42
election of women is good (Jesus)   10/26/06 Vol. 45
election 2000 caused division (Jesus)   11/14/00 Vol. 21
election 2000 choose life (Jesus)   11/17/00 Vol. 21
election 2000 pray for (Jesus)   8/30/00 Vol. 20
election choices battle against abortion (Jesus)   11/3/00 Vol. 21
election of actions between good & evil (Jesus)   1/17/05 Vol. 38
election of God results at the judgment (Jesus)   11/8/00 Vol. 21
election results against Iraq War (Jesus)   11/8/06 Vol. 45
election terrorism being guarded against (Jesus)   10/22/04 Vol. 37
election terrorism Spain, Russia, potential in US (Jesus) 8/25/04 Vol. 36
elections death culture vs. life issues (Jesus)   11/1/04 Vol. 37
elections decision for USA (Jesus)   9/19/96 Vol. 4
elections greed (Jesus)   11/8/94 Vol. 2
elections money vs moral decay (Jesus)   8/19/96 Vol. 4
elections one world control of US (Jesus)   11/7/02 Vol. 29
elections for life small reprieve in disasters (Jesus) 11/30/04 Vol. 37
elections for president parties controlled by rich (Jesus) 10/3/00 Vol. 21
electric lines vulnerable & controlled (Jesus)   2/4/03 Vol. 30
electrical devices Antichrist (Jesus)   10/20/95 Vol. 3
electrical devices communications (Jesus)   8/21/96 Vol. 4
electrical devices gratitude (St. Therese)   6/7/95 Vol. 2
electrical devices idols (Jesus)   6/12/95 Vol. 2
electrical devices rid, Antichrist declaration (Jesus) 11/29/97 Vol. 9
electrical devices wash lines (Jesus)   8/10/94 Vol. 2
electrical power failures and brownouts (Jesus)   6/15/02 Vol. 27
electrical power manipulated (Jesus)   12/29/00 Vol. 21
electrical power more foresight (Jesus)   5/10/01 Vol. 23
electricity power outages (Jesus)   6/26/98 Vol. 11
electricity vulnerable, dependent on (Jesus)   10/25/03 Vol. 33
electricity & devices will not always be available (Jesus) 7/25/02 Vol. 28
electricity & fuel storms and shortages (Jesus)   10/30/97 Vol. 9
electricity & heating fuels are more expensive (Jesus) 12/2/04 Vol. 37
electricity dependence for many things in life (Jesus) 12/15/04 Vol. 37
electricity loss trust in God (Jesus)   1/21/95 Vol. 2
electricity needs conservation & efficiency (Jesus)   7/2/07 Vol. 48

electricity production attacked by terrorists (Jesus)   2/9/04 Vol. 34
electricity, loss of confusion during takeover (Jesus) 9/20/07 Vol. 48
electricity, vulnerable grid failures, ice storms (Jesus) 7/28/07 Vol. 48
electronic connections Antichrist's hypnotism (Jesus)   7/17/96 Vol. 4
electronic connections do away with at tribulation (Jesus) 11/20/97 Vol. 9
electronic devices control of life (Jesus)   12/26/96 Vol. 5
electronic devices do not let them control you (Jesus) 10/22/04 Vol. 37
electronic devices during tribulation (Jesus)   5/29/96 Vol. 3
electronic devices refuse control of your life (Jesus) 6/28/01 Vol. 23
electronic devices run our lives (Jesus)   2/14/98 Vol. 10
electronic gadgets avoid them (Jesus)   11/4/97 Vol. 9
electronic marvels entrap children (Jesus)   12/30/96 Vol. 5
electronic records control of lives (Jesus)   4/15/03 Vol. 31
electronics distractions of evil (Jesus)   3/19/98 Vol. 10
electronics helicopters & satellites (Jesus)   3/18/97 Vol. 6
elements justice (Jesus)   1/3/96 Vol. 3
elevator hiding (Jesus)   1/3/95 Vol. 2
elevator need direction first (Jesus)   8/10/98 Vol. 12
eleventh hour still available to be saved (Jesus)   1/13/00 Vol. 18
Elijah allegience to God or Baal (Jesus)   6/9/04 Vol. 35
Elijah called down fire from God (Jesus)   6/14/06 Vol. 43
Elvera Cappiello funeral message (Jesus)   8/26/03 Vol. 32
emergency manufactured crisis (Jesus)   1/3/01 Vol. 22
emergency martial law planned for surprise (Jesus)   1/4/00 Vol. 18
Emmaus share gifts (Jesus)   3/12/95 Vol. 2
Emmaus, road to disciples hearts burning (Jesus)   4/19/06 Vol. 43
Emmaus, road to Jesus fulfilled prophecies (Jesus)   4/14/04 Vol. 35
Emmaus, road to Scriptures explained (Jesus)   3/30/05 Vol. 38
Emmet Murphy, Msgr funeral (Jesus)   3/1/08 Vol. 50
EMP attack need vacuum tubes (Jesus)   3/6/08 Vol. 50
EMP pulse weapon destorys chip devices (Jesus)   3/24/06 Vol. 42
EMP pulse weapon stops electricity, cars (Jesus)   10/31/06 Vol. 45
EMP threats to chips & electricity (Jesus)   2/4/06 Vol. 42
empathy needed for Iraqi people (Jesus)   4/25/07 Vol. 47
empires rise and fall (Jesus)   1/30/97 Vol. 6
employee giving fair work? (Jesus)   9/18/05 Vol. 40
employees just wages & benefits (Jesus)   9/21/97 Vol. 8
employers to suffer for ill-gotten gains (Jesus)   12/5/98 Vol. 13
employers too greedy stop layoffs,make jobs (Jesus)   11/12/98 Vol. 13
employers, greedy to pay for crimes (Jesus)   1/17/08 Vol. 50
employment being lost abroad (Jesus)   5/22/03 Vol. 31
employment God will provide (Jesus)   2/28/08 Vol. 50
empty cross rose smell   8/22/93 Vol. 1
empty one's heart to make room for Jesus (Jesus)   7/31/00 Vol. 20
empty pews abortion (Jesus)   1/22/95 Vol. 2
empty self to love others (Jesus)   2/4/00 Vol. 18
empty your hearts for indwelling of Jesus' Spirit (Jesus) 5/16/00 Vol. 19

enablers are not helping sinners (Jesus) — 5/9/06 Vol. 43

end days Era of Peace, renewed earth (Jesus) — 11/26/04 Vol. 37

end days evil ones cast into hell (Jesus) — 11/16/03 Vol. 33

end days foretold by recent prophets (Jesus) — 12/20/03 Vol. 33

end days fulfilled in Revelation (Jesus) — 2/2/98 Vol. 10

end days fulfillment of Scripture (Jesus) — 1/25/98 Vol. 10

end days order of events (Jesus) — 11/19/00 Vol. 21

end days prepared with pure soul (Jesus) — 10/22/03 Vol. 33

end days wheat & chaff separated (Jesus) — 5/23/03 Vol. 31

end days signs eclipses, asteroid fly bys (Jesus) — 5/13/04 Vol. 35

end of age separate goats from lambs (Jesus) — 3/3/05 Vol. 38

end of time after Era of Peace (Jesus) — 9/20/99 Vol. 16

end time only God the Father knows (Jesus) — 11/18/07 Vol. 49

end time preparations refuges, food & water (Jesus) — 9/10/05 Vol. 40

end time prophecies must be fulfilled (Jesus) — 4/11/07 Vol. 47

end time signs blindness to big picture (Jesus) — 11/29/02 Vol. 29

end time signs earthquake & tidal waves (Jesus) — 12/26/04 Vol. 37

end time signs earthquakes,epidemics,wars (Jesus) — 8/28/01 Vol. 24

end time signs in front of your eyes (Jesus) — 9/9/04 Vol. 36

end time signs in Hurricane Katrina (Jesus) — 8/30/05 Vol. 40

end times announced by messengers (Jesus) — 1/28/06 Vol. 42

end times are at the door (Jesus) — 11/20/06 Vol. 45

end times battle (Jesus) — 3/27/94 Vol. 1

end times battle of good and evil (Jesus) — 7/20/96 Vol. 4

end times clergy (Jesus) — 5/2/94 Vol. 1

end times conversion time short (Jesus) — 9/20/99 Vol. 16

end times do not fear with God's help (Jesus) — 5/24/98 Vol. 11

end times do not lose heart (Jesus) — 6/27/01 Vol. 23

end times don't worry about dates (Jesus) — 7/6/99 Vol. 16

end times evil to test faith (Jesus) — 1/12/04 Vol. 34

end times freedoms (Jesus) — 5/13/94 Vol. 1

end times in our lifetime (Jesus) — 11/26/01 Vol. 25

end times in your lifetime (Jesus) — 11/19/06 Vol. 45

end times lie at the door (Jesus) — 2/5/98 Vol. 10

end times New Covenant (Jesus) — 4/27/94 Vol. 1

end times pestilence,famine, earthquakes (Jesus) — 8/17/06 Vol. 44

end times pray for grace to endure (Jesus) — 12/31/00 Vol. 21

end times prepare,love God,neighbor (Jesus) — 11/10/96 Vol. 5

end times read about in Bible (Jesus) — 11/28/03 Vol. 33

end times read signs of (Jesus) — 2/5/04 Vol. 34

end times sacramentals (Jesus) — 6/27/94 Vol. 1

end times Scripture fulfilled in warnings (Jesus) — 9/12/04 Vol. 36

end times seeing signs (Jesus) — 10/5/01 Vol. 25

end times signs all around us (Jesus) — 6/7/06 Vol. 43

end times signs in the sun (Jesus) — 6/18/98 Vol. 11

end times signs of (Jesus) — 6/3/04 Vol. 35

end times victory over Satan (Jesus) — 11/19/01 Vol. 25

end times victory, not doom & gloom (Jesus) — 11/17/05 Vol. 41

end times warn of signs of tribulation (Jesus) — 11/23/04 Vol. 37

end times message personal mission (Jesus) — 9/1/06 Vol. 44

end times signs only seen through eyes of faith (Jesus) — 10/11/04 Vol. 37

end times signs repent, purify souls (Jesus) — 12/12/05 Vol. 41

endless love in green wreath symbol (Jesus) — 7/14/00 Vol. 20

endurance in prayer and deeds (Jesus) — 4/13/04 Vol. 35

endurance in life physical & spiritual tests (Jesus) — 1/21/05 Vol. 38

enemies love & forgive (Jesus) — 3/7/05 Vol. 38

enemies love & forgive (Jesus) — 7/11/04 Vol. 36

enemies love and forgive (Jesus) — 6/15/04 Vol. 35

enemies love them (Jesus) — 8/14/03 Vol. 32

enemies love them (Jesus) — 4/27/02 Vol. 27

enemies love them (Jesus) — 2/22/04 Vol. 34

enemies more forgiven, more graces (Jesus) — 9/11/03 Vol. 32

enemies perfection (Jesus) — 7/16/95 Vol. 3

enemies & persecutors love them (Jesus) — 9/12/02 Vol. 28

enemy, determined danger to America (Jesus) — 5/24/07 Vol. 47

energy danger of new form of (Jesus) — 10/9/03 Vol. 33

energy food & spiritual grace (Jesus) — 10/15/05 Vol. 41

energy have extra fuel on hand (Jesus) — 10/31/02 Vol. 29

energy reduce pollution (Jesus) — 6/13/02 Vol. 27

energy & fossil fuels limited, use hydrogen & alcohol (Jesus) — 1/10/02 Vol. 26

energy & fuel price gouging (Jesus) — 1/22/04 Vol. 34

energy & fuel seek new sources (Jesus) — 3/7/07 Vol. 46

energy & fuel supplies being controlled (Jesus) — 7/19/01 Vol. 24

energy & power America consumes too much (Jesus) — 1/4/01 Vol. 22

energy consumption conserve more (Jesus) — 5/24/01 Vol. 23

energy needs alternatives,conserve,efficient (Jesus) — 1/24/07 Vol. 46

energy prices affected by unusual temps (Jesus) — 1/4/07 Vol. 46

energy prices hurting the poor (Jesus) — 12/8/05 Vol. 41

energy production and green house gases (Jesus) — 6/21/01 Vol. 23

energy saving conservation & efficiency (Jesus) — 11/25/07 Vol. 49

energy sources conserve by less demand (Jesus) — 8/23/01 Vol. 24

energy sources protect environment (Jesus) — 7/10/03 Vol. 32

energy sources reduce usage (Jesus) — 2/15/07 Vol. 46

energy sources share with all (Jesus) — 7/27/06 Vol. 44

energy supplies make serious choices (Jesus) — 5/17/01 Vol. 23

energy supply is being strained (Jesus) — 2/5/04 Vol. 34

energy usage must be atmosphere friendly (Jesus) — 8/18/04 Vol. 36

England Common market (Jesus) — 11/7/97 Vol. 9

England elusive peace (Jesus) — 3/13/96 Vol. 3

England keep roots of faith (Jesus) — 7/10/96 Vol. 3

England run by secret government (Jesus) — 7/24/99 Vol. 16

enlightenment will see souls as God does (Jesus) — 4/7/98 Vol. 11

entertainment demand of worldly (Jesus) — 3/29/00 Vol. 18

entertainment distractions of the world (Jesus) — 8/7/97 Vol. 8

entertainment movies and TV (Jesus) — 5/29/96 Vol. 3

entertainment poisoning children's minds (Jesus) — 3/2/98 Vol. 10

enthronement of Sac. H. welcome in home (Jesus) — 6/19/98 Vol. 11

environment balance of nature (Jesus) — 4/11/02 Vol. 27

environment balance of nature (Jesus) — 9/24/02 Vol. 28

environment causes cancers (Jesus) — 1/31/03 Vol. 30

environment clean air (Jesus) — 1/10/02 Vol. 26

environment do not abuse resources (Jesus) — 4/23/98 Vol. 11

environment God's care of the earth (Jesus) — 2/6/97 Vol. 6

environment greenhouse effect (Jesus) — 7/25/02 Vol. 28

environment harder to correct abuses (Jesus) — 9/19/02 Vol. 28

environment keep balance of nature (Jesus) — 12/11/97 Vol. 9

environment keep clean of pollution (Jesus) — 12/6/04 Vol. 37

environment manke makes war on (Jesus) — 12/25/04 Vol. 37

environment protect balance of nature (Jesus) — 2/16/08 Vol. 50

environment protect natural resources (Jesus) — 8/23/01 Vol. 24

environment protect nature & animals (Jesus) — 5/5/05 Vol. 39

environment storms caused by abuse (Jesus) — 2/12/98 Vol. 10

environment threatened by burning fuels (Jesus) — 11/11/04 Vol. 37

environment to be recreated (Jesus) — 3/4/99 Vol. 14

environment war and pollution (Jesus) — 2/13/98 Vol. 10

environment work to improve (Jesus) — 4/7/05 Vol. 39

environment, clean pass on to children (Jesus) — 5/2/07 Vol. 47

environment,destruction cause of problems (Jesus) — 3/1/99 Vol. 14

environmental abuses need correction (Jesus) — 5/15/06 Vol. 43

environmental damage affecting balance of nature (Jesus) — 11/21/03 Vol. 33

environmentalists need numbers verified (Jesus) — 4/27/07 Vol. 47

envy & jealousy temptations over goods,women (Jesus) — 3/1/02 Vol. 26

Ephesus, Turkey seek your own sainthood (Jesus) — 11/1/98 Vol. 13

epidemic from chem trails (Jesus) — 7/5/07 Vol. 48

epidemic from man-made virus (Jesus) — 6/9/07 Vol. 47

epidemic diseases sign of end times (Jesus) — 2/1/01 Vol. 22

epidemic, bombs event for takeover (Jesus) — 9/20/07 Vol. 48

epidemics AIDS,tuberculosis,pneumonia (Jesus) — 3/29/01 Vol. 22

epidemics of disease among man at tribulation (Jesus) — 7/26/01 Vol. 24

epidemics of disease hemorrhaging (Jesus) — 5/4/02 Vol. 27

Epiphany bring gifts for a king (Jesus) — 1/7/01 Vol. 22

Epiphany give adoration & honor (Jesus) — 1/2/99 Vol. 14

Epiphany heal (Jesus) — 1/6/96 Vol. 3

Epiphany heavenly gifts (Jesus) — 1/5/97 Vol. 6

Epiphany keep close in Confession (Jesus) — 1/4/04 Vol. 34

Epiphany Kingship over mankind (Jesus) — 1/6/02 Vol. 26

Epiphany Magi followed star (Jesus) — 1/6/08 Vol. 50

Epiphany sacrifices & homage (Jesus) — 1/5/03 Vol. 30

Epiphany warnings as to wise men (Jesus) — 1/2/00 Vol. 18

Episcopal Church homosexual bishop (Jesus) — 8/7/03 Vol. 32

equal love for all no discrimination (Jesus) — 5/31/00 Vol. 19

equality of all before God (Jesus) — 4/27/02 Vol. 27

Era of Peace after brief suffering (Jesus) — 5/12/98 Vol. 11

Era of Peace after purification (Jesus) — 8/8/97 Vol. 8

Era of Peace after purification (Jesus) — 9/4/97 Vol. 8

Era of Peace after suffering purification (Jesus) — 2/19/99 Vol. 14

Era of Peace after victory over evil (Jesus) — 11/13/03 Vol. 33

Era of Peace after victory over evil (Jesus) — 5/23/02 Vol. 27

Era of Peace all order restored (God the Father) — 8/7/99 Vol. 16

Era of Peace be faithful in tribulation (Jesus) — 5/9/98 Vol. 11

Era of Peace coming soon (Jesus) — 2/17/97 Vol. 6

Era of Peace darkness overcome (Jesus) — 7/16/03 Vol. 32

Era of Peace earth cleansed & renewed (Jesus) — 2/4/08 Vol. 50

Era of Peace earth renewed (Jesus) — 11/16/05 Vol. 41

Era of Peace earth renewed (Jesus) — 9/9/04 Vol. 36

Era of Peace earth renewed (Jesus) — 10/6/06 Vol. 45

Era of Peace end of evil age (Jesus) — 2/17/97 Vol. 6

Era of Peace evil destroyed (Jesus) — 10/5/02 Vol. 29

Era of Peace evil removed (Jesus) — 6/8/02 Vol. 27

Era of Peace faithful enjoy reward (Jesus) — 10/6/03 Vol. 33

Era of Peace faithful raised up (Jesus) — 6/15/99 Vol. 15

Era of Peace free from evil (Jesus) — 10/6/99 Vol. 17

Era of Peace granted to believers (Jesus) — 3/21/03 Vol. 30

Era of Peace grow in Divine Will (Jesus) — 1/7/99 Vol. 14

Era of Peace heaven on earth,Jerusalem (Jesus) — 4/3/00 Vol. 19

Era of Peace hope (Jesus) — 5/10/94 Vol. 1

Era of Peace hope and joy (Jesus) — 6/5/96 Vol. 3

Era of Peace illuminated earth (Jesus) — 10/28/02 Vol. 29

Era of Peace in lifetime (Jesus) — 9/27/96 Vol. 4

Era of Peace Isaiah 40:3 (Jesus) — 11/26/99 Vol. 17

Era of Peace land of milk and honey (Jesus) — 3/23/98 Vol. 10

Era of Peace land of milk and honey (Jesus) — 10/31/97 Vol. 9

Era of Peace lead by resurrected saints (Jesus) — 12/18/97 Vol. 9

Era of Peace life before fall (Jesus) — 8/12/06 Vol. 44

era of peace lifetime (Jesus) — 3/2/94 Vol. 1

Era of Peace like Promised Land (Jesus) — 8/13/03 Vol. 32

Era of Peace live in the Divine Will (Jesus) — 9/30/96 Vol. 4

Era of Peace new heavens and new earth (Jesus) — 11/6/05 Vol. 41

Era of Peace new Jerusalem (Jesus) — 7/2/98 Vol. 12

Era of Peace no evil or pain (Jesus) — 12/3/99 Vol. 17

Era of Peace no evil or wars (Jesus) — 7/3/99 Vol. 16

Era of Peace no evil, no pain (Jesus) — 12/15/99 Vol. 17

Era of Peace no more evil (Jesus) — 6/18/02 Vol. 27

Era of Peace our Easter Sunday (Jesus) — 3/28/98 Vol. 10

Era of Peace paradise recreated (Jesus) — 6/17/99 Vol. 15

Era of Peace prepare by being faithful (Jesus) — 4/9/98 Vol. 11

Era of Peace prepares yourself for heaven (Jesus) — 9/26/98 Vol. 12

Era of Peace purification,original sin (Jesus) — 2/2/97 Vol. 6

St. Therese's Rose

On another pilgrimage to Betania, we took a side trip to Angel Falls. This is the highest water falls in the world, but it is located in the middle of the jungle. The only way to get there is by canoe up the river or by a small plane. We arrived by plane, but took a dug out canoe up the river to climb up to the falls. As we were getting into the canoe, Gerry stumbled on something and when he looked down there was a perfectly fresh long stem red rose. He gave it to us and our friend Marie even saved one of the pedals and eventually put it in plexiglass for us. It is shaped like a monstrance. After returning home, St. Therese gave us a message saying that she gave the rose to us as a gift for Valentine's Day. In the jungle we were not even thinking of what day it was.

St. Therese is also our spiritual director from heaven and she is always trying to guide us on our way to be more perfect with several messages to John.

Message: March 11, 1996 (volume 3)

Era of Peace reign over the earth (Jesus)	2/1/99 Vol. 14	Era of Peace reward for faithful (Jesus)	3/24/03 Vol. 30
Era of Peace renewal,New Jerusalem (Jesus)	4/27/00 Vol. 19	Era of Peace reward for faithful (Jesus)	3/8/99 Vol. 14
Era of Peace renewed earth,fulfill Scripture (Jesus)	4/23/00 Vol. 19	Era of Peace Scripture fulfilled (Jesus)	6/4/02 Vol. 27
Era of Peace reward for faithful (Jesus)	7/1/03 Vol. 32	Era of Peace share in Divine Will (Jesus)	9/15/03 Vol. 32
Era of Peace reward for faithful (Jesus)	5/2/03 Vol. 31	Era of Peace taken up to safe place (Jesus)	4/30/96 Vol. 3
Era of Peace reward for faithful (Jesus)	6/13/02 Vol. 27	Era of Peace triumph over evil (Jesus)	3/9/99 Vol. 14

Era of Peace trust and patience (Jesus) — 9/1/97 Vol. 8
Era of Peace victory after tribulation (Jesus) — 6/2/05 Vol. 39
Era of Peace well worth the wait (Jesus) — 6/10/99 Vol. 15
Era of Peace without abuse,manipulation (Jesus) — 6/11/06 Vol. 43
Era of Peace granted if enough prayed (Jesus) — 6/5/06 Vol. 43
errors forfeit authority & obedience (Jesus) — 9/28/98 Vol. 12
eternal destination heaven or hell (Jesus) — 5/19/06 Vol. 43
eternal destination higher than earthly concerns (Jesus) — 3/14/06 Vol. 42
eternal destination make time to prepare (Jesus) — 3/14/01 Vol. 22
eternal destination man created to be in heaven (Jesus) — 9/13/98 Vol. 12
eternal destination most important subject (Jesus) — 5/4/06 Vol. 43
eternal destiny worth more than long life (Jesus) — 4/20/99 Vol. 15
Eternal Father prayer group dedicated (God the Father) — 8/14/97 Vol. 8
Eternal Father Prayer Group He's greatly pleased (Jesus) — 2/4/04 Vol. 34
eternal life accept Savior, repent (Jesus) — 4/6/06 Vol. 43
eternal life better than earthly desires (Jesus) — 1/27/06 Vol. 42
eternal life choice of heaven or hell (Jesus) — 5/18/05 Vol. 39
eternal life choice of heaven or hell (Jesus) — 11/27/04 Vol. 37
eternal life final judgment (Jesus) — 3/29/95 Vol. 2
eternal life for following His ways (Jesus) — 4/11/04 Vol. 35
eternal life for taking Holy Communion (Jesus) — 4/27/07 Vol. 47
eternal life greater glory for deeds (Jesus) — 9/25/99 Vol. 16
eternal life in Jesus' Body & Blood (Jesus) — 5/21/04 Vol. 35
eternal life in Resurrection (Jesus) — 4/19/01 Vol. 23
eternal life must eat Body, Blood of Jesus (Jesus) — 1/25/06 Vol. 42
eternal life not attainable by riches (Jesus) — 8/2/02 Vol. 28
eternal life now open to every soul (Jesus) — 4/15/00 Vol. 19
eternal life only through Jesus (Jesus) — 4/28/06 Vol. 43
eternal life promise for faithful (Jesus) — 5/4/03 Vol. 31
eternal life Savior, forgiveness of sins (Jesus) — 10/28/03 Vol. 33
eternal life with receiving Eucharist (Jesus) — 5/17/06 Vol. 43
eternal life worth more than news (Jesus) — 11/29/99 Vol. 17
eternal life gamble living in mortal sin risks hell (Jesus) — 8/12/00 Vol. 20
Eternal life in heaven more valuable than earthly life (Jesus) — 3/31/04 Vol. 34
eternal life preparation more valuable than things (Jesus) — 5/18/00 Vol. 19
eternal life,gateway in Eucharist (Jesus) — 3/19/00 Vol. 18
eternal now prepare soul by Confession (Jesus) — 2/18/98 Vol. 10
eternal rest goal of earthly striving (Jesus) — 1/28/05 Vol. 38
eternal salvation requires forgiveness of sins (Jesus) — 8/2/00 Vol. 20
eternity heaven, hell, purgatory (Jesus) — 9/15/00 Vol. 20
eternity prepare for in faith (Jesus) — 7/19/99 Vol. 16
eternity in heaven better than body comforts (Jesus) — 9/5/99 Vol. 16
eternity in hell feeling of how long (Jesus) — 7/21/97 Vol. 8
eternity vs lifetime value of conversion (Jesus) — 8/3/00 Vol. 20
eternity with God better than in hell (Jesus) — 3/23/06 Vol. 42
ethanol & hydrogen alternates to oil (Jesus) — 11/17/04 Vol. 37
ethnic conflicts war is never a solution (Jesus) — 2/18/99 Vol. 14

Eucharist a taste of heaven (Jesus) — 4/15/05 Vol. 39
Eucharist Antichrist (Jesus) — 12/4/94 Vol. 2
Eucharist at Last Supper (Jesus) — 4/8/04 Vol. 35
Eucharist Blessed Sacrament (Jesus) — 3/22/95 Vol. 2
Eucharist bomb — 8/8/93 Vol. 1
Eucharist Bread of Life (Jesus) — 5/21/01 Vol. 23
Eucharist Bread of Life (Jesus) — 5/5/03 Vol. 31
Eucharist breaking bread with Jesus (Jesus) — 6/1/00 Vol. 19
Eucharist center of gathering (Jesus) — 5/22/00 Vol. 19
Eucharist closest to heaven on earth (Jesus) — 10/28/02 Vol. 29
Eucharist Confession (Jesus) — 8/28/94 Vol. 2
Eucharist conquered death and sin (Jesus) — 4/21/96 Vol. 3
Eucharist crib (Jesus) — 12/17/94 Vol. 2
Eucharist daily (Jesus) — 10/3/94 Vol. 2
Eucharist daily spiritual nourishment (Jesus) — 5/13/05 Vol. 39
Eucharist eternal flame of love (Jesus) — 6/26/03 Vol. 31
Eucharist flock (Jesus) — 2/1/94 Vol. 1
Eucharist forgiveness (Jesus) — 4/21/95 Vol. 2
Eucharist freedoms (Jesus) — 11/25/93 Vol. 1
Eucharist fruits of love (Jesus) — 1/22/02 Vol. 26
Eucharist gift of Jesus (Jesus) — 2/7/05 Vol. 38
Eucharist gift of Jesus (Jesus) — 3/24/05 Vol. 38
Eucharist gift of Jesus' Body & Blood (Jesus) — 4/13/00 Vol. 19
Eucharist gift of Jesus to everyone (Jesus) — 2/24/08 Vol. 50
Eucharist gift of love (Jesus) — 4/17/03 Vol. 31
Eucharist gift of Real Presence (Jesus) — 11/30/03 Vol. 33
Eucharist gift of sacramental presence (Jesus) — 11/15/03 Vol. 33
Eucharist gives eternal life (Jesus) — 4/29/04 Vol. 35
Eucharist grace & mercy offered (Jesus) — 3/14/99 Vol. 14
Eucharist grace of strength (Jesus) — 8/19/00 Vol. 20
Eucharist graces to endure life (Jesus) — 3/18/08 Vol. 50
Eucharist great gift from Jesus (Jesus) — 9/10/06 Vol. 44
Eucharist greatest gift FREE (Jesus) — 2/14/98 Vol. 10
Eucharist is a thanksgiving (Jesus) — 11/16/00 Vol. 21
Eucharist is Bread of Life (Jesus) — 4/20/02 Vol. 27
Eucharist is Bread of Life (Jesus) — 4/23/04 Vol. 35
Eucharist is food for soul (Jesus) — 10/15/05 Vol. 41
Eucharist love and obedience (Jesus) — 2/6/96 Vol. 3
Eucharist manna (Jesus) — 10/24/94 Vol. 2
Eucharist most important gift (Jesus) — 4/7/99 Vol. 15
Eucharist most intimate love of creatures (Jesus) — 2/26/02 Vol. 26
Eucharist multiplication of Jesus (Jesus) — 4/28/06 Vol. 43
Eucharist necessary for spiritual life (Jesus) — 10/24/05 Vol. 41
Eucharist needed for eternal life (Jesus) — 12/9/04 Vol. 37
Eucharist preparation (Jesus) — 7/1/95 Vol. 3
Eucharist priests and vocations (Jesus) — 4/4/96 Vol. 3
Eucharist protection and witness (Jesus) — 5/23/96 Vol. 3

Eucharist Real Presence (Jesus) 6/22/03 Vol. 31
Eucharist Real Presence attacked (Jesus) 5/25/03 Vol. 31
Eucharist Real Presence of Jesus (Jesus) 1/9/07 Vol. 46
Eucharist receive all healing needed (Jesus) 10/26/98 Vol. 13
Eucharist renews spiritual life (Jesus) 5/24/01 Vol. 23
Eucharist reverence (Jesus) 4/7/94 Vol. 1
Eucharist reverence needed (Jesus) 11/5/07 Vol. 49
Eucharist sacrilege (Jesus) 3/23/96 Vol. 3
Eucharist satisfies soul forever (Jesus) 1/10/00 Vol. 18
Eucharist source of grace and rest (Jesus) 7/12/01 Vol. 24
Eucharist spiritual bread,food of soul (Jesus) 4/22/99 Vol. 15
Eucharist tabernacles moved aside (Jesus) 8/17/94 Vol. 2
Eucharist taste of heaven, rest (Jesus) 5/20/07 Vol. 47
Eucharist the battle to destroy it (Jesus) 2/6/02 Vol. 26
Eucharist tingling feeling (Jesus) 8/17/03 Vol. 32
Eucharist treasure of Jesus Himself (Jesus) 5/21/04 Vol. 35
Eucharist Tree of life (Jesus) 3/30/03 Vol. 30
Eucharist tribulation (Jesus) 6/19/94 Vol. 1
Eucharist true presence (Jesus) 3/12/97 Vol. 6
Eucharist trust (St. Catherine) 4/29/94 Vol. 1
Eucharist united with Trinity (Jesus) 3/17/06 Vol. 42
Eucharist unity and adoration (Jesus) 10/21/97 Vol. 9
Eucharist until the end of time (Jesus) 1/11/98 Vol. 10
Eucharist we become tabernacles (Jesus) 4/19/98 Vol. 11
Eucharist attacked desecration of Host (Jesus) 5/24/07 Vol. 47
Eucharist in church to be taken away (Jesus) 1/13/00 Vol. 18
Eucharist, miracles of witness of Real Presence (Jesus) 4/12/07 Vol. 47
Eucharist, Year of MOM Conference, Adoration (Jesus) 10/1/04 Vol. 37
Eucharist,Confession provide Light to the soul (Jesus) 7/22/00 Vol. 20
Eucharistic call invites everyone (Jesus) 11/7/06 Vol. 45
Eucharistic Host Real Presence gift (Jesus) 9/28/01 Vol. 24
Eucharistic Hosts need protection (Jesus) 5/18/06 Vol. 43
Eucharistic miracle at Mass, greatest miracle (Jesus) 10/4/04 Vol. 37
Eucharistic miracle Host 2/3 covered in blood (Jesus) 12/11/06 Vol. 45
Eucharistic miracles bleeding Hosts (Jesus) 3/16/99 Vol. 14
Eucharistic miracles proof of Real Presence (Jesus) 11/9/04 Vol. 37
Eucharistic miracles Real Presence (Jesus) 8/13/97 Vol. 8
Eucharistic miracles to believe in Real Presence (Jesus) 6/10/07 Vol. 47
Eucharistic miracles to show Real Presence (Jesus) 10/25/02 Vol. 29
Eucharistic miracles witness Real Presence in Host (Jesus) 5/22/04 Vol. 35
Eucharistic Mystery Body & Blood of Jesus (Jesus) 5/1/04 Vol. 35
Eucharistic visits praise God as the angels (Jesus) 9/3/99 Vol. 16
Euro coin, the symbol of monetary power (Jesus) 5/2/98 Vol. 11
euro currency step to global currency (Jesus) 9/4/01 Vol. 24
Europe events speeding up (Jesus) 2/18/95 Vol. 2
Europe wars (Jesus) 10/7/94 Vol. 2
Europe weather chastisements (Jesus) 8/7/03 Vol. 32

Europe & Asia tested by natural disasters (Jesus) 8/15/02 Vol. 28
Europe rising Antichrist takeover (Jesus) 12/19/02 Vol. 29
European Union gaining in importance (Jesus) 10/27/03 Vol. 33
European Union nations to lose identity (Jesus) 6/19/05 Vol. 39
European Union one world government (Jesus) 6/9/05 Vol. 39
European Union rise to power (Jesus) 7/31/02 Vol. 28
Euro. Union Constitution accept New Age & masons (Jesus) 6/9/05 Vol. 39
euros global currency (Jesus) 8/30/01 Vol. 24
euthanasia in hospital emergencies (Jesus) 10/13/05 Vol. 41
euthanasia Terry Schiavo (Jesus) 3/31/05 Vol. 38
euthanasia, avoid allow purgatory on earth (Jesus) 8/12/02 Vol. 28
euthansia genocide made acceptable (Jesus) 8/5/98 Vol. 12
euthansia protect all life (Jesus) 1/8/97 Vol. 6
evacuations from hurricanes & earthquakes (Jesus) 6/29/06 Vol. 43
evacution plans as year ends (Jesus) 3/3/99 Vol. 14
evangelism how many souls converted (Jesus) 10/22/00 Vol. 21
evangelism needs religious courage (Jesus) 12/30/05 Vol. 41
evangelist calling fishers of men & women (Jesus) 11/30/99 Vol. 17
evangelistic spirit desire to bring souls to God (Jesus) 3/1/01 Vol. 22
evangelists all are called to be (Jesus) 10/8/03 Vol. 33
evangelists bring faith to save souls (Jesus) 8/31/02 Vol. 28
evangelists called by Baptism,Confirmation (Jesus) 8/18/02 Vol. 28
evangelists called to wake people up (Jesus) 1/5/05 Vol. 38
evangelists explain gospel,conversion (Jesus) 4/14/97 Vol. 7
evangelists fishers of men (Jesus) 9/20/07 Vol. 48
evangelists for sainthood (Jesus) 10/26/06 Vol. 45
evangelists save souls (Jesus) 8/3/06 Vol. 44
evangelists waited for Holy Spirit (Jesus) 3/31/97 Vol. 6
evangelists needed to convert sinners (Jesus) 9/15/07 Vol. 48
evangelists of today persecuted for speaking out (Jesus) 5/22/07 Vol. 47
evangelists,all called to save souls (Jesus) 1/23/05 Vol. 38
evangelization all called to (Jesus) 9/4/03 Vol. 32
evangelization all called to do (Jesus) 6/11/05 Vol. 39
evangelization all called to save souls (Jesus) 5/10/04 Vol. 35
evangelization attacked by demons (Jesus) 12/7/01 Vol. 25
evangelization be examples (Jesus) 10/7/01 Vol. 25
evangelization be persistent for souls (Jesus) 6/2/04 Vol. 35
evangelization call of Jesus to everyone (Jesus) 5/17/07 Vol. 47
evangelization called by Baptism (Jesus) 1/8/00 Vol. 18
evangelization despite the risk (Jesus) 4/6/02 Vol. 27
evangelization difficulties leading souls to God (Jesus) 10/9/04 Vol. 37
evangelization everyone's job (Jesus) 2/3/03 Vol. 30
evangelization from power of Holy Spirit (Jesus) 6/8/03 Vol. 31
evangelization give witness (Jesus) 8/16/97 Vol. 8
evangelization grace of mission,shrine (Mother Cabrini) 11/17/96 Vol. 5
evangelization is our mission (Jesus) 9/26/06 Vol. 44
evangelization keep struggling (Jesus) 5/16/01 Vol. 23

evangelization know,love & serve God (Jesus)	4/1/98 Vol. 11	evangelize enthusiasm (Jesus)	1/20/96 Vol. 3
evangelization live message of love (Jesus)	6/18/03 Vol. 31	evangelize especially in family (Holy Spirit)	8/11/96 Vol. 4
evangelization meet resistance of devil (Jesus)	5/27/03 Vol. 31	evangelize especially spiritually lazy (Jesus)	10/24/06 Vol. 45
evangelization mission (Jesus)	5/3/94 Vol. 1	evangelize even if persecuted (Jesus)	4/28/04 Vol. 35
evangelization most important mission (Jesus)	7/9/06 Vol. 44	evangelize even non-Christians (Jesus)	5/27/01 Vol. 23
evangelization most worthy labor of love (Jesus)	7/8/01 Vol. 24	evangelize faith (Jesus)	6/28/94 Vol. 1
evangelization needed for tribulation (Jesus)	7/21/00 Vol. 20	evangelize faith and love (Jesus)	4/15/96 Vol. 3
evangelization of lost sheep (Jesus)	12/7/04 Vol. 37	evangelize fishers of men (Jesus)	2/8/96 Vol. 3
evangelization our mission (Jesus)	5/22/01 Vol. 23	evangelize friends & relatives (Jesus)	7/10/05 Vol. 40
evangelization personal attacks,angels (Jesus)	2/4/97 Vol. 6	evangelize gifts (Jesus)	3/1/94 Vol. 1
evangelization personal mission (Jesus)	10/19/96 Vol. 5	evangelize gospel (St. Luke)	10/18/94 Vol. 2
evangelization preach gospel message (Holy Spirit)	10/28/96 Vol. 5	evangelize gospel message (Jesus)	7/3/98 Vol. 12
evangelization prepare your spiritual life (Jesus)	11/1/98 Vol. 13	evangelize Gospel of love (Jesus)	1/27/02 Vol. 26
evangelization save souls (Jesus)	1/21/01 Vol. 22	evangelize grace for public ministry (Jesus)	3/23/96 Vol. 3
evangelization St. Paul maintained (Jesus)	5/12/98 Vol. 11	evangelize grace of your Baptism (Jesus)	1/9/99 Vol. 14
evangelization through Holy Spirit's power (Jesus)	4/15/04 Vol. 35	evangelize heaven rejoices (Jesus)	8/23/97 Vol. 8
evangelization time is short (Jesus)	1/14/97 Vol. 6	evangelize highest calling (Jesus)	3/2/98 Vol. 10
evangelization time running out (Jesus)	1/19/99 Vol. 14	evangelize in Conferences (Jesus)	9/21/06 Vol. 44
evangelization to save souls with love (Jesus)	4/21/04 Vol. 35	evangelize in persecution (Mark)	12/26/97 Vol. 9
evangelization we are His arms & legs (Jesus)	1/9/03 Vol. 30	evangelize Kingdom of God (Jesus)	10/22/06 Vol. 45
evangelization with love (Jesus)	5/13/03 Vol. 31	evangelize leave your comfort zone (Jesus)	12/8/00 Vol. 21
evangelization work quickly to save souls (Jesus)	1/26/08 Vol. 50	evangelize like Sts. Peter & Paul (Jesus)	6/29/04 Vol. 35
evangelization call after conversion (Jesus)	1/25/08 Vol. 50	evangelize live the Gospel (St. Therese)	2/7/98 Vol. 10
evangelization of souls most important mission (Jesus)	7/17/04 Vol. 36	evangelize love & forgiveness (Jesus)	1/19/97 Vol. 6
evangelization today easier with conveniences (Jesus)	6/11/03 Vol. 31	evangelize messages wakeup call (Jesus)	7/17/97 Vol. 8
evangelize Adelaide (St. Therese)	9/7/95 Vol. 3	evangelize messengers (Jesus)	7/3/96 Vol. 3
evangelize as beacons of faith (Jesus)	6/8/06 Vol. 43	evangelize mission (St. John)	12/27/93 Vol. 1
evangelize as fishers of men (Jesus)	9/5/00 Vol. 20	evangelize most important task (Jesus)	7/27/97 Vol. 8
evangelize as long as you can (Jesus)	8/6/01 Vol. 24	evangelize must act quickly (Jesus)	7/20/97 Vol. 8
evangelize as salt & light of the earth (Jesus)	2/9/02 Vol. 26	evangelize personal call,conversion (Mary)	10/11/97 Vol. 9
evangelize as St.John Baptist (Jesus)	12/24/97 Vol. 9	evangelize personal mission (Mary)	12/8/96 Vol. 5
evangelize Ascension Thursday (Jesus)	5/25/95 Vol. 2	evangelize personal responsibility (Jesus)	1/2/97 Vol. 6
evangelize avoid being hypocrite (Jesus)	11/25/00 Vol. 21	evangelize pray & witness in public (Jesus)	4/21/05 Vol. 39
evangelize be a good example (Jesus)	6/27/98 Vol. 11	evangelize pray for persecutors (Jesus)	12/26/96 Vol. 5
evangelize be good examples (Jesus)	10/23/97 Vol. 9	evangelize pray with people (Jesus)	9/9/96 Vol. 4
evangelize be prayerful and humble (Mother Cabrini)	4/26/98 Vol. 11	evangelize prayer groups (Jesus)	6/29/94 Vol. 1
evangelize be ready for Jesus' return (Jesus)	4/2/97 Vol. 7	evangelize preach Christ crucified (Jesus)	3/25/97 Vol. 6
evangelize beauty of saving souls (Jesus)	9/10/96 Vol. 4	evangelize pride (Jesus)	5/3/95 Vol. 2
evangelize before tribulation (Jesus)	3/27/96 Vol. 3	evangelize quickly (Jesus)	2/5/98 Vol. 10
evangelize before/during tribulation (Jesus)	7/31/96 Vol. 4	evangelize reach out for souls (Jesus)	7/10/99 Vol. 16
evangelize Betania Reunion (Mary)	3/26/94 Vol. 1	evangelize reach out to others (Jesus)	7/24/02 Vol. 28
evangelize by Baptism & Confirmation (Jesus)	1/11/04 Vol. 34	evangelize reach out with help & prayer (Jesus)	7/16/06 Vol. 44
evangelize by serving the rest (Jesus)	5/27/02 Vol. 27	evangelize reachout (Jesus)	2/8/94 Vol. 1
evangelize by touching hearts (Jesus)	6/9/02 Vol. 27	evangelize rejoice to save souls (Jesus)	1/8/98 Vol. 10
evangelize call of everyone (Jesus)	9/28/03 Vol. 32	evangelize religious education (Jesus)	2/25/96 Vol. 3
evangelize call to save souls important (Jesus)	3/22/98 Vol. 10	evangelize responsibility of message (Holy Spirit)	3/31/96 Vol. 3
evangelize conversion time is short (Jesus)	8/24/97 Vol. 8	evangelize responsibility to act (Jesus)	6/23/04 Vol. 35

evangelize rocky road to heaven (Jesus) — 5/24/96 Vol. 3
evangelize rosaries (Jesus) — 10/18/95 Vol. 3
evangelize saint (St.Catherine) — 4/29/95 Vol. 2
evangelize save souls (St. Therese) — 9/20/96 Vol. 4
evangelize save souls (Jesus) — 8/18/97 Vol. 8
evangelize save souls from hell (Holy Spirit) — 5/31/98 Vol. 11
evangelize save souls,carry crosses (Jesus) — 2/15/97 Vol. 6
evangelize serving lost souls (Jesus) — 7/25/97 Vol. 8
evangelize share love and faith (Jesus) — 10/25/97 Vol. 9
evangelize short time, confession (Jesus) — 2/6/97 Vol. 6
evangelize soldiers of Christ (Jesus) — 1/10/96 Vol. 3
evangelize souls from hell (Jesus) — 10/12/06 Vol. 45
evangelize suffering, persecution (Jesus) — 7/1/97 Vol. 8
evangelize time is running out (Jesus) — 3/8/97 Vol. 6
evangelize time is short, angels to help (Jesus) — 4/2/98 Vol. 11
evangelize times have not changed (Jesus) — 1/10/98 Vol. 10
evangelize to bring lost souls to God (Jesus) — 4/19/98 Vol. 11
evangelize to build up Church (Jesus) — 10/26/99 Vol. 17
evangelize to save all souls (Jesus) — 4/18/05 Vol. 39
evangelize to save souls (Jesus) — 11/15/05 Vol. 41
evangelize to save souls (Jesus) — 2/4/07 Vol. 46
evangelize to save souls (Jesus) — 2/1/99 Vol. 14
evangelize to save souls (Jesus) — 11/17/00 Vol. 21
evangelize to the whole world (Jesus) — 3/12/96 Vol. 3
evangelize travel (Jesus) — 6/19/96 Vol. 3
evangelize value of each soul (Jesus) — 4/3/98 Vol. 11
evangelize weaker souls (Jesus) — 10/28/05 Vol. 41
evangelize wherever you go (Jesus) — 6/23/96 Vol. 3
evangelize with double speed (Mary) — 7/13/97 Vol. 8
evangelize with fasting and prayer (Jesus) — 6/11/02 Vol. 27
evangelize with love (Jesus) — 7/7/99 Vol. 16
evangelize with love, not nagging (Jesus) — 4/11/02 Vol. 27
evangelize with power of Holy Spirit (Jesus) — 5/5/05 Vol. 39
evangelize with time & talents (Jesus) — 2/7/02 Vol. 26
evangelize witness the Gospel (Mary) — 3/7/97 Vol. 6
evangelize & pray for neglected souls (Jesus) — 10/13/05 Vol. 41
evangelize (personal) avoid distractions (Jesus) — 5/24/98 Vol. 11
evangelize (personal) love of God, or fear of hell (Jesus) — 4/16/98 Vol. 11
evangelize (personal) many souls touched (Jesus) — 4/22/98 Vol. 11
evangelize (personal) speak out in His Name (Jesus) — 5/17/98 Vol. 11
evangelize nations spread love message (Jesus) — 9/29/99 Vol. 16
evangelize sinners spiritually correct (Jesus) — 9/24/07 Vol. 48
evangelize sinners with Easter Spirit (Jesus) — 5/3/07 Vol. 47
evangelize souls call for all Christians (Jesus) — 8/24/05 Vol. 40
evangelize souls lead them to heaven (Jesus) — 8/7/00 Vol. 20
evangelize souls speak out on evils (Jesus) — 7/6/06 Vol. 44
evangelize souls to keep them from hell (Jesus) — 11/21/06 Vol. 45

evangelize souls with Word of God (Jesus) — 10/18/04 Vol. 37
evangelizing be prepared spiritually (Jesus) — 4/30/02 Vol. 27
evangelizing messages for purifying (Jesus) — 7/28/96 Vol. 4
evangelizing outside of comfort zone (Jesus) — 2/24/08 Vol. 50
evangelizing souls most important job (Jesus) — 9/21/04 Vol. 36
evangelizing souls satisfaction in conversions (Jesus) — 9/8/04 Vol. 36
Eve, New blessing of Guadeloupe (Mary) — 12/12/06 Vol. 45
event timing chosen by God, not man (Jesus) — 10/5/04 Vol. 37
events accelerating out of control (Jesus) — 7/25/03 Vol. 32
events occuring very fast (Jesus) — 1/25/98 Vol. 10
events occurr like a whirlwind (Jesus) — 2/8/99 Vol. 14
events questioned (Father) — 10/8/95 Vol. 3
events speeded up (Jesus) — 11/25/96 Vol. 5
events vigilant (Jesus) — 2/13/94 Vol. 1
events & timing time of mercy granted (Jesus) — 1/3/00 Vol. 18
events increasing fears of the end times (Jesus) — 7/19/96 Vol. 4
events of 2004 disasters, closer to Antichrist (Jesus) — 12/31/03 Vol. 33
events to happen like on a roller coaster (Jesus) — 6/21/01 Vol. 23
events, major can start at any time (Jesus) — 4/16/02 Vol. 27
events, serious about to happen (Jesus) — 8/9/04 Vol. 36
every day of life gift of God (Jesus) — 3/31/00 Vol. 18
evil allowed as a test (Jesus) — 2/19/98 Vol. 10
evil allowed for a test (Jesus) — 7/15/97 Vol. 8
evil allowed for dependence (Jesus) — 5/29/97 Vol. 7
evil battle of good & evil (Jesus) — 2/20/97 Vol. 6
evil darkness of takeover (Jesus) — 4/26/01 Vol. 23
evil demons (Jesus) — 4/26/95 Vol. 2
evil do not give credit to evil (Jesus) — 7/15/97 Vol. 8
evil is conquered by good (Jesus) — 8/6/01 Vol. 24
evil Jesus will be victorious (Jesus) — 8/10/99 Vol. 16
evil speak out against it (Jesus) — 7/21/99 Vol. 16
evil test (Jesus) — 9/10/94 Vol. 2
evil testing and purification (Jesus) — 5/7/96 Vol. 3
evil vanquished from earth (Jesus) — 8/13/04 Vol. 36
evil will be conquered (Jesus) — 10/5/02 Vol. 29
evil age cross (Jesus) — 2/24/94 Vol. 1
evil age forehead (Jesus) — 12/1/93 Vol. 1
evil age injustices,final years (Jesus) — 10/21/96 Vol. 5
evil age justice (Jesus) — 2/23/94 Vol. 1
evil age test of endurance (Jesus) — 3/13/96 Vol. 3
evil age to come worse than ever seen (Jesus) — 2/27/05 Vol. 38
evil battle grand design of (Jesus) — 1/15/04 Vol. 34
evil cities destroyed (Jesus) — 10/12/06 Vol. 45
evil cleansed from face of the earth (Jesus) — 4/30/00 Vol. 19
evil days guardian angel (Mark) — 5/11/94 Vol. 1
evil days remnant (Jesus) — 4/26/94 Vol. 1
evil influence pornography,abortion,casinos (Jesus) — 10/18/05 Vol. 41

evil leaders punished for wicked deed (Jesus)   11/25/97 Vol. 9

evil life can lead to eternal hell (Jesus)   7/2/07 Vol. 48

evil morality speak out against society (Jesus)   7/21/02 Vol. 28

evil of abortion pray to stop or lose blessings (Jesus)   12/13/02 Vol. 29

evil one false witness (Jesus)   8/12/95 Vol. 3

evil one more attacks as souls saved (Jesus)   2/20/98 Vol. 10

evil one's plan to divide and conquer (Jesus)   6/19/05 Vol. 39

evil ones vanquished as Egyptians in desert (Jesus)   3/17/00 Vol. 18

evil people lose possessions,destroyed (Jesus)   4/13/00 Vol. 19

evil people suffer plague of water to blood (Jesus)   10/19/00 Vol. 21

evil power permitted within God's restraint (Jesus)   8/19/99 Vol. 16

evil powers avoid sources of (Jesus)   9/7/07 Vol. 48

evil reign of one world people (Mark)   10/2/06 Vol. 45

evil shadows with drugs & occult (Jesus)   2/22/07 Vol. 46

evil society immorality getting worse, dark (Jesus)   9/30/04 Vol. 36

evil society needs prayer, no death culture (Jesus)   10/26/04 Vol. 37

evil spirit influence TV,movies,evil people (Jesus)   3/27/06 Vol. 42

evil spirits devour souls (Jesus)   9/28/06 Vol. 44

evil spirits fight with spiritual weapons (Jesus)   6/15/06 Vol. 43

evil spirits holy water,sacramentals (Jesus)   3/5/98 Vol. 10

evil spirits Jesus will protect us from (Jesus)   5/1/98 Vol. 11

evil spirits ready to devour us (Jesus)   5/11/98 Vol. 11

evil spirits try to claim souls (Jesus)   7/12/01 Vol. 24

evil spirits trying to mute Church (Jesus)   7/6/06 Vol. 44

evil storm clouds in killings, disasters (Jesus)   4/6/00 Vol. 19

evil succeeds when good do nothing (Jesus)   2/9/08 Vol. 50

evil takeover do not despair (Jesus)   6/24/04 Vol. 35

evil thoughts cleanse with prayer (Jesus)   3/16/00 Vol. 18

evil time trust (St. Michael)   10/29/93 Vol. 1

evil times preparation (Jesus)   5/1/94 Vol. 1

evil times second coming (Jesus)   11/4/95 Vol. 3

evil to be cleansed with wrath of God (Jesus)   8/21/99 Vol. 16

evil trial hope (Jesus)   4/15/94 Vol. 1

evil ways, seeing chance for better spiritual life (Jesus)   9/16/04 Vol. 36

evil, flood of calls for more evangelization (Jesus)   11/22/02 Vol. 29

evil's power insignificant to God's power (Jesus)   9/21/98 Vol. 12

evolution courts pervert the truth (Jesus)   6/12/97 Vol. 7

evolution is theory and not proven fact (Jesus)   11/10/05 Vol. 41

evolution not proven in reality (Jesus)   2/5/07 Vol. 46

evolution vs. creation (Jesus)   9/20/96 Vol. 4

exalted to be humbled (Jesus)   5/25/05 Vol. 39

examination of conscience to avoid sacrilege (Jesus)   12/21/06 Vol. 45

examination, conscience check spiritual progress (Jesus)   7/31/99 Vol. 16

example, good speaks louder than our words (Jesus)   8/21/04 Vol. 36

examples, good of life each day (Jesus)   1/11/01 Vol. 22

excesses, sinful encouraged by the devil (Jesus)   9/12/07 Vol. 48

excuses will get one to heaven (Jesus)   11/4/03 Vol. 33

executive orders UN troops (Jesus)   2/9/97 Vol. 6

existence caused by Jesus' love (Jesus)   6/19/02 Vol. 27

existence His Will maintains (Jesus)   1/5/97 Vol. 6

existence & energy comes from God (Holy Spirit)   5/27/07 Vol. 47

exorcism weapons needed against evil ones (Jesus)   11/1/05 Vol. 41

Exodus complaining (Jesus)   8/11/95 Vol. 3

Exodus forehead (Jesus)   11/13/93 Vol. 1

Exodus miraculous protection (Jesus)   1/2/97 Vol. 6

Exodus modern day (Jesus)   1/10/08 Vol. 50

Exodus modern day (Jesus)   9/27/07 Vol. 48

Exodus of modern day (Jesus)   6/6/05 Vol. 39

Exodus parallel to today (Jesus)   7/23/03 Vol. 32

Exodus plagues (Jesus)   7/11/94 Vol. 2

Exodus plagues and diseases (Jesus)   5/17/95 Vol. 2

Exodus power against Egypt army (Jesus)   10/20/97 Vol. 9

Exodus protection (Jesus)   7/15/95 Vol. 3

Exodus repeated today (Jesus)   4/21/03 Vol. 31

Exodus repeated today (Jesus)   1/10/02 Vol. 26

Exodus repeated today (Jesus)   6/10/99 Vol. 15

Exodus today as in the past (Jesus)   8/13/04 Vol. 36

Exodus we will suffer like them (Jesus)   4/12/98 Vol. 11

Exodus will leave in haste (Jesus)   6/18/99 Vol. 15

Exodus yesterday and today (Jesus)   3/15/05 Vol. 38

Exodus at night down less traveled roads (Jesus)   10/6/98 Vol. 13

Exodus experience led by angels (Jesus)   7/31/97 Vol. 8

Exodus from Antichrist angels to protect refuges (Jesus)   7/19/00 Vol. 20

Exodus manna prefigures the Eucharist (Jesus)   3/11/08 Vol. 50

Exodus manna similar miracles (Jesus)   4/23/99 Vol. 15

Exodus of end times heavenly manna, water (Jesus)   8/7/02 Vol. 28

Exodus slaves new slaves,mark of beast (Jesus)   9/30/99 Vol. 16

Exodus, modern haste with backpacks (Jesus)   4/26/07 Vol. 47

Exodus, modern day hope in protection at refuges (Jesus)   7/23/04 Vol. 36

Exodus, modern day miracles of protection (Jesus)   7/14/05 Vol. 40

Exodus, new linked with Revelation book (Jesus)   4/9/01 Vol. 23

Exodus,modern day to provide food & water (Jesus)   8/17/02 Vol. 28

exorcism need groups, sacramentals (Jesus)   1/29/06 Vol. 42

exorcism prayers, by priest (Jesus)   1/11/06 Vol. 42

exorcism prayers St. Michael prayer (Jesus)   3/2/01 Vol. 22

exorcism, deliverance need constant prayers (Jesus)   6/28/07 Vol. 47

exorcism use crucifix,Name of Jesus (Jesus)   5/6/07 Vol. 47

exorcisms with prayer & fasting (St. Michael)   9/29/05 Vol. 40

exorcisms needed remove demons from possessed (Jesus)   3/7/02 Vol. 26

exorcists needed today (Jesus)   9/2/03 Vol. 32

exorcizing demons from people or houses (Jesus)   11/7/02 Vol. 29

exports, US becoming 3rd world country (Jesus)   1/24/06 Vol. 42

exposition Penance (Jesus)   5/6/95 Vol. 2

extinction events control species (Jesus)   5/15/06 Vol. 43

eye peace (Jesus)	11/28/94 Vol. 2	faith focus on prayer & sacraments (Jesus)	10/14/01 Vol. 25
eye of God used by masons (Jesus)	12/12/99 Vol. 17	faith foundation (Jesus)	8/18/94 Vol. 2
eye protection from occasions of sin (Jesus)	3/20/02 Vol. 26	faith gift with no price (Jesus)	2/21/99 Vol. 14
eyes are windows to the soul (Jesus)	12/13/07 Vol. 49	faith God's most important gift (Jesus)	5/17/07 Vol. 47
eyes prayer time (Jesus)	2/25/95 Vol. 2	faith greatest riches (Jesus)	9/7/00 Vol. 20
eyes protect from evil (Jesus)	5/30/02 Vol. 27	faith guard the children (Jesus)	7/25/03 Vol. 32
eyes of faith born in the Spirit (Jesus)	4/24/06 Vol. 43	faith have firm foundation for (Jesus)	7/7/98 Vol. 12
eyes of faith magnify spiritual needs (Jesus)	11/16/97 Vol. 9	faith have solid foundation (Jesus)	7/21/03 Vol. 32
eyes of faith protect us from sin (Jesus)	10/7/05 Vol. 41	faith important to preserve (Jesus)	1/26/06 Vol. 42
eyes of faith puts life in perspective (Jesus)	7/28/97 Vol. 8	faith in Baptism & Eucharist (Jesus)	7/11/01 Vol. 24
eyes of faith spiritual awareness (Jesus)	12/27/06 Vol. 45	faith in good & bad times (Jesus)	1/6/05 Vol. 38
eyes of faith spiritual blindness (Jesus)	3/30/03 Vol. 30	faith in old Church (Jesus)	9/26/97 Vol. 8
eyes of faith to discern right from wrong (Jesus)	4/6/04 Vol. 35	faith is a valuable pearl (Jesus)	1/7/97 Vol. 6
eyes of faith to help,love neighbor (Jesus)	10/29/00 Vol. 21	faith journey (Jesus)	8/20/95 Vol. 3
eyes of faith to keep on right path (Jesus)	3/28/08 Vol. 50	faith keep childlike (Jesus)	12/4/01 Vol. 25
eyes of faith to know love of God,other (Jesus)	5/4/99 Vol. 15	faith lay strong foundation (Jesus)	5/28/98 Vol. 11
eyes of pilgrims sharing of problems (Jesus)	12/13/07 Vol. 49	faith like a little child (Jesus)	5/6/03 Vol. 31
eyes opened to Jesus (Jesus)	4/5/02 Vol. 27	faith lived in actions (Jesus)	10/10/05 Vol. 41
fabric of life faith holds humans together (Jesus)	12/10/02 Vol. 29	faith living in prayer,Communion (Jesus)	12/8/02 Vol. 29
factories to close will cause banks to fail (Jesus)	9/18/98 Vol. 12	faith lukewarm (Jesus)	11/29/93 Vol. 1
factory owners selling out American workers (Jesus)	6/3/07 Vol. 47	faith Magisterium (Jesus)	11/10/95 Vol. 3
failures, mistakes do not dwell on (Jesus)	12/6/02 Vol. 29	faith maintain with prayer (Jesus)	10/26/99 Vol. 17
failures,forget past build up faith in God (Jesus)	3/19/01 Vol. 22	faith many growing lax in (Jesus)	7/31/03 Vol. 32
faith a treasured gift (Jesus)	10/11/99 Vol. 17	faith more given, more expected (Jesus)	11/22/03 Vol. 33
faith always tested (Jesus)	5/8/04 Vol. 35	faith more simple in country (Jesus)	10/10/03 Vol. 33
faith and trust in God's help (Jesus)	6/25/06 Vol. 43	faith necessary for healings (Jesus)	1/30/01 Vol. 22
faith as an anchor for stability in life (Jesus)	8/23/04 Vol. 36	faith needed for healings (Jesus)	6/25/04 Vol. 35
faith be beacons to shine forth (Jesus)	6/13/05 Vol. 39	faith needs defending in society (Jesus)	3/19/06 Vol. 42
faith be humble and simple (Jesus)	7/14/98 Vol. 12	faith needs good works (Jesus)	9/17/06 Vol. 44
faith build on solid foundation (Jesus)	7/10/03 Vol. 32	faith needs instilling to be saved (Jesus)	11/6/00 Vol. 21
faith build with daily prayer (Jesus)	3/3/05 Vol. 38	faith needs to be shared (Jesus)	2/12/08 Vol. 50
faith built on rock for foundation (Jesus)	9/10/05 Vol. 40	faith new life and love (Jesus)	5/8/96 Vol. 3
faith by following God's Will (Jesus)	7/15/99 Vol. 16	faith nourish in prayer (Jesus)	2/1/03 Vol. 30
faith church & evangelize (Jesus)	5/3/96 Vol. 3	faith nourish with God's Word (God the Father)	1/7/99 Vol. 14
faith come as child for protection (Jesus)	11/28/01 Vol. 25	faith of religious freedom (Jesus)	12/3/99 Vol. 17
faith comes from heart, is lived (Jesus)	6/26/00 Vol. 19	faith our greatest gift (Jesus)	7/10/99 Vol. 16
faith confession (Jesus)	3/12/94 Vol. 1	faith our true riches (Jesus)	6/11/98 Vol. 11
faith cost of martyrdom (Jesus)	2/5/07 Vol. 46	faith pass on to children (Jesus)	7/14/03 Vol. 32
faith deposit (Jesus)	9/24/94 Vol. 2	faith pass on to children (Jesus)	6/19/01 Vol. 23
faith dove (Holy Spirit)	7/8/94 Vol. 2	faith practice by example (Jesus)	10/12/96 Vol. 5
faith dying or growing (Jesus)	10/7/01 Vol. 25	faith prayer and fasting (Jesus)	12/9/99 Vol. 17
faith endurance in (Jesus)	2/4/98 Vol. 10	faith prayer,fasting,sacraments (Jesus)	11/18/98 Vol. 13
faith enhanced by Holy Spirit (Jesus)	7/3/99 Vol. 16	faith prepare (Jesus)	9/5/95 Vol. 3
faith evangelize (Jesus)	3/13/94 Vol. 1	faith responsible to witness to (Jesus)	2/2/04 Vol. 34
faith evangelize (Jesus)	4/12/94 Vol. 1	faith speak out & defend (Jesus)	6/29/04 Vol. 35
faith evangelize everyone (Jesus)	6/9/03 Vol. 31	faith spread Gospel of love (Jesus)	10/31/97 Vol. 9
faith fight the good fight (Jesus)	9/25/97 Vol. 8	faith stand up for beliefs (Mary)	8/28/03 Vol. 32

faith stay rooted in (Jesus) — 3/14/05 Vol. 38
faith take off masks of world (Jesus) — 10/31/96 Vol. 5
faith teach to children (Jesus) — 10/29/02 Vol. 29
faith tested over time (Jesus) — 1/13/04 Vol. 34
faith testing sincerity of (Jesus) — 9/13/03 Vol. 32
faith to get through trials (Jesus) — 1/8/04 Vol. 34
faith to overcome all evil (Jesus) — 2/17/98 Vol. 10
faith to shine not hide (Jesus) — 6/7/05 Vol. 39
faith treasured gift,example (Jesus) — 2/5/97 Vol. 6
faith truth — 9/26/93 Vol. 1
faith witness — 11/16/93 Vol. 1
faith witness in public (Jesus) — 8/9/99 Vol. 16
faith & belief in God needed for heaven (Jesus) — 11/13/07 Vol. 49
faith & healing heal body & soul (Jesus) — 3/22/04 Vol. 34
faith & hope call on Trinity for help (Jesus) — 5/28/03 Vol. 31
faith & love be grounded each day (Jesus) — 1/11/01 Vol. 22
faith & right reason breastplate & helmet (Jesus) — 4/27/99 Vol. 15
faith & sight gifts to our missions (Jesus) — 11/14/05 Vol. 41
faith & trust build on Jesus (Jesus) — 2/13/03 Vol. 30
faith & trust forget pride (Jesus) — 2/14/08 Vol. 50
faith & trust prevails over evil (Jesus) — 7/19/01 Vol. 24
faith affirmation needed for heaven (Jesus) — 11/3/03 Vol. 33
faith and hope Easter message (Jesus) — 4/5/99 Vol. 15
faith as mustard seed all things possible (Jesus) — 11/18/06 Vol. 45
faith as mustard seed can accomplish great things (Jesus) — 1/10/06 Vol. 42
faith calling comes from parents,God (Jesus) — 9/8/07 Vol. 48
faith commitment needed throughout life (Jesus) — 5/22/07 Vol. 47
faith community early Church (Jesus) — 9/19/95 Vol. 3
faith decision serve God or not (Jesus) — 6/27/02 Vol. 27
faith experience shared with everyone (Jesus) — 11/4/00 Vol. 21
faith formation example of parents,teachers (Jesus) — 10/3/06 Vol. 45
faith gift share with everyone (Jesus) — 1/8/06 Vol. 42
faith growing weak few live their faith (Jesus) — 6/21/00 Vol. 19
faith in cures necessary for healing (Jesus) — 12/3/98 Vol. 13
faith in God pass on to children (Jesus) — 6/21/06 Vol. 43
faith in God protection from demons (Jesus) — 1/5/07 Vol. 46
faith in God shout it from the rooftops (Jesus) — 6/30/05 Vol. 39
faith in God will set you free (Jesus) — 4/30/99 Vol. 15
faith in healing better disposition to healing (Jesus) — 12/4/06 Vol. 45
faith in Jesus main priority (Jesus) — 11/13/05 Vol. 41
faith in Jesus needed to be content (Jesus) — 2/19/07 Vol. 46
faith in trials Jesus carries (Jesus) — 9/5/02 Vol. 28
faith in tribulation has a price of suffering (Jesus) — 12/7/98 Vol. 13
faith is as strong as roots (Jesus) — 2/5/06 Vol. 42
faith is a gift to nurture in love of God (Jesus) — 1/12/04 Vol. 34
faith is gift do not squander (Jesus) — 3/10/07 Vol. 46
faith journey cannot stay at base camp (Jesus) — 3/31/03 Vol. 30

faith like wheels easier to come to God (Jesus) — 3/2/00 Vol. 18
faith lived out good example to follow (Jesus) — 10/17/00 Vol. 21
faith lost related to jobs lost (Jesus) — 7/21/05 Vol. 40
faith must grow not just status quo (Jesus) — 3/3/06 Vol. 42
faith needed to overcome the impossible (Jesus) — 10/14/04 Vol. 37
faith needs prayer life,total consecration (Jesus) — 6/27/03 Vol. 31
faith of little children needed to be saved (Jesus) — 4/12/99 Vol. 15
faith progress assessed during Lent (Jesus) — 3/23/00 Vol. 18
faith remnant false gods (Jesus) — 4/10/95 Vol. 2
faith shared call to all Christians (Jesus) — 8/4/05 Vol. 40
faith tested see dependence on God (Jesus) — 9/8/05 Vol. 40
faith trip friends (Jesus) — 8/23/94 Vol. 2
faith, defend out of love, not anger (Jesus) — 11/15/03 Vol. 33
faith, deposit of stand up to heresies (Jesus) — 6/30/98 Vol. 11
faith, genuine not just in name only (Jesus) — 10/18/98 Vol. 13
faith, gift of accepted by free will (Jesus) — 8/10/02 Vol. 28
faith, gift of given by God in grace (Jesus) — 9/3/01 Vol. 24
faith, growth in move forward,more prayer (Jesus) — 9/5/01 Vol. 24
faith, hope, & charity virtues needed by faithful (Jesus) — 10/28/03 Vol. 33
faith, solid pass on to others (Jesus) — 3/21/07 Vol. 46
faith, stale needs fresh air of grace (Jesus) — 11/24/03 Vol. 33
faith, strong to face society's criticisms (Jesus) — 11/7/04 Vol. 37
faith, traditions need to be taught to children (Jesus) — 9/30/06 Vol. 44
faith, traditions of endured over years (Jesus) — 12/13/05 Vol. 41
faith, training in greater than secular (Jesus) — 8/11/05 Vol. 40
faith,focus of life heavenly banquet for faithful (Jesus) — 6/12/00 Vol. 19
faith,gift of tested in life (Jesus) — 2/26/00 Vol. 18
faith,hope, & love calling by God (Jesus) — 5/26/05 Vol. 39
faith,strength of based on teachers,Jesus (Jesus) — 5/4/00 Vol. 19
faithful all can evangelize gospel (Jesus) — 11/25/98 Vol. 13
faithful do not grieve in death (Jesus) — 1/3/98 Vol. 10
faithful emanate faith & love (Jesus) — 8/12/99 Vol. 16
faithful follow God's Will (Jesus) — 8/27/07 Vol. 48
faithful Savior (Jesus) — 3/16/94 Vol. 1
faithful soul (Jesus) — 4/4/94 Vol. 1
faithful target of evil ones (Jesus) — 12/9/05 Vol. 41
faithful trust (Jesus) — 3/23/95 Vol. 2
faithful trust (Jesus) — 3/23/95 Vol. 2
faithful are special for who they are (Jesus) — 8/21/99 Vol. 16
faithful as beacons spread truth,love of God (Jesus) — 10/16/00 Vol. 21
faithful left only hope is in Jesus (Jesus) — 3/21/02 Vol. 26
faithful ones find food&shelter at refuges (Jesus) — 10/6/04 Vol. 37
faithful parents help to convert children (Jesus) — 8/21/07 Vol. 48
faithful people beacons of light in darkness (Jesus) — 4/25/04 Vol. 35
faithful people must speak out (God the Father) — 8/20/03 Vol. 32
faithful people pillars of faith (Jesus) — 1/19/02 Vol. 26
faithful people will not be left orphans (Jesus) — 10/14/99 Vol. 17

faithful persecuted by modern Pharisees (Jesus) — 3/12/04 Vol. 34

faithful remnant call to wilderness protection (Jesus) — 7/19/00 Vol. 20

faithful remnant devy evil authority (Jesus) — 6/22/06 Vol. 43

faithful remnant God's true bride (Jesus) — 9/3/06 Vol. 44

faithful remnant hope (Jesus) — 7/26/94 Vol. 2

faithful remnant left when Jesus returns (Jesus) — 7/20/05 Vol. 40

faithful remnant meet in homes (Jesus) — 8/23/03 Vol. 32

faithful remnant need to build up Kingdom (Jesus) — 7/17/04 Vol. 36

faithful remnant needed to spread Word (Jesus) — 1/28/06 Vol. 42

faithful remnant pass on to future generations (Jesus) — 5/20/00 Vol. 19

faithful remnant persevere in life (Jesus) — 9/17/05 Vol. 40

faithful remnant protected as apostles were (Jesus) — 5/12/05 Vol. 39

faithful remnant protected from demons (Jesus) — 5/18/07 Vol. 47

faithful remnant protected from evil ones (Jesus) — 12/14/05 Vol. 41

faithful remnant spread 'Good News' (Jesus) — 2/13/07 Vol. 46

faithful remnant teach children the faith (Jesus) — 2/21/08 Vol. 50

faithful remnant tested by schismatic church (Jesus) — 11/13/04 Vol. 37

faithful remnant to prevail over Satan (Jesus) — 9/18/07 Vol. 48

faithful remnant to survive Satan (Jesus) — 5/26/04 Vol. 35

faithful remnant to survive tribulation (Jesus) — 7/6/00 Vol. 20

faithful remnant true Church following Jesus (Jesus) — 8/14/02 Vol. 28

faithful remnant work for souls (Jesus) — 8/16/99 Vol. 16

faithful reward peace & rest of Jesus (Jesus) — 4/10/07 Vol. 47

faithful rewarded at end of tunnel in heaven (Jesus) — 7/15/00 Vol. 20

faithful teaching encounter devil's attacks (Jesus) — 6/3/03 Vol. 31

faithful to be persecuted for not following new world order (Jesus) — 9/20/04 Vol. 36

faithful to God not idols (Jesus) — 11/17/06 Vol. 45

faithful today to receive more graces (Jesus) — 7/17/03 Vol. 32

faithful valuable means for spreading Christianity (Jesus) 2/22/02 Vol. 26

faithful vs lost in sin sinners need forgiveness of sin (Jesus) 3/27/04 Vol. 34

faithful vs. lukewarm heaven vs. hell (Jesus) — 5/30/05 Vol. 39

faithful vs. occult spiritual battle (Jesus) — 7/9/07 Vol. 48

faithful vs. unfaithful in families (Jesus) — 10/25/07 Vol. 49

faithfulness fulfillment of destiny (Jesus) — 12/17/96 Vol. 5

faithfulness to God and spouse (Jesus) — 7/3/02 Vol. 28

faithfulness to God's love (Jesus) — 7/23/01 Vol. 24

faith's foundation built on Jesus, not on sand (Jesus) — 5/18/00 Vol. 19

faith's price is worth dying for (Jesus) — 10/6/98 Vol. 13

fall end times (Jesus) — 12/7/94 Vol. 2

Fall events watchful of your souls (Jesus) — 7/17/96 Vol. 4

fall of finances at time of tribulation (Jesus) — 12/17/99 Vol. 17

fall season represents twilight to death (Jesus) — 10/31/00 Vol. 21

fall season think of your judgment (Jesus) — 10/25/07 Vol. 49

falling away from God sign of end times (Jesus) — 8/21/07 Vol. 48

false christs beware of in end days (Jesus) — 5/15/99 Vol. 15

false christs cunning as serpents (Jesus) — 5/4/00 Vol. 19

false christs to teach New Age (Jesus) — 1/4/08 Vol. 50

false gods sports,fame,money (Jesus) — 6/16/99 Vol. 15

false gods worshippers to suffer flames (Jesus) — 9/20/01 Vol. 24

false idols need to be purged (Jesus) — 11/15/99 Vol. 17

false peace Antichrist (Jesus) — 1/25/95 Vol. 2

false prophet fruits (Jesus) — 10/6/94 Vol. 2

false prophet tribulation (Jesus) — 6/17/95 Vol. 2

false prophets avoid idol worship (Jesus) — 6/14/00 Vol. 19

false prophets discern from Scriptures (Jesus) — 6/21/99 Vol. 15

false prophets discern with Holy Spirit (Jesus) — 8/30/03 Vol. 32

false prophets discernment of fruits (Jesus) — 8/5/96 Vol. 4

false prophets test their fruits (Jesus) — 11/16/00 Vol. 21

false shepherds obey God before man (Jesus) — 5/7/00 Vol. 19

false teachers lead many astray (Jesus) — 6/23/04 Vol. 35

false witnesses deceive the faithful (Jesus) — 5/20/97 Vol. 7

false witnesses discern (Jesus) — 3/27/96 Vol. 3

false witnesses discernment (Jesus) — 4/1/96 Vol. 3

false witnesses Mystical Body (Jesus) — 9/17/95 Vol. 3

fame passes tomorrow (Jesus) — 2/9/00 Vol. 18

fame soon forgotten (Jesus) — 10/20/06 Vol. 45

fame & fortune judgment not based on (Jesus) — 8/27/01 Vol. 24

fame & glory fleeting & soon forgotten (Jesus) — 2/20/02 Vol. 26

fame & riches will pass away (Jesus) — 1/26/03 Vol. 30

fame and fortune do not aspire to (Jesus) — 5/19/99 Vol. 15

fame and power fleeting before Triumph (Jesus) — 11/26/98 Vol. 13

fame and riches depend on God (Jesus) — 10/4/02 Vol. 29

fame and riches fade away, focus on service (Jesus) — 2/29/04 Vol. 34

fame and riches store spiritual treasures (Jesus) — 9/4/97 Vol. 8

fame and riches will never equal God's gifts (Jesus) — 12/20/98 Vol. 13

fame vs. humble faithful suffer criticism (Jesus) — 9/30/99 Vol. 16

fame vs. humility cannot seek places of honor (Jesus) — 5/6/00 Vol. 19

fame, power, money gods for some (Jesus) — 9/1/07 Vol. 48

families abortion (David) — 1/12/94 Vol. 1

families are heart of society (Jesus) — 4/26/04 Vol. 35

families communicate, pray together (Jesus) — 12/5/03 Vol. 33

families each member contributes (Jesus) — 11/23/00 Vol. 21

families faith and peace within (Jesus) — 12/28/97 Vol. 9

families happy death (St. Joseph) — 6/21/95 Vol. 2

families have spiritual division (Jesus) — 7/9/03 Vol. 32

families homosexual (Jesus) — 12/26/93 Vol. 1

families imitate Holy Family (Jesus) — 5/13/99 Vol. 15

families keep them together (Jesus) — 5/22/01 Vol. 23

families Mystical Body (Jesus) — 11/23/95 Vol. 3

families of love and prayer (Jesus) — 12/9/99 Vol. 17

families only 1/3rd traditional (Jesus) — 6/14/99 Vol. 15

families part of Mystical Body (Jesus) — 11/11/99 Vol. 17

families Sacred Heart enthroned (Jesus) — 4/10/97 Vol. 7

families seek love and unity (Jesus)	5/4/98 Vol. 11
families seek peace most (Mary)	3/12/98 Vol. 10
families need love stop divorce and abortions (Jesus)	10/10/98 Vol. 13
families, normal environment for children (Jesus)	1/21/06 Vol. 42
family appreciation (Uncle Jim)	2/20/96 Vol. 3
family corrupted (Jesus)	5/29/02 Vol. 27
family love (Jesus)	6/9/94 Vol. 1
family pilgrims of life (Jesus)	6/25/95 Vol. 2
family pray (Adelaide)	8/23/95 Vol. 3
family preserve in society (Jesus)	3/20/97 Vol. 6
family protection and help (St. Joseph)	3/19/96 Vol. 3
Family responsibility (Jesus)	3/28/94 Vol. 1
family sacredness of life (Jesus)	11/18/96 Vol. 5
family under evil attack (Jesus)	7/27/97 Vol. 8
family & society attacked by Satan (Jesus)	8/8/03 Vol. 32
family as model faith needed for children (Jesus)	12/30/94 Vol. 2
family attacked strength of civilization (Jesus)	12/30/01 Vol. 25
family attacks by devil & culture (Jesus)	12/30/07 Vol. 49
family budget suffering higher prices (Jesus)	9/29/05 Vol. 40
family Christmas marriage instead of sin (Jesus)	12/26/02 Vol. 29
family divisions need healing, forgiveness (Jesus)	3/13/04 Vol. 34
family life attacks of the world (Jesus)	5/18/07 Vol. 47
family life have peace & love (Jesus)	7/1/99 Vol. 16
family life love of God & each other (Jesus)	5/13/99 Vol. 15
family life nurture, prayer life (Jesus)	12/29/02 Vol. 29
family life strength of society (Jesus)	8/8/99 Vol. 16
family life breakdown no respect for morality (Jesus)	8/20/99 Vol. 16
family love about caring & sharing (Jesus)	12/30/05 Vol. 41
family members brought back together (Jesus)	11/28/05 Vol. 41
family peace brings peace in world (Jesus)	7/17/06 Vol. 44
family prayer best protection for family (Jesus)	3/3/04 Vol. 34
family prayer can prevent divorce (Jesus)	10/28/04 Vol. 37
family prayer enriches our lives (Jesus)	7/3/06 Vol. 44
family prayer helps stay together (Jesus)	2/27/03 Vol. 30
family prayer keeps family together (Jesus)	2/4/07 Vol. 46
family prayer permanent marriage (Jesus)	5/4/04 Vol. 35
family prayer take time daily (Jesus)	12/4/03 Vol. 33
family prayer to avoid divorce (Jesus)	12/30/07 Vol. 49
family prayer to prevent adultery (Jesus)	1/16/00 Vol. 18
family protection from hatred & division (Jesus)	12/12/02 Vol. 29
family responsibilities physical & spiritual (Jesus)	9/24/00 Vol. 20
family roots hold people together (Jesus)	12/5/02 Vol. 29
family sports do together (Jesus)	12/5/03 Vol. 33
family stress expenses of cars,homes,ed (Jesus)	12/3/04 Vol. 37
family stress from lower incomes (Jesus)	8/18/05 Vol. 40
family support for older & younger members (Jesus)	2/21/08 Vol. 50
family under attack divorce, living together (Jesus)	10/8/00 Vol. 21
family values attacked by communism (Jesus)	4/22/99 Vol. 15
family,core of society breakdown, ruin of USA (Jesus)	10/8/00 Vol. 21
famine and control of food (Jesus)	5/13/99 Vol. 15
famine and food distribution (Jesus)	5/21/03 Vol. 31
famine and unemployment (Jesus)	7/18/99 Vol. 16
famine bread lines (Jesus)	5/9/97 Vol. 7
famine by droughts & plagues (Jesus)	7/12/01 Vol. 24
famine by floods & storms (Jesus)	1/10/01 Vol. 22
famine by weather & control (Jesus)	7/8/99 Vol. 16
famine conditions, disasters (Jesus)	4/11/01 Vol. 23
famine contrived by chips (Jesus)	8/7/06 Vol. 44
famine control of one world people (Jesus)	10/2/03 Vol. 33
famine control of one world people (Jesus)	5/8/05 Vol. 39
famine controlled distribution (Jesus)	6/8/04 Vol. 35
famine controlled distribution with chips (Jesus)	8/12/04 Vol. 36
famine drought in Europe (Jesus)	8/14/03 Vol. 32
famine emergency powers (Jesus)	1/16/97 Vol. 6
famine food and water rationed (Jesus)	7/19/98 Vol. 12
famine food multiplied (Jesus)	8/3/03 Vol. 32
famine food multiplied (Jesus)	1/9/97 Vol. 6
famine food multiplied in (Jesus)	10/1/03 Vol. 33
famine food wasted,controlled (Jesus)	3/10/97 Vol. 6
famine food worth more than oil (Jesus)	5/22/03 Vol. 31
famine from drought & pestilence (Jesus)	7/18/02 Vol. 28
famine from storms and droughts (Jesus)	6/23/98 Vol. 11
famine futures market (Jesus)	9/1/96 Vol. 4
famine God to multiply bread (Jesus)	2/12/00 Vol. 18
famine have food stored (Jesus)	6/30/06 Vol. 43
famine manna provided (Jesus)	10/17/96 Vol. 5
famine news is controlled (Jesus)	12/26/96 Vol. 5
famine no fuel for travel (Jesus)	2/6/03 Vol. 30
famine physical & spiritual (Jesus)	2/6/97 Vol. 6
famine physical and spiritual (Jesus)	5/20/95 Vol. 2
famine plan for food shortages (Jesus)	8/1/96 Vol. 4
famine poor food production (Jesus)	10/23/03 Vol. 33
famine prepare as Joseph (Jesus)	7/14/01 Vol. 24
famine prepare food & water (Jesus)	6/1/02 Vol. 27
famine prepare food and water (Jesus)	7/9/97 Vol. 8
famine prepare food prudently (Jesus)	10/10/96 Vol. 5
famine prepare for emergencies (Jesus)	4/3/97 Vol. 7
famine prepare for shortages (Jesus)	11/14/96 Vol. 5
famine prepare people & nations (Jesus)	8/26/96 Vol. 4
famine result from bee loss (Jesus)	2/29/08 Vol. 50
famine rich (Jesus)	9/30/94 Vol. 2
famine riots and chaos (Jesus)	2/5/97 Vol. 6
famine roving bands in streets (Jesus)	11/26/95 Vol. 3
famine share, food multiplied (Jesus)	5/22/97 Vol. 7

famine sickness & plagues (Jesus) — 1/18/97 Vol. 6
famine sign of tribulation (Jesus) — 8/7/04 Vol. 36
famine sign to go to refuges (Jesus) — 6/1/05 Vol. 39
famine signs of control (Jesus) — 2/20/03 Vol. 30
famine some critical of message (Jesus) — 10/31/96 Vol. 5
famine some will kill for food (Jesus) — 4/21/05 Vol. 39
famine store one year's food (Jesus) — 8/7/96 Vol. 4
famine to ravage America (Jesus) — 8/30/07 Vol. 48
famine tribulation (Jesus) — 8/30/96 Vol. 4
famine weather & controlled markets (Jesus) — 4/4/02 Vol. 27
famine weather and control (Jesus) — 11/10/97 Vol. 9
famine will test the world (Jesus) — 7/17/98 Vol. 12
famine world wide (Jesus) — 8/20/01 Vol. 24
famine & drought prepare food and water (Jesus) — 8/10/99 Vol. 16
famine & droughts threaten food supplies (Jesus) — 8/22/02 Vol. 28
famine & pestilence sign to go to refuges (Jesus) — 2/1/06 Vol. 42
famine and food no hoarding (Jesus) — 10/3/96 Vol. 5
famine and Y2K store 1 yr's food & water (Jesus) — 5/7/99 Vol. 15
famine causes abuses of nature (Jesus) — 3/6/00 Vol. 18
famine coming store food to multiply (Jesus) — 12/20/06 Vol. 45
famine in world food shortages,distribution (Jesus) — 12/23/99 Vol. 17
famine over world droughts,unusual weather (Jesus) — 3/27/00 Vol. 18
famine to cause riots go into hiding as riots start (Jesus) — 8/20/98 Vol. 12
famine world wide tell everyone/governments (Jesus) — 8/19/96 Vol. 4
famine worldwide save food & fresh water (Jesus) — 6/6/00 Vol. 19
famine, world for not taking chip (Jesus) — 12/19/06 Vol. 45
famine, world need chips to buy food (Jesus) — 10/3/02 Vol. 29
famine, world roots for in this year (Jesus) — 5/23/02 Vol. 27
famine, world to start in 2002 (Jesus) — 8/7/02 Vol. 28
famine, world wide control of food (Jesus) — 1/28/03 Vol. 30
famines appreciate gifts (Jesus) — 6/5/96 Vol. 3
famines manna (Jesus) — 5/25/94 Vol. 1
famines universe (Jesus) — 6/1/94 Vol. 1
fanatics cannot love God enough (Jesus) — 5/21/01 Vol. 23
farmers deserve thanks (Jesus) — 8/28/06 Vol. 44
farmers food shortages (Jesus) — 9/21/97 Vol. 8
farmers fuel costs, subsidies (Jesus) — 9/29/05 Vol. 40
farmers last freedom from China (Jesus) — 8/9/07 Vol. 48
farmers need help for our survival (Jesus) — 5/6/04 Vol. 35
farmers need support and subsidies (Jesus) — 7/5/04 Vol. 36
farmers remove small ones (Jesus) — 9/16/00 Vol. 20
farmers small farmers forced out (Jesus) — 12/28/97 Vol. 9
farmers tested by fuel prices (Jesus) — 9/22/05 Vol. 40
farmers threatened by bankruptcy (Jesus) — 6/3/99 Vol. 15
farmers under control (Jesus) — 9/25/00 Vol. 20
farmers disappearing due to bankruptcies (Jesus) — 2/22/01 Vol. 22
farmers lose by low prices (Jesus) — 10/4/07 Vol. 49

farmers, small forced out of business (Jesus) — 9/2/03 Vol. 32
farms controlled by a few (Jesus) — 3/15/06 Vol. 42
farms at refuges self-sufficient in needs (Jesus) — 11/29/05 Vol. 41
fast living slow down to see Jesus (Jesus) — 1/18/05 Vol. 38
fast pace confession (Jesus) — 8/12/94 Vol. 2
fast pace of life no time to meditate (Jesus) — 9/13/99 Vol. 16
fast paced living age of materialism (Jesus) — 2/7/00 Vol. 18
fast torpedoes,mines tested by Iran (Jesus) — 4/8/06 Vol. 43
fasting Consecration (Mary) — 2/20/95 Vol. 2
fasting during Lent (Jesus) — 2/23/07 Vol. 46
fasting help focus on holy life (Jesus) — 6/24/04 Vol. 35
fasting helps control body by soul (Jesus) — 2/8/08 Vol. 50
fasting helps in food shortages (Jesus) — 7/30/00 Vol. 20
fasting means to self-control (Jesus) — 1/5/06 Vol. 42
fasting stengthens your soul (Jesus) — 2/7/08 Vol. 50
fasting train body and soul (Jesus) — 2/23/98 Vol. 10
fasting & prayer restrict body's passions (Jesus) — 3/5/02 Vol. 26
fasting difficult takes stamina,famine prep (Jesus) — 3/8/01 Vol. 22
fasting from desserts Wednesdays,Fridays (Jesus) — 6/15/00 Vol. 19
fasting from sweets controls sin (Jesus) — 6/19/03 Vol. 31
fasting of Jesus preparation for tasks (Jesus) — 3/1/06 Vol. 42
fasting,suffering,grace needed for conversions (Jesus) — 10/9/04 Vol. 37
fate as nation decided by repenting or not (Jesus) — 8/25/01 Vol. 24
Father disgusted by sins (Father) — 6/16/05 Vol. 39
father took to Confession (Jesus) — 7/11/03 Vol. 32
Father & Jesus are One in the Trinity (Jesus) — 5/4/06 Vol. 43
Father & Jesus give good gifts to us (Jesus) — 3/12/04 Vol. 34
father & mother core of society (Jesus) — 6/17/07 Vol. 47
father in old age children need help them (Jesus) — 4/17/97 Vol. 7
Father, Eternal thanks for dedicated chapel (God the Father) — 1/20/08 Vol. 50
Father, God the go through Jesus (Jesus) — 4/30/98 Vol. 11
Father, God the honor on Father's Day (Jesus) — 6/21/98 Vol. 11
Father,God the honored on father's day (Jesus) — 6/18/00 Vol. 19
Father,Our; Glory Be give praise in prayer (God the Father) — 8/4/02 Vol. 28
Fatherly love angel guide to refuge (God the Father) — 6/20/99 Vol. 15
fathers protectors of the family (Jesus) — 6/17/07 Vol. 47
father's day appreciate their efforts (Jesus) — 6/13/97 Vol. 7
Father's Day feast of God the Father (God the Father) — 6/17/04 Vol. 35
Father's day provide food & shelter (God the Father) — 6/20/99 Vol. 15
Father's Day special blessing for (God the Father) — 6/20/04 Vol. 35
Father's Day with a capital F (Jesus) — 6/21/98 Vol. 11
fathers' day lead & support families (Jesus) — 6/17/01 Vol. 23
father's love in helping children (Jesus) — 8/29/07 Vol. 48
fatigue & tiredness makes one weak to sin (Jesus) — 6/1/06 Vol. 43
Fatima 90th anniversary of miracle (Jesus) — 10/11/07 Vol. 49
Fatima annihilation of nations (Jesus) — 6/7/99 Vol. 15
Fatima annihilation of nations (Jesus) — 10/21/99 Vol. 17

Fatima messages about war,communism (Jesus)   5/12/00 Vol. 19
Fatima prophecies several nation annihilated (Jesus)   3/21/99 Vol. 14
Fatima secret salvation is all that matters (Jesus)   5/13/04 Vol. 35
Fatima Statue close of visit in Rochester (Mary)   8/22/97 Vol. 8
faults understand each other's (Jesus)   3/4/06 Vol. 42
fear & anxieties no concern with Jesus (Jesus)   5/8/04 Vol. 35
fear is useless trust in God for needs (Jesus)   1/29/05 Vol. 38
fear killer of the soul unfaithful to face hell (Jesus)   11/24/98 Vol. 13
fear not grandfather clock (Jesus)   7/5/94 Vol. 2
fear not not tested over endurance (Jesus)   11/18/99 Vol. 17
fear of God Holy Spirit gift, evil otherwise (Jesus)   6/25/06 Vol. 43
fear tactics to control people (Jesus)   5/29/03 Vol. 31
fear, have no because you can call on Jesus (Jesus)   3/16/02 Vol. 26
fear, have no Jesus reigns over Satan (Jesus)   6/30/99 Vol. 15
fear, have no of those who kill the body (Jesus)   6/23/02 Vol. 27
fears faith takes away (Jesus)   1/28/06 Vol. 42
feast days fireworks in souls (Jesus)   5/29/96 Vol. 3
feast days reduced to non-events (Jesus)   8/22/01 Vol. 24
Feast of Annunciation Mary gave her 'yes' (Mary)   3/25/98 Vol. 10
Fed,State,Town levels of control (Jesus)   10/30/07 Vol. 49
Federal Reserve answers to central bankers (Jesus)   4/24/02 Vol. 27
Federal Reserve bailing out the rich (Jesus)   11/30/07 Vol. 49
Federal Reserve bails out bankers,brokers (Jesus)   9/18/07 Vol. 48
Federal Reserve exploits money from people (Jesus)   9/23/07 Vol. 48
Federal Reserve notes no gold backing (Jesus)   4/29/04 Vol. 35
Federal Reserve Notes not US, but central bankers (Jesus)   6/7/04 Vol. 35
Federal Reserve,bankers to take control of world (Jesus)   9/3/98 Vol. 12
feed hungry water, clothes to poor (Jesus)   5/7/07 Vol. 47
feed the hungry feeding Jesus (Jesus)   5/6/99 Vol. 15
feed the poor charity stored up in heaven (Jesus)   3/30/00 Vol. 18
feeding the poor charity needed (Jesus)   6/23/06 Vol. 43
feeding tubes discerning life (Jesus)   3/17/05 Vol. 38
feeling,deep of dread twin tower related (Jesus)   7/24/01 Vol. 24
feminists extremists ruin families (Jesus)   9/3/98 Vol. 12
fences removed love neighbors more (Jesus)   3/5/01 Vol. 22
fertility in nations being threatened (Jesus)   1/23/06 Vol. 42
fever pitch for souls required after Warning (Jesus)   7/4/00 Vol. 20
fiat, personal follow Divine Will (Mary)   3/26/07 Vol. 46
fiat, personal follow God's Will (Jesus)   12/20/06 Vol. 45
fiber optic cable control TV & telephones (Jesus)   8/30/01 Vol. 24
fiber optics used for listening devices (Jesus)   1/15/04 Vol. 34
fiber optics used for spying (Jesus)   2/7/07 Vol. 46
fighting stop your killing (Jesus)   3/13/99 Vol. 14
fighting in sports should not be glorified (Jesus)   3/15/01 Vol. 22
fighting over food sign for hiding (Jesus)   2/29/00 Vol. 18
fighting wars between in power, out of power (Jesus)   3/23/04 Vol. 34
final appearance angels will provide manna (Jesus)   6/19/95 Vol. 2

final decision after Warning (Jesus)   1/3/07 Vol. 46
final judgment between heaven or hell (Jesus)   8/23/05 Vol. 40
final judgment body & soul united (Jesus)   2/8/01 Vol. 22
final judgment end of era of peace (Jesus)   8/2/97 Vol. 8
finances & military crumbling from effects of sin (Jesus)   11/7/01 Vol. 25
financial collapse from deficits (Jesus)   1/2/07 Vol. 46
financial collapse North American Union (Jesus)   7/16/07 Vol. 48
financial collapse to be used for takeover (Jesus)   3/17/08 Vol. 50
financial crisis world famine (Jesus)   7/3/02 Vol. 28
financial meltdown greed at any cost (Jesus)   12/25/97 Vol. 9
financial pit good job, sponsor needed (Jesus)   3/19/07 Vol. 46
financial problems burden of sins (Jesus)   9/25/03 Vol. 32
financial problems result of greed & sin (Jesus)   3/13/08 Vol. 50
financial problems result of sin & greed (Jesus)   1/13/05 Vol. 38
financial troubles need trust in God (Jesus)   1/28/99 Vol. 14
financial troubles part of chastisement (Jesus)   1/16/03 Vol. 30
financial upheavals stock market manipulated (Jesus)   3/16/01 Vol. 22
finished the course crown in heaven waiting (Jesus)   1/14/00 Vol. 18
fire purification (Jesus)   1/30/95 Vol. 2
fire alarm urgency to avoid hell (Jesus)   10/15/02 Vol. 29
fire balls on a city America to be tested (Jesus)   7/28/01 Vol. 24
fire from heaven lasers,magic of Antichrist (Jesus)   5/31/02 Vol. 27
fire from planes dropped on cities (Jesus)   9/22/06 Vol. 44
fire in America volcanoes,forest fires,arson (Jesus)   2/25/02 Vol. 26
fire purification choose Me or the world (Jesus)   7/14/96 Vol. 4
fire season summer droughts in west (Jesus)   8/30/01 Vol. 24
fire, wall of terrible deaths in Iraq (Jesus)   12/21/02 Vol. 29
fireball spiritual well-being (Jesus)   4/7/95 Vol. 2
fireplaces fuel needs will vary (Jesus)   9/6/99 Vol. 16
fires and droughts (Jesus)   5/29/03 Vol. 31
fires chaos and looters (Jesus)   2/21/97 Vol. 6
fires chastisements (Jesus)   1/25/95 Vol. 2
fires chastisements for sins (Jesus)   9/11/03 Vol. 32
fires demons (Jesus)   12/25/95 Vol. 3
fires demons (Jesus)   11/3/94 Vol. 2
fires hazards of (Jesus)   6/6/02 Vol. 27
fires in Florida, drought (Jesus)   6/25/98 Vol. 11
fires more building damage this year (Jesus)   6/12/02 Vol. 27
fires people not consumed (Jesus)   1/23/03 Vol. 30
fires physically & spiritually (Jesus)   9/2/02 Vol. 28
fires polluting air (Jesus)   5/23/02 Vol. 27
fires possessions taken (Jesus)   5/17/96 Vol. 3
fires pray for protection from (Jesus)   10/6/05 Vol. 41
fires pray for rain (Jesus)   9/2/04 Vol. 36
fires punishment for sins (Jesus)   7/5/98 Vol. 12
fires signs of times (Jesus)   7/31/03 Vol. 32
fires storms and droughts (Jesus)   6/23/98 Vol. 11

fires taste of hell or purgatory (Jesus) 9/10/98 Vol. 12

fires upset infrastructure (Jesus) 12/5/96 Vol. 5

fires USA (Jesus) 8/3/94 Vol. 2

fires wealth taken away (Jesus) 10/23/96 Vol. 5

fires & droughts for sins of abortion (Jesus) 8/31/00 Vol. 20

fires & droughts to increase from weather (Jesus) 3/1/01 Vol. 22

fires & heat warnings in prophecies (Jesus) 7/20/00 Vol. 20

fires & storms purges for sin (Jesus) 8/17/00 Vol. 20

fires and storms will increase (Jesus) 6/4/98 Vol. 11

fires and wind chastisements to continue (Jesus) 1/12/00 Vol. 18

fires in California chastise movie makers (Jesus) 10/14/99 Vol. 17

fires in Florida stripped of materialism (Jesus) 7/4/98 Vol. 12

fires in Texas unusual in winter (Jesus) 1/5/06 Vol. 42

fires in West natural, punishment for sin (Jesus) 10/30/06 Vol. 45

fires in west noticed with homes lost (Jesus) 9/6/01 Vol. 24

fires of chastisement for abortions,sexual sins (Jesus) 6/29/00 Vol. 19

fires of Hell evil influences on earth (Jesus) 4/15/99 Vol. 15

fires to come in cities and forests (Jesus) 12/30/03 Vol. 33

fires to continue for sins of abortion,flesh (Jesus) 8/26/99 Vol. 16

fires to get worse wrath of God poured out (Jesus) 5/11/00 Vol. 19

fires widespread chastisements for sins (Jesus) 6/15/00 Vol. 19

fires, arson forests & refineries (Jesus) 6/14/03 Vol. 31

fires, California possessions are temporary (Jesus) 10/22/07 Vol. 49

fires, continuing tested by flames (Jesus) 2/7/01 Vol. 22

fires, record amount 9 million acres burned (Jesus) 11/16/06 Vol. 45

fires,storms & floods chastisements (Jesus) 5/3/01 Vol. 23

first & second judgment Purgatory (Jesus) 5/4/95 Vol. 2

First Cause of creation is God (Jesus) 10/6/05 Vol. 41

First Commandment love God, not world (Jesus) 11/8/02 Vol. 29

First Commandment no idols before God (Jesus) 8/22/02 Vol. 28

First Communion reverence & grace (Jesus) 5/12/01 Vol. 23

First Communion thanks for gift (Jesus) 5/19/01 Vol. 23

First Covenant repent (Father) 12/20/93 Vol. 1

First Holy Communion teach by example (Jesus) 5/5/97 Vol. 7

first priority prayer, love of God (Jesus) 2/23/00 Vol. 18

first priority to follow Jesus (Jesus) 9/27/07 Vol. 48

first,second Resurrection first,second deaths (Jesus) 11/29/96 Vol. 5

fish symbol of Christians (Jesus) 1/30/07 Vol. 46

fish ponds refuge food multiplied (Jesus) 11/29/06 Vol. 45

fish supplies and natural disasters (Jesus) 11/3/05 Vol. 41

fisherman Jesus reels in souls by love (Jesus) 1/9/01 Vol. 22

fishermen for souls be prepared (Jesus) 4/30/02 Vol. 27

fishers of men apostles in all nations (Jesus) 11/15/98 Vol. 13

fishers of men gifts of the Holy Spirit (Jesus) 9/25/96 Vol. 4

Fishers of men harvest souls,all nations (Jesus) 4/14/97 Vol. 7

fishers of men new calling of apostles (Jesus) 1/30/07 Vol. 46

fishers of men vocation (Jesus) 3/9/95 Vol. 2

fishers of men,women bringing souls to convert (Jesus) 4/9/99 Vol. 15

fishing depleted by greed (Jesus) 5/29/03 Vol. 31

fishing, over avoid to ruin banks (Jesus) 2/2/08 Vol. 50

flag perdition (Jesus) 7/3/94 Vol. 2

flag of United States united to God in beginning (Jesus) 6/18/98 Vol. 11

flags Antichrist (Jesus) 8/3/94 Vol. 2

flakes found on the floor (Mary) 7/10/97 Vol. 8

flakes near the altar protection (Mary) 12/4/95 Vol. 3

flame love (Jesus) 11/29/93 Vol. 1

flames earth 8/11/93 Vol. 1

flames of destruction fires & computer problems (Jesus) 8/19/99 Vol. 16

flames of fire faith taught to children (Jesus) 1/9/95 Vol. 2

flames of fire inspiration of Holy Spirit (Jesus) 5/11/00 Vol. 19

flames of life are light & love (Jesus) 2/16/03 Vol. 30

flames of love pass on life & faith (Jesus) 9/29/02 Vol. 28

flames on earth plague of fire for evil ones (Jesus) 11/20/99 Vol. 17

flee for life soon after schism (Jesus) 6/15/98 Vol. 11

flesh on cross no longer hollow (Jesus) 1/15/00 Vol. 18

flood of Noah's day injustice to them (Jesus) 6/23/97 Vol. 7

Flood, Patrick reunited with wife, heaven (Jesus) 5/17/99 Vol. 15

flooding abortion and sins (Jesus) 2/7/96 Vol. 3

flooding animal sanctuaries lost (Jesus) 7/24/96 Vol. 4

flooding Baptism, sins of man (Jesus) 4/13/96 Vol. 3

flooding from melting snow (Jesus) 1/22/04 Vol. 34

flooding physical,spiritual stripping (Jesus) 11/2/97 Vol. 9

flooding seek high ground (Jesus) 8/27/98 Vol. 12

flooding sin and events (Jesus) 5/9/97 Vol. 7

flooding when snow melts (Jesus) 2/12/04 Vol. 34

flooding & droughts water & fires (Jesus) 6/16/04 Vol. 35

flooding in Midwest fulfilled prophecy (Jesus) 3/19/08 Vol. 50

flooding in New England enhanced by HAARP (Jesus) 6/3/06 Vol. 43

flooding storms will continue destruction (Jesus) 3/4/06 Vol. 42

floods chastisements (Jesus) 12/31/94 Vol. 2

floods chastisements (Jesus) 12/21/94 Vol. 2

floods destruction 8/30/93 Vol. 1

floods linked to abortion sins (Jesus) 4/22/97 Vol. 7

floods sins and disasters (Jesus) 5/26/97 Vol. 7

floods to affect economy (Jesus) 6/25/02 Vol. 27

floods & crops wather patterns crucial (Jesus) 7/2/04 Vol. 36

floods & droughts cause lost homes, fires (Jesus) 4/6/00 Vol. 19

floods & droughts fulfilling prophecy (Jesus) 8/24/02 Vol. 28

floods & droughts start of famine (Jesus) 5/30/00 Vol. 19

floods & droughts to cause famine (Mary) 5/15/00 Vol. 19

floods & droughts to continue in winter (Jesus) 11/15/07 Vol. 49

floods & fires chastisements (Jesus) 8/16/01 Vol. 24

floods & fires chastisements for sin (Jesus) 8/1/97 Vol. 8

floods & lost power from rain & tornadoes (Jesus) 3/29/06 Vol. 42

floods and storms chastisement of America (Jesus)   8/28/97 Vol. 8

floods in California sign of coming tribulation (Jesus)   1/5/06 Vol. 42

floods, world God's wrath for sin (Jesus)   8/25/05 Vol. 40

Florida hit by huge wave (Jesus)   7/28/06 Vol. 44

Florida unusual tornadoes (Jesus)   2/2/07 Vol. 46

Florida ballots flawed system (Jesus)   11/30/00 Vol. 21

Florida economy damage to crops & property (Jesus)   8/19/04 Vol. 36

Florida vote no settlement,long trials (Jesus)   11/8/00 Vol. 21

Florida,fires in stripped of materialism (Jesus)   7/4/98 Vol. 12

Florida's sins bringing punishment (Jesus)   7/28/06 Vol. 44

flower blooming Holy Spirit empowers confirmed (Jesus) 12/3/04 Vol. 37

flowers we are like them (Jesus)   6/23/97 Vol. 7

flowers' beauty gives glory to God (Jesus)   4/27/06 Vol. 43

flu bugs man-made origin (Jesus)   2/8/08 Vol. 50

flu epidemics possibility raises concerns (Jesus)   12/7/04 Vol. 37

flu shots virus to be put in (Jesus)   2/18/08 Vol. 50

flue scare latest media distraction (Jesus)   12/18/03 Vol. 33

flying cross renewed earth return (Jesus)   10/28/94 Vol. 2

focus love (Jesus)   10/20/95 Vol. 3

focus life on love of God, neighbor (Jesus)   2/9/00 Vol. 18

focus of life God vs. worldly things (Jesus)   12/11/03 Vol. 33

focus of life on love of God & neighbor (Jesus)   5/29/99 Vol. 15

focus on path to heaven (Jesus)   11/22/06 Vol. 45

focus on Jesus even during tribulation (Jesus)   2/24/00 Vol. 18

focus on Jesus for peace and love (Jesus)   12/27/02 Vol. 29

focus on Jesus in and not of the world (Jesus)   11/27/99 Vol. 17

follow the crowd broad road to hell (Jesus)   3/9/00 Vol. 18

food contrived shortages (Jesus)   8/7/96 Vol. 4

food controlled by 1 world men (Jesus)   12/28/97 Vol. 9

food controlled distribution (Jesus)   6/11/02 Vol. 27

food donate to the poor (Jesus)   2/14/02 Vol. 26

food have extra for multiplication (Jesus)   8/12/04 Vol. 36

food more difficult to get (Jesus)   8/7/03 Vol. 32

food more valued than money (Jesus)   7/3/02 Vol. 28

food most valuable possession (Jesus)   7/3/03 Vol. 32

food multiplied (Jesus)   6/1/02 Vol. 27

food multiplied (Jesus)   10/2/03 Vol. 33

food multiplied (Jesus)   1/28/03 Vol. 30

food multiplied (Jesus)   9/7/00 Vol. 20

food multiplied at refuges (Jesus)   4/1/03 Vol. 31

food prepare extra for disasters (Jesus)   1/10/97 Vol. 6

food prepare some (Jesus)   2/5/98 Vol. 10

food set aside for multiplication (Jesus)   7/12/01 Vol. 24

food store for evil times (Jesus)   1/13/04 Vol. 34

food store for famine (Jesus)   6/13/02 Vol. 27

food stored & multiplied (Jesus)   10/20/05 Vol. 41

food to become more expensive (Jesus)   8/11/05 Vol. 40

food to help feed the poor (Jesus)   9/18/03 Vol. 32

food will multiply for others (Jesus)   3/2/99 Vol. 14

food & blessings to be taken away (Jesus)   7/27/00 Vol. 20

food & famine controlled & multiplied (Jesus)   4/21/05 Vol. 39

food & fuel control buying & selling (Jesus)   10/19/00 Vol. 21

food & fuel multiplied (Jesus)   1/8/01 Vol. 22

food & fuel multiplied for needs (Jesus)   9/22/07 Vol. 48

food & fuel stored for power outages, famine (Jesus)   11/25/03 Vol. 33

food & sacramentals ready to leave with (Jesus)   3/16/99 Vol. 14

food & water multiplied & preserved (Jesus)   1/10/02 Vol. 26

food & water multiplied by God (Jesus)   11/16/99 Vol. 17

food & water multiplies at refuges (Jesus)   12/16/00 Vol. 21

food & water prepare reserves (Jesus)   10/21/99 Vol. 17

food & water renew for tribulation (Jesus)   8/15/05 Vol. 40

food & water taken for granted (Jesus)   7/8/06 Vol. 44

food & water thank God for abundance (Jesus)   5/12/07 Vol. 47

food & water will be scarce (Jesus)   3/13/00 Vol. 18

food altered radiation,hybrids to problems (Jesus)   4/5/01 Vol. 23

food and energy do not waste (Jesus)   9/23/00 Vol. 20

food and fuel prepare extra (Jesus)   1/10/08 Vol. 50

food and fuel save extra (Jesus)   9/16/00 Vol. 20

food and shelter Jesus will provide (Jesus)   7/17/96 Vol. 4

food and water one year's supply needed (Jesus)   12/3/98 Vol. 13

food and water prepare for one year (Jesus)   5/13/99 Vol. 15

food and water scarce in famine (Jesus)   5/25/00 Vol. 19

food and water store now (Jesus)   7/19/98 Vol. 12

food at refuges multiplied (Jesus)   1/14/08 Vol. 50

food control by one world people (Jesus)   1/28/03 Vol. 30

food controlled by chips in buying (Jesus)   12/17/03 Vol. 33

food controlled through hybid seeds (Jesus)   5/24/07 Vol. 47

food crisis Antichrist control (Jesus)   8/8/97 Vol. 8

food damage bad weather & insects (Jesus)   7/24/96 Vol. 4

food donations to the poor (Jesus)   11/20/03 Vol. 33

food for poor better than war (Jesus)   1/25/07 Vol. 46

food harvest threatened starting this year (Jesus)   6/20/02 Vol. 27

food industry causing more diseases (Jesus)   3/30/07 Vol. 46

food manipulation chastisements for sin (Jesus)   7/19/01 Vol. 24

food mulitiplied in time of famine (Jesus)   2/28/02 Vol. 26

food multiplied at homes & refuges (Jesus)   10/6/07 Vol. 49

food multiplied at refuges (Jesus)   7/3/03 Vol. 32

food multiplied at refuges (Jesus)   8/11/01 Vol. 24

food multiplied depend on God (Jesus)   9/2/03 Vol. 32

food multiplied during famine (Jesus)   8/1/99 Vol. 16

food multiplied during tribulation (Jesus)   8/26/02 Vol. 28

food multiplied during tribulation (Jesus)   1/18/01 Vol. 22

food multiplied during tribulation (Jesus)   5/29/99 Vol. 15

food multiplied in famine (Jesus)   10/13/02 Vol. 29

St. Anthony Saves Our Luggage

We were in Genoa, Italy to meet Mary's Pilgrims on our way to a cruise to Egypt, Greece, and the Holy Lands for two weeks. We arrived two days early, but none of our luggage arrived with us from Rome, Italy. We spent two days trying to locate it. Finally, in desperation as we were ready to board the ship, we frantically prayed to St. Anthony, even reminding him that we were not far from his town of Padua. As we boarded the ship, we were resigned now to be two weeks in our winter clothes that we were wearing. The gangplank was being lifted, and a lady from the travel bureau came running and shouting to wait. She had just located our luggage at the airport in some back room.

We could write a book on all of the help that we have gotten from St. Anthony.

Message: October 24, 1998 (volume 13)

food multiplied like a fast food restaurant (Jesus)	6/21/05 Vol. 39	food storage need seen in Columbia (Jesus)	1/28/99 Vol. 14
food multiplied miraculous food in trial (Jesus)	4/23/99 Vol. 15	food storage one year supply (Jesus)	8/10/99 Vol. 16
food multiplied so do not take mark beast (Jesus)	10/22/99 Vol. 17	food storage scoffers will regret actions (Jesus)	10/9/97 Vol. 9
food multiplied supplied in need (Jesus)	6/9/98 Vol. 11	food stored for famine & chips (Jesus)	9/2/03 Vol. 32
food multiplied to be shared at refuges (Jesus)	8/20/98 Vol. 12	food stored multiplied (Jesus)	1/11/04 Vol. 34
food multiplied to save souls (Jesus)	1/2/06 Vol. 42	food supplies multiplied (Jesus)	2/6/03 Vol. 30
food multiplied wise & foolish virgins (Jesus)	8/31/01 Vol. 24	food supplies threatened (Jesus)	8/14/03 Vol. 32
food preparation can cause disease to spread (Jesus)	1/20/05 Vol. 38	food to be scarce commodities controlled (Jesus)	2/29/00 Vol. 18
food preparation for disasters (Jesus)	1/22/98 Vol. 10	food wasted in hotels, cruise ships (Jesus)	3/30/06 Vol. 42
food prices hurt farmers (Jesus)	10/4/07 Vol. 49	food, clothes God will provide (Jesus)	2/29/00 Vol. 18
food prices to go higher (Jesus)	8/8/02 Vol. 28	food, drug industry money is incentive (Jesus)	1/31/07 Vol. 46
food prices controlled to bankrupt small farmers (Jesus)	8/12/99 Vol. 16	food, plentiful share with poor (Jesus)	4/12/07 Vol. 47
food production more important than tech jobs (Jesus)	4/5/01 Vol. 23	food, water world famine,mark in hand (Jesus)	9/23/99 Vol. 16
food rations one world contrived (Jesus)	12/4/97 Vol. 9	food, water needed for famine,chip in the hand (Jesus)	12/25/99 Vol. 17
food reserves needed famine,control of food (Jesus)	3/30/00 Vol. 18	food, water, & fuel prepare extra (Jesus)	10/22/99 Vol. 17
food saved for world famine (Jesus)	4/4/00 Vol. 19	food,fighting over sign for hiding (Jesus)	2/29/00 Vol. 18
food set aside to be multiplied (Jesus)	4/4/02 Vol. 27	food,water & fuel have prepared (Jesus)	10/7/99 Vol. 17
food shelves for homeless (Jesus)	2/14/08 Vol. 50	food,water needed to prepare for Y2K trials (Jesus)	9/22/99 Vol. 16
food shortage manipulated by price (Jesus)	6/3/99 Vol. 15	food,water, & fuel multiplied, so share (Jesus)	10/28/99 Vol. 17
food shortages food multiplied (Jesus)	8/11/97 Vol. 8	food,water,heat needed in power outages (Jesus)	12/26/98 Vol. 13
food shortages help provided at refuges (Jesus)	8/19/99 Vol. 16	foods, fast adulterated and abused (Jesus)	4/30/02 Vol. 27
food shortages natural and man made (Jesus)	5/29/96 Vol. 3	foods, natural focus on good health (Jesus)	4/30/02 Vol. 27
food shortages riots, contrived (Jesus)	9/2/97 Vol. 8	foolish man depends on himself (Jesus)	2/8/00 Vol. 18
food shortages set aside food (Jesus)	6/21/07 Vol. 47	foolish virgins did not prepare (Jesus)	4/9/99 Vol. 15
food shortages weather, one world (Jesus)	7/3/97 Vol. 8	foolish virgins like the lukewarm (Jesus)	1/12/02 Vol. 26
food storage help others, multiply (Jesus)	6/9/99 Vol. 15	football mesmerized by desires (Jesus)	9/30/97 Vol. 8
food storage like wise virgins (Mary)	10/16/97 Vol. 9	football season September to January (Jesus)	7/2/05 Vol. 40

footprints of Jesus imitate Jesus' life (Jesus)	12/11/05 Vol. 41
footsoldiers family (Mary)	8/20/94 Vol. 2
footstep Divine Wine (Jesus)	8/16/94 Vol. 2
footsteps follow & imitate Jesus (Jesus)	8/16/01 Vol. 24
footsteps rejection (Jesus)	2/21/95 Vol. 2
footstool of God man's place to serve God (Jesus)	3/9/04 Vol. 34
foreclosures, home rich bailed out (Jesus)	10/4/07 Vol. 49
forehead mark of the beast (Holy Spirit)	11/6/93 Vol. 1
forehead crosses will detect spies without (Jesus)	8/13/98 Vol. 12
foreign ownership of ports questioned (Jesus)	2/23/06 Vol. 42
foreign troops control our cities (Jesus)	5/7/02 Vol. 27
foreign troops to help in martial law (Jesus)	9/28/06 Vol. 44
forgive all loving (Jesus)	3/13/95 Vol. 2
forgive and be forgiven (Jesus)	4/18/04 Vol. 35
forgive graces	9/15/93 Vol. 1
forgive each other before you die (Jesus)	5/17/07 Vol. 47
forgive enemies do not exact revenge (Jesus)	8/12/04 Vol. 36
forgive injustices love those hating you (Jesus)	8/25/99 Vol. 16
forgive without grudges admit being wrong (Jesus)	6/21/00 Vol. 19
forgiveness 70 times 7 times (Jesus)	8/16/01 Vol. 24
forgiveness and restitution (Jesus)	5/26/02 Vol. 27
forgiveness and sacrifice of cross (Jesus)	3/5/05 Vol. 38
forgiveness as you forgive (Jesus)	8/12/99 Vol. 16
forgiveness ask humbly for (Jesus)	9/18/03 Vol. 32
forgiveness beauty of creation (Jesus)	6/14/96 Vol. 3
forgiveness endless love for all (Jesus)	3/17/01 Vol. 22
forgiveness even in hard cases (Jesus)	6/18/01 Vol. 23
forgiveness evil destroyed (Jesus)	2/25/97 Vol. 6
forgiveness for killers & abortionists (Jesus)	9/4/03 Vol. 32
forgiveness for self and others (Jesus)	3/19/06 Vol. 42
forgiveness from God & neighbor (Jesus)	1/19/08 Vol. 50
forgiveness from God & to others (Jesus)	1/27/05 Vol. 38
forgiveness gives peace (Jesus)	9/11/03 Vol. 32
forgiveness in Confession (Jesus)	9/14/96 Vol. 4
forgiveness in divorces (Jesus)	6/30/04 Vol. 35
forgiveness in families (Jesus)	3/7/05 Vol. 38
forgiveness Jarice Hogan (Jarice Hogan)	9/2/00 Vol. 20
forgiveness love enemies (Jesus)	9/8/02 Vol. 28
forgiveness need white robe for heaven (Jesus)	11/7/00 Vol. 21
forgiveness needed before Communion (Jesus)	3/3/00 Vol. 18
forgiveness needed for heaven (Jesus)	3/2/08 Vol. 50
forgiveness needed in Confession (Jesus)	11/8/99 Vol. 17
forgiveness needs an open heart (Jesus)	10/11/05 Vol. 41
forgiveness needs work (Jesus)	6/21/07 Vol. 47
forgiveness of enemies (Jesus)	10/24/02 Vol. 29
forgiveness of enemies (Jesus)	8/14/03 Vol. 32
forgiveness of everyone (Jesus)	12/4/00 Vol. 21
forgiveness repent of sins (Jesus)	3/1/97 Vol. 6
forgiveness seventy times seven (Jesus)	5/19/99 Vol. 15
forgiveness seventy times seven times (Jesus)	9/15/02 Vol. 28
forgiveness should not have limits (Jesus)	9/12/99 Vol. 16
forgiveness sought from grave (Maggie Vest)	11/2/02 Vol. 29
forgiveness train of life (Jesus)	3/1/96 Vol. 3
forgiveness way back to Jesus (Jesus)	3/31/07 Vol. 46
forgiveness & repentance calling of Jesus (Jesus)	12/14/04 Vol. 37
forgiveness & Savior to get to heaven (Jesus)	9/3/01 Vol. 24
forgiveness for all even enemies, hard cases (Jesus)	9/11/05 Vol. 40
forgiveness in Confession flow of graces (Jesus)	1/2/02 Vol. 26
forgiveness in Confession needed to save souls (Jesus)	4/11/99 Vol. 15
forgiveness needed for most grievous sins (Jesus)	7/9/04 Vol. 36
forgiveness needed in Confession (Jesus)	7/29/05 Vol. 40
forgiveness needed in family & for others (Jesus)	3/13/04 Vol. 34
forgiveness needed to heal grudges (Jesus)	10/27/07 Vol. 49
forgiveness of others takes faith & growth in spirit (Jesus)	11/13/00 Vol. 21
forgiveness of self harder than God's forgiveness (Jesus)	11/13/00 Vol. 21
forgiveness of sin needed to enter heaven (Jesus)	7/1/00 Vol. 20
forgiveness of sinners required for heaven (Jesus)	4/1/01 Vol. 23
forgiveness of sins needed before death (Jesus)	12/17/04 Vol. 37
forgiveness of sins needed to enter heaven (Jesus)	9/14/05 Vol. 40
forgiveness of sins needed to enter heaven (Jesus)	3/20/08 Vol. 50
forgiveness of sins needed to gain heaven (Jesus)	8/26/05 Vol. 40
forgiveness of sins or wish never to be born (Jesus)	4/12/98 Vol. 11
forgiveness of sins provided in Confession (Jesus)	10/26/00 Vol. 21
forgiveness of sins to keep pure soul for death (Jesus)	11/13/04 Vol. 37
forgiveness of souls frees bonds of sins (Jesus)	3/5/08 Vol. 50
forgiveness, without you will wither and die (Jesus)	12/19/98 Vol. 13
forgiveness,endless needs no bounds (Jesus)	3/20/01 Vol. 22
forgiveness,Savior needed for heaven (Jesus)	3/14/00 Vol. 18
forgiving is Christmas spirit (Jesus)	12/21/00 Vol. 21
forgiving heart to forgive others (Jesus)	3/28/00 Vol. 18
forgiving neighbor do not seek vengeance (Jesus)	4/10/00 Vol. 19
forgotten souls prisoners,lukewarm,displaced (Jesus)	3/30/08 Vol. 50
fornication a mortal sin (Jesus)	4/30/98 Vol. 11
fornication confess before Communion (Jesus)	8/12/05 Vol. 40
fornication need gentle counseling (Jesus)	3/1/07 Vol. 46
fornication serious sin (Jesus)	10/2/01 Vol. 25
fornication sin against the body (Jesus)	1/16/00 Vol. 18
fornication speak out against it (Jesus)	7/30/05 Vol. 40
fornication & adultery against 6th Commandment (Jesus)	1/14/07 Vol. 46
fornication acts speak out to relatives (Jesus)	8/29/05 Vol. 40
foundation in faith fertile ground, open (Jesus)	1/29/00 Vol. 18
foundation of faith built on prayer,deeds (Jesus)	8/27/99 Vol. 16
foundation of faith count the costs (Jesus)	1/9/07 Vol. 46
foundation of faith in Word of God (Jesus)	3/22/07 Vol. 46

foundations spiritual and physical (Jesus) — 11/14/05 Vol. 41

four angels sounding trumpets (Jesus) — 10/24/95 Vol. 3

four lampstands angels — 9/5/93 Vol. 1

Fr. Bonsignore's 25th Latin High Mass (Jesus) — 5/21/06 Vol. 43

Fr. Charlie St. Anthony (St. Anthony) — 6/16/03 Vol. 31

Fr. Elmer Heindl's funeral message (Jesus) — 7/22/06 Vol. 44

Fr. Gagnier installation Mass (Jesus) — 6/26/07 Vol. 47

Fr. Luke Zimmer petition for healing (K. Tekakwitha) — 7/28/96 Vol. 4

Fr. Solanus Casey keep simple faith (Jesus) — 10/13/03 Vol. 33

Fran Pierce funeral example of love (Jesus) — 2/28/07 Vol. 46

France deaths from heat (Jesus) — 8/14/03 Vol. 32

Franciscan life model for living close to God (Jesus) — 9/5/01 Vol. 24

free time family (Jesus) — 5/28/95 Vol. 2

free trade decimating manufacturing (Jesus) — 7/31/03 Vol. 32

free trade in NAFTA & GATT (Jesus) — 6/19/05 Vol. 39

free trade policy cause of job losses (Jesus) — 9/4/03 Vol. 32

free will called to love God (Jesus) — 6/30/00 Vol. 19

free will chance to choose life over death (Jesus) — 8/17/07 Vol. 48

free will choice to love God (Jesus) — 7/2/07 Vol. 48

free will choose narrow road to heaven (Jesus) — 4/11/03 Vol. 31

free will choose to love (Jesus) — 6/10/04 Vol. 35

free will choose to love God (Jesus) — 12/20/05 Vol. 41

free will controls door to heart (Jesus) — 9/25/03 Vol. 32

free will determines eternal destination (Jesus) — 1/9/04 Vol. 34

free will die to self (Jesus) — 9/18/97 Vol. 8

free will follow Divine Will (Jesus) — 8/22/04 Vol. 36

free will given to angels and us (Jesus) — 6/20/97 Vol. 7

free will gives yes or no to everything (Jesus) — 10/29/03 Vol. 33

free will God does not violate (Jesus) — 7/11/06 Vol. 44

free will love, but not forced (Jesus) — 4/27/98 Vol. 11

free will means to open heart to God (Jesus) — 9/11/01 Vol. 24

free will of man and angels (Jesus) — 2/2/98 Vol. 10

free will still must choose Jesus (Jesus) — 10/25/03 Vol. 33

free will to open door to our heart (Jesus) — 3/1/99 Vol. 14

free will to reason and choose (Jesus) — 7/21/01 Vol. 24

free will choice God's order vs. devil's chaos (Jesus) — 8/21/03 Vol. 32

free will choice heaven vs hell (Jesus) — 8/7/00 Vol. 20

free will choice to choose heaven (Jesus) — 10/4/98 Vol. 13

free will to God to shape mission (Jesus) — 7/31/07 Vol. 48

free will, gift of consecration to God needed (Jesus) — 8/13/00 Vol. 20

freedom physical & spiritual (Jesus) — 4/10/03 Vol. 31

freedom poor (St. Joseph) — 8/23/93 Vol. 1

freedom revolutions for repression (Jesus) — 3/25/99 Vol. 14

freedom spiritual & physical (Jesus) — 6/20/96 Vol. 3

freedom spiritual choices (Jesus) — 8/7/06 Vol. 44

freedom from sin Confession looses bonds (Jesus) — 3/16/01 Vol. 22

freedom of desires growth in perfection (Jesus) — 3/7/06 Vol. 42

freedom of religion attacked by New Agers (Jesus) — 7/4/06 Vol. 44

freedom of religion take advantage to save souls (Jesus) — 2/24/02 Vol. 26

freedom of speech attacked in abortion protests (Jesus) — 11/2/00 Vol. 21

freedom of spirit freedom from body's desires (Jesus) — 2/27/01 Vol. 22

freedom of worship most important (Jesus) — 9/7/00 Vol. 20

freedom of worship taken away in tribulation (Jesus) — 3/4/01 Vol. 22

freedom, physical thanks to veterans (Jesus) — 11/11/07 Vol. 49

freedom, spiritual thanks to Jesus (Jesus) — 11/11/07 Vol. 49

freedom, struggle for desire to be uncontrolled (Jesus) — 7/4/05 Vol. 40

freedoms are slipping away (Jesus) — 5/28/99 Vol. 15

freedoms challenged in security (Jesus) — 1/16/02 Vol. 26

freedoms compromised by terrorism (Jesus) — 1/10/02 Vol. 26

freedoms do not sell out for security (Jesus) — 7/4/06 Vol. 44

freedoms have a price (Jesus) — 9/25/03 Vol. 32

freedoms lost by fiat laws (Jesus) — 6/19/98 Vol. 11

freedoms lost from decay (Jesus) — 9/12/00 Vol. 20

freedoms lost to government (Jesus) — 10/20/06 Vol. 45

freedoms not worth giving up (Jesus) — 12/16/03 Vol. 33

freedoms religious (Jesus) — 7/4/02 Vol. 28

freedoms slipping away (Jesus) — 9/9/00 Vol. 20

freedoms spiritual & physical (Jesus) — 9/9/02 Vol. 28

freedoms spiritual and physical (Jesus) — 7/3/97 Vol. 8

freedoms stripped (Jesus) — 6/22/02 Vol. 27

freedoms taken away (Jesus) — 11/12/01 Vol. 25

freedoms taken away (Jesus) — 6/6/02 Vol. 27

freedoms taken away (Jesus) — 9/7/00 Vol. 20

freedoms to be taken in name of security (Jesus) — 5/25/02 Vol. 27

freedoms at risk from terrorism, war (Jesus) — 12/18/02 Vol. 29

freedoms at risk in state of emergency (Jesus) — 9/15/01 Vol. 24

freedoms at risk unless change of lifestyles (Jesus) — 6/14/03 Vol. 31

freedoms in America right to worship important (Jesus) — 7/2/00 Vol. 20

freedoms lost both secular & religious (Jesus) — 8/6/00 Vol. 20

freedoms lost under guise of security (Jesus) — 1/3/02 Vol. 26

freedoms taken chastisements continue (Jesus) — 9/6/99 Vol. 16

freedoms threatened by new laws (Jesus) — 10/12/06 Vol. 45

freedoms threatened by terrorism, ID chip (Jesus) — 9/14/01 Vol. 24

freemasons desire to destroy the Church (Jesus) — 6/22/00 Vol. 19

frequent Confession keeps soul from neglect (Jesus) — 6/19/03 Vol. 31

frequent Confession maintenance for the soul (Jesus) — 6/30/05 Vol. 39

fresh water becoming scarce (Jesus) — 5/27/04 Vol. 35

fresh water difficult to distribute (Jesus) — 5/19/05 Vol. 39

fresh water harder to find everywhere (Jesus) — 11/19/07 Vol. 49

fresh water keep unpolluted (Jesus) — 9/19/05 Vol. 40

fresh water necessary for physical life (Jesus) — 10/24/05 Vol. 41

fresh water needed in poor countries (Jesus) — 3/22/06 Vol. 42

fresh water needs protection (Jesus) — 3/21/01 Vol. 22

fresh water to become more valuable (Jesus) — 5/15/00 Vol. 19

fresh water control do not give in to Antichrist (Jesus)   2/15/01 Vol. 22
fresh water needed supply problems in drought (Jesus)   8/3/02 Vol. 28
fresh water scarce cause of famine (Jesus)   2/3/00 Vol. 18
fresh water scarce water to be expensive (Jesus)   3/30/00 Vol. 18
fresh water shortage lack of rain,drought,crop threat (Jesus) 3/15/02 Vol. 26
fresh water,food one world control (Jesus)   3/14/00 Vol. 18
friend, a true help in serious illness (Jesus)   11/6/99 Vol. 17
friends true and abusive (Jesus)   3/16/03 Vol. 30
friends, true stick by you till your death (Jesus)   7/22/04 Vol. 36
friendship love over hate (Jesus)   8/14/97 Vol. 8
friendship of God & neighbor (Jesus)   2/28/03 Vol. 30
friendship, barriers to be friendly, hospitable (Jesus)   10/30/00 Vol. 21
friendships,build rather than killing in war (Jesus)   4/9/00 Vol. 19
fruit of person determining good or bad (Jesus)   5/3/07 Vol. 47
fruit, vegetable prices higher because of hurricanes (Jesus) 10/21/04 Vol. 37
fruits of actions determine good or evil (Jesus)   9/10/05 Vol. 40
fuel be grateful for (Jesus)   5/1/03 Vol. 31
fuel in short supply (Jesus)   3/19/98 Vol. 10
fuel & electricity higher prices (Jesus)   8/15/00 Vol. 20
fuel & electricity one world people control (Jesus)   2/1/01 Vol. 22
fuel & light devices multiplied in winter (Jesus)   6/21/05 Vol. 39
fuel & power threatened by cost & outages (Jesus)   10/21/05 Vol. 41
fuel and heat have alternate sources (Jesus)   10/12/06 Vol. 45
fuel at refuge to be multiplied (Jesus)   1/16/07 Vol. 46
fuel backup for power shortages (Jesus)   2/16/06 Vol. 42
fuel choices environment, new choice (Jesus)   1/10/06 Vol. 42
fuel consumption gives higher standard of living (Jesus) 10/21/04 Vol. 37
fuel costs, high stressing the poor (Jesus)   11/18/04 Vol. 37
fuel depots buring (Jesus)   2/6/03 Vol. 30
fuel losses accidents, arsonists (Jesus)   12/22/05 Vol. 41
fuel multiplied in long power outage (Jesus)   12/21/07 Vol. 49
fuel preparation other sources of fuel (Jesus)   9/9/99 Vol. 16
fuel prices effect on US economy (Jesus)   10/9/00 Vol. 21
fuel prices controlled to lower standard of living (Jesus) 7/12/00 Vol. 20
fuel prices high result of disasters (Jesus)   9/9/05 Vol. 40
fuel prices, high will reduce living standards (Jesus)   9/23/04 Vol. 36
fuel shortage have alternate ready (Jesus)   12/22/05 Vol. 41
fuel shortages and higher prices (Jesus)   10/4/05 Vol. 41
fuel shortages could require bikes (Jesus)   3/12/06 Vol. 42
fuel shortages from disasters, inflation (Jesus)   12/21/05 Vol. 41
fuel sources all have risks (Jesus)   6/12/03 Vol. 31
fuel supplies threatened by Iraq war (Jesus)   11/14/02 Vol. 29
fuel supplies at risk have alternate fuel ready (Jesus)   9/26/01 Vol. 24
fuel, alternate needed for power outages (Jesus)   10/23/03 Vol. 33
fuel, alternate to keep warm in winter (Jesus)   12/16/06 Vol. 45
fuels contrived prices (Jesus)   5/10/01 Vol. 23
fuels & electricity needed for comforts (Jesus)   9/22/05 Vol. 40

fuels, alternate ethanol & hydgrogen (Jesus)   11/17/04 Vol. 37
fuels, alternate have ready (Jesus)   12/3/07 Vol. 49
fuels, alternate hydrogen,alcohol,wood (Jesus)   11/20/03 Vol. 33
fuels, alternate needed for cost (Jesus)   2/2/06 Vol. 42
fuels, alternative needed to replace oil (Jesus)   12/6/04 Vol. 37
fuels, renewable to replace gas & oil (Jesus)   9/16/05 Vol. 40
full trust in God needed in tribulation (Jesus)   3/20/00 Vol. 18
fundraisers fraudulant percentages (Jesus)   3/2/03 Vol. 30
funeral body's mortal nature (Jesus)   1/24/99 Vol. 14
funeral gratitude (Uncle Jim)   5/14/94 Vol. 1
funeral message from Mary Ellen Frisch (Mary Ellen)   11/26/05 Vol. 41
funerals a wake up call (Jesus)   9/12/03 Vol. 32
funerals promise of Resurrection (Jesus)   4/15/04 Vol. 35
funerals reflect on our own mortality (Jesus)   7/8/04 Vol. 36
funerals reminder of our own death (Jesus)   3/5/99 Vol. 14
fusion experiments secrets threaten life (Jesus)   1/6/00 Vol. 18
fusion, radioactivity pray for protection (Jesus)   9/6/05 Vol. 40
future God will instruct direction (Jesus)   6/6/95 Vol. 2
future events don't be anxious for dates (Jesus)   11/3/97 Vol. 9
future saints prayer,fasting,& good works (Jesus)   8/11/98 Vol. 12
G 7 meeting planning monetary control (Jesus)   5/10/98 Vol. 11
Gabriel's message Light comes into world (Jesus)   12/19/99 Vol. 17
gaining heaven most important goal on earth (Jesus)   2/24/02 Vol. 26
Gamaliel test of prophet (Jesus)   4/27/01 Vol. 23
gamble, avoid with soul, seek heaven (Jesus)   6/26/03 Vol. 31
gambling addiction to (Jesus)   7/24/03 Vol. 32
gambling addictions control your life (Jesus)   6/17/06 Vol. 43
gambling bad for money & soul (Jesus)   10/23/03 Vol. 33
gambling for greed and power (Jesus)   8/15/01 Vol. 24
gambling know your limit (Jesus)   10/21/07 Vol. 49
gambling money (Jesus)   8/10/94 Vol. 2
gambling pride, habits a problem (Jesus)   9/27/99 Vol. 16
gambling with life and soul, avoid (Jesus)   4/28/05 Vol. 39
gambling addicts need counseling (Jesus)   1/22/06 Vol. 42
gambling cities near occasion of sin (Jesus)   9/21/07 Vol. 48
gambling risks lose of money and lives (Jesus)   8/12/00 Vol. 20
gambling with soul without conversion (Jesus)   11/24/03 Vol. 33
game life (Jesus)   10/21/94 Vol. 2
game obsessions limit time,emotions (Jesus)   9/27/99 Vol. 16
games and sports have become gods (Jesus)   1/27/00 Vol. 18
games of chance can be occasion of sin (Jesus)   10/21/07 Vol. 49
games people play no way to fool God (Jesus)   11/27/99 Vol. 17
Garcia grotto pulsating crucifix (Jesus)   7/20/96 Vol. 4
Garden of Eden Divine Will (Jesus)   3/17/97 Vol. 6
Garden of Eden Era of Peace,triumph (Jesus)   5/6/97 Vol. 7
Garden of Eden to Era of Peace (Jesus)   2/23/99 Vol. 14
Garden of Eden tree of good & evil (Jesus)   11/21/00 Vol. 21

Garden of Eden trees of life and knowledge (Jesus) 4/30/98 Vol. 11
Garden of Eden Triumph (Jesus) 11/15/95 Vol. 3
Garden of Gethsemene watch with Jesus one hour (Jesus) 12/27/00 Vol. 21
gas & electric manipulated control (Jesus) 8/28/03 Vol. 32
gas & electric stripped of convenience (Jesus) 5/30/01 Vol. 23
gas & electricity not available (Jesus) 1/18/97 Vol. 6
gas & oil prices controlled,manipulated (Jesus) 1/25/01 Vol. 22
gas & oil prices pray to help poor (Jesus) 11/10/05 Vol. 41
gas and oil controlled (Jesus) 9/28/00 Vol. 20
gas and oil manipulated for control (Jesus) 9/14/00 Vol. 20
gas chambers diabolical influence (Jesus) 4/24/07 Vol. 47
gas price increase terrorism in oil, refineries (Jesus) 5/26/04 Vol. 35
gas shortage contrived one world government (St. Therese) 11/15/95 Vol. 3
gasoline endangered in war (Jesus) 1/25/98 Vol. 10
gasoline shortages in Mideast (Jesus) 5/25/98 Vol. 11
gasoline and oil manipulated shortages (Jesus) 8/31/00 Vol. 20
gasoline prices controlled by supply,fears of war (Jesus) 3/14/02 Vol. 26
gasoline shortage rationing,bicycles needed (Jesus) 4/7/99 Vol. 15
gasoline supplies shortages cause problems (Jesus) 4/5/01 Vol. 23
gasoline truck accident terrorists could use (Jesus) 4/29/03 Vol. 31
gate to heaven many photographed (Jesus) 5/14/98 Vol. 11
gate to heaven seek forgiveness,Savior (Jesus) 6/3/03 Vol. 31
gatekeeper Jesus lights our way (Jesus) 9/2/02 Vol. 28
gatekeeper in Jesus special key to heaven (Jesus) 3/25/00 Vol. 18
gatekeepers follow the light (Mary) 7/1/96 Vol. 3
gates of heaven need good deeds,perfection (Jesus) 9/20/01 Vol. 24
Gates of heaven open through Jesus (Jesus) 4/22/04 Vol. 35
gates of heaven opened by Jesus' Blood (Jesus) 3/27/01 Vol. 22
gates of heaven opened by Jesus' death (Jesus) 9/8/07 Vol. 48
gates of heaven opened by Jesus's sacrifice (Jesus) 3/17/08 Vol. 50
Gates of Heaven require open door to soul (Jesus) 10/26/98 Vol. 13
gates of heaven require pure soul to enter (Jesus) 11/14/99 Vol. 17
gates of Heaven welcome to my adorers (Jesus) 4/21/99 Vol. 15
gates of heaven open allows souls to enter (Jesus) 8/22/07 Vol. 48
gates of heaven open long waiting before Christ (Jesus) 3/27/02 Vol. 26
gates of hell not to prevail over Church (Jesus) 6/14/02 Vol. 27
gates of hell not to prevail over Church (Jesus) 5/26/04 Vol. 35
gates of hell will not prevail against Church (Jesus) 5/13/00 Vol. 19
Gates of Jerusalem at every refuge (Jesus) 7/31/05 Vol. 40
Gates of Paradise open to worthy souls (Jesus) 4/16/06 Vol. 43
gateway to eternal life in Eucharist (Jesus) 3/19/00 Vol. 18
gay marriage law snow storm, 3.0 earthquake (Jesus) 12/27/02 Vol. 29
gay marriages sinful & abhorrent to God (Jesus) 12/29/02 Vol. 29
gay parades calling down of God's wrath (Jesus) 4/28/06 Vol. 43
Gaza takeover threat to Israel (Jesus) 6/14/07 Vol. 47
Gehenna living dead (Jesus) 6/18/95 Vol. 2
gene manipulation abomination to creation (Jesus) 6/26/97 Vol. 7

gene manipulation cause for concern (Jesus) 9/16/97 Vol. 8
gene manipulation same as Hitler (Jesus) 3/24/00 Vol. 18
gene manipulation will make things worse (Jesus) 8/5/00 Vol. 20
genealogy roots of Messiah (Jesus) 12/15/97 Vol. 9
genealogy of Jesus from Adam & Eve (Jesus) 12/17/03 Vol. 33
geneology of Jesus (Jesus) 7/10/99 Vol. 16
generation lost abortions,family planning (Jesus) 6/14/99 Vol. 15
generation, every warned of sinful lives (Jesus) 3/8/06 Vol. 42
generosity more given/more expected (Jesus) 8/4/96 Vol. 4
generosity share to gain heaven (Jesus) 5/29/03 Vol. 31
generosity with time & money (Jesus) 9/22/02 Vol. 28
generosity needed physically & spiritually (Jesus) 11/14/07 Vol. 49
generosity with gifts be loving, even when rejected (Jesus) 12/31/07 Vol. 49
genetic engineering devastating results (Jesus) 3/14/00 Vol. 18
genocide of Christians by Muslims (Jesus) 7/26/06 Vol. 44
genocide in abortions not just in Kosovo (Jesus) 4/8/99 Vol. 15
genuflecting give glory to God (Jesus) 7/10/98 Vol. 12
genuflecting gives honor and glory (Jesus) 9/5/98 Vol. 12
George Albert a witness of faith (Jesus) 3/12/98 Vol. 10
Georges, hurricane violence in weather,spiritual (Jesus) 11/10/98 Vol. 13
germ warfare of one world (Jesus) 3/26/98 Vol. 10
germ warfare spread by military (Jesus) 9/1/98 Vol. 12
germ warfare start epidemics (Jesus) 3/27/98 Vol. 10
Geyssens, Al funeral thoughts (Jesus) 12/20/04 Vol. 37
gift buying do not be disturbed in stores (Jesus) 12/8/02 Vol. 29
gift buying keep calm, be thankful (Jesus) 12/1/05 Vol. 41
gift giving spirit of Magi (Jesus) 11/29/01 Vol. 25
gift of life always precious (Jesus) 9/5/02 Vol. 28
gift of life give thanks each day (Jesus) 11/23/00 Vol. 21
gift of life know, love and serve (Jesus) 3/3/97 Vol. 6
gift of life love (Jesus) 3/14/94 Vol. 1
gift of life most precious gift (Jesus) 5/16/99 Vol. 15
gift of life praise God for (Jesus) 3/22/05 Vol. 38
gift of life reach out to others (Jesus) 6/17/04 Vol. 35
gift of life salvation (Jesus) 6/26/95 Vol. 2
gift of life taken back by God (Jesus) 8/28/02 Vol. 28
gift of life to everyone (Jesus) 6/21/03 Vol. 31
gift of life treasure love and life (Jesus) 2/3/98 Vol. 10
gift of life worthy of thanks to God (Jesus) 1/20/00 Vol. 18
gift of self to God & others (Jesus) 12/5/04 Vol. 37
gift of the Spirit trials (Jesus) 3/15/94 Vol. 1
gifts apostles (Jesus) 9/21/94 Vol. 2
gifts be grateful for gift of life (Jesus) 4/3/97 Vol. 7
gifts Divine Will (Jesus) 5/2/94 Vol. 1
gifts family (Father) 6/22/94 Vol. 1
gifts for praise & glory of God (Jesus) 1/29/04 Vol. 34
gifts free will (Jesus) 12/6/94 Vol. 2

gifts gift of self (Jesus) — 12/24/94 Vol. 2
gifts more given, more expected (Jesus) — 3/2/07 Vol. 46
gifts need to thank the giver (Jesus) — 11/25/04 Vol. 37
gifts of self most important (Jesus) — 12/18/97 Vol. 9
gifts passed on to children (Jesus) — 5/22/96 Vol. 3
gifts rainbows,spinning sun (Mary) — 7/10/96 Vol. 3
gifts & talents more given, more expected (Jesus) — 4/27/02 Vol. 27
gifts & talents to heal & evangelize (Jesus) — 1/6/05 Vol. 38
gifts accountable how used at judgement (Jesus) — 12/16/05 Vol. 41
gifts and talents give God credit for (Jesus) — 4/20/02 Vol. 27
gifts at Christmas thank giver, & Jesus (Jesus) — 11/25/03 Vol. 33
gifts of God creation,health,life (Jesus) — 5/30/99 Vol. 15
gifts of God like a water mill (Jesus) — 9/10/03 Vol. 32
gifts of God worthy of thanks (Jesus) — 11/22/07 Vol. 49
gifts of Holy Spirit use to save souls (Jesus) — 11/30/99 Vol. 17
gifts of Spirit need to be shared (Holy Spirit) — 5/15/05 Vol. 39
gifts of the heart desired by Jesus (Jesus) — 12/17/98 Vol. 13
gifts of the Holy Spirit graces (Jesus) — 6/3/95 Vol. 2
gifts of the Holy Spirit prayer (Holy Spirit) — 5/24/95 Vol. 2
gifts of the Spirit claim in Jesus' name (Jesus) — 2/11/02 Vol. 26
gifts to God do for others from heart (Jesus) — 1/7/01 Vol. 22
gifts to God gold, frankincense, myrrh (Jesus) — 12/21/04 Vol. 37
gifts without returns gain merits in heaven (Jesus) — 8/8/02 Vol. 28
gifts, personal use to help others (Jesus) — 8/5/01 Vol. 24
give of your love to gain heaven for your soul (Jesus) — 12/20/98 Vol. 13
give thanks,praise to One True God (Jesus) — 11/21/99 Vol. 17
giver of gifts more valuable than gifts (Jesus) — 12/16/04 Vol. 37
glasses to see in dark spying electrical devices (Jesus) — 10/3/96 Vol. 5
glitter of things faded empty promises (Jesus) — 12/30/99 Vol. 17
global control trade,currency,governance (Jesus) — 9/4/01 Vol. 24
global warming alarmists extreme science (Jesus) — 11/17/07 Vol. 49
global warming melting ice shelves (Jesus) — 12/29/06 Vol. 45
global warming more factors than CO2 (Jesus) — 2/27/08 Vol. 50
global warming need independent study (Jesus) — 4/27/07 Vol. 47
global warming raise sea level (Jesus) — 6/4/02 Vol. 27
global warming results in storms (Jesus) — 2/2/07 Vol. 46
global warming testing of temperatures (Jesus) — 5/16/02 Vol. 27
globalists solutions by one world people (Jesus) — 11/17/07 Vol. 49
globalization of North America (Jesus) — 9/22/06 Vol. 44
globe in monstrance released from sin by Jesus (Jesus) — 12/13/99 Vol. 17
glorified bodies as intended (Jesus) — 2/26/04 Vol. 34
glorified bodies at final judgment (Jesus) — 4/5/05 Vol. 39
glorified bodies at last judgment (Jesus) — 7/11/99 Vol. 16
glorified bodies at our resurrection (Jesus) — 3/30/08 Vol. 50
glorified bodies beauty of Resurrection (Jesus) — 1/21/00 Vol. 18
glorified bodies given at the resurrection (Jesus) — 4/12/00 Vol. 19
glorified bodies if we follow His Will (Jesus) — 4/16/98 Vol. 11

glorified bodies in heaven (Jesus) — 2/17/08 Vol. 50
glorified bodies mediatrix of graces (Mary) — 8/15/94 Vol. 2
glorified bodies price of suffering for (Jesus) — 5/19/98 Vol. 11
glorified bodies resurrected like angels (Mary) — 6/4/97 Vol. 7
glorified bodies washed robes in heaven (Jesus) — 1/25/99 Vol. 14
glorified bodies will be had in heaven (Jesus) — 8/6/98 Vol. 12
glorified bodies young with no restraints (Jesus) — 1/24/01 Vol. 22
glorified body after death sin is purified (Jesus) — 5/3/99 Vol. 15
glorified body at last judgment (Jesus) — 4/16/01 Vol. 23
glorified body at our own resurrection (Jesus) — 7/14/06 Vol. 44
glorified body at resurrection (Jesus) — 11/12/02 Vol. 29
glorified body if live faith in love & action (Jesus) — 4/19/04 Vol. 35
glorified body in Resurrection (Jesus) — 2/21/07 Vol. 46
glorified body Jesus and us (Jesus) — 6/6/02 Vol. 27
glorified body like our future resurrection (Jesus) — 8/6/07 Vol. 48
glorified body received by faithful (Jesus) — 6/28/05 Vol. 39
glorified body shown in Jesus' Resurrection (Jesus) — 8/6/02 Vol. 28
glorified body test for eternity (Jesus) — 6/21/97 Vol. 7
glory and fame will pass away (Jesus) — 9/21/00 Vol. 20
glory of God over glory of man (Jesus) — 9/3/02 Vol. 28
glory to God for all He accomplished (Jesus) — 9/30/99 Vol. 16
gluttony overweight people (Jesus) — 2/13/04 Vol. 34
goal in life to win heaven (Jesus) — 8/28/04 Vol. 36
goal of heaven worth persistence to win (Jesus) — 10/27/98 Vol. 13
goals in life Jesus is only hope (Jesus) — 12/15/97 Vol. 9
goals in life spiritual goal primary (Jesus) — 4/15/02 Vol. 27
goals, realistic to avoid stress, frustration (Jesus) — 12/13/03 Vol. 33
goats & sheep evil ones & faithful remnant (Jesus) — 5/10/05 Vol. 39
goats and lambs separated at schism (Jesus) — 11/4/98 Vol. 13
God being removed from public (Jesus) — 7/4/07 Vol. 48
God is a jealous God (Jesus) — 4/26/04 Vol. 35
God wants our dependence (Jesus) — 3/8/07 Vol. 46
God & money trust God for care (Jesus) — 10/30/99 Vol. 17
God & saints,heroes more than movie stars (Jesus) — 3/9/00 Vol. 18
God blamed for trials all to test our faith (Jesus) — 3/7/00 Vol. 18
God first in life over everything else (Jesus) — 1/25/07 Vol. 46
God first in our life prayer & consecration (Jesus) — 7/22/07 Vol. 48
God is all love died for our sins (Jesus) — 6/4/07 Vol. 47
God is love,peace does not advocate killing (Jesus) — 9/14/01 Vol. 24
God is perfect love shared with all mankind (Jesus) — 6/18/00 Vol. 19
God not mocked laws need following (Jesus) — 3/31/00 Vol. 18
God on your side no one can threaten you (Jesus) — 11/8/99 Vol. 17
God or money cannot have two masters (Jesus) — 11/7/03 Vol. 33
God provides for all of our needs (Jesus) — 7/19/04 Vol. 36
God the Creator leads us through life (Jesus) — 11/4/99 Vol. 17
God the Father all love on Father's Day (God the Father) — 6/16/07 Vol. 47
God the Father blessing for New Year (God the Father) — 1/3/08 Vol. 50

God the Father blowing wind on earth (Jesus) 10/21/05 Vol. 41

God the Father gold light,Transfiguration (God the Father) 8/4/02 Vol. 28

God the Father holy ground Presence (Jesus) 5/26/06 Vol. 43

God the Father honor as creator (Jesus) 6/17/01 Vol. 23

God the Father love of human family (Jesus) 8/29/07 Vol. 48

God the Father prayer for belief (Jesus) 5/6/06 Vol. 43

God the Father sent Jesus for our sins (God the Father) 4/6/07 Vol. 47

God the Father Ten Commandments (God the Father) 8/20/03 Vol. 32

God the Father Three Persons in One God (God the Father)6/3/07 Vol. 47

God the Father Trinity 8/31/93 Vol. 1

God the Father worthy of worship (God the Father) 2/22/98 Vol. 10

God the Father Confer. special blessings given (Jesus) 8/7/99 Vol. 16

God the Father conferenc needs word of repentance (God the Father)
10/9/98 Vol. 13

God the Father's gifts shelter us as farmer with animals (Jesus)
3/8/02 Vol. 26

God vs. world heaven vs hell (Jesus) 9/23/01 Vol. 24

God vs. devil heaven vs. hell (Jesus) 3/20/01 Vol. 22

God vs. self world election of destination (Jesus) 11/6/02 Vol. 29

God vs. worldly things choice in this earthly life (Jesus) 10/13/04 Vol. 37

God, important guest please God more than man (Jesus) 7/13/00 Vol. 20

God, love of everything revolves around (Jesus) 10/5/02 Vol. 29

God, priority for should be first (Jesus) 5/8/07 Vol. 47

God, serving more important than ourselves (Jesus) 4/22/07 Vol. 47

God, worship first not earthly things (Jesus) 4/26/07 Vol. 47

God-centered actions more accomplished (Jesus) 1/29/07 Vol. 46

God-centered goals instead of self-centered goals (Jesus) 8/8/00 Vol. 20

God-righteous vs. self-righteous (Jesus) 11/11/06 Vol. 45

God's agenda better than ours (Jesus) 2/14/05 Vol. 38

God's attributes seen in Trinity (Jesus) 3/30/99 Vol. 14

God's concern loved man to die for our sins (Jesus) 6/16/00 Vol. 19

God's glory proclaim from rooftops (Jesus) 12/9/04 Vol. 37

God's help needed over our own efforts (Jesus) 9/3/99 Vol. 16

God's infinite love demands man's love response (Jesus) 8/10/00 Vol. 20

God's intentions better than our own (Jesus) 5/4/06 Vol. 43

God's intervention to change our lives (Jesus) 12/1/06 Vol. 45

God's intervention to defeat evil ones (Jesus) 8/31/06 Vol. 44

God's judgment knows all the facts (Jesus) 5/28/06 Vol. 43

God's love are we living it? (Jesus) 11/10/06 Vol. 45

God's love death on cross, Real Presence (Jesus) 10/26/04 Vol. 37

God's love equal to everyone (Jesus) 10/28/04 Vol. 37

God's mission planned for every soul (Jesus) 12/28/03 Vol. 33

God's Name removed from public (Jesus) 11/20/07 Vol. 49

God's peace better than man's (Jesus) 4/19/07 Vol. 47

God's peace vs man's peace lasting vs. fleeting (Jesus) 12/31/01 Vol. 25

God's peace,justice needed in the world (Jesus) 9/19/99 Vol. 16

God's place in our lives, see need (Jesus) 3/23/04 Vol. 34

God's plan means for souls to heaven (Jesus) 11/10/00 Vol. 21

God's success love for God & mankind (Jesus) 12/16/05 Vol. 41

God's success love of God & others (Jesus) 9/2/06 Vol. 44

God's ways better than man's ways (Jesus) 6/9/00 Vol. 19

God's ways contrary to man's ways (Jesus) 3/9/00 Vol. 18

God's ways test your comfort zone (Jesus) 4/16/99 Vol. 15

God's ways versus man's ways (Jesus) 1/23/03 Vol. 30

God's ways vs man's ways pride to not follow God (Jesus) 11/20/02 Vol. 29

God's Will always pray in (Jesus) 7/25/06 Vol. 44

God's Will better than man's failures (Jesus) 2/7/00 Vol. 18

God's Will better then personal agenda (Jesus) 2/18/01 Vol. 22

God's Will follow to be saved (Jesus) 10/24/03 Vol. 33

God's Will is best for our soul (Jesus) 3/6/08 Vol. 50

God's Will path to perfection (Jesus) 8/23/99 Vol. 16

God's Will should control our lives (Jesus) 10/25/07 Vol. 49

God's Will followed lose earthly life for heaven (Jesus) 4/9/00 Vol. 19

gold icon statue of Fatima, help (Mary) 8/2/97 Vol. 8

gold in sacramentals miracles,sign of supernatural (Jesus) 5/13/00 Vol. 19

gold pyramid cross 8/3/93 Vol. 1

gold,frankincense,myrrh foretell Era of Peace (Jesus) 7/12/98 Vol. 12

golden calf bull of stock market (Jesus) 8/25/03 Vol. 32

golden calf hiding (Jesus) 11/29/94 Vol. 2

golden calf possessions & stock markets (Jesus) 8/25/01 Vol. 24

Golden Compass leads to atheism (Jesus) 12/3/07 Vol. 49

golden opportunity to change Supreme Court (Jesus) 11/3/04 Vol. 37

golden tongue to confront the evil one (Jesus) 12/20/97 Vol. 9

golf clubs cross (Jesus) 9/14/95 Vol. 3

golf courses take water from farmers (Jesus) 8/23/01 Vol. 24

good & bad thoughts heavenly or worldly (Jesus) 10/20/03 Vol. 33

good & evil each soul decides (Jesus) 10/24/02 Vol. 29

good & evil life is a contest of (Jesus) 9/16/02 Vol. 28

good & evil mingle in life (Jesus) 11/14/02 Vol. 29

good & evil deeds determine judgment (Jesus) 11/15/99 Vol. 17

good deeds balance off sins (Jesus) 3/29/08 Vol. 50

good deeds gain treasure in heaven (Jesus) 8/4/02 Vol. 28

good deeds heavenly treasures (Jesus) 7/9/99 Vol. 16

good deeds many opportunities given (Jesus) 7/12/07 Vol. 48

good deeds opportunities given by God (Jesus) 9/13/07 Vol. 48

good deeds store treasure in heaven (Jesus) 2/26/06 Vol. 42

good deeds in secret gain more merits in heaven (Jesus) 3/11/02 Vol. 26

good example shown to heaven & earth (Jesus) 12/6/02 Vol. 29

good example to save souls (Jesus) 7/10/99 Vol. 16

good example, give do not be hypocrites (Jesus) 7/10/03 Vol. 32

Good Friday cruelty of soldiers (Jesus) 4/14/06 Vol. 43

Good Friday death on the cross (Jesus) 4/18/03 Vol. 31

Good Friday everyone must suffer (Jesus) 5/10/06 Vol. 43

Good Friday gates of heaven opened (Jesus) 4/13/01 Vol. 23

Good Friday love (Jesus)   4/1/94 Vol. 1
Good Friday meaning of crucifixion (Jesus)   4/5/96 Vol. 3
Good Friday prayer (Jesus)   4/14/95 Vol. 2
Good Friday salvation from sins (Jesus)   3/28/97 Vol. 6
Good Friday tradition veneration of crucifix needed (Jesus) 3/21/02 Vol. 26
good fruit bear in our lives (Jesus)   10/2/05 Vol. 41
Good News believe & remove doubt (Jesus)   4/14/07 Vol. 47
Good News Holy Spirit inspired teaching of (Jesus)   3/28/05 Vol. 38
Good News of salvation most important (Jesus)   11/16/05 Vol. 41
Good News salvation of mankind (Jesus)   12/23/06 Vol. 45
Good News share with all nations (Jesus)   3/27/05 Vol. 38
Good News shout from the rooftops (Jesus)   3/21/05 Vol. 38
Good News shout from the rooftops (Jesus)   4/20/06 Vol. 43
Good News spread to all nations (Jesus)   9/21/07 Vol. 48
Good News spread to all nations (Jesus)   9/25/07 Vol. 48
Good News of Jesus hope of future life (Jesus)   11/8/03 Vol. 33
Good News vs man's news life vs. death (Jesus)   12/31/01 Vol. 25
Good Samaritan give time & money (Jesus)   7/15/01 Vol. 24
Good Samaritan help neighbor, no payment (Jesus)   7/15/07 Vol. 48
Good Samaritan help the poor (Jesus)   10/6/03 Vol. 33
Good Samaritan help with no pay (Jesus)   2/18/03 Vol. 30
Good Sam. in physical & spiritual needs (Mother Cabrini)7/12/98 Vol. 12
Good Samaritan reach out to help (Jesus)   8/9/99 Vol. 16
Good Samaritan share time,talent,treasure (Jesus)   10/2/06 Vol. 45
Good Samaritans helping flood victims (Jesus)   9/8/05 Vol. 40
Good Shepherd chastisement   9/3/93 Vol. 1
Good Shepherd do not follow false shepherds (Jesus)   5/7/00 Vol. 19
Good Shepherd hear Jesus' voice (Jesus)   7/23/06 Vol. 44
Good Shepherd Jesus cares for us (Jesus)   5/2/04 Vol. 35
Good Shepherd light (Jesus)   12/24/95 Vol. 3
Good Shepherd looking for lost sheep (Jesus)   8/17/99 Vol. 16
Good Shepherd repent (Jesus)   10/3/95 Vol. 3
Good Shepherd searching for lost sheep (Jesus)   3/30/06 Vol. 42
Good Shepherd seeks lost sheep (Jesus)   1/14/02 Vol. 26
Good Shepherd seeks out last sheep (Jesus)   7/17/05 Vol. 40
Good Shepherd to all faiths (Jesus)   4/18/05 Vol. 39
good works count most with God (Jesus)   11/20/00 Vol. 21
good works do in secret (Jesus)   4/23/98 Vol. 11
good works, faith needed to witness love (Jesus)   8/9/00 Vol. 20
goodness see gift of others (Jesus)   10/21/02 Vol. 29
Gospa House 6th anniversary (Jesus)   2/24/07 Vol. 46
Gospa House pleases Our Lady,4th anniv (Blessed Mother)2/24/05 Vol. 38
Gospel choose God (Jesus)   2/13/97 Vol. 6
Gospel daily walk with Jesus (Jesus)   8/7/96 Vol. 4
Gospel follow & imitate (Jesus)   5/27/02 Vol. 27
Gospel live it every day (Jesus)   9/17/00 Vol. 20
Gospel love God & neighbor (Jesus)   6/22/01 Vol. 23

Gospel one of joy and hope (Jesus)   5/26/99 Vol. 15
Gospel power of His Word (Jesus)   2/8/98 Vol. 10
Gospel proclaim from rooftops (Jesus)   3/25/97 Vol. 6
Gospel put into practice (Jesus)   1/18/98 Vol. 10
Gospel in heart live your faith (Jesus)   6/23/99 Vol. 15
Gospel message proclaim with courage (Jesus)   5/24/01 Vol. 23
Gospel message Word of love from rooftops (Jesus)   7/11/02 Vol. 28
Gospel message&laws eternal life (Jesus)   10/1/99 Vol. 17
Gospel of love evangelize all (Jesus)   4/2/02 Vol. 27
Gospel of love make waves (Jesus)   6/8/01 Vol. 23
Gospel preached by prayer and action (Jesus)   4/12/02 Vol. 27
Gospel values be a good witness (Jesus)   5/15/01 Vol. 23
Gospel Word witness God to souls (Jesus)   10/28/98 Vol. 13
Gospel,live the inspires conversions (Jesus)   3/2/00 Vol. 18
Gospels savor His love (Jesus)   8/16/01 Vol. 24
Gospels & Epistles avoid distractions,pay attention (Jesus) 11/6/03 Vol. 33
Gospels on boats used to teach lessons of faith (Jesus)   3/27/02 Vol. 26
gossip avoid slander of neighbor (Jesus)   6/5/97 Vol. 7
gossip curb your tongue (Jesus)   1/26/98 Vol. 10
gossip destroys reputations (Jesus)   9/30/03 Vol. 32
gossip do not do (Jesus)   5/15/98 Vol. 11
gossip live in the truth (Jesus)   9/20/97 Vol. 8
gossip ruining reputations (Jesus)   7/19/03 Vol. 32
gossip ruins reputations (Jesus)   6/21/04 Vol. 35
gossip & bad language venting of complaints (Jesus)   6/26/02 Vol. 27
gossip & lies ruin reputations (Jesus)   6/10/03 Vol. 31
gossip & talking avoid before Blessed Sacrament (Jesus) 10/31/04 Vol. 37
gossip ruins lives guard speech,reputations (Jesus)   10/21/98 Vol. 13
gossiping destroys one's reputation (Jesus)   6/21/05 Vol. 39
gossiping ruining reputations (Jesus)   6/23/03 Vol. 31
government 3 levels of control (Jesus)   10/30/07 Vol. 49
government deceivers of disinformation (Jesus)   10/14/06 Vol. 45
government downfall through traitors (Jesus)   7/3/99 Vol. 16
government knees (Jesus)   11/20/93 Vol. 1
government peace (Jesus)   12/16/95 Vol. 3
government prepared for catastrophes (Jesus)   8/27/04 Vol. 36
government rights eliminated (Jesus)   2/20/97 Vol. 6
government attack for imprisonment (Jesus)   3/31/08 Vol. 50
government control by chips and cameras (Jesus)   6/25/07 Vol. 47
Government leaders bankers (Jesus)   8/28/96 Vol. 4
government leaders hide from these killers (Jesus)   7/17/96 Vol. 4
government leaders moral decay (Jesus)   4/10/96 Vol. 3
government officials actions mean more than words (Jesus) 5/10/07 Vol. 47
government officials to leave positions (Jesus)   5/11/06 Vol. 43
government support lowering with less taxes (Jesus)   5/13/06 Vol. 43
governments fall & takeover (Jesus)   1/30/03 Vol. 30
governments not stable much longer (Jesus)   2/5/98 Vol. 10

governments,finances to suffer chaos from Y2K (Jesus)   4/29/99 Vol. 15
grace as air for spiritual life (Jesus)   8/19/07 Vol. 48
grace brings light to the soul (Jesus)   3/1/04 Vol. 34
grace fresh air to the soul (Jesus)   10/27/01 Vol. 25
grace gives life to the soul (Jesus)   2/14/02 Vol. 26
grace lifeblood of the soul (Jesus)   3/20/07 Vol. 46
grace like rain to nourish soul (Jesus)   6/5/05 Vol. 39
grace Mediatrix (Mary)   4/24/96 Vol. 3
grace necessary for life of soul (Jesus)   5/10/00 Vol. 19
grace needed to endure trials (Jesus)   4/27/05 Vol. 39
grace refreshes the soul (Jesus)   5/15/03 Vol. 31
grace sufficient for life (Jesus)   3/11/05 Vol. 38
grace & Communion spiritual life blood (Jesus)   6/30/05 Vol. 39
grace & faith means to heaven (Jesus)   11/20/99 Vol. 17
grace given to save each soul (Jesus)   2/19/04 Vol. 34
grace gives strength in temptations (Jesus)   3/23/07 Vol. 46
grace like a falls prayer,good deeds,sacraments (Jesus)   11/19/03 Vol. 33
grace needed lifeblood of soul (Jesus)   4/4/01 Vol. 23
grace of God shield from demons (Jesus)   5/13/07 Vol. 47
grace of understanding to know God's Word (Jesus)   2/26/00 Vol. 18
grace opportunity in Warning (Jesus)   11/8/06 Vol. 45
grace to souls as water to life (Jesus)   5/8/03 Vol. 31
grace vs water soul vs body (Jesus)   8/13/00 Vol. 20
grace, ask for to be a saint (Jesus)   4/19/06 Vol. 43
grace, given to endure trials (Jesus)   9/17/07 Vol. 48
grace, loss of as loss of electricity (Jesus)   9/16/07 Vol. 48
grace, oasis of we reflect image of God (Jesus)   9/8/01 Vol. 24
grace,opportunities for in helping others (Jesus)   2/16/00 Vol. 18
grace,places of Confession,Eucharist,prayer (Jesus)   11/16/98 Vol. 13
graces baptism & confession (Jesus)   9/24/97 Vol. 8
graces be grateful to God (Jesus)   12/14/00 Vol. 21
graces from Eucharist in tabernacles (Jesus)   10/25/05 Vol. 41
graces give security (Jesus)   7/23/99 Vol. 16
graces given in Holy Communion (Jesus)   11/3/02 Vol. 29
graces given to do God's Will (Jesus)   12/30/00 Vol. 21
graces lifeblood of the soul (Jesus)   2/22/01 Vol. 22
graces pilgrims (Holy Spirit)   3/13/94 Vol. 1
graces will (Jesus)   3/10/94 Vol. 1
graces & blessings multiplied (Jesus)   1/8/08 Vol. 50
graces & blesssings a spiritual life raft (Jesus)   5/20/99 Vol. 15
graces for all souls to fulfill their mission (Jesus)   12/27/07 Vol. 49
graces in wave poured out every day (Jesus)   12/31/99 Vol. 17
graces, abundant available to everyone (Jesus)   3/11/08 Vol. 50
graces, endless like endless river flow (Jesus)   2/21/01 Vol. 22
graces, endless needed to renew souls (Jesus)   4/10/01 Vol. 23
graces, open flow of by prayer, fasting, sacraments (Jesus) 10/20/03 Vol. 33
graduation heaven is real one (Jesus)   6/16/04 Vol. 35

graduation from life knowledge (Jesus)   1/19/95 Vol. 2
grandchildren protected (David)   5/6/96 Vol. 3
grandchildren watch over and guide (David)   4/10/96 Vol. 3
grandparents look out for grandchildren (Jesus)   7/26/02 Vol. 28
grapes of wrath in natural disasters (Jesus)   8/31/05 Vol. 40
grateful for food enjoy plenty now (Jesus)   3/21/00 Vol. 18
gratitude for what we have (Jesus)   1/10/02 Vol. 26
grave, time in resurrection at final judgment (Jesus)   3/30/02 Vol. 26
gravestone death (Jesus)   3/6/95 Vol. 2
Great Chastisement cannot be diverted (Jesus)   5/13/02 Vol. 27
Great Chastisement comet striking the earth (Jesus)   3/17/04 Vol. 34
Great Chastisement evil destroyed (Jesus)   2/18/04 Vol. 34
Great Chastisement is victory by fire over evil (Jesus)   6/27/05 Vol. 39
Great Chastisement prepare yourselves (Jesus)   8/14/97 Vol. 8
Great Chastisement tidal wave,eastern shore (Jesus)   4/11/97 Vol. 7
Great Chastisement to defeat all evil (Jesus)   10/31/07 Vol. 49
Great Chastisement to rid evil ones (Jesus)   8/9/05 Vol. 40
Great Chastisement victory over evil (Jesus)   6/4/02 Vol. 27
Great Chastisement when all appears hopeless (Jesus)   9/26/02 Vol. 28
greed envy, selfishness (Jesus)   2/28/97 Vol. 6
greed & war cause financial problems (Jesus)   1/27/05 Vol. 38
greed for money behind drugs,abortions (Jesus)   4/22/99 Vol. 15
greed for resources abuse to the land (Jesus)   3/6/00 Vol. 18
greed in corporations could cause market crash (Jesus)   8/2/02 Vol. 28
green eyes Antichrist   8/10/93 Vol. 1
green pastures spiritual satisfaction in Jesus (Jesus)   6/16/07 Vol. 47
green vs dry prosperity vs tribulation (Jesus)   7/14/00 Vol. 20
greenhouses at refuges (Jesus)   1/14/08 Vol. 50
greeters share warmth of Church (Jesus)   8/31/02 Vol. 28
grieving give consolation (Jesus)   8/14/97 Vol. 8
grieving process souls in purgatory (Jesus)   2/8/01 Vol. 22
grieving the dead comfort dead & dying (Jesus)   2/2/01 Vol. 22
grotto during tribulation healing water for sick (Jesus)   10/16/98 Vol. 13
grottos of water at places of refuge (Jesus)   12/27/01 Vol. 25
growth in faith sacraments,prayer,reading (Jesus)   8/29/01 Vol. 24
grudges don't bear,ask forgiveness (Jesus)   3/9/99 Vol. 14
Guadalupe second coming (Mary)   12/12/95 Vol. 3
Guadalupe sign against abortion (Mary)   12/12/98 Vol. 13
Guadalupe abortion bishop   12/9/93 Vol. 1
Guadalupe treasures (Mary)   12/12/94 Vol. 2
Guadalupe refuge protected by angel (Jesus)   8/21/06 Vol. 44
Guadalupe statue stop abortions (Jesus)   12/28/06 Vol. 45
Guadalupe, Lady of Mother of all Americas (Mary)   12/11/07 Vol. 49
Guadalupe, Our Lady of miracles in Clearwater, Robstown (Jesus)
    8/15/04 Vol. 36
Guadalupe Image miracles for faithful (Jesus)   12/12/05 Vol. 41
guard souls an everyday battle (Jesus)   3/23/00 Vol. 18

guard time of reflection salvation at stake (Jesus)   12/31/98 Vol. 13

guardian angel be good example (Mark)   10/6/05 Vol. 41

guardian angel Blessed Sacrament (Mark)   10/2/93 Vol. 1

guardian angel call on for help (Mark)   1/2/97 Vol. 6

guardian angel call on for help (Jesus)   12/28/00 Vol. 21

Guardian angel crosses (Jesus)   10/11/94 Vol. 2

Guardian angel dates (Mark)   10/2/94 Vol. 2

guardian angel demons (Jesus)   5/25/94 Vol. 1

guardian angel encourage holiness (Mark)   10/2/03 Vol. 33

Guardian Angel evil days (Jesus)   5/17/94 Vol. 1

guardian angel free will (Mark)   10/2/95 Vol. 3

Guardian Angel given at conception (Jesus)   9/24/06 Vol. 44

Guardian Angel gives counsel (Mark)   10/2/02 Vol. 29

guardian angel hard to help while in sin (Jesus)   1/5/08 Vol. 50

Guardian Angel holiness (Mark)   4/25/94 Vol. 1

guardian angel host (Mark)   10/2/93 Vol. 1

guardian angel Mark (Jesus)   9/1/94 Vol. 2

Guardian Angel materialism   9/2/93 Vol. 1

guardian angel power (Jesus)   10/2/95 Vol. 3

guardian angel prompt us to do good (Jesus)   4/25/03 Vol. 31

guardian angel prompts to do good (Jesus)   2/12/01 Vol. 22

guardian angel underground city (Jesus)   8/27/95 Vol. 3

Guardian Angel Mark personal message (Mark)   10/2/06 Vol. 45

guardian angels appointed at conception (Mark)   10/2/99 Vol. 17

guardian angels ask for help in speech (Jesus)   1/26/01 Vol. 22

guardian angels ask to battle evil ones (Jesus)   10/19/03 Vol. 33

guardian angels assigned at parents' wedding (Jesus)   9/5/98 Vol. 12

guardian angels call on for help (Jesus)   5/11/98 Vol. 11

guardian angels call on for help (Jesus)   5/14/99 Vol. 15

guardian angels call on for help (Jesus)   2/18/99 Vol. 14

guardian angels call on them for help (Mark)   4/25/98 Vol. 11

guardian angels caves dug out (Jesus)   10/21/95 Vol. 3

Guardian angels do not waste time (Mark)   10/2/04 Vol. 37

guardian angels food, water, protection (Jesus)   8/21/01 Vol. 24

guardian angels given at conception (Jesus)   10/2/03 Vol. 33

guardian angels help more with soul in grace (Jesus)   2/22/07 Vol. 46

guardian angels hiding (Jesus)   8/21/95 Vol. 3

guardian angels keep close (Jesus)   1/2/98 Vol. 10

guardian angels lead to caves & holy ground (Jesus)   5/4/98 Vol. 11

guardian angels lead to refuges (Jesus)   8/22/01 Vol. 24

guardian angels lead to refuges (Jesus)   3/24/03 Vol. 30

guardian angels lead to refuges (Mark)   10/2/01 Vol. 25

guardian angels lead to refuges (Jesus)   11/3/05 Vol. 41

guardian angels lead to refuges by sign (Jesus)   2/3/03 Vol. 30

guardian angels lead to refuges, protection (Jesus)   11/21/00 Vol. 21

guardian angels lead to safety (Mark)   6/6/98 Vol. 11

guardian angels lead us to refuge (Jesus)   2/2/02 Vol. 26

guardian angels lead us to refuges (Jesus)   7/6/01 Vol. 24

guardian angels love & service to God (Jesus)   10/2/00 Vol. 21

guardian angels love is center of life (Mark)   10/2/98 Vol. 13

guardian angels make us close to Jesus (Jesus)   5/17/97 Vol. 7

guardian angels people invisible at refuges (Jesus)   7/19/07 Vol. 48

Guardian angels power, protection (Mark)   10/2/97 Vol. 9

guardian angels pray for help, personal (Mark)   5/21/97 Vol. 7

guardian angels protect & guide (Mark)   10/6/05 Vol. 41

guardian angels protect children (Jesus)   12/30/96 Vol. 5

Guardian Angels protect you from evil Angel (Mark)   10/2/96 Vol. 5

guardian angels protection (Jesus)   2/20/97 Vol. 6

guardian angels protection in tribulation (Jesus)   10/2/00 Vol. 21

guardian angels protection of (Jesus)   1/13/98 Vol. 10

guardian angels provide food and shelter (Jesus)   9/3/98 Vol. 12

guardian angels show you the way (Mark)   9/11/97 Vol. 8

guardian angels to care for us (Jesus)   5/2/04 Vol. 35

guardian angels to guide us in Era of Peace (Mark)   11/3/98 Vol. 13

guardian angels to lead & protect us (Mark)   10/2/07 Vol. 49

guardian angels to lead us in hiding (Jesus)   2/22/99 Vol. 14

guardian angels to lead you to refuge (Jesus)   6/9/05 Vol. 39

guardian angels to make us invisible (Jesus)   1/16/08 Vol. 50

guardian angels will lead us into hiding (Jesus)   7/2/98 Vol. 12

guardian angels will lead you to safety (Jesus)   12/17/97 Vol. 9

Guest of honor Jesus in tabernacle (Jesus)   1/15/02 Vol. 26

guide Confession (Jesus)   4/4/95 Vol. 2

Guillotine killings used for public example (Jesus)   1/18/07 Vol. 46

Guillotines being prepared (Jesus)   9/5/02 Vol. 28

Guillotines in public executions (Jesus)   6/18/01 Vol. 23

Guillotines public martyrdom (Jesus)   8/7/03 Vol. 32

guilt seek Confession (Jesus)   6/16/98 Vol. 11

gun removal stept to world control (Jesus)   6/28/00 Vol. 19

guns removed, so defenseless (Jesus)   3/15/03 Vol. 30

guns vs crucifixes sacramentals more powerful (Jesus)   3/2/00 Vol. 18

Gysel, Camiel funeral Mass (Camiel Gysel)   9/9/05 Vol. 40

Gysel, Roger funeral (Jesus)   7/4/03 Vol. 32

HAARP affects minds (Jesus)   2/25/03 Vol. 30

HAARP controlling,enhancing weather (Jesus)   8/24/07 Vol. 48

HAARP enhance weather (Jesus)   1/8/04 Vol. 34

HAARP enhances storms (Jesus)   10/28/06 Vol. 45

HAARP enhancing storms (Jesus)   6/9/06 Vol. 43

HAARP stronger beams for weather (Jesus)   11/18/03 Vol. 33

HAARP weather modification (Jesus)   5/14/02 Vol. 27

HAARP machine affecting jet streams (Jesus)   2/10/06 Vol. 42

HAARP machine can enhance disasters (Jesus)   7/5/06 Vol. 44

HAARP machine capable of power outages (Jesus)   8/23/03 Vol. 32

HAARP machine causing severe weather (Jesus)   12/5/07 Vol. 49

HAARP machine creates disasters (Jesus)   9/26/03 Vol. 32

HAARP machine four times more powerful (Jesus) — 6/3/06 Vol. 43
HAARP machine holding jet streams in place (Jesus) — 12/29/06 Vol. 45
HAARP machine makes weather worse (Jesus) — 1/11/05 Vol. 38
HAARP machine manipulating weather (Jesus) — 12/29/00 Vol. 21
HAARP machine use in weather control (Jesus) — 1/9/97 Vol. 6
HAARP machine weather & earthquakes (Jesus) — 2/13/06 Vol. 42
HAARP machine worsens ice storms (Jesus) — 11/16/06 Vol. 45
HAARP machines enhance weather (Jesus) — 6/12/06 Vol. 43
HAARP machines intensifying hurricanes (Jesus) — 9/27/05 Vol. 40
HAARP machines manipulating weather (Jesus) — 5/31/00 Vol. 19
HAARP machines source of severe weather (Jesus) — 5/25/04 Vol. 35
habits, bad break by Confession (Jesus) — 7/8/04 Vol. 36
habits, bad pray to be strong (Jesus) — 10/8/99 Vol. 17
habits, sinful change lifestyle (Jesus) — 2/15/02 Vol. 26
habitual sin hardest to break (Jesus) — 8/24/04 Vol. 36
habitual sin remove bonds of sin (Jesus) — 1/27/06 Vol. 42
habitual sin ways to correct (Jesus) — 4/8/02 Vol. 27
habitual sins need conversion (Jesus) — 3/3/01 Vol. 22
habitual sins worst infection of (Jesus) — 9/23/02 Vol. 28
Haiti revolt for injustice (Jesus) — 2/28/04 Vol. 34
Hale Bopp comet sign of Antichrist (Jesus) — 7/20/99 Vol. 16
Hale-Bopp comet sign of Antichrist (Jesus) — 3/27/97 Vol. 6
Hale-Bopp Comet sign of Antichrist on earth (Jesus) — 9/12/02 Vol. 28
Hale-Bopp comet sign of Antichrist on earth (Jesus) — 9/3/04 Vol. 36
Hale-Bopp comet sign of Antichrist's coming (Jesus) — 9/22/99 Vol. 16
Hall, Jack funeral message (Jesus) — 10/18/06 Vol. 45
Halloween avoid evil disguises (Jesus) — 10/23/03 Vol. 33
Halloween contrast God over demons (Jesus) — 11/26/00 Vol. 21
Halloween demons glorify evil (Jesus) — 10/26/04 Vol. 37
Halloween evil symbols glorified (Jesus) — 10/28/04 Vol. 37
Halloween feastday of occult (Jesus) — 10/31/01 Vol. 25
Halloween focus on All Saints Day (Jesus) — 10/12/06 Vol. 45
Halloween shopkeepers celebrate evil feast (Jesus) — 10/30/03 Vol. 33
Halloween witches and evil spirits (Jesus) — 10/23/97 Vol. 9
Halloween & Christmas battle of good & evil (Jesus) — 10/6/01 Vol. 25
Halloween storm sign of end times (Jesus) — 10/25/06 Vol. 45
hand writing on the wall for America's demise (Jesus) — 1/1/02 Vol. 26
handgun abuse better not to have guns (Jesus) — 8/25/99 Vol. 16
handicapped and caregivers (Jesus) — 2/14/08 Vol. 50
handicapped help physically,spiritually (Jesus) — 1/22/98 Vol. 10
handicapped need empathy & help (Jesus) — 5/10/04 Vol. 35
handicapped suffering purgatory on earth (Jesus) — 7/14/05 Vol. 40
handicapped & elderly give help to (Jesus) — 12/14/01 Vol. 25
handicapped people physically & spiritually (Jesus) — 9/25/00 Vol. 20
happiness love God and neighbor (Jesus) — 4/3/98 Vol. 11
happiness & love show to everyone (Jesus) — 6/14/01 Vol. 23
hard road suffering (Jesus) — 11/7/94 Vol. 2

hard times,troubles call on God to lift spirit (Jesus) — 3/19/01 Vol. 22
hardships tests of faith (Jesus) — 12/3/99 Vol. 17
hardships in life learn from them (Jesus) — 2/11/04 Vol. 34
harmony of earth destroyed by greed & pride (Jesus) — 12/25/04 Vol. 37
harmony with God creation as ordered (Jesus) — 6/13/07 Vol. 47
Harry Potter avoid witchcraft (Jesus) — 12/18/06 Vol. 45
Harry Potter corrupts children with evil (Jesus) — 11/20/01 Vol. 25
Harry Potter headaches caused by reading (Jesus) — 10/30/03 Vol. 33
Harry Potter leads to occult (Jesus) — 6/24/03 Vol. 31
Harry Potter leads to witchcraft (Jesus) — 12/3/07 Vol. 49
Harry Potter misleading childen & adults (Jesus) — 11/15/02 Vol. 29
Harry Potter misleading to evil (Jesus) — 1/23/03 Vol. 30
Harry Potter New Age Movement (Jesus) — 2/4/03 Vol. 30
Harry Potter occasions of sin (Jesus) — 6/20/03 Vol. 31
Harry Potter protect children from evil (Jesus) — 4/6/02 Vol. 27
Harry Potter question source of power (Jesus) — 8/8/02 Vol. 28
Harry Potter rid from houses (Jesus) — 10/12/06 Vol. 45
Harry Potter teaches New Age & occult (Jesus) — 9/5/03 Vol. 32
Harry Potter books avoid witchcraft influence (Jesus) — 5/16/05 Vol. 39
Harry Potter books lead to witchcraft, occult (Jesus) — 7/27/05 Vol. 40
Harry Potter influence no good and bad witches (Jesus) — 2/20/02 Vol. 26
Harry Potter things remove from houses (Jesus) — 4/30/06 Vol. 43
Harry Potter, New Age keep from children (Jesus) — 9/13/07 Vol. 48
Harry Potter, occult protect children from (Jesus) — 9/30/06 Vol. 44
harvest farmers move to new land (Jesus) — 10/24/96 Vol. 5
harvest protection (St. Michael) — 8/13/95 Vol. 3
harvest master call to faithful to evangelize (Jesus) — 12/7/02 Vol. 29
harvest masters gather wheat and tares (Jesus) — 9/26/98 Vol. 12
harvest of grapes angels to gather up (Jesus) — 1/24/00 Vol. 18
harvest of souls grapes to winepress, helll (Jesus) — 5/19/07 Vol. 47
harvest of souls prepare for purification (Jesus) — 10/3/96 Vol. 5
harvest of souls separate wheat from weeds (Jesus) — 9/6/01 Vol. 24
harvest of souls time is short (Jesus) — 3/21/98 Vol. 10
harvest of souls wheat to barn, heaven (Jesus) — 5/19/07 Vol. 47
harvest of souls with few laborers (Jesus) — 5/28/99 Vol. 15
harvesting souls convert to dying day (Jesus) — 10/20/96 Vol. 5
harvests, poor from droughts, floods (Jesus) — 8/7/02 Vol. 28
haste prayer (Jesus) — 11/27/93 Vol. 1
haste in agenda follow the Lord's plan (Jesus) — 11/4/99 Vol. 17
hate & revenge spreads evil in world (Jesus) — 1/9/04 Vol. 34
hate crimes increase mirrors society (Jesus) — 9/16/99 Vol. 16
hate vs reason focus on love of God (Holy Spirit) — 9/24/01 Vol. 24
Hawthorn & herbs for improving immune system (Jesus) — 2/18/08 Vol. 50
hawthorn & vitamines to build up immunity (Jesus) — 12/5/03 Vol. 33
hawthorn & vitamins to help immune system (Jesus) — 2/22/03 Vol. 30
hawthorn herbs,vitamins protect from symptoms (Jesus) — 10/17/02 Vol. 29
Haw.,herbs,vitamins protect from man-made viruses (Jesus) — 12/5/07 Vol. 49

hding signs to go (Jesus)   9/26/00 Vol. 20

head of state assassination attempt (Jesus)   11/4/07 Vol. 49

Head of state future funeral of (Jesus)   1/10/07 Vol. 46

head of state killed by one world people (Jesus)   3/3/04 Vol. 34

healed by crucifix & Confession (Jesus)   9/14/03 Vol. 32

Healer, Great in Jesus of body & soul (Jesus)   5/29/05 Vol. 39

healers & prophets to prepare way (Jesus)   7/26/03 Vol. 32

healing end time miracles (Jesus)   4/17/96 Vol. 3

healing faith (Holy Spirit)   11/12/94 Vol. 2

healing faith in Jesus needed (Jesus)   2/19/07 Vol. 46

healing gifts (Holy Spirit)   6/4/95 Vol. 2

healing give glory only to God (Jesus)   5/10/04 Vol. 35

healing have faith and trust (Mary)   7/23/98 Vol. 12

healing in body and spirit (Jesus)   2/26/97 Vol. 6

healing in Name of Jesus (Jesus)   1/3/07 Vol. 46

healing involves soul & body (Jesus)   2/17/00 Vol. 18

healing miracles (Jesus)   4/23/94 Vol. 1

healing more faith, greater gifts (Jesus)   5/29/98 Vol. 11

healing occurs in body and soul (Jesus)   3/18/02 Vol. 26

healing of body & soul (Jesus)   5/14/01 Vol. 23

healing of body and soul (Jesus)   4/16/04 Vol. 35

healing physical & spiritual (Jesus)   10/30/95 Vol. 3

healing physically & spiritually (Jesus)   1/18/98 Vol. 10

healing requires faith (Jesus)   2/7/00 Vol. 18

healing requires faith in healed (Jesus)   11/6/00 Vol. 21

healing requires faith in Jesus (Jesus)   9/11/06 Vol. 44

healing soul first, then body (Jesus)   10/31/07 Vol. 49

healing spiritual and physical (Holy Spirit)   10/28/97 Vol. 9

healing spiritually & physically (Jesus)   4/21/01 Vol. 23

healing through His servants (Jesus)   1/14/04 Vol. 34

healing use gifts or loose them (Mary)   2/11/97 Vol. 6

healing at refuges from looking at cross (Jesus)   5/5/00 Vol. 19

healing at refuges of diseases (Jesus)   11/26/06 Vol. 45

healing body, soul in Confession (Jesus)   8/31/04 Vol. 36

healing diseases herbs,vitamins,luminous cross (Jesus)   11/6/02 Vol. 29

healing gifts to cure epidemics (Jesus)   6/18/03 Vol. 31

healing in America needed for elections (Jesus)   11/3/04 Vol. 37

healing Jesus helps hurts & troubles (Jesus)   8/29/99 Vol. 16

healing ministry evangelize all (Jesus)   3/6/97 Vol. 6

healing miracles going on even today (Mary)   8/5/98 Vol. 12

healing of faults in grace of Confession (Jesus)   3/20/00 Vol. 18

healing of sick by God's Will (Jesus)   7/2/06 Vol. 44

healing power if not used, will dry up (Jesus)   4/21/97 Vol. 7

healing power in laying on of hands (Jesus)   12/26/02 Vol. 29

healing prayers spiritual and physical (Jesus)   3/22/04 Vol. 34

healing prerequisites invoking Jesus' Name,faith in (Jesus) 3/18/02 Vol. 26

healing requests what is best for soul (Jesus)   11/5/06 Vol. 45

healing springs, cross to cure diseases (Jesus)   6/9/07 Vol. 47

Healing Tree in Concepcion, Texas (Jesus)   8/22/06 Vol. 44

healing waters at refuges (Jesus)   10/20/01 Vol. 25

healing waters in caves (Jesus)   4/9/05 Vol. 39

healing waters provided by Mary (Jesus)   6/12/99 Vol. 15

healings at luminous crosses,caves (Jesus)   9/1/98 Vol. 12

healings call on His Name (Jesus)   5/20/97 Vol. 7

healings faith necessary in healed (Jesus)   6/25/04 Vol. 35

healings faith needed for (Jesus)   3/12/07 Vol. 46

healings forgive sins first, then body (Jesus)   2/11/04 Vol. 34

healings heal spirit and body (Jesus)   6/26/98 Vol. 11

healings in Jesus' name (Jesus)   5/8/96 Vol. 3

healings in Jesus' Will and Name (Jesus)   6/25/05 Vol. 39

healings miraculously answered (Jesus)   12/1/96 Vol. 5

healings must heal souls first (Jesus)   7/31/96 Vol. 4

healings need belief in (Holy Spirit)   6/4/06 Vol. 43

healings of body & soul (Jesus)   7/1/06 Vol. 44

healings of Jesus (Jesus)   2/9/07 Vol. 46

healings physical & spiritual (Jesus)   1/30/01 Vol. 22

healings pray for (Jesus)   12/21/06 Vol. 45

healings spiritual and physical (Mary)   2/11/98 Vol. 10

healings spiritual and physical (Jesus)   6/5/96 Vol. 3

healings spiritual first/God's Will (Jesus)   10/8/96 Vol. 5

healings spiritual most important (Jesus)   1/11/08 Vol. 50

healings spiritual,physical,mind (Jesus)   2/3/98 Vol. 10

healings suffering servants/cures (Jesus)   5/22/96 Vol. 3

healings through faith (Jesus)   2/11/02 Vol. 26

healings to come to this place (Jesus)   2/28/05 Vol. 38

healings trust in God (Jesus)   5/25/01 Vol. 23

healings with faith (Jesus)   7/7/03 Vol. 32

healings with rose petals (Jesus)   2/23/07 Vol. 46

healings at refuges springs, luminous cross,healers (Jesus) 10/15/03 Vol. 33

healings today through Name of Jesus (Jesus)   2/7/00 Vol. 18

healings, faith in Kateri Tekakwitha, Jesus power (Kateri) 5/16/04 Vol. 35

healings, refuge at springs,luminous crosses (Jesus)   9/14/07 Vol. 48

health gift to be thankful for (Jesus)   11/14/07 Vol. 49

health stress,food,technology (Jesus)   1/13/97 Vol. 6

health care industry abuses & expenses (Jesus)   1/27/04 Vol. 34

health industry making money on patients (Jesus)   3/30/07 Vol. 46

health problems caused by stress (Jesus)   1/26/01 Vol. 22

health, God's gift thank Him for it (Jesus)   5/11/07 Vol. 47

heart attention (Jesus)   9/25/94 Vol. 2

heart corrupt and pure (Jesus)   2/29/96 Vol. 3

heart disciple (Jesus)   1/18/94 Vol. 1

heart Divine Will,trust,faith (Jesus)   3/11/96 Vol. 3

heart fasting (Mary)   6/10/94 Vol. 1

heart love (Jesus)   3/8/94 Vol. 1

heart source of love for God (Jesus)	6/24/03 Vol. 31	heaven complete peace & love (Jesus)	5/7/03 Vol. 31
heart what comes out is problem (Jesus)	10/4/03 Vol. 33	heaven description of (Jesus)	11/1/06 Vol. 45
heart recessed empty heart (Jesus)	3/4/95 Vol. 2	heaven description of presence (Jesus)	7/6/07 Vol. 48
heart, door to not always open to Jesus (Jesus)	9/6/07 Vol. 48	heaven distractions (St. Agnes)	1/21/94 Vol. 1
heart, door to opens only from inside (Jesus)	9/4/01 Vol. 24	heaven earth (Jesus)	5/27/95 Vol. 2
heart, pray with in addition to prayers on lips (Mary)	10/7/04 Vol. 37	heaven eternal now,young forever (Jesus)	7/6/98 Vol. 12
heart, think with your so love shows forth (Mary)	5/31/99 Vol. 15	heaven evangelization (Jesus)	2/4/96 Vol. 3
heart,crack open let in Jesus' graces (Jesus)	11/20/98 Vol. 13	heaven experience & level of love (Jesus)	6/7/06 Vol. 43
heart,unforgiving needs purging, love (Jesus)	3/20/01 Vol. 22	heaven few go straight after death (Jesus)	6/20/01 Vol. 23
hearts empty selfishness (Jesus)	8/16/01 Vol. 24	heaven focus priorities (Jesus)	8/22/00 Vol. 20
hearts ice cold, melt with love (Jesus)	11/8/96 Vol. 5	heaven for the faithful (Jesus)	8/3/01 Vol. 24
hearts melt away hardness (Jesus)	3/2/07 Vol. 46	heaven gem of great value (Jesus)	12/2/01 Vol. 25
hearts open to mercy & love (Jesus)	7/24/96 Vol. 4	heaven goal for everyone (Jesus)	12/20/05 Vol. 41
hearts time	10/3/93 Vol. 1	heaven goal of our souls (Jesus)	2/23/99 Vol. 14
hearts trust (Mary)	2/23/94 Vol. 1	Heaven goal of your soul (Jesus)	4/12/99 Vol. 15
hearts weather (Jesus)	7/27/95 Vol. 3	heaven goal of your soul (Jesus)	8/9/00 Vol. 20
heart's door let Jesus come in (Jesus)	12/10/07 Vol. 49	heaven graduation from purgatory (Jesus)	7/3/07 Vol. 48
heart's intentions outside covers up evil (Jesus)	11/29/97 Vol. 9	heaven greeted by known souls (Jesus)	3/11/99 Vol. 14
heart's intentions pure following God's Will (Jesus)	6/19/00 Vol. 19	heaven guided by faith,hope & truth (Jesus)	4/15/04 Vol. 35
heart's intentions read by Jesus (Jesus)	4/7/01 Vol. 23	heaven harmony (Jesus)	4/27/94 Vol. 1
hearts need opening in order to be saved (Jesus)	9/4/01 Vol. 24	heaven has different levels (Jesus)	7/15/98 Vol. 12
hearts need opening make room for Jesus (Jesus)	3/14/01 Vol. 22	heaven has many mansions (Jesus)	11/16/00 Vol. 21
hearts of stone love of God decides fate (Jesus)	6/6/97 Vol. 7	heaven His Key (Jesus)	4/17/96 Vol. 3
hearts of stone turn to love and joy (Jesus)	10/6/05 Vol. 41	heaven in the eternal now (Jesus)	7/8/04 Vol. 36
hearts open advance in spirituality (Jesus)	8/8/98 Vol. 12	heaven is birth in the spirit (Jesus)	7/23/04 Vol. 36
hearts opened spiritual spring cleaning (Jesus)	8/5/97 Vol. 8	heaven is our first goal (Jesus)	3/30/04 Vol. 34
hearts purified from worldly desires (Jesus)	6/26/00 Vol. 19	heaven is watching & cheering us (Jesus)	8/4/06 Vol. 44
hearts, cold faithful need to reach out to (Jesus)	10/14/00 Vol. 21	heaven life (Jesus)	5/22/94 Vol. 1
hearts, icy need warming by love of God (Jesus)	3/2/01 Vol. 22	heaven little child (Jesus)	1/11/96 Vol. 3
hearts, icy cold melt with love & prayers (Jesus)	12/2/05 Vol. 41	heaven love in the eternal now (Jesus)	7/22/99 Vol. 16
hearts, locked key needed to open to God (Jesus)	3/6/08 Vol. 50	heaven love is the focus (Jesus)	7/26/99 Vol. 16
hearts, locked need openness to Jesus (Jesus)	11/7/00 Vol. 21	heaven mercy (Jesus)	3/5/94 Vol. 1
hearts, locked to be opened to Jesus (Jesus)	2/21/04 Vol. 34	heaven most precious moment in (Jesus)	7/11/99 Vol. 16
hearts, loving turn from icy hearts (Jesus)	11/15/03 Vol. 33	heaven must be perfected (Jesus)	1/7/99 Vol. 14
heat,strong winds more disasters in summer (Jesus)	3/15/01 Vol. 22	Heaven nature (Mary)	8/15/95 Vol. 3
heating bills higher by manipulated prices (Jesus)	9/21/00 Vol. 20	heaven new Creation (Jesus)	3/21/94 Vol. 1
heating devices,alternate have working for outages (Jesus)	12/16/06 Vol. 45	heaven no space or time (Jesus)	4/20/01 Vol. 23
heating homes help neighbor with expenses (Jesus)	12/14/00 Vol. 21	heaven only through Jesus (Jesus)	5/1/07 Vol. 47
heatwave deaths in Europe (Jesus)	8/14/03 Vol. 32	heaven prepare for spiritual battle (Jesus)	1/14/02 Vol. 26
heaven accept Savior,pardon sins (Jesus)	11/24/00 Vol. 21	heaven Prodigal Son (Jesus)	7/20/94 Vol. 2
heaven angels (Mary)	12/22/93 Vol. 1	heaven pure love,peace,music (Jesus)	11/11/05 Vol. 41
heaven as a precious gem (Jesus)	2/13/99 Vol. 14	heaven reach by carrying crosses (Jesus)	8/1/01 Vol. 24
heaven banquet table (Jesus)	9/24/01 Vol. 24	heaven requires God's graces (Jesus)	11/19/03 Vol. 33
heaven beatific vision (Jesus)	5/5/96 Vol. 3	Heaven salvation (Jesus)	8/12/95 Vol. 3
heaven by following God's Will (Jesus)	4/6/04 Vol. 35	heaven seek higher places (Jesus)	11/27/06 Vol. 45
heaven choice (Jesus)	2/7/94 Vol. 1	heaven seven levels of glory (Jesus)	12/14/00 Vol. 21
heaven come with wedding garment (Jesus)	1/16/02 Vol. 26	heaven souls watch everything (Jesus)	6/15/01 Vol. 23

heaven special place for martyrs (Jesus) — 8/14/01 Vol. 24

heaven special places (Jesus) — 4/2/02 Vol. 27

heaven spiritual freedom (Jesus) — 3/29/03 Vol. 30

heaven steps to each day (Jesus) — 8/6/03 Vol. 32

heaven submit to Jesus' Will (Jesus) — 5/6/01 Vol. 23

heaven the faithful will rise (Jesus) — 3/7/99 Vol. 14

heaven the road is bumpy,suffer (Jesus) — 5/23/97 Vol. 7

heaven travel spiritually in next life (Jesus) — 6/10/04 Vol. 35

heaven trust in God's help (Jesus) — 7/12/04 Vol. 36

heaven warning (Jesus) — 4/17/94 Vol. 1

heaven watching souls on earth (Jesus) — 12/1/00 Vol. 21

heaven will I be bored? All praising (Jesus) — 8/31/98 Vol. 12

heaven your only choice to be (Jesus) — 11/12/99 Vol. 17

heaven & hell only ultimate destinations (Jesus) — 11/27/06 Vol. 45

heaven & hell you send yourself (Jesus) — 12/10/01 Vol. 25

heaven as graduation takes effort, hard work (Jesus) — 2/22/01 Vol. 22

heaven bound renounce attachments to world (Jesus) — 11/1/03 Vol. 33

heaven calling souls to eternal life (Jesus) — 12/14/03 Vol. 33

heaven on earth Adam (Jesus) — 5/19/94 Vol. 1

heaven on earth angels (Jesus) — 1/15/94 Vol. 1

heaven on earth angels & safe havens (Jesus) — 9/13/96 Vol. 4

heaven on earth beauty and peace (Jesus) — 3/20/96 Vol. 3

heaven on earth end of time (Jesus) — 1/31/94 Vol. 1

heaven on earth Garden of Eden (Jesus) — 5/14/95 Vol. 2

Heaven on earth light — 9/25/93 Vol. 1

heaven on earth peace,love,harmony (Jesus) — 6/12/96 Vol. 3

heaven on earth reward for labors (Jesus) — 1/6/98 Vol. 10

heaven on earth with Eucharist (Jesus) — 12/18/04 Vol. 37

heaven only by doing God's Will (Jesus) — 5/16/03 Vol. 31

heaven opened good souls to heaven (Jesus) — 4/16/00 Vol. 19

heaven opened to cheers from the dead (Jesus) — 11/29/01 Vol. 25

heaven or hell biggest choice of life (Jesus) — 8/22/01 Vol. 24

heaven or hell choice of a lifetime (Jesus) — 11/7/02 Vol. 29

heaven or hell choice of life (Jesus) — 10/27/04 Vol. 37

heaven or hell choose in every action (Jesus) — 12/30/02 Vol. 29

heaven or hell decided by our actions (Jesus) — 3/11/08 Vol. 50

heaven or hell free will choice (Jesus) — 4/10/03 Vol. 31

heaven or hell real choice by free will (Jesus) — 11/6/02 Vol. 29

Heaven picture Transfiguration — 8/6/93 Vol. 1

Heaven rejoices as souls enter as saints (Jesus) — 4/25/99 Vol. 15

heaven sees all actions nothing is hidden (Jesus) — 8/24/02 Vol. 28

heaven vs hell compare descriptions of each (Jesus) — 8/9/00 Vol. 20

heaven vs. hell choose Jesus (Jesus) — 12/19/06 Vol. 45

heaven vs. hell destination of choices (Jesus) — 5/3/06 Vol. 43

heaven vs. hell die to self,follow God's Will (Jesus) — 8/21/98 Vol. 12

heaven vs. hell life long decision in actions (Jesus) — 10/23/03 Vol. 33

heaven vs. hell love vs. hate (Jesus) — 11/19/98 Vol. 13

heaven vs. hell spiritual choice in actions (Jesus) — 11/8/07 Vol. 49

heaven watches actions & intentions (Jesus) — 2/10/04 Vol. 34

heaven, attaining seems overwhelming at first (Jesus) — 12/19/05 Vol. 41

heaven, goal of purpose in life (Jesus) — 3/24/01 Vol. 22

heaven, in transition live consecration (Jesus) — 12/16/02 Vol. 29

heaven, levels of Adoration,help poor,suffering (Jesus) — 3/30/04 Vol. 34

heaven, levels of response to God's love (Jesus) — 10/28/04 Vol. 37

heaven, levels of seek higher levels of faith (Jesus) — 11/14/04 Vol. 37

heaven, path to requires payment of suffering (Jesus) — 7/26/01 Vol. 24

heaven, purgatory, hell various levels of (Jesus) — 6/29/07 Vol. 47

heaven, salvation in purchased by Blood of Jesus (Jesus) — 7/27/05 Vol. 40

heaven, steps to cross,consecration,trust in God (Jesus) — 8/19/04 Vol. 36

heaven, taste of in Holy Communion (Jesus) — 5/5/00 Vol. 19

heaven, vision of peace & love of Jesus (Jesus) — 6/7/07 Vol. 47

heaven, vision of total peace,rest in love (Jesus) — 3/29/01 Vol. 22

heaven,descriptions rid time & earthly comforts (Jesus) — 4/3/00 Vol. 19

heaven,hell,purgatory love determines judgment (Jesus) — 12/6/98 Vol. 13

heaven,levels of by faithfulness in testing (Jesus) — 2/3/00 Vol. 18

heaven,struggle for best prize of all (Jesus) — 6/7/03 Vol. 31

heavenly agenda more important than our own (Jesus) — 9/5/01 Vol. 24

heavenly armies massing for Battle of Armageddon (Jesus) — 9/28/06 Vol. 44

heavenly banker Jesus blesses (Jesus) — 6/10/02 Vol. 27

heavenly banquet come properly dressed (Jesus) — 8/11/01 Vol. 24

heavenly banquet purify and prepare (Jesus) — 2/25/99 Vol. 14

heavenly banquet treated as royalty (Jesus) — 10/3/02 Vol. 29

heav. conversations light beams & thought waves (Jesus) — 12/15/06 Vol. 45

heavenly description God's ceaseless praises (Jesus) — 11/12/99 Vol. 17

heavenly destination hinges on soul's purity (Jesus) — 8/8/02 Vol. 28

heavenly direction Truth & Way of Jesus (Jesus) — 5/21/00 Vol. 19

heavenly ectasy in Holy Communion (Jesus) — 2/24/00 Vol. 18

heavenly experience in receiving Holy Communion (Jesus) — 8/1/04 Vol. 36

heavenly food satisfies soul more (Jesus) — 8/3/98 Vol. 12

heavenly goal grace and angels help (Jesus) — 3/13/03 Vol. 30

heavenly goal must die to self here (Jesus) — 7/8/00 Vol. 20

heavenly goals better than earthly goals (Jesus) — 1/6/00 Vol. 18

heavenly home has many mansions (Jesus) — 6/25/06 Vol. 43

heavenly life desire for all souls (Jesus) — 4/23/07 Vol. 47

heavenly life worth more than earthly (Jesus) — 11/29/06 Vol. 45

heavenly music greater than earthly (Jesus) — 12/11/04 Vol. 37

heavenly music love and harmony (Jesus) — 5/5/07 Vol. 47

heavenly path souls suffer, purified (Jesus) — 4/9/06 Vol. 43

heavenly path ultimate home (Jesus) — 12/3/06 Vol. 45

heavenly preparations sacraments and love (Jesus) — 8/18/00 Vol. 20

heavenly priorities come before earthly ones (Jesus) — 8/23/02 Vol. 28

heavenly reward matches efforts on earth (Jesus) — 11/14/04 Vol. 37

heavenly riches better than earthly things (Jesus) — 6/24/99 Vol. 15

heavenly riches better to store up than money (Jesus) — 12/28/01 Vol. 25

heavenly riches desired over Satan's lies (Jesus) — 10/20/98 Vol. 13

heavenly riches greater than earthly riches (Jesus) — 6/26/03 Vol. 31

heavenly riches last forever (Jesus) — 12/22/01 Vol. 25

heavenly struggle through complete surrender (Jesus) — 5/13/04 Vol. 35

heavenly things shine in God's eyes (Jesus) — 12/18/03 Vol. 33

heavenly things spend more time on (Jesus) — 11/3/03 Vol. 33

heavenly thoughts better than man's ways (Jesus) — 12/3/02 Vol. 29

heavenly treasure better than possessions (Jesus) — 11/15/99 Vol. 17

heavenly treasure determines final destination (Jesus) — 12/30/02 Vol. 29

heavenly treasure for helping hurricane victims (Jesus) — 9/17/04 Vol. 36

heavenly treasure for helping others (Jesus) — 4/21/07 Vol. 47

heavenly treasure helps at your judgment (Jesus) — 9/19/04 Vol. 36

heavenly treasure more valuable than money (Jesus) — 2/11/05 Vol. 38

heavenly treasures last forever (Jesus) — 1/24/01 Vol. 22

heavenly treasures more important than earthly (Jesus) — 1/18/00 Vol. 18

heavenly treasures never lost (Jesus) — 6/6/02 Vol. 27

heavenly treasures secret deeds,not repayment (Jesus) — 9/20/98 Vol. 12

heavenly treasures will never lose (Jesus) — 1/5/04 Vol. 34

heavenly treasures will satisfy your soul more (Jesus) — 8/23/04 Vol. 36

heavenly treasures worth more than possessions (Jesus) — 5/4/00 Vol. 19

heaven's climb needs advance in holiness (Jesus) — 2/25/06 Vol. 42

heaven's entrance comes only through Jesus (Jesus) — 4/20/00 Vol. 19

heaven's gates worth all of life's trials (Jesus)   11/8/02 Vol. 29

heaven's key love God and neighbor (Jesus)   7/15/99 Vol. 16

heaven's mansions by accepting Savior, good deeds (Jesus) 7/29/04 Vol. 36

heaven's mansions different levels (Jesus)   6/7/05 Vol. 39

heaven's path keep focused on (Jesus)   7/12/03 Vol. 32

heaven's path like train on track (Jesus)   1/11/01 Vol. 22

heaven's requirements love God,accept as Savior (Jesus) 3/25/00 Vol. 18

heaven's req. totally perfect,no earthly desires (Jesus) 12/4/02 Vol. 29

heaven's road suffering & persecution (Jesus)   5/26/03 Vol. 31

heaven's stairway life is short (Jesus)   8/29/06 Vol. 44

Helen Hogan funeral Mass (Jesus)   3/25/08 Vol. 50

helicopters investigating people (Jesus)   11/14/96 Vol. 5

helicopters mapping targets (Jesus)   7/26/97 Vol. 8

helicopters more active roll (Jesus)   3/12/98 Vol. 10

helicopters & satellites means of searching (Jesus)   10/29/96 Vol. 5

hell as lake of fire (Jesus)   6/15/06 Vol. 43

hell Auriesville (Kateri T.)   9/10/93 Vol. 1

hell danger to the soul (St. Therese)   12/10/04 Vol. 37

hell description of levels (Jesus)   1/14/08 Vol. 50

hell disguised by evil one (Jesus)   10/29/05 Vol. 41

hell eternity without hope (Jesus)   11/2/05 Vol. 41

hell evil destroyed (Jesus)   5/11/97 Vol. 7

hell fall unsuspectingly (Jesus)   12/22/97 Vol. 9

hell fire of (Jesus)   5/31/05 Vol. 39

hell fires a preparation for (Jesus)   7/5/98 Vol. 12

hell flames forever (Jesus)   8/29/06 Vol. 44

hell for corrupt leaders (Jesus)   3/9/99 Vol. 14

hell for evil clergy (Jesus)   7/17/02 Vol. 28

hell for refusing God (Jesus)   11/15/00 Vol. 21

hell for spiritually lazy (Jesus)   5/19/03 Vol. 31

hell for those in mortal sin (Jesus)   7/8/03 Vol. 32

hell for those refusing convert (Jesus)   6/17/99 Vol. 15

hell for those who refuse God (Jesus)   12/20/97 Vol. 9

hell go on free choice (Jesus)   10/9/03 Vol. 33

hell has a broad road (Jesus)   5/9/03 Vol. 31

hell horrific alternative to heaven (Jesus)   3/29/01 Vol. 22

hell made for defiant angels (Jesus)   12/29/96 Vol. 5

hell many choose by free will (Jesus)   2/9/04 Vol. 34

hell many souls falling into (Jesus)   3/22/98 Vol. 10

hell many souls going there (Jesus)   10/3/01 Vol. 25

hell no grace or love in heart (Jesus)   8/13/03 Vol. 32

hell or listen to warnings (Jesus)   6/13/98 Vol. 11

hell path full of good intentions (Jesus)   7/25/97 Vol. 8

hell repent of laziness (Jesus)   9/24/97 Vol. 8

hell rich man (Jesus)   3/16/95 Vol. 2

hell sins (Jesus)   3/19/94 Vol. 1

hell souls refuse to serve God (Jesus)   2/21/08 Vol. 50

hell suffering flames, hate (Jesus)   5/7/03 Vol. 31

hell television can lead to (Jesus)   6/10/02 Vol. 27

hell threat to souls in abyss of sin (Jesus)   5/17/04 Vol. 35

hell understanding eternity (Jesus)   7/21/97 Vol. 8

hell unleashed in tribulation (Jesus)   2/1/99 Vol. 14

hell viewed in Warning (Jesus)   6/8/05 Vol. 39

hell where evil ones are sent (Jesus)   11/25/05 Vol. 41

hell whirlpool (Jesus)   8/29/94 Vol. 2

hell world (Jesus)   11/22/93 Vol. 1

hell & purgatory description of each (Jesus)   5/2/07 Vol. 47

hell & purgatory for those chosing earthly things (Jesus) 11/8/03 Vol. 33

hell bound souls lack love of God (Jesus)   11/29/03 Vol. 33

hell bound souls reaching for your prayers (Jesus)   5/16/06 Vol. 43

hell for Satan for refusal to serve God (Jesus)   8/21/02 Vol. 28

hell in levels justice in degrees (Jesus)   12/6/98 Vol. 13

hell on earth desire death vs. flames (Jesus)   5/25/06 Vol. 43

hell on earth evil ones not consumed (Jesus)   12/2/05 Vol. 41

hell on earth fire,scorpions,plagues (Jesus)   7/18/98 Vol. 12

hell on earth for unfaithful, take mark (Jesus)   11/20/99 Vol. 17

hell on earth plague for condemned (Jesus)   7/5/07 Vol. 48

hell on earth for lost evil cleansed from the earth (Jesus) 8/21/98 Vol. 12

hell, fires of Jesus fireman for souls (Jesus)   10/17/07 Vol. 49

hell, forever no turning back (Jesus)   7/25/07 Vol. 48

hell, gates to more souls in hell than heaven (Jesus)   9/3/01 Vol. 24

hell, many going to for breaking 6th Commandment (Jesus) 6/17/02 Vol. 27

hell, vision of inspiration to save souls (Jesus)   9/26/04 Vol. 36

hell,heaven,purgatory judgment decides for soul (Jesus) 11/8/98 Vol. 13

help neighbor do not be selfish (Jesus)   4/20/01 Vol. 23

help of Jesus needed through life (Jesus)   5/2/00 Vol. 19

help others without looking for a reward (Jesus)   5/10/04 Vol. 35

help out of love than for personal gain (Jesus)   2/19/02 Vol. 26

help the poor before theft & fighting (Jesus)   5/3/00 Vol. 19

help the sick corporal work of mercy (Jesus)   3/30/00 Vol. 18

helping others purifies your love (Jesus)   2/26/06 Vol. 42

helping people better than wasting time (Jesus)   11/20/03 Vol. 33

herald remnant (Mary)   7/10/94 Vol. 2

herald second coming (Mary)   12/23/94 Vol. 2

herbs discern physically&spiritually (Jesus)   12/6/03 Vol. 33

herbs & vitamins better long term cure (Jesus)   1/16/06 Vol. 42

herbs & vitamins better than unnatural drugs (Jesus) 10/12/04 Vol. 37

herbs & vitamins for protection (Jesus)   5/26/03 Vol. 31

heresies speak out against (Jesus)   1/2/97 Vol. 6

heresy cross   8/18/93 Vol. 1

Herod, Hitler killed the children (Jesus)   12/28/98 Vol. 13

heroic measures determined by family (Jesus)   7/22/04 Vol. 36

Hezbollah firing rockets (Jesus)   7/31/06 Vol. 44

hibernation in tribulation for protection (Jesus)   1/21/04 Vol. 34

hibernation means of protection (Jesus) — 6/7/96 Vol. 3

hiding angel as in Exodus (Jesus) — 11/6/94 Vol. 2

hiding apostasy (Jesus) — 11/14/95 Vol. 3

hiding as events unfold (Jesus) — 12/5/96 Vol. 5

hiding as Pope John Paul II leaves (Jesus) — 12/8/98 Vol. 13

hiding because of persecution (Jesus) — 5/1/07 Vol. 47

hiding best protection (Jesus) — 9/1/97 Vol. 8

hiding books (Jesus) — 11/3/95 Vol. 3

hiding car and possessions (Jesus) — 4/30/96 Vol. 3

hiding caves (Jesus) — 8/31/94 Vol. 2

hiding caves,mines,refuges (Jesus) — 5/11/96 Vol. 3

hiding detention/mark of beast (Jesus) — 7/31/96 Vol. 4

hiding electrical devices (Jesus) — 5/12/97 Vol. 7

hiding electrical devices (Jesus) — 10/31/95 Vol. 3

hiding faith in protection (Jesus) — 1/9/97 Vol. 6

hiding health,safety in danger (Jesus) — 5/8/97 Vol. 7

hiding holy weapons,essentials (Jesus) — 1/3/97 Vol. 6

hiding in caves or holy ground (Jesus) — 6/11/98 Vol. 11

hiding moving south (Jesus) — 10/8/94 Vol. 2

hiding necessary for faith in secret (Jesus) — 10/19/98 Vol. 13

hiding necessities (Jesus) — 12/14/94 Vol. 2

hiding persecution (Jesus) — 1/14/94 Vol. 1

hiding pope leaving, sign to flee (Jesus) — 12/31/97 Vol. 9

hiding prepare sacramentals (Jesus) — 7/23/01 Vol. 24

hiding prepare spiritually,physically (Jesus) — 7/30/01 Vol. 24

hiding protect loss of faith (Jesus) — 1/9/97 Vol. 6

hiding protection (Jesus) — 3/24/95 Vol. 2

hiding protection and angels (Jesus) — 6/17/96 Vol. 3

hiding protection of angels (Jesus) — 3/12/98 Vol. 10

hiding Real Presence with us (Jesus) — 4/7/98 Vol. 11

hiding refuges and angels (Jesus) — 10/17/96 Vol. 5

hiding refuges or caves (Jesus) — 9/4/98 Vol. 12

hiding renewed earth (Jesus) — 11/3/94 Vol. 2

hiding shovel (Jesus) — 11/24/94 Vol. 2

hiding sign on the forehead (Jesus) — 6/9/95 Vol. 2

hiding signs to go into (Jesus) — 10/27/99 Vol. 17

hiding signs to leave (Jesus) — 6/18/99 Vol. 15

hiding small groups (Jesus) — 11/11/94 Vol. 2

hiding some martyred/protected (Jesus) — 7/25/96 Vol. 4

hiding soon forced to believe (Jesus) — 2/22/99 Vol. 14

hiding survival in wilderness (Jesus) — 3/30/96 Vol. 3

hiding tabernacle & monstrance (Jesus) — 2/13/97 Vol. 6

hiding testing (Jesus) — 12/11/94 Vol. 2

hiding to be protected from slavery (Jesus) — 4/2/98 Vol. 11

hiding to escape diseases (Jesus) — 3/27/98 Vol. 10

hiding to save life (Jesus) — 5/25/02 Vol. 27

hiding tunnels,angels to lead (Jesus) — 11/24/96 Vol. 5

hiding underground home (Jesus) — 9/7/94 Vol. 2

hiding urge to flee,blind eyes (Jesus) — 5/14/96 Vol. 3

hiding warning when pope leaves (Jesus) — 4/17/98 Vol. 11

hiding when Antichrist comes (Jesus) — 7/9/01 Vol. 24

hiding when pope is exiled (Jesus) — 1/7/99 Vol. 14

hiding when pope is exiled (Jesus) — 6/16/99 Vol. 15

hiding woods (Jesus) — 8/10/94 Vol. 2

hiding conditions warning,Antipope,chip (Jesus) — 11/29/97 Vol. 9

hiding from sin God sees all (Jesus) — 3/18/07 Vol. 46

hiding from sins guilt of sin before God (Jesus) — 3/15/04 Vol. 34

hiding in tribulation need miraculous help of God (Jesus) — 4/12/00 Vol. 19

hiding or captivity faithful to be protected (Jesus) — 4/21/99 Vol. 15

hiding out of homes avoid prison,Antichrist (Jesus) — 11/14/98 Vol. 13

hiding places food,water,shelter provided (Jesus) — 9/16/98 Vol. 12

hiding places multiplied food, no fear (Jesus) — 4/27/00 Vol. 19

hiding places needed at interim refuges (Jesus) — 12/29/07 Vol. 49

hiding places to avoid persecution (Jesus) — 2/10/00 Vol. 18

hiding preparations blankets,food,sacramentals (Jesus) — 7/30/00 Vol. 20

hiding preparations vulnerable in houses (Jesus) — 12/15/99 Vol. 17

hiding refuges to escape being martyrs (Jesus) — 4/27/00 Vol. 19

hiding time food riots,chip in hand (Jesus) — 8/18/99 Vol. 16

hiding time when Pope John Paul II exile (Jesus) — 9/17/98 Vol. 12

hiding time when pope John Paul leaves (Jesus) — 10/6/98 Vol. 13

hiding with manna mark of the beast (Jesus) — 9/27/95 Vol. 3

hiding, help chip vs Jesus (Jesus) — 3/13/00 Vol. 18

hiding, refuge before death camps (Jesus) — 3/15/99 Vol. 14

hiding,led by angel into Exodus likeness (Jesus) — 9/28/95 Vol. 3

high definition TV listening devices in (Jesus) — 11/20/97 Vol. 9

high oil cost threatens fuel supply (Jesus) — 2/15/05 Vol. 38

high place in heaven for those using gifts (Jesus) — 6/11/07 Vol. 47

higher powers union heart&soul in prayer (Jesus) — 11/18/02 Vol. 29

higher spiritual road more given, more expected (Jesus) — 4/8/00 Vol. 19

highway Samaritan (Jesus) — 3/11/95 Vol. 2

historical mistakes destruction from within (Jesus) — 9/2/99 Vol. 16

history no learning from past (Jesus) — 1/6/99 Vol. 14

history of kingdoms fall from inside decadence (Jesus) — 7/18/00 Vol. 20

history of man no learning from mistakes (Jesus) — 9/19/03 Vol. 32

history of mistakes will continue without God (Jesus) — 5/10/99 Vol. 15

history of wars live to repeat them (Jesus) — 3/25/99 Vol. 14

Hitler aghast at killings (Jesus) — 1/8/99 Vol. 14

Hitler controlled by fear (Jesus) — 4/15/01 Vol. 23

Hitler to form master race (Jesus) — 8/2/01 Vol. 24

holidays keep spirit through year (Jesus) — 12/22/97 Vol. 9

holidays & feasts taken over by secular (Jesus) — 10/3/03 Vol. 33

holiness called to follow His Will (Jesus) — 1/4/02 Vol. 26

holiness learn from mistakes (Jesus) — 3/27/06 Vol. 42

holiness & perfection overcome little trials (Jesus) — 1/1/02 Vol. 26

holiness in families needed by Confession (Jesus)   8/18/05 Vol. 40

holiness, growth in in Holy Communion (Jesus)   4/17/07 Vol. 47

holiness,advances in constant struggle in life (Jesus)   8/10/00 Vol. 20

HOLLYWOOD sign   7/23/93 Vol. 1

Hollywood movies conditioning bad morals (Jesus)   3/28/00 Vol. 18

Holocaust of abortion killing most evil sin (Jesus)   12/21/98 Vol. 13

Holocaust victims revered by pope (Jesus)   3/24/00 Vol. 18

Holy Communion angels adore Jesus (St. Michael)   9/29/07 Vol. 48

Holy Communion bridge to spiritual life (Jesus)   9/2/96 Vol. 4

Holy Communion closest to heaven (Jesus)   3/20/07 Vol. 46

Holy Communion craving of soul (Jesus)   6/5/99 Vol. 15

Holy Communion do not receive in mortal sin (Jesus)   7/12/02 Vol. 28

Holy Communion grace for the day (Jesus)   8/5/01 Vol. 24

Holy Communion heals harm done by sin (Jesus)   3/5/08 Vol. 50

Holy Communion Jesus present 15 minutes (Jesus)   6/24/05 Vol. 39

Holy Communion means to grow in faith (Jesus)   11/28/99 Vol. 17

Holy Communion mingling our spirit with God (Jesus)   7/8/04 Vol. 36

Holy Communion most precious gift (Jesus)   2/15/03 Vol. 30

Holy Communion multiplied for everyone (Jesus)   2/7/06 Vol. 42

Holy Communion need purity to receive Jesus (Jesus)   3/26/01 Vol. 22

Holy Communion needed to fight Satan (Jesus)   11/18/99 Vol. 17

Holy Communion no mortal sin in receiving (Jesus)   8/3/98 Vol. 12

Holy Communion our spirits glow in (Jesus)   9/16/06 Vol. 44

Holy Communion precious moments with Jesus (Jesus)   10/26/00 Vol. 21

Holy Communion presence & blessing (Jesus)   5/1/96 Vol. 3

Holy Communion Real Presence (Jesus)   1/8/08 Vol. 50

Holy Communion Real Presence of Jesus (Jesus)   6/1/03 Vol. 31

Holy Communion receive without mortal sin (Jesus)   5/28/05 Vol. 39

Holy Communion receive without mortal sin (Jesus)   1/29/07 Vol. 46

Holy Communion requires confessing mortal sins (Jesus)   9/18/04 Vol. 36

Holy Communion reverence for Real Presence (Jesus)   10/27/98 Vol. 13

Holy Communion sacred union (Jesus)   3/2/97 Vol. 6

Holy Communion share intimate love of God (Jesus)   7/17/05 Vol. 40

Holy Communion spend time to listen after (Jesus)   12/21/97 Vol. 9

Holy Communion spiritual oasis (Jesus)   7/23/02 Vol. 28

Holy Communion take extra time to pray (Jesus)   5/25/99 Vol. 15

Holy Communion taste of heaven (Jesus)   5/22/03 Vol. 31

Holy Communion taste of heaven (Jesus)   7/27/06 Vol. 44

Holy Communion taste of heaven (Jesus)   10/27/07 Vol. 49

Holy Communion taste of heaven (Jesus)   6/26/99 Vol. 15

Holy Communion tingling of spirit (Jesus)   10/28/02 Vol. 29

Holy Communion union of spirits (Jesus)   3/7/98 Vol. 10

Holy Communion we are arks of the covenant (Jesus)   4/5/04 Vol. 35

Holy Communion, First awe of Real Presence (Jesus)   5/4/02 Vol. 27

Holy Communion, First we are tabernacles (Jesus)   4/14/02 Vol. 27

Holy Comm.,tongue reverence for Real Presence (Jesus)   9/17/98 Vol. 12

Holy days of obligation for Mass (Jesus)   1/1/04 Vol. 34

Holy Family example of life (Jesus)   12/9/99 Vol. 17

Holy Family example to imitate (Jesus)   1/9/99 Vol. 14

Holy Family focus on (Jesus)   12/4/03 Vol. 33

Holy Family imitate a simple life (Jesus)   3/3/05 Vol. 38

Holy Family is our example (Jesus)   4/19/01 Vol. 23

Holy Family model for all families (Jesus)   12/30/05 Vol. 41

Holy Family model for society (Jesus)   12/28/96 Vol. 5

Holy Family pray to them all year (Jesus)   8/1/02 Vol. 28

Holy Family reverence families (Jesus)   12/29/96 Vol. 5

holy ground Abbey of Our Lady, Trinity (Jesus)   9/13/97 Vol. 8

holy ground caves and refuges (Jesus)   4/29/98 Vol. 11

holy ground cure ills,provide manna (Jesus)   1/13/98 Vol. 10

holy ground Marmora healing place (Mary)   9/8/99 Vol. 16

holy ground Mt. Sinai,holy spots (Jesus)   7/7/97 Vol. 8

holy ground places of protection (Jesus)   10/14/99 Vol. 17

holy ground presence in Host (God the Father)   3/22/98 Vol. 10

Holy hr. in Adoration listen to God,Scripture,rosary (Jesus)   10/24/04 Vol. 37

holy hours share love & thanks with God (Jesus)   12/27/00 Vol. 21

Holy Innocents abortion (Jesus)   12/28/95 Vol. 3

Holy Innocents abortion (Jesus)   12/26/96 Vol. 5

Holy Innocents in abused,aborted infants (Jesus)   12/28/99 Vol. 17

Holy Innocents in modern day abortions (Jesus)   7/24/00 Vol. 20

Holy Innocents Jeremiah prophecy (Jesus)   12/28/05 Vol. 41

Holy Innocents killed to protect Herod (Jesus)   12/22/06 Vol. 45

Holy Innocents suffering for little ones (Jesus)   12/28/96 Vol. 5

Holy Innocents uses of fetuses (Jesus)   12/28/00 Vol. 21

Holy Lands battle for religious sites (Jesus)   10/19/00 Vol. 21

Holy Lands no peace at Christmas (Jesus)   12/13/01 Vol. 25

Holy Lands pray for peace (Jesus)   10/10/96 Vol. 5

Holy Lands fighting Israel vs Palestinians (Jesus)   3/25/04 Vol. 34

holy life prayer, free will to God (Jesus)   11/13/03 Vol. 33

holy lives by total consecration (Jesus)   6/24/04 Vol. 35

Holy Name 40th anniv. crucifix on altar (Jesus)   10/18/07 Vol. 49

Holy Name crucifix all commended for work (Jesus)   12/2/07 Vol. 49

Holy Name of Jesus Bible quotes (Jesus)   1/3/07 Vol. 46

Holy Name of Jesus called on to heal (Jesus)   5/7/05 Vol. 39

Holy Name of Jesus feast eternal life through Him (Jesus)   1/3/04 Vol. 34

Holy of Holies in Blessed Sacrament (Jesus)   7/29/07 Vol. 48

Holy of Holies is holy ground (Jesus)   4/6/97 Vol. 7

Holy of Holies reverence, Ark of Covenant (Jesus)   9/5/98 Vol. 12

Holy Orders grace to forgive sins (Jesus)   9/13/00 Vol. 20

holy pictures inspiration for life (Jesus)   12/5/98 Vol. 13

holy places & shrines graces of protection (Jesus)   7/23/98 Vol. 12

Holy Rosary feast pray family rosary (Mary)   10/3/96 Vol. 5

Holy Saturday second Resurrection (Jesus)   4/15/95 Vol. 2

Holy Sepulcher protect and preserve holy places (Jesus)   9/9/04 Vol. 36

Holy Shroud burst of Jesus' Light (Jesus)   4/22/00 Vol. 19

Holy Shroud energy flashed the image (Jesus) 3/15/98 Vol. 10
Holy Spirit and angels for protection (Jesus) 6/8/02 Vol. 27
Holy Spirit angels (Mark) 6/4/95 Vol. 2
Holy Spirit animates our souls (Jesus) 5/6/02 Vol. 27
Holy Spirit ask for courage, strength (Jesus) 5/17/07 Vol. 47
Holy Spirit be baptized in (Jesus) 1/8/98 Vol. 10
Holy Spirit Betania reunion (Holy Spirit) 8/11/96 Vol. 4
Holy Spirit call on for help (Jesus) 5/29/01 Vol. 23
Holy Spirit call on help in trials (Holy Spirit) 3/4/99 Vol. 14
Holy Spirit conception of Mary & Jesus (Mary) 12/8/05 Vol. 41
Holy Spirit empowered at Confirmation (Jesus) 6/8/03 Vol. 31
Holy Spirit empowers preaching,courage (Jesus) 5/5/05 Vol. 39
Holy Spirit empowers teaching of faith (Holy Spirit) 5/15/05 Vol. 39
Holy Spirit enabled apostles in grace (Jesus) 6/1/00 Vol. 19
Holy Spirit every soul is lovable (Jesus) 12/20/05 Vol. 41
Holy Spirit fire empowers evangelism (Jesus) 4/26/99 Vol. 15
Holy Spirit flames of love (Holy Spirit) 5/19/02 Vol. 27
Holy Spirit gave apostles courage in speech (Jesus) 9/21/03 Vol. 32
Holy Spirit gave gifts of healing, speaking (Jesus) 8/24/04 Vol. 36
Holy Spirit gifts to the Blessed Mother (Mary) 5/21/98 Vol. 11
Holy Spirit gives courage to speak out (Jesus) 5/1/05 Vol. 39
Holy Spirit gives courage to speak out (Jesus) 4/28/05 Vol. 39
Holy Spirit gives life (Holy Spirit) 1/14/98 Vol. 10
Holy Spirit gives power to evangelize (Jesus) 4/15/04 Vol. 35
Holy Spirit gives strength to speak out (Jesus) 5/10/04 Vol. 35
Holy Spirit gives us strength (Jesus) 5/20/99 Vol. 15
Holy Spirit God of love,Pentecost (Holy Spirit) 5/3/01 Vol. 23
Holy Spirit help in presentations (Holy Spirit) 7/10/97 Vol. 8
Holy Spirit help in speaking (Holy Spirit) 1/14/98 Vol. 10
Holy Spirit help to speak out (Jesus) 4/24/06 Vol. 43
Holy Spirit help,grace for evangelizing (Jesus) 5/20/04 Vol. 35
Holy Spirit helped write Gospels (Jesus) 4/25/06 Vol. 43
Holy Spirit helping with talks, messages (Jesus) 9/26/04 Vol. 36
Holy Spirit helps evangelize souls (Jesus) 5/16/02 Vol. 27
Holy Spirit helps in messages & talks (Jesus) 2/4/04 Vol. 34
Holy Spirit helps to evangelize (Jesus) 4/5/02 Vol. 27
Holy Spirit in Baptism & Confirmation (Jesus) 4/19/04 Vol. 35
Holy Spirit infinite love by (Jesus) 1/8/98 Vol. 10
Holy Spirit invoke and preach (Jesus) 6/7/96 Vol. 3
Holy Spirit Jesus-birth, resurrection (Jesus) 5/21/07 Vol. 47
Holy Spirit leads souls to judgment (Jesus) 11/20/99 Vol. 17
Holy Spirit life (Mary) 6/5/95 Vol. 2
Holy Spirit love in dissent against war (Holy Spirit) 7/18/07 Vol. 48
Holy Spirit love of Father and Son (Holy Spirit) 6/4/06 Vol. 43
Holy Spirit power of peace & love (Jesus) 1/13/98 Vol. 10
Holy Spirit power to heal and convert (Jesus) 4/16/04 Vol. 35
Holy Spirit protect souls with love (Jesus) 3/12/98 Vol. 10

Holy Spirit protection at refuges (Jesus) 3/7/05 Vol. 38
Holy Spirit rains down graces,blessings (Holy Spirit) 7/23/07 Vol. 48
Holy Spirit source of power over demons (Jesus) 5/27/04 Vol. 35
Holy Spirit Spirit of life (Holy Spirit) 2/28/96 Vol. 3
Holy Spirit Spouse of Mary (Jesus) 5/15/97 Vol. 7
Holy Spirit spread Gospel of love (Jesus) 4/6/05 Vol. 39
Holy Spirit the sin against (Jesus) 5/26/02 Vol. 27
Holy Spirit transformed apostles (Jesus) 8/6/01 Vol. 24
Holy Spirit trust in spiritual power (Holy Spirit) 10/28/97 Vol. 9
Holy Spirit upholds remnant Church (Jesus) 9/18/96 Vol. 4
Holy Spirit will give what to say (Jesus) 7/18/03 Vol. 32
Holy Spirit will speak through us (Jesus) 8/9/03 Vol. 32
Holy Spirit will strengthen,speak for you (Jesus) 3/26/98 Vol. 10
Holy Spirit year dedicated to (Holy Spirit) 7/20/98 Vol. 12
Holy Spirit at refuge protection against demons (Jesus) 2/8/05 Vol. 38
Holy Spirit gifts evangelizes souls (Jesus) 4/27/06 Vol. 43
Holy Spirit, Confirmation seven gifts needed (Jesus) 12/3/04 Vol. 37
Holy Spirit, power of for evangelization (Jesus) 3/10/06 Vol. 42
Holy Spirit,sin against unforgiving spirit in soul (Jesus) 10/21/00 Vol. 21
Holy Spirit's call comforts our wounds,sorrows (Holy Spirit)9/24/01 Vol. 24
Holy Spirit's gifts need to be used or lost (Jesus) 5/30/04 Vol. 35
Holy Spirit's gifts seven gifts granted (Jesus) 3/12/04 Vol. 34
Holy Spirit's power wind in your sails (Jesus) 9/16/99 Vol. 16
Holy Stairs Jesus' steps to Pilate (Jesus) 3/28/98 Vol. 10
Holy Thursday keep traditional church visits (Jesus) 3/13/08 Vol. 50
Holy Thursday presence (Jesus) 4/13/95 Vol. 2
Holy Trinity unity of three persons (Jesus) 6/7/98 Vol. 11
Holy water power, take into hiding (Jesus) 7/22/97 Vol. 8
holy water sign of the cross (Jesus) 9/14/97 Vol. 8
Holy water weapon against demons (Jesus) 1/29/06 Vol. 42
holy water aquifer feeds tree (Jesus) 10/2/07 Vol. 49
holy water in cars spiritual protection (Jesus) 11/12/07 Vol. 49
Holy Week attend services (Jesus) 4/6/06 Vol. 43
Holy Week most important of year (Jesus) 3/22/05 Vol. 38
Holy Week Scripture fulfilled (Jesus) 4/2/04 Vol. 35
home in heaven vs. home on earth (Jesus) 6/30/02 Vol. 27
home Masses during persecution (Jesus) 11/9/99 Vol. 17
home Masses during schism (Jesus) 2/2/99 Vol. 14
home physical protection blessed medals, scapulars (Jesus) 11/30/06 Vol. 45
home protection medals,scapular,blessed salt (Jesus) 1/29/08 Vol. 50
home schooling a special grace (Jesus) 8/7/97 Vol. 8
home spiritual protection holy water, scapulars (Jesus) 11/30/06 Vol. 45
home, selling losing an old friend (Jesus) 9/24/02 Vol. 28
home, warm thank God for blessing (Jesus) 12/9/03 Vol. 33
Homeland defense increased power over privacy (Jesus) 11/23/02 Vol. 29
Homeland Security vehicle of one world people (Jesus) 4/14/05 Vol. 39
homeless help feed & clothe (Jesus) 6/2/07 Vol. 47

homeless help find shelter (Jesus)	10/15/03 Vol. 33
homeless help to survive (Jesus)	2/14/08 Vol. 50
homeless need prayer & help (Jesus)	12/11/03 Vol. 33
homeless need quick help for shelter (Jesus)	9/23/04 Vol. 36
homeless relatives, less fortunate (Jesus)	11/21/96 Vol. 5
homeless & hungry need help (Jesus)	3/1/07 Vol. 46
homeless need shelter help those needing a home (Jesus)	3/14/02 Vol. 26
homeless people need charity (Jesus)	11/29/07 Vol. 49
homeless,unemployed need food,water & not criticism (Jesus)	2/28/02 Vol. 26
homes food & religious articles (Jesus)	8/7/97 Vol. 8
homes have pictures, statues about (Jesus)	6/25/06 Vol. 43
homes have religious pictures (Jesus)	7/6/98 Vol. 12
homes have religious signs on walls (Jesus)	4/28/98 Vol. 11
homes live in safe areas (Jesus)	9/26/05 Vol. 40
homes destroyed by fiery chastisement (Jesus)	10/30/03 Vol. 33
homes destroyed punishment for sins (Jesus)	2/28/02 Vol. 26
homilies discern for errors (Jesus)	10/16/03 Vol. 33
homosexual birth control (Jesus)	11/19/95 Vol. 3
homosexual activity places of destruction (Jesus)	4/28/06 Vol. 43
homosexual acts mortal sin (Jesus)	12/1/99 Vol. 17
homosexual acts mortal sins, unnatural (Jesus)	10/22/00 Vol. 21
homosexual acts still mortal sins (Jesus)	3/15/04 Vol. 34
homosexual bishop in Episcopal Church (Jesus)	8/7/03 Vol. 32
homosexual marriages devil's perversion (Jesus)	7/31/03 Vol. 32
homosexual marriages living in sin (Jesus)	2/5/04 Vol. 34
homosexual marriages Pope against (Jesus)	3/4/04 Vol. 34
homosexual marriages speak out against (Jesus)	2/4/05 Vol. 38
homosexual marriages vote against (Jesus)	5/19/05 Vol. 39
homosexual sins speak out against (Jesus)	7/6/04 Vol. 36
homosexual unions abomination in God's sight (Jesus)	12/27/98 Vol. 13
homosexual unions abomination, calls God's wrath (Jesus)	7/15/04 Vol. 36
homosexual unions avoid this lifestyle (Jesus)	4/30/98 Vol. 11
homosexual,heterosexual sin destroying society (Jesus)	3/25/04 Vol. 34
homosexuality & living together (Jesus)	1/31/01 Vol. 22
homosexuality led to pedophilia (Jesus)	6/5/02 Vol. 27
homosexuality taught in seminaries (Jesus)	5/2/02 Vol. 27
homosexuality and sex is our downfall (Jesus)	3/26/98 Vol. 10
homosexuality flaunted brings God's blazing wrath (Jesus)	1/23/08 Vol. 50
homosexuals no right to marry (Jesus)	7/11/01 Vol. 24
honesty needed in all you do (Jesus)	12/25/00 Vol. 21
honoring Sunday reverence for day of rest (Jesus)	7/27/01 Vol. 24
hope Armageddon (Jesus)	7/2/95 Vol. 3
hope hearts joined,daylight (Mary)	3/5/97 Vol. 6
hope in adversity (Jesus)	10/25/96 Vol. 5
hope in life of the spirit (Jesus)	1/24/99 Vol. 14
hope persecution (Jesus)	8/10/95 Vol. 3
hope sinner (Jesus)	4/5/94 Vol. 1
hope witness (Jesus)	5/2/95 Vol. 2
hope & courage in trials (Jesus)	1/4/01 Vol. 22
hope & faith in Resurrection (Jesus)	2/19/04 Vol. 34
hope & trust in Jesus to solve all problems (Jesus)	5/27/00 Vol. 19
hope and trust evil will be destroyed (Jesus)	9/16/97 Vol. 8
hopeless upset and weary (Jesus)	6/1/96 Vol. 3
horoscopes & occult do not sell soul for (Jesus)	6/21/02 Vol. 27
horses of Revelation seals revealed (Jesus)	10/7/06 Vol. 45
hospice to bring souls to Jesus (Jesus)	7/16/06 Vol. 44
hospitality give and accept (Jesus)	7/9/02 Vol. 28
hospitality got God & neighbor (Jesus)	7/29/97 Vol. 8
hospitality loving & cheeful to all (Jesus)	2/21/00 Vol. 18
hospitality offer to serve others (Jesus)	6/13/05 Vol. 39
hospitality to neighbor,love for God (Jesus)	10/8/96 Vol. 5
hospitality to those who come (Jesus)	10/10/06 Vol. 45
hospitality for neighbors rewarded in heaven (Jesus)	4/9/01 Vol. 23
hospitality to travelers patience with facilities (Jesus)	7/18/04 Vol. 36
Host in bread gift of Real Presence in Eucharist (Jesus)	3/8/02 Vol. 26
Hosts reflection of love (Jesus)	7/23/98 Vol. 12
Hosts, consecrated protect from black masses (Jesus)	8/2/07 Vol. 48
hot & cold weather to cause wind, ice storms (Jesus)	3/12/08 Vol. 50
Hotel chapel Cross (Jesus)	2/11/95 Vol. 2
hound of heaven follow His Will (Jesus)	2/1/97 Vol. 6
hound of Heaven hunter (Jesus)	10/31/94 Vol. 2
Hound of Heaven Jesus seeks souls (Jesus)	12/29/05 Vol. 41
hour of evil earthquakes a sign (Jesus)	9/2/05 Vol. 40
house chores prayer (Jesus)	7/29/94 Vol. 2
House of Loreto imitate Holy Family (Jesus)	11/6/97 Vol. 9
House of Prayer refuge in Leander,Texas (Jesus)	8/18/06 Vol. 44
houses will be harder to afford (Jesus)	10/14/04 Vol. 37
housing for the poor (Jesus)	7/20/06 Vol. 44
housing more difficult (Jesus)	5/29/03 Vol. 31
housing needs demand after hurricanes (Jesus)	10/21/04 Vol. 37
huge crater white cross	8/2/93 Vol. 1
huge crevass earthquake	7/30/93 Vol. 1
human condition difficulties (Jesus)	7/28/95 Vol. 3
human garbage of dead babies (Jesus)	6/5/03 Vol. 31
human perfection purified in life,purgatory (Jesus)	3/7/01 Vol. 22
human race limit to destruction (Jesus)	8/2/01 Vol. 24
'human' unborn determined by science (Jesus)	1/18/07 Vol. 46
humanitarian aid to poor, help Jesus (Jesus)	3/21/03 Vol. 30
Humanity & Divinity God's love, Redeemer (Jesus)	12/31/02 Vol. 29
humanity of unborn not debatable (Jesus)	1/22/05 Vol. 38
humble faith (St. Charles)	11/4/93 Vol. 1
humble man's pride (Jesus)	10/19/06 Vol. 45
humble meek inherit the earth (Jesus)	11/25/96 Vol. 5
humble messages (Jesus)	6/27/95 Vol. 2

humble will be exalted (Jesus) 3/15/06 Vol. 42

humble life simple, full obedience (Jesus) 9/26/07 Vol. 48

humble servant in order to reach heaven (Jesus) 11/4/00 Vol. 21

humility as sinners (Jesus) 10/28/07 Vol. 49

humility boast in Lord only (Jesus) 10/31/05 Vol. 41

humility conform to Divine Will (Jesus) 9/23/97 Vol. 8

humility contemplation (Jesus) 10/4/94 Vol. 2

humility depend on Jesus (Jesus) 8/29/00 Vol. 20

humility do not belittle people (Jesus) 12/24/04 Vol. 37

humility do not let pride mislead you (Jesus) 8/29/04 Vol. 36

humility give God praise, not self (Jesus) 5/11/98 Vol. 11

humility imperfections keep us in (Jesus) 4/25/98 Vol. 11

humility in all accomplishments (Jesus) 1/10/04 Vol. 34

humility in being supervised (Jesus) 6/19/00 Vol. 19

humility in face of our sins (Jesus) 3/1/08 Vol. 50

humility meekness (St. Therese) 10/1/93 Vol. 1

humility needed before God (Jesus) 11/29/04 Vol. 37

humility needed in actions (Jesus) 2/7/06 Vol. 42

humility not easy for man (Jesus) 9/11/07 Vol. 48

humility path to heaven (Jesus) 9/11/97 Vol. 8

humility please God only (Jesus) 9/1/96 Vol. 4

humility replaces pride by wisdom (Jesus) 1/10/00 Vol. 18

humility serve & give witness (Jesus) 4/8/97 Vol. 7

humility submit to authority (Jesus) 6/10/02 Vol. 27

humility & service needed for high place in heaven (Jesus) 2/27/02 Vol. 26

hungry feed them in charity (Jesus) 6/1/07 Vol. 47

hungry of world crying out for help (Jesus) 10/18/03 Vol. 33

hungry of world hard to find food (Jesus) 12/11/03 Vol. 33

hurricane threatens America (Jesus) 9/5/07 Vol. 48

hurricane cities restoring infrastructures (Jesus) 9/29/05 Vol. 40

hurricane damage effect on economy (Jesus) 10/21/05 Vol. 41

hurricane damage more sin could bring storms (Jesus) 1/18/06 Vol. 42

hurricane foretold wrath of God for sins (Jesus) 9/13/05 Vol. 40

Hurricane Fran chastisement (Jesus) 9/4/96 Vol. 4

Hurricane Isabel people help each other (Jesus) 9/17/03 Vol. 32

Hurricane Isabel test faith, chastisement (Jesus) 9/16/03 Vol. 32

Hurricane Ivan testing rebuilding, insurance co. (Jesus) 9/15/04 Vol. 36

Hurricane Katrina sexual sins, gambling (Jesus) 8/30/05 Vol. 40

Hurricane Lilli prayer lessened storm (Jesus) 10/3/02 Vol. 29

hurricane records, 2005 devastation in New Orleans (Jesus) 11/30/05 Vol. 41

hurricane recovery slow as sin remains (Jesus) 1/12/06 Vol. 42

hurricane relief how to pay for? (Jesus) 9/23/05 Vol. 40

hurricane victims need on going help (Jesus) 10/6/05 Vol. 41

hurricane victims need prayer,money,food,water (Jesus) 9/17/04 Vol. 36

hurricane victims receive little relief (Jesus) 2/23/06 Vol. 42

Hurricane Wilma lowest pressure (Jesus) 10/19/05 Vol. 41

Hurricane Wilma postponed Fantasy Fest (Jesus) 10/27/05 Vol. 41

hurricanes brace for this summer (Jesus) 6/30/04 Vol. 35

hurricanes damage still needs repair (Jesus) 4/30/07 Vol. 47

hurricanes destruction in Southern states (Jesus) 9/7/04 Vol. 36

hurricanes disasters increasing (Jesus) 8/28/06 Vol. 44

hurricanes do not rebuild places of sin (Jesus) 10/27/05 Vol. 41

hurricanes find safety (Jesus) 6/7/07 Vol. 47

hurricanes influencing economy down (Jesus) 10/14/04 Vol. 37

hurricanes punishment for sin (Jesus) 8/31/06 Vol. 44

hurricanes record damage in dollars (Jesus) 9/21/05 Vol. 40

hurricanes set record number of storms (Jesus) 10/17/05 Vol. 41

hurricanes strain economy (Jesus) 10/5/05 Vol. 41

hurricanes & earthquakes to continue for sins (Jesus) 7/23/05 Vol. 40

hurricanes & storms taken to the next level (Jesus) 7/15/03 Vol. 32

hurricanes & tsunamis to cause damage from sea (Jesus) 5/15/07 Vol. 47

hurricanes & waves to cause some flooding (Jesus) 6/20/00 Vol. 19

hurricane's destruction gets your attention (Jesus) 9/15/99 Vol. 16

hurricanes in 2004 getting our attention (Jesus) 9/13/04 Vol. 36

hurricanes, fires testing people (Jesus) 2/16/06 Vol. 42

hurricanes, intense warming, weather machines (Jesus) 9/27/05 Vol. 40

hurricanes, parade of US to knees for its sins (Jesus) 9/2/04 Vol. 36

hurricanes, severe linked to warmer oceans (Jesus) 9/16/05 Vol. 40

hurricanes, severe will be increasing (Jesus) 3/23/06 Vol. 42

hurricanes, tornadoes wrath of God for sin (Jesus) 8/9/05 Vol. 40

hurts, let go stop grudges (Jesus) 1/27/05 Vol. 38

husband praying (Alice N.) 11/16/95 Vol. 3

Hussein pray for leaders (Jesus) 2/9/98 Vol. 10

Hussein weapons hidden in hills (Jesus) 2/12/98 Vol. 10

Hussein, Saddam needed for more wars (Jesus) 1/29/02 Vol. 26

hygiene, good to protect from diseases (Jesus) 12/6/03 Vol. 33

hypocrite Christ like (Jesus) 3/14/95 Vol. 2

hypocrites be clean in & out (Jesus) 10/11/05 Vol. 41

hypocrites do not make judgments (Jesus) 2/26/99 Vol. 14

hypocrites give good example (Jesus) 9/13/02 Vol. 28

hypocrites have spiritual house in order (Jesus) 6/25/01 Vol. 23

hypocrites not all say Lord, Lord (Jesus) 10/24/97 Vol. 9

hypocrites practice what preached (Jesus) 12/23/97 Vol. 9

hypocrites practice what you preach (Jesus) 6/21/04 Vol. 35

hypocrites should follow God's plan (Jesus) 7/25/99 Vol. 16

hypocrites will (Jesus) 4/3/96 Vol. 3

hypocritical behavior live in truth & not a lie (Jesus) 10/12/04 Vol. 37

I AM kingdom has no beginning or end (God the Father) 3/21/02 Vol. 26

I AM warning (Father) 11/5/93 Vol. 1

ice packs melting pollution effects (Jesus) 12/27/98 Vol. 13

ice storm enhanced by weather machines (Jesus) 4/10/03 Vol. 31

ice storm fulfilled prophecy (Jesus) 12/26/98 Vol. 13

ice storm in Canada (Jesus) 1/15/98 Vol. 10

ice storms becoming more common (Jesus) 1/28/07 Vol. 46

ice storms continue for sins (Jesus)   1/31/02 Vol. 26
ice storms frequent in warming trend (Jesus)   11/16/06 Vol. 45
ice storms more frequent than before (Jesus)   1/17/07 Vol. 46
ice storms on trees with leaves (Jesus)   10/19/07 Vol. 49
ice storms power outages in South (Jesus)   12/16/05 Vol. 41
ice storms in America from warm winter (Jesus)   1/15/07 Vol. 46
icon turned to gold at home (Mary)   7/31/97 Vol. 8
ID cards go into force (Jesus)   9/10/02 Vol. 28
identification Christian for death camps (Jesus)   10/22/96 Vol. 5
identify theft use chips & smart cards (Jesus)   12/1/03 Vol. 33
identity theft new crime threatens security (Jesus)   12/28/03 Vol. 33
identity theft to force chips in body (Jesus)   6/9/05 Vol. 39
identity theft with electronics (Jesus)   2/18/04 Vol. 34
idol worship abuse of pleasures & needs (Jesus)   3/9/02 Vol. 26
idol worship fame, money, success (Jesus)   2/12/08 Vol. 50
idol worship in place of God (Jesus)   2/27/05 Vol. 38
idol worship lukewarm far from God (Jesus)   2/9/06 Vol. 42
idol worship money, things, fame, success (Jesus)   9/28/04 Vol. 36
idol worship no worship of earth gods (Jesus)   7/1/99 Vol. 16
idol worship of material things (Jesus)   5/30/02 Vol. 27
idol worship riches, fame & sports (Jesus)   7/9/99 Vol. 16
idol worship still tests us (Jesus)   2/11/06 Vol. 42
idol worshipers avoid fortunetellers, occult (Jesus)   6/27/02 Vol. 27
idol worshipers broad road to hell (Jesus)   3/13/00 Vol. 18
idol worshipers punished on earth, in hell (Jesus)   7/30/07 Vol. 48
idols cannot give love (Jesus)   4/23/98 Vol. 11
idols electronics, sex & movies (Jesus)   7/7/04 Vol. 36
idols money,fame,sports (Jesus)   12/18/97 Vol. 9
idols obsession of money,sports,drugs (Jesus)   8/22/02 Vol. 28
idols of money & electronics (Jesus)   6/1/04 Vol. 35
idols of money and stocks (Jesus)   8/17/00 Vol. 20
idols possessions (Jesus)   9/10/94 Vol. 2
idols sports and finance (Jesus)   4/23/98 Vol. 11
idols sports,money,possessions (Jesus)   9/16/02 Vol. 28
idols TV and technology (Jesus)   3/21/96 Vol. 3
idols TV,sports,technology (Jesus)   7/9/96 Vol. 3
idols & earthly gods money,sports,computers (Jesus)   8/16/99 Vol. 16
idols before God possessions,entertainment (Jesus)   1/25/07 Vol. 46
idols destroyed to show power of God (Jesus)   5/3/04 Vol. 35
idols of the world need avoiding (Jesus)   5/25/04 Vol. 35
idols of worship money,sports,computers (Jesus)   3/30/00 Vol. 18
idols, control avoid mind control (Jesus)   11/3/06 Vol. 45
illegal immigrants National ID chips in licences (Jesus) 3/31/05 Vol. 38
image of beast on altars (Jesus)   8/23/03 Vol. 32
image of beast to be forced on altars (Jesus)   7/24/00 Vol. 20
image of beast worshiped on altars (Jesus)   9/22/00 Vol. 20
Image of God reflection of Creator (Jesus)   8/18/02 Vol. 28

image of God seen in every man (Jesus)   5/1/00 Vol. 19
image of God seen in poor (Jesus)   9/27/00 Vol. 20
image of Jesus focus on Him, one Body (Jesus)   10/5/96 Vol. 5
image of the beast adored by condemned (Jesus)   1/12/01 Vol. 22
image of the beast choice of good and evil (Jesus)   11/20/97 Vol. 9
image of the beast digital displays (Jesus)   5/28/03 Vol. 31
image of the beast in many public places (Jesus)   6/16/00 Vol. 19
image of the beast on church altars (Jesus)   4/18/99 Vol. 15
image of the beast on our altars (Jesus)   1/5/02 Vol. 26
image of the beast praised as a god (Jesus)   1/6/01 Vol. 22
image of the beast seeks worship of all (Jesus)   3/21/00 Vol. 18
image of the beast worship demanded (Jesus)   10/1/98 Vol. 13
image of the beast worshiped (Jesus)   2/6/99 Vol. 14
image of the beast worshiped on altars (Jesus)   12/15/98 Vol. 13
image of the beast worshipped on altars (Jesus)   9/8/03 Vol. 32
imitate Christ in love and service (Jesus)   1/21/01 Vol. 22
imitate Jesus,Mary by Christian example (Jesus)   9/18/99 Vol. 16
Imitation of Christ practical virtues (Jesus)   12/4/00 Vol. 21
Imitation of Jesus reflected in your actions (Jesus)   2/4/05 Vol. 38
Immaculate Conception (Mary)   12/8/95 Vol. 3
Immaculate Conception affirmed in Lourdes (Mary)   2/11/00 Vol. 18
Immaculate Conception consecration to Mary,Jesus (Mary) 12/8/06 Vol. 45
Immaculate Conception give praise and thanks (Mary)   12/8/97 Vol. 9
Immaculate Conception image of Church in America (Jesus) 12/6/01 Vol. 25
Immaculate Conception leads to Jesus (Mary)   12/8/96 Vol. 5
Immaculate Conception Mary is new Eve for world (Jesus) 12/8/04 Vol. 37
Immaculate Conception mission as Mother of God (Mary)   7/5/97 Vol. 8
Immaculate Conception model of Divine Mercy (Mary)   12/8/01 Vol. 25
Immaculate Conception overturn abortion (Mary)   12/8/00 Vol. 21
Immaculate Conception patroness of America (Jesus)   9/11/03 Vol. 32
Immaculate Conception plan of the Father (Jesus)   12/8/03 Vol. 33
Immaculate Conception sinless life (Mary)   12/8/99 Vol. 17
Immaculate Conception special, national feast (Mary)   2/11/99 Vol. 14
Immaculate Heart give 'yes' to God's Will (Jesus)   6/19/04 Vol. 35
Immaculate Heart Mary's love for Jesus (Mary)   6/15/96 Vol. 3
Immaculate Heart prayer intentions (Our Lady)   6/16/07 Vol. 47
Immaculate Heart rejoice in love (Jesus)   6/23/06 Vol. 43
Immaculate Heart share in love (Mary)   6/12/99 Vol. 15
Immaculate Heart two hearts as one (Jesus)   6/4/05 Vol. 39
Immaculate Heart Mary do not mock (Mary)   6/20/98 Vol. 11
Immaculate Heart Mary no original sin (Jesus)   6/23/01 Vol. 23
Immaculate Heart of Mary united with Jesus (Jesus)   6/8/02 Vol. 27
immigrants, illegal seeking jobs (Jesus)   3/28/06 Vol. 42
Immigration problem greedy employers (Jesus)   9/4/06 Vol. 44
immoral society divorce,fornication,homosexuals (Jesus) 11/28/05 Vol. 41
immoral society stand up against sins (Jesus)   3/12/08 Vol. 50
immorality abortion/evils in society (Jesus)   6/9/96 Vol. 3

immorality birth control (Jesus) 4/22/95 Vol. 2
immorality darkness of sin (Jesus) 7/20/05 Vol. 40
immorality downfall of America (Jesus) 3/12/05 Vol. 38
immorality in society speak out against (Jesus) 4/7/05 Vol. 39
immortal souls drowning in sins, cares (Jesus) 11/28/98 Vol. 13
immortality found in soul in next life (Jesus) 6/16/05 Vol. 39
impatience dealing with (Jesus) 3/17/03 Vol. 30
impatience lesson on imperfections (St. Therese) 6/2/97 Vol. 7
imperfection of man from original sin (Jesus) 4/19/07 Vol. 47
imperfections in life (Jesus) 12/23/01 Vol. 25
imperfections healed through sacraments (Jesus) 12/19/98 Vol. 13
imperfections,weakness be good examples (Jesus) 4/24/98 Vol. 11
imprisonment be willing to die for God (Jesus) 11/6/97 Vol. 9
improvements needed determined by faults (Jesus) 12/31/01 Vol. 25
inauguration gallows or change of laws (Jesus) 11/27/00 Vol. 21
Incarnation Blessed Trinity present (Jesus) 7/18/05 Vol. 40
Incarnation Conception (Holy Spirit) 1/1/94 Vol. 1
Incarnation depth of His love (Jesus) 1/4/99 Vol. 14
Incarnation free will (Jesus) 12/24/93 Vol. 1
Incarnation hearts as one (Mary) 3/25/98 Vol. 10
Incarnation Jesus had our pains (Jesus) 12/24/98 Vol. 13
Incarnation Jesus to serve, not be served (Jesus) 12/15/01 Vol. 25
Incarnation light (Jesus) 1/8/94 Vol. 1
Incarnation mystery in man & Divine (Jesus) 6/29/00 Vol. 19
Incarnation of Jesus as a man (Jesus) 12/21/06 Vol. 45
Incarnation purpose for saving man (Jesus) 4/23/07 Vol. 47
Incarnation shared in the Eucharist (Jesus) 12/23/01 Vol. 25
Incarnation St. John the Baptist (Jesus) 6/24/94 Vol. 1
Incarnation worm of a man (Jesus) 5/2/97 Vol. 7
Incarnation worm of a man,empathy (Jesus) 12/11/97 Vol. 9
Incarnation as a man love of Jesus for mankind (Jesus) 12/20/07 Vol. 49
Incarnation as man joy in heaven on Christmas (Jesus) 12/24/99 Vol. 17
Incarnation mystery Jesus,Mary models of life (Jesus) 12/24/04 Vol. 37
Incarnation of Jesus foreshadowed by Mary (Jesus) 12/8/04 Vol. 37
Incarnation of Jesus hard for man to accept (Jesus) 7/21/00 Vol. 20
Incarnation of Jesus human & spiritual natures (Jesus) 1/9/07 Vol. 46
Incarnation of Jesus means of salvation (Mary) 12/17/98 Vol. 13
Incarnation of Jesus necessary to die for man's sins (Jesus) 10/11/04 Vol. 37
Incarnation of Jesus people refused to believe (Jesus) 8/30/04 Vol. 36
Incarnation of Jesus sign of salvation (Jesus) 11/28/03 Vol. 33
income needs cause of recession fears (Jesus) 3/24/04 Vol. 34
incorruptible body reward of faith, holiness (Jesus) 8/16/07 Vol. 48
India earthquake thousands killed (Jesus) 2/1/01 Vol. 22
Indian Ocean earthquake plates still unstable (Jesus) 3/29/05 Vol. 38
Indian tidal waves death & disease (Jesus) 12/28/04 Vol. 37
Indians claims for land (Jesus) 6/8/05 Vol. 39
Indians discerning spirits (Jesus) 3/8/96 Vol. 3

Indians love and protection (Mary) 5/31/97 Vol. 7
indifference offends Jesus (Jesus) 2/8/99 Vol. 14
indifferent souls Jesus loathes the most (Jesus) 1/31/02 Vol. 26
individual judgment Book of Life (Jesus) 1/6/96 Vol. 3
individual responsibility for life's actions (Jesus) 5/20/05 Vol. 39
industrial-military inventions for military (Jesus) 4/19/00 Vol. 19
industries job failures (Jesus) 10/3/97 Vol. 9
industry not respecting workers (Jesus) 6/20/02 Vol. 27
Infancy of Jesus novenas, petitions (Jesus) 12/25/05 Vol. 41
Infancy of Jesus worshiped by some (Jesus) 1/7/07 Vol. 46
Infant Jesus equally available as adult (Jesus) 12/4/03 Vol. 33
infant Jesus important to love (Jesus) 12/5/02 Vol. 29
Infant Jesus praise of angels (Jesus) 1/1/06 Vol. 42
Infant Jesus salvation (St. Theresa) 1/5/94 Vol. 1
Infant Jesus statue novena before Christmas (Jesus) 6/7/07 Vol. 47
Infant King scepter at birth (Jesus) 12/25/07 Vol. 49
Infant King special devotion (Jesus) 1/10/04 Vol. 34
Infant of Prague as infant king (Jesus) 4/27/98 Vol. 11
Infant of Prague Eucharist (Jesus) 12/25/93 Vol. 1
Infant of Prague sinners (Jesus) 8/20/93 Vol. 1
infant shots possible mercury poisoning (Jesus) 12/18/03 Vol. 33
infants preciousness of life (Mary) 9/11/97 Vol. 8
infants killed Antichrist (Jesus) 1/11/95 Vol. 2
infidelity in marriage avoid sins of (Jesus) 11/17/06 Vol. 45
infinite love heart (Jesus) 10/9/95 Vol. 3
infinite love knowledge (Jesus) 4/29/95 Vol. 2
infinite love shared with Trinity (Jesus) 6/15/03 Vol. 31
infinite love,mercy,peace all sinners can be forgiven (Jesus) 10/4/98 Vol. 13
infinite mercy God's desire to save all souls (Jesus) 2/25/02 Vol. 26
informal prayer tell God how we love Him (Jesus) 9/11/04 Vol. 36
informal, quiet prayer deeper love for God (Jesus) 5/10/07 Vol. 47
infrastructure attacked RR,fuel,nuclear plants (Jesus) 10/24/02 Vol. 29
inheritance do not fight over possessions (Jesus) 7/22/04 Vol. 36
inheritance of heaven restored in Resurrection (Jesus) 12/17/99 Vol. 17
injustices blinded by one worlders (Jesus) 3/29/99 Vol. 14
injustices suffer for Jesus' sake (Jesus) 3/25/99 Vol. 14
injustices & hurts how to react to (Jesus) 3/9/99 Vol. 14
innocent victims help with alms (Jesus) 2/26/98 Vol. 10
insects do not manipulate (Jesus) 4/25/02 Vol. 27
insects protect environment (Jesus) 4/11/02 Vol. 27
insects,grasshoppers attacking food supply (Jesus) 4/29/99 Vol. 15
inside appearance can be beautiful as outside (Jesus) 2/23/00 Vol. 18
insurance companies high risk in Gulf (Jesus) 9/21/05 Vol. 40
insurgent warfare uses road, suicide bombs (Jesus) 9/3/07 Vol. 48
intelligent design politically correct on Creator (Jesus) 11/10/05 Vol. 41
intentions God looks into hearts (Jesus) 9/28/97 Vol. 8
intentions Jesus knows all (Jesus) 11/29/00 Vol. 21

intentions Jesus sees the heart (Jesus)	11/15/00 Vol. 21
intentions seen by God (Jesus)	12/30/97 Vol. 9
intentions in heart for sins committed (Jesus)	6/6/07 Vol. 47
intentions in heart harbors good or evil (Jesus)	7/25/02 Vol. 28
intentions in heart how we will be judged (Jesus)	8/21/04 Vol. 36
intentions in heart read by Jesus (Jesus)	8/24/02 Vol. 28
intentions of heart determine our actions (Jesus)	2/8/06 Vol. 42
intentions of heart determine our destiny (Jesus)	2/6/00 Vol. 18
intentions of heart Jesus considers most (Mary)	5/31/99 Vol. 15
intentions of heart most important (St. Therese)	10/1/05 Vol. 41
intentions of heart seen by Jesus (Jesus)	9/1/02 Vol. 28
intentions of heart to correct faults (Jesus)	1/25/01 Vol. 22
intentions of the heart God reads all actions by (Jesus)	10/29/03 Vol. 33
intentions,real cannot fool Jesus (Jesus)	4/7/01 Vol. 23
intercede spiritual gifts (St. Anthony)	6/13/95 Vol. 2
intercessors saints will help (St. Therese)	9/29/07 Vol. 48
intercessors, use for prayers to Jesus (Jesus)	11/5/06 Vol. 45
intercessory prayer for innocent souls (Jesus)	5/8/06 Vol. 43
interim refuge protection on way to refuge (Jesus)	2/25/08 Vol. 50
interim refuges and caves (Jesus)	7/7/01 Vol. 24
interim refuges little sleeping space (Jesus)	3/6/08 Vol. 50
interim refuges people hiding in attics (Jesus)	6/19/07 Vol. 47
International companies elimination of middle class (Jesus)	7/21/07 Vol. 48
international companies exporting jobs (Jesus)	11/11/03 Vol. 33
international companies jobs exported overseas (Jesus)	11/13/03 Vol. 33
Internet Antichrist (Jesus)	5/15/96 Vol. 3
Internet control of people (Jesus)	3/30/97 Vol. 6
Internet mark of the beast (Jesus)	8/1/95 Vol. 3
Internet virtural reality (Jesus)	2/5/96 Vol. 3
internet web of control (Jesus)	10/16/01 Vol. 25
internet, kids on be watchful of predators (Jesus)	7/21/07 Vol. 48
intervention rejection (Jesus)	5/2/95 Vol. 2
inventions for killing weapons of war threaten life (Jesus)	9/13/98 Vol. 12
inventory purified (Jesus)	11/7/94 Vol. 2
inventory of sins needed for Confession (Jesus)	8/28/99 Vol. 16
invisible shield from the angels (Jesus)	10/17/07 Vol. 49
invisible to captors pray to avoid capture (Jesus)	8/10/07 Vol. 48
invisible to refuges angel protection from evil (Jesus)	7/31/07 Vol. 48
invitation to faith call to lost souls (Jesus)	11/9/99 Vol. 17
Iran challenging right to A bomb (Jesus)	9/7/06 Vol. 44
Iran making nuclear weapons (Jesus)	1/17/06 Vol. 42
Iran new source of nuclear terror (Jesus)	1/12/06 Vol. 42
Iran posturing for attack (Jesus)	2/1/07 Vol. 46
Iran threat of new war (Jesus)	10/18/07 Vol. 49
Iran threat of new war (Jesus)	2/3/07 Vol. 46
Iran & Iraq do not escalate (Jesus)	2/12/07 Vol. 46
Iran & North Korea nuclear threats (Jesus)	2/4/06 Vol. 42
Iran government stockpiling, spreading arms (Jesus)	5/10/07 Vol. 47
Iran nuclear weapons possible world confrontation (Jesus)	6/20/06 Vol. 43
Iran sanctions UN proposals (Jesus)	8/31/06 Vol. 44
Iran threat for nuclear arms (Jesus)	2/2/06 Vol. 42
Iran War possible conflict (Jesus)	5/4/06 Vol. 43
Iran war pray to prevent (Jesus)	3/27/07 Vol. 46
Iran War threatened by one world people (Jesus)	5/14/07 Vol. 47
Iranian sanctions possible war (Jesus)	8/23/06 Vol. 44
Iraq air threat,doubt helpful (Jesus)	11/12/98 Vol. 13
Iraq America needs to leave (Jesus)	11/28/06 Vol. 45
Iraq control of oil (Jesus)	5/22/03 Vol. 31
Iraq cost of restoring (Jesus)	4/28/03 Vol. 31
Iraq costing lives and money (Jesus)	10/23/03 Vol. 33
Iraq do not go to war (Jesus)	9/10/02 Vol. 28
Iraq do not start a war (Jesus)	9/5/02 Vol. 28
Iraq exit strategy needed (Jesus)	11/6/03 Vol. 33
Iraq exit strategy needed (Jesus)	12/16/03 Vol. 33
Iraq means to New World Order (Jesus)	11/30/98 Vol. 13
Iraq miscalculated war (Jesus)	1/30/98 Vol. 10
Iraq more dictators still possible (Jesus)	12/15/03 Vol. 33
Iraq no peace among car bombs (Jesus)	11/13/03 Vol. 33
Iraq oil interests (Jesus)	10/3/02 Vol. 29
Iraq one world order and oil (Jesus)	1/28/98 Vol. 10
Iraq potential for wider war (Jesus)	12/17/98 Vol. 13
Iraq pray for healing,rebuilding (Jesus)	4/10/03 Vol. 31
Iraq pray for peace (Jesus)	10/24/02 Vol. 29
Iraq pray to end crisis (Jesus)	9/12/02 Vol. 28
Iraq pray to stop war (Jesus)	2/8/07 Vol. 46
Iraq prayer to limit killing (Jesus)	11/22/02 Vol. 29
Iraq reasons for war (Jesus)	9/20/02 Vol. 28
Iraq target of US war on terrorism (Jesus)	2/18/02 Vol. 26
Iraq threatens more conflict (Jesus)	12/28/98 Vol. 13
Iraq took liberties with weakness (Jesus)	1/25/98 Vol. 10
Iraq war later than sooner (Jesus)	4/3/02 Vol. 27
Iraq weapons shipped from friends (Jesus)	12/11/02 Vol. 29
Iraq & Israel potential war near oil (Jesus)	8/30/01 Vol. 24
Iraq & Israel pray for peace (Jesus)	9/6/02 Vol. 28
Iraq & Kosovo challenging America (Jesus)	1/22/99 Vol. 14
Iraq bombers not stopped by surge (Jesus)	4/19/07 Vol. 47
Iraq double standard vs. Iran & No. Korea (Jesus)	2/18/06 Vol. 42
Iraq exit strategy needed to stop deficits (Jesus)	10/14/04 Vol. 37
Iraq explosives unguarded question (Jesus)	10/28/04 Vol. 37
Iraq insurrection problems in leaving (Jesus)	5/21/04 Vol. 35
Iraq military threat miscalculation,cause of war (Jesus)	8/6/98 Vol. 12
Iraq occupation causing hatred from Arabs (Jesus)	5/11/04 Vol. 35
Iraq oil threatened by insurgents (Jesus)	12/22/05 Vol. 41
Iraq oil lines vulnerable to terrorists (Jesus)	11/6/03 Vol. 33

Iraq War admit it is a mistake (Jesus) — 1/31/08 Vol. 50

Iraq War America-where is benefit? (Jesus) — 8/16/02 Vol. 28

Iraq war Arabs unite to help (Jesus) — 3/20/03 Vol. 30

Iraq war begin serious consequences (Jesus) — 11/4/02 Vol. 29

Iraq war billions spent on wars (Jesus) — 11/11/02 Vol. 29

Iraq war cost in dollars & lives (Jesus) — 8/8/02 Vol. 28

Iraq war could have many deaths (Jesus) — 3/27/03 Vol. 30

Iraq War death & destruction (Jesus) — 2/2/03 Vol. 30

Iraq War destroying economy,military (Jesus) — 3/18/08 Vol. 50

Iraq War destroying military,economy (Jesus) — 11/6/07 Vol. 49

Iraq war dissent (Jesus) — 9/26/02 Vol. 28

Iraq war double standard for WMD (Jesus) — 3/8/04 Vol. 34

Iraq War expenditures too high (Jesus) — 2/9/06 Vol. 42

Iraq war extent of destruction unsure (Jesus) — 11/29/02 Vol. 29

Iraq war financial burden (Jesus) — 3/5/03 Vol. 30

Iraq War gain for the rich (Jesus) — 10/11/07 Vol. 49

Iraq war high cost, little gain (Jesus) — 1/25/07 Vol. 46

Iraq War how long to fight? (Jesus) — 5/30/06 Vol. 43

Iraq War if not enough prayer (Jesus) — 2/6/03 Vol. 30

Iraq war leaving now a problem (Jesus) — 3/23/05 Vol. 38

Iraq war make problems worse (Jesus) — 2/17/98 Vol. 10

Iraq war many deaths (Jesus) — 3/18/03 Vol. 30

Iraq war many deaths if expanded (Jesus) — 3/14/03 Vol. 30

Iraq war many deaths, count cost (Jesus) — 9/25/02 Vol. 28

Iraq War mistake to start (Jesus) — 9/15/07 Vol. 48

Iraq War need exit strategy (Jesus) — 5/20/05 Vol. 39

Iraq War needs God's peace (Holy Spirit) — 7/18/07 Vol. 48

Iraq War needs to be stopped (Jesus) — 10/23/07 Vol. 49

Iraq war no support (Jesus) — 9/25/02 Vol. 28

Iraq war nuclear weapons threatened (Jesus) — 12/18/02 Vol. 29

Iraq War oil for one worlders (Jesus) — 1/2/03 Vol. 30

Iraq war one world people (Jesus) — 3/27/03 Vol. 30

Iraq War one world people profit from (Jesus) — 7/30/07 Vol. 48

Iraq War one worlders vs. people (Jesus) — 6/14/07 Vol. 47

Iraq war our troops stretched thin (Jesus) — 2/6/98 Vol. 10

Iraq War paralyzed like snowstorm (Jesus) — 2/16/03 Vol. 30

Iraq War place of hate, killing (Jesus) — 11/16/06 Vol. 45

Iraq war plan to destroy US (Jesus) — 1/24/03 Vol. 30

Iraq War pray for an end (Jesus) — 6/2/07 Vol. 47

Iraq war pray for dead (Jesus) — 3/23/03 Vol. 30

Iraq war pray MDW are not used (Jesus) — 11/14/02 Vol. 29

Iraq war prayer needed most (Jesus) — 3/21/03 Vol. 30

Iraq war preparations being made (Jesus) — 9/30/02 Vol. 28

Iraq War preparations made (Jesus) — 2/20/03 Vol. 30

Iraq war quagmire of trouble (Jesus) — 2/15/98 Vol. 10

Iraq war question of cost,casualties (Jesus) — 8/19/02 Vol. 28

Iraq war resistance is gaining (Jesus) — 1/25/07 Vol. 46

Iraq war risk for soldiers & civilians (Jesus) — 12/28/02 Vol. 29

Iraq War ruining US economy (Jesus) — 5/5/04 Vol. 35

Iraq war spread terrorism (Jesus) — 2/24/03 Vol. 30

Iraq war surprises on both sides (Jesus) — 3/19/03 Vol. 30

Iraq war troop increase unpopular (Jesus) — 1/11/07 Vol. 46

Iraq war US desperate for victory (Jesus) — 3/31/03 Vol. 30

Iraq War victory not defined (Jesus) — 6/21/07 Vol. 47

Iraq war wearing down troops (Jesus) — 6/12/04 Vol. 35

Iraq War withdrawal questioned (Jesus) — 6/22/06 Vol. 43

Iraq war would like to hit Israel (Jesus) — 3/17/03 Vol. 30

Iraq War cost decided by voters (Jesus) — 5/2/06 Vol. 43

Iraq war deaths determined by weapons used (Jesus) — 11/15/02 Vol. 29

Iraq War, stop Congress refuses funds (Jesus) — 11/15/07 Vol. 49

Iraq weapons causing war tensions (Jesus) — 11/24/98 Vol. 13

Iraq withdrawal stop losses (Jesus) — 5/30/06 Vol. 43

Iraq, leaving problem to leave or stay (Jesus) — 5/12/04 Vol. 35

Iraqi caves harder to find weapons (Jesus) — 11/15/02 Vol. 29

Iraqi leader will be a militant on exit (Jesus) — 1/1/05 Vol. 38

Iraqi occupation causing more killings (Jesus) — 3/29/04 Vol. 34

Iraqi people to decide own government (Jesus) — 12/4/03 Vol. 33

Iraqi side of war do not force democracy (Jesus) — 4/25/07 Vol. 47

Iraqi war biological weapons (Jesus) — 10/16/02 Vol. 29

Iraqi War cannot force by guns (Jesus) — 4/15/04 Vol. 35

Iraqi war consequencesq (Jesus) — 10/29/02 Vol. 29

Iraqi War costs were not counted (Jesus) — 9/5/04 Vol. 36

Iraqi war could lead to WWIII (Jesus) — 10/30/02 Vol. 29

Iraqi war democracy difficult (Jesus) — 1/1/05 Vol. 38

Iraqi war difficult exit strategy (Jesus) — 8/19/04 Vol. 36

Iraqi War for oil interests (Jesus) — 4/8/03 Vol. 31

Iraqi war is a losing battle (Jesus) — 10/1/05 Vol. 41

Iraqi war killing is not the answer (Jesus) — 10/16/02 Vol. 29

Iraqi war no victory (Jesus) — 2/4/07 Vol. 46

Iraqi War not enough troops (Jesus) — 7/31/03 Vol. 32

Iraqi War nothing won (Jesus) — 7/10/03 Vol. 32

Iraqi War oil control sought (Jesus) — 1/29/03 Vol. 30

Iraqi war one world people forcing (Jesus) — 10/10/02 Vol. 29

Iraqi War Pope John Paul II against (Jesus) — 3/3/07 Vol. 46

Iraqi war pray for peace (Jesus) — 10/7/02 Vol. 29

Iraqi War pray to stop (Jesus) — 11/17/05 Vol. 41

Iraqi War prayers answered (Jesus) — 4/10/03 Vol. 31

Iraqi War still many questions (Jesus) — 4/10/03 Vol. 31

Iraqi War time to leave overdue (Jesus) — 10/27/05 Vol. 41

Iraqi War timetable for withdrawal (Jesus) — 3/16/07 Vol. 46

Iraqi War troops vs. insurgents (Jesus) — 3/16/07 Vol. 46

Ireland churches closed (Mary) — 7/2/96 Vol. 3

Ireland personal visit (St. Patrick) — 6/12/96 Vol. 3

Ireland reach out in love (Jesus) — 7/1/99 Vol. 16

Ireland shared faith experience (Jesus) — 3/15/98 Vol. 10

Isaiah's prophecies about Era of Peace (Jesus) — 12/10/98 Vol. 13

Islam has a desire to control world (Jesus) — 3/11/02 Vol. 26

Islam militant against Christians (Jesus) — 5/10/01 Vol. 23

Islam wants world domination (Jesus) — 4/4/02 Vol. 27

Islam war with West (Jesus) — 12/18/01 Vol. 25

Islamic states more faithful to prayer (Jesus) — 3/20/03 Vol. 30

Islamic states sympathetic to terrorists (Jesus) — 12/13/01 Vol. 25

Islamic terrorists goal to destroy US (Jesus) — 8/25/04 Vol. 36

Israel Arabs, gas, wars (Jesus) — 4/23/96 Vol. 3

Israel conflict for land (Jesus) — 10/19/06 Vol. 45

Israel conquered when fallen away (Jesus) — 2/7/04 Vol. 34

Israel how to respond (Jesus) — 10/30/02 Vol. 29

Israel Jews vs. Palestinians (Jesus) — 12/29/03 Vol. 33

Israel stop the war on both sides (Jesus) — 10/30/01 Vol. 25

Israel & Palestinians hostilities (Jesus) — 8/13/01 Vol. 24

Israel conflict no compromise,no love (Jesus) — 3/29/01 Vol. 22

Israel fighting peace not in hearts (Jesus) — 9/6/01 Vol. 24

Israel link to Iraq could cause wider war (Jesus) — 8/19/02 Vol. 28

Israel vs Moslems possible war in Middle East (Jesus) — 10/7/00 Vol. 21

Israel vs. America destruction & takeover (Jesus) — 9/22/05 Vol. 40

Israelites lost & found God (Jesus) — 6/14/06 Vol. 43

Israelites lost homes for sins (Jesus) — 6/30/98 Vol. 11

Israelites condemned 40 yrs for doubting God's power (Jesus) — 8/3/05 Vol. 40

Italian plane crash wake up call into building (Jesus) — 4/18/02 Vol. 27

Italy, Vatican attacks on churches (Jesus) — 11/21/02 Vol. 29

Jack Hall funeral message (Jesus) — 10/18/06 Vol. 45

Jack Shea's House rosary (Mary) — 9/8/95 Vol. 3

Jacob's ladder saints, angels up & down (Jesus) — 7/9/07 Vol. 48

jail for standing up to the world (Jesus) — 6/22/02 Vol. 27

jail ministry help prisoners have faith (Jesus) — 2/14/08 Vol. 50

Jakus,Irena gratitude for pictures (Jesus) — 7/23/98 Vol. 12

Jane's Mass gold wedding garment (Jane) — 10/11/00 Vol. 21

Japan emperors (Jesus) — 5/10/95 Vol. 2

Japan warning smart cards monitoring (Jesus) — 1/3/96 Vol. 3

Japanese earthquakes 8.0 scale sign of end times (Jesus) — 10/30/03 Vol. 33

Jarice Hogan cannot deprive rest from dead (Jesus) — 11/5/00 Vol. 21

Jarice Hogan love God & neighbor (Jarice Hogan) — 9/2/00 Vol. 20

jaws of death always be prepared (Jesus) — 10/14/97 Vol. 9

Jean Dayton's funeral her mission in life (Jesus) — 6/30/04 Vol. 35

Jeremiah persecuted & protected (Jesus) — 7/31/04 Vol. 36

Jerusalem control of land (Jesus) — 4/9/97 Vol. 7

Jerusalem finding in temple, mission (Jesus) — 12/29/03 Vol. 33

Jerusalem golden gate (Jesus) — 12/5/99 Vol. 17

Jerusalem unsettled peace (Jesus) — 3/9/06 Vol. 42

Jerusalem destroyed as America to be punished (Jesus) — 7/27/01 Vol. 24

Jerusalem destroyed as America will be (Jesus) — 12/7/03 Vol. 33

Jerusalem sites contested by various faiths (Jesus) — 8/10/00 Vol. 20

Jesus always with us (Jesus) — 1/15/96 Vol. 3

Jesus as guest of honor (Jesus) — 1/15/02 Vol. 26

Jesus ask before doing anything (Jesus) — 3/11/05 Vol. 38

Jesus ask daily help (Jesus) — 6/16/02 Vol. 27

Jesus authority over universe (Jesus) — 1/11/99 Vol. 14

Jesus calls us to love Him (Jesus) — 7/10/02 Vol. 28

Jesus center of our lives (Jesus) — 8/4/05 Vol. 40

Jesus center of our lives (Jesus) — 12/9/07 Vol. 49

Jesus center of universe (Jesus) — 6/15/07 Vol. 47

Jesus conductor of events (Jesus) — 2/8/99 Vol. 14

Jesus cornerstone of Church (Jesus) — 5/21/07 Vol. 47

Jesus events of His youth (Jesus) — 12/31/00 Vol. 21

Jesus first priority in life (Jesus) — 11/22/04 Vol. 37

Jesus is first priority (Jesus) — 5/5/06 Vol. 43

Jesus is King, Master, Savior (Jesus) — 8/14/03 Vol. 32

Jesus is the oars in our lives (Jesus) — 7/21/05 Vol. 40

Jesus Light of the world (Jesus) — 12/25/01 Vol. 25

Jesus mercy vs. justice (Jesus) — 9/27/03 Vol. 32

Jesus needs to be part of our life (Jesus) — 12/27/07 Vol. 49

Jesus oasis of living water (Jesus) — 1/8/04 Vol. 34

Jesus only means of salvation (Jesus) — 5/18/05 Vol. 39

Jesus our beacon of light (Jesus) — 5/25/99 Vol. 15

Jesus permits evil to go so far (Jesus) — 6/25/02 Vol. 27

Jesus spiritual authority (Jesus) — 11/26/06 Vol. 45

Jesus spiritual garbage man (Jesus) — 2/20/06 Vol. 42

Jesus tested by Satan 3 times (Jesus) — 7/10/03 Vol. 32

Jesus the Light of the world (Jesus) — 11/16/00 Vol. 21

Jesus use for praise, not in vain (Jesus) — 1/3/08 Vol. 50

Jesus victory over evil (Jesus) — 2/7/04 Vol. 34

Jesus will defeat evil (Jesus) — 4/29/05 Vol. 39

Jesus & Mary models of perfection (Jesus) — 7/25/04 Vol. 36

Jesus & Mary new Adam & Eve (Jesus) — 2/8/07 Vol. 46

Jesus & people parallel of gifts to children (Jesus) — 12/30/02 Vol. 29

Jesus & saints models of holiness (Jesus) — 9/7/06 Vol. 44

Jesus' appearance proof of Divinity (Jesus) — 4/27/06 Vol. 43

Jesus' appearance real flesh and blood (Jesus) — 4/22/06 Vol. 43

Jesus' appearances flesh and blood proof (Jesus) — 12/27/06 Vol. 45

Jesus as cornerstone rejected (Jesus) — 4/6/05 Vol. 39

Jesus as God St. Peter,Isaiah scroll,at well (Jesus) — 3/4/02 Vol. 26

Jesus as groom Church as bride (Jesus) — 4/11/07 Vol. 47

Jesus as judge choose life (Jesus) — 3/2/95 Vol. 2

Jesus as King not accepted as Messiah (Jesus) — 1/23/06 Vol. 42

Jesus as king power in creation,death,etc. (Jesus) — 6/3/00 Vol. 19

Jesus as man amazed angels (Jesus) — 12/24/98 Vol. 13

Jesus as servant washed apostles' feet (Jesus) — 4/13/06 Vol. 43

Jesus carried off leadership needed in faith (Jesus) — 3/21/00 Vol. 18

Jesus comes to bring order & love (Jesus) — 12/21/00 Vol. 21

Jesus coming in my lifetime (Jesus) — 8/12/07 Vol. 48

Jesus coming to chain evil ones in hell (Jesus) — 3/29/04 Vol. 34

Jesus cornerstone strength in faith (Jesus) — 2/5/00 Vol. 18

Jesus' death all sinners to blame (Jesus) — 2/26/04 Vol. 34

Jesus' death arranged in prophecy (Jesus) — 2/16/04 Vol. 34

Jesus' death for all peoples (Jesus) — 9/27/99 Vol. 16

Jesus' death price of our sins (Jesus) — 3/21/08 Vol. 50

Jesus denied to avoid changes in lives (Jesus) — 12/14/98 Vol. 13

Jesus' face on tree to pray for crimes (Jesus) — 10/27/05 Vol. 41

Jesus forgets forgiven sins (Jesus) — 6/25/07 Vol. 47

Jesus' glorified Body hope for our resurrection (Jesus) — 4/6/99 Vol. 15

Jesus' healing whole person,body & soul (Jesus) — 3/14/08 Vol. 50

Jesus' help better than man's ideas (Jesus) — 6/15/00 Vol. 19

Jesus' help earthly burdens,temptations (Jesus) — 8/31/01 Vol. 24

Jesus' help necessary to save souls (Jesus) — 4/24/99 Vol. 15

Jesus' help needed throughout life (Jesus) — 3/20/00 Vol. 18

Jesus' image grows large to help everyone (Jesus) — 12/26/02 Vol. 29

Jesus in every thought at start of each project (Jesus) — 5/23/00 Vol. 19

Jesus in life greatest gift (Jesus) — 9/10/06 Vol. 44

Jesus in poor needs our help always (Jesus) — 9/22/04 Vol. 36

Jesus increases we decrease (Jesus) — 1/12/08 Vol. 50

Jesus invites you let Jesus into your heart (Jesus) — 12/20/98 Vol. 13

Jesus is bridge from earth to heaven (Jesus) — 11/23/07 Vol. 49

Jesus knocks on doors to sinners (Jesus) — 11/21/06 Vol. 45

Jesus like snowplow for calls of help (Jesus) — 2/19/00 Vol. 18

Jesus' love for man & God the Father (Jesus) — 5/23/04 Vol. 35

Jesus' love shown in death for all (Jesus) — 12/14/04 Vol. 37

Jesus' mission fulfilled Isaiah prophecies (Jesus) — 2/9/07 Vol. 46

Jesus' Name invoke to avoid Satan's influence (Jesus) — 5/17/04 Vol. 35

Jesus' Name kneel and genuflect (Jesus) — 5/5/99 Vol. 15

Jesus' Name protection against Satan (Jesus) — 5/4/06 Vol. 43

Jesus' Name the demons flee (Jesus) — 2/4/08 Vol. 50

Jesus' pain share in own lives (Jesus) — 3/17/07 Vol. 46

Jesus' Presence real presence in Host (Jesus) — 7/12/97 Vol. 8

Jesus ransomed sinners opened gates of heaven (Jesus) — 2/9/01 Vol. 22

Jesus' Real Presence a mystery in Host (Jesus) — 4/7/06 Vol. 43

Jesus rejected by Jews & today's people (Jesus) — 10/2/05 Vol. 41

Jesus saves in storms of life (Jesus) — 4/22/04 Vol. 35

Jesus seeks us as hound of heaven (Jesus) — 2/21/04 Vol. 34

Jesus' Star is Light of the world (Jesus) — 2/3/08 Vol. 50

Jesus' suffering for our sins (Jesus) — 1/22/01 Vol. 22

Jesus' teachings all need to follow (Jesus) — 4/28/07 Vol. 47

Jesus the healer of both soul & body (Jesus) — 1/12/07 Vol. 46

Jesus' victory past, present, & future (Jesus) — 9/21/98 Vol. 12

Jesus' victory wolf without teeth (Jesus) — 3/26/08 Vol. 50

Jesus vs Antichrist trust in God vs. riches (Jesus) — 5/6/00 Vol. 19

Jesus vs pit of hell choice for eternity (Jesus) — 8/31/02 Vol. 28

Jesus vs. Antichrist worship only Jesus (Jesus) — 6/1/00 Vol. 19

Jesus vs. money choice of masters (Jesus) — 5/3/06 Vol. 43

Jesus waits for us despite sins, He loves us (Jesus) — 2/23/01 Vol. 22

Jesus' ways of love hard to love enemies (Jesus) — 9/19/07 Vol. 48

Jesus' Word mission to all to spread (Jesus) — 9/26/06 Vol. 44

Jesus, cornerstone of His Church (Jesus) — 11/22/99 Vol. 17

Jesus, first priest sacrifice of the Mass (Jesus) — 10/30/98 Vol. 13

Jesus, forgiveness only way to eternal life (Jesus) — 10/30/98 Vol. 13

Jesus, king over the universe (Jesus) — 11/26/06 Vol. 45

Jesus, Light in darkness of sin (Jesus) — 6/18/07 Vol. 47

Jesus, ruler over Satan & demons (Jesus) — 7/10/07 Vol. 48

Jesus, search for in Blessed Sacrament,hearts (Jesus) — 12/15/02 Vol. 29

Jesus, Son of God believe it (God the Father) — 4/6/07 Vol. 47

Jesus, Son of God proclaimed by St. Peter (Jesus) — 8/21/05 Vol. 40

Jesus, spiritual guide on path to heaven (Jesus) — 3/28/08 Vol. 50

Jesus, trust in for life's decisions (Jesus) — 2/3/08 Vol. 50

Jesus, who is Messiah by St. Peter (Jesus) — 8/25/02 Vol. 28

Jesus,focus on even during tribulation (Jesus) — 2/24/00 Vol. 18

Jesus,gateway only way to heaven (Jesus) — 6/29/00 Vol. 19

Jesus,life preserver from physical, spiritual death (Jesus) — 11/26/07 Vol. 49

Jesus,no abandonment refuges by sign of angels (Jesus) — 12/22/99 Vol. 17

jet streams manipulated (Jesus) — 8/7/03 Vol. 32

jet streams unusual cause of snow storms (Jesus) — 12/29/06 Vol. 45

jewels of God tears of joy & sorrow (Jesus) — 12/5/02 Vol. 29

Jewish critics of Passion (Jesus) — 2/26/04 Vol. 34

Jewish leaders tried to hide Resurrection (Jesus) — 4/10/07 Vol. 47

Jewish lives lost in another war (Jesus) — 7/1/99 Vol. 16

Jews & Palestinians killing begets more killing (Jesus) — 1/24/02 Vol. 26

Job test of faith (Jesus) — 9/30/96 Vol. 4

Job tested by My blessings (Jesus) — 7/28/98 Vol. 12

job loss gain for the rich (Jesus) — 1/13/05 Vol. 38

job losses affect taxes (Jesus) — 9/4/03 Vol. 32

job markets hard for middle class and poor (Jesus) — 8/7/04 Vol. 36

jobless support Sorrowful Mother (Mary) — 12/2/97 Vol. 9

jobs are disappearing for greed (Jesus) — 7/16/98 Vol. 12

jobs declining standard of living (Jesus) — 10/31/02 Vol. 29

jobs do not seek riches (Jesus) — 1/14/99 Vol. 14

jobs endangered by competition (Jesus) — 8/28/03 Vol. 32

jobs feel like prisoners (Jesus) — 1/7/98 Vol. 10

jobs gone abroad (Jesus) — 9/22/03 Vol. 32

jobs gone overseas (Jesus) — 5/23/02 Vol. 27

jobs good paying, hard to find (Jesus) — 12/11/03 Vol. 33

jobs in jeopardy from layoffs (Jesus) — 9/5/05 Vol. 40

jobs labor exploited (Jesus) — 10/30/97 Vol. 9

jobs lower standard of living (Jesus) — 1/12/02 Vol. 26

jobs lower standard of living (Jesus) — 10/23/97 Vol. 9

jobs lower standard of living (Jesus)	2/12/98 Vol. 10
jobs more service & technology (Jesus)	6/20/02 Vol. 27
jobs persecutions, less pay (Jesus)	10/17/97 Vol. 9
jobs smart cards & chips (Jesus)	1/2/01 Vol. 22
jobs threatened by greed (Jesus)	6/25/98 Vol. 11
jobs too much pressure (Jesus)	12/12/97 Vol. 9
jobs & cost of living trust in God (Jesus)	1/28/04 Vol. 34
jobs & economy with lower standard of living (Jesus)	7/21/05 Vol. 40
jobs & freedoms not abused by rich (Jesus)	12/2/04 Vol. 37
jobs & manufacturing exported & lost (Jesus)	2/20/04 Vol. 34
jobs & manufacturing exported out of US (Jesus)	11/8/07 Vol. 49
jobs & manufacturing going to foreign countries (Jesus)	4/18/02 Vol. 27
jobs & manufacturing threatened to foreign countries (Jesus)	2/24/04 Vol. 34
jobs & unemployment effect on economy (Jesus)	7/3/03 Vol. 32
jobs & unemployment free trade causes (Jesus)	1/22/04 Vol. 34
jobs / anarchy Antichrist (Jesus)	8/9/95 Vol. 3
jobs by mark of beast book of life (Jesus)	10/13/95 Vol. 3
jobs exported free trade abused (Jesus)	6/14/03 Vol. 31
jobs exported unfair trade practices (Jesus)	2/15/07 Vol. 46
jobs exported will be downfall of U.S. (Jesus)	12/17/04 Vol. 37
jobs in America lost by trade agreements (Jesus)	2/15/07 Vol. 46
jobs lost lower standard of living (Jesus)	12/11/97 Vol. 9
jobs lost to manufacturing overseas (Jesus)	4/27/01 Vol. 23
jobs lost overseas by companies greedy for profits (Jesus)	9/6/04 Vol. 36
jobs lost,deaths challenges in life (Jesus)	2/18/05 Vol. 38
Job's reward faithful,reward in heaven (Jesus)	4/5/00 Vol. 19
jobs slow growth blamed on corporate greed (Jesus)	3/26/04 Vol. 34
Job's testing in loss of possessions (Jesus)	4/5/00 Vol. 19
jobs, manufacturing lost to overseas (Jesus)	1/13/05 Vol. 38
jobs, manufacturing lost to slave labor (Jesus)	2/5/04 Vol. 34
Jocelyn read St. Bernadette's life (St. Bernadette)	2/2/08 Vol. 50
Jocelyn, granddaughter Confirmation message (Jesus)	1/15/08 Vol. 50
Joe Murray's funeral seek reward in heaven (Jesus)	2/17/99 Vol. 14
Joe Norman parents (Jesus)	10/4/95 Vol. 3
Joe Trunfio witness of faith (Jesus)	2/24/98 Vol. 10
John Lydia's son (Jesus)	8/11/06 Vol. 44
John Hogan funeral cup of suffering (Jesus)	1/30/07 Vol. 46
John Miller funeral Mass (John Miller)	12/17/05 Vol. 41
John Paul II Antichrist (Jesus)	5/30/94 Vol. 1
John Paul II leader, inspiration to youth (Jesus)	11/9/02 Vol. 29
John Paul II missionaries (Jesus)	10/11/95 Vol. 3
John Paul II pope (Mary)	2/22/95 Vol. 2
John Paul II rising	8/13/93 Vol. 1
John Paul II shooting	8/14/93 Vol. 1
John Paul II tortured (Jesus)	7/27/94 Vol. 2
Jonah a reluctant prophet (Jesus)	10/3/05 Vol. 41
Jonah asked people to repent (Jesus)	7/18/01 Vol. 24
Jonah called but frustrated (Jesus)	10/8/03 Vol. 33
Jonah host (Jesus)	7/12/94 Vol. 2
Jonah lead people like (Jesus)	4/22/98 Vol. 11
Jonah messengers preach as (Jesus)	9/29/97 Vol. 8
Jonah only sign given (Jesus)	7/6/01 Vol. 24
Jonah symbolic 40 days now (Jesus)	7/22/98 Vol. 12
Jonah warning of purification (Jesus)	11/18/96 Vol. 5
Jonah, sign of call to repent (Jesus)	2/13/08 Vol. 50
Joseph predicted the famine (Jesus)	7/8/99 Vol. 16
Joseph sold for 30 pieces of silver (Jesus)	3/21/03 Vol. 30
Joseph & Jesus bold sold for money (Jesus)	3/12/04 Vol. 34
Joseph famine will repeat today (Jesus)	7/9/97 Vol. 8
joy bloom in heart (Jesus)	3/27/03 Vol. 30
joy slavery to sin ended (Jesus)	9/26/97 Vol. 8
joy of God vs. joy of earth (Jesus)	7/10/06 Vol. 44
joy vs despair in trials of life (Jesus)	10/26/00 Vol. 21
joy, love of God signs of saint (Jesus)	2/21/06 Vol. 42
Joyce Wagner Eternal Father seal (Jesus)	3/27/08 Vol. 50
joyfulness rejoice in victory (Jesus)	5/21/98 Vol. 11
Jubilee 2000 yrs of testing (Jesus)	12/28/99 Vol. 17
Jubilee 2000 pope criticizes killing (Jesus)	1/28/99 Vol. 14
Jubilee celebration after 2000 yrs from birth (Jesus)	12/24/99 Vol. 17
Jubilee indulgence take advantage of (Jesus)	1/4/01 Vol. 22
Jubilee indulgence take advantage of graces (Jesus)	8/10/00 Vol. 20
Jubilee year commemorates Christianity (Jesus)	1/1/00 Vol. 18
Jubilee Year uncomfortable to live truth (Jesus)	5/7/00 Vol. 19
Judas' betrayal means for salvation (Jesus)	4/12/06 Vol. 43
judged living (Jesus)	11/26/93 Vol. 1
judged on managing money, time, love (Jesus)	9/19/04 Vol. 36
judgement account for every minute (Jesus)	3/17/05 Vol. 38
judgements good intentions,humble (Jesus)	1/17/97 Vol. 6
judges taking God out of public (Jesus)	12/30/05 Vol. 41
judges, lawyers ruling America (Jesus)	9/15/05 Vol. 40
judging and criticizing (Jesus)	1/16/01 Vol. 22
judging God alone can judge (Jesus)	6/21/04 Vol. 35
judging God is only judge (Jesus)	6/21/05 Vol. 39
judging leave only to God (Jesus)	7/19/03 Vol. 32
judging leave to God (Jesus)	7/17/99 Vol. 16
judging left only to God (Jesus)	8/14/03 Vol. 32
judging only for God (Jesus)	9/30/03 Vol. 32
judging only God can do right (Jesus)	4/3/97 Vol. 7
judging owner of the vineyard (Jesus)	8/20/97 Vol. 8
judging spiritually & physically (Jesus)	1/4/98 Vol. 10
judging & vengeance belong to God only (Jesus)	3/14/02 Vol. 26
judging events need time, big picture (Jesus)	11/18/02 Vol. 29
judging goes to God adultress forgiven (Jesus)	4/10/00 Vol. 19
judging others only by Jesus (Jesus)	6/21/99 Vol. 15

St. Anthony, Finder of Lost Objects

In March of 1995 our daughter, Jeanette, woke up and realized that her wedding rings were missing. Since she never takes them off, she retraced her steps of the previous day to try and find them, but to no avail. Now she remembers that there was someone to pray to for lost things, but she thought it was St. Joseph. The next morning at Mass she prayed a second time to St. Joseph and she said that she would give him another chance to find the rings. After returning home, her husband, Brad, went for a walk. On the way back home, he heard a man's voice speak to him and it said: "Go to the mailbox." Brad looked and saw nothing in the mailbox. He started up the driveway and the voice said: "Go back and look again." This time he sees the rings under the mailbox on top of the snowbank ready to melt into the sewer. Jeanette said that she took her gloves off to get the mail and her cold fingers made them loose enough for the rings to fall off. Now Jeanette was home visiting us on June 13, 1995, the feast day of St. Anthony. John had a vision of St. Anthony and then Jeanette. St. Anthony said that people have asked him to find things, and even some who do not remember who he is.

Message: June 13, 1995 (volume 2)

judgment abortion (Jesus)	11/14/93 Vol. 1	judgment convert today (Jesus)	8/9/96 Vol. 4
judgment abortions in the USA (Jesus)	12/18/95 Vol. 3	judgment determine pass to heaven (Jesus)	6/27/99 Vol. 15
judgment account for every hour of life (Jesus)	4/16/04 Vol. 35	judgment did we love God & neighbor (Jesus)	12/19/01 Vol. 25
judgment accountable to help others (Jesus)	6/23/06 Vol. 43	judgment do good deeds for day of (Jesus)	2/14/08 Vol. 50
judgment accounting for time,wealth (Jesus)	10/22/00 Vol. 21	judgment earthly vs. heavenly things (Jesus)	3/26/99 Vol. 14
judgment accounting of life (Jesus)	1/10/99 Vol. 14	judgment forgiveness of sins (Jesus)	1/3/04 Vol. 34
judgment all are equal at the (Jesus)	5/17/98 Vol. 11	judgment forgiveness,prodigal son (Jesus)	11/12/96 Vol. 5
judgment always be ready (Jesus)	6/6/05 Vol. 39	judgment free will to choose (Jesus)	11/14/01 Vol. 25
judgment answer for our deeds (Jesus)	4/3/98 Vol. 11	judgment God of love, no worry (Jesus)	11/4/99 Vol. 17
judgment based on love, souls saved (Jesus)	5/27/07 Vol. 47	judgment graces (Jesus)	4/17/95 Vol. 2
judgment be always ready (Jesus)	7/4/03 Vol. 32	judgment harvest of souls (Jesus)	3/18/96 Vol. 3
judgment be at heavenly banquet (Jesus)	1/18/04 Vol. 34	judgment have good deeds in hands (Jesus)	7/12/04 Vol. 36
judgment be prepared (Jesus)	5/20/98 Vol. 11	judgment have souls prepared (Jesus)	5/11/02 Vol. 27
judgment be prepared for (Jesus)	7/16/05 Vol. 40	judgment heaven,hell,purgatory (Jesus)	3/11/99 Vol. 14
judgment beatific vision (Jesus)	12/10/93 Vol. 1	judgment heavenly treasures valuable (Jesus)	10/26/05 Vol. 41
judgment belongs to God (Jesus)	5/7/06 Vol. 43	judgment huge price for killers (Jesus)	2/6/98 Vol. 10
judgment Blessed Mother intercedes (Jesus)	7/20/06 Vol. 44	judgment hungry,sick,dying (Jesus)	3/16/06 Vol. 42
judgment Cabrini Shrine (Father)	6/30/94 Vol. 1	judgment injustices & killings (Jesus)	6/23/97 Vol. 7
judgment choice of heaven or hell (Jesus)	11/1/01 Vol. 25	judgment life (Jesus)	11/24/93 Vol. 1
judgment confession,be prepared (Jesus)	9/12/97 Vol. 8	judgment life preparation in purity (Jesus)	11/3/03 Vol. 33
judgment convert before death (Jesus)	3/31/99 Vol. 14	judgment love (Father)	11/7/93 Vol. 1

judgment love God & neighbor (Jesus)   5/8/01 Vol. 23

judgment mortal sin (Jesus)   1/3/94 Vol. 1

judgment need wedding garment (Jesus)   4/4/99 Vol. 15

judgment new earth (Jesus)   9/18/94 Vol. 2

judgment of souls & nations (Jesus)   11/17/04 Vol. 37

judgment on love of God,neighbor (Jesus)   6/22/99 Vol. 15

judgment particular and final (Jesus)   7/22/04 Vol. 36

judgment peace (Jesus)   4/19/94 Vol. 1

judgment perfect   10/30/93 Vol. 1

judgment prayers and deeds (Jesus)   5/23/95 Vol. 2

judgment prepare and evangelize (Jesus)   2/28/96 Vol. 3

judgment prepare quickly (Jesus)   6/5/04 Vol. 35

judgment prepare soul in confession (Jesus)   12/5/96 Vol. 5

judgment prepare with good deeds (Jesus)   8/26/04 Vol. 36

judgment pure souls to heaven (Jesus)   5/19/07 Vol. 47

judgment Purgatory (Jesus)   9/6/94 Vol. 2

judgment remnant (Mary)   11/19/93 Vol. 1

judgment repent and prepare (Jesus)   9/26/96 Vol. 4

judgment requires prepared souls (Jesus)   11/16/03 Vol. 33

judgment saved and condemned (Jesus)   5/22/96 Vol. 3

judgment separate sheep & goats (Jesus)   2/24/07 Vol. 46

judgment separate sheep from goats (Jesus)   6/19/98 Vol. 11

judgment separate wheat and tares (Jesus)   8/23/98 Vol. 12

judgment sin   10/13/93 Vol. 1

judgment souls live on for eternity (Jesus)   4/1/98 Vol. 11

judgment spiritual preparation (Jesus)   8/21/97 Vol. 8

judgment stand alone before God (Jesus)   5/20/05 Vol. 39

judgment stand in His Light (Jesus)   1/15/98 Vol. 10

judgment state of your soul (Jesus)   10/16/97 Vol. 9

judgment table not set yet (Jesus)   6/7/05 Vol. 39

judgment testing (Jesus)   1/30/94 Vol. 1

judgment use of talents (Jesus)   9/2/96 Vol. 4

judgment wheat & tares separated (Jesus)   1/18/02 Vol. 26

judgment wheat & tares separated (Jesus)   2/13/03 Vol. 30

judgment with mercy (Jesus)   3/1/07 Vol. 46

judgment witnesses (Jesus)   3/20/95 Vol. 2

judgment & heaven change outlook on earthly things (Jesus) 9/5/05 Vol. 40

judgment by Jesus separation of good & evil (Jesus)   7/26/01 Vol. 24

judgment day be prepared for (Jesus)   10/23/04 Vol. 37

judgment day be prepared with pure soul (Jesus)   11/18/07 Vol. 49

judgment day have souls pure, ready (Jesus)   11/15/07 Vol. 49

judgment day love of God & neighbor (Jesus)   5/3/97 Vol. 7

judgment day reunited with body (Jesus)   2/18/98 Vol. 10

Judgment Day unrepentant sinners need fear (Jesus)   11/23/04 Vol. 37

judgment decision Jesus or the world (Jesus)   12/22/06 Vol. 45

judgment destinations heaven,purgartory,hell (Jesus)   4/25/06 Vol. 43

judgment helps good deeds,charities,prayers (Jesus)   8/11/07 Vol. 48

judgment of Jesus repent & prepare for this day (Jesus)   11/26/04 Vol. 37

judgment of others only for God (Jesus)   3/1/08 Vol. 50

judgment of souls accounting for actions (Jesus)   11/9/06 Vol. 45

judgment of souls bad to hell,good share God (Jesus)   6/17/00 Vol. 19

judgment preparation do not assume tomorrow (Jesus)   1/18/07 Vol. 46

judgment preparation love God & neighbor (Jesus)   9/24/05 Vol. 40

judgment preparation no excuses,keep close to God (Jesus) 10/12/04 Vol. 37

judgment question how you loved others (Jesus)   12/10/05 Vol. 41

judgment seen level of hell,purgatory (Jesus)   5/31/05 Vol. 39

judgment time have friend in Jesus (Jesus)   10/10/00 Vol. 21

judgment time hell or heaven (Jesus)   11/27/98 Vol. 13

judgment, at life is passed before you (Jesus)   7/22/04 Vol. 36

judgment,mini direction soul is headed (Jesus)   10/28/00 Vol. 21

judgments are left for only God (Jesus)   9/3/04 Vol. 36

judgments God only to judge (Jesus)   12/23/97 Vol. 9

judgments leave to God only (Jesus)   1/11/01 Vol. 22

judgments love every one (Jesus)   9/17/00 Vol. 20

judgments only God judges (Jesus)   1/26/98 Vol. 10

judgments original sin, pride (Jesus)   10/8/97 Vol. 9

judgments without the facts (Jesus)   8/18/99 Vol. 16

judgments, refuse Jesus only true judge (Jesus)   6/25/07 Vol. 47

just wages should raise minimum wage (Jesus)   11/9/06 Vol. 45

justice about to fall (God the Father)   6/7/01 Vol. 23

justice based on love (Jesus)   3/1/03 Vol. 30

justice done in next life (Jesus)   10/7/99 Vol. 17

justice end evil age (Jesus)   2/17/97 Vol. 6

justice evil removed from earth (Jesus)   9/5/97 Vol. 8

justice God's vs man's judgments (Jesus)   9/5/96 Vol. 4

justice heavenly treasures (Jesus)   2/27/97 Vol. 6

justice man's vs. God's (Jesus)   9/3/05 Vol. 40

justice of love over killing (Jesus)   7/3/99 Vol. 16

justice on those selfish souls (Jesus)   1/1/99 Vol. 14

justice prayer groups   10/5/93 Vol. 1

justice reparation (Jesus)   6/12/94 Vol. 1

justice spiritual, in heaven or hell (Jesus)   10/19/06 Vol. 45

justice & mercy unquestioned (Jesus)   7/12/05 Vol. 40

justice for killing murder (Jesus)   10/4/95 Vol. 3

justice not found justice at second coming (Jesus)   1/20/00 Vol. 18

justice of God overflowing,America destroyed (Jesus)   12/30/03 Vol. 33

justice of God overwhelmed by too much sin (Jesus)   2/21/05 Vol. 38

justice only on Jesus' return (Jesus)   2/28/06 Vol. 42

justice or mercy choice of man's free will (Jesus)   12/31/04 Vol. 37

justice system collapse with injustices (Jesus)   3/7/98 Vol. 10

justice system corrupt in its practices (Jesus)   1/21/99 Vol. 14

justice system corrupted by money (Jesus)   3/19/98 Vol. 10

justice system not just (Jesus)   5/7/98 Vol. 11

justice system not true justice (Jesus)   2/26/98 Vol. 10

justice warped abortion,atheism,devil worship (Jesus) 3/9/01 Vol. 22

justice, cup of overflowing due to many sins (Jesus) 8/25/01 Vol. 24

justice, mercy of God accountable for actions (Jesus) 5/26/06 Vol. 43

justice, moment of separate evil from righteous (Jesus) 11/14/98 Vol. 13

justice,mercy of God at the judgment (Jesus) 11/26/06 Vol. 45

Justin David birth message (grandson) (Jesus) 2/4/02 Vol. 26

Kateri Tekakwitha cared for the sick (Jesus) 7/14/04 Vol. 36

Kateri Tekakwitha faith in healing power of Jesus (Kateri)5/16/04 Vol. 35

Kateri Tekakwitha intercessor for prayer (Jesus) 3/24/07 Vol. 46

Kateri Tekakwitha interview preparation (Kateri T.) 3/1/95 Vol. 2

Kateri Tekakwitha persecuted for her faith (Jesus) 7/14/07 Vol. 48

Kateri Tekakwitha,Bl example & inspirational (Jesus) 7/14/05 Vol. 40

Katrina financial effects worse (Jesus) 9/15/05 Vol. 40

Katrina infrastructures big trouble (Jesus) 9/15/05 Vol. 40

Katrina who pays for damage (Jesus) 9/15/05 Vol. 40

Katrina looters held up relief (Jesus) 9/8/05 Vol. 40

Katrina water contamination of environment (Jesus) 9/7/05 Vol. 40

Keenan, Michael funeral (Jesus) 3/15/03 Vol. 30

kerocene lamps needed as wise virgins (Jesus) 9/3/99 Vol. 16

keys to Heaven priests offer forgiveness (Jesus) 4/26/97 Vol. 7

keystone blueprint (Jesus) 3/21/95 Vol. 2

killers of people have heavy reparation (Jesus) 12/27/07 Vol. 49

killing abhorrent to Jesus (Jesus) 12/7/01 Vol. 25

killing abortions, war, homicides (Jesus) 10/10/96 Vol. 5

killing against God's plan for lives (Jesus) 2/22/04 Vol. 34

killing arrogance of power (Jesus) 2/6/98 Vol. 10

killing cannot be condoned (Jesus) 8/22/02 Vol. 28

killing denies God's purpose for life (Jesus) 4/22/07 Vol. 47

killing Divine Will (Jesus) 1/14/96 Vol. 3

killing do not glorify the act of (Jesus) 5/27/99 Vol. 15

killing harvest of evil (Jesus) 5/23/02 Vol. 27

killing in wars & abortions (Jesus) 1/3/04 Vol. 34

killing is blood money (Jesus) 3/15/07 Vol. 46

killing Lord of life and death (Jesus) 8/27/96 Vol. 4

killing manage anger and hate (Jesus) 8/26/04 Vol. 36

killing offends God the most (Jesus) 7/22/99 Vol. 16

killing repent of (Jesus) 4/4/02 Vol. 27

killing serious sin offends God (Jesus) 6/12/97 Vol. 7

killing the worst sin (Jesus) 5/18/99 Vol. 15

killing throughout history (Jesus) 1/31/01 Vol. 22

killing tool of devil to destroy man (Jesus) 8/10/06 Vol. 44

killing trap of Satan (Jesus) 7/22/02 Vol. 28

killing violates commandments (Jesus) 1/28/99 Vol. 14

killing will not solve problems (Jesus) 1/29/02 Vol. 26

killing & destruction not answer for peace (Mary) 3/25/99 Vol. 14

killing & sexual sins speak out against (Jesus) 3/15/04 Vol. 34

killing & stealing one world people (Jesus) 4/4/07 Vol. 47

killing & suicide against God's plan (Jesus) 5/30/07 Vol. 47

killing & wars all life is precious (Jesus) 6/20/02 Vol. 27

killing children indifference to abortion,disasters (Jesus) 3/14/02 Vol. 26

killing children not a choice,mortal sin (Jesus) 7/24/00 Vol. 20

killing for food sign to go to refuges (Jesus) 12/17/03 Vol. 33

killing from Satan love and life from God (Jesus) 9/13/98 Vol. 12

killing in abortion death warrant for all (Jesus) 3/30/00 Vol. 18

killing in wars unnecessary fo US (Jesus) 1/29/05 Vol. 38

killing lives is not an option (Jesus) 2/3/06 Vol. 42

killing machines to control people (Jesus) 6/15/06 Vol. 43

killing of babies by mothers of abortions (Jesus) 11/7/01 Vol. 25

killing of civilians by militant terrorists (Jesus) 11/7/01 Vol. 25

killing of man stirred up by Satan (Jesus) 9/21/01 Vol. 24

killing, a mortal sin brings death to the soul (Jesus) 12/2/98 Vol. 13

killing, abortions mortal sin, needs Confession (Jesus) 10/19/04 Vol. 37

killing, worst sin against love of God (Jesus) 2/1/00 Vol. 18

killing,senseless against law of God (Jesus) 9/21/01 Vol. 24

killings abortion,wars,euthanasia (Jesus) 10/9/05 Vol. 41

killings all serious sins (Jesus) 5/10/03 Vol. 31

killings defilement of God's plans (Jesus) 12/28/06 Vol. 45

killings justice will come (Jesus) 12/20/96 Vol. 5

killings mother of five children (Jesus) 6/27/01 Vol. 23

killings turn to Jesus for help (Jesus) 10/16/97 Vol. 9

killings, abortions, wars calling down God's justice (Jesus) 11/15/04 Vol. 37

kindness requested playing cards,driving cars (Jesus) 2/24/01 Vol. 22

king Antichrist (Jesus) 1/4/95 Vol. 2

king single camel (Mary) 12/18/94 Vol. 2

King & Creator humble servant of God (Jesus) 11/12/04 Vol. 37

King of all Nations created us out of love (Jesus) 7/31/02 Vol. 28

King of All Nations demons acknowledge power (Jesus) 1/10/04 Vol. 34

King of All Nations King of Creation (Jesus) 1/6/03 Vol. 30

King of All Nations Lord over earth (Jesus) 4/4/02 Vol. 27

King of All Nations power of resurrection (Jesus) 4/27/01 Vol. 23

King of All Nations Redeemer (Jesus) 10/29/07 Vol. 49

King of All Nations Shrine at Marcy, N.Y. (Jesus) 4/30/06 Vol. 43

King of the Universe 2nd coming preparation (Jesus) 11/23/97 Vol. 9

King of the Universe deserves all praise (Jesus) 4/17/96 Vol. 3

King of the Universe give glory and praise (Jesus) 1/4/98 Vol. 10

King of the Universe he guides everything (Jesus) 3/12/98 Vol. 10

King of the Universe honor & respect (Jesus) 7/6/97 Vol. 8

King of the Universe kingship,final judgment (Jesus) 11/24/96 Vol. 5

King of the Universe lift bondage of our sins (Jesus) 12/24/96 Vol. 5

King of the Universe love/dog (Jesus) 12/21/93 Vol. 1

King of the Universe personal (St. Therese) 9/27/95 Vol. 3

King of the Universe praise and glory (Jesus) 1/5/97 Vol. 6

King of the Universe test of life (Jesus) 4/23/95 Vol. 2

King of the Universe triumph (Jesus) 7/8/95 Vol. 3

King of the Universe triumph (Jesus) — 2/6/97 Vol. 6
King of Universe glorified bodies (Jesus) — 11/26/95 Vol. 3
King of Universe willed all creation (Jesus) — 4/4/98 Vol. 11
King of Universe worthy of praise (Jesus) — 3/29/98 Vol. 10
kingdom Adam's fall (Jesus) — 12/3/93 Vol. 1
kingdom devil tempts (Jesus) — 11/25/95 Vol. 3
kingdom king of the universe (Jesus) — 11/19/94 Vol. 2
Kingdom signs (Father) — 7/25/95 Vol. 3
kingdom of God awaits repentant sinners (Jesus) — 9/16/99 Vol. 16
Kingdom of God brought to earth (Jesus) — 4/16/07 Vol. 47
kingdom of God by accepting Jesus in heart (Jesus) — 11/22/98 Vol. 13
Kingdom of God images in Gospels (Jesus) — 10/30/07 Vol. 49
Kingdom of God in His Presence (Jesus) — 5/9/01 Vol. 23
Kingdom of God in Real Presence of Host (Jesus) — 11/25/07 Vol. 49
Kingdom of God is at hand (Jesus) — 7/7/04 Vol. 36
Kingdom of God is upon you (Jesus) — 11/21/04 Vol. 37
Kingdom of God needs to be proclaimed (Jesus) — 9/26/07 Vol. 48
Kingdom of God present in Jesus (Jesus) — 12/16/04 Vol. 37
Kingdom of God present in Jesus (Jesus) — 1/13/05 Vol. 38
Kingdom of God seek first (Jesus) — 6/11/07 Vol. 47
Kingdom of God seek first (Jesus) — 12/10/00 Vol. 21
Kingdom of God worth more than money (Jesus) — 5/14/07 Vol. 47
kingdom of heaven goal of the soul (Jesus) — 5/23/04 Vol. 35
Kingdom of heaven is at hand (Jesus) — 7/8/04 Vol. 36
Kingdom of heaven pearl of great price (Jesus) — 7/27/05 Vol. 40
Kingdom of Heaven pearl of great value (Jesus) — 2/20/08 Vol. 50
Kingdom of heaven seek first, all will be provided (Jesus) — 10/24/06 Vol. 45
Kingdom, spiritual not earthly king (Jesus) — 12/22/04 Vol. 37
kingdoms crumbling lack of God causes ruin (Jesus) — 11/25/97 Vol. 9
kingship every knee must bend (Jesus) — 11/22/97 Vol. 9
kingship free will (Jesus) — 10/30/94 Vol. 2
Kingship Infant of Prague (Jesus) — 1/6/03 Vol. 30
kingship Jesus came to suffer (Jesus) — 12/20/01 Vol. 25
kingship reverence (Jesus) — 10/29/95 Vol. 3
Kingship acknowledged praying at Adoration of Jesus (Jesus) — 9/9/04 Vol. 36
kingship mocked Real Presence lip service (Jesus) — 9/16/99 Vol. 16
Kingship of Jesus honor, glory, & praise (Jesus) — 9/27/07 Vol. 48
Kingship of Jesus personal relationship with God (Jesus) — 11/23/03 Vol. 33
kingship of Jesus power over evil (Jesus) — 10/5/00 Vol. 21
Kingship of Jesus reveals power over all (Jesus) — 7/20/04 Vol. 36
kitchen table share (Jesus) — 11/8/94 Vol. 2
kneel Blessed Sacrament — 9/29/93 Vol. 1
kneel in prayer gives praise to God (Jesus) — 3/28/01 Vol. 22
kneeling most reverent prayer (Jesus) — 3/13/03 Vol. 30
kneeling proper posture praying (Jesus) — 9/11/99 Vol. 16
kneeling posture most conducive to prayer,thanks (Jesus) — 3/25/02 Vol. 26
knees will bend testing time (Mary) — 10/22/93 Vol. 1

knees will bend to God at judgment (Jesus) — 9/11/99 Vol. 16
knock on hearts come out of isolation (Jesus) — 8/23/99 Vol. 16
knowledge experts (Jesus) — 1/25/94 Vol. 1
knowledge faith (Jesus) — 7/29/95 Vol. 3
knowledge internet,chips,satellites (Jesus) — 11/4/97 Vol. 9
knowledge man's pride in science (Jesus) — 11/22/96 Vol. 5
knowledge pride (Jesus) — 4/6/95 Vol. 2
knowledge pride (Jesus) — 2/18/94 Vol. 1
knowledge will never be complete (Jesus) — 5/10/99 Vol. 15
knowledge increase sign of end times (Jesus) — 3/8/98 Vol. 10
knowledge of man only scratches the surface (Jesus) — 7/29/03 Vol. 32
knowledge, full more learning in era of peace (Jesus) — 12/4/98 Vol. 13
Kosovo avoid starting a war (Jesus) — 3/23/99 Vol. 14
Kosovo pray for compromise (Jesus) — 6/3/99 Vol. 15
Kosovo pray for peace (Jesus) — 5/27/99 Vol. 15
Kosovo preview to tribulation (Jesus) — 4/8/99 Vol. 15
Kosovo shown dead bodies (Jesus) — 3/29/99 Vol. 14
Kosovo war begets war (Jesus) — 8/5/99 Vol. 16
Kosovo unrest pray for peace (Jesus) — 10/11/98 Vol. 13
Kosovo war crossroads to stop (Jesus) — 3/22/99 Vol. 14
Kosovo,NATO threatens troops asked to leave (Jesus) — 10/12/98 Vol. 13
labor & management need to work together fairly (Jesus) — 9/6/04 Vol. 36
labor and jobs have good attitude (Jesus) — 9/4/00 Vol. 20
Labor Day use talents wisely (Jesus) — 9/2/02 Vol. 28
labor, cheap cause of job losses (Jesus) — 9/6/01 Vol. 24
ladder to heaven life's trials (Jesus) — 2/1/05 Vol. 38
ladder to heaven way to forgiveness (Jesus) — 2/28/07 Vol. 46
lake levels going down (Jesus) — 6/14/07 Vol. 47
lamb of Christ offered for our sins (Jesus) — 3/20/99 Vol. 14
Lamb of God & Good Shepherd images (Jesus) — 12/15/05 Vol. 41
Lamb of God saved by Precious Blood (Jesus) — 1/10/98 Vol. 10
lampstands remnant (Jesus) — 7/12/95 Vol. 3
land control of one world people (Jesus) — 9/28/00 Vol. 20
land,wealth,power cause of many wars (Jesus) — 7/18/00 Vol. 20
landscapes God vs. man's art (Jesus) — 9/25/99 Vol. 16
Las Vegas modern Sodom & Gomorrah (Jesus) — 9/21/07 Vol. 48
laser beams used as a weapon (Jesus) — 2/18/99 Vol. 14
lasers, blue blind or destroy missiles (Jesus) — 2/21/01 Vol. 22
lasers, magic tricks of the Antichrist (Jesus) — 5/31/02 Vol. 27
last days events rapid succession (Jesus) — 12/13/97 Vol. 9
last days punishment & plagues (Jesus) — 9/25/97 Vol. 8
last days events to come true by the Bible (Jesus) — 11/24/98 Vol. 13
Last Judgment after Era of Peace (Jesus) — 2/23/99 Vol. 14
Last Judgment did you answer need in poor (Jesus) — 9/27/06 Vol. 44
last judgment heaven or hell (Jesus) — 6/3/04 Vol. 35
Latin High Mass favored over Novus Ordo (Jesus) — 5/21/06 Vol. 43
Latin Mass more access by pope (Jesus) — 7/10/07 Vol. 48

launchers use for good (Jesus) — 9/12/02 Vol. 28

lava forms new earth taken up from earth (Jesus) — 11/17/95 Vol. 3

law spirit of love (God the Father) — 7/23/99 Vol. 16

law spirit over letter of (Jesus) — 6/16/05 Vol. 39

Law followed to gain heaven (Jesus) — 8/2/05 Vol. 40

laws God's versus man's (Jesus) — 12/28/96 Vol. 5

laws mercy with justice (Jesus) — 10/25/99 Vol. 17

laws to remove God & prayer (Jesus) — 8/29/03 Vol. 32

laws & regulations difficult to know,follow (Jesus) — 11/23/02 Vol. 29

laws against God supported by evil authorities (Jesus) — 3/4/00 Vol. 18

laws mocked taste God's wrath (Jesus) — 10/12/03 Vol. 33

laws of God give peace & harmony (Jesus) — 9/19/03 Vol. 32

laws of God see consequences (Jesus) — 10/13/97 Vol. 9

laws, man's on displaying holy objects (Jesus) — 8/3/04 Vol. 36

laws, men's against God's laws (Jesus) — 5/4/04 Vol. 35

lawyers criticized by Jesus (Jesus) — 3/10/08 Vol. 50

lawyers greed for money (Jesus) — 2/26/98 Vol. 10

lawyers lay heavy burdens on innocent (Jesus) — 8/26/02 Vol. 28

lawyers money (Jesus) — 10/30/94 Vol. 2

lawyers & leaders will be judged (Jesus) — 9/18/00 Vol. 20

laxity in faith from evil society (Jesus) — 12/13/05 Vol. 41

laying on of hands for healing (Jesus) — 4/16/04 Vol. 35

layoffs in factory from stockholder greed (Jesus) — 11/18/97 Vol. 9

Lazarus raised by God the Father (Jesus) — 5/24/01 Vol. 23

Lazarus & rich man alms for the poor (Jesus) — 3/11/04 Vol. 34

laziness to work waste of talents (Jesus) — 6/7/03 Vol. 31

lazy holy (Jesus) — 4/25/95 Vol. 2

lazy avoiding Confession carry out improvement plan (Jesus) 3/17/00 Vol. 18

leaders also corrupted (Jesus) — 3/14/05 Vol. 38

leaders called to high moral order (Jesus) — 7/15/97 Vol. 8

leaders conflicts (Jesus) — 5/29/95 Vol. 2

leaders fight for power (Jesus) — 6/13/02 Vol. 27

leaders good ones to be purged (Jesus) — 9/2/04 Vol. 36

leaders have a double standard (Jesus) — 5/14/98 Vol. 11

leaders people should refuse war (Jesus) — 12/4/97 Vol. 9

leaders power and control (Jesus) — 6/19/98 Vol. 11

leaders pray for spiritual & secular (Jesus) — 1/20/98 Vol. 10

leaders pray for them (Jesus) — 2/6/97 Vol. 6

leaders pray to have peace (Jesus) — 2/26/98 Vol. 10

leaders servants to all (Jesus) — 3/15/06 Vol. 42

leaders spiritual, physical (Jesus) — 3/9/99 Vol. 14

leaders stepping down (Jesus) — 6/2/98 Vol. 11

leaders to lose positions to Antichrist (Jesus) — 2/18/00 Vol. 18

leaders to set stage for tribulation (Jesus) — 12/14/99 Vol. 17

leaders world governments (Jesus) — 11/21/95 Vol. 3

leaders cause wars greed and power reasons (Jesus) — 8/7/98 Vol. 12

leaders of government misleading people on morals (Jesus) 6/24/02 Vol. 27

leaders' own laws protected from conviction (Jesus) — 6/17/06 Vol. 43

leader's power influence by one world (Jesus) — 2/17/00 Vol. 18

leaders, evil risk judgment in hell (Jesus) — 11/22/03 Vol. 33

leaders, ruthless need prayer (Jesus) — 4/29/99 Vol. 15

leadership steward (Jesus) — 9/2/94 Vol. 2

leadership of God seek direction from God (Jesus) — 6/29/97 Vol. 7

leaking roof sign of weak faith (Jesus) — 2/4/00 Vol. 18

learn from mistakes both past & present (Jesus) — 9/19/99 Vol. 16

Leary, Ray needs prayers (Jesus) — 2/16/05 Vol. 38

Lebanon & Israel pray not to expand war (Jesus) — 8/12/06 Vol. 44

Lebanon War effect on gas prices (Jesus) — 7/20/06 Vol. 44

Lebanon War killing civilians (Jesus) — 7/27/06 Vol. 44

Lebanon War new weapons displayed (Jesus) — 7/31/06 Vol. 44

legacy of faith from dead faithful (Jesus) — 8/23/07 Vol. 48

leisure time spend wisely for God,others (Jesus) — 4/7/05 Vol. 39

leisure time take time for God (Jesus) — 1/13/97 Vol. 6

leisure time use for prayer,evangelize (Jesus) — 2/12/99 Vol. 14

leisure time use wisely for God (Jesus) — 6/15/02 Vol. 27

leisure time wasted on entertainment (Jesus) — 9/20/06 Vol. 44

leisure time who is your master? (Mary) — 3/20/98 Vol. 10

Lent battle of bodily desires (Jesus) — 2/20/07 Vol. 46

Lent confusion (Jesus) — 2/15/94 Vol. 1

Lent desert experience (Jesus) — 2/23/98 Vol. 10

Lent grace (Jesus) — 3/7/94 Vol. 1

Lent graces for year (Jesus) — 4/2/04 Vol. 35

Lent heal habitual sins (Jesus) — 3/6/07 Vol. 46

Lent improve spiritual life (Jesus) — 3/3/05 Vol. 38

Lent improve spiritual life, penance (Jesus) — 2/25/04 Vol. 34

Lent improves spiritual life (Jesus) — 3/16/06 Vol. 42

Lent keep soul healthy (Jesus) — 2/22/07 Vol. 46

Lent mortify the body (Jesus) — 2/10/97 Vol. 6

Lent our desert experience (Jesus) — 2/15/99 Vol. 14

Lent pray & help your neighbor (Jesus) — 1/31/08 Vol. 50

Lent prayer & Divine Will (Jesus) — 3/6/03 Vol. 30

Lent prayer and self-denial (Jesus) — 2/26/98 Vol. 10

Lent preparation for tribulation (Jesus) — 2/12/02 Vol. 26

Lent prepare resolutions (Jesus) — 1/14/99 Vol. 14

Lent prepare while time (Jesus) — 3/1/99 Vol. 14

Lent prune earthly failings (Mary) — 3/18/98 Vol. 10

Lent prune occasions of sin (Jesus) — 3/4/98 Vol. 10

Lent puts focus back on God (Jesus) — 3/13/02 Vol. 26

Lent renew spiritual lives (Jesus) — 3/2/98 Vol. 10

Lent renews spiritual life (Jesus) — 2/6/08 Vol. 50

Lent self-denial for penance (Jesus) — 1/26/06 Vol. 42

Lent share in suffering (Jesus) — 3/8/03 Vol. 30

Lent share with the poor (Jesus) — 2/13/08 Vol. 50

Lent special preparation (Jesus) — 2/6/97 Vol. 6

Lent spiritual progress (Jesus) — 3/28/94 Vol. 1
Lent suffer as Jesus (Jesus) — 3/16/98 Vol. 10
Lent time for fasting (Jesus) — 2/23/07 Vol. 46
Lent time for renewal (Jesus) — 2/19/07 Vol. 46
Lent time for spiritual renewal (Jesus) — 2/23/04 Vol. 34
Lent time to correct faults (Jesus) — 2/26/99 Vol. 14
Lent time to suffer the body (Jesus) — 2/16/99 Vol. 14
Lent to improve spiritual life (Jesus) — 4/4/07 Vol. 47
Lent unite with Jesus' suffering (Jesus) — 3/1/07 Vol. 46
Lent witness (Mary) — 2/28/94 Vol. 1
Lent, middle of renew original intentions (Jesus) — 3/24/01 Vol. 22
Lenten decisions fasting, prayer, habits (Jesus) — 3/6/03 Vol. 30
Lenten desire live as last Lent (Jesus) — 2/21/07 Vol. 46
Lenten devotions make holier people (Jesus) — 3/5/06 Vol. 42
Lenten devotions need remembering & renewal (Jesus) — 2/28/02 Vol. 26
Lenten devotions preparing for tribulation (Jesus) — 4/19/00 Vol. 19
Lenten devotions renew for Holy Week (Jesus) — 3/27/04 Vol. 34
Lenten focus on heaven, not world (Jesus) — 2/12/04 Vol. 34
Lenten goals to improve spiritual life (Jesus) — 3/1/01 Vol. 22
Lenten intentions be faithful to (Jesus) — 2/19/04 Vol. 34
Lenten intentions prayer, healing bad habits (Jesus) — 3/18/04 Vol. 34
Lenten intentions prepare for now (Jesus) — 1/6/05 Vol. 38
Lenten intentions put on spiritual track (Jesus) — 2/13/02 Vol. 26
Lenten meditation time as Jesus in desert (Jesus) — 3/18/00 Vol. 18
Lenten opportunity spiritual growth (Jesus) — 3/13/08 Vol. 50
Lenten penances be persistent (Jesus) — 2/28/08 Vol. 50
Lenten penances improve spiritual life (Jesus) — 3/13/07 Vol. 46
Lenten penances need reminders,keep focused (Jesus) — 2/20/02 Vol. 26
Lenten penances plan for (Jesus) — 1/27/05 Vol. 38
Lenten prayers heaven (Jesus) — 4/6/96 Vol. 3
Lenten preparations to improve spiritual life (Jesus) — 1/29/04 Vol. 34
Lenten regimen good for the soul (Jesus) — 3/9/06 Vol. 42
Lenten resolution penance, increase prayer (Jesus) — 2/21/07 Vol. 46
Lenten resolutions new spiritual resolutions (Jesus) — 1/17/08 Vol. 50
Lenten resolve refocus lives on Jesus (Jesus) — 4/11/00 Vol. 19
Leo Remacle preparations thanked for (Jesus) — 1/2/99 Vol. 14
leper, returned all should be thanking God (Jesus) — 11/27/03 Vol. 33
leper's cure as cure of our sins (Jesus) — 2/13/00 Vol. 18
leprosy, spiritual change from unclean (Jesus) — 2/12/06 Vol. 42
Leroy in heaven (Jesus) — 8/12/02 Vol. 28
letter of the law vs. spirit of the law (Jesus) — 2/12/02 Vol. 26
letters of acceptance truth by your actions (Jesus) — 6/11/97 Vol. 7
letters,cards,calls rainbows in mailbox (Jesus) — 2/27/07 Vol. 46
letting go give will over to God's Will (Jesus) — 10/31/03 Vol. 33
levees not strong enough (Jesus) — 11/3/05 Vol. 41
levels of heaven by faithfulness in testing (Jesus) — 2/3/00 Vol. 18
levitation from deep union with God (Jesus) — 4/9/07 Vol. 47

libation difficulties in life (Jesus) — 6/30/95 Vol. 2
liberation theology priests (Jesus) — 9/3/96 Vol. 4
Liberty bell our freedoms removed (Jesus) — 9/9/02 Vol. 28
license plates tracking devices (Jesus) — 2/20/97 Vol. 6
license tags smart card IDS (Jesus) — 8/21/03 Vol. 32
life abortion (Jesus) — 9/9/94 Vol. 2
Life abortion/mercy killing (Jesus) — 5/8/96 Vol. 3
life analogy in seasons (Jesus) — 9/5/02 Vol. 28
life appreciate each soul (Jesus) — 5/17/01 Vol. 23
life as an opportunity and joy (Jesus) — 1/23/02 Vol. 26
life be simple (Jesus) — 8/17/00 Vol. 20
life big picture of life (Jesus) — 6/12/96 Vol. 3
life birth and death (Jesus) — 6/6/05 Vol. 39
life blooms like a flower (Jesus) — 4/12/04 Vol. 35
life circle of (Jesus) — 9/23/06 Vol. 44
life equality (Jesus) — 12/28/94 Vol. 2
life Eucharist (Jesus) — 4/22/96 Vol. 3
life faith (Jesus) — 8/14/94 Vol. 2
life fragile, vulnerable (Jesus) — 11/4/03 Vol. 33
life give praise and glory for (Jesus) — 5/27/98 Vol. 11
life God's plan for each (Jesus) — 8/26/00 Vol. 20
life God's plan for each person (Jesus) — 5/18/01 Vol. 23
life has plan and purpose (Jesus) — 6/11/99 Vol. 15
life important to protect (Jesus) — 4/3/07 Vol. 47
life in the fast lane (Jesus) — 12/29/96 Vol. 5
life is a test of love (Jesus) — 4/12/03 Vol. 31
life is fragile to death (Jesus) — 7/16/05 Vol. 40
life is like a book (Jesus) — 5/3/01 Vol. 23
life is most precious gift (Jesus) — 9/7/98 Vol. 12
life is preparation for death (Jesus) — 11/20/00 Vol. 21
life like a basement to heaven (Jesus) — 4/2/04 Vol. 35
life like a merry-go-round (Jesus) — 2/8/01 Vol. 22
life like innings in ballgame (Jesus) — 6/6/01 Vol. 23
life love will set you free (Jesus) — 11/28/98 Vol. 13
life most precious gift (Jesus) — 11/22/01 Vol. 25
life needs protection (Jesus) — 2/3/06 Vol. 42
life new signs in spring (Jesus) — 5/17/01 Vol. 23
life new starts at birth & death (Jesus) — 2/7/02 Vol. 26
life order to God's plan (Father) — 6/12/96 Vol. 3
life pilgrimage through suffering (Jesus) — 12/2/99 Vol. 17
life plan for us and others (Jesus) — 7/29/02 Vol. 28
Life position & meaning (Jesus) — 5/15/96 Vol. 3
life procreate (Jesus) — 9/13/94 Vol. 2
life protect all life, plan (Jesus) — 10/11/97 Vol. 9
life protect in all forms (Jesus) — 5/6/02 Vol. 27
life rebirth of new (St. Therese) — 5/7/98 Vol. 11
life rejoice in gift of (Jesus) — 4/24/03 Vol. 31

life satisfied with lot given (Jesus) 5/25/05 Vol. 39
life should not be violated (Jesus) 10/9/99 Vol. 17
life stages of (Jesus) 6/3/02 Vol. 27
life test on earth (Jesus) 9/15/00 Vol. 20
life testing of our love (Jesus) 6/3/98 Vol. 11
life through God's eyes (Jesus) 1/16/96 Vol. 3
life too precious to kill (Jesus) 12/17/05 Vol. 41
life views (Jesus) 3/26/95 Vol. 2
life with overactive agendas (Jesus) 5/19/03 Vol. 31
life with patience & love (Jesus) 2/12/04 Vol. 34
life & death of body & soul (Jesus) 10/27/04 Vol. 37
life & death choices God vs. self (Jesus) 11/24/03 Vol. 33
life & death everyday in hands of God (Jesus) 7/19/04 Vol. 36
life about love of God and neighbor (Jesus) 12/11/99 Vol. 17
life and death the battle of (Jesus) 8/21/00 Vol. 20
life appreciation precious time,pray for soul (Jesus) 12/29/99 Vol. 17
life as a race death means to next life (Jesus) 12/11/99 Vol. 17
life changed mercy for those who choose God (Jesus) 3/15/02 Vol. 26
life choices broad & narrow roads (Jesus) 3/11/03 Vol. 30
life currents do God's Will (Jesus) 10/4/06 Vol. 45
life cycle here a short time (Jesus) 3/9/98 Vol. 10
life each day gift of God (Jesus) 3/31/00 Vol. 18
life for God over our own personal glory (Jesus) 8/23/04 Vol. 36
life given to Jesus as He gave us His (Jesus) 6/1/06 Vol. 43
Life here is a test of suffering (Jesus) 1/25/01 Vol. 22
life in heaven better than earthly gains (Jesus) 12/9/98 Vol. 13
life in soul forgive,accept Jesus (Jesus) 6/7/00 Vol. 19
life in souls gift of God to us (Jesus) 12/2/04 Vol. 37
Life in Spirit after Resurrection (Jesus) 4/28/00 Vol. 19
life is a stage intentions of heart seen (Jesus) 2/28/01 Vol. 22
life is a test accept responsibilities (Jesus) 4/15/03 Vol. 31
life is a test of loving God and neighbor (Jesus) 9/8/98 Vol. 12
life is a test physical vs. spiritual (Jesus) 5/11/03 Vol. 31
life is a test woven like Persian rug (Jesus) 4/16/01 Vol. 23
life is short Baptism,annointing (Jesus) 1/31/00 Vol. 18
life is struggle need sacraments, consecration (Jesus) 12/23/02 Vol. 29
life is vulnerable disposed to sudden death (Jesus) 11/11/99 Vol. 17
life issues at stake in elections (Jesus) 10/15/04 Vol. 37
life issues fight laws against (Jesus) 2/5/07 Vol. 46
life issues in elections (Jesus) 10/21/04 Vol. 37
life lines electricity,water,gas,phone (Jesus) 3/6/02 Vol. 26
life lines spiritual, physical (Jesus) 12/6/99 Vol. 17
life long commitment to obey commandments (Jesus) 6/28/99 Vol. 15
life more bearable through Jesus' help (Jesus) 7/13/00 Vol. 20
life needs rebuilding from rubble of sins (Jesus) 9/13/01 Vol. 24
life of each one affects us decisions (Jesus) 9/11/95 Vol. 3
life of soul not worth worldly gain (Jesus) 8/29/99 Vol. 16

life on earth a test of faith (Jesus) 11/25/00 Vol. 21
life on earth a time of testing (Jesus) 6/20/01 Vol. 23
life on earth preparation for your death (Jesus) 11/12/04 Vol. 37
life on earth time running out (Jesus) 9/4/97 Vol. 8
life preserved Good Friday,love needed (Jesus) 4/2/99 Vol. 15
life rafts saved from sins (Jesus) 9/30/01 Vol. 24
life restored by one Man, Jesus (Jesus) 3/29/02 Vol. 26
life review choose 8/31/93 Vol. 1
life review heaven,hell,purgatory (Jesus) 7/2/99 Vol. 16
life review judgment shown in Warning (Jesus) 1/9/06 Vol. 42
life review see sins of omission (Jesus) 1/20/07 Vol. 46
life review test of love (Jesus) 6/3/02 Vol. 27
life review coming will give people a 2nd chance (Jesus) 10/11/98 Vol. 13
life style seek calm, not to be busy (Jesus) 7/9/98 Vol. 12
life through Jesus only means to heaven (Jesus) 3/21/99 Vol. 14
life vs. death love vs. sword (Jesus) 6/27/02 Vol. 27
life vs. death culture presidential choices (Jesus) 10/13/04 Vol. 37
life, every is a gift to us (Jesus) 12/2/06 Vol. 45
life, is short is like a race (Jesus) 11/30/05 Vol. 41
life, love of lost sensitivity (Jesus) 9/20/02 Vol. 28
life, new is precious to God & family (Jesus) 2/4/02 Vol. 26
life, new physically & spiritually (Jesus) 4/22/04 Vol. 35
life, new spiritual and physical (Jesus) 4/3/02 Vol. 27
life, our like construction blueprint (Jesus) 9/21/02 Vol. 28
life, road of meet many people as flowers (Jesus) 6/25/03 Vol. 31
life, simple easier to focus on God (Jesus) 5/13/04 Vol. 35
life, stages of experience life every moment (Jesus) 7/6/05 Vol. 40
life, test of faith not place of rest,pleasures (Jesus) 7/16/00 Vol. 20
life, valuable lack of love causing wars (Jesus) 11/8/00 Vol. 21
life, voyage of need grace for ups & downs (Jesus) 3/19/04 Vol. 34
life, vulnerable be thankful to God each day (Jesus) 12/11/03 Vol. 33
life,race to finish line struggle for heaven (Jesus) 10/27/98 Vol. 13
life's choices between God & Satan (Jesus) 11/27/04 Vol. 37
life's choices to heaven or hell (Jesus) 3/9/05 Vol. 38
life's cycles prepare for death (Jesus) 10/30/01 Vol. 25
life's decisions determine heaven or hell (Jesus) 3/25/08 Vol. 50
life's events change your life (Jesus) 12/19/04 Vol. 37
life's experiences help you grow in faith (Jesus) 12/7/99 Vol. 17
life's experiences in different rooms (Jesus) 6/16/02 Vol. 27
life's experiences teach about love (Jesus) 11/27/99 Vol. 17
life's focus on love of God,neighbor (Jesus) 2/9/00 Vol. 18
life's meaning love of God & neighbor (Jesus) 8/9/00 Vol. 20
life's milestones celebrated in families (Jesus) 8/23/05 Vol. 40
life's mission time is short (Jesus) 8/25/06 Vol. 44
life's mission use gifts and talents (Jesus) 6/14/05 Vol. 39
life's opportunity to serve God (Jesus) 12/11/05 Vol. 41
life's plan train to a destination (Jesus) 10/12/96 Vol. 5

life's problems trust in God (Jesus) — 3/15/07 Vol. 46
life's purpose know, love & serve God (Jesus) — 9/16/02 Vol. 28
life's purpose to know love and serve (Jesus) — 9/6/00 Vol. 20
life's stages has its own struggles (Jesus) — 12/16/02 Vol. 29
life's struggles Jesus is strength (Jesus) — 1/27/03 Vol. 30
life's struggles physical and spiritual (Jesus) — 2/14/02 Vol. 26
life's trials accept God's Will (Jesus) — 12/30/00 Vol. 21
life's trials heaven watches reaction (Jesus) — 1/1/02 Vol. 26
life's ups & downs requires daily trust in God (Jesus) — 11/13/99 Vol. 17
life's ups & downs tested by trials (Jesus) — 1/30/05 Vol. 38
life's value beyond earthly comforts (Jesus) — 4/22/99 Vol. 15
lifestyle will be simpler (Jesus) — 4/25/02 Vol. 27
lifestyle keep simple and natural (Jesus) — 4/30/02 Vol. 27
lifestyle adjustment improves spiritual life (God the Father) — 11/24/99 Vol. 17
lifestyles be simple & prayerful (Jesus) — 1/31/02 Vol. 26
lifestyles of evil,divorce,abortion,gays (Jesus) — 1/9/05 Vol. 38
lifestyles sinful ways (Jesus) — 5/22/01 Vol. 23
lifestyles vulnerable to natural disasters (Jesus) — 9/16/99 Vol. 16
lifetime to see His glory (Jesus) — 10/5/01 Vol. 25
lifetime trust in triumph (Jesus) — 11/20/95 Vol. 3
lifetime ups and downs of life (Jesus) — 6/11/96 Vol. 3
lifetime stages on escalator (Jesus) — 4/23/05 Vol. 39
lift up depressed seek eternal joy in heaven (Jesus) — 8/21/99 Vol. 16
light breath of life (Holy Spirit) — 12/15/93 Vol. 1
light darkness (Jesus) — 9/23/94 Vol. 2
light faith (Jesus) — 12/16/94 Vol. 2
light holy people give off (Jesus) — 2/22/07 Vol. 46
light hope (Jesus) — 10/24/95 Vol. 3
light judgment (Jesus) — 3/24/95 Vol. 2
light light of the world (Jesus) — 11/30/98 Vol. 13
light love (David) — 1/5/94 Vol. 1
light martyrdom (St. Lucy) — 12/13/93 Vol. 1
light peace/love (Jesus) — 12/19/93 Vol. 1
light salvation (Jesus) — 11/15/93 Vol. 1
light scriptures (Jesus) — 1/7/96 Vol. 3
light second coming (Jesus) — 11/27/94 Vol. 2
light sin (Mary) — 1/27/94 Vol. 1
light sinners (Jesus) — 9/6/94 Vol. 2
light & water needed for physical survival (Jesus) — 3/31/02 Vol. 26
light and love daily Mass (Jesus) — 12/16/95 Vol. 3
Light at death drawn to God over Satan (Jesus) — 7/20/04 Vol. 36
light beam for moving objects (Jesus) — 2/19/06 Vol. 42
light dispels darkness Easter ultimate feast day (Jesus) — 4/5/99 Vol. 15
light in the darkness devil talking in your ears (Jesus) — 7/13/96 Vol. 4
Light in the world asks faithful to be (Jesus) — 4/18/04 Vol. 35
Light of Christ lamp to the soul's life (Jesus) — 4/3/00 Vol. 19
light of Christ way to salvation (Jesus) — 3/11/99 Vol. 14

Light of creation warmth, love of God (Jesus) — 3/7/07 Vol. 46
Light of faith Light of Jesus (Jesus) — 12/17/02 Vol. 29
Light of faith, grace shine on all people (Jesus) — 6/12/07 Vol. 47
light of faithful beacons of faith (Jesus) — 11/5/04 Vol. 37
Light of God dispels darkness (Jesus) — 4/19/03 Vol. 31
Light of God needed each day (Jesus) — 2/10/00 Vol. 18
Light of God seen at Warning, death (Jesus) — 1/8/06 Vol. 42
light of grace out in souls as blackouts (Jesus) — 2/22/01 Vol. 22
light of Jesus at 1st & 2nd coming (Jesus) — 11/30/99 Vol. 17
Light of Jesus avoid other gods,religions (Jesus) — 1/1/00 Vol. 18
Light of Jesus direction for life (Jesus) — 1/19/05 Vol. 38
Light of Jesus dispels darkness of sin (Jesus) — 12/13/03 Vol. 33
Light of Jesus dispels darkness of sin (Jesus) — 11/5/04 Vol. 37
Light of Jesus follow & discern Will (Jesus) — 4/25/03 Vol. 31
Light of Jesus gives hope, witness of love (Jesus) — 12/9/04 Vol. 37
Light of Jesus illuminates saints (Jesus) — 1/1/07 Vol. 46
Light of Jesus in coming Warning (Jesus) — 3/27/08 Vol. 50
Light of Jesus make life decisions by (Jesus) — 3/25/08 Vol. 50
Light of Jesus path to heaven (Jesus) — 3/9/00 Vol. 18
Light of Jesus takes away darkness of sin (Jesus) — 12/14/04 Vol. 37
Light of Jesus vs. darkness of Satan (Jesus) — 4/28/03 Vol. 31
Light of Jesus vs. darkness of sin (Jesus) — 11/19/07 Vol. 49
Light of Jesus walk in (Jesus) — 7/9/04 Vol. 36
Light of Life puts love in hearts (Jesus) — 5/28/98 Vol. 11
Light of salvation call sinners to repent (Jesus) — 4/15/04 Vol. 35
Light of the World bless candles (Jesus) — 2/2/07 Vol. 46
Light of the world conquer sin & death (Jesus) — 12/6/96 Vol. 5
Light of the world eternal light of Jesus (Jesus) — 1/25/99 Vol. 14
Light of the world have no fear of Antichrist (Jesus) — 12/28/99 Vol. 17
Light of the World in Jesus (Jesus) — 9/24/07 Vol. 48
Light of the World is Jesus (Jesus) — 2/16/03 Vol. 30
Light of the World Jesus calls all to Himself (Jesus) — 11/4/97 Vol. 9
Light of the world Jesus dispels the darkness (Jesus) — 7/20/04 Vol. 36
Light of the world Jesus leads us to heaven (Jesus) — 1/3/02 Vol. 26
Light of the world Jesus' vast Presence (Jesus) — 7/30/01 Vol. 24
Light of the world physical and spiritual (Jesus) — 7/1/02 Vol. 28
Light of the world shines for all to see (Jesus) — 6/19/04 Vol. 35
Light of the world that pierces the darkness (Jesus) — 12/24/01 Vol. 25
Light of the world to dispel the darkness (Jesus) — 9/29/02 Vol. 28
Light of truth in Commandments,God's Will (Jesus) — 6/22/00 Vol. 19
light of victory hope in Jesus (Jesus) — 8/19/99 Vol. 16
Light of Word St. John's Gospel (Jesus) — 12/22/04 Vol. 37
Light of world cannot hide from Jesus (Jesus) — 5/9/03 Vol. 31
Light of world dispelled darkness of sin (Jesus) — 2/11/01 Vol. 22
Light of world in Easter candle of Baptism (Jesus) — 11/30/02 Vol. 29
Light of world to dispel the darkness (Jesus) — 4/22/04 Vol. 35
light vs darkness Jesus vs Satan (Jesus) — 3/11/00 Vol. 18

Light vs. darkside spiritual battle (Jesus) 4/18/07 Vol. 47

Light, Paschal Candle dispels darkness of sin (Jesus) 3/20/07 Vol. 46

Light,not under basket let Blessed Sacrament be seen (Jesus) 8/8/02 Vol. 28

Light,salt of earth be witness of faith (Jesus) 2/5/05 Vol. 38

lightning central focus (Jesus) 2/26/95 Vol. 2

limits for evil God always in control (Jesus) 2/14/01 Vol. 22

Lincoln, Abraham Civil War and abortion (Jesus) 5/31/01 Vol. 23

line of grace kept open through sacraments (Jesus) 3/6/02 Vol. 26

lineage peace (St. Joseph) 12/22/93 Vol. 1

lion image of courage to convert sinners (Jesus) 8/24/99 Vol. 16

Lise's father in purgatory (Jesus) 5/31/05 Vol. 39

listen person (Jesus) 6/24/94 Vol. 1

listening yet? one disaster after another (Jesus) 9/23/03 Vol. 32

Listening, seeing devices lost privacy for security (Jesus) 4/17/97 Vol. 7

lists for extermination of those agains new world order (Jesus) 9/29/06 Vol. 44

litigation justice system favors rich (Jesus) 8/26/02 Vol. 28

litigation for money mean spirited people using (Jesus) 8/12/04 Vol. 36

little things do not be upset by them (Jesus) 8/31/07 Vol. 48

Little Way distractions (St. Therese) 10/11/95 Vol. 3

Littleton deaths compared to abortions (Jesus) 4/26/99 Vol. 15

Littleton killings TV,virtual reality,Internet (Jesus) 4/22/99 Vol. 15

liturgy of hours,psalms lifts hearts in meditation (Jesus) 6/8/00 Vol. 19

Liturgy of the Hours daily psalms in readings (Jesus) 3/5/04 Vol. 34

Liturgy of the Hours good daily prayer (Jesus) 6/9/04 Vol. 35

live faith in your actions (Jesus) 3/22/07 Vol. 46

live in trust than worrying about problems (Jesus) 5/10/00 Vol. 19

live lives simply & humbly (Jesus) 3/12/07 Vol. 46

live the Gospel inspires conversions (Jesus) 3/2/00 Vol. 18

lives affect each other (Jesus) 4/16/03 Vol. 31

lives need simpler, helpful (Jesus) 8/26/04 Vol. 36

lives in life help you,means to heaven (Jesus) 6/25/03 Vol. 31

lives of family gifts from God (Jesus) 11/23/06 Vol. 45

lives, changed miracle of grace in Warning (Jesus) 10/17/03 Vol. 33

lives, our let God run by His plan (Jesus) 5/5/02 Vol. 27

living bread strength to reach heaven (Jesus) 7/8/97 Vol. 8

living dead those with mortal sin (Jesus) 4/17/00 Vol. 19

living presence holiness (Jesus) 3/15/94 Vol. 1

living Scriptures in actions is important (Jesus) 2/25/06 Vol. 42

living soul kingship (Jesus) 1/8/95 Vol. 2

living things man cannot make (Jesus) 2/15/07 Vol. 46

living together cause of mortal sin (Jesus) 9/6/99 Vol. 16

living together mortal sin (Jesus) 6/20/98 Vol. 11

living together,homosexuals destroying the family (Jesus) 12/30/01 Vol. 25

living water always available (Jesus) 7/17/03 Vol. 32

Living Water and eternal life (Jesus) 5/6/01 Vol. 23

Living Water Eucharistic eternal life (Jesus) 6/10/07 Vol. 47

Living Water grace from sacraments (Jesus) 1/28/05 Vol. 38

living water graces and blessings (Jesus) 6/6/96 Vol. 3

living water in Eucharist (Jesus) 4/1/03 Vol. 31

Living Water in Eucharist (Jesus) 7/3/03 Vol. 32

living water in Eucharist (Jesus) 1/10/00 Vol. 18

living water in grace of Jesus,sacraments (Jesus) 3/3/02 Vol. 26

Living Water Jesus' power over death (Jesus) 2/5/08 Vol. 50

living water lasts forever (Jesus) 1/13/01 Vol. 22

Living Water love in Eucharist (Jesus) 8/9/03 Vol. 32

Living Water of Eucharist (Jesus) 4/22/01 Vol. 23

living water peace (Jesus) 9/23/94 Vol. 2

Living Water spiritual food, Eucharist (Jesus) 2/24/08 Vol. 50

Living Water to refresh soul (Jesus) 7/22/01 Vol. 24

Living Water of God grace, peace & rest (Jesus) 2/23/06 Vol. 42

living water,manna no survival without Jesus (Jesus) 6/28/99 Vol. 15

Living waters of grace (Jesus) 7/7/03 Vol. 32

loan crisis Fed bailing out the rich (Jesus) 1/31/08 Vol. 50

loaves & fish multiplied, 7 & 12 used (Jesus) 2/7/06 Vol. 42

local church family sacraments (Jesus) 5/18/06 Vol. 43

local church needs your support (Jesus) 5/18/06 Vol. 43

locust infestation sign of end times in Africa (Jesus) 9/27/04 Vol. 36

locust infestations at Biblical proportion (Jesus) 12/7/04 Vol. 37

locust swarms Africa, consuming crops (Jesus) 8/8/04 Vol. 36

locusts threaten food crops (Jesus) 3/5/05 Vol. 38

lodging open to those in need (Jesus) 12/20/99 Vol. 17

London killings abhorrent to Jesus (Jesus) 7/7/05 Vol. 40

London's royalty symbol secret government (Jesus) 9/4/99 Vol. 16

London's terrorism for involvement in Iraq (Jesus) 7/23/05 Vol. 40

loneliness friend in Jesus (Jesus) 4/21/07 Vol. 47

longer lives from better care (Jesus) 2/4/01 Vol. 22

looters shooting at relief workers (Jesus) 9/15/05 Vol. 40

looting & energy with desperate people (Jesus) 10/13/05 Vol. 41

looting and stealing after natural disaster, LA (Jesus) 10/3/05 Vol. 41

looting for food time to go into hiding (Jesus) 4/9/99 Vol. 15

Lord of the Universe every knee should bend (Jesus) 4/9/99 Vol. 15

Lord's coming repent (St. John Baptist) 12/23/93 Vol. 1

Lord's Ranch, The feeds the poor (Holy Spirit) 5/31/98 Vol. 11

Loretta's funeral emptiness in hearts at loss (Jesus) 12/23/04 Vol. 37

lost & lukewarm need saving (Jesus) 1/24/00 Vol. 18

lost objects how to pray (St. Anthony) 6/12/96 Vol. 3

lost souls need evangelizing (Jesus) 11/9/99 Vol. 17

lost souls need to find Jesus (Jesus) 12/15/05 Vol. 41

Louch Derg walk in Jesus' footsteps (Jesus) 7/12/99 Vol. 16

Lough Derg we walked road to Calvary (Jesus) 7/14/99 Vol. 16

Lourdes 150th Anniversary (Jesus) 2/10/08 Vol. 50

Lourdes faith to be healed (Jesus) 2/11/04 Vol. 34

Lourdes healing waters & refuge (Jesus) 2/4/08 Vol. 50

Lourdes healing from miraculous waters (Mary) 2/10/00 Vol. 18

love of self & neighbor (Jesus) — 6/3/04 Vol. 35
love angels (Jesus) — 12/26/95 Vol. 3
love basis of life (Jesus) — 8/18/00 Vol. 20
love be disciples of (Jesus) — 5/13/01 Vol. 23
love binds hearts together (Jesus) — 10/5/03 Vol. 33
love by death on the cross (Jesus) — 1/28/01 Vol. 22
love by living the Gospel (Jesus) — 6/15/99 Vol. 15
love call on Jesus for help (Jesus) — 1/27/98 Vol. 10
love central to Divine Will (Jesus) — 3/17/98 Vol. 10
love Christmas (Jesus) — 12/22/93 Vol. 1
love communication (Jesus) — 4/26/94 Vol. 1
love Communion (Mary) — 1/5/94 Vol. 1
love confounds enemies (Jesus) — 1/9/04 Vol. 34
love conquers evil with good (Jesus) — 4/20/04 Vol. 35
love covenant (God the Father) — 4/12/95 Vol. 2
love Covenant of commands (Jesus) — 2/24/96 Vol. 3
love death on cross,marriage (Jesus) — 5/3/97 Vol. 7
love Divine Mercy (Jesus) — 3/26/94 Vol. 1
love everyone, even enemies (Jesus) — 6/14/05 Vol. 39
love feelings (Jesus) — 5/31/95 Vol. 2
love focus on God & neighbor (Jesus) — 9/18/02 Vol. 28
love focus on His joy (Jesus) — 1/15/98 Vol. 10
love follow His Will (Jesus) — 9/18/96 Vol. 4
love for life of perfection (Jesus) — 10/8/01 Vol. 25
love fruits (St. Francis) — 9/20/93 Vol. 1
Love gift of a rose (St. Therese) — 3/11/96 Vol. 3
love God & neighbor (Jesus) — 2/13/03 Vol. 30
love God and neighbor (Jesus) — 11/19/00 Vol. 21
love Gospel message (Jesus) — 2/6/04 Vol. 34
love graces (Jesus) — 4/3/95 Vol. 2
love greatest message of Jesus (Jesus) — 1/24/05 Vol. 38
love harmony of life & time (Jesus) — 3/4/05 Vol. 38
love harmony with God's Will (Jesus) — 7/21/96 Vol. 4
love heart (Jesus) — 10/24/94 Vol. 2
love holds families together (Jesus) — 12/5/02 Vol. 29
love humility and equality (Father) — 2/15/96 Vol. 3
love is answer to problems (Jesus) — 4/8/02 Vol. 27
love is connected through prayer (Jesus) — 1/23/02 Vol. 26
love is core of belief and life (Jesus) — 10/23/05 Vol. 41
love is the only answer (Jesus) — 9/20/03 Vol. 32
Love is to soul as water is to soil (Jesus) — 8/20/01 Vol. 24
love Jesus cries tears of (Jesus) — 1/17/98 Vol. 10
love Jesus' gift of (Jesus) — 1/1/01 Vol. 22
love Jesus' heart burns for us (Jesus) — 4/8/98 Vol. 11
love judgment (Jesus) — 11/21/93 Vol. 1
love keep focused on (Jesus) — 7/30/03 Vol. 32
love keep hearts open to (Jesus) — 5/22/99 Vol. 15

love key to entering heaven (Jesus) — 12/20/05 Vol. 41
love key to life (Jesus) — 11/28/98 Vol. 13
love knowledge (Jesus) — 7/10/95 Vol. 3
love lesson of life (Jesus) — 9/5/00 Vol. 20
love life (Jesus) — 4/10/94 Vol. 1
love makes the world go round (Jesus) — 10/29/06 Vol. 45
love marriage (Jesus) — 2/14/94 Vol. 1
love more important than success (Jesus) — 1/9/00 Vol. 18
love mortar of society (Jesus) — 8/25/97 Vol. 8
love must be focus in life (Jesus) — 9/9/06 Vol. 44
love must permeate whole life (Jesus) — 4/20/04 Vol. 35
love of God and neighbor (Jesus) — 6/11/05 Vol. 39
love of God and neighbor (Jesus) — 10/23/06 Vol. 45
love of God and neighbor (Jesus) — 2/14/96 Vol. 3
love of God, neighbor vs. things (Jesus) — 4/17/04 Vol. 35
love of Jesus & neighbor (Jesus) — 5/6/01 Vol. 23
love of spouse, God & others (Jesus) — 2/14/04 Vol. 34
Love of spouses & God (Jesus) — 5/26/05 Vol. 39
love open hearts to God (Jesus) — 7/10/01 Vol. 24
love open our hearts (Jesus) — 6/13/99 Vol. 15
love passion and death (Jesus) — 4/3/96 Vol. 3
love peace (Jesus) — 1/30/94 Vol. 1
love perfection (Jesus) — 6/6/94 Vol. 1
love perfection for heaven (Jesus) — 5/22/02 Vol. 27
love prayer (Jesus) — 1/29/94 Vol. 1
Love prayer & communication (Jesus) — 2/13/97 Vol. 6
love prodigal son (Jesus) — 1/14/96 Vol. 3
love rejoice in His (Jesus) — 6/17/98 Vol. 11
love replace stony hearts (Jesus) — 5/18/02 Vol. 27
love reverence (Jesus) — 3/4/94 Vol. 1
love saints (Jesus) — 11/17/95 Vol. 3
love share or shrivel up (Jesus) — 6/23/97 Vol. 7
love share unconditionally (Jesus) — 10/12/97 Vol. 9
love share with everyone (Jesus) — 9/25/98 Vol. 12
love study scriptures for Will (Jesus) — 1/29/97 Vol. 6
Love thankgiving (Jesus) — 6/5/94 Vol. 1
love the core of life (Holy Spirit) — 5/31/98 Vol. 11
love the core of the Trinity (Jesus) — 5/30/99 Vol. 15
love to balance evil (Jesus) — 9/11/00 Vol. 20
love to conquer all (Jesus) — 1/23/03 Vol. 30
love unconditional & infinite (Jesus) — 1/12/98 Vol. 10
love unconditionally (Jesus) — 1/12/04 Vol. 34
love unconditionally (Jesus) — 7/27/99 Vol. 16
love will (Jesus) — 6/5/94 Vol. 1
love win souls to Jesus (St. Therese) — 5/22/96 Vol. 3
love work in God's service (Jesus) — 6/21/97 Vol. 7
love your enemies (Jesus) — 11/15/05 Vol. 41

love your neighbor (Jesus) 1/10/02 Vol. 26

love & Baptism symbols in hot water (Jesus) 12/29/06 Vol. 45

love & good deeds have for heaven (Jesus) 6/24/03 Vol. 31

love & good deeds make you holy (Jesus) 7/13/06 Vol. 44

love & good works better than wealth (Jesus) 3/9/00 Vol. 18

love & happiness improves our lives (Jesus) 1/3/05 Vol. 38

love & joy heal & help others (Jesus) 4/16/03 Vol. 31

love & mercy for neighbor (Jesus) 9/13/07 Vol. 48

love & mercy of God awaits every sinner (Jesus) 11/27/02 Vol. 29

love & obedience mission from God (Jesus) 12/28/03 Vol. 33

love & peace seek to be holy (Jesus) 5/31/06 Vol. 43

love & peace of God all that is needed (Jesus) 11/22/04 Vol. 37

love & sharing way to heaven (Jesus) 12/22/04 Vol. 37

love & worship of God needed for heaven (Jesus) 11/25/04 Vol. 37

love (true) for God without fear of punishment (Jesus) 1/28/07 Vol. 46

love and actions determine your destination (Jesus) 7/6/05 Vol. 40

love and joy make peaceful hearts (Jesus) 12/13/03 Vol. 33

love and mercy fulfilled in Jesus (Jesus) 2/27/08 Vol. 50

love at Christmas in family and world (Jesus) 12/13/01 Vol. 25

love brings peace not by man's fighting (Jesus) 3/19/99 Vol. 14

love capacities use ability to love God more (Jesus) 7/13/00 Vol. 20

love enemies treat everyone equal (Jesus) 6/19/03 Vol. 31

love everyone despite bombings (Jesus) 11/20/03 Vol. 33

love everyone everyday of the year (Jesus) 2/9/06 Vol. 42

love everyone show your care for others (Jesus) 3/13/01 Vol. 22

love for God agape love (Jesus) 2/14/06 Vol. 42

love from heart needed in our actions (Jesus) 10/24/07 Vol. 49

love from the heart in prayers & actions (Jesus) 10/16/07 Vol. 49

love generously think from heart (Jesus) 10/6/07 Vol. 49

love God & man more desire things less (Jesus) 3/22/04 Vol. 34

love God & neighbor for salvation (Jesus) 8/10/03 Vol. 32

love God & neighbor reward great in heaven (Jesus) 10/2/03 Vol. 33

Love God always not just in obligation or need (Jesus) 7/19/04 Vol. 36

love God vs love world cannot have two masters (Jesus) 7/16/00 Vol. 20

love God, neighbor determines destiny (Jesus) 11/2/07 Vol. 49

love God, neighbor most valuable (Jesus) 11/24/07 Vol. 49

love in actions needed to show God (Jesus) 5/1/04 Vol. 35

love in daily prayers will gain eternal life (Jesus) 11/22/00 Vol. 21

love in heart gives order and peace (Jesus) 8/31/03 Vol. 32

love in heart necessary to enter heaven (Jesus) 12/23/98 Vol. 13

love in heart no room for anger (Jesus) 2/27/03 Vol. 30

love in heart true to follow law (Jesus) 10/31/98 Vol. 13

love in heart worth more than decorations (Jesus) 12/17/98 Vol. 13

love in voice avoid harsh judging,criticism (Jesus) 12/12/04 Vol. 37

love is missing in world of constant wars (Jesus) 3/20/04 Vol. 34

love letters prayers for petitions (Jesus) 11/15/97 Vol. 9

love link to God destroyed by sin (Jesus) 3/22/01 Vol. 22

love lived action needed to be perfected (Jesus) 2/24/02 Vol. 26

love message we limit His love (Jesus) 10/3/96 Vol. 5

love needed of God & neighbor (Jesus) 10/17/04 Vol. 37

love needed to gain heaven (Jesus) 1/13/05 Vol. 38

love needs reciprocation between man and God (Jesus) 5/11/00 Vol. 19

love neighbors instead of fighting them (Jesus) 12/27/01 Vol. 25

love not forced accommodate,tolerate others (Jesus) 6/19/03 Vol. 31

Love of God agape love (Jesus) 3/26/08 Vol. 50

love of God better than fear of punishment (Jesus) 1/5/05 Vol. 38

love of God create burning hearts of love (Jesus) 1/21/05 Vol. 38

love of God eternal, always available (Jesus) 3/4/04 Vol. 34

Love of God experienced in heaven (Jesus) 7/6/07 Vol. 48

love of God fulfilled in heaven (Jesus) 2/3/00 Vol. 18

Love of God give joy & peace (Jesus) 5/22/03 Vol. 31

love of God gives us everything (Jesus) 12/19/01 Vol. 25

love of God great enough to die for man (Jesus) 3/31/01 Vol. 22

love of God greatest desire of soul (Jesus) 2/22/06 Vol. 42

Love of God in gift of life (Jesus) 2/25/05 Vol. 38

love of God in suffering & death (Jesus) 10/20/05 Vol. 41

love of God like a marriage (Jesus) 2/1/03 Vol. 30

love of God measure of importance (Jesus) 11/14/07 Vol. 49

love of God more than world can offer (Jesus) 12/5/02 Vol. 29

love of God needed everyday of life (Jesus) 11/4/99 Vol. 17

Love of God needed more by mankind (Jesus) 3/21/04 Vol. 34

love of God root of all our desires (Jesus) 10/3/99 Vol. 17

love of God seeks us under every rock (Jesus) 3/11/01 Vol. 22

love of God shared in good example (Jesus) 7/20/00 Vol. 20

love of God sign of true Christian (Jesus) 1/14/00 Vol. 18

love of God sought, not punishment (Jesus) 4/11/07 Vol. 47

Love of God suffers for our sins (Jesus) 4/5/98 Vol. 11

love of God teach others by actions (Jesus) 1/20/05 Vol. 38

love of God through His Word (Jesus) 6/16/01 Vol. 23

Love of God vs. hate of Satan (God the Father) 11/24/99 Vol. 17

love of God & neighbor how life is judged (Jesus) 3/22/02 Vol. 26

love of God & neighbor needed for heaven (Jesus) 1/18/07 Vol. 46

love of God & others opportunity in each day for (Jesus) 3/18/04 Vol. 34

Love of God for man also permanent relationship (Jesus) 8/13/04 Vol. 36

love of God vs self live as a true Christian (Jesus) 2/11/01 Vol. 22

Love of God, family most important in life (Jesus) 2/20/08 Vol. 50

love of God, true requires Sunday worship,praise (Jesus) 3/27/04 Vol. 34

love of God,souls return God's love (Jesus) 6/16/00 Vol. 19

love of Jesus Do you love Me? (Jesus) 8/3/96 Vol. 4

love of Jesus heart of St.John's gospel (St. John) 11/1/98 Vol. 13

love of Jesus is unconditional (Jesus) 8/6/06 Vol. 44

love of Jesus love everyone, even enemies (Jesus) 12/21/03 Vol. 33

love of Jesus more peace & satisfaction (Jesus) 5/5/06 Vol. 43

love of Jesus only love to satisfy soul (Jesus) 4/5/99 Vol. 15

Love of Jesus protection from evil (Jesus)	9/13/06 Vol. 44
love of Jesus shown in death for sins (Jesus)	3/13/08 Vol. 50
love of neighbor accountable at judgment (Jesus)	11/16/07 Vol. 49
love of neighbor melts hate in hearts (Jesus)	7/20/00 Vol. 20
love of neighbor tested in helping their needs (Jesus)	5/31/00 Vol. 19
love of neighbor time, talent, money (Jesus)	11/5/07 Vol. 49
love of the Lord always on fire (Jesus)	12/29/07 Vol. 49
love of two persons needs to be unconditional (Jesus)	8/28/99 Vol. 16
love one another do not kill each other (Jesus)	8/12/04 Vol. 36
love relationship God chose us (Jesus)	2/25/01 Vol. 22
love relationships, building with God & neighbor (Jesus)	1/22/07 Vol. 46
love unconditionally gift of Christmas (Jesus)	12/20/00 Vol. 21
love unconditionally to follow Jesus (Jesus)	2/19/04 Vol. 34
love vs. hate Jesus vs. Satan (Jesus)	7/28/01 Vol. 24
love without self needed for perfection (Jesus)	9/14/99 Vol. 16
love your enemies difficult in the flesh (Jesus)	9/18/99 Vol. 16
love your enemies even terrorists (Jesus)	11/15/01 Vol. 25
love your enemies heal divisions (Jesus)	3/31/05 Vol. 38
love your neighbor and love your enemies (Jesus)	5/11/00 Vol. 19
love your persecutors encouraged by Jesus (Jesus)	11/6/99 Vol. 17
love your persecutors speak truth without fear (Jesus)	6/30/97 Vol. 7
love, binding force holds creation together (Jesus)	10/5/02 Vol. 29
love, bond of hold Church together (Jesus)	11/12/02 Vol. 29
love, conditional people need trust (Jesus)	2/28/07 Vol. 46
love, God & neighbor covenant of love (Jesus)	11/12/06 Vol. 45
love, quality of in heart for God important (Jesus)	5/20/04 Vol. 35
love, serve God to gain heaven (Jesus)	4/9/07 Vol. 47
love, shared cannot keep love to yourself (God the Father)	7/15/00 Vol. 20
love, unconditional Adoration, Communion (Jesus)	1/7/03 Vol. 30
love, unconditional even love persecutors (Jesus)	9/9/00 Vol. 20
love, unconditional return His love (Jesus)	7/30/01 Vol. 24
love, words of need for God & neighbor (Jesus)	2/13/05 Vol. 38
love,basis of life both spiritual, physical (Jesus)	9/14/99 Vol. 16
love,heavenly free will decision (Jesus)	4/2/99 Vol. 15
love,spread than anger, complaints (Jesus)	2/18/00 Vol. 18
loved by God all equally (Jesus)	5/8/03 Vol. 31
love's meanings erotic,filial,spiritual (Jesus)	2/14/01 Vol. 22
loving & hospitable to those in life (Jesus)	9/10/01 Vol. 24
loving vs. mean eyes satisfy soul or body (Jesus)	6/15/97 Vol. 7
low pay, no benefits employers called to justice (Jesus)	12/5/98 Vol. 13
lukewarm avoid being weak (Jesus)	7/19/04 Vol. 36
lukewarm easier to bring back (Jesus)	10/24/06 Vol. 45
lukewarm evangelize (St. Patrick)	7/1/96 Vol. 3
lukewarm God vomits from His mouth (Jesus)	6/9/04 Vol. 35
lukewarm lifeless,neither hot nor cold (Jesus)	7/26/98 Vol. 12
lukewarm need conversion, prayers (Jesus)	5/19/07 Vol. 47
lukewarm need love in your heart (Jesus)	12/29/07 Vol. 49

lukewarm on broad road to hell (Jesus)	11/19/98 Vol. 13
lukewarm only faithful to gain heaven (Jesus)	12/11/98 Vol. 13
lukewarm refuge Jesus' dinner (Jesus)	11/21/06 Vol. 45
lukewarm risk loss of soul in hell (Jesus)	8/9/02 Vol. 28
lukewarm souls present on Easter (Jesus)	4/20/06 Vol. 43
lukewarm spewed from His mouth (Jesus)	6/21/05 Vol. 39
lukewarm spewed out (Jesus)	10/9/05 Vol. 41
lukewarm & converts help to save souls (Jesus)	11/15/07 Vol. 49
lukewarm & weak sifted by the evil one (Jesus)	5/9/05 Vol. 39
lukewarm in danger those away from Mass (Jesus)	12/23/99 Vol. 17
lukewarm in faith spew from His mouth (Jesus)	1/5/04 Vol. 34
lukewarm priests responsible for souls (Jesus)	12/2/04 Vol. 37
lukewarm souls need prayers to return (Jesus)	5/17/07 Vol. 47
lukewarm souls not a part time God (Jesus)	1/12/02 Vol. 26
Luminous Cross give thanks and praise (Jesus)	3/20/06 Vol. 42
luminous cross healing at refuges (Jesus)	4/4/06 Vol. 43
luminous cross healing at refuges (Jesus)	2/25/07 Vol. 46
luminous cross healing at refuges (Jesus)	5/4/00 Vol. 19
luminous cross in Thermal, California (Jesus)	11/21/05 Vol. 41
luminous cross in Thermal, California (Jesus)	2/25/07 Vol. 46
luminous cross sign over refuges (Jesus)	2/25/08 Vol. 50
luminous cross Thermal, Calif., miracle (Jesus)	10/4/04 Vol. 37
Luminous Cross, Ca. gift shared with all (Jesus)	11/13/06 Vol. 45
Luminous Cross, Ca. third anniversary (Jesus)	2/9/05 Vol. 38
Luminous Cross, Ca. three crosses for Trinity (Jesus)	2/28/05 Vol. 38
luminous crosses at refuges (Jesus)	6/7/01 Vol. 23
luminous crosses at refuges (Jesus)	5/25/01 Vol. 23
luminous crosses at refuges for healing (Jesus)	8/15/03 Vol. 32
luminous crosses at refuges of protection (Jesus)	11/17/05 Vol. 41
luminous crosses healed by looking at (Jesus)	8/13/04 Vol. 36
luminous crosses healed when looked upon (Jesus)	11/4/05 Vol. 41
luminous crosses healings at refuges (Jesus)	7/20/05 Vol. 40
luminous crosses look at to be healed (Jesus)	6/21/05 Vol. 39
luminous crosses look at to be healed (Jesus)	5/5/05 Vol. 39
luminous crosses over protected refuges (Jesus)	9/26/00 Vol. 20
luminous crosses over refuges (Jesus)	3/15/05 Vol. 38
luminous crosses over refuges (Jesus)	2/4/08 Vol. 50
luminous crosses over refuges with healing (Jesus)	10/19/01 Vol. 25
luminous crosses protect refuges (Jesus)	9/6/03 Vol. 32
luminous crosses sign of hope & healing (Jesus)	4/17/03 Vol. 31
luminous crosses throughout tribulation (Jesus)	9/14/03 Vol. 32
luminous crosses will heal illnesses (Jesus)	9/7/06 Vol. 44
Luminous Mysteries attention to rosary (Jesus)	11/19/02 Vol. 29
lunar eclipse bad omen for America (Jesus)	10/27/04 Vol. 37
lunar eclipse sign of events to begin (Jesus)	6/7/01 Vol. 23
lung ailments spread by evil people (Jesus)	2/22/01 Vol. 22
lure of sin from Satan's lies (Jesus)	11/18/06 Vol. 45

Lyon, John Paul death of young child (Jesus)   2/4/06 Vol. 42

Maastrat Treaty the beast   8/19/93 Vol. 1

mad cow disease media scare on meat (Jesus)   12/25/03 Vol. 33

mad cow,foot & mouth spread to cause chaos (Jesus)   3/21/01 Vol. 22

Magesterium of Church to interpret Scripture (Jesus)   3/30/01 Vol. 22

Maggie Vest Carol's aunt (Maggie Vest)   11/2/02 Vol. 29

Magi gifts (Jesus)   1/2/94 Vol. 1

Magi gifts for Infant King (Jesus)   1/7/07 Vol. 46

Maginn, Ray funeral serve others while you can (Jesus)   10/30/06 Vol. 45

magisterium always obey (Jesus)   9/29/97 Vol. 8

Magisterium apostasy (Jesus)   6/3/94 Vol. 1

magisterium Church fathers (Jesus)   10/4/97 Vol. 9

magisterium commandments,traditions (Jesus)   10/20/97 Vol. 9

magnetic pole shifts spread Northern Lights (Jesus)   1/12/06 Vol. 42

Magnificat Ark of the Covenant (Jesus)   5/31/06 Vol. 43

Magnificat in liturgy of hours (Jesus)   5/31/01 Vol. 23

Magnificat of Mary evening prayer (Jesus)   5/31/07 Vol. 47

major event coming in fall season (Jesus)   8/4/07 Vol. 48

man custodian of the earth (Jesus)   12/6/04 Vol. 37

man as god with new computer chips (Jesus)   3/3/00 Vol. 18

man destroying nature abuses for money (Jesus)   6/4/07 Vol. 47

man returns to dust focus on heaven more (Jesus)   8/2/02 Vol. 28

mandatory chips avoid mind control (Jesus)   4/26/07 Vol. 47

mandatory chips control buying & selling (Jesus)   8/15/02 Vol. 28

mandatory chips rely on stored food (Jesus)   8/20/05 Vol. 40

mandatory chips in body time for refuge (Jesus)   3/28/08 Vol. 50

mandatory smart cards then chips in the body (Jesus)   8/31/06 Vol. 44

mandatory smart cards vote against (Jesus)   5/19/05 Vol. 39

manipulated prices by one world people (Jesus)   9/21/00 Vol. 20

manipulation of chips for buying and selling (Jesus)   12/27/99 Vol. 17

mankind has not changed (Jesus)   7/25/99 Vol. 16

man-made diseases for global control (Jesus)   11/5/03 Vol. 33

man-made diseases increased healing gifts (Jesus)   6/4/03 Vol. 31

man-made diseases to control population (Jesus)   11/8/05 Vol. 41

man-made event could trigger martial law (Jesus)   11/15/06 Vol. 45

man-made events near (Jesus)   8/4/07 Vol. 48

man-made incidents to come (Jesus)   6/20/07 Vol. 47

man-made old diseases population control, America (Jesus)   7/5/07 Vol. 48

man-made viruses threats to control people (Jesus)   12/12/05 Vol. 41

manna and food multiplied (Jesus)   12/28/97 Vol. 9

manna and food multiplied (Jesus)   6/17/99 Vol. 15

manna angels bring communion (Jesus)   2/8/98 Vol. 10

manna angels will provide (Jesus)   2/14/98 Vol. 10

manna at refuges (Jesus)   1/20/04 Vol. 34

manna brought by angels (Jesus)   8/8/97 Vol. 8

manna brought by angels (Jesus)   3/7/99 Vol. 14

manna by angels at refuges (Jesus)   5/8/02 Vol. 27

manna delivered by angels (Jesus)   5/12/97 Vol. 7

manna distributed by angels (Jesus)   4/11/01 Vol. 23

Manna fed miraculously at refuges (Jesus)   6/8/04 Vol. 35

manna from angels (Jesus)   3/24/03 Vol. 30

manna given by angels (Jesus)   8/3/03 Vol. 32

manna in hiding,detention centers (Jesus)   10/21/96 Vol. 5

manna in real presence (Jesus)   2/19/98 Vol. 10

manna in spiritual communion (Jesus)   1/12/01 Vol. 22

manna in tribulation (Jesus)   7/31/03 Vol. 32

manna in tribulation (Jesus)   8/17/97 Vol. 8

manna provided by angels (Jesus)   5/22/98 Vol. 11

manna provided by the angels (Jesus)   3/26/97 Vol. 6

manna provided in tribulation (Jesus)   10/9/97 Vol. 9

manna spiritual & physical food (Jesus)   7/18/97 Vol. 8

manna Spiritual Communion (Jesus)   1/12/98 Vol. 10

manna spiritual hunger,new earth (Jesus)   11/6/96 Vol. 5

manna spiritual weapons (Jesus)   5/11/96 Vol. 3

manna underground Masses (Jesus)   7/4/96 Vol. 3

manna when no Masses (Jesus)   2/2/99 Vol. 14

manna & water provided for survival (Jesus)   1/28/03 Vol. 30

manna & water provided in tribulation (Jesus)   7/31/01 Vol. 24

manna vs. chip trust in God,not Antichrist (Jesus)   12/2/97 Vol. 9

manna, heavenly eager to feed your soul (Jesus)   3/17/99 Vol. 14

manna, heavenly food for soul (Jesus)   11/7/02 Vol. 29

manna,water,meat at refuges (Jesus)   10/6/06 Vol. 45

Manning, Anne funeral (Jesus)   4/24/03 Vol. 31

man's abuses nature rebels (Jesus)   3/24/06 Vol. 42

man's beauty more than sunsets,mountains (Jesus)   3/22/01 Vol. 22

man's building nothing to God's creation (Jesus)   12/3/05 Vol. 41

man's call listen for God's voice (Jesus)   1/15/06 Vol. 42

man's free choice but accept consequences (Jesus)   12/5/05 Vol. 41

man's hands are imperfect (Jesus)   4/25/05 Vol. 39

man's justice corrupt,has no mercy (Jesus)   9/3/05 Vol. 40

man's justice less merciful than Jesus (Jesus)   6/21/99 Vol. 15

man's laws vs. God's laws (Jesus)   12/5/05 Vol. 41

man's pollution physical and spiritual (Jesus)   12/15/05 Vol. 41

man's pride in tall buildings (Jesus)   12/3/05 Vol. 41

man's sufferings joined with Jesus (Jesus)   4/6/06 Vol. 43

man's violence reflected in nature (Jesus)   10/25/07 Vol. 49

man's ways vs. God's ways (Jesus)   7/7/05 Vol. 40

mantle of protection by intercessory prayer (Mary)   5/9/99 Vol. 15

mantle of protection offered by Mary (Mary)   9/8/99 Vol. 16

mantle of protection over Mary's children (Mary)   8/15/99 Vol. 16

mantle of protection takes away your fear (Mary)   10/29/98 Vol. 13

manufacturers selling out workers (Jesus)   1/17/08 Vol. 50

manufacturers of today cutting corners on quality (Jesus)   5/24/02 Vol. 27

manufacturing base is lost (Jesus)   5/10/02 Vol. 27

manufacturing effected by war (Jesus)   2/6/03 Vol. 30
manufacturing decline from debts, wars, taxes (Jesus)   3/24/04 Vol. 34
manufacturing job loss causing lower wages (Jesus)   5/1/06 Vol. 43
manufacturing job losses could cause riots (Jesus)   2/2/06 Vol. 42
manufacturing jobs being destroyed by US policies (Jesus) 1/24/06 Vol. 42
manufacturing jobs decimated by free trade (Jesus)   8/22/02 Vol. 28
manufacturing jobs going to China (Jesus)   4/15/02 Vol. 27
manufacturing jobs lost to cheap labor (Jesus)   2/17/05 Vol. 38
manufacturing jobs moving to other countries (Jesus)   3/1/01 Vol. 22
manufacturing jobs lost because of companies' greed (Jesus) 7/25/02 Vol. 28
manufacturing layoffs still causing job losses (Jesus)   11/4/04 Vol. 37
maps for local roads (Jesus)   10/20/06 Vol. 45
maps of back roads to avoid check points (Jesus)   8/10/07 Vol. 48
Maracay incorrupt body warning (Jesus)   2/10/95 Vol. 2
Marci's holy ground (Mary)   6/23/95 Vol. 2
Margaret Farnand funeral Mass (Jesus)   10/20/07 Vol. 49
Margaret Mary Shine Baptism (Jesus)   4/28/07 Vol. 47
Maria Esperanza bless with rose petals (Jesus)   2/23/07 Vol. 46
Maria Esperanza death is a sign (Jesus)   8/12/04 Vol. 36
Maria Esperanza doing more in heaven (Maria E.)   8/14/07 Vol. 48
Maria Esperanza grace (Jesus)   2/26/94 Vol. 1
Maria Esperanza love (Jesus)   2/21/94 Vol. 1
Maria Esperanza poor (Jesus)   3/3/94 Vol. 1
Maria Esperanza unite in Communion of Saints (Maria Esperanza)
                                                               12/10/06 Vol. 45
Maria Fallone funeral message (Jesus)   4/13/04 Vol. 35
Maria intercessor water, rose pedals (Jesus)   12/21/06 Vol. 45
Marian Movement of priests pray for priests (Jesus)   5/2/02 Vol. 27
Marie Esperanza present to family, guests (Blessed Mother) 2/24/05 Vol. 38
marital law police state (Jesus)   3/14/03 Vol. 30
marital life help each other to salvation (Jesus)   8/11/00 Vol. 20
Mark give thanks for protection (Mark)   10/2/06 Vol. 45
Mark my guardian angel (Mark)   10/6/05 Vol. 41
Mark my guardian angel (Mark)   10/2/07 Vol. 49
Mark praise & adoration of God (Mark,angel)   6/28/01 Vol. 23
mark beast,smart cards set up by one world people (Jesus) 4/23/98 Vol. 11
mark of beast Antichrist's means of control (Jesus)   6/24/00 Vol. 19
mark of beast chips in passports,licenses (Jesus)   8/31/07 Vol. 48
mark of beast refuse chip in body (Jesus)   9/24/07 Vol. 48
mark of beast shown in Warning (Jesus)   1/6/05 Vol. 38
mark of beast to be worshipped in Church (Jesus)   7/13/01 Vol. 24
mark of the beast Advent OL of Mt. Carmel   11/29/95 Vol. 3
mark of the beast and mind control (Jesus)   11/3/05 Vol. 41
mark of the beast and smart cards (Jesus)   4/19/01 Vol. 23
mark of the beast angels and hiding (Jesus)   2/5/97 Vol. 6
mark of the beast Antichrist takeover (Jesus)   2/9/97 Vol. 6
mark of the beast avoid Antichrist's control (Jesus)   1/13/00 Vol. 18

mark of the beast avoid, at refuges (Jesus)   12/21/05 Vol. 41
mark of the beast buying & selling (Jesus)   3/30/97 Vol. 6
mark of the beast buying food (Jesus)   9/4/96 Vol. 4
mark of the beast chip gives Satan control (Jesus)   8/20/96 Vol. 4
mark of the beast chip in the body (Jesus)   6/22/04 Vol. 35
mark of the beast chip in the body (Jesus)   12/16/04 Vol. 37
mark of the beast chips are in place for (Jesus)   5/29/02 Vol. 27
mark of the beast chips for buying and selling (Jesus)   7/15/04 Vol. 36
mark of the beast chips in the hand (Jesus)   5/2/02 Vol. 27
mark of the beast computers (Jesus)   3/17/95 Vol. 2
mark of the beast control by Antichrist (Jesus)   5/10/03 Vol. 31
mark of the beast control the weak (Jesus)   1/5/02 Vol. 26
mark of the beast control through food (Jesus)   10/9/97 Vol. 9
mark of the beast crosses on foreheads (Jesus)   6/21/96 Vol. 3
mark of the beast designed to control people (Jesus)   9/21/98 Vol. 12
mark of the beast detention for Christians (Jesus)   12/16/99 Vol. 17
mark of the beast do not accept (Jesus)   2/22/99 Vol. 14
mark of the beast do not take (Jesus)   6/18/01 Vol. 23
mark of the beast do not take (Jesus)   6/1/02 Vol. 27
mark of the beast do not take (Jesus)   6/9/99 Vol. 15
mark of the beast do not take (Jesus)   7/27/99 Vol. 16
mark of the beast do not take chips (Jesus)   4/15/03 Vol. 31
mark of the beast do not take for food,etc. (Jesus)   2/18/99 Vol. 14
mark of the beast do not take it (Jesus)   1/5/98 Vol. 10
mark of the beast do not take it (Jesus)   9/3/98 Vol. 12
mark of the beast do not take to buy and sell (Jesus)   4/16/98 Vol. 11
mark of the beast don't take or worship (Jesus)   6/10/99 Vol. 15
mark of the beast electrical control (Jesus)   2/13/97 Vol. 6
Mark of the Beast electronic buying & selling (Jesus)   10/6/96 Vol. 5
Mark of the Beast electronic chips (Jesus)   12/22/96 Vol. 5
mark of the beast flee into hiding,refuse mark (Jesus)   11/12/98 Vol. 13
mark of the beast for buying & selling (Jesus)   10/7/99 Vol. 17
mark of the beast for buying & selling (Jesus)   7/1/99 Vol. 16
mark of the beast for buying and selling (Jesus)   6/2/01 Vol. 23
mark of the beast for buying food (Jesus)   7/8/99 Vol. 16
mark of the beast for identity theft (Jesus)   12/1/03 Vol. 33
mark of the beast for money and food (Jesus)   7/18/99 Vol. 16
mark of the beast for the worldly (Jesus)   8/20/01 Vol. 24
mark of the beast forced to worship (Jesus)   1/14/99 Vol. 14
Mark of the beast gestapo tactics (Jesus)   10/19/96 Vol. 5
mark of the beast hell on earth & below (Jesus)   8/15/99 Vol. 16
mark of the beast hiding (Jesus)   6/20/94 Vol. 1
mark of the beast hiding and signs (Jesus)   3/22/96 Vol. 3
mark of the beast hiding in caves (Jesus)   5/16/94 Vol. 1
mark of the beast hiding, detention centers (Jesus)   12/19/95 Vol. 3
mark of the beast in computer chips (Jesus)   1/31/00 Vol. 18
mark of the beast is real from Antichrist (Jesus)   10/1/98 Vol. 13

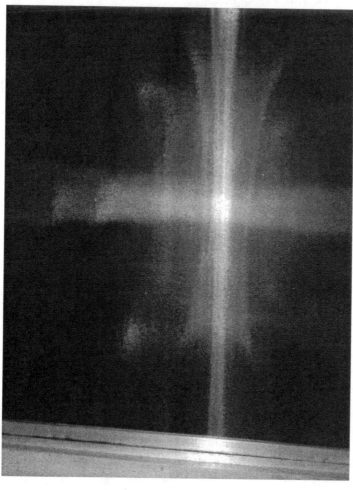

The Luminous Cross

mark of the beast leads people to hell (Jesus)	10/27/99 Vol. 17	mark of the beast persecution (Jesus)	5/8/94 Vol. 1
mark of the beast linked to chip in the hand (Jesus)	6/14/00 Vol. 19	mark of the beast prison camps,martial law (Jesus)	11/18/99 Vol. 17
mark of the beast lost forever if taken (Jesus)	3/28/03 Vol. 30	mark of the beast puppet on a string (Jesus)	9/20/99 Vol. 16
mark of the beast mandatory, refuge time (Jesus)	6/19/06 Vol. 43	mark of the beast ready to be deployed (Jesus)	2/3/97 Vol. 6
mark of the beast martyrs for speaking against (Jesus)	7/18/02 Vol. 28	mark of the beast refuse at all costs (Jesus)	5/14/99 Vol. 15
mark of the beast mind control (Jesus)	8/24/00 Vol. 20	mark of the beast refuse chip in the hand (Jesus)	11/20/97 Vol. 9
mark of the beast new forbidden fruit (Jesus)	6/7/97 Vol. 7	mark of the beast refuse chips in hand (Jesus)	9/7/99 Vol. 16
mark of the beast new forbidden fruit (Jesus)	2/12/99 Vol. 14	mark of the beast refuse even if killed (Jesus)	6/16/06 Vol. 43
mark of the beast new money system (Jesus)	3/2/99 Vol. 14	mark of the beast refuse even if martyred (Jesus)	11/30/00 Vol. 21
mark of the beast or chips in the hand (Jesus)	6/24/04 Vol. 35	mark of the beast refuse even if martyred (Jesus)	10/6/98 Vol. 13
mark of the beast outlaws if you refuse to take (Jesus)	4/30/98 Vol. 11	mark of the beast refuse even to death (Jesus)	2/3/03 Vol. 30
mark of the beast owners to suffer hell on earth (Jesus)	7/18/98 Vol. 12	mark of the beast refuse for buying & selling (Jesus)	6/13/02 Vol. 27
mark of the beast people will suffer most (Jesus)	2/10/99 Vol. 14	mark of the beast refuse on hand,forehead (Jesus)	4/18/99 Vol. 15
mark of the beast persecuted for refusing (Jesus)	10/18/99 Vol. 17	mark of the beast refuse or be lost (Jesus)	7/8/05 Vol. 40

mark of the beast refuse smart chip in body (Jesus) — 11/24/99 Vol. 17
mark of the beast refuse to take chip (Jesus) — 11/16/05 Vol. 41
mark of the beast refuse,lose of possessions (Jesus) — 5/6/00 Vol. 19
mark of the beast resisting, foolish to world (Jesus) — 2/2/00 Vol. 18
mark of the beast revealed in the Warning (Jesus) — 10/12/99 Vol. 17
mark of the beast same chip as smart card (Jesus) — 5/28/99 Vol. 15
mark of the beast take or imprisoned,tortured (Jesus) — 7/2/98 Vol. 12
mark of the beast taking,road to hell (Jesus) — 3/8/00 Vol. 18
mark of the beast test of faith,persecution (Jesus) — 3/27/96 Vol. 3
mark of the beast the new apple (Jesus) — 2/20/99 Vol. 14
mark of the beast time of hiding (Jesus) — 8/18/99 Vol. 16
mark of the beast to buy and sell (Jesus) — 8/8/97 Vol. 8
mark of the beast to buy and sell (Jesus) — 4/26/01 Vol. 23
Mark of the Beast to buy and sell (Jesus) — 1/7/99 Vol. 14
mark of the beast to control minds & souls (Jesus) — 8/24/01 Vol. 24
mark of the beast to control the people (Jesus) — 6/17/99 Vol. 15
mark of the beast to restrict travel (Jesus) — 1/21/00 Vol. 18
mark of the beast under control of Antichrist (Jesus) — 6/8/98 Vol. 11
mark of the beast used to buy and sell (Jesus) — 6/4/98 Vol. 11
mark of the beast vulnerable to interference (Jesus) — 9/18/98 Vol. 12
mark of the beast warning, hiding (Jesus) — 5/15/97 Vol. 7
mark of the beast will cause loss of soul (Jesus) — 2/11/00 Vol. 18
mark of the beast will suffer hell on earth (Jesus) — 5/21/99 Vol. 15
mark of the beast will suffer the most (Jesus) — 6/18/99 Vol. 15
mark of the beast will try to force on all (Jesus) — 1/27/01 Vol. 22
mark of the beast worship of Antichrist (Jesus) — 3/16/96 Vol. 3
mark of the beast,chips do not take (Jesus) — 8/4/06 Vol. 44
mark, famine reason for food reserves (Jesus) — 3/27/00 Vol. 18
mark,accepted suffering here and in hell (Jesus) — 11/9/00 Vol. 21
Mark,angel personal protection (Mark) — 6/29/01 Vol. 23
mark,chip needed in hand for jobs,buying (Jesus) — 4/7/99 Vol. 15
marked by angels trumpets for plagues (Jesus) — 3/12/99 Vol. 14
markets manipulated to steal retirement money (Jesus) — 8/22/02 Vol. 28
Marmora Greenside's farm a refuge (Jesus) — 6/5/05 Vol. 39
Marmora holy ground place (Mary) — 2/22/98 Vol. 10
Marmora Our Lady of Mt. Carmel (Mary) — 9/6/97 Vol. 8
Marmora grotto verified by rain (Mary) — 9/8/99 Vol. 16
Marmora pilgrimage Mary's birthday (Mary) — 9/8/99 Vol. 16
Marmora, Canada a refuge place (Jesus) — 10/6/06 Vol. 45
Marmora, Canada holy ground (Mary) — 10/11/96 Vol. 5
marriage a lifetime commitment (Jesus) — 2/25/00 Vol. 18
marriage as Christ loves the Church (Jesus) — 1/26/02 Vol. 26
marriage as God loves the Church (Jesus) — 8/27/97 Vol. 8
marriage as permanent commitment (Jesus) — 8/13/04 Vol. 36
marriage avoid sinful relationships (Jesus) — 8/17/07 Vol. 48
marriage churches (Jesus) — 5/5/94 Vol. 1
marriage commitment to vows (Jesus) — 3/2/00 Vol. 18

marriage constant renewal of faith (Jesus) — 7/3/06 Vol. 44
marriage Covenant relationships (Mary) — 7/19/97 Vol. 8
marriage do not defile,sacred union (Jesus) — 8/18/06 Vol. 44
marriage do not violate sacredness (Jesus) — 1/9/99 Vol. 14
marriage endures with love of God,spouse (Jesus) — 1/18/04 Vol. 34
marriage example of God's love (Jesus) — 8/24/03 Vol. 32
marriage family — 11/6/93 Vol. 1
marriage for only man & woman (Jesus) — 1/14/07 Vol. 46
marriage for procreation of human race (Jesus) — 10/22/00 Vol. 21
marriage God as third person (Jesus) — 8/11/00 Vol. 20
marriage God's love relationship (Jesus) — 1/7/99 Vol. 14
marriage graces of (Jesus) — 7/3/02 Vol. 28
marriage intended by God (Jesus) — 10/5/03 Vol. 33
marriage Jim & Lill Anniversary (Jesus) — 8/25/95 Vol. 3
marriage keep Jesus as center (Jesus) — 10/15/01 Vol. 25
marriage lessons for success (Jesus) — 8/11/96 Vol. 4
marriage life (Jesus) — 5/13/95 Vol. 2
marriage love spouse as they are (Jesus) — 5/15/05 Vol. 39
marriage need full commitment (Jesus) — 11/10/02 Vol. 29
marriage need to be preserved in love (Jesus) — 9/12/98 Vol. 12
marriage needs loving communication (Jesus) — 1/13/05 Vol. 38
marriage only for man & woman (Jesus) — 7/16/05 Vol. 40
marriage place of Jesus' 1st miracle (Jesus) — 1/7/06 Vol. 42
marriage priesthood (Jesus) — 8/12/94 Vol. 2
marriage respect & be committed (Jesus) — 6/2/99 Vol. 15
marriage stay faithful to vows (Jesus) — 6/10/01 Vol. 23
marriage torn by divorce,living together (Jesus) — 2/22/01 Vol. 22
marriage total commitment in love (Jesus) — 7/4/04 Vol. 36
marriage trust between spouses,true love (Jesus) — 10/24/04 Vol. 37
marriage union,gift of love to spouses (Jesus) — 7/29/98 Vol. 12
marriage unity in family (Jesus) — 7/3/97 Vol. 8
Marriage use grace of sacrament (Jesus) — 2/16/99 Vol. 14
marriage vocations, love (Jesus) — 2/9/97 Vol. 6
marriage ways to make it work (Jesus) — 10/8/06 Vol. 45
marriage & divorce life commitment needed (Jesus) — 2/24/06 Vol. 42
marriage & faith not taken lightly (Jesus) — 9/17/05 Vol. 40
marriage & family perpetuates the faith (Jesus) — 8/24/05 Vol. 40
marriage bed for love and not lust (Jesus) — 7/16/05 Vol. 40
marriage bond Church as spouse (Jesus) — 6/22/96 Vol. 3
marriage bond do not violate (Jesus) — 4/30/98 Vol. 11
marriage bond love of God & spouse (Jesus) — 5/27/00 Vol. 19
marriage defended in election vote (Jesus) — 11/3/04 Vol. 37
marriage grace protects the couple (Jesus) — 7/8/00 Vol. 20
marriage is for life faithful instead of divorce (Jesus) — 5/27/00 Vol. 19
marriage mockery committing adultery (Jesus) — 2/28/01 Vol. 22
marriage mockery same sex,divorces,US ruin (Jesus) — 9/30/98 Vol. 12
marriage need daily commitment (Jesus) — 5/20/06 Vol. 43

marriage, attacks on infidelity,abuse,drunkenness (Jesus) 8/18/05 Vol. 40
marriage, enduring my 40th anniversary (Jesus) 7/3/05 Vol. 40
marriage, long example of true love (Jesus) 5/15/05 Vol. 39
marriage, relic family,society's blueprint (Jesus) 12/27/98 Vol. 13
marriages be true to vows (Jesus) 2/27/03 Vol. 30
marriages God as third partner (Jesus) 6/7/01 23
marriages place in God's hands (Jesus) 6/1/05 Vol. 39
marriages pray for (Jesus) 6/4/99 Vol. 15
marriages stay faithful (Jesus) 2/11/07 Vol. 46
marriages of love faithful to vocation (Jesus) 4/26/05 Vol. 39
marriages, quick less chance of lasting (Jesus) 10/31/06 Vol. 45
married in grace instead of fornication (Jesus) 8/12/05 Vol. 40
married life only place for relations (Jesus) 12/11/07 Vol. 49
married love deepest emotions (Jesus) 9/4/04 Vol. 36
married love like God has for His Church (Jesus) 4/29/05 Vol. 39
married love like God's love of Church (Jesus) 11/4/01 Vol. 25
married love self-giving, nothing in return (Jesus) 10/26/04 Vol. 37
married spouses blessed to have each other (Jesus) 11/4/01 Vol. 25
marry in Church than live in fornication (Jesus) 2/24/06 Vol. 42
Mars closeness sign of war (Jesus) 8/27/03 Vol. 32
Mars man as spec in space (Jesus) 7/6/97 Vol. 8
Mars rocks in perspective to earth (Jesus) 2/12/04 Vol. 34
Mars & moon appreciate creation (Jesus) 1/7/04 Vol. 34
Martha & Mary faith and works (Jesus) 10/10/06 Vol. 45
Martha & Mary love of God & neighbor (Jesus) 7/18/04 Vol. 36
martial law after EMP attack (Jesus) 10/31/06 Vol. 45
martial law after storms & layoffs (Jesus) 9/29/98 Vol. 12
martial law against patriots & religious (Jesus) 11/9/04 Vol. 37
martial law beginning of takeover (God the Father) 11/13/00 Vol. 21
martial law being prepared for (Jesus) 6/10/99 Vol. 15
martial law by created emergency (Jesus) 2/12/00 Vol. 18
martial law come to your home (Jesus) 1/7/99 Vol. 14
martial law coming takeover of America (Jesus) 4/14/05 Vol. 39
martial law control of main highways (Jesus) 8/10/07 Vol. 48
martial law could be initiated (Jesus) 2/4/99 Vol. 14
martial law create an incident for (Jesus) 8/10/06 Vol. 44
martial law end of America (Jesus) 11/27/07 Vol. 49
martial law excuses for emergency (Jesus) 7/19/01 Vol. 24
martial law fiat tyranny (Jesus) 7/4/98 Vol. 12
martial law forced chips in body (Jesus) 4/23/07 Vol. 47
martial law foreign troops of UN deployed (Jesus) 10/19/00 Vol. 21
martial law fortunate to have elections (Jesus) 9/20/07 Vol. 48
martial law freedoms taken away (Jesus) 11/23/98 Vol. 13
martial law from chem trail epidemic (Jesus) 7/5/07 Vol. 48
martial law from created event (Jesus) 10/17/07 Vol. 49
martial law from financial collapse (Jesus) 1/2/07 Vol. 46
martial law implement executive orders (Jesus) 9/20/98 Vol. 12

martial law in takeover of country (Jesus) 10/4/06 Vol. 45
martial law insurance & federal aid (Jesus) 1/6/97 Vol. 6
martial law is close (Jesus) 7/25/03 Vol. 32
martial law leave for refuges (Jesus) 2/8/08 Vol. 50
martial law leave for refuges (Jesus) 10/3/07 Vol. 49
martial law leave home ahead of (Jesus) 2/7/08 Vol. 50
martial law lives are in danger (Jesus) 10/15/07 Vol. 49
martial law more authority to military (Jesus) 10/3/05 Vol. 41
martial law need prayers for peace (Jesus) 10/7/00 Vol. 21
martial law no rights under (Jesus) 2/5/08 Vol. 50
martial law one world takeover (Jesus) 4/8/06 Vol. 43
martial law police state for order (Jesus) 4/29/99 Vol. 15
martial law possible before presidential vote (Jesus) 7/30/06 Vol. 44
martial law prepare to leave for refuges (Jesus) 11/21/07 Vol. 49
martial law prepared lists for prison (Jesus) 8/25/07 Vol. 48
martial law pretext of one worlders (Jesus) 9/22/06 Vol. 44
martial law punishment for sins (Jesus) 2/3/00 Vol. 18
martial law remove religious & patriots (Jesus) 4/14/05 Vol. 39
martial law requires emergency declared (Jesus) 7/7/00 Vol. 20
martial law result of major insurrection (Jesus) 12/4/98 Vol. 13
martial law secret capture of leaders before (Jesus) 4/15/05 Vol. 39
martial law start of Antichrist takeover (Jesus) 1/28/99 Vol. 14
martial law takeover coming quickly (Jesus) 8/24/06 Vol. 44
martial law takeover in disaster (Jesus) 7/5/06 Vol. 44
martial law terrorism & looting (Jesus) 1/15/99 Vol. 14
martial law through weather,food shortage (Jesus) 5/31/00 Vol. 19
martial law time for refuge (Jesus) 3/28/08 Vol. 50
martial law time for refuges (Jesus) 7/28/07 Vol. 48
martial law time to go to refuges (Jesus) 11/15/06 Vol. 45
martial law to being police state (Jesus) 10/27/99 Vol. 17
martial law to control riots (Jesus) 6/9/99 Vol. 15
martial law to control travel (Jesus) 10/18/04 Vol. 37
martial law to force chips in the body (Jesus) 8/20/05 Vol. 40
martial law to takeover country (Jesus) 2/7/08 Vol. 50
martial law to threaten Christians (Jesus) 11/17/99 Vol. 17
martial law to use electricity, shutdown (Jesus) 7/28/07 Vol. 48
martial law tribulation to follow soon (Jesus) 10/28/99 Vol. 17
martial law warning of start coming (Jesus) 11/29/06 Vol. 45
martial law when economy collapses (Jesus) 1/4/04 Vol. 34
martial law will strike quickly (Jesus) 10/3/03 Vol. 33
martial law pickup before & after declaration (Jesus) 6/8/07 Vol. 47
martial law preparations made by one world people (Jesus) 9/22/04 Vol. 36
martial law takeover already planned (Jesus) 5/30/07 Vol. 47
martial law, chips end of America (Jesus) 11/28/07 Vol. 49
martial law, chips time to flee to refuges (Jesus) 11/2/07 Vol. 49
martial law,national ID path to Antichrist control (Jesus) 9/27/01 Vol. 24
martial law,UN troops one world control (Jesus) 3/21/00 Vol. 18

martyr better to die than be lost (Jesus) — 6/18/99 Vol. 15

martyr mark of the beast (Jesus) — 12/2/94 Vol. 2

martyr willingness to be one (Jesus) — 12/28/99 Vol. 17

martyrdom a call to sainthood (Jesus) — 10/17/99 Vol. 17

martyrdom are willing to die for your faith? (Jesus) — 6/22/05 Vol. 39

martyrdom as early Christians (Jesus) — 1/6/01 Vol. 22

martyrdom better than loss of soul (Jesus) — 2/18/99 Vol. 14

martyrdom by public execution (Jesus) — 9/5/02 Vol. 28

martyrdom came to some prophets (Jesus) — 8/7/07 Vol. 48

martyrdom challenge during evil control (Jesus) — 11/1/02 Vol. 29

martyrdom disciples tested again (Jesus) — 4/27/04 Vol. 35

martyrdom do not be afraid (Jesus) — 4/20/98 Vol. 11

martyrdom for defending the faith (Jesus) — 12/16/97 Vol. 9

martyrdom for faithful (Jesus) — 3/1/07 Vol. 46

martyrdom for those faithful not hiding (Jesus) — 4/2/98 Vol. 11

martyrdom given endurance, saints (Jesus) — 3/13/03 Vol. 30

martyrdom given grace to endure (Jesus) — 5/9/98 Vol. 11

martyrdom great tidal wave (Jesus) — 7/4/96 Vol. 3

martyrdom heresies, modernists (Jesus) — 6/2/03 Vol. 31

martyrdom in evangelization (Jesus) — 7/25/02 Vol. 28

martyrdom inspires our faith (Jesus) — 6/3/06 Vol. 43

martyrdom instant heavenly reward (Jesus) — 3/20/99 Vol. 14

martyrdom instant sainthood (Jesus) — 6/29/03 Vol. 31

martyrdom instant saints (Jesus) — 7/16/03 Vol. 32

martyrdom messengers & prophets (Jesus) — 10/17/96 Vol. 5

martyrdom pain will be softened (Jesus) — 7/23/98 Vol. 12

martyrdom possible for faith (Jesus) — 6/22/06 Vol. 43

martyrdom prophets persecuted (Jesus) — 1/14/98 Vol. 10

martyrdom public executions (Jesus) — 10/7/03 Vol. 33

martyrdom real possibility in future (Jesus) — 8/29/03 Vol. 32

martyrdom some called to (Jesus) — 9/2/97 Vol. 8

martyrdom souls given grace to endure (Jesus) — 8/12/04 Vol. 36

martyrdom strengthened by faith (Jesus) — 2/12/04 Vol. 34

martyrdom strengthened to endure (Jesus) — 10/19/02 Vol. 29

martyrdom suffering (Jesus) — 10/7/95 Vol. 3

martyrdom test of faith (Jesus) — 4/30/01 Vol. 23

martyrdom to stay faithful (Jesus) — 3/26/98 Vol. 10

martyrdom was through heavenly gates (Jesus) — 5/4/06 Vol. 43

martyrdom when example to others (Jesus) — 9/26/03 Vol. 32

martyrdom will lessen pain (Jesus) — 6/18/99 Vol. 15

martyrdom with courage & bravery (Jesus) — 7/8/03 Vol. 32

martyrdom for faith be prepared to die for faith (Jesus) — 9/9/01 Vol. 24

martyrdom for faith better to be saint than in hell (Jesus) — 10/12/00 Vol. 21

martyrdom in tribulation pray for endurance (Jesus) — 8/20/05 Vol. 40

martyrdom or hell choice in tribulation (Jesus) — 5/31/04 Vol. 35

martyrdom threat from Antichrist in tribulation (Jesus) — 3/28/07 Vol. 46

martyrdom,persecution for His Name's sake (Jesus) — 3/10/99 Vol. 14

martyred choose — 10/10/93 Vol. 1

martyred & tortured for not taking mark (Jesus) — 3/2/99 Vol. 14

martyrs and refuges for others (Jesus) — 1/2/06 Vol. 42

martyrs are instant saints (Jesus) — 2/18/07 Vol. 46

martyrs Auriesville (Kateri T.) — 9/16/93 Vol. 1

martyrs become instant saints (Jesus) — 1/9/08 Vol. 50

martyrs beheaded (Jesus) — 6/9/05 Vol. 39

martyrs beheadings,killing Christians (Jesus) — 11/24/04 Vol. 37

martyrs born and unborn (Jesus) — 10/12/02 Vol. 29

martyrs die before taking chips (Jesus) — 9/9/99 Vol. 16

martyrs during tribulation (Jesus) — 7/10/02 Vol. 28

martyrs examples to the rest (Jesus) — 5/2/02 Vol. 27

martyrs for belief in Jesus (Jesus) — 6/16/05 Vol. 39

martyrs for God not terrorism (Jesus) — 12/3/03 Vol. 33

martyrs for the faith (Jesus) — 6/22/04 Vol. 35

martyrs for those not leaving soon (Jesus) — 1/15/04 Vol. 34

martyrs go immediately to heaven (Jesus) — 5/29/97 Vol. 7

martyrs hiding (Jesus) — 6/30/95 Vol. 2

martyrs in new era of peace (Jesus) — 10/7/97 Vol. 9

martyrs in New Jerusalem (Jesus) — 6/18/01 Vol. 23

martyrs in persecution (Jesus) — 7/21/98 Vol. 12

martyrs in tribulation (Jesus) — 9/28/00 Vol. 20

martyrs instant saints (Jesus) — 2/5/03 Vol. 30

martyrs instant saints (Jesus) — 4/7/05 Vol. 39

martyrs instant saints (Jesus) — 4/20/99 Vol. 15

martyrs life (St. Josephat) — 11/12/93 Vol. 1

martyrs many to give lives (Jesus) — 6/13/02 Vol. 27

martyrs may have to die for faith (Jesus) — 1/13/06 Vol. 42

martyrs North American, rewarded (Jesus) — 10/19/06 Vol. 45

martyrs price of faith (Jesus) — 1/18/01 Vol. 22

martyrs raised in glorified bodies (Jesus) — 11/25/97 Vol. 9

martyrs raised up in Era of Peace (Jesus) — 7/18/98 Vol. 12

martyrs receive instant sainthood (Jesus) — 1/21/04 Vol. 34

martyrs redemptive suffering (Jesus) — 6/20/02 Vol. 27

martyrs saints for God (Jesus) — 8/14/02 Vol. 28

martyrs special place in heaven (Jesus) — 8/14/01 Vol. 24

martyrs to come in tribulation (Jesus) — 8/10/98 Vol. 12

martyrs witnesses of faith (Jesus) — 7/23/98 Vol. 12

martyrs would we die for Jesus? (Jesus) — 2/5/07 Vol. 46

martyrs & faithful go straight to heaven (Jesus) — 10/8/04 Vol. 37

martyrs' blood religious persecution (Jesus) — 12/16/99 Vol. 17

martyrs for Christ proclaim faith over death (Jesus) — 5/18/00 Vol. 19

martyrs for Christ victims of persecution (Jesus) — 8/24/99 Vol. 16

martyrs for faith Christian killed today (Jesus) — 10/19/04 Vol. 37

mar. in tribulation for not worshiping beast,no mark (Jesus) 9/1/04 Vol. 36

martyrs in tribulation religious & patriots sought (Jesus) — 7/5/05 Vol. 40

martyrs of tribulation to suffer little pain (Jesus) — 12/22/99 Vol. 17

martyrs today pray for strength (Jesus) — 11/24/01 Vol. 25

martyrs vindicated in Rome and judgment (Jesus) — 12/1/04 Vol. 37

martyrs, protected at refuges (Jesus) — 5/24/00 Vol. 19

Mary as new Eve (Mary) — 2/13/99 Vol. 14

Mary fewer visits,purpose done (Mary) — 7/23/98 Vol. 12

Mary graces of the Holy Spirit (Mary) — 5/21/98 Vol. 11

Mary intercedes for us (Mary) — 5/6/98 Vol. 11

Mary intercedes for us (Mary) — 8/14/99 Vol. 16

Mary our heavenly mother (Jesus) — 9/12/06 Vol. 44

Mary protect during tribulation (Jesus) — 6/12/99 Vol. 15

Mary rosary — 8/11/93 Vol. 1

Mary thanks for rosaries,pictures (Mary) — 6/18/98 Vol. 11

Mary & Zachariah response to angel messages (Jesus) — 6/23/07 Vol. 47

Mary and John Behold your mother (Jesus) — 8/27/93 Vol. 1

Mary and Martha faith and trust (Jesus) — 7/19/98 Vol. 12

Mary Ann Magin Stewart funeral (Jesus) — 7/12/06 Vol. 44

Mary as New Eve to defeat Satan (Jesus) — 10/5/98 Vol. 13

Mary Bistrica Shrine Croatian refuge (Jesus) — 7/12/02 Vol. 28

Mary Burke funeral right to life defender (Jesus) — 1/6/07 Vol. 46

Mary dressed in sun from Jesus in womb (Mary) — 4/24/97 Vol. 7

Mary Ellen Frisch funeral message (Mary Ellen) — 11/26/05 Vol. 41

Mary Magdalene be persistent as her in faith (Jesus) — 7/22/04 Vol. 36

Mary Magdalene heresy in Divinci Code (Jesus) — 5/19/06 Vol. 43

Mary not coming mission of warning waning (Jesus) — 4/1/00 Vol. 19

Mary Reilich Carmelite friends (Jesus) — 4/18/06 Vol. 43

Mary, Blessed Mother imitate her life (Jesus) — 10/7/03 Vol. 33

Mary, Blessed Virgin handmaid of God (Jesus) — 8/22/05 Vol. 40

Mary, new Eve lived in Divine Will (Jesus) — 8/15/02 Vol. 28

Mary, new Eve mother of mankind (Mary) — 2/11/00 Vol. 18

Mary, sinless no predisposition to sin (Jesus) — 12/9/02 Vol. 29

Mary,prophets announcing 2nd coming (Jesus) — 6/24/99 Vol. 15

Mary-free of sin original and actual (Mary) — 12/8/98 Vol. 13

Mary's birth crown of purity (Mary) — 12/8/98 Vol. 13

Mary's encouragement take rosaries,not arms (Mary) — 3/23/06 Vol. 42

Mary's mantle in rosary & scapular (Jesus) — 5/18/06 Vol. 43

Mary's mantle protection through rosary (Jesus) — 3/21/00 Vol. 18

Mary's Pilgrims be good example (Jesus) — 12/1/00 Vol. 21

Mary's Pilgrims protected in China (Jesus) — 10/9/01 Vol. 25

Mary's Pilgrims to China,Russia,Japan (Jesus) — 4/16/01 Vol. 23

Mary's Triumph preparing to battle Antichrist (Jesus) — 10/5/98 Vol. 13

Mary's Triumph Satan's head crushed (Mary) — 10/3/98 Vol. 13

Mary's yes braved stoning (Jesus) — 12/18/07 Vol. 49

Mary's yes no mere accident (Jesus) — 3/25/00 Vol. 18

Mary's Yes ripple throughout history (Jesus) — 12/19/99 Vol. 17

masks needed protect from virus (Jesus) — 11/17/06 Vol. 45

masonic elements to remove real presence (Jesus) — 11/9/98 Vol. 13

Masonic elements undermining the Church (Jesus) — 10/25/98 Vol. 13

masonic order central bankers,one worlders (Jesus) — 12/21/03 Vol. 33

masons abuse power and money (Jesus) — 1/24/02 Vol. 26

masons among clergy (Mary) — 9/8/98 Vol. 12

masons as politicians (Jesus) — 5/17/03 Vol. 31

masons attack in Church (Jesus) — 6/4/04 Vol. 35

masons attacking the Church (Jesus) — 12/12/99 Vol. 17

masons behind removing reverence (Jesus) — 7/4/02 Vol. 28

masons changes in Church (Jesus) — 1/12/99 Vol. 14

masons control banks & leaders (Jesus) — 12/7/00 Vol. 21

masons control by one world people (Jesus) — 5/23/98 Vol. 11

masons control government & money (Jesus) — 7/31/02 Vol. 28

masons controls US as punishment (Jesus) — 4/25/03 Vol. 31

masons Egypt (Dina C.) — 11/15/95 Vol. 3

masons encouraging wars (Jesus) — 7/7/03 Vol. 32

masons evil influence in Church (Jesus) — 8/20/04 Vol. 36

masons get power from Satan (Jesus) — 11/1/05 Vol. 41

masons hide evil deeds (Jesus) — 7/7/02 Vol. 28

masons in Church,New Age,homosexuals (Jesus) — 8/16/04 Vol. 36

masons in the Church (Jesus) — 7/15/02 Vol. 28

masons inside church (Jesus) — 9/7/03 Vol. 32

masons leading clergy away (Jesus) — 2/14/03 Vol. 30

masons one world control (Jesus) — 10/26/97 Vol. 9

masons One World Order (Jesus) — 6/4/98 Vol. 11

masons plan for world takeover (Jesus) — 4/14/03 Vol. 31

masons power and money (Jesus) — 6/17/96 Vol. 3

masons profit from killing (Jesus) — 11/25/02 Vol. 29

masons run schismatic church (Jesus) — 7/15/03 Vol. 32

masons secret meeting plans (Jesus) — 1/21/04 Vol. 34

masons seek worldly power (Jesus) — 4/23/98 Vol. 11

masons sharing wealth is real value (Jesus) — 8/13/98 Vol. 12

masons stripped churches (Jesus) — 4/25/03 Vol. 31

masons stripping churches (Jesus) — 4/15/05 Vol. 39

masons to take over the world (Jesus) — 10/10/06 Vol. 45

masons try to control Vatican (Jesus) — 6/16/99 Vol. 15

masons trying to destroy Church (Jesus) — 7/20/02 Vol. 28

masons use war,economy,& terrorism (Jesus) — 7/24/03 Vol. 32

masons want US military neutralized (Jesus) — 12/17/01 Vol. 25

masons will control food & jobs (Jesus) — 6/23/02 Vol. 27

masons work with the Antichrist (Jesus) — 5/22/98 Vol. 11

masons worship Satan (God the Father) — 8/20/03 Vol. 32

masons worship the demonic (Jesus) — 3/8/01 Vol. 22

masons & bankers fund dictators (Jesus) — 3/7/03 Vol. 30

masons & central bankers behind wars for money (Jesus) — 4/29/04 Vol. 35

masons & New Age in European Union (Jesus) — 6/9/05 Vol. 39

masons & rich to take over the world (Jesus) — 12/21/01 Vol. 25

masons in Church removing statues, tabernacles (Jesus) — 1/14/05 Vol. 38

masons in tribulation planned evil force (Jesus) — 3/2/00 Vol. 18

mason's New World financial,military takeover (Jesus)   9/30/99 Vol. 16
masons vs. God God's power prevails over (Jesus)   3/8/01 Vol. 22
masons, central bankers leaders in control (Jesus)   6/16/05 Vol. 39
masons, one worlders to take over America (Jesus)   6/30/06 Vol. 43
Mass attend on Sunday (Jesus)   2/18/03 Vol. 30
Mass Covenant (Jesus)   1/23/96 Vol. 3
Mass disasters   10/25/93 Vol. 1
Mass family (Jesus)   12/18/95 Vol. 3
Mass get out what you bring to it (Jesus)   10/20/05 Vol. 41
Mass gift of love and Presence (Jesus)   12/11/99 Vol. 17
Mass gift of transubstantiation (Jesus)   6/5/99 Vol. 15
Mass give praise,glory,thanks (Jesus)   6/17/99 Vol. 15
Mass goes underground (Jesus)   5/11/97 Vol. 7
Mass goes underground (Jesus)   9/27/97 Vol. 8
Mass government (Jesus)   11/19/93 Vol. 1
Mass greatest prayer (Jesus)   12/17/01 Vol. 25
Mass Heavenly bread (Jesus)   9/26/95 Vol. 3
Mass held underground (Jesus)   3/24/03 Vol. 30
Mass is the greatest prayer (Jesus)   10/27/05 Vol. 41
Mass memorial of Jesus' death (Jesus)   6/1/00 Vol. 19
Mass miracle of Consecration (Jesus)   3/6/99 Vol. 14
Mass most important prayer (Jesus)   10/11/06 Vol. 45
Mass multiplication of Bread (Jesus)   12/16/04 Vol. 37
Mass not with us much longer (Jesus)   6/17/02 Vol. 27
Mass participate with heart (Jesus)   7/26/98 Vol. 12
Mass place to celebrate life (Jesus)   4/30/07 Vol. 47
Mass prayer of thanksgiving (Jesus)   3/7/06 Vol. 42
Mass preserve it (Jesus)   9/7/00 Vol. 20
Mass preserve proper words (Jesus)   2/19/98 Vol. 10
Mass preserve traditions (Jesus)   9/28/96 Vol. 4
Mass repeats death,rising of Jesus (Jesus)   4/28/00 Vol. 19
Mass reverence & respect for (Jesus)   9/8/03 Vol. 32
Mass reverence in dress (Jesus)   3/20/97 Vol. 6
Mass sacrifice (Jesus)   1/17/96 Vol. 3
Mass sacrifice of Body & Blood (Jesus)   2/28/97 Vol. 6
Mass should be an inspiration (Jesus)   10/27/02 Vol. 29
Mass suffering, not comfort (Jesus)   3/13/03 Vol. 30
Mass taken away in tribulation (Jesus)   4/10/97 Vol. 7
Mass the greatest prayer (Jesus)   10/10/02 Vol. 29
Mass treasure Communion (Jesus)   3/15/07 Vol. 46
Mass treasure daily Presence (Jesus)   4/29/03 Vol. 31
Mass unbloody crucifixion (Jesus)   3/29/99 Vol. 14
Mass unbloody sacrifice (Jesus)   9/25/03 Vol. 32
Mass under seige (Jesus)   5/16/02 Vol. 27
Mass underground (Jesus)   2/4/94 Vol. 1
Mass underground in tribulation (Jesus)   10/24/01 Vol. 25
Mass union of Jesus with us (Jesus)   8/18/97 Vol. 8

Mass will satisfy your soul (Jesus)   7/12/01 Vol. 24
Mass & Eucharist treasure now (Jesus)   8/16/00 Vol. 20
Mass attendance declining (Jesus)   8/23/01 Vol. 24
Mass attendance decreasing (Jesus)   7/29/05 Vol. 40
Mass attendance low with no leadership (Jesus)   5/2/00 Vol. 19
Mass attendance needs active participants (Jesus)   10/19/00 Vol. 21
Mass attendance spiritual priority (Jesus)   3/13/03 Vol. 30
mass destruction weapons of (Jesus)   10/24/00 Vol. 21
mass destruction arms question to world in Iraq (Jesus)   12/11/02 Vol. 29
mass destruction tools if not enough prayers (Jesus)   3/21/99 Vol. 14
mass destruction weapons do not use (Jesus)   10/24/02 Vol. 29
Mass for Betania trip pilgrimage (Jesus)   1/6/95 Vol. 2
Mass for dead memory of those passed on (Jesus)   11/5/00 Vol. 21
Mass' importance open hearts to be fulfilled (Jesus)   12/11/99 Vol. 17
Mass important miracle of Body & Blood (Jesus)   4/18/99 Vol. 15
Mass in homes at religious persecution (Jesus)   12/23/99 Vol. 17
Mass in homes brief before need for refuges (Jesus)   9/25/04 Vol. 36
Mass on Sunday cold hearts need warming (Jesus)   12/12/02 Vol. 29
Mass on Sunday do not miss (Jesus)   3/4/07 Vol. 46
Mass on Sunday golden rain of graces (Jesus)   2/5/02 Vol. 26
Mass on Sunday invite people back (Jesus)   2/3/03 Vol. 30
Mass on Sunday is greatest prayer (Jesus)   6/8/06 Vol. 43
Mass on Sunday remember God all week (Jesus)   10/6/05 Vol. 41
Mass preparations from persecutions (Jesus)   6/17/02 Vol. 27
Mass preparations in homes for tribulation (Jesus)   4/29/02 Vol. 27
Mass reverence kneeling at Consecration (Jesus)   11/7/02 Vol. 29
Mass reverence on time,quiet,attentive (Jesus)   6/9/00 Vol. 19
Mass taken away prophecy being fulfilled (Jesus)   3/15/00 Vol. 18
Mass vs. movies heaven vs. world (Jesus)   5/20/07 Vol. 47
Mass, come to out of love than obligation (Jesus)   11/17/02 Vol. 29
Mass, daily is blessing of grace (Jesus)   4/26/04 Vol. 35
Mass, daily people are very special (Jesus)   11/30/01 Vol. 25
Mass, daily reward in heaven (Jesus)   12/5/99 Vol. 17
Mass, First sacrifice of Jesus in Eucharist (Jesus)   7/20/07 Vol. 48
Mass, intentions at worship & obey God (Jesus)   11/17/02 Vol. 29
Mass, invalid when Consecration changed (Jesus)   4/15/05 Vol. 39
Mass, old acceptable today (Jesus)   5/17/07 Vol. 47
Mass, Sacrifice of the reverence to Real Presence (Jesus)   1/20/08 Vol. 50
Mass, Sunday attendance down (Jesus)   3/26/03 Vol. 30
Masses at homes & refuges (Jesus)   8/14/06 Vol. 44
Masses churches closed (Jesus)   8/14/97 Vol. 8
Masses eventually underground (Jesus)   8/31/04 Vol. 36
Masses held in secret (Jesus)   10/25/99 Vol. 17
Masses in homes (Jesus)   11/24/01 Vol. 25
Masses in homes eventually (Jesus)   1/4/08 Vol. 50
Masses outlawed (Jesus)   2/27/03 Vol. 30
Masses remnant in underground (Jesus)   1/12/98 Vol. 10

Masses underground (Jesus) — 4/28/05 Vol. 39
Masses valid and invalid (Jesus) — 1/8/98 Vol. 10
Masses will go into the homes (Jesus) — 6/22/02 Vol. 27
Masses for living more valuable (Jesus) — 9/2/99 Vol. 16
Masses for the dead leave in will (Jesus) — 6/20/05 Vol. 39
Masses for you in your will (Jesus) — 10/8/07 Vol. 49
masses gone hiding (Jesus) — 8/30/94 Vol. 2
Masses in hiding away from Antichrist (Jesus) — 3/15/00 Vol. 18
Masses in home early Christians and now (Jesus) — 5/2/05 Vol. 39
Masses in homes foreshadows tribulation (Jesus) — 1/16/01 Vol. 22
Masses, home have Mass kit (Jesus) — 1/24/08 Vol. 50
Masses,underground held secretly in homes (Jesus) — 10/11/99 Vol. 17
Master builder blueprint for all creation (Jesus) — 3/8/01 Vol. 22
master builder of Church in Jesus (Jesus) — 12/6/02 Vol. 29
material commercialism more important than Christmas (Jesus) — 12/27/01 Vol. 25
material desires have no lasting meaning (Jesus) — 2/19/02 Vol. 26
material desires imperfect, seek perfect in God (Jesus) — 3/8/01 Vol. 22
material gods things,sports,craving flesh (Jesus) — 4/28/97 Vol. 7
material possessions gone tomorrow (Jesus) — 9/26/00 Vol. 20
material things become obsolete,out of fashion (Jesus) — 2/19/02 Vol. 26
material things never satisfy the soul (Jesus) — 4/24/00 Vol. 19
material things lost do not worship possessions (Jesus) — 7/30/98 Vol. 12
materialism be God-centered (Jesus) — 3/6/97 Vol. 6
materialism be purified (Jesus) — 2/13/97 Vol. 6
materialism breakdown of the family (Jesus) — 8/8/99 Vol. 16
materialism cannot satisfy the soul (Jesus) — 2/25/99 Vol. 14
materialism decay of our country (Jesus) — 1/27/97 Vol. 6
materialism do not amass wealth (Jesus) — 10/27/01 Vol. 25
materialism fast paced living (Jesus) — 2/7/00 Vol. 18
materialism give it up (Jesus) — 11/10/01 Vol. 25
materialism go to oasis of prayer (Jesus) — 11/23/01 Vol. 25
materialism gods of money, sports (Jesus) — 10/27/96 Vol. 5
materialism keep spiritual priorities (Jesus) — 6/1/04 Vol. 35
materialism life (Jesus) — 5/30/94 Vol. 1
materialism prayer life (Jesus) — 9/16/94 Vol. 2
materialism priorities (Jesus) — 11/25/93 Vol. 1
materialism science and money (Jesus) — 10/28/97 Vol. 9
materialism selfishness & control (Jesus) — 1/6/98 Vol. 10
materialism set priorities (Jesus) — 12/12/97 Vol. 9
materialism share with others (Jesus) — 2/25/04 Vol. 34
materialism storms, jobs lost (Jesus) — 12/9/97 Vol. 9
materialism strip your idols (Jesus) — 7/17/97 Vol. 8
materialism stripped of possessions (Jesus) — 7/2/98 Vol. 12
materialism unborn (Mary) — 12/12/93 Vol. 1
materialism we will be stripped of (Jesus) — 5/22/98 Vol. 11
materialism will be stripped of things (Jesus) — 3/9/98 Vol. 10

mat. & comforts deal with Christian suffering (Jesus) — 10/15/98 Vol. 13
materialism & sin fall of America (Jesus) — 2/12/04 Vol. 34
Mauer, Dick funeral Mass (Jesus) — 1/5/06 Vol. 42
Maximillian Kolbe Shrine survived atomic blast (Jesus) — 10/15/01 Vol. 25
'me' generation recognize Me (Jesus) — 1/24/94 Vol. 1
medals & scapulars for house protection (Jesus) — 5/29/06 Vol. 43
medals of Marian shrines evangelize and convert (Jesus) — 7/15/96 Vol. 4
media brainwashing viewers (Jesus) — 12/1/05 Vol. 41
media censored to protect evil ones (Jesus) — 8/13/98 Vol. 12
media controlled by one worlders (Jesus) — 10/6/06 Vol. 45
media controlled,press present (Jesus) — 7/31/96 Vol. 4
media drumbeats for war (Jesus) — 8/27/03 Vol. 32
media twists facts (Jesus) — 5/16/02 Vol. 27
media blamed for displaying constant violence (Jesus) — 4/19/07 Vol. 47
media hidden agenda to control people (Jesus) — 5/23/00 Vol. 19
media, used by rich brainwash people to wars (Jesus) — 8/16/05 Vol. 40
media's misleading polls refuted by election (Jesus) — 11/4/04 Vol. 37
Mediatrix of all graces intercession (Mary) — 6/12/96 Vol. 3
Mediatrix of grace blessings (Mary) — 2/21/96 Vol. 3
Mediatrix of graces Mary as intercessor (Jesus) — 8/15/05 Vol. 40
Mediatrix, Mary is of graces (Jesus) — 8/22/05 Vol. 40
medicine bad side effects (Jesus) — 2/5/07 Vol. 46
medicine to help 3rd world (Jesus) — 8/23/01 Vol. 24
medicines for third world poor (Jesus) — 9/4/03 Vol. 32
medicines natural and modern (Jesus) — 6/14/01 Vol. 23
medicines vs. natural remedies (Jesus) — 1/31/03 Vol. 30
medicines,artificial side effects (Jesus) — 6/1/02 Vol. 27
meditate on Jesus remove distractions (Jesus) — 12/22/06 Vol. 45
meditation Father (Jesus) — 5/8/95 Vol. 2
meditation listen for His Will (Jesus) — 2/15/99 Vol. 14
meditation time prepare for Jesus' coming (Jesus) — 12/1/98 Vol. 13
Medjugorje conversion (Mary) — 12/8/96 Vol. 5
Medjugorje personal message revisited (Mary) — 7/14/02 Vol. 28
Medjugorje pray for peace (Mary) — 2/6/97 Vol. 6
Medjugorje share message of love (Mary) — 7/20/02 Vol. 28
Medjugorje mission Fr. Shamon influence (Jesus) — 11/25/03 Vol. 33
Medjugorje,Yugoslavia many wars started there (Mary) — 3/25/99 Vol. 14
Melissa's Wedding permanence in marriage (Jesus) — 5/20/06 Vol. 43
Memorial Day be grateful to soldiers (Jesus) — 5/30/01 Vol. 23
Memorial Day cost of wars (Jesus) — 5/29/06 Vol. 43
men converted through women (Mary) — 8/14/99 Vol. 16
men in black to implement martial law (Jesus) — 4/14/05 Vol. 39
men of wealth blood money for weapons (Jesus) — 4/19/00 Vol. 19
mene,tekel,peres fate of America like Babylon (Jesus) — 11/26/03 Vol. 33
mercury poisoning effect on infants, from fish (Jesus) — 12/18/03 Vol. 33
mercy falls like sunlight on all (Jesus) — 4/27/03 Vol. 31
mercy for least repentant sinner (Jesus) — 3/11/99 Vol. 14

mercy forgive 70 x 7 times (Jesus)   9/15/96 Vol. 4
mercy given more time to repent (Jesus)   9/26/98 Vol. 12
mercy is endless (Jesus)   9/15/02 Vol. 28
mercy last chance in warning (Jesus)   2/2/99 Vol. 14
mercy witness to everyone (Jesus)   7/17/99 Vol. 16
mercy & forgiveness needed to follow Christian life (Jesus) 2/25/02 Vol. 26
mercy & grace gains peace and rest (Jesus)   7/27/07 Vol. 48
mercy desired over sacrifice (Jesus)   3/18/99 Vol. 14
mercy in Warning from God to save souls (Jesus)   11/24/05 Vol. 41
mercy is endless always time to repent (Jesus)   1/29/99 Vol. 14
mercy killing death culture promoted (Jesus)   8/5/98 Vol. 12
mercy of God in 2nd chance to change (Jesus)   2/20/06 Vol. 42
mercy of Warning to see need to repent (Jesus)   1/20/07 Vol. 46
Mercy Sunday accept forgiveness (Jesus)   4/7/02 Vol. 27
Mercy Sunday Blessed Sacrament (Jesus)   4/4/97 Vol. 7
Mercy Sunday chances for graces,blessings (Jesus)   4/30/00 Vol. 19
Mercy Sunday in Toronto,for conference 2003 (Jesus)   4/11/02 Vol. 27
Mercy Sunday love (Jesus)   4/23/95 Vol. 2
Mercy Sunday love (Jesus)   4/22/95 Vol. 2
Mercy Sunday love,mercy,graces given (Jesus)   4/19/98 Vol. 11
mercy, justice of God tested by man (Jesus)   11/25/05 Vol. 41
mercy, time of justice postponed for prayer (Jesus)   7/30/98 Vol. 12
mercy, works of in visiting sick & aged (Jesus)   11/19/02 Vol. 29
mergers less competition, jobs (Jesus)   6/3/99 Vol. 15
mergers to take money out of US (Jesus)   5/1/01 Vol. 23
Merida Cathedral rising spirit (Jesus)   2/8/95 Vol. 2
Merry Christmas shunned in stores (Jesus)   12/26/02 Vol. 29
merry-go-round life seek forgiveness of sins (Jesus)   2/8/01 Vol. 22
merry-go-round of life fast moving society (Jesus)   7/3/00 Vol. 20
merry-go-rounds get off,proper priorities (Jesus)   9/13/99 Vol. 16
message call to evangelize (Jesus)   7/16/99 Vol. 16
message funeral (Jean P.)   12/30/93 Vol. 1
message funeral (Mary Harris)   1/10/94 Vol. 1
message personal in Medjugorje (Mary)   7/14/02 Vol. 28
message personal information (Jesus)   8/11/99 Vol. 16
message personal mission (Jesus)   8/11/99 Vol. 16
message of repentance prepare souls (Jesus)   7/19/99 Vol. 16
messages about to end for Mary (Mary)   1/1/98 Vol. 10
messages act on them daily (Jesus)   2/4/98 Vol. 10
messages by Mary to stop (Mary)   2/5/98 Vol. 10
messages concern over dates (Jesus)   9/12/96 Vol. 4
messages conferences & books (Jesus)   9/5/96 Vol. 4
messages convert many (Jesus)   5/17/98 Vol. 11
messages distribution to be attacked (Jesus)   6/21/99 Vol. 15
messages encourage faith in end times (Jesus)   12/12/03 Vol. 33
messages end times (Jesus)   2/12/94 Vol. 1
messages evangelize (Jesus)   6/19/96 Vol. 3

messages evangelize in book (Jesus)   3/1/96 Vol. 3
messages evangelize with books (Jesus)   10/1/96 Vol. 5
messages given deaf ear (Jesus)   9/9/00 Vol. 20
messages help of Holy Spirit (Jesus)   5/6/97 Vol. 7
messages humble (St. Therese)   7/17/95 Vol. 3
messages Maria E. (Padre Pio)   10/26/95 Vol. 3
messages Mary waning,Jesus incr (Mary)   7/30/96 Vol. 4
messages mission (Jesus)   9/3/95 Vol. 3
messages near fulfillment (Mary)   7/29/99 Vol. 16
messages not listened to (Jesus)   5/6/98 Vol. 11
messages personal difficulties (Jesus)   1/25/97 Vol. 6
messages personal evangelization (Jesus)   9/9/96 Vol. 4
messages personal mission (Jesus)   6/19/97 Vol. 7
messages personal mission (Mark)   8/16/96 Vol. 4
messages personal mission (Jesus)   8/30/96 Vol. 4
messages personal responsibilities (Jesus)   8/17/96 Vol. 4
messages personal submission (Jesus)   7/7/99 Vol. 16
messages personal,time is short (Jesus)   4/2/98 Vol. 11
messages personal/books/speaking (Jesus)   7/26/96 Vol. 4
messages preach peace,love,convert (Jesus)   10/18/96 Vol. 5
messages proclaim from rooftops (Holy Spirit)   11/22/96 Vol. 5
messages publicized (Jesus)   11/26/93 Vol. 1
messages publish & give talks (Jesus)   2/20/97 Vol. 6
messages re-read in light of events (Mary)   9/6/98 Vol. 12
messages responsibility (Mary)   1/12/94 Vol. 1
messages save souls,Holy Spirit (Jesus)   12/27/96 Vol. 5
messages seek conversion of souls (Jesus)   8/6/96 Vol. 4
messages seek help to save souls (Jesus)   3/26/96 Vol. 3
messages shout from the rooftops (Jesus)   12/12/96 Vol. 5
messages speak truth (Jesus)   9/3/96 Vol. 4
messages tell of love,hope & trust (Jesus)   12/7/96 Vol. 5
messages wake up soon (Mary)   3/13/96 Vol. 3
messages warning and preparation (Mary)   7/24/96 Vol. 4
messages will cease, trust (Mary)   10/16/97 Vol. 9
messages & miracles less from Blessed Mother (Jesus)   8/12/99 Vol. 16
messages & talks with help of Holy Spirit (Jesus)   2/4/04 Vol. 34
messages from prophets gifts of God to faithful (Jesus)   7/16/00 Vol. 20
messages given by Jesus are being fulfilled (Jesus)   1/21/07 Vol. 46
messages not heeded imitate Jesus (Mary)   6/12/97 Vol. 7
messages, apparitions threat to authorities (Jesus)   4/6/05 Vol. 39
messages, visions need testing in Spirit (Jesus)   3/29/05 Vol. 38
messages,apparitions about to end (Mary)   6/12/99 Vol. 15
messages,apparitions need testing of time for truth (Jesus) 5/13/00 Vol. 19
messenger healing (Jesus)   8/9/94 Vol. 2
messenger perfection (Mary)   1/1/95 Vol. 2
messenger prayer (St. Theresa)   10/1/94 Vol. 2
messenger rosary (Mary)   10/7/94 Vol. 2

messenger serve (Mary) 10/26/95 Vol. 3
messenger soul's destination (Jesus) 8/24/94 Vol. 2
messenger spotlight (Jesus) 2/16/95 Vol. 2
messenger time management (St. Theresa) 1/20/95 Vol. 2
messenger warning (Jesus) 2/3/95 Vol. 2
messenger witness (Holy Spirit) 2/18/95 Vol. 2
messengers abortions & weather (Jesus) 1/18/97 Vol. 6
messengers abused for telling the truth (Jesus) 7/31/98 Vol. 12
messengers called to prepare people (Jesus) 10/28/99 Vol. 17
messengers called to proclaim Gospel (Jesus) 3/22/00 Vol. 18
messengers called to say yes (Jesus) 1/23/00 Vol. 18
messengers continue warnings (Jesus) 1/2/00 Vol. 18
messengers discern,test false witnesses (Jesus) 11/10/98 Vol. 13
messengers end time events (Jesus) 2/10/03 Vol. 30
messengers evangelize lost souls (Jesus) 7/21/02 Vol. 28
messengers face serious opposition (Jesus) 8/2/96 Vol. 4
messengers faith (Jesus) 9/24/94 Vol. 2
messengers false witnesses (Jesus) 6/8/96 Vol. 3
messengers feed the people (Jesus) 3/31/98 Vol. 10
messengers gift of His Word (Jesus) 3/6/96 Vol. 3
messengers given gifts of healing in tribulation (Jesus) 10/5/01 Vol. 25
messengers given spiritual stamina (Jesus) 10/8/03 Vol. 33
messengers harassed (Jesus) 4/30/95 Vol. 2
messengers have different missions (Jesus) 11/19/03 Vol. 33
messengers help in today's trials (Jesus) 1/29/04 Vol. 34
messengers knowledge (Jesus) 6/15/94 Vol. 1
messengers messages mostly from Jesus (Jesus) 4/1/00 Vol. 19
messengers ministries (Jesus) 9/25/94 Vol. 2
messengers never look back;forward (Jesus) 4/15/97 Vol. 7
messengers no right to stop (Jesus) 9/29/97 Vol. 8
messengers open ears to repent (Jesus) 1/13/03 Vol. 30
messengers persecutions (Jesus) 7/28/94 Vol. 2
messengers personal (Mother Cabrini) 11/13/95 Vol. 3
messengers personal witness (Jesus) 5/31/96 Vol. 3
messengers pray for strength (Jesus) 4/24/02 Vol. 27
messengers preach Gospel to all nations (Jesus) 4/24/02 Vol. 27
messengers prepare for tribulation (Jesus) 3/21/98 Vol. 10
messengers protected by Holy Spirit (Jesus) 5/16/02 Vol. 27
messengers repent (Jesus) 3/8/95 Vol. 2
messengers Satan attacking more (Jesus) 9/17/01 Vol. 24
messengers sent from town to town (Jesus) 6/29/02 Vol. 27
messengers spiritual attacks (Jesus) 5/24/96 Vol. 3
messengers suffering (Jesus) 12/27/94 Vol. 2
messengers test the spirit (Jesus) 2/11/02 Vol. 26
messengers to prepare the people (Jesus) 10/18/01 Vol. 25
messengers to spread love&Gospel (Jesus) 10/6/99 Vol. 17
messengers travel sea of life (Jesus) 7/11/02 Vol. 28

messengers watched by one worlders (Jesus) 10/5/01 Vol. 25
messengers will be vindicated (Jesus) 2/5/04 Vol. 34
messengers will suffer hardships (Jesus) 7/16/96 Vol. 4
messengers witness (Jesus) 4/7/95 Vol. 2
messengers witness to messages (Jesus) 1/2/97 Vol. 6
messengers & prophets anoint for service (Jesus) 1/19/03 Vol. 30
messengers & prophets call to feed lambs (Jesus) 7/15/06 Vol. 44
messengers & prophets prepare the people (Jesus) 8/29/96 Vol. 4
messengers,conversion urgent time for converting (Jesus) 4/18/97 Vol. 7
messengers,prophets witness Word to all nations (Jesus) 10/28/98 Vol. 13
Messiah Jews did not believe (Jesus) 8/22/99 Vol. 16
Messiah rejected by His own people (Jesus) 12/13/02 Vol. 29
Messiah witness of Jesus as God (Jesus) 3/4/02 Vol. 26
Messiah & Redeemer foretold by prophets of old (Jesus) 12/20/03 Vol. 33
Messiah in Jesus not accepted by Jews (Jesus) 4/10/07 Vol. 47
Messiah in Jesus not accepted by Jews (God the Father) 4/6/01 Vol. 23
Messiah of Christmas Lamb to slaughter (Jesus) 11/23/99 Vol. 17
Messiah on earth fulfilled promise (Jesus) 12/28/06 Vol. 45
Messiah prophecies fulfilled in Jesus (Jesus) 12/21/05 Vol. 41
Messiah's coming to save mankind (Jesus) 7/26/01 Vol. 24
metamorphosis, spiritual earthly life to eternal life (Jesus) 10/13/04 Vol. 37
meteors & asteroids signs in the sky (Jesus) 7/24/01 Vol. 24
Mexico chips leaders taking chips in body (Jesus) 7/15/04 Vol. 36
Mexico wall little help (Jesus) 1/25/07 Vol. 46
Michelle Davis message in death (Michelle Davis) 2/14/08 Vol. 50
microchip do not be controlled by (Jesus) 10/19/01 Vol. 25
microchips control of people (Jesus) 6/9/97 Vol. 7
microchips destroyed by nuclear weapons (Jesus) 11/14/01 Vol. 25
microchips in passports & licenses (Jesus) 11/3/05 Vol. 41
microphone second coming (Jesus) 12/19/94 Vol. 2
microwave antenna monitor chips in body (Jesus) 5/9/06 Vol. 43
microwave gun power outages (Jesus) 8/23/03 Vol. 32
microwave machines control brain waves (Jesus) 11/1/01 Vol. 25
microwave pollution danger to brain, insects (Jesus) 11/9/07 Vol. 49
microwave pulses trigger epidemic diseases (Jesus) 3/1/06 Vol. 42
microwaves control minds (Jesus) 8/24/00 Vol. 20
microwaves in weather & earthquakes (Jesus) 3/21/05 Vol. 38
microwaves to track chips (Jesus) 1/14/00 Vol. 18
middle class attack on by one worlders (Jesus) 5/26/07 Vol. 47
middle class being destroyed by rich (Jesus) 7/7/06 Vol. 44
middle class shrinking to poor class (Jesus) 1/24/08 Vol. 50
middle class Wall Street, corporation atttack (Jesus) 7/11/07 Vol. 48
mid. class elimination by international corporations (Jesus) 7/21/07 Vol. 48
middle class jobs being eliminated (Jesus) 6/3/07 Vol. 47
Middle East and terrorism (Jesus) 4/11/02 Vol. 27
Middle East could ignite a war (Jesus) 8/18/01 Vol. 24
Middle East fighting over land, oil (Jesus) 2/16/05 Vol. 38

Middle East needs increased prayer,stop hate (Jesus)	3/14/02 Vol. 26
Middle East pray for peace (Jesus)	10/26/06 Vol. 45
Middle East pray for peace (Jesus)	10/14/99 Vol. 17
Middle East pray for peace (Jesus)	7/1/99 Vol. 16
Middle East snow to cool anger (Jesus)	2/26/03 Vol. 30
Middle East terrorists control oil (Jesus)	9/14/00 Vol. 20
Middle East conflict more war on horizon (Jesus)	2/18/02 Vol. 26
Middle East fighting avoid wasting of lives (Jesus)	10/26/00 Vol. 21
Middle East nations in constant turmoil (Jesus)	11/11/04 Vol. 37
Middle East war pray for peace (Jesus)	8/31/00 Vol. 20
Middle East war precipitate justice (Jesus)	3/17/03 Vol. 30
Middle East war threatens more countries (Jesus)	1/19/06 Vol. 42
Middle-East conflicts over greed,power (Jesus)	6/3/99 Vol. 15
Middle-East control of rich (Jesus)	11/6/97 Vol. 9
Middle-East pray for peace (Jesus)	4/9/97 Vol. 7
Middle-East prayers for peace (Jesus)	3/13/97 Vol. 6
Mid-east pray for peace, pride (Jesus)	10/16/97 Vol. 9
Mid-East war (Jesus)	12/21/94 Vol. 2
Mid-East without peace war widens (Jesus)	10/3/96 Vol. 5
Mid-east war destruction, no winners (Jesus)	1/29/98 Vol. 10
Mid-east war many nations involved (Jesus)	10/9/97 Vol. 9
Midnight Mass joy in singing (Jesus)	12/16/04 Vol. 37
Miguel Pro, Blessed martyrs to occur in tribulation (Jesus)	8/12/04 Vol. 36
Miguel Pro,Blessed work till you cannot move (Jesus)	4/19/97 Vol. 7
militant Islamists fight against Israel (Jesus)	7/7/07 Vol. 48
militant Moslems are seeking a world war (Jesus)	11/6/01 Vol. 25
militants cause wars,contrived (Jesus)	11/25/97 Vol. 9
military depleted (Jesus)	9/22/03 Vol. 32
military do not take pride in (Jesus)	12/6/01 Vol. 25
military troops stretched thin (Jesus)	1/16/02 Vol. 26
military buildup could spark a war (Jesus)	9/27/01 Vol. 24
military leaders threat to peace (Jesus)	2/18/01 Vol. 22
military of US one worlders to break (Jesus)	2/1/07 Vol. 46
military overseas little defense home (Jesus)	9/21/01 Vol. 24
military services part of the UN (Jesus)	11/18/99 Vol. 17
military weapons to destroy satellites (Jesus)	9/29/04 Vol. 36
military/industrial complex profit from wars (Jesus)	6/15/06 Vol. 43
military-industrial complex profit from wars (Jesus)	10/4/07 Vol. 49
Miller, John vision of heaven beautiful (John Miller)	12/17/05 Vol. 41
millstone around neck for those hurting children (Jesus)	10/4/01 Vol. 25
millstone on neck for hurting little children (Jesus)	11/7/05 Vol. 41
miltary creating secret weapons (Jesus)	10/31/05 Vol. 41
mind control by chips in body (Jesus)	6/4/03 Vol. 31
mind control by electrical devices (Jesus)	4/19/02 Vol. 27
mind control from chips (Jesus)	7/7/06 Vol. 44
mind control from chips in body (Jesus)	5/9/06 Vol. 43
mind control from chips in body (Jesus)	5/24/06 Vol. 43
mind control gold robots (Jesus)	8/10/94 Vol. 2
mind control in chips in the body (Jesus)	11/13/02 Vol. 29
mind control microwaves & contrails (Jesus)	5/26/03 Vol. 31
mind control rid TV watching (Jesus)	12/4/06 Vol. 45
mind control risk of chips in body (Jesus)	5/9/05 Vol. 39
mind control through chips (Jesus)	8/24/00 Vol. 20
mind control through chips in body (Jesus)	6/16/06 Vol. 43
mind control through chips in body (Jesus)	8/29/06 Vol. 44
mind control through electrical devices (Jesus)	2/18/99 Vol. 14
mind control through microwaves (Jesus)	11/1/01 Vol. 25
mine disaster learning to improve safety (Jesus)	8/11/07 Vol. 48
mine violations to be investigated (Jesus)	1/4/06 Vol. 42
minerals needed for good health (Jesus)	3/21/01 Vol. 22
miners' deaths not revealed properly (Jesus)	1/4/06 Vol. 42
miners killed West Virginia tragedy (Jesus)	1/4/06 Vol. 42
mines, mudslides need safety improvements (Jesus)	2/23/06 Vol. 42
mini judgment life review of good,bad actions (Jesus)	3/15/02 Vol. 26
mini-judgment preview of final judgment (Jesus)	1/3/07 Vol. 46
mining slaves (Jesus)	8/24/94 Vol. 2
mining disasters vs.dangers to spiritual life (Jesus)	12/9/04 Vol. 37
mining metals Armageddon (Jesus)	8/30/94 Vol. 2
Minneapolis bridge sign to fix old bridges (Jesus)	8/2/07 Vol. 48
miracle of Resurrection & Mass (Jesus)	6/28/05 Vol. 39
miracle growing crops miracle growth of faith (Jesus)	5/25/06 Vol. 43
miracle icons,satutues lift up faith (Jesus)	9/11/97 Vol. 8
miracle of Cana provide in tribulation (Jesus)	5/21/98 Vol. 11
miracle of the Eucharist suffering (Jesus)	2/25/94 Vol. 1
Miracle of the Eucharist suffering (Jesus)	2/10/95 Vol. 2
miracle picture prayer answered,wedding (St. Therese)	9/11/97 Vol. 8
miracles continue today in faith (Jesus)	4/16/04 Vol. 35
miracles gift of faith (Jesus)	7/6/98 Vol. 12
miracles have faith in (Jesus)	1/9/08 Vol. 50
miracles help belief in God (Jesus)	3/25/04 Vol. 34
miracles hope for salvation (Jesus)	10/20/99 Vol. 17
miracles of grace and trust (Jesus)	4/27/02 Vol. 27
miracles of the Eucharist (Jesus)	5/7/97 Vol. 7
miracles performed today (Jesus)	5/29/98 Vol. 11
miracles possible with Jesus (Jesus)	12/18/06 Vol. 45
miracles provided in tribulation (Jesus)	12/27/01 Vol. 25
miracles witness supernatural events (Mary)	8/5/98 Vol. 12
miracles at refuges believe and have faith (Jesus)	6/25/05 Vol. 39
miracles at refuges will make believers (Jesus)	6/6/07 Vol. 47
miracles in boats taught trust in Jesus (Jesus)	3/27/02 Vol. 26
miracles in prayer Lepanto,fall of communism (Jesus)	11/5/01 Vol. 25
miracles of deception Satan to mislead souls (Jesus)	6/21/99 Vol. 15
Miracles of Eucharist help belief in Real Presence (Jesus)	8/16/07 Vol. 48
miracles of Eucharist in Real Presence (Jesus)	4/18/01 Vol. 23

miracles of Eucharist proof of Real Presence (Jesus) 11/23/05 Vol. 41

mir.of Eucharist prove Real Presence to doubters (Jesus) 2/25/05 Vol. 38

miracles of faith tilma still preserved (Mary) 12/12/98 Vol. 13

miracles of Jesus from faith in Jesus' power (Jesus) 3/22/04 Vol. 34

miracles of Jesus to emphasize points of faith (Jesus) 5/5/04 Vol. 35

miracles of protection at refuges in tribulation (Jesus) 4/6/00 Vol. 19

miracles of protection at refuges in wilderness (Jesus) 8/20/02 Vol. 28

miracles of the Eucharist to help believers (Jesus) 6/18/06 Vol. 43

miracles of the Eucharist truth of Real Presence (Jesus) 4/5/98 Vol. 11

miracles, believe in calming waters,walking on (Jesus) 8/11/02 Vol. 28

miracles, seeing less worry at refuges (Jesus) 10/6/07 Vol. 49

miraculous intervention needed to mitigate war (Jesus) 2/24/03 Vol. 30

miraculous signs to be seen at refuges (Jesus) 11/1/02 Vol. 29

mirror combat evil temptations (Jesus) 1/11/95 Vol. 2

mirrors opposite faith passed on to future (Jesus) 11/29/99 Vol. 17

missile attack could trigger war (Jesus) 5/14/07 Vol. 47

missile defense one world people (Jesus) 4/26/01 Vol. 23

missile program work on peace (Jesus) 6/28/01 Vol. 23

missiles secrets to China & Russia (Jesus) 10/19/99 Vol. 17

missiles spreading to other nations (Jesus) 11/18/04 Vol. 37

missiles in Israel Iraq to cause war (Jesus) 6/14/97 Vol. 7

mission converson, urgent (St.John Neumann) 2/8/97 Vol. 6

mission demanding, Holy Spirit (Jesus) 4/28/97 Vol. 7

mission everyone called by God (Jesus) 1/22/06 Vol. 42

mission experience of grace (Jesus) 10/23/95 Vol. 3

mission no hesitation to accept (Jesus) 7/1/07 Vol. 48

mission offer up each day (St. Therese) 1/24/97 Vol. 6

mission personal difficulties (Jesus) 2/11/97 Vol. 6

mission personal urgency, omens (Jesus) 1/7/97 Vol. 6

mission prepare for tribulation (Jesus) 11/29/07 Vol. 49

mission prepare the people (Jesus) 1/18/97 Vol. 6

mission save souls (Jesus) 2/7/97 Vol. 6

mission spread His Word (Jesus) 9/21/96 Vol. 4

mission time is short, pray (Jesus) 3/20/97 Vol. 6

mission unique for each life (Jesus) 6/23/04 Vol. 35

Mission churches need financial,physical help (Jesus) 10/20/04 Vol. 37

Mission churches, CA US becoming mission land (Jesus) 7/1/05 Vol. 40

mission in life accept or reject God (Jesus) 10/3/05 Vol. 41

mission in life charity,not humanistic (Jesus) 9/20/01 Vol. 24

mission in life directed by Holy Spirit (Holy Spirit) 6/11/00 Vol. 19

mission in life directed by Jesus (Jesus) 11/12/03 Vol. 33

mission in life discern with God (Jesus) 12/30/06 Vol. 45

mission in life each person is unique (Jesus) 7/25/04 Vol. 36

mission in life follow God's Will (Jesus) 6/16/04 Vol. 35

mission in life follow inspiration for (Jesus) 8/9/06 Vol. 44

mission in life given to each person (Jesus) 1/13/06 Vol. 42

mission in life grace given for (Jesus) 8/25/06 Vol. 44

mission in life in total consecration (Jesus) 6/28/05 Vol. 39

mission in life know,love,serve God (Jesus) 8/8/01 Vol. 24

mission in life path to heaven (Jesus) 3/6/05 Vol. 38

mission in life prayers & good deeds (Jesus) 8/10/06 Vol. 44

mission in life talents given for (Jesus) 7/13/06 Vol. 44

mission in life talents,special from God (Jesus) 5/25/05 Vol. 39

mission in life to save souls (Jesus) 6/12/05 Vol. 39

mission in life use gifts & talents (Jesus) 6/13/06 Vol. 43

mission of faithful save souls from hell (Jesus) 8/30/02 Vol. 28

mission of life encouraged by Olena (Olena Terelya) 11/20/04 Vol. 37

mission on earth carry your cross (Jesus) 7/25/07 Vol. 48

mission on earth do not seek praise (Jesus) 2/20/03 Vol. 30

mission plan how best to serve God (Jesus) 1/13/07 Vol. 46

mission purpose instill faith for end days (Jesus) 9/4/07 Vol. 48

Mission to preach save souls,not free ticket (Jesus) 4/13/97 Vol. 7

mission, important save souls from hell (Jesus) 3/18/06 Vol. 42

mission, personal preparation for tribulation (Jesus) 12/27/03 Vol. 33

mission, unique each given unique gifts (Jesus) 1/13/05 Vol. 38

missionaries courageous & selfless (Jesus) 5/27/03 Vol. 31

missionaries evangelize the Gospel (Jesus) 10/10/99 Vol. 17

missionaries find Jesus in poor (Jesus) 11/12/98 Vol. 13

missionaries help and pray for (Jesus) 10/22/06 Vol. 45

missionaries needed to spread Gospel (Jesus) 6/26/03 Vol. 31

missionaries opportunity to reach nations (Jesus) 11/25/98 Vol. 13

missionaries rock (Jesus) 5/9/95 Vol. 2

missionaries to Indians in America (Jesus) 10/19/02 Vol. 29

missionaries of love to save souls (Jesus) 3/3/99 Vol. 14

missionary USA (St. Francis) 12/3/93 Vol. 1

missions responsibility (Jesus) 10/9/95 Vol. 3

missions, personal trust in God's help (Jesus) 11/15/07 Vol. 49

Mississippi casinos could be destroyed again (Jesus) 10/27/05 Vol. 41

mistakes faults (Jesus) 1/28/96 Vol. 3

mistakes learn to correct (Jesus) 10/21/03 Vol. 33

mistakes & weaknesses learn from them (Jesus) 6/19/04 Vol. 35

mobile society causes distractions,anxieties (Jesus) 8/8/00 Vol. 20

mockery of Blessed Mother (Mary) 6/20/98 Vol. 11

models in life Jesus & Mary (Jesus) 8/17/02 Vol. 28

modern art misleads some people (Mary) 5/15/97 Vol. 7

modern churches made for utility vs glory to God (Jesus) 3/7/02 Vol. 26

modern day Exodus water, manna, deer (Jesus) 9/27/07 Vol. 48

modern music influenced by Satan (Jesus) 2/17/00 Vol. 18

modern weapons efficient killers (Jesus) 4/25/00 Vol. 19

modernism change for its own sake (Jesus) 6/24/05 Vol. 39

modernism foundation for apostasy (Jesus) 1/29/00 Vol. 18

modernism influencing churces (Jesus) 5/19/05 Vol. 39

modernism leads to New Age mentality (Jesus) 8/16/02 Vol. 28

modernism less reverence to Host (Jesus) 1/12/99 Vol. 14

modernism lost faith in traditions (Jesus)   6/10/06 Vol. 43
modernism materialism (Jesus)   12/12/95 Vol. 3
modernism remove statues,crucifixes (Jesus)   10/21/99 Vol. 17
modernism schismatic Church (Jesus)   12/27/97 Vol. 9
modernism scripture (Jesus)   7/23/94 Vol. 2
modernism in Church avoid evil changes (Jesus)   10/25/98 Vol. 13
modernism vs remnant schism in the Church (Jesus)   10/5/96 Vol. 5
modernism vs. tradition remnant,underground Mass (Jesus) 11/9/98 Vol. 13
modernism, infiltration trying to destroy Church (Jesus) 10/12/07 Vol. 49
modernist false teaching follow Catechism,Bible (Jesus)   6/2/03 Vol. 31
modernists control content in churches (Jesus)   5/4/00 Vol. 19
modernists have lost their faith (Jesus)   11/15/04 Vol. 37
modest living example in Jesus' life (Jesus)   12/20/99 Vol. 17
Molloc worship by government officials (Jesus)   4/26/07 Vol. 47
Molly refuge blessed (Jesus)   1/13/01 Vol. 22
MOM Conference Year of Eucharist, Adoration (Jesus)   10/1/04 Vol. 37
MOM priests pray for (Jesus)   2/24/07 Vol. 46
monasteries holy ground refuges (Jesus)   7/13/05 Vol. 40
monasteries places of holy ground (Jesus)   1/17/08 Vol. 50
monasteries places of hospitality (Jesus)   3/13/08 Vol. 50
monasteries safe havens (Jesus)   1/13/98 Vol. 10
monasteries safe havens, refuges (Jesus)   3/13/08 Vol. 50
Monastery protected by an angel (Jesus)   8/31/97 Vol. 8
monastic life free of the world (Jesus)   12/4/00 Vol. 21
monastic life keeps focus on Jesus (Jesus)   6/1/07 Vol. 47
monastic life of silence (Jesus)   1/2/08 Vol. 50
monastic life quiet & prayerful (Jesus)   12/5/07 Vol. 49
monastic life St. Anthony started (Jesus)   1/17/08 Vol. 50
monastic life strip earthly desires (Jesus)   3/12/07 Vol. 46
monastic lifestyle need simpler life for holiness (Jesus) 8/1/00 Vol. 20
monastic prayer life keeps focus on Jesus (Jesus)   2/10/06 Vol. 42
monastic retreats removes distractions (Jesus)   3/16/06 Vol. 42
money better spent on infrastructure (Jesus)   6/26/03 Vol. 31
money can control your life (Jesus)   7/6/07 Vol. 48
money cannot serve 2 masters (Jesus)   8/3/96 Vol. 4
money cannot take past grave (Jesus)   6/15/01 Vol. 23
money choice of God vs. money (Jesus)   7/10/97 Vol. 8
money control by masters of evil (Jesus)   7/1/99 Vol. 16
money control by one worlders (Jesus)   4/25/01 Vol. 23
money do not idolize it (Jesus)   8/8/04 Vol. 36
money do not put trust in (Jesus)   10/30/01 Vol. 25
money electronic devices (Jesus)   10/5/94 Vol. 2
money evolution of (Jesus)   9/24/07 Vol. 48
money for necessities, not idol (Jesus)   8/21/03 Vol. 32
money God (Jesus)   3/27/95 Vol. 2
money greed to be rich (Jesus)   7/16/98 Vol. 12
money judgment (Jesus)   1/8/94 Vol. 1

money justice Trinity   3/16/94 Vol. 1
money love Jesus instead, one Master (Jesus)   11/27/04 Vol. 37
money makes prisoners of greedy (Jesus)   12/28/01 Vol. 25
money no price for your soul (Jesus)   12/12/98 Vol. 13
money no real backing,artificial (Jesus)   4/24/02 Vol. 27
money not means to be saved (Jesus)   2/5/00 Vol. 18
money not worth chasing after (Jesus)   1/7/00 Vol. 18
money only for survival (Jesus)   8/4/01 Vol. 24
money root of all evil (Jesus)   6/11/98 Vol. 11
money seek heaven (Jesus)   9/19/97 Vol. 8
money sharing in charity (Jesus)   9/30/07 Vol. 48
money use for charity (Jesus)   9/23/07 Vol. 48
money wasted on wars (Jesus)   2/13/03 Vol. 30
money will mean nothing (Jesus)   9/27/97 Vol. 8
money & fame will not get you to heaven (Jesus)   6/14/05 Vol. 39
money & possessions blind one spiritually (Jesus)   10/27/03 Vol. 33
money & wealth do not make idols of (Jesus)   8/1/03 Vol. 32
money & wealth not help at judgment (Jesus)   1/11/02 Vol. 26
money & wealth not our god (Jesus)   2/25/99 Vol. 14
money and excesses do not be rich for yourself (Jesus)   8/18/98 Vol. 12
money and profits woshiped as a god (Jesus)   1/26/99 Vol. 14
money and riches seek Kingdom of God first (Jesus)   4/2/98 Vol. 11
money and riches trust in God (Jesus)   7/31/97 Vol. 8
money and wealth only touch like a feather (Jesus)   1/30/02 Vol. 26
money as a god for gamblers in Las Vegas (Jesus)   10/30/00 Vol. 21
money as a god worshiped more than God (Jesus)   7/10/00 Vol. 20
money as idol against God's law (Jesus)   7/6/07 Vol. 48
money changers money,sports,shopping (Jesus)   12/2/96 Vol. 5
money chaos unsettled governments (Jesus)   6/3/04 Vol. 35
money desires are distraction from God (Jesus)   2/27/06 Vol. 42
money for war better spent on homeless (Jesus)   10/1/05 Vol. 41
money from wills causes family division (Jesus)   4/5/06 Vol. 43
money in tribulation will have no value for faithful (Jesus) 8/8/04 Vol. 36
money system world control (Jesus)   4/26/01 Vol. 23
money system,Antichrist chips only to buy and sell (Jesus) 10/22/98 Vol. 13
money to poor train to live with less (Jesus)   8/1/00 Vol. 20
money vs God cannot have two masters (Jesus)   4/8/01 Vol. 23
money vs God only one can be your master (Jesus)   11/11/00 Vol. 21
money vs. God elusive wealth not trusted (Jesus)   9/20/98 Vol. 12
money vs. God only one master-God (Jesus)   11/1/07 Vol. 49
money vs. God transitory vs. everlasting (Jesus)   6/12/97 Vol. 7
money, colored track buying & selling (Jesus)   5/13/04 Vol. 35
money, possessions do not make gods (Jesus)   1/27/06 Vol. 42
money,new system mark of the beast (Jesus)   3/2/99 Vol. 14
monied men Sodom & Gomorah (Jesus)   7/1/97 Vol. 8
monkey spiritual devotions (Jesus)   12/20/94 Vol. 2
monstrance time speeded up (Jesus)   7/20/94 Vol. 2

monstrance,tabernacle for Blessed Sacrament (Jesus) 4/21/97 Vol. 7

moon blood red, sign (Jesus) 9/19/96 Vol. 4

moon renewed earth (Jesus) 1/25/95 Vol. 2

moon trips via space station (Jesus) 1/10/07 Vol. 46

moon, red color sign for wars, end days (Jesus) 11/9/00 Vol. 21

moral backbone America rivals Sodom,Gomorrah (Jesus) 11/7/01 Vol. 25

moral bankruptcy need for conversions (Jesus) 2/1/01 Vol. 22

moral decadence to erode US wealth (Jesus) 9/14/06 Vol. 44

moral decay in man's laws (Jesus) 8/16/04 Vol. 36

moral decay in society (Jesus) 6/5/04 Vol. 35

moral decisions not on emotions (Jesus) 5/15/98 Vol. 11

moral decline in US downfall of America (Jesus) 5/5/04 Vol. 35

moral degradation why civilizations are lost (Jesus) 12/11/03 Vol. 33

moral ground,higher needed to fight temptations (Jesus) 11/16/03 Vol. 33

moral issues speak out on (Jesus) 4/18/07 Vol. 47

moral issues speak out publicly (Jesus) 10/29/04 Vol. 37

moral people vs. masons moral values vs. control (Jesus) 11/16/04 Vol. 37

moral teaching important to children (Jesus) 9/8/07 Vol. 48

moral values decided election (Jesus) 11/4/04 Vol. 37

morality in America also declining (Jesus) 2/17/06 Vol. 42

morally corrupt society in America (Jesus) 5/29/04 Vol. 35

morals bankrupt in America (Jesus) 2/5/99 Vol. 14

morals of society are bad (Jesus) 2/28/04 Vol. 34

morals screen children's movies (Jesus) 1/30/03 Vol. 30

morals degraded from 50 yrs. Ago (Jesus) 7/7/06 Vol. 44

morals lost many rely on themselves (Jesus) 4/7/00 Vol. 19

morals polluted by example of sin (Jesus) 11/5/99 Vol. 17

morning offering direct your life (Jesus) 5/17/01 Vol. 23

morning,night prayers need right priorities,focus (Jesus) 4/8/00 Vol. 19

mortal bodies immortal souls (Jesus) 3/8/00 Vol. 18

mortal body immortal soul (Jesus) 3/1/95 Vol. 2

mortal life not extended one moment (Jesus) 7/8/00 Vol. 20

mortal sin cleansed in Confession (Jesus) 3/3/00 Vol. 18

mortal sin Confession before Communion (Jesus) 4/10/06 Vol. 43

mortal sin death for the soul (Jesus) 10/9/00 Vol. 21

mortal sin death to soul,need Confession (Jesus) 3/17/02 Vol. 26

mortal sin demons (Jesus) 8/21/95 Vol. 3

mortal sin devoid of grace, soul dead (Jesus) 2/5/04 Vol. 34

mortal sin difficult to receive help (Jesus) 1/5/08 Vol. 50

mortal sin don't receive Communion (Jesus) 2/26/99 Vol. 14

mortal sin experience hell in warning (Jesus) 12/20/97 Vol. 9

mortal sin hard to hear good prompts (Jesus) 2/12/01 Vol. 22

mortal sin in sex outside of marriage (Jesus) 2/28/01 Vol. 22

mortal sin like barren trees of winter (Jesus) 3/23/01 Vol. 22

mortal sin lose light of grace (Jesus) 1/16/98 Vol. 10

mortal sin only healed by forgiveness (Jesus) 4/7/06 Vol. 43

mortal sin prevents worthy Communion (Jesus) 5/25/00 Vol. 19

mortal sin requires grace in living water (Jesus) 1/28/05 Vol. 38

mortal sin risk hell, sacrileges (Jesus) 3/21/04 Vol. 34

mortal sin risk the fires of hell (Jesus) 10/28/00 Vol. 21

mortal sin sacriligious Communion (Jesus) 3/5/97 Vol. 6

mortal sin separates soul from Vine (Jesus) 5/17/06 Vol. 43

mortal sin sex before marriage (Jesus) 1/7/01 Vol. 22

mortal sin spiritual death (Jesus) 5/19/03 Vol. 31

mortal sin spiritual death (Jesus) 7/8/04 Vol. 36

mortal sins death to the soul (Jesus) 1/3/05 Vol. 38

mortal sins fornication,homosexual act (Jesus) 12/1/99 Vol. 17

mortal sins like a power outage (Jesus) 4/9/03 Vol. 31

mortal sins sexual sins (Jesus) 10/9/99 Vol. 17

mortal sins spiritually dead to God (Jesus) 8/30/01 Vol. 24

mortality always be ready to die (Jesus) 9/4/97 Vol. 8

mortality of body seen at funerals, sicknesses (Jesus) 10/22/03 Vol. 33

mortgage crisis could lead to a takeover (Jesus) 2/7/08 Vol. 50

mortgage deception causes poor lose of homes (Jesus) 9/18/07 Vol. 48

mortgage foreclosures unsettling credit markets (Jesus) 11/3/07 Vol. 49

mortgage industry foreclosure problem (Jesus) 8/30/07 Vol. 48

Moses bronze serpent on pole (Jesus) 11/21/05 Vol. 41

Moses bronze serpent, cross (Jesus) 2/26/04 Vol. 34

Moses burning bush (Jesus) 2/4/99 Vol. 14

Moses greater than Moses here (Jesus) 9/5/98 Vol. 12

Moses lifted bronze serpent (Jesus) 3/15/05 Vol. 38

Moses lifted serpent on a pole (Jesus) 3/18/97 Vol. 6

Moses missed promised land (Jesus) 8/13/03 Vol. 32

Moses mother saved his life (Jesus) 1/22/01 Vol. 22

Moses raised bronze serpent (Jesus) 6/7/01 Vol. 23

Moses & Elijah sign of glory to come (Jesus) 2/18/99 Vol. 14

Moses' bronze serpent prefigure of Jesus' cross (Jesus) 3/27/07 Vol. 46

Moses' cry Let My People Go (Jesus) 4/9/06 Vol. 43

Moses with Burning Bush on holy ground (Jesus) 4/26/04 Vol. 35

Moslem backlash American Islam threatened (Jesus) 9/17/01 Vol. 24

Moslem confrontation with the West (Jesus) 7/1/07 Vol. 48

Moslems defeated at Lepanto (Jesus) 10/7/03 Vol. 33

Moslems genocide of Christians (Jesus) 7/26/06 Vol. 44

Moslems killing Christians (Jesus) 3/30/06 Vol. 42

Moslems may unite against US (Jesus) 11/27/01 Vol. 25

Moslems nations growning (Jesus) 2/20/03 Vol. 30

Moslems united against us (Jesus) 10/30/01 Vol. 25

Moslems vs Catholics militants will be persecutors (Jesus) 3/14/02 Vol. 26

mother heart,focal point of family (Jesus) 5/6/99 Vol. 15

mother Our Lady (Mary) 5/8/94 Vol. 1

mother sorrow 9/15/93 Vol. 1

Mother Angelica Conference (Jesus) 9/26/95 Vol. 3

Mother Angelica temple to Blessed Sacrament (Jesus) 10/21/00 Vol. 21

Mother Angelica TV (Mary) 7/9/95 Vol. 3

M. Cabrini morality vs. material things (Mother Cabrini) 11/13/98 Vol. 13

Mother Cabrini reach out in love (Mother Cabrini)   11/13/97 Vol. 9

Mother Cabrini visit shrine (Mother Cabrini)   9/19/96 Vol. 4

Mother Cabrini will help in mission (Mother Cabrini)   4/26/98 Vol. 11

M. Cabrini Shrine love God and neighbor (Mother Cabrini) 7/12/98 Vol. 12

Mother Cabrini Shrine protected by angels (Mother Cabrini) 9/7/97 Vol. 8

Mother Cabrini Shrine visit healing waters (Mother Cabrini) 8/14/96 Vol. 4

Mother Cabrini's Denver refuge, spring water (Jesus)   3/9/04 Vol. 34

Mother of Sorrows joy (Mary)   9/15/95 Vol. 3

Mother of Sorrows suffered loss of Jesus (Jesus)   9/15/98 Vol. 12

Mother Teresa help poor souls (Mary)   9/18/97 Vol. 8

Mother Teresa works of mercy (St. Therese)   10/2/97 Vol. 9

mothers give thanks for (Jesus)   4/24/03 Vol. 31

mothers have no rights to kill infants (Jesus)   1/22/05 Vol. 38

mothers need save children's souls (Jesus)   5/8/99 Vol. 15

mothers (single parent) help spiritually,physically (Jesus) 10/30/97 Vol. 9

mother's day day for Mary (Mary)   5/14/00 Vol. 19

Mother's Day honor Mary, mothers (Jesus)   5/13/07 Vol. 47

Mother's Day remember the Blessed Mother (Jesus)   5/12/02 Vol. 27

Mother's Day respect life (Jesus)   5/10/97 Vol. 7

Mother's Day view of Mom & Dad (Mary)   5/14/06 Vol. 43

mothers of aborted blood on hands as doctors (Jesus)   10/13/00 Vol. 21

mothers of abortions face judgment for killing (Jesus)   4/13/99 Vol. 15

mother's value has no price (Jesus)   9/13/99 Vol. 16

motive of love lets peace reign in your heart (Jesus)   2/16/02 Vol. 26

mountain top testing (Jesus)   8/6/94 Vol. 2

mountain top joy protection of Jesus (Jesus)   1/30/05 Vol. 38

mountaintop experience Listen to Jesus (Jesus)   3/7/04 Vol. 34

move forward in faith direction to gain heaven (Jesus)   4/11/00 Vol. 19

move inland justice   10/10/93 Vol. 1

movie maker Priest movie (Jesus)   4/19/95 Vol. 2

movies avoid bad ones (Jesus)   9/18/02 Vol. 28

movies corrupt many souls (Jesus)   6/5/97 Vol. 7

movies possessions (Jesus)   11/11/93 Vol. 1

movies & entertainment avoid 'R' rated, limit (Jesus)   1/2/04 Vol. 34

movies & plays mock marriage,Word of God (Jesus)   12/14/05 Vol. 41

movies & TV avoid evil temptations (Jesus)   12/3/03 Vol. 33

movies & TV avoid 'R' rated (Jesus)   6/10/04 Vol. 35

movies & TV have corrupted souls (Jesus)   5/29/04 Vol. 35

movies & TV pulse of evil morals (Jesus)   1/30/03 Vol. 30

movies & video choose clean, good ones (Jesus)   10/14/99 Vol. 17

movies and songs avoid violence,obscenities (Jesus)   3/15/01 Vol. 22

movies and TV corruption of society (Jesus)   2/11/98 Vol. 10

movies corrupt minds better to avoid (Jesus)   6/26/97 Vol. 7

movies in Hollywood avoid violence & sex (Jesus)   1/2/03 Vol. 30

movies of, Hollywood avoid support of filth (Jesus)   5/20/06 Vol. 43

movies on Jesus good at Christmas,Easter (Jesus)   12/23/05 Vol. 41

movies, bad avoid watching (Jesus)   3/28/00 Vol. 18

movies, disgraceful violence,nudity,swearing (Jesus)   5/20/06 Vol. 43

movies, modern avoid violence & sex (Jesus)   9/29/01 Vol. 24

movies, pornography bringing God's justice (Jesus)   11/7/05 Vol. 41

movies, 'R' actors live near fires (Jesus)   9/30/05 Vol. 40

movies, 'R' avoid watching, supporting (Jesus)   5/26/05 Vol. 39

movies, 'R' avoid, do not support (Jesus)   12/18/04 Vol. 37

movies, TV contaminate young minds (Jesus)   10/23/03 Vol. 33

movies, TV violence, evil influence (Jesus)   6/17/03 Vol. 31

movies,TV,books Satan's trash in living room (Jesus)   6/8/00 Vol. 19

movies,TV,friends bad influence on children (Jesus)   3/12/06 Vol. 42

Mt. Carmel House corporal acts of mercy (Jesus)   7/15/94 Vol. 2

Mt. Carmel House service (Mary)   11/13/93 Vol. 1

Mt. Carmel House tribute to hospice (Jesus)   7/16/06 Vol. 44

Mugavero, Ann funeral message (Jesus)   12/2/06 Vol. 45

multinational corporations cause low pay, benefits (Jesus)   9/6/07 Vol. 48

multiplication of food like in Exodus (Jesus)   6/13/02 Vol. 27

multiplied prayers offset evil of world (Jesus)   7/5/07 Vol. 48

mundane tasks blessing (Jesus)   5/5/95 Vol. 2

murders, mass voices of suggestion (Jesus)   5/2/02 Vol. 27

Muriel family message (Muriel)   8/15/97 Vol. 8

music His gift to us (Jesus)   9/4/98 Vol. 12

music instilled in composers (Jesus)   9/3/03 Vol. 32

music will leave God out (Jesus)   5/29/01 Vol. 23

music & singing uplifts the soul (Jesus)   10/23/99 Vol. 17

music & song practice for heaven (Jesus)   2/27/03 Vol. 30

music abused avoid evil lyrics,lewd conduct (Jesus)   6/8/00 Vol. 19

music in heaven better than Messiah (Jesus)   12/11/04 Vol. 37

music of youth leads to drugs & alcohol (Jesus)   3/26/03 Vol. 30

music,form of prayer means to praise God (Jesus)   10/14/00 Vol. 21

music,hard rock avoid evil lyrics, sounds (Jesus)   2/17/01 Vol. 22

music,modern influenced by Satan (Jesus)   2/17/00 Vol. 18

music,sensuous leads to drugs & sex (Jesus)   9/20/01 Vol. 24

musicians,performers should depend on God (Jesus)   1/12/08 Vol. 50

Muslim extremists need love not hate (Jesus)   2/6/07 Vol. 46

Muslim leaders leading people to war (Jesus)   9/17/98 Vol. 12

Muslim persecution of Christians to continue (Jesus)   11/30/06 Vol. 45

Muslims Antichrist & other gods (Jesus)   2/28/96 Vol. 3

Muslims persecuting Christians (Jesus)   4/6/02 Vol. 27

Muslims war/gas (Mary/Jesus)   8/16/95 Vol. 3

Muslims vs. Christians clash for converts (Jesus)   2/6/07 Vol. 46

mustard seed, pearl Kingdom of God (Jesus)   10/30/07 Vol. 49

My Lord & My God belief in Resurrection (Jesus)   3/30/08 Vol. 50

myrrh sign of death, burial (Jesus)   1/3/00 Vol. 18

myrrh symbol of suffering (Jesus)   12/21/06 Vol. 45

Mystical Body all share in pain (Jesus)   2/12/98 Vol. 10

Mystical Body be a light to the world (Jesus)   2/7/99 Vol. 14

Our Lady in Venezuela Saved Our Lives

We were encouraged to bring a group of pilgrims to Venezuela by our missionary friend there, Fr. Tarsicio Moreta, S.J. He said, he would call up Maria Esperanza and see if she would see us. He called from a phone in the country which was a miracle itself because he said they never work. She answered and said her heart was filled with love for our group, and that she would see us at her private home in Caracas. She welcomed us and spoke to us for six hours. During this time she prayed with Beverly, a lady in our group that had breast cancer. Maria never touched her but asked her to turn around and told her that her cancer had started ten years before from a sudden shock. She started to inhale deeply, made a bad face, and then spit something out in the bushes. She told her that she was healed. She is still alive today ten years later. Maria literally inhaled the cancer out of her before our eyes.

As we were about to leave, she went over to John and said: "Thank God for the miracle of your gift. You will be going to evangelize in many nations." Then she said: "I will come to you on Thursday." We did not understand since we were going to be leaving on Monday. What we did not know is that for almost three years on Thursdays at Mass she would be spiritually united with John at Communion time. She would offer a little word of praise or thanks to God as John would see her praying in her private chapel.

The next day we went to the National Shrine of Our Lady of Coromoto which was more south and went through the Andes Mountains. It was 9:00 p.m. and very misty and darkness was setting in. There were no guard rails on the road as we looked thousands of feet down over the edge. As we rounded a hairpin curve, three military vehicles were rapidly heading into us with no place to go. Everyone screamed and prayed for God's help. As the bus finally stopped you could have put a piece of paper between us. The bus driver said that it was a miracle that the bus stopped because under those conditions, he would have needed to apply both brakes to stop, and he only had time to apply one. As we began our trip, the Blessed Mother gave a message saying: "I will be watching over your safety on your trip."

(January 28, 1994 - volume 1)

Mystical body Church,saints,souls in purgatory (Jesus)	2/19/08 Vol. 50	Mystical Body justice (Jesus) 4/25/94 Vol. 1
Mystical Body drawn in at Baptism (Jesus)	1/7/99 Vol. 14	Mystical Body lights of each soul (Jesus) 12/24/01 Vol. 25
Mystical Body gift of life (Holy Spirit)	5/1/96 Vol. 3	Mystical Body reflection of Jesus (Jesus) 2/9/98 Vol. 10
Mystical Body helped by service (Mary)	5/28/98 Vol. 11	Mystical Body rooted in Trinity (Jesus) 9/27/99 Vol. 16
Mystical Body in Holy Communion (Jesus)	5/16/99 Vol. 15	Mystical Body saints, souls on earth,purgatory (Jesus) 11/1/04 Vol. 37
Mystical Body inheritance of new Adam (Jesus)	4/14/06 Vol. 43	Mystical Body second coming (Jesus) 12/1/95 Vol. 3
Mystical Body joined in worthy Holy Communion (Jesus) 5/6/05 Vol. 39		Mystical Body share in new life (Jesus) 4/14/98 Vol. 11

Mystical Body shared in Eucharist (Jesus)	6/6/99 Vol. 15
Mystical Body to build up people (Jesus)	3/3/99 Vol. 14
Mystical Body together in love (Jesus)	6/17/98 Vol. 11
Mystical Body unite in love (Jesus)	1/5/98 Vol. 10
Mystical Body will (Father)	9/11/95 Vol. 3
Mystical Body woven together (Jesus)	7/3/03 Vol. 32
Mystical suffering Jesus for all of mankind (Jesus)	7/24/07 Vol. 48
NAFTA Treaty cause of lost jobs (Jesus)	7/11/07 Vol. 48
Nagasaki pray for peace (Jesus)	11/8/01 Vol. 25
Nagasaki,Japan the effect of WWII (Blessed Mother)	10/14/01 Vol. 25
name each are called by (Jesus)	7/22/03 Vol. 32
Name of Jesus every knee should bend (Jesus)	5/5/99 Vol. 15
Name of Jesus key to unlock graces (Jesus)	1/3/08 Vol. 50
Name of Jesus overwhelming power (St. Michael)	7/20/97 Vol. 8
Name of Jesus power in healing (Jesus)	5/6/07 Vol. 47
Name of Jesus power in healing, vs. demons (Jesus)	6/24/07 Vol. 47
Names for God God always exists (Jesus)	11/26/99 Vol. 17
names of people stay for eternity (Jesus)	1/3/08 Vol. 50
narrow gate faith tested (Jesus)	11/27/97 Vol. 9
narrow gate free will (Jesus)	10/28/94 Vol. 2
narrow gate only way to heaven (Jesus)	8/26/01 Vol. 24
narrow path to heaven give our will to God (Jesus)	3/27/01 Vol. 22
narrow road everlasting vs. temporary (Jesus)	8/22/04 Vol. 36
narrow road need suffering,humility,frugal (Jesus)	3/2/02 Vol. 26
narrow road straight road to heaven (Jesus)	7/26/05 Vol. 40
narrow road vs broad road to hell (Jesus)	8/17/99 Vol. 16
narrow road to God desire of soul (Jesus)	11/5/03 Vol. 33
narrow road to heaven detach from possessions (Jesus)	4/9/00 Vol. 19
narrow road to heaven vs broad road to hell (Jesus)	12/7/05 Vol. 41
narrow vs broad road heaven vs hell (Jesus)	7/20/00 Vol. 20
National Debt expanding with wars (Jesus)	11/24/06 Vol. 45
national emergency preplanned event to cause (Jesus)	5/25/07 Vol. 47
National ID chips in hand (Jesus)	9/9/02 Vol. 28
National ID chips in licences coming (Jesus)	3/31/05 Vol. 38
National ID mandatory smart card,security (Jesus)	8/22/02 Vol. 28
national ID smart cards (Jesus)	5/29/03 Vol. 31
national ID threatened by chaos (Jesus)	9/26/01 Vol. 24
national ID & chips forced in desperation (Jesus)	4/4/02 Vol. 27
national ID card due to war & security (Jesus)	9/20/01 Vol. 24
national ID cards backed by central bankers (Jesus)	3/16/02 Vol. 26
national ID cards for security (Jesus)	7/25/03 Vol. 32
national ID cards refuse this & chips in hand (Jesus)	9/28/01 Vol. 24
national ID cards smart cards and chips (Jesus)	11/12/01 Vol. 25
national ID cards tighter security (Jesus)	10/24/02 Vol. 29
National ID chips loss of freedoms (Jesus)	10/4/01 Vol. 25
national ID chips to buy & sell (Jesus)	11/8/01 Vol. 25
national ID smart card future buying & selling (Jesus)	9/18/01 Vol. 24
National ID smart card identify true citizens (Jesus)	9/4/06 Vol. 44
National ID systems to control people (Jesus)	11/24/99 Vol. 17
national ids for security (Jesus)	5/17/03 Vol. 31
national ids forced for security (Jesus)	5/12/03 Vol. 31
national IDS in many forms (Jesus)	5/2/02 Vol. 27
national IDS mandatory smart cards first (Jesus)	5/21/02 Vol. 27
National Shrine Immaculate Conception (Mary)	7/5/97 Vol. 8
nations destroyed who do not follow God (Jesus)	8/19/05 Vol. 40
nations will fall to power of Antichrist (Jesus)	7/20/00 Vol. 20
nations, rich help poor nations (Jesus)	4/11/02 Vol. 27
nations, rich should share with poor (Jesus)	10/3/02 Vol. 29
Native Americans respect and pray for (Jesus)	7/27/06 Vol. 44
Native Indians do not criticize (Jesus)	7/14/05 Vol. 40
Nativity make room for Jesus (Jesus)	12/31/94 Vol. 2
Nativity Church enhances faith (Jesus)	5/16/02 Vol. 27
Nativity scene continue focus on Jesus (Jesus)	12/21/00 Vol. 21
Nativity scene honors Christ's birth (Jesus)	11/25/04 Vol. 37
Nativity scene in prayer room (Jesus)	1/4/07 Vol. 46
Nativity scene no longer in public (Jesus)	12/19/96 Vol. 5
Nativity scene should be more public (Jesus)	12/9/04 Vol. 37
Nativity scenes as year around altar (Jesus)	1/6/02 Vol. 26
Nativity scenes celebrate all year (Jesus)	1/10/04 Vol. 34
Nativity scenes display throughout the year (Jesus)	12/4/03 Vol. 33
Nativity scenes displayed more now (Jesus)	1/1/07 Vol. 46
Nativity Scenes keep on altar all year long (Jesus)	12/28/00 Vol. 21
Nativity scenes rejected (Jesus)	12/7/03 Vol. 33
Nativity secularized Santa Claus, Xmas (Jesus)	12/18/99 Vol. 17
Nativity, religious objects be not afraid to display (Jesus)	12/18/03 Vol. 33
Nativity,crucifixes meet persecution, criticism (Jesus)	11/26/03 Vol. 33
NATO force of European Union (Jesus)	6/23/99 Vol. 15
natural balance of earth abused for greed (Jesus)	6/15/98 Vol. 11
natural disaster and economy (Jesus)	10/16/02 Vol. 29
natural disaster could trigger martial law (Jesus)	11/15/06 Vol. 45
natural disaster near (Jesus)	8/4/07 Vol. 48
natural disasters abuse of nature (Jesus)	8/5/99 Vol. 16
natural disasters affect delivering essentials (Jesus)	1/23/08 Vol. 50
natural disasters affecting economy (Jesus)	10/21/04 Vol. 37
natural disasters and man-made problems (Jesus)	8/28/03 Vol. 32
natural disasters as chastisements (Jesus)	4/24/05 Vol. 39
natural disasters avoid oceanfront property (Jesus)	6/12/06 Vol. 43
natural disasters Brazil & Europe (Jesus)	1/6/00 Vol. 18
natural disasters bring us to our knees (Jesus)	4/22/04 Vol. 35
natural disasters chastisement for abortions (Jesus)	8/5/02 Vol. 28
natural disasters chastisements for sin (Jesus)	4/4/03 Vol. 31
natural disasters defy one world people (Jesus)	8/13/98 Vol. 12
natural disasters destroying parts of America (Jesus)	9/23/04 Vol. 36
natural disasters events waiting to happen (Jesus)	4/14/05 Vol. 39

natural disasters financial burden (Jesus)   2/2/07 Vol. 46

natural disasters financial losses adding up (Jesus)   1/15/07 Vol. 46

natural disasters from chaos of nature (Jesus)   9/9/03 Vol. 32

natural disasters have food & fuel (Jesus)   1/28/07 Vol. 46

natural disasters help neighbors (Jesus)   1/31/08 Vol. 50

natural disasters increase after June '06 (Jesus)   5/23/06 Vol. 43

natural disasters increase intensity,frequency (Jesus)   9/22/98 Vol. 12

natural disasters more severe (Jesus)   6/30/06 Vol. 43

natural disasters moving to next level (Jesus)   1/18/03 Vol. 30

natural disasters one after another in end times (Jesus)   3/30/05 Vol. 38

natural disasters pray for displaced people (Jesus)   8/29/07 Vol. 48

natural disasters pray for protection from (Jesus)   7/13/06 Vol. 44

natural disasters pray for victims (Jesus)   5/11/06 Vol. 43

natural disasters prayer to ease (Jesus)   9/12/07 Vol. 48

natural disasters punishment for sins (Jesus)   2/24/03 Vol. 30

natural disasters punishment for sins (Jesus)   5/8/02 Vol. 27

natural disasters rain,fire,droughts (Jesus)   7/2/98 Vol. 12

natural disasters reacting to our sins (Jesus)   6/29/04 Vol. 35

natural disasters reflection of man's violence (Jesus)   8/28/07 Vol. 48

natural disasters sign of end times (Jesus)   4/11/06 Vol. 43

natural disasters sign of end times (Jesus)   10/15/07 Vol. 49

natural disasters signs of end times (Jesus)   2/13/07 Vol. 46

natural disasters some payment for abortions (Jesus)   8/24/07 Vol. 48

natural disasters string occurring (Jesus)   8/23/07 Vol. 48

natural disasters suffering to continue (Jesus)   9/13/05 Vol. 40

natural disasters taking on biblical proportions (Jesus)   6/24/02 Vol. 27

natural disasters testing America (Jesus)   9/14/06 Vol. 44

natural disasters threat to crops (Jesus)   5/10/07 Vol. 47

natural disasters threatened in America for sins (Jesus)   3/18/02 Vol. 26

natural disasters tidal wave (Jesus)   5/3/04 Vol. 35

natural disasters to affect transportation (Jesus)   1/23/08 Vol. 50

natural disasters to bring us to our knees (Jesus)   6/11/02 Vol. 27

natural disasters to come to America (Jesus)   12/30/06 Vol. 45

natural disasters to intensify (Jesus)   3/5/08 Vol. 50

natural disasters to strip our possessions (Jesus)   4/13/98 Vol. 11

natural disasters to test people (Jesus)   10/18/07 Vol. 49

natural disasters tornadoes, hurricanes, snow (Jesus)   9/13/03 Vol. 32

natural disasters turning world upside down (Jesus)   12/21/07 Vol. 49

natural disasters wake up call (Jesus)   9/22/03 Vol. 32

natural disasters wherever you live (Jesus)   1/27/05 Vol. 38

natural disturbances reflect man's wars (Jesus)   5/24/04 Vol. 35

Natural Family Planning accepted birth control by Chruch (Jesus)   5/4/05 Vol. 39

Natural Family Planning accepted by Church (Jesus)   1/22/07 Vol. 46

natural gas fuels under stress (Jesus)   12/29/03 Vol. 33

natural gas lower cost when warmer (Jesus)   1/26/06 Vol. 42

natural resources are a blessing (Jesus)   8/28/06 Vol. 44

natural resources need proper management (Jesus)   6/12/03 Vol. 31

natural resources protect as a gift (Jesus)   7/10/06 Vol. 44

natural resources share oil wealth (Jesus)   10/4/07 Vol. 49

nat. resources finite preserve for future generations (Jesus) 8/19/04 Vol. 36

nature abused balance of (Jesus)   3/26/98 Vol. 10

nature balance of (Jesus)   6/1/02 Vol. 27

nature fits together perfectly (Jesus)   8/2/01 Vol. 24

nature gives glory to God in creation (Jesus)   11/22/00 Vol. 21

nature reacting to man's abuses (Jesus)   4/30/07 Vol. 47

nature reflects violence of sin (Jesus)   7/29/04 Vol. 36

nature saint (St. Francis)   10/4/93 Vol. 1

nature stones (Jesus)   12/16/94 Vol. 2

nature teaches us God's plan (Jesus)   6/5/06 Vol. 43

nature will fight back (Jesus)   5/4/01 Vol. 23

nature & creation beauty of (Jesus)   7/27/06 Vol. 44

nature & creation like an orchestra (Jesus)   9/3/03 Vol. 32

nature abused leads to destruction (Jesus)   8/2/01 Vol. 24

nature abused by man needs to be curbed (Jesus)   1/4/07 Vol. 46

nature corrupted by man's manipulations (Jesus)   11/18/03 Vol. 33

nature despoiled by man's manipulation (Jesus)   2/16/06 Vol. 42

nature in storms reacting to man's abuses (Jesus)   9/16/04 Vol. 36

nature manipulated man will pay (Jesus)   2/13/06 Vol. 42

nature rebelling against abuses (Jesus)   10/13/05 Vol. 41

nature rebelling for abuse of nature (Jesus)   3/8/05 Vol. 38

nature violated abortion pills,cloning,DNA (Jesus)   3/10/01 Vol. 22

nature violated hybrids,clones,pesticides (Jesus)   2/26/01 Vol. 22

nature vs. man parallel of violence (Jesus)   5/10/07 Vol. 47

nature, order of follows God's Will (Jesus)   8/29/04 Vol. 36

nature, population confirming evil of abortion (Jesus)   1/23/06 Vol. 42

nature's abuses causing diseases, cancer (Jesus)   11/9/06 Vol. 45

nature's beauty gives glory to God (Jesus)   3/8/02 Vol. 26

nature's life process do not tamper with (Jesus)   8/23/01 Vol. 24

nature's paintbrush colors in leaves, animals (Jesus)   10/16/07 Vol. 49

Navy ships war (Jesus)   1/26/94 Vol. 1

near death experience second chance for conversion (Jesus) 12/26/03 Vol. 33

necessities of life competition between people (Jesus)   6/12/03 Vol. 31

necessities of life struggle for (Jesus)   11/6/06 Vol. 45

need for food many problems,new year (Jesus)   11/11/99 Vol. 17

need Jesus' help throughout life (Jesus)   3/20/00 Vol. 18

needs of others opportunities for graces (Jesus)   3/22/06 Vol. 42

needs of today have more distractions (Jesus)   10/25/07 Vol. 49

neighbor love of (Jesus)   5/17/01 Vol. 23

neighbor talking about others (Jesus)   9/16/94 Vol. 2

neighbor, helping builds bonds of friendship (Jesus)   5/20/04 Vol. 35

neighborly assistance give time,money all year (Mother Cabrini)   11/13/98 Vol. 13

neighborly help help & love someone (Jesus)   9/1/99 Vol. 16

neighbors help each other (Jesus) 1/16/03 Vol. 30
neighbors help physically & spiritually (Jesus) 5/24/03 Vol. 31
neighbors reach out in love (Jesus) 3/15/98 Vol. 10
neighbors reach out in love to (Jesus) 4/24/04 Vol. 35
nervous habits plucking eyelashes (Jesus) 2/21/07 Vol. 46
New Adam New Eve (Jesus) 5/6/03 Vol. 31
New Adam who conquers sin (Jesus) 7/29/06 Vol. 44
New Adam & Eve sin & death conquered (Jesus) 8/15/01 Vol. 24
New Age cleanse from Church (Jesus) 11/6/07 Vol. 49
New Age electrical devices (Jesus) 8/26/95 Vol. 3
New Age evil in churches (Jesus) 9/25/06 Vol. 44
New Age humanism in church (Jesus) 9/18/02 Vol. 28
New Age idols & thinking in Church (Jesus) 7/20/02 Vol. 28
New Age images in churches (Jesus) 9/8/03 Vol. 32
New Age in churches (Jesus) 9/17/03 Vol. 32
New Age influence on churches (Jesus) 8/28/03 Vol. 32
New Age mark of the beast (Jesus) 5/31/94 Vol. 1
New Age monuments to worship (Jesus) 9/11/03 Vol. 32
New Age occult & atheism (Jesus) 10/8/03 Vol. 33
New Age one world religion (Jesus) 2/12/04 Vol. 34
New Age pagan gods of the earth (Jesus) 8/15/98 Vol. 12
New Age remnant to meet in homes (Jesus) 6/4/04 Vol. 35
New Age scriptures 10/18/93 Vol. 1
New Age shape renovations (Jesus) 9/18/03 Vol. 32
New Age we must choose God only (Jesus) 7/16/01 Vol. 24
New Age worship of beast in churches (Jesus) 7/4/02 Vol. 28
New Age worships man and earth (Jesus) 4/29/97 Vol. 7
New Age worships natural gods (Jesus) 7/1/04 Vol. 36
New Age & modernism effect on Church (Jesus) 4/23/02 Vol. 27
New Age & occult cause demon possession (Jesus) 9/2/03 Vol. 32
New Age & occult do not get involved in (Jesus) 9/28/06 Vol. 44
New Age & occult lead to demon possession (Jesus) 9/12/05 Vol. 40
New Age & occult need prayer,sacramentals, saints (Jesus) 3/17/04 Vol. 34
New Age & occult take on evil influence (Jesus) 9/24/03 Vol. 32
New Age & occult to take over in churches (Jesus) 9/22/03 Vol. 32
New Age & U.N. control of religion in world (Jesus) 10/8/04 Vol. 37
New Age banners beginning entry into churches (Jesus) 3/18/04 Vol. 34
New Age believers to test the faithful (Jesus) 5/7/06 Vol. 43
New Age charms avoid (Jesus) 10/15/97 Vol. 9
New Age curiosities blessed sacramentals needed (Jesus) 10/13/05 Vol. 41
New Age designs brought into churches (Jesus) 7/19/07 Vol. 48
New Age display glory to evil, not God (Jesus) 12/16/04 Vol. 37
New Age ecumenism coming worship of Antichrist (Jesus) 8/6/00 Vol. 20
New Age idols do not follow (Jesus) 5/28/01 Vol. 23
New Age idols evil influences in Churches (Jesus) 1/20/04 Vol. 34
New Age idols in churches (Jesus) 1/4/01 Vol. 22
New Age idols remove from church (Jesus) 1/14/05 Vol. 38

New Age idols replace statues (Jesus) 10/22/02 Vol. 29
New Age in Church false teachings of worldly (Jesus) 10/18/03 Vol. 33
New Age influence entering churches (Jesus) 10/28/04 Vol. 37
New Age influences attempt to destroy Church (Jesus) 4/15/05 Vol. 39
New Age influences worship of gods & goddesses (Jesus) 5/14/05 Vol. 39
New Age movement a false religion of evil (Jesus) 7/29/00 Vol. 20
New Age Movement Antichrist head,one world (Jesus) 12/26/97 Vol. 9
New Age movement attacking children (Jesus) 7/11/00 Vol. 20
New Age Movement believe in gods of nature (Jesus) 5/14/99 Vol. 15
New Age Movement calling down God's wrath (Jesus) 11/4/00 Vol. 21
New Age Movement creeping into churches (Jesus) 5/1/03 Vol. 31
New Age Movement deny sexual sins (Jesus) 7/15/03 Vol. 32
New Age Movement do not be fooled by (Jesus) 3/17/99 Vol. 14
New Age Movement do not follow (Jesus) 1/17/01 Vol. 22
New Age Movement evil signs & illusions (Jesus) 1/2/98 Vol. 10
New Age movement false ecumenism (Jesus) 6/4/00 Vol. 19
New Age Movement forced on people (Jesus) 6/6/03 Vol. 31
New Age Movement Harry Potter (Jesus) 2/4/03 Vol. 30
New Age Movement in churches (Jesus) 1/2/01 Vol. 22
New Age Movement in our churches (Jesus) 5/25/01 Vol. 23
New Age movement in stripped churches (Jesus) 7/23/01 Vol. 24
New Age movement influence in churches (Jesus) 4/19/01 Vol. 23
New Age Movement leads to pagan gods (Jesus) 12/31/97 Vol. 9
New Age movement linked to modernism (Jesus) 8/16/02 Vol. 28
New Age Movement occult,crystals,pentagram (Jesus) 2/12/99 Vol. 14
New Age movement one world religion (Jesus) 7/6/04 Vol. 36
New Age movement one world religion (Jesus) 8/24/00 Vol. 20
New Age Movement only religion to be accepted (Jesus) 10/28/03 Vol. 33
New Age Movement refuse to follow (Jesus) 5/12/02 Vol. 27
New Age Movement religion in churches (Jesus) 4/19/01 Vol. 23
New Age Movement sacramentals (Jesus) 6/21/94 Vol. 1
New Age movement spiritual arm of Antichrist (Jesus) 7/5/00 Vol. 20
New Age movement to destroy the churches (Jesus) 7/13/01 Vol. 24
New Age movement world religion forced on us (Jesus) 9/20/01 Vol. 24
New Age movement worship deities of nature (Jesus) 4/13/00 Vol. 19
New Age Movement worship of earthly gods (Jesus) 5/7/98 Vol. 11
New Age Movement worships alien gods (Jesus) 6/27/01 Vol. 23
New Age religion avoid idols, alien gods (Jesus) 10/25/98 Vol. 13
New Age religion New World Order (Jesus) 4/22/03 Vol. 31
New Age religion uses Egyptian gods of evil (Jesus) 3/15/01 Vol. 22
New Age Religions gods of the earth (Jesus) 8/17/00 Vol. 20
New Age songs avoid in church (Jesus) 1/20/05 Vol. 38
New Age symbols evil influence in church (Jesus) 8/23/03 Vol. 32
New Age symbols Satanic sacramentals (Jesus) 3/5/98 Vol. 10
New Age teaching avoid where taught (Jesus) 10/12/07 Vol. 49
New Age teaching confusion & unrest (Jesus) 9/16/06 Vol. 44
New Age teaching taught in churches (Jesus) 8/24/06 Vol. 44

New Age teachings coming into the Church (Jesus) 7/30/05 Vol. 40

New Age teachings to come into churches (Jesus) 2/12/06 Vol. 42

New Age thinking schismatic church (Jesus) 7/7/02 Vol. 28

New Age, modernism undermining traditions (Jesus) 1/19/08 Vol. 50

New Age, occult in our churches (Jesus) 8/23/03 Vol. 32

New Age,occult from Satan (Jesus) 3/13/00 Vol. 18

new cars & homes attracting loans (Jesus) 8/15/02 Vol. 28

New creation Messiah (Jesus) 12/6/93 Vol. 1

new currency to make current money invalid (Jesus) 8/20/02 Vol. 28

new earth abyss 9/20/93 Vol. 1

new earth demons (Jesus) 4/17/94 Vol. 1

new earth first fruit (Jesus) 11/29/94 Vol. 2

new earth follow Divine Will (Jesus) 2/2/98 Vol. 10

new earth love (Jesus) 5/18/95 Vol. 2

New Era radiance of His love (God the Father) 3/22/98 Vol. 10

New era Satan chained (Jesus) 10/9/97 Vol. 9

New Eve yes (Mary) 12/8/93 Vol. 1

new flags New World Order states (Jesus) 12/3/98 Vol. 13

new heavens and new earth (Jesus) 11/4/05 Vol. 41

new heavens & earth Era of Peace (Jesus) 11/19/06 Vol. 45

new heavens & new earth Jesus victor over Antichrist (Jesus) 5/6/07 Vol. 47

new heavens, new earth in New Jerusalem (Jesus) 7/19/07 Vol. 48

New heavens,new earth renew face of the earth (Jesus) 12/15/99 Vol. 17

new heaves & new earth after chastisement (Jesus) 1/26/07 Vol. 46

New Jerusalem at Era of Peace (Jesus) 9/20/07 Vol. 48

New Jerusalem description in Revelation (Jesus) 7/19/07 Vol. 48

New Jerusalem evil influence removed (Jesus) 9/14/98 Vol. 12

New Jerusalem final preparation for heaven (God the Father)2/22/98 Vol. 10

New Jerusalem Golden Gate 8/17/93 Vol. 1

New Jerusalem live to see it (Jesus) 5/20/01 Vol. 23

New Jerusalem recreate the earth (Jesus) 11/26/99 Vol. 17

New Jerusalem triumph of two hearts (Jesus) 6/6/97 Vol. 7

New Jerusalem witness of His glory (Jesus) 10/31/99 Vol. 17

New Jerusalem, The rare stones and light (Jesus) 6/11/98 Vol. 11

new life available in Confession (Jesus) 4/17/01 Vol. 23

new life children (Jesus) 12/25/95 Vol. 3

new life faith (Jesus) 4/18/94 Vol. 1

new life new birth in the Spirit (Jesus) 4/24/06 Vol. 43

new life in Jesus after death (Jesus) 3/8/00 Vol. 18

New Orleans call for charity (Jesus) 9/8/05 Vol. 40

New Orleans long term help needed (Jesus) 9/8/05 Vol. 40

New Orleans needs to repent of sins (Jesus) 3/2/06 Vol. 42

New Orleans rebuilding questionable (Jesus) 9/7/05 Vol. 40

New Orleans return to evil, more destruction (Jesus) 9/7/05 Vol. 40

New Orleans sins brought destruction (Jesus) 10/20/05 Vol. 41

New Orleans still cleaning up (Jesus) 1/18/06 Vol. 42

New Orleans debt city under sea level questioned (Jesus) 9/14/05 Vol. 40

New Orleans troops parallel to tribulation (Jesus) 9/3/05 Vol. 40

New Orleans water treatment plants need help (Jesus) 9/20/05 Vol. 40

new self image rid old habits (Jesus) 3/30/00 Vol. 18

New Testament Messiah fulfills prophesy (Jesus) 5/4/07 Vol. 47

New World Government possible martyrs for faith (Jesus) 6/22/99 Vol. 15

New World Order and New Age Movement (Jesus) 4/30/98 Vol. 11

New World Order by financial collapse,wars (Jesus) 12/1/98 Vol. 13

New World Order cannot conquer will,spirit (Jesus) 7/17/98 Vol. 12

New World Order changes in leadership (Jesus) 6/21/01 Vol. 23

new world order concentration camps (Jesus) 2/1/07 Vol. 46

New World Order control banks and stocks (Jesus) 8/24/98 Vol. 12

New World Order controlled by money (Jesus) 4/6/99 Vol. 15

new world order crematoriums prepared (Jesus) 3/10/05 Vol. 38

New World Order destruction, persecution (Jesus) 8/17/98 Vol. 12

New World Order enemies imprisoned (Jesus) 3/15/99 Vol. 14

New World Order financial & political turmoil (Jesus) 6/2/98 Vol. 11

New World Order gulag of prisons (Jesus) 10/17/96 Vol. 5

New World Order killing lists,religious,patriots (Jesus) 9/20/98 Vol. 12

new world order lose freedoms (Jesus) 4/19/01 Vol. 23

New World Order Nazi tactics for persecution (Jesus) 10/22/98 Vol. 13

new world order obey or lose money (Jesus) 5/31/04 Vol. 35

new world order opposing will bring prison (Jesus) 2/7/08 Vol. 50

new world order people ruthless as Nazis (Jesus) 6/8/07 Vol. 47

New World Order police state (Jesus) 1/20/03 Vol. 30

New World Order preparing for Antichrist (Jesus) 6/5/01 Vol. 23

New World Order prison for not going along with (Jesus) 7/17/01 Vol. 24

New World Order threats via food & medicine (Jesus) 8/12/98 Vol. 12

New World Order to prepare for emergency (Jesus) 6/21/01 Vol. 23

New World religion to be forced on us (Jesus) 1/6/00 Vol. 18

new year need spiritual improvements (Jesus) 12/31/03 Vol. 33

New Year spiritual resolutions (Jesus) 12/28/06 Vol. 45

New Year watch events in the Church (Jesus) 12/31/00 Vol. 21

new year preparation improve spiritual life (Jesus) 12/30/03 Vol. 33

New Year resolutions improve spiritual life (Jesus) 1/10/08 Vol. 50

New Year's Eve opportunity for disaster (Jesus) 5/23/02 Vol. 27

New Year's resolution spend more time with Jesus (Jesus) 12/18/98 Vol. 13

New Year's resolutions gifts for Jesus (Jesus) 12/29/00 Vol. 21

New Year's resolutions improve spiritual lives (Jesus) 12/31/96 Vol. 5

New York trade buildings being rebuilt (Jesus) 5/27/04 Vol. 35

newer translations from obtuse spirit (Jesus) 9/26/99 Vol. 16

news secular vs. religious (Jesus) 6/9/02 Vol. 27

news seek heavenly treasures (Jesus) 1/13/97 Vol. 6

news attractions are old tomorrow (Jesus) 11/16/05 Vol. 41

news media is very censored (Jesus) 2/3/04 Vol. 34

news, gadgets time away from prayer (Jesus) 3/6/08 Vol. 50

newspaper curiosity seek Good News instead (Jesus) 11/29/99 Vol. 17

newspapers wrong presumed winner too soon (Jesus) 11/9/00 Vol. 21

Nineveh repented (Jesus) — 3/12/03 Vol. 30

Noah followed God's Word (Jesus) — 4/1/03 Vol. 31

Noah rainbow covenant (Jesus) — 8/14/97 Vol. 8

Noah scoffers face judgment (Jesus) — 4/12/97 Vol. 7

Noah, like days of scoffers of saving food (Jesus) — 3/15/00 Vol. 18

Noah, Sodom & Gomorrah evil as today (Father) — 6/16/05 Vol. 39

Noah, as in days of evil society of today, sexual sins (Jesus) 3/22/02 Vol. 26

Noah, as in the time of sacramentals, food, water (Jesus) — 4/8/99 Vol. 15

Noah, days of show wrath of God on evil (Jesus) — 2/13/01 Vol. 22

Noah's Ark flood for evils of the day (Jesus) — 2/13/07 Vol. 46

Noah's Ark purification — 8/16/93 Vol. 1

Noah's critics as critics of food storage (Jesus) — 7/20/00 Vol. 20

Noah's day as today, ignored signs (Jesus) — 2/5/04 Vol. 34

Noah's Day as today's signs (Jesus) — 10/16/06 Vol. 45

Noah's day like today (Jesus) — 2/13/03 Vol. 30

Noah's day lost sense of sin (Jesus) — 5/13/99 Vol. 15

Noah's day repeated today (Jesus) — 10/30/02 Vol. 29

Noah's scoffers died as will unrepentant (Jesus) — 2/24/00 Vol. 18

Noah's time as when Jesus comes again (Jesus) — 11/28/04 Vol. 37

Noah's time justice (Jesus) — 2/17/97 Vol. 6

nomads persecutor (Jesus) — 10/25/94 Vol. 2

Noreen Eich's funeral (Jesus) — 1/22/02 Vol. 26

North American martyrs persecuted & tortured (Jesus) — 10/19/05 Vol. 41

North American Union American takeover (Jesus) — 7/4/07 Vol. 48

North American Union Amero new currency (Jesus) — 1/18/07 Vol. 46

North American Union beginning of end of America (Jesus) 10/1/06 Vol. 45

North American Union big media event on (Jesus) — 4/20/07 Vol. 47

North American Union chips in the body (Jesus) — 7/28/07 Vol. 48

North American Union demise of America (Jesus) — 3/22/07 Vol. 46

North American Union favored by corporations (Jesus) — 7/21/07 Vol. 48

North American Union financial collapse (Jesus) — 7/16/07 Vol. 48

North American Union for our takeover (Jesus) — 2/7/08 Vol. 50

North American Union new highways (Jesus) — 5/25/07 Vol. 47

North American Union takeover of America (Jesus) — 12/1/07 Vol. 49

North American Union threat to rights & liberties (Jesus) 3/13/08 Vol. 50

North American Union to remove sovereignty (Jesus) — 2/1/07 Vol. 46

North American Union Trojan horse in NAFTA (Jesus) — 8/9/07 Vol. 48

North Korea also has weapons (Jesus) — 2/16/03 Vol. 30

North Korea nuclear brinkmanship (Jesus) — 1/15/03 Vol. 30

North Korea nuclear tests (Jesus) — 10/19/06 Vol. 45

North Korea nuclear threat (Jesus) — 4/5/03 Vol. 31

North Korea nuclear weapons, double standard (Jesus) — 1/2/03 Vol. 30

North Korea & Iran threats to world peace (Jesus) — 1/17/06 Vol. 42

North Korea & Iraq double standard (Jesus) — 2/6/03 Vol. 30

Norton, Sue vocation Mass (Jesus) — 9/7/02 Vol. 28

nothing, we are without God (Jesus) — 8/3/04 Vol. 36

nothing, we are without God's Presence (Jesus) — 12/7/06 Vol. 45

Notre Dame, Montreal feast of Annunciation (Mary) — 3/26/07 Vol. 46

novena for crucifix on altar (Jesus) — 8/9/07 Vol. 48

novena for crucifix on altar (Jesus) — 7/26/07 Vol. 48

Novena of prayer before Pentecost (Jesus) — 5/17/07 Vol. 47

novenas & fasting temporal punishments (Jesus) — 9/24/97 Vol. 8

nuclear accident nuclear plants (Jesus) — 9/19/97 Vol. 8

nuclear bombs pray to stop wars (Jesus) — 8/7/03 Vol. 32

nuclear effect on microchips (Jesus) — 11/14/01 Vol. 25

nuclear encounter hold up hands in prayer (Jesus) — 7/30/98 Vol. 12

nuclear plant leaks of radiation (Jesus) — 1/4/00 Vol. 18

nuclear plants threat of radiation leak (Jesus) — 12/14/99 Vol. 17

nuclear power plants and computer problems (Jesus) — 10/28/99 Vol. 17

nuclear powers more money on weapons (Jesus) — 9/23/99 Vol. 16

nuclear radiation threat on plants, ships, weapons (Jesus) — 2/26/02 Vol. 26

nuclear reactors pray for protection (Jesus) — 9/12/02 Vol. 28

nuclear secrets government sold out (Jesus) — 5/20/99 Vol. 15

nuclear terrorism more potential from theft (Jesus) — 1/25/05 Vol. 38

nuclear threat requires prayer for leaders (Jesus) — 8/10/00 Vol. 20

nuclear war can be mitigated (Jesus) — 8/14/99 Vol. 16

nuclear war pray consecration (Jesus) — 8/14/97 Vol. 8

nuclear war pray to mitigate (Jesus) — 2/19/98 Vol. 10

nuclear war purification (Jesus) — 6/19/94 Vol. 1

nuclear war sign of preparation (Jesus) — 8/29/97 Vol. 8

nuclear war some nations annihilated (Holy Spirit) — 6/4/98 Vol. 11

nuclear war too dangerous (Jesus) — 3/9/06 Vol. 42

nuclear war wasteland on earth (Jesus) — 1/27/98 Vol. 10

nuclear war will not be permitted in total (Jesus) — 10/24/00 Vol. 21

nuclear warfare will not destroy world (Jesus) — 1/26/01 Vol. 22

nuclear weapons and power plants (Jesus) — 7/10/03 Vol. 32

nuclear weapons could threaten earthly life (Jesus) — 6/1/04 Vol. 35

nuclear weapons do not proliferate (Jesus) — 4/10/03 Vol. 31

nuclear weapons launched accidentally (Jesus) — 6/7/99 Vol. 15

nuclear weapons pray not to use (Jesus) — 6/3/99 Vol. 15

nuclear weapons pray they are not used (Jesus) — 10/28/99 Vol. 17

nuclear weapons pray they are not used (Jesus) — 10/21/99 Vol. 17

nuclear weapons threat in war (Jesus) — 2/28/03 Vol. 30

nuclear weapons threat to the world (Jesus) — 5/11/99 Vol. 15

nuclear weapons threat to Western civilization (Jesus) — 11/6/01 Vol. 25

nuclear weapons used in chemical or bio attack (Jesus) — 3/14/03 Vol. 30

nuclear weapons world an armed camp (Jesus) — 12/15/03 Vol. 33

nuns contemplative, assist dying (Jesus) — 8/6/98 Vol. 12

nuns encouraged in faith (St. Therese) — 8/16/98 Vol. 12

nuns role of women (Jesus) — 8/14/96 Vol. 4

nuns praying Divine Will (Jesus) — 7/5/94 Vol. 2

nuns, cloistered balance sin with their prayer (Jesus) — 7/4/04 Vol. 36

nurses & doctors be thankful for service (Jesus) — 2/4/01 Vol. 22

nurses & doctors to help people (Jesus) — 1/29/04 Vol. 34

oasis of grace in confessional (Jesus) 9/28/02 Vol. 28

oasis of love graces for fallen souls (Jesus) 11/16/98 Vol. 13

obedience according to God's Will (Jesus) 10/24/07 Vol. 49

obedience homage (Jesus) 1/16/96 Vol. 3

obedience needed to God,advisor (Jesus) 9/17/07 Vol. 48

obedience to Commandments (Jesus) 5/22/03 Vol. 31

obedience to God's Will (Jesus) 4/7/04 Vol. 35

obedience to higher authority needed (Jesus) 3/1/02 Vol. 26

obedience & suffering Jesus lived life of (Jesus) 4/25/04 Vol. 35

obe. to God's laws needed to enter heaven (God the Father)4/6/01 Vol. 23

obey God instead of man (Jesus) 5/1/07 Vol. 47

obey God rather than men (Jesus) 8/14/02 Vol. 28

obey God's laws and not man's corrupt laws (Jesus) 8/3/04 Vol. 36

object of all love soul's thirst for the Divine (Jesus) 8/21/96 Vol. 4

obsession for things takes time away from God (Jesus) 12/30/99 Vol. 17

occasions of sin avoid (Jesus) 6/10/01 Vol. 23

occasions of sin avoid like falling off a cliff (Jesus) 3/16/02 Vol. 26

occasions of sin avoid temptations (Jesus) 2/22/07 Vol. 46

occasions of sin avoid them (Jesus) 7/5/04 Vol. 36

occasions of sin avoiding sin, best cure (Jesus) 11/2/00 Vol. 21

occasions of sin control your lives (Jesus) 9/17/99 Vol. 16

occasions of sin in sports & entertainment (Jesus) 9/23/02 Vol. 28

occasions of sin prostitution,gambling,porno (Jesus) 10/26/00 Vol. 21

occasions of sin remove temptations (Jesus) 1/30/04 Vol. 34

occult and mind control (Jesus) 1/18/01 Vol. 22

occult avoid Harry Potter things (Jesus) 6/24/03 Vol. 31

Occult channels of evil (Jesus) 6/25/98 Vol. 11

occult curiosity opens door to evil (Jesus) 7/6/06 Vol. 44

occult do not seek other powers (Jesus) 9/26/96 Vol. 4

Occult evil powers (Jesus) 9/20/95 Vol. 3

occult evil spirits/false witness (Jesus) 7/31/96 Vol. 4

occult leads to demon possession (Jesus) 5/19/05 Vol. 39

occult relies on tarot cards, ouijar board (Jesus) 10/31/01 Vol. 25

occult Satan's lies (Jesus) 2/22/07 Vol. 46

occult & witchcraft forbidden by Church (Jesus) 1/16/02 Vol. 26

occult & witchcraft protect children from (Jesus) 4/23/02 Vol. 27

occult activities aovid participating in (Jesus) 5/24/06 Vol. 43

occult deceptions need faith to withstand (Jesus) 10/18/03 Vol. 33

occult meetings avoid curiosity in influence (Jesus) 4/17/06 Vol. 43

occult societies secret demon power (Jesus) 4/17/06 Vol. 43

occult things remove from your house (Jesus) 11/15/02 Vol. 29

occult things to avoid Reiki,yoga,astrology, seances (Jesus) 10/30/03 Vol. 33

occult, New Age in California (Jesus) 9/10/07 Vol. 48

occult, witchcraft roots in gods of underworld (Jesus) 2/21/02 Vol. 26

occupation church bells ring (Jesus) 10/26/06 Vol. 45

octuplets born mother's refusal of abortion (Jesus) 12/21/98 Vol. 13

offer pain,suffering atone for sin in world (Jesus) 3/16/00 Vol. 18

offer up pain gain more merits in heaven (Jesus) 5/8/00 Vol. 19

offering pain to God as a prayer (Jesus) 5/22/00 Vol. 19

oil blow to economy (Jesus) 8/3/06 Vol. 44

oil fuel threatened (Jesus) 1/19/98 Vol. 10

oil sources of wars (Jesus) 12/6/04 Vol. 37

oil used as a weapon (Jesus) 4/11/02 Vol. 27

oil & chemical fires from wars and Y2K (Jesus) 10/12/99 Vol. 17

oil & drug interests cause for war (Jesus) 2/6/03 Vol. 30

oil & drug money behind Iraq War (Jesus) 8/3/07 Vol. 48

oil & drugs behind war (Jesus) 2/17/07 Vol. 46

oil & fuel problems with demand (Jesus) 2/15/08 Vol. 50

oil & fuels shortages in war (Jesus) 9/5/02 Vol. 28

oil & gas shortages (Jesus) 2/5/03 Vol. 30

oil & gasoline prices rising (Jesus) 4/7/05 Vol. 39

oil & gasoline shortages could change lifestyles (Jesus) 2/15/05 Vol. 38

oil & wars pray for ease of (Jesus) 7/6/06 Vol. 44

oil and fuel shortages from Y2K (Jesus) 3/4/99 Vol. 14

oil and gas being sought inland (Jesus) 11/30/05 Vol. 41

oil embargoes vulnerable to shortages (Jesus) 4/25/02 Vol. 27

oil fields burned as last resort (Jesus) 3/6/03 Vol. 30

oil fields goal of Iraq war (Jesus) 12/26/02 Vol. 29

oil fuel prices make other fuels attractive (Jesus) 11/29/04 Vol. 37

oil in lamps store for power outages (Jesus) 11/6/03 Vol. 33

oil increases due to government deficits (Jesus) 11/17/07 Vol. 49

oil industry controlling fuel choices (Jesus) 11/29/04 Vol. 37

oil interests in Iraq (Jesus) 5/22/03 Vol. 31

oil lamps light needed in darkness (Jesus) 9/3/99 Vol. 16

oil money controlled by rich (Jesus) 3/21/03 Vol. 30

oil of Arabs may hold West hostage (Jesus) 8/25/04 Vol. 36

oil price hikes spills,destroyed pipelines (Jesus) 12/9/04 Vol. 37

oil price increases threats to oil production (Jesus) 11/3/07 Vol. 49

oil prices before election (Jesus) 10/5/06 Vol. 45

oil refineries terrorist attack on (Jesus) 12/30/04 Vol. 37

oil rigs, refineries vulnerable to each storm (Jesus) 9/24/05 Vol. 40

oil shortages beginning of shortages (Jesus) 3/21/00 Vol. 18

oil shortages possible if war expands (Jesus) 12/20/01 Vol. 25

oil stranglehold on fuel sources (Jesus) 4/17/05 Vol. 39

oil supplies behind war (Jesus) 12/12/02 Vol. 29

oil supplies endangered by terrorists (Jesus) 3/29/01 Vol. 22

oil supplies needed for war machines (Jesus) 4/4/02 Vol. 27

oil supplies problem in Iraqi war (Jesus) 10/31/02 Vol. 29

oil supplies sabbotaged (Jesus) 10/21/06 Vol. 45

oil supplies under attack by terrorists (Jesus) 5/26/04 Vol. 35

oil supplies at risk with war in Middle East (Jesus) 10/12/00 Vol. 21

oil, gasoline prices high, increased demand (Jesus) 4/14/05 Vol. 39

oiling objects sign of holiness,blessings (Jesus) 9/20/07 Vol. 48

oiling statues raise our faith (Jesus) 1/15/98 Vol. 10

Old & New Testaments promises & covenants (Jesus) 3/21/07 Vol. 46

Old Testament foretelling of Messiah (Jesus) 5/4/07 Vol. 47

Old Testament fulfilled in Jesus (Jesus) 5/24/03 Vol. 31

Old Testament fulfilled in Jesus (Jesus) 4/6/06 Vol. 43

old vs new things less money available (Jesus) 8/15/02 Vol. 28

Old, New Testaments prophecies fulfilled (Jesus) 3/4/07 Vol. 46

olive tree miraculous healings (Jesus) 10/2/07 Vol. 49

Olympic games love in family of nations (Jesus) 1/15/98 Vol. 10

Olympic judging needs spirit of love,not bickering (Jesus) 2/21/02 Vol. 26

Olympic pride remain humble & obedient (Jesus) 6/13/97 Vol. 7

Olympic year sports (Jesus) 11/7/95 Vol. 3

Olympics focal point of love (Jesus) 7/24/96 Vol. 4

Olympics good will on even playing field (Jesus) 8/19/04 Vol. 36

Olympics preparation for Antichrist (Jesus) 3/10/96 Vol. 3

Olympics smart card,terrorism (Jesus) 8/14/96 Vol. 4

Olympics technology mark beast (Jesus) 7/17/96 Vol. 4

omens comets, asteroids, eclipses (Jesus) 12/26/02 Vol. 29

omens in the sky on day of Warning (Jesus) 10/4/02 Vol. 29

omens in the sky sign of major events (Jesus) 3/5/03 Vol. 30

omens in the sky stop desire for war (Jesus) 10/16/02 Vol. 29

omission, sins of passed up chances for charity (Jesus) 9/23/07 Vol. 48

omission, sins of time & money for poor (Jesus) 3/16/06 Vol. 42

omissions will be held accountable (Jesus) 7/12/04 Vol. 36

one world & UN mergers & jobs (Jesus) 4/26/01 Vol. 23

one world agents forcing chips (Jesus) 5/1/02 Vol. 27

one world bankers behind wars,debts,diseases (Jesus) 4/6/03 Vol. 31

one world bankers control governments (Jesus) 2/11/03 Vol. 30

one world bankers control money & governments (Jesus) 4/24/02 Vol. 27

One World Bankers dictate to leaders (Jesus) 5/20/99 Vol. 15

One World Bankers planning control of money (Jesus) 6/24/99 Vol. 15

one world control control buying & selling (Jesus) 1/14/05 Vol. 38

one world goal total control of population (Jesus) 11/26/02 Vol. 29

one world government accepted by EU (Jesus) 6/9/05 Vol. 39

one world government advocates free trade (Jesus) 4/27/01 Vol. 23

one world government Antichrist (Jesus) 3/9/94 Vol. 1

one world government battle line (Jesus) 9/16/95 Vol. 3

one world government control elections (Jesus) 1/3/08 Vol. 50

one world government control food,fuel,money (Jesus) 1/26/97 Vol. 6

one world government control of people (Jesus) 2/5/97 Vol. 6

one world government detention centers (Jesus) 2/3/97 Vol. 6

one world government European Union & UN joined (Jesus) 6/19/05 Vol. 39

One world government leaders and election (Jesus) 11/7/96 Vol. 5

one world government money, jobs and food (Jesus) 1/20/97 Vol. 6

one world government profits from debts and wars (Jesus) 3/16/02 Vol. 26

One world government take over by UN troops (Jesus) 10/19/96 Vol. 5

one world government takeover of U.S. (Jesus) 1/6/97 Vol. 6

one world government UN control by Antichrist (Jesus) 6/20/95 Vol. 2

one world killing little value for life (Jesus) 4/24/07 Vol. 47

one world leaders no earthly peace (Jesus) 12/29/94 Vol. 2

one world manipulation stripping factory jobs (Jesus) 11/18/97 Vol. 9

one world order reduce population (Jesus) 3/26/98 Vol. 10

One world order rule for Antichrist (Jesus) 5/16/97 Vol. 7

one world people abuse weather & diseases (Jesus) 5/15/03 Vol. 31

one world people agenda for takeover (Jesus) 9/20/02 Vol. 28

one world people are running America (Jesus) 2/17/06 Vol. 42

One World People are using Clinton (Jesus) 1/23/98 Vol. 10

one world people attacking Church in and out (Jesus) 6/22/02 Vol. 27

one world people attempt to destrory Church (Jesus) 6/17/02 Vol. 27

one world people bankruptcy by wars (Jesus) 8/23/06 Vol. 44

one world people bankrupting America (Jesus) 2/20/04 Vol. 34

one world people behind coming attack (Jesus) 9/22/06 Vol. 44

one world people behind continuing wars (Jesus) 12/25/03 Vol. 33

one world people behind demise of America (Jesus) 1/20/06 Vol. 42

one world people behind diseases & weather (Jesus) 5/7/03 Vol. 31

One World People behind evil crimes (Jesus) 8/27/98 Vol. 12

one world people behind Iraqi war (Jesus) 4/8/03 Vol. 31

one world people behind terrorism (Jesus) 11/3/05 Vol. 41

one world people behind wars (Jesus) 2/5/08 Vol. 50

one world people behind wars (Jesus) 10/14/06 Vol. 45

one world people behind wars (Jesus) 7/26/06 Vol. 44

one world people behind wars for profit (Jesus) 8/12/05 Vol. 40

one world people blood money from wars (Jesus) 6/5/06 Vol. 43

one world people bring on war (Jesus) 11/8/01 Vol. 25

one world people bringing America down (Jesus) 10/29/02 Vol. 29

one world people bully wars & control (Jesus) 1/15/04 Vol. 34

one world people cause disasters for control (Jesus) 6/3/06 Vol. 43

one world people cause diseases (Jesus) 1/31/03 Vol. 30

one world people cause of dictators, wars (Jesus) 12/20/02 Vol. 29

one world people cause of terrorism for war (Jesus) 9/14/01 Vol. 24

one world people cause of wars (Jesus) 2/21/05 Vol. 38

one world people cause war for money (Jesus) 4/7/03 Vol. 31

one world people cause wars (Jesus) 7/2/06 Vol. 44

one world people cause wars (Jesus) 6/16/06 Vol. 43

one world people causing bankruptcy (Jesus) 5/2/06 Vol. 43

one world people challenged on ports (Jesus) 3/9/06 Vol. 42

one world people charting our destruction (Jesus) 10/2/03 Vol. 33

one world people control all leaders (Jesus) 2/15/07 Vol. 46

One World People control armies,governments (Jesus) 4/12/98 Vol. 11

One World People control aspects of our lives (Jesus) 4/13/98 Vol. 11

one world people control both parties (Jesus) 5/17/03 Vol. 31

one world people control by electronic devices (Jesus) 2/7/07 Vol. 46

one world people control communications (Jesus) 10/6/99 Vol. 17

one world people control Congress (Jesus) 2/16/07 Vol. 46

one world people control countries by debts (Jesus) 3/6/03 Vol. 30

one world people control debts, war, terrorism (Jesus) 12/19/03 Vol. 33

one world people control food (Jesus) 5/21/03 Vol. 31

one world people control food (Jesus) 7/19/98 Vol. 12

one world people control food (Jesus) 9/16/00 Vol. 20

one world people control food,money,health (Jesus) 3/16/01 Vol. 22

one world people control for greed (Jesus) 3/15/07 Vol. 46

one world people control government from behind (Jesus) 8/14/06 Vol. 44

one world people control governments,Church (Jesus) 6/22/07 Vol. 47

one world people control media (Jesus) 10/6/06 Vol. 45

one world people control money (Jesus) 1/2/08 Vol. 50

one world people control money, weapons (Jesus) 6/8/01 Vol. 23

one world people control news (Jesus) 8/24/06 Vol. 44

one world people control of food (Jesus) 5/22/03 Vol. 31

one world people control presidents (Jesus) 12/7/00 Vol. 21

one world people control through chips (Jesus) 9/18/03 Vol. 32

one world people control through chips (Jesus) 1/13/04 Vol. 34

one world people control us (Jesus) 9/5/02 Vol. 28

one world people control wars, & leaders (Jesus) 7/24/03 Vol. 32

one world people control weather (Jesus) 5/3/01 Vol. 23

one world people control world (Jesus) 8/24/00 Vol. 20

one world people control world finances (Jesus) 7/19/01 Vol. 24

one world people create financial chaos (Jesus) 6/3/04 Vol. 35

one world people create hate (Jesus) 9/11/02 Vol. 28

one world people creating war frenzy (Jesus) 2/6/03 Vol. 30

one world people death culture (Jesus) 5/14/02 Vol. 27

one world people desire fear (Jesus) 1/1/03 Vol. 30

one world people desire wars for money (Jesus) 5/30/05 Vol. 39

one world people destroyed Argentina (Jesus) 12/20/01 Vol. 25

one world people destroying finances,military (Jesus) 3/18/06 Vol. 42

one world people directing attack on churches (Jesus) 6/14/02 Vol. 27

one world people doing away with freedoms (Jesus) 7/4/98 Vol. 12

one world people electronics, Antichrist (Jesus) 10/26/97 Vol. 9

one world people encourage constant wars (Jesus) 9/5/04 Vol. 36

one world people encouraging wars (Jesus) 2/21/03 Vol. 30

one world people exploit computer crisis (Jesus) 10/27/99 Vol. 17

one world people exploit recession (Jesus) 5/1/01 Vol. 23

one world people exploit terrorism for control (Jesus) 11/10/05 Vol. 41

One World People exploit Y2K (Jesus) 5/29/99 Vol. 15

one world people exploiting war (Jesus) 10/4/01 Vol. 25

one world people fear patriots & religious people (Jesus) 1/27/05 Vol. 38

one world people finance candidates in high offices (Jesus) 1/22/04 Vol. 34

one world people finance terrorists & dictators (Jesus) 6/15/06 Vol. 43

one world people financial control (Jesus) 1/16/02 Vol. 26

one world people financial control (Jesus) 10/17/97 Vol. 9

one world people food manipulated (Jesus) 1/10/01 Vol. 22

one world people force chips for control (Jesus) 8/28/03 Vol. 32

one world people force transponders in cars (Jesus) 8/24/06 Vol. 44

one world people force us into wars (Jesus) 7/26/03 Vol. 32

One World People forcing New World Order (Jesus) 12/15/98 Vol. 13

one world people forcing war (Jesus) 2/6/03 Vol. 30

one world people fronted money for satellites (Jesus) 5/29/02 Vol. 27

one world people getting us into wars (Jesus) 4/28/03 Vol. 31

one world people have created wars (Jesus) 9/5/06 Vol. 44

one world people have created wars (Jesus) 12/26/07 Vol. 49

one world people instigate religious differences (Jesus) 8/2/03 Vol. 32

one world people invoke a police state (Jesus) 1/4/04 Vol. 34

one world people involved in war (Jesus) 2/9/98 Vol. 10

one world people leaders selling out to (Jesus) 7/7/98 Vol. 12

one world people made themselves rich (Jesus) 10/7/99 Vol. 17

One World People make us a police state (Jesus) 9/3/98 Vol. 12

one world people make working poor slaves (Jesus) 2/15/07 Vol. 46

one world people manipulate disasters (Jesus) 9/26/03 Vol. 32

one world people manipulate fuel (Jesus) 8/15/00 Vol. 20

one world people manipulate money, stocks (Jesus) 7/26/07 Vol. 48

one world people manipulate stock market (Jesus) 9/26/02 Vol. 28

one world people manipulate weather for control (Jesus) 7/28/04 Vol. 36

one world people most rich & powerful (Jesus) 10/5/01 Vol. 25

one world people oil and control (Jesus) 1/15/03 Vol. 30

one world people oppress & enslave (Jesus) 4/21/03 Vol. 31

one world people orchestrate wars (Jesus) 7/30/06 Vol. 44

one world people orchestrating wars (Jesus) 4/3/02 Vol. 27

one world people pay terrorists (Jesus) 5/29/03 Vol. 31

one world people paying terrorists (Jesus) 5/2/03 Vol. 31

one world people perpetuate wars for profit (Jesus) 11/6/04 Vol. 37

one world people perpetuate wars for profit (Jesus) 2/28/08 Vol. 50

one world people pillaging our wealth (Jesus) 7/16/98 Vol. 12

one world people plan for takeover (Jesus) 10/4/06 Vol. 45

one world people plan to destroy U.S. (Jesus) 4/14/03 Vol. 31

one world people planning Antichrist takeover (Jesus) 6/25/02 Vol. 27

one world people planning new war (Jesus) 10/10/07 Vol. 49

One World People planning our captivity (Jesus) 6/25/98 Vol. 11

One World People planning our demise (Jesus) 6/17/99 Vol. 15

One World People planning takeover (Jesus) 5/23/98 Vol. 11

one world people planning takeover of America (Jesus) 11/9/04 Vol. 37

one world people planning war (Jesus) 12/18/01 Vol. 25

one world people power not impressive as God (Jesus) 1/21/04 Vol. 34

one world people prepare shelters for them (Jesus) 10/14/99 Vol. 17

one world people preparing concentration camps (Jesus) 6/24/04 Vol. 35

one world people preparing for Antichrist (Jesus) 10/28/02 Vol. 29

one world people preparing for battle (Jesus) 11/8/01 Vol. 25

one world people pressure Bush on war (Jesus) 9/25/02 Vol. 28

one world people problem & war solutions (Jesus) 2/3/07 Vol. 46

one world people profit from war (Jesus) 9/10/02 Vol. 28

one world people profit from war and disease (Jesus) 11/8/05 Vol. 41

one world people profit from wars (Jesus)	2/2/03 Vol. 30	one world people to kill head of state (Jesus)	3/3/04 Vol. 34
one world people profit from wars (Jesus)	1/29/02 Vol. 26	one world people to put Antichrist in power (Jesus)	3/27/03 Vol. 30
one world people profit from wars (Jesus)	3/9/06 Vol. 42	one world people to reduce population (Jesus)	9/19/02 Vol. 28
one world people profit from wars (Jesus)	3/29/07 Vol. 46	one world people to take over America (Jesus)	7/24/03 Vol. 32
one world people profit from wars (Jesus)	7/6/06 Vol. 44	one world people trade agreements controlled (Jesus)	2/11/03 Vol. 30
one world people profit from wars (Jesus)	5/29/06 Vol. 43	one world people traitors to America (Jesus)	7/31/03 Vol. 32
One World People promote death culture (Jesus)	4/21/98 Vol. 11	one world people trying to destroy middle class (Jesus)	1/24/06 Vol. 42
one world people promoting death culture (Jesus)	4/12/03 Vol. 31	one world people UN and NATO (Jesus)	10/23/97 Vol. 9
one world people promoting war (Jesus)	12/5/01 Vol. 25	one world people UN, vehicle for takeover (Jesus)	12/29/01 Vol. 25
one world people protect churches from (Jesus)	1/4/08 Vol. 50	one world people use diseases for takeover (Jesus)	12/2/03 Vol. 33
one world people provoke wars & fear (Jesus)	5/20/03 Vol. 31	one world people use information on us (Jesus)	2/18/04 Vol. 34
one world people pushing for war (Jesus)	1/2/03 Vol. 30	one world people use surveillance on us (Jesus)	10/1/06 Vol. 45
one world people ready for takeover (Jesus)	1/3/01 Vol. 22	one world people use terrorism (Jesus)	4/15/04 Vol. 35
one world people reduce our military (Jesus)	4/30/03 Vol. 31	one world people use TV cable & phones (Jesus)	1/15/04 Vol. 34
one world people refuse to go to war (Jesus)	7/27/97 Vol. 8	one world people using Islamic militants (Jesus)	8/4/06 Vol. 44
one world people run death camps (Jesus)	3/2/07 Vol. 46	one world people using our president (Jesus)	5/16/03 Vol. 31
one world people secretly preparing takeover (Jesus)	8/2/00 Vol. 20	one world people using terrorism for control (Jesus)	10/22/02 Vol. 29
one world people seek drugs,oil,arms sales (Jesus)	8/29/02 Vol. 28	one world people using terrorism, security (Jesus)	10/27/05 Vol. 41
one world people seek global control (Jesus)	1/26/04 Vol. 34	one world people using UN (Jesus)	9/11/03 Vol. 32
one world people sell weapons to both sides (Jesus)	1/20/04 Vol. 34	one world people using US to fight battles (Jesus)	11/5/02 Vol. 29
one world people sold souls to Satan (Jesus)	2/15/07 Vol. 46	one world people usurp rights (Jesus)	9/12/00 Vol. 20
one world people sold us lies on war (Jesus)	2/1/07 Vol. 46	one world people vs. American people (Jesus)	1/11/07 Vol. 46
one world people spy on phones (Jesus)	7/19/02 Vol. 28	one world people vs. the people (Jesus)	2/17/07 Vol. 46
one world people staging an attack (Jesus)	2/7/08 Vol. 50	one world people want chips in everyone (Jesus)	1/7/06 Vol. 42
one world people stop at nothing for control (Jesus)	2/9/04 Vol. 34	one world people want to bankrupt us (Jesus)	5/29/03 Vol. 31
one world people stripping defenses of US (Jesus)	7/17/97 Vol. 8	one world people want to control the US (Jesus)	12/20/01 Vol. 25
one world people struggle to control oil (Jesus)	11/24/98 Vol. 13	one world people want to destroy America (Jesus)	2/13/03 Vol. 30
one world people suppress truth of deeds (Jesus)	4/22/03 Vol. 31	one world people want to destroy America (Jesus)	8/16/02 Vol. 28
one world people take advantage of shortages (Jesus)	7/2/98 Vol. 12	one world people want to track us (Jesus)	1/16/08 Vol. 50
one world people take freedoms from us (Jesus)	10/17/99 Vol. 17	one world people want US bankruptcy,takeover (Jesus)	10/23/07 Vol. 49
one world people take over America (Jesus)	10/3/07 Vol. 49	one world people want wars to bankrupt America (Jesus)	5/18/04 Vol. 35
one world people take over in bankruptcies (Jesus)	1/14/04 Vol. 34	one world people war to weaken Americaq (Jesus)	10/16/02 Vol. 29
one world people take over with martial law (Jesus)	10/12/99 Vol. 17	one world people war to weaken military (Jesus)	3/23/03 Vol. 30
one world people takeover by greed,comforts (Jesus)	7/12/00 Vol. 20	one world people war, means of takeover (Jesus)	11/5/02 Vol. 29
one world people takeover cities (Jesus)	12/7/03 Vol. 33	one world people will take over president (Jesus)	11/17/00 Vol. 21
one world people takeover of America (Jesus)	2/18/07 Vol. 46	one world people world war takeover (Jesus)	2/1/98 Vol. 10
one world people takeover the world by chips (Jesus)	7/7/04 Vol. 36	one world people worship Satan (Jesus)	10/8/03 Vol. 33
one world people tested and persecuted (Jesus)	2/6/97 Vol. 6	one world people Y2K used by (Jesus)	2/4/99 Vol. 14
one world people tighten control (Jesus)	10/1/02 Vol. 29	one world people & media pushing war (Jesus)	2/26/03 Vol. 30
one world people to bring Antichrist's control (Jesus)	9/1/00 Vol. 20	one world peopleq planning next war (Jesus)	8/27/03 Vol. 32
one world people to cause pandemic (Jesus)	2/18/08 Vol. 50	one world plan deplete troops & money (Jesus)	9/30/02 Vol. 28
one world people to control food supply (Jesus)	5/8/05 Vol. 39	one world plan to destroy America (Jesus)	7/31/03 Vol. 32
one world people to destroy America (Jesus)	10/2/03 Vol. 33	one world plan to grab power (Jesus)	1/3/02 Vol. 26
one world people to destroy America by wars (Jesus)	3/3/07 Vol. 46	One World Religion Antichrist's coming (Jesus)	3/14/97 Vol. 6
one world people to eliminate power of US (Jesus)	11/30/01 Vol. 25	One World Religion assisted by Antipope (Jesus)	4/6/99 Vol. 15
one world people to establish Antichrist (Jesus)	2/1/07 Vol. 46	one world religion attack the spirit (Jesus)	9/7/00 Vol. 20
one world people to finance Antichrist (Jesus)	8/24/06 Vol. 44	one world religion avoid New Age idolatry (Jesus)	7/29/00 Vol. 20

one world religion based on New Age (Jesus) 6/24/05 Vol. 39

one world religion by religious war (Jesus) 10/4/01 Vol. 25

One World Religion controlled by Antichrist (Jesus) 4/20/99 Vol. 15

one world religion defend your beliefs (Jesus) 1/20/00 Vol. 18

one world religion drives faithful underground (Jesus) 5/14/05 Vol. 39

One World religion from New World Order (Jesus) 12/22/99 Vol. 17

One World Religion in churches (Jesus) 9/27/02 Vol. 28

One World Religion joined by Antipope (Jesus) 6/16/99 Vol. 15

one world religion leads to Antichrist (Jesus) 10/19/01 Vol. 25

one world religion New Age forced on everyone (Jesus) 7/5/05 Vol. 40

One World Religion New Age forced on people (Jesus) 8/31/06 Vol. 44

one world religion New Age idols (Jesus) 9/9/00 Vol. 20

one world religion New Age-Eastern mysticism (Jesus) 10/8/04 Vol. 37

one world religion Satan is core of (Jesus) 9/13/00 Vol. 20

one world religion spiritual arm of new order (Jesus) 6/1/01 Vol. 23

One World Religion supported by U.N. (Jesus) 5/14/99 Vol. 15

one world religion to control churches (Jesus) 1/13/00 Vol. 18

one world religion to force views of Antichrist (Jesus) 7/24/00 Vol. 20

one world religion to worship beast, Antichrist (Jesus) 7/28/04 Vol. 36

one world religion will demand worship of beast (Jesus) 3/16/00 Vol. 18

one world religion without worship of God (Jesus) 11/6/03 Vol. 33

One World Religion worship gods of earth (Jesus) 5/15/99 Vol. 15

One World Religion worship sun,moon,earth (Jesus) 8/15/98 Vol. 12

one world takeover bankruptcy,weakened military (Jesus) 10/13/04 Vol. 37

one world takeover rich people planning for years (God the Father)

11/13/00 Vol. 21

one world takeover with modern technology (Jesus) 7/5/05 Vol. 40

oneness perfection (Mary) 11/21/94 Vol. 2

open heart sin (Jesus) 10/8/94 Vol. 2

open hearts needed for Jesus to enter (Jesus) 11/10/03 Vol. 33

open hearts needed to let Jesus in (Jesus) 11/15/03 Vol. 33

open hearts to God require letting go (Jesus) 3/13/06 Vol. 42

open mind to God needed for change (Jesus) 2/5/05 Vol. 38

open soul needed to be molded (Jesus) 5/25/04 Vol. 35

open to new things can improve or mislead (Jesus) 8/17/99 Vol. 16

open window selfishness (Jesus) 9/2/94 Vol. 2

openness needed for Divine Love (Jesus) 2/27/05 Vol. 38

openness to God in eyes, hearts, souls (Jesus) 3/16/04 Vol. 34

Ophelia flooding, power outages (Jesus) 9/15/05 Vol. 40

opportunities in Warning (Jesus) 6/12/02 Vol. 27

opportunities for grace in helping others (Jesus) 2/16/00 Vol. 18

opportunities in life offered by God (Jesus) 12/1/06 Vol. 45

opportunities in life test our faith (Jesus) 1/7/02 Vol. 26

opportunity for love help people (Jesus) 12/21/04 Vol. 37

opportunity,daily to improve spiritual life (Jesus) 11/13/03 Vol. 33

orange-red object coming towards the earth (Jesus) 3/28/04 Vol. 34

orchestra of lives each has a contribution (Jesus) 12/6/98 Vol. 13

order of creation in God's plan for each life (Jesus) 3/24/04 Vol. 34

orders of nuns visited continue dedication to vows (St. Therese)

8/16/98 Vol. 12

Original Sin all inherited weakness to sin (Jesus) 12/15/00 Vol. 21

Original Sin atoned for by Jesus (Jesus) 12/17/99 Vol. 17

Original Sin baptism (Father) 1/9/94 Vol. 1

original sin baptize infants (Jesus) 3/16/97 Vol. 6

original sin be baptized into Light (Jesus) 1/13/98 Vol. 10

original sin beauty of creation (Jesus) 9/24/95 Vol. 3

Original Sin caused sickness & death (Jesus) 7/22/99 Vol. 16

Original sin causes your weaknesses (Jesus) 5/3/99 Vol. 15

Original Sin cleansed by Baptism (Jesus) 1/24/99 Vol. 14

original sin death a consequence (Jesus) 3/20/05 Vol. 38

Original Sin effects removed by Jesus (Jesus) 2/10/01 Vol. 22

original sin freed, heaven opened (Jesus) 1/8/07 Vol. 46

Original Sin grace of Baptism (Jesus) 1/9/99 Vol. 14

original sin made less than perfect (Jesus) 10/11/97 Vol. 9

Original Sin pain & death,result of (Jesus) 2/9/01 Vol. 22

original sin redeemed from (Jesus) 1/31/04 Vol. 34

original sin removed by Baptism (Jesus) 1/8/05 Vol. 38

Original sin salvation, forgiveness (Jesus) 10/26/96 Vol. 5

Original Sin of Adam effects removed,resurrection (Jesus) 4/14/00 Vol. 19

orphanages help children in (Jesus) 7/22/04 Vol. 36

orphans need love in presents (Jesus) 12/26/06 Vol. 45

Our Father always present (God the Father) 8/14/97 Vol. 8

Our Father example of prayer by Jesus (Jesus) 8/6/04 Vol. 36

Our Father perfect prayer (Father) 6/16/05 Vol. 39

Our Father thy Will be done (Jesus) 6/19/03 Vol. 31

Our Father, The nourish prayer life (Father) 2/27/96 Vol. 3

Our Father's House Corpus Christi,Texas (Jesus) 8/22/06 Vol. 44

Our Lady of Guadalupe image on building (Mary) 2/28/98 Vol. 10

Our Lady of Guadalupe many conversions (Mary) 12/12/97 Vol. 9

Our Lady of Guadalupe prepare for Advent (Mary) 12/11/97 Vol. 9

Our Lady of Guadalupe protector and patroness (Jesus) 12/12/00 Vol. 21

Our Lady of Guadeloupe unites Americas (Jesus) 12/12/01 Vol. 25

Our Lady of Guadelupe protect children (Mary) 5/3/02 Vol. 27

Our Lady of Lourdes Immaculate Conception (Blessed Mother)

2/14/05 Vol. 38

Our Lady of Lourdes Immaculate Conception (Mary) 2/11/97 Vol. 6

Our Lady of Mt. Carmel Heavenly Hill refuge (Blessed Mother)

7/16/07 Vol. 48

Our Lady of Peace fall on knees in prayer (Mary) 8/28/03 Vol. 32

Our Lady of Sinj physical & spiritual healings (Jesus) 7/15/02 Vol. 28

Our Lady of Sorrows endure pain & suffering (Jesus) 9/15/03 Vol. 32

Our Lady of Sorrows salvation (Mary) 9/15/97 Vol. 8

Our Lady of the Pillar Zaragosa, Spain (Mary) 10/5/97 Vol. 9

our will needs to follow God's Will (Jesus) 3/2/00 Vol. 18

out of body spiritual experience (Jesus) — 7/4/07 Vol. 48

outside of life vs. inside in soul (Jesus) — 4/6/06 Vol. 43

overkill weapons better to spend money on poor (Jesus) — 3/14/04 Vol. 34

ownership all belongs to God (Jesus) — 11/1/03 Vol. 33

oxygen needed space,on earth,under water (Jesus) — 12/2/04 Vol. 37

Pacific coastline earthquakes,volcanoes (Jesus) — 2/14/01 Vol. 22

Pacific coastline Seattle earthquake (Jesus) — 3/1/01 Vol. 22

Pacific Ocean Orient (Jesus) — 1/30/95 Vol. 2

Pacific Ring of Fire earthquake & tsunami (Jesus) — 12/15/06 Vol. 45

Padre Pio don't waste pain or complain (Padre Pio) — 4/6/98 Vol. 11

Padre Pio pray for Pope,shroud cloth (Padre Pio) — 9/11/97 Vol. 8

Padre Pio stigmata (Jesus) — 6/11/95 Vol. 2

Padre Pio thanks for Steve's art (Jesus) — 5/8/03 Vol. 31

Padre Pio wear crucifixes publicly (Padre Pio) — 8/7/01 Vol. 24

Padre Pio, St. great confessor (Jesus) — 9/23/06 Vol. 44

pagan practices human sacrifices, idol worship (Jesus) — 1/30/06 Vol. 42

pain folding chairs yellow wall (Jesus) — 1/13/95 Vol. 2

pain has redemptive value (Jesus) — 9/30/00 Vol. 20

pain humble (St. Theresa) — 10/15/94 Vol. 2

pain spiritual benefits from (Jesus) — 9/15/05 Vol. 40

pain suffering (Jesus) — 10/13/94 Vol. 2

pain & discomfort price to help body & soul (Jesus) — 5/20/04 Vol. 35

pain & sickness have redemptive value (Jesus) — 7/2/06 Vol. 44

pain & suffering blessing or a curse (Jesus) — 10/26/03 Vol. 33

pain & suffering offered atone for sin in world (Jesus) — 3/16/00 Vol. 18

pain and suffering pray for the sick (Jesus) — 3/18/99 Vol. 14

pain eased even for martyrs (Jesus) — 9/9/99 Vol. 16

pain, constant hard to cope with (Jesus) — 2/6/01 Vol. 22

pain, offer up as redemptive suffering (Jesus) — 8/14/05 Vol. 40

pain, undesirable people do not want to suffer (Jesus) — 2/15/02 Vol. 26

Pakistan & India pray for peace (Jesus) — 6/6/02 Vol. 27

Palm Sunday avoid making Jesus suffer (Jesus) — 3/29/07 Vol. 46

Palm Sunday signs (Jesus) — 3/27/94 Vol. 1

pandemic diseases to come from chem trails (Jesus) — 3/24/08 Vol. 50

pandemic flu from chem trails (Jesus) — 2/28/08 Vol. 50

pandemic virus from chem trails (Jesus) — 3/2/08 Vol. 50

Pandora's box opened by scientists (Jesus) — 8/2/01 Vol. 24

Papal Mass graces given (Mary) — 2/11/96 Vol. 3

papal teaching Antichrist (Jesus) — 5/3/95 Vol. 2

parables gifts how to live (Jesus) — 7/23/00 Vol. 20

parables of Jesus explained by evangelists (Jesus) — 4/20/07 Vol. 47

parables,analogies for better spiritual lives (Jesus) — 11/2/99 Vol. 17

paralytic in gospel cured by faith (Jesus) — 12/3/98 Vol. 13

parental duty shaping spiritual lives (Jesus) — 4/17/97 Vol. 7

parental responsibility for children's faith (Jesus) — 9/13/06 Vol. 44

parental responsibility teach children (Jesus) — 7/6/06 Vol. 44

parents educate children in faith (Jesus) — 5/8/99 Vol. 15

parents encourage faith & vocations (Jesus) — 4/21/02 Vol. 27

parents help care for willingly (Jesus) — 10/19/99 Vol. 17

parents judged on parenting (Jesus) — 7/14/05 Vol. 40

parents judged on teaching faith (Jesus) — 9/5/03 Vol. 32

parents love your children (Jesus) — 5/18/99 Vol. 15

parents need care in old age (Jesus) — 7/22/04 Vol. 36

parents need to teach the faith (Jesus) — 8/18/05 Vol. 40

parents obligation to care for (Jesus) — 2/10/07 Vol. 46

parents responsibility of children (Jesus) — 1/30/97 Vol. 6

parents responsible for children's souls (Jesus) — 12/26/01 Vol. 25

parents responsible for children's souls (Jesus) — 7/12/07 Vol. 48

parents responsible to God for children (Jesus) — 4/26/04 Vol. 35

parents & children help in their need (Jesus) — 1/7/01 Vol. 22

parent's bond same as Jesus for us (Jesus) — 2/1/00 Vol. 18

parents' good example models for children (Jesus) — 8/13/05 Vol. 40

parents' help schooling,wedding,mortgage (Jesus) — 9/26/05 Vol. 40

parents needed to teach the faith (Jesus) — 7/26/07 Vol. 48

parent's responsibility teach faith to children (Jesus) — 7/5/06 Vol. 44

parents' responsibility to teach faith to children (Jesus) — 8/13/05 Vol. 40

parents responsible for children's souls (Jesus) — 3/15/08 Vol. 50

parents to children pass legacy of faith on (Jesus) — 8/24/05 Vol. 40

parents, elderly need care (Jesus) — 11/1/07 Vol. 49

parish involvement for parish survival (Jesus) — 11/13/07 Vol. 49

parish priests need support,prayers (Jesus) — 5/12/00 Vol. 19

partial birth abortion banned by Congress, Bush (Jesus) — 10/22/03 Vol. 33

partial birth abortion Supreme Court upholds (Jesus) — 4/19/07 Vol. 47

particular judgment after death (Jesus) — 12/5/06 Vol. 45

particular judgment at death (Jesus) — 7/22/04 Vol. 36

particular judgment prepare soul for (Jesus) — 4/19/07 Vol. 47

particular judgment prepare soul for (Jesus) — 9/28/00 Vol. 20

passing events fulfilling prophecies (Jesus) — 9/15/99 Vol. 16

Passion is greatest love (Jesus) — 4/22/04 Vol. 35

Passion Movie more truth than Hollywood (Jesus) — 3/18/04 Vol. 34

Passion Movie prophecy fulfilled (Jesus) — 2/26/04 Vol. 34

Passion Movie reflection of Passion, love (Jesus) — 2/26/04 Vol. 34

Passion Movie religious view vs. violence (Jesus) — 3/4/04 Vol. 34

Passion Movie Scripture fulfilled (Jesus) — 1/22/04 Vol. 34

Passion movie suffered for love of us (Jesus) — 4/6/04 Vol. 35

Passion of the Christ critics faded, Word eternal (Jesus) — 4/29/04 Vol. 35

Passion Week prayer and meditation (Jesus) — 3/20/97 Vol. 6

Passion week world's purification (Jesus) — 3/31/96 Vol. 3

passions & appetites need control by Commandments (Jesus) — 3/9/02 Vol. 26

passions & appetites need fasting,prayer,almsgiving (Jesus) — 3/2/02 Vol. 26

Passover changed to the Mass (Jesus) — 4/13/06 Vol. 43

Passover Mass preview (Jesus) — 7/20/07 Vol. 48

passports put in aluminum foil, lead (Jesus) — 1/16/08 Vol. 50

passports to require smart cards (Jesus) — 1/6/06 Vol. 42

past & future should not control you (Jesus) — 8/14/05 Vol. 40

pastor responsible for souls of parish (Jesus) — 12/26/01 Vol. 25

pastor's duties encourage Confession (Jesus) — 10/15/00 Vol. 21

patent protection not honored overseas (Jesus) — 2/17/05 Vol. 38

path to heaven through forgiveness of sin (Jesus) — 4/3/00 Vol. 19

pathway to Heaven testing (Jesus) — 11/11/94 Vol. 2

patience control your temper (Jesus) — 8/19/98 Vol. 12

patience in driving (Jesus) — 1/25/02 Vol. 26

patience tested throughout life (Jesus) — 4/21/06 Vol. 43

patience while driving your car (Jesus) — 7/17/99 Vol. 16

patience & peace by trusting in God (Jesus) — 6/28/04 Vol. 35

patience needed until Jesus returns (Jesus) — 3/27/08 Vol. 50

patient complaint (Jesus) — 12/30/95 Vol. 3

patriots & religious attacked by men in black (Jesus) — 11/9/04 Vol. 37

patriots & religious target of one world people (Jesus) — 12/25/04 Vol. 37

patriots, religious targets of one world people (Jesus) — 5/10/06 Vol. 43

Paul persecution (Jesus) — 1/25/94 Vol. 1

peace angels (Jesus) — 12/17/93 Vol. 1

peace Antichrist (Jesus) — 8/19/95 Vol. 3

peace build bridges for (Jesus) — 7/8/06 Vol. 44

peace by love and obedience (Jesus) — 7/17/06 Vol. 44

peace change comfortable lives (Mary) — 1/2/97 Vol. 6

peace comes with love in hearts (Jesus) — 4/9/00 Vol. 19

peace do not let Satan divide (Jesus) — 8/9/01 Vol. 24

peace faith in tribulation (Jesus) — 12/20/97 Vol. 9

peace families (Jesus) — 6/13/94 Vol. 1

peace fear (Jesus) — 2/24/95 Vol. 2

peace graces (Jesus) — 6/28/95 Vol. 2

peace hope (Jesus) — 4/18/95 Vol. 2

peace humble (Jesus) — 11/17/94 Vol. 2

peace if hostilities are removed (Jesus) — 10/30/00 Vol. 21

peace in families & world (Jesus) — 7/1/99 Vol. 16

peace in family and nations (Jesus) — 3/10/03 Vol. 30

peace intervention (Jesus) — 12/17/93 Vol. 1

peace love (Jesus) — 1/1/94 Vol. 1

peace love God and neighbor (Holy Spirit) — 5/26/96 Vol. 3

peace only found in Jesus (Jesus) — 4/7/06 Vol. 43

peace only through prayer (Jesus) — 11/29/01 Vol. 25

peace pray 15 decades for (Jesus) — 11/1/99 Vol. 17

peace pray and compromise (Jesus) — 12/6/01 Vol. 25

peace pray and make amends (Mary) — 3/13/97 Vol. 6

peace pray for (Jesus) — 9/26/02 Vol. 28

peace pray for (Jesus) — 5/31/01 Vol. 23

peace pray for (Jesus) — 7/6/06 Vol. 44

peace pray for (Jesus) — 12/19/96 Vol. 5

peace pray for (Jesus) — 9/14/00 Vol. 20

peace pray for (Jesus) — 12/9/99 Vol. 17

peace pray for (Jesus) — 8/14/99 Vol. 16

peace pray for leaders (Jesus) — 5/15/96 Vol. 3

peace pray for or more war (Jesus) — 1/24/02 Vol. 26

peace pray for strongly (Holy Spirit) — 6/4/98 Vol. 11

peace pray for unity (Jesus) — 5/4/98 Vol. 11

peace pray for, stop fighting (Jesus) — 8/30/97 Vol. 8

peace pray hard for (Jesus) — 1/2/03 Vol. 30

peace pray three rosaries (Mary) — 2/21/97 Vol. 6

peace pray three rosaries (Mary) — 6/21/97 Vol. 7

peace pray to stop wars (Jesus) — 6/8/05 Vol. 39

peace pray to stop world war III (Jesus) — 1/28/97 Vol. 6

peace pray, greed and war (Jesus) — 10/31/96 Vol. 5

peace prayer is best to stop (Jesus) — 7/12/06 Vol. 44

peace prayers for pride (Jesus) — 8/28/96 Vol. 4

peace prayers to stop killing (Jesus) — 8/4/98 Vol. 12

Peace requires anger out of hearts (Jesus) — 10/28/98 Vol. 13

peace stained glass — 7/31/93 Vol. 1

peace starts in the family (Jesus) — 12/24/07 Vol. 49

peace weapons (Jesus) — 9/15/95 Vol. 3

peace weapons and love (Jesus) — 2/26/96 Vol. 3

peace with self and others (Jesus) — 11/14/96 Vol. 5

peace & joy share with others in church (Jesus) — 10/27/02 Vol. 29

peace & love better than war & hatred (Jesus) — 5/24/04 Vol. 35

peace & love better than wars & hate (Jesus) — 1/9/06 Vol. 42

peace & love defies devil's plans (Jesus) — 1/20/04 Vol. 34

peace & love manage time wisely (Jesus) — 1/24/02 Vol. 26

peace & love needed among neighbors,nations (Jesus) — 8/22/07 Vol. 48

peace & love needed in your lives (Jesus) — 2/5/05 Vol. 38

peace & love overcome sin & hate (Jesus) — 11/21/99 Vol. 17

peace & prayer to stop wars (Jesus) — 5/30/05 Vol. 39

peace and love start in the home (Jesus) — 2/23/06 Vol. 42

peace and love what heaven is about (Jesus) — 12/17/98 Vol. 13

Peace be with you love & forgive (Jesus) — 4/18/04 Vol. 35

peace found only in God (Jesus) — 2/27/05 Vol. 38

peace in Advent through Jesus' love,grace (Jesus) — 11/19/98 Vol. 13

peace in families set aside difficulties (Jesus) — 12/20/98 Vol. 13

peace in heart no event should unsettle (Jesus) — 2/16/02 Vol. 26

peace in Middle East pray for (Jesus) — 11/11/04 Vol. 37

peace in soul by loving everyone (Jesus) — 12/8/03 Vol. 33

peace in soul only found in Jesus (Jesus) — 11/4/99 Vol. 17

peace in world by family prayer (Jesus) — 3/23/04 Vol. 34

peace in world pray the rosary for (Jesus) — 7/2/06 Vol. 44

peace in world starts with individual love (Jesus) — 2/4/05 Vol. 38

peace needed pray for peace to stop war (Jesus) — 9/10/04 Vol. 36

peace of Bethlehem lost in war, fear (Jesus) — 12/25/02 Vol. 29

peace of God needed among nations (Jesus) — 12/12/04 Vol. 37

peace of God puts minds at rest (Jesus) — 7/3/00 Vol. 20

peace of Jesus lasts forever (Jesus)	4/24/00 Vol. 19	Pentecost power to evangelize (Jesus)	5/15/97 Vol. 7
peace of Jesus lasts forever (Jesus)	3/12/00 Vol. 18	Pentecost preach the Gospel (Holy Spirit)	5/25/96 Vol. 3
peace of Jesus more than man's peace (Jesus)	3/19/99 Vol. 14	Pentecost rosary and Mass (Mary)	5/22/96 Vol. 3
peace on earth give up greed, wars (Jesus)	12/25/99 Vol. 17	Pentecost Temples of Holy Spirit (Holy Spirit)	5/27/07 Vol. 47
peace on earth in freedom of religion (Jesus)	12/22/99 Vol. 17	Pentecost the fire of love (Holy Spirit)	5/23/99 Vol. 15
peace on earth only through love (Jesus)	12/19/01 Vol. 25	Pentecost Sundays celebrate gifts of Holy Spirit (Jesus)	5/20/04 Vol. 35
peace on earth vs. peace in heaven (Jesus)	4/26/05 Vol. 39	perfect as heavenly Father is (Jesus)	6/14/05 Vol. 39
peace to war world dictatorship coming (Jesus)	11/25/97 Vol. 9	perfected, being no fear being incomplete (Jesus)	6/19/99 Vol. 15
peace vs. war compromise vs. destruction (Jesus)	11/11/98 Vol. 13	perfection accept corrections (Jesus)	10/9/02 Vol. 29
peace, bridges of president desires war (Jesus)	12/28/02 Vol. 29	perfection almsgiving,prayer,fasting (Jesus)	6/15/05 Vol. 39
peace, God's only satisfies souls (Jesus)	12/27/02 Vol. 29	perfection as heavenly Father (Jesus)	6/18/98 Vol. 11
peace, inner do not let it be disturbed (Jesus)	8/6/06 Vol. 44	perfection as heavenly Father is (Jesus)	6/21/02 Vol. 27
peace, love of Jesus satisfies more than sin (Jesus)	9/16/07 Vol. 48	perfection as the saints (Jesus)	3/6/03 Vol. 30
peace, pray for pray to take hate out of hearts (Jesus)	3/23/02 Vol. 26	perfection by daily consecration (Jesus)	1/24/03 Vol. 30
peace, pray for to avoid wars (Jesus)	8/12/05 Vol. 40	perfection by detaching self (Jesus)	7/13/05 Vol. 40
peace, rest calms chaos of sin (Jesus)	4/20/06 Vol. 43	perfection by following Jesus Will (Jesus)	5/2/01 Vol. 23
peace, seek than constant wars (Jesus)	3/28/07 Vol. 46	perfection by grace of sacraments (Jesus)	8/13/03 Vol. 32
peace, spiritual restored in Confession (Jesus)	4/20/06 Vol. 43	perfection by purifying our wills (Jesus)	6/17/04 Vol. 35
peace, true with God's intervention (Jesus)	2/16/05 Vol. 38	perfection commitment (Jesus)	6/13/94 Vol. 1
peace, world requires constant prayer (Jesus)	12/15/03 Vol. 33	perfection detach from earthly things (Jesus)	11/4/06 Vol. 45
peace,prayers for unending need for God's help (Jesus)	10/3/00 Vol. 21	perfection do God's Will (Jesus)	2/9/04 Vol. 34
peacekeeping needed pray for end of killing (Jesus)	10/22/98 Vol. 13	perfection faith is like a garden (Jesus)	10/4/99 Vol. 17
peacemakers call to heal divisions (Jesus)	1/9/06 Vol. 42	perfection fast, pray, give money (Jesus)	9/12/96 Vol. 4
peacemakers do not discriminate (Jesus)	12/16/99 Vol. 17	perfection grace to improve (Jesus)	3/31/03 Vol. 30
peacemakers do not kill (Jesus)	5/24/01 Vol. 23	perfection in daily holiness (Jesus)	11/16/00 Vol. 21
peacemakers in nations and families (Jesus)	5/27/99 Vol. 15	perfection in Divine Will (Jesus)	6/19/01 Vol. 23
peacemakers needed in families, nations (Jesus)	12/24/07 Vol. 49	perfection in Era of Peace (Jesus)	6/4/98 Vol. 11
peacemakers needed to stop wars (Jesus)	8/22/07 Vol. 48	perfection in obedience to His Will (Jesus)	12/4/99 Vol. 17
peacemakers no war to force your ideas (Jesus)	5/6/99 Vol. 15	perfection Jesus seeks it in us (Jesus)	1/30/99 Vol. 14
peacemakers not part of the problem (Jesus)	6/23/03 Vol. 31	perfection love your enemies (Jesus)	3/3/07 Vol. 46
peacemakers reach compromises (Jesus)	8/4/99 Vol. 16	perfection love your enemies (Jesus)	9/20/97 Vol. 8
peacemakers needed heal wrongs,injustices (Jesus)	4/25/00 Vol. 19	perfection needed for sainthood (Jesus)	10/15/03 Vol. 33
peacemakers needed to compromise wars (Jesus)	6/19/03 Vol. 31	perfection offer each day to Jesus (Jesus)	10/16/99 Vol. 17
peacemakers, be than war makers (Jesus)	3/2/06 Vol. 42	perfection open, 'yes' to God (Jesus)	6/22/06 Vol. 43
Pentagon power hollow force controlled (Jesus)	4/25/00 Vol. 19	perfection persevere in faith (Jesus)	2/16/04 Vol. 34
Pentecost await the Holy Spirit (Jesus)	5/7/05 Vol. 39	perfection purified in fire (Jesus)	2/10/98 Vol. 10
Pentecost Body of Christ (Holy Spirit)	5/22/94 Vol. 1	perfection requires God at center of life (Jesus)	5/26/00 Vol. 19
Pentecost call on gifts and graces (Holy Spirit)	5/14/98 Vol. 11	perfection requires soul's purification (Jesus)	12/3/06 Vol. 45
Pentecost call on gifts of Holy Spirit (Jesus)	5/28/98 Vol. 11	perfection requires work every day (Jesus)	12/9/04 Vol. 37
Pentecost call on Holy Spirit (Jesus)	6/2/01 Vol. 23	perfection rid every worldly desire (Jesus)	2/5/04 Vol. 34
Pentecost call on Holy Spirit's gifts (Jesus)	5/24/07 Vol. 47	perfection service (Jesus)	6/14/94 Vol. 1
Pentecost celebrate indwelling of Holy Spirit (Jesus)	5/5/05 Vol. 39	perfection sin as impediment (Jesus)	9/15/96 Vol. 4
Pentecost gifts of Baptism,Confirmation (Holy Spirit)	6/11/00 Vol. 19	perfection temptations & prayer (Jesus)	7/5/96 Vol. 3
Pentecost gifts of Spirit, mission (Holy Spirit)	5/18/97 Vol. 7	perfection to advance spiritually (Jesus)	5/15/03 Vol. 31
Pentecost gifts of the Holy Spirit (Holy Spirit)	5/19/02 Vol. 27	perfection with patience & peace (Jesus)	6/28/04 Vol. 35
Pentecost gifts of the Holy Spirit (Jesus)	6/4/06 Vol. 43	perfection for heaven with fasting & prayer (Jesus)	1/24/05 Vol. 38
Pentecost love God and neighbor (Holy Spirit)	5/31/98 Vol. 11	perfection for sainthood requires God's help (Jesus)	4/19/07 Vol. 47

perfection in nature being abused by man (Jesus)   3/6/02 Vol. 26

perf. in spiritual life analyze progress over time (Jesus)   11/17/05 Vol. 41

perfection is goal call to extraordinary deeds (Jesus)   4/8/00 Vol. 19

perfection needed improve spiritual life for heaven (Jesus) 3/26/02 Vol. 26

perfection needed to be a saint (Jesus)   5/25/04 Vol. 35

perfection of God cannot be improved on (Jesus)   2/26/01 Vol. 22

perfection on earth goal for spiritual life (Jesus)   12/20/04 Vol. 37

perfection required to gain heaven by Jesus (Jesus)   4/29/00 Vol. 19

perfection, spiritual improvements or purgatory (Jesus)   6/20/07 Vol. 47

permanent sign hope   10/1/93 Vol. 1

permanent sign Moses and cross (Jesus)   5/4/96 Vol. 3

permanent sign places of refuge (Jesus)   2/16/96 Vol. 3

permanent sign refuges of protection (Jesus)   8/19/97 Vol. 8

permanent sign supernatural (Jesus)   11/14/93 Vol. 1

permanent sign supernatural event   10/16/93 Vol. 1

permanent sign tribulation & new earth (Jesus)   3/2/96 Vol. 3

permanent signs safe haven (Jesus)   11/22/95 Vol. 3

permanent signs trust in protection (Jesus)   8/25/96 Vol. 4

permanent signs white cross protection (Jesus)   6/21/96 Vol. 3

permissive society do not follow sins of others (Jesus)   3/15/04 Vol. 34

Perna, Joan's funeral (Jesus)   8/18/03 Vol. 32

Perpetual Adoration blessing on parish (Jesus)   8/28/97 Vol. 8

perpetual adoration encourage priests (Jesus)   6/1/97 Vol. 7

perpetual adoration power and grace (Jesus)   10/25/02 Vol. 29

perpetual prayer vigil candles in prayer room (Jesus)   11/10/03 Vol. 33

perpetural adoration channel of grace (Jesus)   6/11/98 Vol. 11

persecution a test of faith and love (Jesus)   8/2/99 Vol. 16

persecution abortion (Jesus)   1/31/96 Vol. 3

persecution about to begin (Jesus)   9/20/00 Vol. 20

persecution and rejection (Jesus)   5/13/03 Vol. 31

persecution apostasy in Church (Jesus)   9/13/96 Vol. 4
persecution as souls are saved (Jesus)   10/6/97 Vol. 9
persecution at border crossings (Jesus)   2/27/04 Vol. 34
persecution by Arabs of Islam (Jesus)   7/2/01 Vol. 24
persecution by Romans,catacomb refuge (Jesus)   10/26/05 Vol. 41
persecution call on our angels (Jesus)   10/10/96 Vol. 5
persecution churches locked by authorities (Jesus)   8/14/06 Vol. 44
persecution clergy, test of faith (Jesus)   10/13/97 Vol. 9
persecution coming for Christians (Jesus)   8/24/06 Vol. 44
persecution continue in mission (Jesus)   9/29/97 Vol. 8
persecution continue to witness (Jesus)   10/10/99 Vol. 17
persecution do not be fearful (Jesus)   8/7/99 Vol. 16
persecution do not want to hear Word (Jesus)   9/28/97 Vol. 8
persecution do not worry about (Jesus)   4/21/04 Vol. 35
persecution Eucharist (Jesus)   2/7/94 Vol. 1
persecution evil taking over countries (Jesus)   6/26/07 Vol. 47
persecution flee into hiding (Jesus)   12/17/97 Vol. 9
persecution for being a Christian (Jesus)   11/23/02 Vol. 29
persecution for belief in Jesus (Jesus)   10/18/99 Vol. 17
persecution for belief in Jesus (Jesus)   1/14/99 Vol. 14
persecution for beliefs (Jesus)   8/29/00 Vol. 20
persecution for celebrating Christmas (Jesus)   12/3/98 Vol. 13
persecution for fighting sexual sins (Jesus)   10/26/05 Vol. 41
persecution for following Jesus (Jesus)   5/21/98 Vol. 11
persecution for His Name's sake (Jesus)   5/21/99 Vol. 15
persecution for preaching Christ (Jesus)   4/12/02 Vol. 27
persecution for proclaiming Gospel (Jesus)   4/21/01 Vol. 23
persecution for speaking of religion in public (Jesus)   11/24/04 Vol. 37
persecution for speaking out (Jesus)   2/6/04 Vol. 34
persecution for speaking out on sins (Jesus)   6/14/06 Vol. 43
persecution for speaking out on sins (Jesus)   6/29/06 Vol. 43
persecution for the Gospel (Jesus)   11/14/00 Vol. 21
persecution for those who follow God (Jesus)   3/12/08 Vol. 50
persecution forced to flee (Jesus)   3/7/98 Vol. 10
persecution from one world people (Jesus)   4/23/06 Vol. 43
persecution give public witness to Jesus (Jesus)   11/27/01 Vol. 25
persecution go into hiding (Jesus)   7/9/01 Vol. 24
persecution go into hiding (Jesus)   6/16/98 Vol. 11
persecution Holy Spirit our defense (Jesus)   5/27/99 Vol. 15
persecution in public places (Jesus)   1/19/99 Vol. 14
persecution in Russia & China (Jesus)   6/30/01 Vol. 23
persecution in tribulation (Jesus)   7/8/03 Vol. 32
persecution in tribulation (Jesus)   8/29/05 Vol. 40
persecution in tribulation (Jesus)   9/12/00 Vol. 20
persecution in tribulation will be short (Jesus)   5/27/04 Vol. 35
persecution in underground Masses (Jesus)   2/19/98 Vol. 10
persecution manna from heaven (Jesus)   2/28/96 Vol. 3

persecution mass graves in America (Jesus)   10/7/97 Vol. 9
persecution messages (Jesus)   1/21/96 Vol. 3
persecution mission (Jesus)   3/15/97 Vol. 6
persecution never deny Jesus in (Jesus)   3/26/98 Vol. 10
persecution now and later (Jesus)   1/20/01 Vol. 22
persecution of Christian groups (Jesus)   4/21/98 Vol. 11
persecution of Christians (Jesus)   11/1/05 Vol. 41
persecution of Christians (Jesus)   10/19/05 Vol. 41
persecution of Christians and freedoms (Jesus)   10/30/01 Vol. 25
persecution of Christians increasing (Jesus)   2/3/04 Vol. 34
persecution of religious, patriots (Jesus)   8/30/06 Vol. 44
persecution persevere in mission (Jesus)   9/26/03 Vol. 32
persecution preach the Gospel (Jesus)   5/28/96 Vol. 3
persecution preserve church things (Jesus)   3/20/97 Vol. 6
persecution pride (Jesus)   5/4/94 Vol. 1
persecution protected areas (Jesus)   6/22/94 Vol. 1
persecution remnant (Jesus)   5/20/94 Vol. 1
persecution returns as earlier years (Jesus)   5/14/05 Vol. 39
persecution seek God's protection (Jesus)   8/1/97 Vol. 8
persecution short for sake of elect (Jesus)   4/3/97 Vol. 7
persecution sign for Antichrist (Jesus)   10/9/03 Vol. 33
persecution speak out about faith (Jesus)   2/3/05 Vol. 38
persecution stadium (Jesus)   11/15/94 Vol. 2
persecution stand up for faith (Jesus)   10/30/97 Vol. 9
persecution still speak out under (Jesus)   6/13/05 Vol. 39
persecution suffer as Jesus did (Jesus)   4/27/04 Vol. 35
persecution test of faith (Jesus)   2/9/98 Vol. 10
persecution test of faith (Jesus)   7/8/96 Vol. 3
persecution test of tribulation (Jesus)   6/16/99 Vol. 15
persecution tested (Jesus)   11/10/94 Vol. 2
persecution the price to save souls (Jesus)   5/26/99 Vol. 15
persecution threatened with martyrdom (Jesus)   4/16/98 Vol. 11
persecution to increase for Christians (Jesus)   3/2/07 Vol. 46
persecution to test our faith shortly (Jesus)   4/15/98 Vol. 11
persecution trust (Jesus)   1/27/95 Vol. 2
persecution underground Church (Jesus)   1/2/98 Vol. 10
persecution underground Church (Jesus)   12/31/97 Vol. 9
persecution underground Mass (Jesus)   6/15/94 Vol. 1
persecution unsafe to walk the streets (Jesus)   2/28/04 Vol. 34
persecution when proclaiming Jesus (Jesus)   4/11/05 Vol. 39
persecution & suffering is the narrow road (Jesus)   6/21/05 Vol. 39
persecution & suffering road to heaven (Jesus)   5/26/03 Vol. 31
persecution as Jesus public suffering for Jesus (Jesus)   8/21/02 Vol. 28
persecution for abortion suffer for belief in Jesus (Jesus)   4/15/99 Vol. 15
persecution of Catholics to worsen (Jesus)   5/11/05 Vol. 39
pers. of Christians for not worshiping Antichrist (Jesus)   3/19/01 Vol. 22
persecution of Christians martyrs refuse Antichrist (Jesus)   6/30/97 Vol. 7

pers. of Christians widespread by Antichrist (Jesus) 12/13/99 Vol. 17
pers.of Christians will become threatening again (Jesus) 1/26/06 Vol. 42
persecution of Church in tribulation (Jesus) 6/6/03 Vol. 31
persecution of faithful reason for refuges (Jesus) 6/22/07 Vol. 47
persecution suffered protesting abortion (Jesus) 2/28/01 Vol. 22
persecution to increase during tribulation (Jesus) 4/7/01 Vol. 23
persecution,harder test choose Jesus over this life (Jesus) 7/4/00 Vol. 20
persecutions pray for persecutors (Jesus) 5/17/98 Vol. 11
persecutors love your enemies (Jesus) 11/21/97 Vol. 9
persevere faith (Jesus) 4/4/94 Vol. 1
perseverence in faith faith nurtured, maintained (Jesus) 11/18/98 Vol. 13
Persian Gulf War threat to oil (Jesus) 5/11/06 Vol. 43
Persion Gulf Oil threatened by Iran War (Jesus) 4/8/06 Vol. 43
persistence in faith accomplish amazing things (Jesus) 10/14/04 Vol. 37
persistence in faith answers prayer requests (Jesus) 12/3/98 Vol. 13
persistence in faith determines endurance (Jesus) 8/27/99 Vol. 16
persistence in faith God's Word, foundation (Jesus) 10/18/98 Vol. 13
persistence in faith required for trials (Jesus) 11/13/99 Vol. 17
personal (Jesus) 1/16/94 Vol. 1
personal advice (St. Therese) 10/1/07 Vol. 49
personal called as prophet (Jesus) 1/16/08 Vol. 50
personal Catherine (K. Tekakwitha) 10/19/95 Vol. 3
personal consolation (Jesus) 1/7/03 Vol. 30
personal daughter's family to Rochester (Jesus) 7/21/05 Vol. 40
personal evangelist calling (Jesus) 9/21/05 Vol. 40
personal for messengers (Jesus) 2/10/03 Vol. 30
personal Guardian Angel (Mark) 10/2/02 Vol. 29
personal heaven helps (Jesus) 10/1/02 Vol. 29
personal help & consolation (Jesus) 7/30/99 Vol. 16
personal increased persecution (Jesus) 5/26/99 Vol. 15
personal love and trust more (St. Theresa) 10/1/01 Vol. 25
personal message of angel (Mark) 10/2/07 Vol. 49
personal messages (Jesus) 8/13/95 Vol. 3
personal messages (Jesus) 10/10/95 Vol. 3
personal messages protected (Jesus) 2/11/08 Vol. 50
personal mission (Jesus) 8/29/95 Vol. 3
personal mission of preparation (Jesus) 8/27/04 Vol. 36
personal public harassment (Jesus) 8/29/95 Vol. 3
personal purification (Mary) 3/25/94 Vol. 1
personal spiritual weapons (Jesus) 10/15/95 Vol. 3
personal turning points in faith (Jesus) 9/17/04 Vol. 36
per. choice of Jesus need loving relationship to God (Jesus) 11/30/05 Vol. 41
per. commitment necessary to Jesus to be saved (Jesus) 5/20/04 Vol. 35
personal commitment to follow Jesus (Jesus) 4/8/07 Vol. 47
personal cross way to heaven (Jesus) 5/19/00 Vol. 19
personal feeling of many deaths (Jesus) 2/13/03 Vol. 30
personal God loves us despite our sins (Jesus) 11/26/99 Vol. 17

personal information being sought (Jesus) 3/10/99 Vol. 14
personal message 12th anniversary messages (Jesus) 7/21/05 Vol. 40
personal message attacks on credibility (Jesus) 3/31/08 Vol. 50
personal message attacks on trips (Jesus) 4/17/02 Vol. 27
personal message call on for gifts (Holy Spirit) 6/3/01 Vol. 23
personal message messages fulfilled (Jesus) 7/3/02 Vol. 28
personal message mission from God (Jesus) 1/14/04 Vol. 34
personal message of protection (Mark) 6/29/01 Vol. 23
personal message pray for safe travel (Jesus) 1/4/08 Vol. 50
personal message responsibility for actions (Jesus) 12/19/00 Vol. 21
personal message spreading God's Word (Jesus) 12/3/00 Vol. 21
personal message to continue mission (Jesus) 10/13/99 Vol. 17
personal message to evangelize (Jesus) 10/18/01 Vol. 25
personal message to meet in secret (Jesus) 4/28/04 Vol. 35
personal message wasting time (Jesus) 5/3/02 Vol. 27
personal mission bring people closer to Eucharist (Jesus) 8/16/07 Vol. 48
personal mission consolation (St. Therese) 1/18/96 Vol. 3
personal mission end times message (Jesus) 9/1/06 Vol. 44
personal mission prepare people for end days (Jesus) 1/21/07 Vol. 46
personal pride overcome it to see paradise (Jesus) 12/10/98 Vol. 13
personal relationship needed with God (Jesus) 10/20/03 Vol. 33
personal relationship with Jesus in His Word (Jesus) 5/5/04 Vol. 35
personal response needed in heart (Jesus) 3/1/00 Vol. 18
personal suffering for souls (Jesus) 8/30/07 Vol. 48
personal touch more meaning than donation (Jesus) 2/19/02 Vol. 26
personal treasure box tears of joy & sorrow (Jesus) 6/12/00 Vol. 19
personnel locators send signals to locate men (Jesus) 10/13/98 Vol. 13
pestilence swarms of locusts (Jesus) 8/8/04 Vol. 36
pestilence & famine as Revelation proceeds (Jesus) 8/10/06 Vol. 44
pet animals bring to refuge (Jesus) 1/11/07 Vol. 46
Peter & Paul apostles were martyred (Jesus) 6/29/03 Vol. 31
Peter's denial Baptism of the HolySpirit (Jesus) 1/8/96 Vol. 3
petitions make in faith by God's Will (Jesus) 5/8/03 Vol. 31
petitions answered as best for the soul (Mary) 6/11/98 Vol. 11
petitions given to Jesus by Maria Esperanza (Maria E.) 12/9/07 Vol. 49
petitions in prayer ask for help (Jesus) 4/5/03 Vol. 31
pets welcomed at refuges (Jesus) 1/13/00 Vol. 18
Pharisees denied Jesus' Divinity (Jesus) 3/2/08 Vol. 50
Pharisees, lawyers ignored John & Jesus (Jesus) 12/9/05 Vol. 41
phone conversations evil ones listening (Jesus) 9/20/07 Vol. 48
phone, internet intercepted conversations (Jesus) 9/29/06 Vol. 44
phones tapped to find Christians (Jesus) 7/19/02 Vol. 28
physical appearance many spend time & money on (Jesus) 3/12/02 Vol. 26
physical appearances lead to sins of pleasure (Jesus) 6/27/02 Vol. 27
physical body mirror of faults (Jesus) 4/22/96 Vol. 3
physical life vs. spiritual life (Jesus) 3/11/99 Vol. 14
physical talents shared with others in need (Jesus) 11/14/99 Vol. 17

physical,financial losses we will not recover from (Jesus) 6/28/01 Vol. 23

physical,spiritual events how they help souls (Jesus)   2/5/01 Vol. 22

picnic food appropriate for Y2K (Jesus)   11/17/99 Vol. 17

picnic food in time of need (Jesus)   12/26/99 Vol. 17

picture of life, big misfortune causes conversions (Jesus) 11/18/02 Vol. 29

pictures best memory of deceased (Jesus)   1/11/07 Vol. 46

pictures freeze points of time (Jesus)   10/14/05 Vol. 41

pictures show life's progress (Jesus)   11/26/04 Vol. 37

pictures of dead keep memory of souls (Jesus)   11/1/07 Vol. 49

pictures of people snapshot of that life (Jesus)   12/5/98 Vol. 13

pictures, old signs of spiritual progress (Jesus)   6/19/99 Vol. 15

pictures, statues Jesus, saints in rooms of home (Jesus)   12/5/02 Vol. 29

pieta humble lamb (Mary)   3/13/95 Vol. 2

Pilgrim Statue of Fatima thanks to workers (Mary)   8/28/97 Vol. 8

pilgrimage repentance (Jesus)   7/7/94 Vol. 2

pilgrimage on cruise daily bread in Jesus (Jesus)   11/28/99 Vol. 17

pilgrimages gain graces & protection (Jesus)   2/22/08 Vol. 50

pilgrimages give better focus (Jesus)   6/26/01 Vol. 23

pilgrimages prayer & sacramentals (Jesus)   9/21/06 Vol. 44

pilgrimages,called prayers for peace needed (Mary)   4/8/99 Vol. 15

pilgrimmages spiritual travel vs for pleasure (Jesus)   3/18/04 Vol. 34

Pilgrims difficulties surviving (Jesus)   11/22/06 Vol. 45

pillar of Church example to others (Jesus)   12/20/04 Vol. 37

pillar of flame purification (Mary)   7/10/94 Vol. 2

pillars of Church Jesus & Mary (Jesus)   8/17/02 Vol. 28

pillars of Church maintain Church traditions (Jesus)   11/15/04 Vol. 37

pillars of Church models of faith to others (Jesus)   3/3/06 Vol. 42

pillars of faith teach faith to children (Jesus)   12/15/05 Vol. 41

Pillars of God's Word Gospels,prophetic word (Jesus)   7/6/00 Vol. 20

pillars of salt for unbelievers (Jesus)   2/7/99 Vol. 14

pine tree praying hands (Jesus)   2/2/95 Vol. 2

pink lightning Antichrist (Jesus)   11/1/94 Vol. 2

place pray for leaders (Jesus)   8/28/97 Vol. 8

place of dead where Jesus went first (Jesus)   4/16/00 Vol. 19

plagues angels to bring against evil (Jesus)   11/17/05 Vol. 41

plagues biological weapons (Jesus)   11/13/97 Vol. 9

plagues during tribulation (Jesus)   2/10/99 Vol. 14

plagues for those condemned (Jesus)   2/18/99 Vol. 14

plagues in tribulation (Jesus)   10/27/97 Vol. 9

plagues living hell (Jesus)   1/14/99 Vol. 14

plagues new era (Jesus)   1/13/96 Vol. 3

plagues of revelation (Jesus)   11/5/97 Vol. 9

plagues of Revelation (Jesus)   10/7/99 Vol. 17

plagues on those who reject Jesus (Jesus)   4/9/98 Vol. 11

plagues snakes and purification (Jesus)   2/3/96 Vol. 3

plagues unfaithful to suffer most (Jesus)   11/25/97 Vol. 9

plagues & diseases to increase before tribulation (Jesus)   3/15/01 Vol. 22

plagues & fire evil ones will suffer at end times (Jesus)   11/28/04 Vol. 37

plagues for evil ones living hell on earth (Jesus)   2/3/00 Vol. 18

plagues of Egypt unfaithful to suffer from (Jesus)   4/9/01 Vol. 23

plagues on evil ones in end days (Jesus)   8/13/04 Vol. 36

plagues on unfaithful will be an earthly hell (Jesus)   9/23/99 Vol. 16

plan eternal destination as you plan education (Jesus)   6/15/00 Vol. 19

plan for life follow Jesus' blueprint (Jesus)   1/8/04 Vol. 34

plan for life use talents & follow Will (Jesus)   1/23/03 Vol. 30

plan for life use unique talents (Jesus)   11/17/02 Vol. 29

plan for takeover destruction, power outage (Jesus)   10/4/06 Vol. 45

plan of God follow for each soul (Jesus)   7/23/00 Vol. 20

plan of God know,love, & serve Him (Jesus)   8/3/00 Vol. 20

plan of God violated by earthly desires (Jesus)   2/17/01 Vol. 22

plane accidents increase with Y2K events (Jesus)   10/28/99 Vol. 17

plane crash a witness in prayer (Jesus)   7/24/96 Vol. 4

plane crash worry (Jesus)   7/31/94 Vol. 2

plane crashes suspicious causes (Jesus)   8/17/05 Vol. 40

planes & pilots pray for (Jesus)   10/12/06 Vol. 45

planet rings resurrection (Jesus)   8/27/94 Vol. 2

planned accidents avoid acts of killing (Jesus)   6/5/97 Vol. 7

plant diseases to allow world control of food (Jesus)   12/15/02 Vol. 29

plants & animals desire life in house (Jesus)   11/25/03 Vol. 33

plasma, fusion danger in experiments (Jesus)   9/6/05 Vol. 40

plastination of cadavers (Jesus)   7/2/06 Vol. 44

pleasing God better than ourselves (Jesus)   11/21/06 Vol. 45

pleasures & possessions lost sense of sin (Jesus)   12/18/04 Vol. 37

Pledge of Allegiance attacked by atheists (Jesus)   7/4/02 Vol. 28

Pledge of Allegiance struggle to remove God (Jesus)   9/15/05 Vol. 40

pocketbook threatened by disasters (Jesus)   6/24/02 Vol. 27

point source spotlight   8/5/93 Vol. 1

poisoned water potential by terrorists (Jesus)   12/18/03 Vol. 33

polar shift by God's intervention (Jesus)   10/9/03 Vol. 33

polarization of good & evil Armageddon (Jesus)   1/24/95 Vol. 2

police avoid working with UN (Jesus)   8/13/98 Vol. 12

police state America like Germany (Jesus)   5/20/03 Vol. 31

police state as result of terrorism (Jesus)   11/10/05 Vol. 41

police state by UN and New World Order (Jesus)   8/14/98 Vol. 12

police state caused by riots in streets (Jesus)   12/10/98 Vol. 13

police state coming soon (Jesus)   7/4/99 Vol. 16

police state control food,fuel,airports (Jesus)   8/12/99 Vol. 16

police state freedoms stripped (Jesus)   7/3/03 Vol. 32

police state military to take power (Jesus)   9/27/01 Vol. 24

police state of one world people (Jesus)   5/16/03 Vol. 31

police state smart cards & chips (Jesus)   9/10/02 Vol. 28

police state through smart cards,chips (Jesus)   10/24/99 Vol. 17

police state to prevent terrorism (Jesus)   3/7/98 Vol. 10

police state UN troops (Jesus)   5/10/97 Vol. 7

police state will be America's downfall (Jesus) 11/21/00 Vol. 21

police state with UN troops (Jesus) 9/26/00 Vol. 20

police,foreign infiltrators with UN,capture resistors (Jesus) 9/22/98 Vol. 12

Polish traditions love of Adoration (Jesus) 11/9/02 Vol. 29

political leaders pray for them, corruption (Jesus) 5/22/97 Vol. 7

political polls abortion favored by people (Jesus) 2/15/00 Vol. 18

politicians & money selling your rights (Jesus) 3/18/99 Vol. 14

politicians,immoral elected by those for abortion (Jesus) 10/11/00 Vol. 21

Polizzi, Rose funeral message (Rose Polizzi) 4/25/05 Vol. 39

polls manipulated control people by media (Jesus) 3/9/00 Vol. 18

pollution air needs protection (Jesus) 8/18/04 Vol. 36

pollution keep balance of nature (Jesus) 1/24/07 Vol. 46

pollution killing plants,animals (Jesus) 3/4/99 Vol. 14

pollution nature (Jesus) 10/13/95 Vol. 3

pollution ruins balance of nature (Jesus) 8/31/06 Vol. 44

pollution upsets balance of nature (Jesus) 4/18/01 Vol. 23

pollution and evil destroyed and renewed (Jesus) 7/6/01 Vol. 24

pollution by man affecting the atmosphere (Jesus) 11/21/03 Vol. 33

pollution of fuels melting the icecaps (Jesus) 1/18/07 Vol. 46

pollution of man chem trails,microwaves (Jesus) 7/19/07 Vol. 48

pollution of nature no room for abuse (Jesus) 10/15/98 Vol. 13

pollution, fuel affecting environment (Jesus) 3/30/06 Vol. 42

pollution,trees out causing storms,mudslides (Jesus) 4/27/00 Vol. 19

pollution-air,water balance of nature threat (Jesus) 8/1/07 Vol. 48

pool of water living water (Jesus) 1/10/95 Vol. 2

poor care for needs of (Jesus) 9/27/06 Vol. 44

poor charity & help (Jesus) 1/29/04 Vol. 34

poor clothe & feed always (Jesus) 2/1/04 Vol. 34

poor compassion (Jesus) 6/25/94 Vol. 1

poor Denver (Mother Cabrini) 11/17/93 Vol. 1

poor donations (Mother Seton) 1/3/94 Vol. 1

poor feed spiritually,physically (Jesus) 3/6/07 Vol. 46

poor help food,time,money (Jesus) 3/27/96 Vol. 3

poor help with housing for (Jesus) 7/1/04 Vol. 36

poor lonely (Jesus) 12/4/93 Vol. 1

poor neighbors (St. Martin) 11/3/93 Vol. 1

poor relic (St. Eliz Seton) 1/4/96 Vol. 3

poor rich (Jesus) 9/22/95 Vol. 3

poor share (St. Elizabeth) 11/17/93 Vol. 1

poor share corporal works of mercy (Jesus) 11/5/07 Vol. 49

poor share gifts with (Jesus) 12/17/98 Vol. 13

poor & aged see Jesus in them (Jesus) 12/10/05 Vol. 41

poor & homeless need supplies to survive (Jesus) 12/28/04 Vol. 37

poor & hungry need your shared food (Jesus) 3/27/08 Vol. 50

poor in Middle East brainwashed to hate (Jesus) 7/27/06 Vol. 44

poor in spirit even in rich (Jesus) 9/27/00 Vol. 20

poor man appreciates God's gifts (Jesus) 3/18/00 Vol. 18

poor need donations all year long (Jesus) 11/9/06 Vol. 45

poor need charity heavenly treasure in charity (Jesus) 9/6/01 Vol. 24

poor need help and not criticism (Jesus) 2/28/02 Vol. 26

poor people can still help church (Jesus) 3/2/03 Vol. 30

poor people cannot repay you (Jesus) 12/18/97 Vol. 9

poor people everyone's responsibility (Jesus) 1/29/98 Vol. 10

poor people give alms, food, clothes (Jesus) 2/25/04 Vol. 34

poor people give charity to (Jesus) 9/27/00 Vol. 20

poor people give help (Mary) 1/22/98 Vol. 10

poor people help cheerfully (Jesus) 2/27/04 Vol. 34

poor people help generously (Jesus) 5/4/01 Vol. 23

poor people help in any way,shrine (Mother Cabrini) 11/13/96 Vol. 5

poor people help Jesus in the poor (Jesus) 12/28/00 Vol. 21

poor people help physically, financially (Jesus) 2/11/07 Vol. 46

poor people help them (Jesus) 6/19/96 Vol. 3

poor people help to feed (Jesus) 7/21/05 Vol. 40

poor people help with food & clothes (Jesus) 11/15/01 Vol. 25

poor people help with prayers, money (Jesus) 1/22/98 Vol. 10

poor people help with time & money (Jesus) 12/9/99 Vol. 17

poor people lack of self worth (Jesus) 2/19/07 Vol. 46

poor people money & suffering (Jesus) 8/25/96 Vol. 4

poor people need help (Jesus) 3/10/03 Vol. 30

poor people need sharing of wealth (Jesus) 11/18/04 Vol. 37

poor people need works of mercy (Jesus) 3/17/07 Vol. 46

poor people pass on old clothes,computers (Jesus) 11/20/03 Vol. 33

poor people pray and help (Jesus) 1/31/97 Vol. 6

poor people pray for and help (Jesus) 10/5/06 Vol. 45

poor people share and help (Jesus) 1/21/97 Vol. 6

poor people share and help with them (Jesus) 3/2/98 Vol. 10

poor people share instead of criticize (Jesus) 12/26/02 Vol. 29

poor people share love,faith & alms (Jesus) 5/21/98 Vol. 11

poor sick people need charity organizations (Jesus) 3/29/08 Vol. 50

poor sinners pray for lost souls (Jesus) 3/18/06 Vol. 42

poor, alms for Lenten devotion (Jesus) 3/11/04 Vol. 34

poor, gifts to store heavenly treasures (Jesus) 11/30/06 Vol. 45

poor, needs of money better spent on (Jesus) 10/14/04 Vol. 37

poor, uninsured help with health problems (Jesus) 5/11/07 Vol. 47

pope 15 decade rosary (Mary) 10/4/95 Vol. 3

pope blood 8/10/93 Vol. 1

Pope Church (Jesus) 9/13/95 Vol. 3

pope cross 8/7/93 Vol. 1

pope death 7/27/93 Vol. 1

pope exiled (Jesus) 5/18/96 Vol. 3

pope given teaching authority (Jesus) 11/9/02 Vol. 29

pope John Paul II (Jesus) 11/17/94 Vol. 2

Pope John Paul II and successor (Jesus) 4/7/05 Vol. 39

pope keys given by Jesus (Jesus) 8/21/05 Vol. 40

pope regarding Muslim faith (Jesus) — 9/21/06 Vol. 44

Pope salvation (Jesus) — 10/5/95 Vol. 3

pope schism — 10/20/93 Vol. 1

pope (St. Joseph) — 11/3/93 Vol. 1

Pope teaching authority of Church (Jesus) — 2/22/05 Vol. 38

pope dying pray for good leadership (Jesus) — 3/31/05 Vol. 38

Pope evangelizes vocations (Jesus) — 1/5/96 Vol. 3

pope exiled remnant forced out (Jesus) — 6/7/97 Vol. 7

Pope in Turkey with Muslims (Jesus) — 11/30/06 Vol. 45

Pope John Paul II against Iraqi War (Jesus) — 3/3/07 Vol. 46

Pope John Paul II apostasy (Jesus) — 3/6/96 Vol. 3

Pope John Paul II being protected (Jesus) — 2/19/05 Vol. 38

Pope John Paul II carry crosses in life (Jesus) — 12/10/96 Vol. 5

Pope John Paul II deeply tested (Jesus) — 11/22/94 Vol. 2

Pope John Paul II do not follow the antipope (Jesus) — 10/24/97 Vol. 9

Pope John Paul II example of evangelization (Jesus) — 1/23/98 Vol. 10

Pope John Paul II exile and schism (Jesus) — 2/22/97 Vol. 6

Pope John Paul II exiled (Jesus) — 2/8/99 Vol. 14

Pope John Paul II exiled (Jesus) — 5/21/99 Vol. 15

Pope John Paul II exiled and schism (Jesus) — 6/16/99 Vol. 15

Pope John Paul II exiled,knife in chair (Jesus) — 2/22/99 Vol. 14

Pope John Paul II few listen on abortion (Jesus) — 1/27/99 Vol. 14

Pope John Paul II follow commandments (Jesus) — 5/15/99 Vol. 15

Pope John Paul II follow him (Jesus) — 8/24/00 Vol. 20

Pope John Paul II follow him & magisterium (Jesus) — 2/28/98 Vol. 10

Pope John Paul II follow his teachings (Jesus) — 3/7/97 Vol. 6

Pope John Paul II follow his teachings (Jesus) — 11/13/97 Vol. 9

Pope John Paul II follow his teachings (Jesus) — 9/6/98 Vol. 12

Pope John Paul II follow in faith & morals (Jesus) — 1/2/97 Vol. 6

Pope John Paul II follow My vicar (Jesus) — 1/13/03 Vol. 30

Pope John Paul II follow teachings of (Jesus) — 4/23/02 Vol. 27

Pope John Paul II forced to leave (Jesus) — 1/5/99 Vol. 14

Pope John Paul II give prayer support (Mary) — 1/8/98 Vol. 10

Pope John Paul II go into hiding when exiled (Jesus) — 2/27/99 Vol. 14

Pope John Paul II health affected,evil men (Jesus) — 12/31/97 Vol. 9

Pope John Paul II his accomplishments (Jesus) — 4/10/05 Vol. 39

Pope John Paul II hope for faithful (Jesus) — 2/17/05 Vol. 38

Pope John Paul II lead remnant Church (Jesus) — 3/20/97 Vol. 6

Pope John Paul II lead remnant,rosaries (Mary) — 5/29/97 Vol. 7

Pope John Paul II lead, in hiding (Jesus) — 1/4/97 Vol. 6

Pope John Paul II leads remnant,exiled (Jesus) — 3/22/97 Vol. 6

Pope John Paul II listen on faith & morals (Jesus) — 1/29/01 Vol. 22

Pope John Paul II major pronouncement (Jesus) — 5/25/00 Vol. 19

Pope John Paul II needs our prayers (Jesus) — 11/11/04 Vol. 37

Pope John Paul II obey him during schism (Jesus) — 4/26/00 Vol. 19

Pope John Paul II pope of end times (Jesus) — 12/6/96 Vol. 5

Pope John Paul II pray and support (Jesus) — 4/26/98 Vol. 11

Pope John Paul II pray for and follow (Jesus) — 1/7/02 Vol. 26

Pope John Paul II pray for him (Jesus) — 12/12/96 Vol. 5

Pope John Paul II pray to strengthen (Mary) — 9/8/98 Vol. 12

Pope John Paul II pray,tested by peers (Mary) — 1/14/99 Vol. 14

Pope John Paul II rejected by China (Jesus) — 8/9/99 Vol. 16

Pope John Paul II replaced for health,age (Jesus) — 1/7/99 Vol. 14

Pope John Paul II rock of faith (Jesus) — 10/21/99 Vol. 17

Pope John Paul II speaks out on sin (Jesus) — 9/29/97 Vol. 8

Pope John Paul II stay faithful to his teachings (Jesus) — 7/24/98 Vol. 12

Pope John Paul II stay faithful to his teachings (Jesus) — 4/17/98 Vol. 11

Pope John Paul II suffering servant (Jesus) — 6/2/02 Vol. 27

Pope John Paul II supports call for peace (Jesus) — 1/1/02 Vol. 26

Pope John Paul II teaching authority (Jesus) — 4/30/97 Vol. 7

Pope John Paul II teachings & authority (Jesus) — 2/1/97 Vol. 6

Pope John Paul II to lead remnant Church (Jesus) — 12/16/97 Vol. 9

Pope John Paul II tries to stop war (Jesus) — 3/5/03 Vol. 30

Pope John Paul II will flee when he's exiled (Jesus) — 8/4/97 Vol. 8

Pope John Paul II's cup share the Mass (Jesus) — 5/26/05 Vol. 39

pope, leader of Church on social issues (Jesus) — 11/18/04 Vol. 37

popes errors, authority, obedience (Jesus) — 9/28/98 Vol. 12

popes set up by Jesus (Jesus) — 8/21/07 Vol. 48

pope's infallibility on decisions of faith (Jesus) — 6/22/00 Vol. 19

population increasing problems (Jesus) — 6/1/05 Vol. 39

population control abortion and wars (Jesus) — 4/21/98 Vol. 11

population control by diseases (Jesus) — 6/7/01 Vol. 23

population control by monied people (Jesus) — 8/12/99 Vol. 16

population control by one world diseases (Jesus) — 11/6/02 Vol. 29

population control in poor countries (Jesus) — 8/23/01 Vol. 24

population control man-made diseases (Jesus) — 6/18/03 Vol. 31

population control to reduce by diseases (Jesus) — 4/9/02 Vol. 27

population decrease need confidence in God (Jesus) — 2/21/08 Vol. 50

porno, 'R' movies away from children (Jesus) — 12/18/06 Vol. 45

pornography avoid, fight against (Jesus) — 11/20/05 Vol. 41

pornography misused by priests (Jesus) — 3/10/05 Vol. 38

pornography rampant in America (Jesus) — 1/26/07 Vol. 46

port selling to Arabs security questioned (Jesus) — 3/9/06 Vol. 42

possession can be by multiple demons (Jesus) — 1/30/06 Vol. 42

possession salvation (Jesus) — 12/1/95 Vol. 3

possession time (Jesus) — 1/17/95 Vol. 2

possessions as gods (Jesus) — 5/8/96 Vol. 3

possessions as gods, destroyed in storms (Jesus) — 10/26/05 Vol. 41

possessions be good stewards of (Jesus) — 10/12/03 Vol. 33

possessions become obsolete (Jesus) — 4/23/01 Vol. 23

possessions can interfere with mission (Mary) — 5/14/06 Vol. 43

possessions can survive on little (Jesus) — 1/1/99 Vol. 14

possessions cannot take them to grave (Jesus) — 6/3/98 Vol. 11

possessions detach from them in life (Jesus) — 10/21/04 Vol. 37

possessions detachment & trust (Jesus)   11/7/96 Vol. 5

possessions do not be attached to them (Jesus)   11/22/00 Vol. 21

possessions do not let them run your life (Jesus)   6/9/06 Vol. 43

possessions do not love much (Jesus)   10/15/06 Vol. 45

possessions do not make idols of them (Jesus)   6/20/03 Vol. 31

possessions do not put before God (Jesus)   11/25/04 Vol. 37

possessions drop to follow Jesus (Jesus)   8/16/01 Vol. 24

possessions excess baggage (Jesus)   1/12/95 Vol. 2

possessions given & taken away (Jesus)   1/28/00 Vol. 18

possessions hard to leave, control (Jesus)   1/7/05 Vol. 38

possessions may be lost (Jesus)   9/25/98 Vol. 12

possessions riches (Jesus)   9/5/94 Vol. 2

possessions stripped (Jesus)   8/5/99 Vol. 16

possessions stripped at death (Jesus)   11/4/06 Vol. 45

possessions stripped from us (Jesus)   5/16/01 Vol. 23

possessions stripped from us (Jesus)   2/24/99 Vol. 14

possessions temporary, no attachments to (Jesus)   12/28/07 Vol. 49

possessions to be taken away (Jesus)   3/5/07 Vol. 46

possessions trust (Jesus)   2/9/96 Vol. 3

possessions trust (Jesus)   8/3/94 Vol. 2

possessions wealth (Jesus)   1/29/95 Vol. 2

possessions will be stripped (Jesus)   2/11/99 Vol. 14

possessions will not last (Jesus)   5/23/01 Vol. 23

possessions worldly (Jesus)   9/27/94 Vol. 2

possessions worldly delights, fame (Jesus)   11/8/96 Vol. 5

possessions & money show us no love (Jesus)   1/17/03 Vol. 30

pos. & powers lost tomorrow, only stewards of (Jesus)   8/17/04 Vol. 36

possessions & talents use for God's Will (Jesus)   8/3/99 Vol. 16

possessions & wealth hard to leave (Jesus)   9/20/06 Vol. 44

possessions left on way to refuge (Jesus)   2/7/05 Vol. 38

possessions lost by wars and nature (Jesus)   2/3/00 Vol. 18

possessions lost corrode, get old (Jesus)   3/20/01 Vol. 22

possessions of today destroyed tomorrow (Jesus)   5/18/00 Vol. 19

possessions removed to awake complacency (Jesus)   8/25/99 Vol. 16

possessions shared build up heavenly treasure (Jesus)   12/7/00 Vol. 21

possessions stripped by destruction & power loss (Jesus)   9/10/98 Vol. 12

possessions stripped by storms and finances (Jesus)   8/31/98 Vol. 12

possessions stripped by weather chastisements (Jesus)   12/18/98 Vol. 13

possessions stripped easier for full trust (Jesus)   6/10/03 Vol. 31

possessions vs. heaven choices in this life (Jesus)   2/19/05 Vol. 38

possessions, more harder to give up (Jesus)   3/14/06 Vol. 42

possessions, not idols worship only God (Jesus)   8/16/05 Vol. 40

possessions,affluence leave empty souls (Jesus)   3/25/99 Vol. 14

possessions,temporary not to take pride in (Jesus)   5/25/00 Vol. 19

possible vs impossible slow down fast paced living (Jesus)   8/8/00 Vol. 20

pot holes like sin in life (Jesus)   3/3/03 Vol. 30

poverty evangelize (Jesus)   2/21/94 Vol. 1

poverty help spiritual & physical (Jesus)   12/30/97 Vol. 9

poverty reach out to help (Jesus)   3/26/98 Vol. 10

poverty rich in spirit (Jesus)   12/19/94 Vol. 2

poverty of saints seek graces vs. riches (Jesus)   6/15/00 Vol. 19

poverty test opportunity to do better (Jesus)   12/23/02 Vol. 29

power corruption of leaders (Jesus)   4/3/98 Vol. 11

power good and evil (Jesus)   10/31/96 Vol. 5

power greed (Jesus)   8/14/95 Vol. 3

power seek heaven, not control (Jesus)   8/28/97 Vol. 8

power & energy all comes from God (Jesus)   9/7/07 Vol. 48

power & money become idols & gods (Jesus)   8/19/03 Vol. 32

power & water controlled by evil ones (Jesus)   7/24/01 Vol. 24

power grid failures weak links like dominoes (Jesus)   9/9/99 Vol. 16

power grids, fuel depots targets of terrorists (Jesus)   1/20/06 Vol. 42

power of God devil as grain of sand (Jesus)   9/29/06 Vol. 44

power of God greater than all demons (Jesus)   1/14/06 Vol. 42

power of God hard to comprehend (Jesus)   5/9/07 Vol. 47

Power of God just, merciful, loving (Jesus)   6/28/07 Vol. 47

power of prayer greater than military weapons (Jesus)   11/5/01 Vol. 25

power outage plan for takeover (Jesus)   10/4/06 Vol. 45

power outage used in takeover (Jesus)   11/2/07 Vol. 49

power outage, major to cause great stress (Jesus)   12/15/04 Vol. 37

power outages a chastisement (Jesus)   12/27/00 Vol. 21

power outages and fuel supply (Jesus)   3/10/05 Vol. 38

power outages at risk by terrorists (Jesus)   11/7/05 Vol. 41

power outages be prepared for (Jesus)   9/18/03 Vol. 32

power outages cause a simpler life (Jesus)   5/12/99 Vol. 15

power outages difficult to work for support (Jesus)   9/16/04 Vol. 36

power outages for sins (Jesus)   1/4/01 Vol. 22

power outages from ice & snow (Jesus)   12/30/04 Vol. 37

power outages have fuels ready (Jesus)   12/21/07 Vol. 49

power outages have oil in lamps (Jesus)   6/12/05 Vol. 39

power outages have preparations (Jesus)   3/2/05 Vol. 38

power outages hurricanes,grid down,wind storms (Jesus)   10/15/03 Vol. 33

power outages in Canada & States (Jesus)   8/14/03 Vol. 32

power outages in coming winter months (Jesus)   12/3/98 Vol. 13

power outages keep extra food, fuel (Jesus)   1/20/05 Vol. 38

power outages microwave gun, HAARP machine (Jesus)   8/23/03 Vol. 32

power outages more frequent (Jesus)   1/8/98 Vol. 10

power outages pray for victims (Jesus)   1/2/07 Vol. 46

power outages prepare as wise virgins (Jesus)   6/24/99 Vol. 15

power outages requires alternate heating (Jesus)   8/23/99 Vol. 16

power outages suffer for greed (Jesus)   1/12/99 Vol. 14

power outages & energy more scarce and expensive (Jesus)   7/2/03 Vol. 32

power plants need for improving (Jesus)   5/26/01 Vol. 23

power plants, new where to get more fuel (Jesus)   9/6/01 Vol. 24

power plants, ports subject to foreign ownership (Jesus)   8/9/07 Vol. 48

power shortages cause simpler lives (Jesus) — 10/24/02 Vol. 29

power shortages lifestyle changed (Jesus) — 6/10/99 Vol. 15

power supplies keep for famine, trial (Jesus) — 2/10/00 Vol. 18

praise of God only (Jesus) — 2/10/03 Vol. 30

praise & glorify God in a simple life (Jesus) — 6/26/05 Vol. 39

praise & glory to God alone (Jesus) — 1/25/01 Vol. 22

praise and glory seek God first (Jesus) — 3/10/98 Vol. 10

praise and thanksgiving live your 'yes' to Jesus (Mary) — 12/8/97 Vol. 9

praise God every day (Jesus) — 8/4/03 Vol. 32

praise God with many titles (Jesus) — 4/4/04 Vol. 35

praise in song harmony of love (Jesus) — 2/27/03 Vol. 30

praise to God for all of our gifts (Jesus) — 11/22/00 Vol. 21

pray deceased souls (Jesus) — 11/3/96 Vol. 5

pray for daily strength (Jesus) — 6/6/02 Vol. 27

pray for peace (Jesus) — 2/4/07 Vol. 46

pray one hour with Me (Jesus) — 4/12/01 Vol. 23

Pray sinners,stop abortions,etc. (Jesus) — 5/6/98 Vol. 11

pray time (Mary) — 12/12/93 Vol. 1

pray daily preparation for heaven (Jesus) — 10/11/06 Vol. 45

pray for John Paul II intercessors in older popes (Jesus) — 12/28/99 Vol. 17

pray for peace and strength (Jesus) — 8/28/00 Vol. 20

pray for peace as Satan's time is up (Jesus) — 5/11/99 Vol. 15

pray for peace constantly against war (Jesus) — 3/15/07 Vol. 46

pray for peace daily intention (Jesus) — 6/7/01 Vol. 23

pray for peace double prayer effort (Jesus) — 8/8/06 Vol. 44

pray for peace in war on terrorism (Jesus) — 11/15/01 Vol. 25

pray for peace no solutions in war (Jesus) — 6/12/03 Vol. 31

pray for peace not war (Jesus) — 2/18/99 Vol. 14

pray for peace or nations to be annihilated (Jesus) — 5/12/00 Vol. 19

pray for peace to avoid destruction (Jesus) — 1/17/00 Vol. 18

pray for peace to stop wars (Jesus) — 10/1/05 Vol. 41

pray for the pope salvation history (Jesus) — 4/19/95 Vol. 2

pray kneeling to train body,concentrate on God (Jesus) — 3/25/02 Vol. 26

pray one hour with Jesus as apostles (Jesus) — 4/30/00 Vol. 19

pray persistently is price of souls (Jesus) — 7/12/99 Vol. 16

pray the rosary make time for prayer (Jesus) — 12/30/98 Vol. 13

pray to avoid mark lukewarm will be lost (Jesus) — 9/9/99 Vol. 16

pray, to stop chemical & biological arms (Jesus) — 11/16/02 Vol. 29

prayer a higher calling (Jesus) — 6/17/97 Vol. 7

prayer allows things to go easier (Jesus) — 1/29/07 Vol. 46

prayer an oasis of refreshment (Jesus) — 5/5/98 Vol. 11

prayer and free will (Jesus) — 6/17/04 Vol. 35

prayer answered (Father) — 1/9/96 Vol. 3

prayer Antichrist — 9/19/93 Vol. 1

prayer avoid distractions (Jesus) — 9/4/97 Vol. 8

prayer be persistent and humble (Jesus) — 8/27/98 Vol. 12

prayer communication with Jesus (Jesus) — 5/30/05 Vol. 39

prayer consecration (Mary) — 11/28/93 Vol. 1

prayer contemplative,adoration (Jesus) — 11/5/96 Vol. 5

prayer daily communication (Jesus) — 5/15/03 Vol. 31

prayer deed (St. Bernard) — 8/20/94 Vol. 2

prayer different kinds of (Jesus) — 2/12/08 Vol. 50

prayer do not waste time (Jesus) — 9/22/96 Vol. 4

prayer focus on loving God (Jesus) — 7/5/07 Vol. 48

prayer for conversion of sinners (Jesus) — 6/18/98 Vol. 11

prayer graces (Mary) — 2/19/94 Vol. 1

prayer humility,focus on God (Jesus) — 3/28/01 Vol. 22

prayer is best communication (Jesus) — 6/10/04 Vol. 35

prayer is weapon of choice (Jesus) — 4/7/03 Vol. 31

prayer kinds of prayer (Jesus) — 2/4/07 Vol. 46

prayer letters of love to Jesus (Jesus) — 7/31/05 Vol. 40

prayer levels of intimacy (Jesus) — 12/5/99 Vol. 17

prayer listen for God's plan (Jesus) — 7/9/98 Vol. 12

prayer make time for (Jesus) — 2/24/98 Vol. 10

prayer many needs for (Jesus) — 3/10/05 Vol. 38

prayer mission (Jesus) — 11/14/93 Vol. 1

prayer need persistence (Jesus) — 10/14/03 Vol. 33

prayer need private moments to think (Jesus) — 9/7/04 Vol. 36

prayer one hour a day (Jesus) — 5/14/95 Vol. 2

prayer one hour each day (Jesus) — 5/5/98 Vol. 11

prayer Our Lady's intentions (Mary) — 9/7/96 Vol. 4

prayer persevere in faith (Jesus) — 2/13/99 Vol. 14

prayer power in a group (Mary) — 3/20/97 Vol. 6

prayer priorities (Jesus) — 7/17/95 Vol. 3

prayer priority of time (St. Therese) — 1/24/97 Vol. 6

prayer private and group (Jesus) — 1/12/96 Vol. 3

prayer quiet time necessary (Jesus) — 4/28/02 Vol. 27

prayer removed from the schools (Jesus) — 4/7/98 Vol. 11

prayer reparation (Jesus) — 4/14/94 Vol. 1

prayer rosary and scapular (Mary) — 1/1/98 Vol. 10

prayer rosary, Scripture, Liturgy Hours (Jesus) — 10/4/05 Vol. 41

prayer satisfy all your needs (Jesus) — 10/3/99 Vol. 17

prayer Scriptures (Jesus) — 2/5/94 Vol. 1

prayer short time for conversion (Jesus) — 4/2/96 Vol. 3

prayer sign of love (Jesus) — 8/28/97 Vol. 8

prayer strength for mission (St.Theresa/Avila) — 10/15/96 Vol. 5

prayer to all three Persons (Jesus) — 5/22/05 Vol. 39

prayer unites heart with God (Jesus) — 3/15/07 Vol. 46

prayer way to lighten burdens (Jesus) — 1/13/05 Vol. 38

prayer will (Jesus) — 12/5/93 Vol. 1

prayer & Adoration rest for soul (Jesus) — 1/25/07 Vol. 46

prayer & charity needed in life (Jesus) — 11/21/06 Vol. 45

prayer & charity take earthly desires away (Jesus) — 11/24/03 Vol. 33

prayer & Confession needed over money & power (Jesus) — 11/8/01 Vol. 25

prayer & Confession spiritual strength for tribulation (Jesus) 8/10/07 Vol. 48

prayer & faith foundation for heaven (Jesus) 8/18/00 Vol. 20

prayer & fasting for conversions (Jesus) 10/30/05 Vol. 41

prayer & fasting for spiritual lives (Jesus) 2/27/03 Vol. 30

prayer & fasting help in tribulation (Jesus) 10/22/02 Vol. 29

prayer & fasting powerful to answer petitions (Jesus) 7/2/05 Vol. 40

prayer & fasting spiritual training (Jesus) 8/25/05 Vol. 40

prayer & fasting to maintain faith (Jesus) 2/21/99 Vol. 14

prayer & fasting to rid demons, addictions (Jesus) 5/16/05 Vol. 39

prayer & good actions helpful at judgment (Jesus) 7/28/05 Vol. 40

prayer & meditation better out in nature (Jesus) 6/12/07 Vol. 47

prayer & sharing needed to be saved (Jesus) 12/2/04 Vol. 37

prayer & suffering road map to heaven (Jesus) 2/27/01 Vol. 22

prayer and fasting needed to save souls (Jesus) 5/12/98 Vol. 11

prayer answered as best for soul (Jesus) 10/12/06 Vol. 45

prayer for Kosovo to stop spread of war (Jesus) 4/22/99 Vol. 15

prayer for obstinate long & persistent (Jesus) 3/13/03 Vol. 30

prayer for peace African action,cycle of killing (Jesus) 8/20/98 Vol. 12

prayer for peace Holy Thursday,Confession (Jesus) 4/1/99 Vol. 15

prayer for peace lessen disasters, change lives (Jesus) 2/12/05 Vol. 38

prayer for peace to change course of history (Jesus) 8/18/01 Vol. 24

prayer for peace to stop Iraq war (Jesus) 11/29/02 Vol. 29

prayer from the heart and Lord of life (Jesus) 10/18/01 Vol. 25

prayer group 25th Anniversary (Mary) 5/28/98 Vol. 11

prayer group 32nd year anniversary (Jesus) 6/10/04 Vol. 35

prayer group blessed by adoration (Jesus) 12/21/00 Vol. 21

prayer group dedicated to Eternal Father (God the Father) 6/17/04 Vol. 35

prayer group dedication to Father (God the Father) 4/17/99 Vol. 15

prayer group grateful for Adoration (Jesus) 1/3/02 Vol. 26

prayer group held in secret (Jesus) 10/9/03 Vol. 33

prayer group Jesus in our midst (Jesus) 12/15/05 Vol. 41

prayer group source of strength (Mary) 11/6/97 Vol. 9

prayer group The Father's thanks (God the Father) 12/18/97 Vol. 9

prayer group to meet in secret (Jesus) 4/28/04 Vol. 35

prayer groups & sacramentals to defend faith (Jesus) 10/18/03 Vol. 33

prayer groups and spiritual communion (Jesus) 11/24/01 Vol. 25

prayer groups backbone of traditions (Jesus) 12/13/05 Vol. 41

prayer groups beginning of refuges (Jesus) 7/21/02 Vol. 28

prayer groups chance to share faith (Jesus) 2/1/05 Vol. 38

prayer groups comfort in tribulation (Jesus) 2/27/03 Vol. 30

prayer groups crucifix (St. Therese) 7/20/94 Vol. 2

prayer groups discern protection (Mark) 10/2/01 Vol. 25

prayer groups encourage faith (Jesus) 8/21/06 Vol. 44

prayer groups fewer come, remnants left (Jesus) 1/24/02 Vol. 26

prayer groups for spiritual support (Jesus) 3/2/05 Vol. 38

prayer groups help each other,tribulation (Jesus) 9/22/97 Vol. 8

prayer groups help for faithful (Jesus) 12/27/07 Vol. 49

prayer groups help hiding/unify people (Jesus) 7/27/96 Vol. 4

prayer groups in homes (Jesus) 9/25/06 Vol. 44

prayer groups make us stronger (Jesus) 10/6/01 Vol. 25

prayer groups Mass in homes (Jesus) 9/27/02 Vol. 28

prayer groups meet in homes (Jesus) 2/12/04 Vol. 34

prayer groups persevere in smaller numbers (Jesus) 10/12/06 Vol. 45

prayer groups small in number (Jesus) 4/3/03 Vol. 31

prayer groups source of strength (Jesus) 4/7/02 Vol. 27

prayer groups source of strength (Jesus) 1/24/02 Vol. 26

prayer groups source of strength (Jesus) 8/25/97 Vol. 8

prayer groups stay true to Scripture (Jesus) 11/7/97 Vol. 9

prayer groups support when no Masses (Jesus) 5/15/99 Vol. 15

prayer groups thanks for prayers (God the Father) 6/7/01 Vol. 23

prayer groups to endure persecution (Jesus) 2/26/98 Vol. 10

prayer groups to fight battle (Jesus) 3/22/98 Vol. 10

prayer groups very powerful (Mary) 3/19/98 Vol. 10

prayer groups & refuges gather for protection (Jesus) 9/28/02 Vol. 28

prayer groups persecuted to go underground (Jesus) 5/5/05 Vol. 39

prayer groups smaller stay faithful (Jesus) 2/15/07 Vol. 46

prayer habits attend to all year (Jesus) 5/3/07 Vol. 47

prayer in Lent severity of chastisement (Jesus) 3/30/96 Vol. 3

prayer in the schools separation of church & state (Jesus) 5/22/98 Vol. 11

prayer intentions best for souls (Jesus) 6/30/05 Vol. 39

prayer intentions call on Father,Son,Holy Spirit (Holy Spirit)6/4/06 Vol. 43

prayer intentions candles in church (Jesus) 9/28/05 Vol. 40

prayer intentions needed for the world (Our Lady) 6/16/07 Vol. 47

prayer intentions peace,sinners,stop abortions (Jesus) 12/31/98 Vol. 13

prayer leaflets Divine Mercy and rosary (Jesus) 11/16/02 Vol. 29

prayer life always go forward (Jesus) 5/10/98 Vol. 11

prayer life and busy schedules (Jesus) 1/6/02 Vol. 26

prayer life communication with God (Jesus) 1/30/05 Vol. 38

prayer life daily actions (Jesus) 7/9/95 Vol. 3

prayer life disasters (Jesus) 10/21/93 Vol. 1

prayer life do not forget it (Jesus) 1/30/02 Vol. 26

prayer life do not short change (Jesus) 10/8/02 Vol. 29

prayer life focus on daily (Jesus) 6/19/04 Vol. 35

prayer life important to teach children (Jesus) 11/16/02 Vol. 29

prayer life keep focused (Jesus) 2/8/99 Vol. 14

prayer life Lenten devotions (Jesus) 3/11/99 Vol. 14

prayer life mainstay of life (Jesus) 12/30/03 Vol. 33

prayer life more important than things (Jesus) 3/20/01 Vol. 22

prayer life needed to face life (Jesus) 6/21/06 Vol. 43

prayer life needed to fight Satan (Jesus) 5/17/05 Vol. 39

prayer life nothing should interfere with (Jesus) 11/1/98 Vol. 13

prayer life refreshes soul (Jesus) 4/3/03 Vol. 31

prayer life refreshes soul (Jesus) 6/26/01 Vol. 23

prayer life strength (Jesus) 1/30/96 Vol. 3

prayer life teach to children (Jesus)	9/9/06 Vol. 44
prayer life first need to leave time for Jesus (Jesus)	10/5/00 Vol. 21
prayer life needed to overcome life's anxieties (Jesus)	11/4/02 Vol. 29
prayer life, faith needed to endure life's trials (Jesus)	11/29/03 Vol. 33
prayer lives to keep faith (Jesus)	2/25/03 Vol. 30
prayer needed for electing faithful people (Jesus)	11/3/00 Vol. 21
prayer needed for every task, avoid pride (Jesus)	12/10/03 Vol. 33
prayer needed for people of America to repent (Jesus)	9/20/04 Vol. 36
prayer needed for protection against demons (Jesus)	2/22/02 Vol. 26
prayer needed for rain in droughts (Jesus)	11/19/07 Vol. 49
prayer needed or further destruction (Jesus)	9/13/01 Vol. 24
prayer needed overcome difficulties of life (Jesus)	12/30/07 Vol. 49
prayer needed to mitigate chastisements (Jesus)	12/25/00 Vol. 21
prayer needed to stop nuclear war (Jesus)	2/10/06 Vol. 42
prayer needed to stop war in Iraq (Mary)	11/21/02 Vol. 29
prayer needed to stop war,terrorism (Jesus)	12/12/02 Vol. 29
prayer petition how answered (Jesus)	10/11/07 Vol. 49
prayer petitions Jesus wants trust (Jesus)	12/6/00 Vol. 21
prayer preparation rid worldly distractions (Jesus)	10/24/04 Vol. 37
prayer preparation strength for everyday trials (Jesus)	10/6/04 Vol. 37
prayer priority should be first on list (Jesus)	9/24/99 Vol. 16
prayer purpose petition,thanks,sorrow,praise (Jesus)	3/6/01 Vol. 22
prayer time do when rested (Jesus)	6/1/06 Vol. 43
prayer time early so you do not fall asleep (Jesus)	9/11/04 Vol. 36
prayer time first priority (Jesus)	9/9/07 Vol. 48
prayer time focus,not on our plans (Jesus)	7/5/00 Vol. 20
prayer time is spiritual priority (Jesus)	3/12/07 Vol. 46
prayer time keep close to God, necessary (Jesus)	9/30/04 Vol. 36
prayer time make priority for (Jesus)	7/29/04 Vol. 36
prayer time make up missed next day (Jesus)	7/5/07 Vol. 48
prayer time needed daily,Church,home (Jesus)	4/8/00 Vol. 19
prayer time needed for peace with God (Jesus)	7/15/04 Vol. 36
prayer time nothing more important than (Jesus)	5/19/00 Vol. 19
prayer time priorities (Jesus)	2/13/96 Vol. 3
prayer time priorities needed (Jesus)	2/18/05 Vol. 38
prayer time should equal earthly cares (Jesus)	5/7/04 Vol. 35
prayer time should not be forgotten (Jesus)	7/29/05 Vol. 40
prayer time to slow down & think (Jesus)	8/1/03 Vol. 32
prayer time, peace protect from outside events (Jesus)	5/2/06 Vol. 43
prayer vs. demons contemplative prayer (Jesus)	9/8/06 Vol. 44
prayer vs. entertainment how free time is spent (Jesus)	3/4/02 Vol. 26
prayer warriors all called, few listen (Jesus)	11/7/96 Vol. 5
prayer warriors dying off, no replacements (Jesus)	4/18/06 Vol. 43
prayer warriors fight the good fight (Jesus)	1/3/98 Vol. 10
prayer warriors from heart in tribulation (Jesus)	6/21/07 Vol. 47
prayer warriors holding back total destruction (Jesus)	1/12/05 Vol. 38
prayer warriors open door for Jesus (Jesus)	1/5/08 Vol. 50
prayer warriors placed in each family (Jesus)	10/13/05 Vol. 41
prayer warriors warning (Jesus)	6/26/94 Vol. 1
prayer, constant needed for sins of world (Jesus)	11/10/03 Vol. 33
prayer, daily pray early for tasks (Jesus)	7/7/05 Vol. 40
prayer, persistent all possible with God (Jesus)	1/10/06 Vol. 42
prayer, persistent can accomplish impossible (Jesus)	8/11/02 Vol. 28
prayer, reasons for adore,bless,petition,forgive (Jesus)	3/7/06 Vol. 42
prayer, sufficient needed to stop wars (Jesus)	6/22/06 Vol. 43
prayer, wayward souls persistent in faith (Jesus)	12/8/03 Vol. 33
prayer,best weapon rosaries to battle evil ones (Jesus)	10/5/00 Vol. 21
prayer,contemplative as Jesus in mountains (Jesus)	12/14/02 Vol. 29
prayer,distractions to use Lenten devotions (Jesus)	3/16/00 Vol. 18
prayer,fasting,almsgiving to gain heaven (Jesus)	6/15/05 Vol. 39
prayers answered by God's Will (Jesus)	4/29/01 Vol. 23
prayers answered in His Will (Jesus)	2/24/99 Vol. 14
prayers answered yes or no (Jesus)	7/25/06 Vol. 44
prayers best weapons for peace (Jesus)	12/16/03 Vol. 33
prayers conversion of sinners (Mary)	3/27/96 Vol. 3
prayers do not rush through them (Jesus)	4/26/01 Vol. 23
prayers examine intentions (Jesus)	3/6/01 Vol. 22
prayers family many	3/23/94 Vol. 1
prayers for peace (Mary)	4/3/97 Vol. 7
prayers for sinners,purgatory (Mary)	2/20/97 Vol. 6
prayers good intentions count (Jesus)	1/24/98 Vol. 10
prayers have faith in (Jesus)	7/17/06 Vol. 44
prayers humble,contrite heart (Jesus)	1/5/97 Vol. 6
prayers messages (Mark)	4/25/95 Vol. 2
prayers morning & evening,remember (Jesus)	2/14/02 Vol. 26
prayers need help and petitions (Jesus)	7/6/02 Vol. 28
prayers persistent in requests (Mary)	5/8/97 Vol. 7
prayers personal mission (Mother Cabrini)	11/7/96 Vol. 5
prayers petitions as love letters (Jesus)	11/15/97 Vol. 9
prayers power for good over sins (Jesus)	5/27/05 Vol. 39
prayers reparation (Jesus)	11/22/93 Vol. 1
prayers will be answered (Jesus)	7/29/07 Vol. 48
prayers will be answered (Jesus)	9/17/07 Vol. 48
prayers & devotions spiritual treasures (Jesus)	1/19/01 Vol. 22
prayers & fasting for sins of the world (Jesus)	6/28/07 Vol. 47
prayers & Masses move souls up (Jesus)	3/4/08 Vol. 50
prayers & rosaries need more fervor (Jesus)	9/11/04 Vol. 36
prayers answered give thanks (Jesus)	6/13/06 Vol. 43
prayers answered need thanksgiving (Jesus)	10/11/07 Vol. 49
prayers for bishops for proper priest teaching (Jesus)	4/13/99 Vol. 15
prayers for messengers to carry out mission (Jesus)	11/19/03 Vol. 33
prayers for peace constantly needed (Jesus)	12/27/07 Vol. 49
prayers for peace or WWIII could start (Jesus)	10/4/01 Vol. 25
prayers for relatives in Purgatory (Jesus)	3/27/99 Vol. 14

prayers for the dead never wasted (Jesus)   6/20/05 Vol. 39
prayers needed by soul in purgatory (Jesus)   11/2/04 Vol. 37
prayers needed for evangelization trips (Jesus)   7/26/07 Vol. 48
prayers vs. weapons against evil in tribulation (Jesus)   10/11/07 Vol. 49
prayers, donations needed for disaster victims (Jesus)   9/22/04 Vol. 36
prayers, fasting spiritual armor (Jesus)   11/6/99 Vol. 17
prayers, reparation will be multiplied (Jesus)   9/12/07 Vol. 48
preaching practice what you do (Jesus)   9/13/02 Vol. 28
Precious Blood sacrifice for all time (Jesus)   4/15/04 Vol. 35
Precious Blood victim (Jesus)   10/31/95 Vol. 3
Precious Blood washes our sins (Jesus)   3/23/05 Vol. 38
Precious Blood wine consecrated at Mass (Jesus)   6/7/07 Vol. 47
predators vs. prey demons vs. souls (Jesus)   9/19/07 Vol. 48
pre-emptive attack oil is goal in Iraq (Jesus)   11/21/02 Vol. 29
pre-emptive war uncertainty of deaths (Jesus)   11/29/02 Vol. 29
pregnancies, problem encourage adoption,keeping (Jesus)   7/12/07 Vol. 48
pregnancies, unwed pray to seek forgiveness (Jesus)   12/18/07 Vol. 49
pregnancies,abortion prayer to stop abortion (Jesus)   10/7/00 Vol. 21
pre. help centers support to encourage adoption (Jesus)   11/16/07 Vol. 49
preparation death (Jesus)   12/11/93 Vol. 1
preparation like five wise virgins (Jesus)   8/27/04 Vol. 36
preparation sacramentals (Jesus)   8/9/95 Vol. 3
preparation spiritual weapons,blanket (Jesus)   12/26/96 Vol. 5
preparation as Noah refuse the mark of the beast (Jesus)   10/8/98 Vol. 13
preparation for death souls need to be cleansed (Jesus)   11/4/99 Vol. 17
preparations for tribulation (Jesus)   10/7/05 Vol. 41
preparations needed soon (Jesus)   1/29/01 Vol. 22
preparations physical & spiritual (Jesus)   1/15/01 Vol. 22
preparations sacramentals,food,water (Jesus)   3/3/99 Vol. 14
preparations spiritual & physical (Jesus)   12/25/07 Vol. 49
preparations spiritual & physical (Jesus)   7/8/99 Vol. 16
preparations spiritual and physical (Jesus)   5/11/99 Vol. 15
prep. for heaven serve God,no worldly desires (Jesus)   8/20/07 Vol. 48
preparations needed for the end times (Jesus)   4/11/06 Vol. 43
preparations, heavenly praise God (Jesus)   4/25/06 Vol. 43
prepare Blessed Sacrament   10/11/93 Vol. 1
prepare fire   9/21/93 Vol. 1
prepare food, water, fuel (Jesus)   6/1/99 Vol. 15
prepare protection (Jesus)   7/22/95 Vol. 3
prepare punishment (Jesus)   12/28/93 Vol. 1
prepare purification (Jesus)   10/1/95 Vol. 3
prepare repent (Jesus)   11/3/95 Vol. 3
prepare with mercy and protection (Jesus)   4/4/97 Vol. 7
prepare with sacraments & rosary (Jesus)   9/27/96 Vol. 4
prepare for 2nd coming sinners are not ready (Jesus)   11/14/97 Vol. 9
prepare for tribulation sacramental,warm clothes (Jesus)   11/4/99 Vol. 17
prepared for death? many are not ready (Jesus)   5/19/07 Vol. 47

presence will (Jesus)   4/13/94 Vol. 1
Presence of God only seen by Holy Spirit gift (Jesus)   4/11/98 Vol. 11
Presence of Jesus in Holy Communion (Jesus)   5/25/06 Vol. 43
present moment live in the (Jesus)   8/14/05 Vol. 40
present moment live in, not tomorrow (Jesus)   8/12/07 Vol. 48
present moment live today,not past or future (Jesus)   11/7/04 Vol. 37
present moment no worries on past or future (Jesus)   11/4/03 Vol. 33
present, live in following God's Will (Jesus)   9/15/04 Vol. 36
Presentation mission (Jesus)   2/2/94 Vol. 1
Presentation in Temple by Mary & St. Joseph (Jesus)   1/3/08 Vol. 50
Presentation in Temple Jesus' Light in world (Jesus)   2/2/06 Vol. 42
Presentation in Temple naming Jesus (Jesus)   2/2/07 Vol. 46
Presentation of Mary by St. Ann & St. Joachim (Jesus)   11/21/03 Vol. 33
presentation of Mary no original sin (Jesus)   11/21/02 Vol. 29
Presentation of Mary St. Ann, St. Joachim (Mary)   11/21/98 Vol. 13
preserve Church Remnant,on narrow road (Jesus)   4/21/97 Vol. 7
preserve the Church guard Bible from changes (Jesus)   10/17/98 Vol. 13
President abortions (Jesus)   3/29/94 Vol. 1
president threat to our rights (Jesus)   11/8/07 Vol. 49
President to flee to safety (Jesus)   2/7/08 Vol. 50
President Bush following one world directives (Jesus)   7/3/03 Vol. 32
President Bush involving us in war (Jesus)   7/25/03 Vol. 32
president,new set new moral course (Jesus)   2/19/01 Vol. 22
presidential candidates break promises (Jesus)   2/19/04 Vol. 34
presidential candidates favor death culture (Jesus)   3/3/08 Vol. 50
presidential election controlled by one worlders (Jesus)   1/3/08 Vol. 50
presidential election fortunate to have another (Jesus)   7/4/98 Vol. 12
presidential election out of control on icy spot (Jesus)   11/21/00 Vol. 21
presidential election vote for pro-life candidates (Jesus)   7/29/04 Vol. 36
presidential vote fairness needed in election (Jesus)   11/9/00 Vol. 21
presidents pray for them, tested in office (Jesus)   6/10/04 Vol. 35
price of conversions prayer,fasting,example (Jesus)   1/25/00 Vol. 18
price of soul ransomed by Jesus (Jesus)   3/9/00 Vol. 18
price of souls few prayers or fasting (Jesus)   6/3/03 Vol. 31
price of souls higher for addicts (Jesus)   5/16/06 Vol. 43
prices of commodities controlling consumers (Jesus)   3/3/01 Vol. 22
prices,jobs,wars controlled by the rich (Jesus)   10/9/00 Vol. 21
pride accept advice (Jesus)   9/23/97 Vol. 8
pride be a humble sinner (Jesus)   2/2/02 Vol. 26
pride be humble, thank God (Jesus)   5/17/05 Vol. 39
pride blessings (Jesus)   2/12/94 Vol. 1
pride block to spiritual success (Jesus)   7/10/00 Vol. 20
pride body's mortality/testing (Jesus)   8/20/96 Vol. 4
pride brings us to ruin (Jesus)   10/7/99 Vol. 17
pride disaster   10/28/93 Vol. 1
pride do not get puffed up (Jesus)   6/16/98 Vol. 11
pride do not seek fame (Jesus)   4/23/98 Vol. 11

pride fear of embarrassment (Jesus)   9/23/96 Vol. 4
pride first will be last (Jesus)   10/4/97 Vol. 9
pride follow God's Will (Jesus)   9/20/97 Vol. 8
pride follow God's Will (Jesus)   5/13/96 Vol. 3
pride give credit to God (Jesus)   2/20/07 Vol. 46
pride give glory to God instead (Jesus)   3/12/07 Vol. 46
pride give glory to God instead (Jesus)   6/9/00 Vol. 19
pride give thanks for gifts (Jesus)   8/16/97 Vol. 8
pride holds us back (Jesus)   10/9/02 Vol. 29
pride humility (Jesus)   4/8/95 Vol. 2
pride in traveling (Jesus)   1/25/01 Vol. 22
pride keep soul pure (Jesus)   9/17/02 Vol. 28
pride leads to self-righteousness (Jesus)   5/2/02 Vol. 27
pride love God and neighbor (Jesus)   3/4/97 Vol. 6
pride man small in universe (Jesus)   9/29/97 Vol. 8
pride no interference with love (Jesus)   12/31/07 Vol. 49
pride proud are humbled (Jesus)   8/2/98 Vol. 12
pride rationalize our sins (Jesus)   9/18/03 Vol. 32
pride the devil's weapon (Jesus)   9/14/99 Vol. 16
pride the root of other sins (Jesus)   1/24/98 Vol. 10
pride will and gifts (Jesus)   4/26/96 Vol. 3
pride & comforts take mind off of God (Jesus)   10/26/07 Vol. 49
pride & cover-up causes more sin (Jesus)   3/15/04 Vol. 34
pride & curiosity used by devil to distract (Jesus)   12/27/06 Vol. 45
pride & fame be humble & serve (Jesus)   3/13/03 Vol. 30
pride & fame impediments in spiritual life (Jesus)   2/27/02 Vol. 26
pride & fame quickly forgotten (Jesus)   9/3/02 Vol. 28
pride & greed leaves no room for Jesus (Jesus)   10/27/03 Vol. 33
pride & money do not judge (Jesus)   4/11/02 Vol. 27
pride & money man's downfall (Jesus)   12/20/00 Vol. 21
pride & power will come to ruin (Jesus)   2/20/03 Vol. 30
pride & selfishness hold back love (Jesus)   2/27/06 Vol. 42
pride and greed sin of Adam in U.S. (Jesus)   11/17/98 Vol. 13
pride and privacy tear down walls to neighbor (Jesus)   3/15/98 Vol. 10
pride in being first need good example (Jesus)   3/14/01 Vol. 22
pride, an impediment Jesus' help needed in everything (Jesus)
                                                             12/10/03 Vol. 33
pride, envy tools of the devil (Jesus)   9/26/05 Vol. 40
priest prayer life (Jesus)   9/13/94 Vol. 2
priest service (Jesus)   9/27/94 Vol. 2
priest vocations (Jesus)   12/4/93 Vol. 1
priest calling Adoration,prayers,parents (Jesus)   1/27/08 Vol. 50
priest needed to forgive sins through Jesus (Jesus)   4/2/01 Vol. 23
priest scandal and scam artists (Jesus)   4/7/02 Vol. 27
priest scandals lawsuits for sexual offenses (Jesus)   2/17/02 Vol. 26
priest scandals test and a threat (Jesus)   5/27/02 Vol. 27
priest shortage artificial,discouraged vocation (Jesus)   5/2/00 Vol. 19

priest shortage encouragement,role models (Jesus)   10/27/00 Vol. 21
priest shortage need priest models (Jesus)   2/24/01 Vol. 22
priest shortage pray for more priests (Jesus)   10/10/00 Vol. 21
priesthood discernment (Jesus)   3/5/96 Vol. 3
priesthood flourishes by Adoration (Jesus)   6/14/02 Vol. 27
priesthood gift of sacraments (Jesus)   4/15/04 Vol. 35
priesthood great example (Jesus)   7/22/06 Vol. 44
priesthood respect office,pray for (Jesus)   4/21/02 Vol. 27
priesthood undermined (Jesus)   9/7/03 Vol. 32
Priesthood, Holy picture in honor of (Jesus)   12/9/06 Vol. 45
priestly vocations need encouragement (Jesus)   6/8/00 Vol. 19
priests accountable for false teaching (Jesus)   10/16/03 Vol. 33
priests attacked by evil one (Jesus)   7/17/02 Vol. 28
priests attacked by Satan (Jesus)   10/11/02 Vol. 29
priests attacked by Satan (Jesus)   4/21/02 Vol. 27
priests befriend loyal ones (Jesus)   5/12/98 Vol. 11
priests Blessed Sacrament (Jesus)   2/24/95 Vol. 2
priests build up spiritually (Jesus)   4/3/03 Vol. 31
priests discern teachings (Jesus)   2/14/03 Vol. 30
priests discourage rosary,adoring (Jesus)   2/3/99 Vol. 14
priests do not complain about (Jesus)   7/21/99 Vol. 16
priests errors, authority, obedience (Jesus)   9/28/98 Vol. 12
priests Eucharist (Jesus)   12/9/93 Vol. 1
priests first victims of Antichrist (Jesus)   10/24/99 Vol. 17
priests forgive sins through Jesus (Jesus)   8/21/05 Vol. 40
priests founders of orders (Jesus)   8/14/96 Vol. 4
priests get attacked by demons (Jesus)   10/24/01 Vol. 25
priests gift to provide sacraments (Jesus)   12/9/06 Vol. 45
priests help in Mass,homilies (Holy Spirit)   11/11/96 Vol. 5
priests indifference (Jesus)   1/6/95 Vol. 2
priests Jesus acts through them (Jesus)   4/13/96 Vol. 3
priests life blood of soul (Jesus)   1/21/95 Vol. 2
priests lost faith in Real Presence (Jesus)   10/25/02 Vol. 29
priests love,prayers & respect (Jesus)   8/28/96 Vol. 4
priests lukewarm separated (Jesus)   12/27/05 Vol. 41
priests martryed (Mary)   9/17/93 Vol. 1
priests more given,more expected (Jesus)   10/22/97 Vol. 9
priests need prayer themselves, others (Jesus)   10/16/03 Vol. 33
priests need prayers to keep holy (Jesus)   2/17/05 Vol. 38
priests need to encourage Confession (Jesus)   8/1/02 Vol. 28
priests need to stress Confession (Jesus)   8/3/02 Vol. 28
priests order of Melchisedech (Jesus)   1/18/99 Vol. 14
priests persecuted (Jesus)   4/9/94 Vol. 1
priests pray for (Jesus)   6/5/02 Vol. 27
priests pray for (Jesus)   3/10/05 Vol. 38
priests pray for (Jesus)   12/5/96 Vol. 5
priests pray for courage for (Jesus)   7/19/03 Vol. 32

priests pray for daily (Jesus) — 5/9/05 Vol. 39

priests pray for support (Jesus) — 10/5/99 Vol. 17

priests pray for them (Jesus) — 2/15/03 Vol. 30

priests pray for them (Jesus) — 11/7/97 Vol. 9

priests pray for them and protect them (Jesus) — 7/25/04 Vol. 36

priests pray for vocations (Jesus) — 10/25/01 Vol. 25

priests pray for vocations (Jesus) — 3/24/96 Vol. 3

priests preach boldly (Jesus) — 10/27/96 Vol. 5

priests prepare for Warning (Jesus) — 4/10/97 Vol. 7

priests prizes worth prayer (Jesus) — 1/9/00 Vol. 18

priests protect them (Jesus) — 3/1/07 Vol. 46

priests representatives on earth (Jesus) — 9/25/97 Vol. 8

priests respect in Jesus' place (Jesus) — 2/15/03 Vol. 30

priests responsibilites in Confession (Jesus) — 8/28/03 Vol. 32

priests responsibility to save souls (Jesus) — 5/1/02 Vol. 27

priests responsible for souls (Jesus) — 2/26/99 Vol. 14

priests sacraments (Jesus) — 6/27/95 Vol. 2

priests sacraments — 9/17/93 Vol. 1

priests scandal in sexual sins (Jesus) — 7/17/02 Vol. 28

priests second coming (Mary) — 3/2/94 Vol. 1

priests sexual offenses (Jesus) — 1/30/03 Vol. 30

priests sexual scandals (Jesus) — 5/18/06 Vol. 43

priests should encourage confession (Jesus) — 5/9/98 Vol. 11

priests show way to salvation (Jesus) — 3/3/97 Vol. 6

priests some lost prayer life (Jesus) — 5/1/02 Vol. 27

priests some misled (Jesus) — 6/23/04 Vol. 35

priests speak out on Real Presence (Jesus) — 7/8/02 Vol. 28

priests stay faithful (Jesus) — 5/22/98 Vol. 11

priests support and correct gently (Jesus) — 5/15/98 Vol. 11

priests support and pray for (Jesus) — 3/11/99 Vol. 14

priests support parish priest (Jesus) — 12/11/96 Vol. 5

priests support, Masses (Jesus) — 4/10/97 Vol. 7

priests to be persecuted (Jesus) — 10/11/99 Vol. 17

priests underground Masses (Jesus) — 1/13/96 Vol. 3

priests uphold the Gospel,faith (Jesus) — 7/7/97 Vol. 8

priests urge to have adoration (Jesus) — 2/15/99 Vol. 14

priests vocations (St. John N.) — 1/5/94 Vol. 1

priests vocations & sacraments (Jesus) — 2/5/96 Vol. 3

priests will need protection (Jesus) — 4/24/01 Vol. 23

priests & bishops need financial & spiritual support (Jesus) — 5/11/04 Vol. 35

priests & bishops pray for (Jesus) — 4/7/02 Vol. 27

priests & bishops support and pray for (Jesus) — 7/13/99 Vol. 16

priests & prophets leaders sent to people (Jesus) — 5/7/06 Vol. 43

priests & sacraments needed for spiritual life (Jesus) — 5/25/00 Vol. 19

priests abuse vocations lost (Jesus) — 4/13/02 Vol. 27

priests' abuses could bankrupt the Church (Jesus) — 10/14/04 Vol. 37

priests' abuses pray to protect from (Jesus) — 2/22/07 Vol. 46

priests as victim souls persecuted as Jesus was (Jesus) — 5/12/00 Vol. 19

priests' errors preach confession, about sin (Jesus) — 11/3/98 Vol. 13

priests in prison need our prayers (Jesus) — 5/11/06 Vol. 43

priest's problems need more prayer (Jesus) — 4/18/02 Vol. 27

priests' responsibilities pray for them (Jesus) — 1/25/04 Vol. 34

priests' scandal attack of Satan (Jesus) — 6/5/02 Vol. 27

priests' scandals do not loose faith (Jesus) — 5/14/02 Vol. 27

priests, bishops need prayers of protection (Jesus) — 7/17/07 Vol. 48

priests, evil teach sexual sins not sins (Jesus) — 10/18/02 Vol. 29

priests, good pray for, needed (Jesus) — 8/30/07 Vol. 48

priests, inspiration needed for vocations (Jesus) — 3/1/08 Vol. 50

priests, lukewarm accountable to God (Jesus) — 12/2/04 Vol. 37

priests, Marian given extra protection (Jesus) — 5/2/02 Vol. 27

primary campaign personal attacks (Jesus) — 3/13/08 Vol. 50

Princess Diana remember we are mortals (Jesus) — 9/4/97 Vol. 8

Principalities & Powers battle with evil (Jesus) — 10/26/06 Vol. 45

principalities & powers dignitaries (Jesus) — 6/22/95 Vol. 2

principalities & powers fight with angel (Holy Spirit) — 7/20/98 Vol. 12

principalities and powers sacraments our weapons (Jesus) — 4/20/98 Vol. 11

principalities and powers suffer (Jesus) — 6/29/95 Vol. 2

printed word not trusted as Gospel Word (Jesus) — 6/12/03 Vol. 31

priorities analyze time for prayer (Jesus) — 4/4/98 Vol. 11

priorities and full commitment (Jesus) — 1/28/03 Vol. 30

priorities budget time & charity (Jesus) — 6/6/06 Vol. 43

priorities discernment (Jesus) — 9/17/95 Vol. 3

priorities Divine Will (Jesus) — 5/26/95 Vol. 2

priorities do not be selfish (Jesus) — 1/4/98 Vol. 10

priorities examine values in life (Jesus) — 12/15/96 Vol. 5

priorities follow Jesus on narrow road (Jesus) — 8/10/98 Vol. 12

priorities for a simple life (Jesus) — 3/16/05 Vol. 38

priorities get rid of excess baggage (Jesus) — 11/6/97 Vol. 9

priorities God is first priority (Jesus) — 12/10/00 Vol. 21

priorities God over entertainment (Jesus) — 3/13/07 Vol. 46

priorities heavenly vs earthly things (Jesus) — 11/3/99 Vol. 17

priorities help others (Jesus) — 5/16/02 Vol. 27

priorities homosexual (Jesus) — 4/13/94 Vol. 1

priorities love God and neighbor (Jesus) — 12/13/97 Vol. 9

priorities love God first (Jesus) — 7/10/06 Vol. 44

priorities of daily prayer (Jesus) — 12/2/99 Vol. 17

priorities of love & help others (Jesus) — 3/3/05 Vol. 38

priorities of prayer & good deeds (Jesus) — 7/29/04 Vol. 36

priorities pray to discern (Jesus) — 10/8/02 Vol. 29

priorities pray to discern (Jesus) — 6/1/06 Vol. 43

priorities prayer first (Jesus) — 9/9/02 Vol. 28

priorities prayer life first (Jesus) — 6/20/03 Vol. 31

priorities prayers,Confession,works (Jesus) — 3/16/00 Vol. 18

priorities protection (Jesus) — 9/4/95 Vol. 3

priorities Scriptures (Jesus)   2/1/94 Vol. 1
priorities serve (St. Therese)   5/22/95 Vol. 2
priorities should involve God (Jesus)   2/20/00 Vol. 18
priorities & direction change toward heavenly goals (Jesus) 5/16/04 Vol. 35
priorities in life centered around God,not world (Jesus)   7/15/04 Vol. 36
priorities in life evangelize (Mary)   8/2/97 Vol. 8
priorities in life need analyzing to improve (Jesus)   4/11/00 Vol. 19
priorities in life seek heaven, not riches (Jesus)   7/28/02 Vol. 28
priorities in life will lead to heaven (Jesus)   1/1/99 Vol. 14
priorities of day prayer first (Jesus)   3/27/03 Vol. 30
priorities of life daily prayer (Jesus)   8/20/03 Vol. 32
priorities of time put God first in prayer life (Jesus)   9/6/04 Vol. 36
priorities, life's directed toward goal of heaven (Jesus)   3/13/02 Vol. 26
prioritize time love God & neighbor (Jesus)   9/27/03 Vol. 32
priority 1st in heaven soul's destination (Jesus)   9/11/01 Vol. 24
priority,first prayer,love of God (Jesus)   2/23/00 Vol. 18
prison torture (Jesus)   6/12/95 Vol. 2
prison camps all over America (Jesus)   12/26/06 Vol. 45
prison camps for refusing mark of beast (Jesus)   11/2/00 Vol. 21
prison camps of Antichrist (Jesus)   1/10/01 Vol. 22
prison chains for refusing mark in hand (Jesus)   12/16/99 Vol. 17
prisoners need hope in the Spirit (Jesus)   1/13/05 Vol. 38
prisoners need visiting & forgiveness (Jesus)   2/28/02 Vol. 26
prisoners pray for and visit (Jesus)   10/9/06 Vol. 45
prisoners,visit need conversion (Jesus)   2/24/00 Vol. 18
prisoners,visit need conversion (Jesus)   2/24/00 Vol. 18
prisons overcrowded released prisoners trouble (Jesus)   9/6/01 Vol. 24
privacy compromised by technology (Jesus)   11/13/02 Vol. 29
privacy invasion of by government (Jesus)   5/8/97 Vol. 7
privacy challenged by smart cards (Jesus)   2/3/06 Vol. 42
privacy freedoms threatened by false security (Jesus)   11/6/03 Vol. 33
privacy invaded by RFID chips (Jesus)   1/11/04 Vol. 34
privacy invaded identity theft,spyware (Jesus)   10/20/04 Vol. 37
privacy vs. security Patriot Act, wire tapping (Jesus)   12/23/05 Vol. 41
private revelation enhancement of faith (Jesus)   9/10/03 Vol. 32
private revelation requires discernment (Jesus)   8/1/05 Vol. 40
private time is not employer's time (Jesus)   1/7/00 Vol. 18
problem solving pray to God first (Jesus)   12/9/00 Vol. 21
problem, solution means of control (Jesus)   2/3/01 Vol. 22
problems God's Will in life (Jesus)   3/20/96 Vol. 3
problems & trials pray first for help (Jesus)   5/30/03 Vol. 31
problems of life help with Jesus (Jesus)   1/1/04 Vol. 34
problems, difficulties seek help from Jesus (Jesus)   11/20/98 Vol. 13
proclaim the Gospel to help sinners, lukewarm (Jesus)   1/20/00 Vol. 18
proclaim the Gospel witness Jesus' rising to life (Jesus)   1/12/00 Vol. 18
Proclamation of Blessed Mother announcement by pope (Jesus)
                                                                10/3/04 Vol. 37

prodigal son confess your sins (Jesus)   10/30/01 Vol. 25
Prodigal son Father awaits our return (Jesus)   7/2/02 Vol. 28
Prodigal Son lost, now found in mercy (Jesus)   9/11/04 Vol. 36
prodigal son repent now (Jesus)   2/8/03 Vol. 30
Prodigal Son repentance needed (Jesus)   3/10/07 Vol. 46
Prodigal Son return to the Father (Jesus)   7/9/04 Vol. 36
prodigal son sin and forgiveness (Father)   3/9/96 Vol. 3
Prodigal Son, The heaven rejoices (Jesus)   3/14/98 Vol. 10
prodigal son's father reaches out to worst sinners (Jesus) 10/16/98 Vol. 13
product's quality and spiritual life (Jesus)   3/4/03 Vol. 30
profit, share of more to CEO & stockholders (Jesus)   1/18/07 Vol. 46
Progress of man balance of nature lost (Jesus)   2/6/06 Vol. 42
promised land Moses and future (Jesus)   7/19/01 Vol. 24
promises decisions (Jesus)   1/28/95 Vol. 2
promises God always keeps (Jesus)   2/19/04 Vol. 34
promises of God will be always fulfilled (Jesus)   2/15/01 Vol. 22
promotions follow moral law (Jesus)   6/2/03 Vol. 31
prompting of angels to help spiritual lives (Jesus)   1/18/00 Vol. 18
prophecies fulfilled (Jesus)   5/16/98 Vol. 11
prophecies Isaiah fulfilled (Jesus)   12/10/96 Vol. 5
prophecies second coming (Jesus)   7/18/94 Vol. 2
prophecies before are coming to pass (Jesus)   5/3/00 Vol. 19
prophecies fulfilled from Old Testament (Jesus)   4/19/06 Vol. 43
prophecies fulfilled in Jesus' birth (Jesus)   12/22/00 Vol. 21
prophecy affirm personal gift (Jesus)   9/28/97 Vol. 8
prophecy fulfilled in Scripture (Jesus)   2/19/99 Vol. 14
prophecy Redeemer (Jesus)   12/21/94 Vol. 2
prophecy sources (Jesus)   11/18/94 Vol. 2
prophecy fulfilled in Resurrection of Jesus (Jesus)   3/30/02 Vol. 26
prophecy of the Bible fulfilled in Second Coming (Jesus) 4/26/00 Vol. 19
prophesy fulfilled (Jesus)   12/24/96 Vol. 5
prophet messenger (Jesus)   12/10/94 Vol. 2
prophet messengers (Jesus)   8/29/94 Vol. 2
prophet not accepted in own town (Jesus)   2/9/07 Vol. 46
prophet test fruit,love of God in words (Jesus)   6/14/00 Vol. 19
prophet willing to accept mission (Jesus)   7/1/07 Vol. 48
prophetic writings given throughout history (Jesus)   4/25/06 Vol. 43
prophets apostles (Jesus)   7/3/94 Vol. 2
prophets being rejected (Jesus)   3/21/03 Vol. 30
prophets examples (Jesus)   1/28/95 Vol. 2
prophets given for every age (Jesus)   4/18/07 Vol. 47
prophets hometown lacks faith in (Jesus)   3/12/07 Vol. 46
prophets instrument (Jesus)   1/29/95 Vol. 2
prophets killed and persecuted (Jesus)   6/9/98 Vol. 11
prophets messengers (Jesus)   7/30/94 Vol. 2
prophets not to criticize, God's duty (Jesus)   7/31/98 Vol. 12
prophets of end times (Jesus)   1/10/08 Vol. 50

St. Michael the Archangel

We had been invited to speak in Trinidad by Barbara on Perpetual Adoration. In fact she had forty Masses offered for us to speak in many churches in Trinidad with the Bishop's permission. Due to a severe snowstorm in Rochester, N.Y. our plane was very late in arriving in JFK Airport in New York City. The terminal was closing up for the night. It was 11:45 p.m. and our charter flight was leaving at midnight. The woman was leaving her desk as we ran up. She said, "Where do you think you are going?" We told her to Trinidad. She said: "You are too late, the gate and security are closed and you cannot get another flight for three days." This meant that we would miss about four talks including the Cathedral. We pleaded with her as she kept shutting everything off. Finally, I asked her if the plane was still on the ground, and she said it was. I pleaded in the Name of God and bowed my head asking for the intercession of St. Michael for a change of heart as we had several speaking engagements. I looked at her with tears in my eyes and intense prayer in my heart. She looked at me a moment, picked up the phone and called the captain in the plane. She said: "I have two people here who need to go on this flight for some big shindig at the Cathedral." He said we could come but not our luggage. This time we endured Trinidad's high temperatures for three days in our winter clothes. From that trip we were instrumental in eight new chapels of Perpetual Adoration starting.

In the vision of a message, there was a chandelier showing in an Adoration chapel. We were shocked to hear the story from the priest of what happened there. In their Adoration chapel as the adorers were there one night, a man came in wielding a machete. One brave man stood up to him and said: "Would you kill us in front of Jesus?" When he said the Holy Name of Jesus, the man dropped his machete and ran. As a result the bishop closed down that chapel, but now they were going to open another one closer to the church. The hole in the ceiling was too big to fill, so the contractor offered to put up a huge chandelier to cover the hole.

All of the talks were to fourteen packed churches and the eight new Adoration chapels were an inspiration. We know the evil one tried to stop this work, but Jesus and St. Michael over came them.

Message: January 7, 2003 (volume 30)

prophets persecuted for evangelizing (Jesus)	7/31/04 Vol. 36	prophets role of, discern (Jesus)	8/5/03 Vol. 32
prophets persecuted for word of reform (Jesus)	4/28/98 Vol. 11	prophets second coming (Jesus)	6/24/95 Vol. 2
prophets persecuted then & now (Jesus)	6/14/06 Vol. 43	prophets sent to warn people (Jesus)	9/3/07 Vol. 48
prophets persecution (Jesus)	3/31/95 Vol. 2	prophets showing US doomed future (Jesus)	4/25/03 Vol. 31
prophets persecution (Jesus)	7/2/98 Vol. 12	prophets test the fruits (Jesus)	9/28/97 Vol. 8
prophets preparing for second coming (Jesus)	12/23/00 Vol. 21	prophets vindicated by events (Jesus)	6/4/02 Vol. 27

prophets warn of events and to repent (Jesus) 6/30/98 Vol. 11

prophets & messengers face possible martyrdom (Jesus) 2/20/08 Vol. 50

prophets & messengers instruments of the Word (Jesus) 6/5/98 Vol. 11

prophets & messengers special mission for faithful (Jesus) 9/28/03 Vol. 32

prophets & messengers suffer persecution (Jesus) 4/21/01 Vol. 23

prophets & messengers truth,humility,no money (Jesus) 7/9/98 Vol. 12

prophets & messengers warn of this age (Jesus) 2/6/99 Vol. 14

prophets and saints given miraculous help (Jesus) 1/21/98 Vol. 10

prophets' faith dare to be martyrs (Jesus) 3/28/07 Vol. 46

prophets in history spread messages in suffering (Jesus) 8/7/07 Vol. 48

prophets killed in Old & New Testament (Jesus) 4/26/00 Vol. 19

prophets' message people need to be open (Jesus) 8/4/00 Vol. 20

prophet's mission follow God's Will in yes (Jesus) 7/16/00 Vol. 20

prophets' mission question to carry out (Jesus) 3/7/01 Vol. 22

prophets of God given in all ages (Jesus) 6/21/06 Vol. 43

prophets of today defending the faith (Jesus) 6/21/06 Vol. 43

prophets of today prepare for tribulation (Jesus) 1/24/07 Vol. 46

prophets of today rejected for pride (Jesus) 7/13/03 Vol. 32

prophets persecuted love message needs hearing (Jesus) 10/17/00 Vol. 21

prophet's reward for messenger or priest (Jesus) 7/13/06 Vol. 44

prophet's reward for those who receive one (Jesus) 7/7/99 Vol. 16

prophet's reward in adoring Blessed Sacrament (Jesus) 6/8/00 Vol. 19

prophet's reward servant's reward (Jesus) 1/1/04 Vol. 34

prophets sent through all ages (Jesus) 5/3/07 Vol. 47

prophets sent to give up idols,evil ways (Jesus) 8/14/00 Vol. 20

prophets, end times instructing preparations (Jesus) 8/1/05 Vol. 40

prophets, messengers give warning, preparation (Jesus) 12/3/98 Vol. 13

prophets, messengers sent for each age, people (Jesus) 3/29/05 Vol. 38

prophets, modern need people listening to love (Jesus) 8/14/00 Vol. 20

prophets, today's not believed, call to repent (Jesus) 7/18/04 Vol. 36

prophets, true know by their fruits (Jesus) 4/25/06 Vol. 43

prophets,messengers call to wedding feast (Jesus) 1/14/99 Vol. 14

prophets,teachers called to preach Gospel (Jesus) 12/7/02 Vol. 29

protect environment from pollution (Jesus) 1/19/00 Vol. 18

protection angel, faith, trust (Mary) 5/1/97 Vol. 7

protection Battle of Armageddon (St. Michael) 6/1/96 Vol. 3

protection by angels at refuges (Jesus) 7/3/98 Vol. 12

protection end times (Jesus) 6/18/94 Vol. 1

protection for those with faith and trust (Jesus) 7/16/98 Vol. 12

protection have hope in His Word (Jesus) 2/28/99 Vol. 14

protection holy ground and caves (Jesus) 6/6/98 Vol. 11

protection keep faithful,do not fear (Jesus) 5/27/99 Vol. 15

protection of souls from demons (Jesus) 1/11/99 Vol. 14

protection physical and spiritual (Jesus) 8/28/96 Vol. 4

protection rosary and scapular (Mary) 8/21/96 Vol. 4

protection spiritual & physical (Jesus) 2/6/08 Vol. 50

protection with faith in His Name (Jesus) 5/29/98 Vol. 11

protection with Our Lady's mantle (Jesus) 6/6/06 Vol. 43

protection at refuges trust in God (Jesus) 6/13/03 Vol. 31

protection for children physical & spiritual (Jesus) 3/11/04 Vol. 34

protection from harm at refuges (Jesus) 8/28/01 Vol. 24

protection, weapons of holy water, blessed salt (Jesus) 5/31/07 Vol. 47

protection,miracles of by God and angels (Jesus) 10/13/00 Vol. 21

protestants critical of Mary (Mary) 6/20/98 Vol. 11

psalms for every occasion,meditation (Jesus) 8/27/01 Vol. 24

psalms songs of praise (Jesus) 9/4/98 Vol. 12

psalms songs of praise from David (Jesus) 8/27/01 Vol. 24

Psalms for Lent good spiritual reading (Jesus) 3/5/04 Vol. 34

psalms of David songs of praise (Jesus) 10/14/00 Vol. 21

public executions for refusing mark of beast (Jesus) 4/13/00 Vol. 19

public executions to instill fear for control (Jesus) 6/18/99 Vol. 15

public ministry messengers (Jesus) 3/14/96 Vol. 3

public ministry personal mission (Jesus) 10/18/96 Vol. 5

public ministry pray for help (St. Therese) 3/13/96 Vol. 3

public proclamation of sins of this generation (Jesus) 8/29/02 Vol. 28

public witness against sinful lifestyles (Jesus) 11/18/04 Vol. 37

public witness for belief in God (Jesus) 2/4/00 Vol. 18

public witness needed for heaven (Jesus) 6/1/00 Vol. 19

public witness on moral issues (Jesus) 3/14/07 Vol. 46

public witness personal (Jesus) 11/13/95 Vol. 3

public witness to faith, is demanding (Jesus) 12/10/05 Vol. 41

public witness of God needed to be saved (Jesus) 1/3/06 Vol. 42

public witness of Jesus acceptance by the Father (Jesus) 1/1/07 Vol. 46

public witness to faith will risk your life (Jesus) 1/29/05 Vol. 38

publican vs. pharisee seek pardon,not praise (Jesus) 6/10/00 Vol. 19

publication of messages persecution (Jesus) 11/19/95 Vol. 3

publications not telling whole truth (Jesus) 8/5/99 Vol. 16

publishing evangelize (Jesus) 7/21/95 Vol. 3

publishing money people (Jesus) 8/9/95 Vol. 3

pulpits preach real faith (Jesus) 10/27/96 Vol. 5

pulse nuclear bombs could destroy chips (Jesus) 8/3/05 Vol. 40

pulse shock waves destroy microchips (Jesus) 6/20/06 Vol. 43

punishment for sin in natural disasters (Jesus) 9/4/05 Vol. 40

puppets on strings avoid Satan's lies (Jesus) 9/20/99 Vol. 16

pure heart as young child (Jesus) 4/19/06 Vol. 43

pure soul no excuse not to have (Jesus) 12/16/06 Vol. 45

purification needed to enter heaven (Jesus) 12/19/00 Vol. 21

purgatory a cleansing time (Jesus) 11/15/00 Vol. 21

Purgatory abortion (Jesus) 12/27/95 Vol. 3

purgatory better to do here (Jesus) 2/8/01 Vol. 22

Purgatory better to suffer here (Jesus) 11/1/97 Vol. 9

Purgatory better to suffer on earth (Jesus) 5/9/98 Vol. 11

purgatory cleanse last blemishes (Jesus) 6/19/01 Vol. 23

purgatory do more good deeds (Jesus) 10/22/01 Vol. 25

Purgatory do reparation here (Jesus) — 3/28/98 Vol. 10
purgatory during tribulation (Jesus) — 7/29/01 Vol. 24
purgatory during tribulation of Antichrist (Jesus) — 6/19/02 Vol. 27
Purgatory earthquake (Jesus) — 1/3/96 Vol. 3
purgatory here or hereafter (Jesus) — 6/7/04 Vol. 35
purgatory journey to heaven (Jesus) — 3/4/08 Vol. 50
purgatory levels of (Jesus) — 5/31/05 Vol. 39
purgatory lower levels like hell (Jesus) — 6/20/05 Vol. 39
Purgatory may suffer here (Jesus) — 6/10/99 Vol. 15
purgatory most go there (Jesus) — 12/10/01 Vol. 25
purgatory needed for many souls (Jesus) — 2/8/00 Vol. 18
purgatory needed purification (Jesus) — 8/19/03 Vol. 32
purgatory now or next life (Jesus) — 5/26/01 Vol. 23
purgatory offer pain up for souls (Jesus) — 9/14/00 Vol. 20
Purgatory offer up sufferings (Jesus) — 3/5/99 Vol. 14
purgatory offer your suffering now (Jesus) — 9/3/98 Vol. 12
purgatory on earth (Jesus) — 4/2/03 Vol. 31
purgatory on earth in tribulation (Jesus) — 5/10/01 Vol. 23
purgatory only level that changes (Jesus) — 6/29/07 Vol. 47
purgatory perfected for heaven (Jesus) — 6/5/01 Vol. 23
purgatory place of purification (Jesus) — 5/6/01 Vol. 23
Purgatory poor souls (Jesus) — 11/2/95 Vol. 3
purgatory pray for friends & relatives (Jesus) — 7/22/04 Vol. 36
Purgatory pray for poor souls in (Jesus) — 9/25/97 Vol. 8
purgatory pray for relatives in (Jesus) — 10/8/07 Vol. 49
Purgatory pray for relatives while time (Jesus) — 11/15/98 Vol. 13
purgatory pray for relatives,others (Jesus) — 11/2/03 Vol. 33
purgatory pray for souls (Jesus) — 7/8/02 Vol. 28
Purgatory pray for souls (Mary) — 10/30/97 Vol. 9
purgatory pray for souls (Mary) — 10/31/96 Vol. 5
purgatory pray for souls in (Jesus) — 4/14/03 Vol. 31
purgatory pray for souls in (Jesus) — 4/2/02 Vol. 27
purgatory pray for souls in (Jesus) — 9/28/05 Vol. 40
purgatory pray for souls in (Jesus) — 11/10/07 Vol. 49
purgatory pray for souls there (Jesus) — 3/17/05 Vol. 38
purgatory pray for souls there (Jesus) — 6/13/06 Vol. 43
purgatory pray for souls,lessen pain (Jesus) — 11/2/99 Vol. 17
purgatory pray for suffering souls (Jesus) — 12/1/00 Vol. 21
purgatory pray for the dead (Jesus) — 1/31/00 Vol. 18
purgatory pray much for souls (Jesus) — 4/7/02 Vol. 27
Purgatory prayer (Uncle Jim) — 5/11/94 Vol. 1
purgatory prayers never wasted (Jesus) — 3/15/07 Vol. 46
purgatory purification (Jesus) — 6/4/01 Vol. 23
purgatory purification of worldly desires (Jesus) — 10/24/03 Vol. 33
purgatory purifies earthly desires (Jesus) — 11/12/05 Vol. 41
purgatory purifies earthly desires (Jesus) — 10/18/06 Vol. 45
purgatory purify earthly desires (Jesus) — 7/9/04 Vol. 36

purgatory purify earthly desires (Jesus) — 8/29/06 Vol. 44
purgatory purify worldly cravings (Jesus) — 11/2/05 Vol. 41
Purgatory relatives (Jesus) — 11/6/94 Vol. 2
Purgatory relatives need prayers (Jesus) — 3/27/99 Vol. 14
purgatory reparation for souls,pray (Jesus) — 11/2/96 Vol. 5
purgatory souls cry out for prayers (Jesus) — 9/26/06 Vol. 44
purgatory souls purified on earth or there (Jesus) — 5/16/03 Vol. 31
Purgatory suffer Calvary here (Jesus) — 6/17/99 Vol. 15
purgatory suffer fire,loss of God's presence (Jesus) — 7/25/02 Vol. 28
purgatory suffer now or later (Jesus) — 9/30/03 Vol. 32
purgatory suffer now or later (Jesus) — 10/25/02 Vol. 29
Purgatory suffer now or later (Jesus) — 1/12/98 Vol. 10
Purgatory suffer now or later (Jesus) — 1/2/99 Vol. 14
purgatory suffered here in tribulation (Jesus) — 1/20/01 Vol. 22
purgatory suffered in tribulation (Jesus) — 11/19/01 Vol. 25
Purgatory suffering on earth (Jesus) — 1/8/97 Vol. 6
purgatory temporal punishment (Jesus) — 1/31/98 Vol. 10
Purgatory temporal punishment (Jesus) — 3/5/95 Vol. 2
Purgatory Thanksgiving (Father) — 11/22/95 Vol. 3
purgatory to cleanse earthly desires (Jesus) — 7/13/05 Vol. 40
purgatory to perfect & cleanse (Jesus) — 7/22/05 Vol. 40
Purgatory to suffer on earth is better (Jesus) — 9/25/98 Vol. 12
purgatory until perfection reached (Jesus) — 8/13/03 Vol. 32
purgatory urges to pray for person (Jesus) — 10/26/06 Vol. 45
purgatory vision of (Jesus) — 11/2/06 Vol. 45
Purgatory vs. suffer pain on earth (Jesus) — 11/15/97 Vol. 9
Purgatory & Hell do exist (Jesus) — 2/12/99 Vol. 14
purgatory and hell suffering of souls (Jesus) — 11/2/05 Vol. 41
purgatory choice suffer here than there (Jesus) — 2/12/06 Vol. 42
purgatory description ladder,cesspool of fire (Jesus) — 9/15/01 Vol. 24
purgatory description upper and lower (Jesus) — 6/5/07 Vol. 47
purgatory needed few go straight to heaven (Jesus) — 11/2/04 Vol. 37
purgatory needed perfects souls to saints (Jesus) — 11/1/00 Vol. 21
purgatory on earth during tribulation (Jesus) — 12/4/02 Vol. 29
purgatory on earth during tribulation (Jesus) — 9/15/01 Vol. 24
purgatory on earth during tribulation (Jesus) — 11/27/06 Vol. 45
purgatory on earth during tribulation (Jesus) — 1/7/00 Vol. 18
purgatory on earth during tribulation (Jesus) — 11/28/00 Vol. 21
purgatory on earth life in tribulation (Jesus) — 1/8/02 Vol. 26
purgatory on earth tribulation (Jesus) — 7/30/03 Vol. 32
purgatory time set for unrepentant sin (Jesus) — 8/13/06 Vol. 44
purgatory time short by suffering,good deeds (Jesus) — 3/4/08 Vol. 50
Purgatory(upper) pray for relatives (Jesus) — 6/16/97 Vol. 7
purgatory, living during tribulation (Jesus) — 12/14/06 Vol. 45
purgatory, souls in crying for our prayers (Jesus) — 4/4/00 Vol. 19
purgatory, souls in pray by name best (Jesus) — 5/29/07 Vol. 47
purgatory, souls in prayer group intentions (Jesus) — 9/29/07 Vol. 48

purification abortion (Jesus) — 2/4/96 Vol. 3

purification cleanse the earth of sin (Jesus) — 12/28/96 Vol. 5

purification during the tribulation (Jesus) — 11/15/06 Vol. 45

purification earth will be made clean (Jesus) — 7/24/96 Vol. 4

purification Garden of Eden (Jesus) — 5/22/96 Vol. 3

purification here & in purgatory (Jesus) — 4/22/01 Vol. 23

Purification must come to remove evil (Jesus) — 4/12/97 Vol. 7

purification of earth by fire (Jesus) — 2/13/03 Vol. 30

purification of faults and habits (Jesus) — 5/19/97 Vol. 7

purification on earth & purgatory (Jesus) — 2/27/03 Vol. 30

purification persecution & protection (Jesus) — 1/11/97 Vol. 6

purification prepare spiritually (Jesus) — 1/14/97 Vol. 6

purification rich & poor tested (Jesus) — 3/16/97 Vol. 6

purification save souls in family (Jesus) — 8/18/96 Vol. 4

purification Scripture fulfilled (Jesus) — 8/19/97 Vol. 8

purification signs (Jesus) — 9/18/95 Vol. 3

purification signs and disasters (Jesus) — 5/3/97 Vol. 7

purification to be perfected (Jesus) — 1/20/02 Vol. 26

purification to perfect us for heaven (Jesus) — 9/3/98 Vol. 12

purification tribulation,Era of Peace (Jesus) — 9/3/06 Vol. 44

purification volcanoes and fires (Jesus) — 8/12/96 Vol. 4

purification of souls by life's progress (Jesus) — 5/21/06 Vol. 43

purified to enter heaven (Jesus) — 6/18/98 Vol. 11

purify as refiner tested by difficulties (Jesus) — 6/26/00 Vol. 19

purify ourselves with love and mercy (Jesus) — 2/25/99 Vol. 14

purity young adult (Mary) — 9/18/94 Vol. 2

purity of soul come as a little child (Jesus) — 9/20/03 Vol. 32

purple over statues traditions of Lent (Jesus) — 3/30/01 Vol. 22

purpose in life following God' Will (Jesus) — 3/12/01 Vol. 22

purpose in life glorify God and not man (Jesus) — 3/2/01 Vol. 22

purpose in life in world, not of it (Jesus) — 10/16/01 Vol. 25

purpose in life know, love, & serve God (Jesus) — 5/9/03 Vol. 31

purpose in life to serve, love God (Jesus) — 1/11/00 Vol. 18

pyramid Masons (Jesus) — 9/7/94 Vol. 2

pyramid new golden calf (Jesus) — 6/11/98 Vol. 11

pyramid one world order (Jesus) — 10/29/94 Vol. 2

pyramid one world order (Jesus) — 10/18/94 Vol. 2

pyramid one world symbol of evil (Jesus) — 7/11/97 Vol. 8

pyramid triumph (Jesus) — 11/20/94 Vol. 2

quality time count for Jesus (Jesus) — 3/6/00 Vol. 18

quality time for God need proper priorities (Jesus) — 3/26/01 Vol. 22

Quebec,Canada Americas as one government (Jesus) — 4/26/01 Vol. 23

Queen of heaven one with Jesus (Jesus) — 11/21/03 Vol. 33

Queenship hearts are one (Mary) — 8/22/97 Vol. 8

Queenship mother (Mary) — 8/22/94 Vol. 2

Queenship signs of the times (Mary) — 8/22/95 Vol. 3

Queenship of Mary as Queen of heaven (Jesus) — 8/22/06 Vol. 44

Queenship of Mary follow His Will (Mary) — 8/22/98 Vol. 12

Queenship of Mary heart as one with Jesus (Mary) — 8/22/96 Vol. 4

Queenship of Mary Mother to all (Jesus) — 8/22/03 Vol. 32

Queenship of Mary New Ark of the Covenenat (Jesus) — 8/22/05 Vol. 40

Queenship of Mary Our Lady's message (Mary) — 8/28/05 Vol. 40

Queenship of Mary special place in heaven (Jesus) — 8/22/02 Vol. 28

Queenship of Mary Virgin birth,sinless gift (Mary) — 8/22/98 Vol. 12

quick wealth not mastered by money (Jesus) — 2/24/00 Vol. 18

quiet time for nature and retreats (Jesus) — 1/31/02 Vol. 26

quiet time for true prayer (Jesus) — 4/26/07 Vol. 47

quiet time in prayer needed each day (Jesus) — 12/14/02 Vol. 29

quiet time with God in prayer (Jesus) — 7/8/07 Vol. 48

quiet time with Jesus needed (Jesus) — 1/6/06 Vol. 42

'R' movies bad for adults & children (Jesus) — 12/3/07 Vol. 49

race for eternal life judgment is finish line (Jesus) — 7/7/05 Vol. 40

radio frequency chips RFID, invasion of privacy (Jesus) — 1/11/04 Vol. 34

railcars for prisoners in place for tribulation (Jesus) — 9/21/99 Vol. 16

railroads carry dangerous chemicals (Jesus) — 1/19/05 Vol. 38

rain blessings of life (Jesus) — 6/3/02 Vol. 27

rain food shortages (Jesus) — 3/27/96 Vol. 3

rainbow around moon Blessed Mother's protection (Jesus) — 2/8/01 Vol. 22

rainbow people those saved in God (Jesus) — 3/23/06 Vol. 42

rainbows Mt. Tabor (Jesus) — 7/5/96 Vol. 3

rainstorms damage on East coast (Jesus) — 11/20/03 Vol. 33

rationalizing sin to obtain things illegally (Jesus) — 3/1/02 Vol. 26

rationed water bought with mark (Jesus) — 3/26/99 Vol. 14

Ray Maginn funeral illnesses of elderly (Jesus) — 10/30/06 Vol. 45

razor wire for detention centers (Jesus) — 2/11/00 Vol. 18

reading, spiritual Bible, lives of the saints (Jesus) — 9/1/03 Vol. 32

ready for death? use daily prayers,Confession (Jesus) — 3/23/02 Vol. 26

Real Presence adoration (Jesus) — 9/11/98 Vol. 12

Real Presence at Masses all over world (Jesus) — 2/17/00 Vol. 18

Real Presence attack to remove tabernacles (Jesus) — 11/10/04 Vol. 37

Real Presence blessed to believe in (Jesus) — 7/3/04 Vol. 36

Real Presence breaking of bread,eyes open (Jesus) — 4/18/01 Vol. 23

Real Presence center of our life (Jesus) — 5/4/02 Vol. 27

real presence civilization (Jesus) — 11/8/95 Vol. 3

Real Presence daily bread (Jesus) — 6/14/98 Vol. 11

Real Presence disbelief in (Jesus) — 5/1/04 Vol. 35

Real Presence do not hide (Jesus) — 10/1/02 Vol. 29

real presence Eucharist (Jesus) — 1/2/95 Vol. 2

Real Presence Eucharist not just a meal (Jesus) — 7/30/98 Vol. 12

Real Presence experience heat and power (Jesus) — 7/3/01 Vol. 24

Real Presence faith & reverence (Jesus) — 7/3/99 Vol. 16

Real Presence faithful witness to God (Jesus) — 11/5/99 Vol. 17

Real Presence few believe in (Jesus) — 11/19/99 Vol. 17

Real Presence found in Eucharist (Jesus) — 2/25/05 Vol. 38

Real Presence give honor a & praise (Jesus) 7/20/99 Vol. 16
Real Presence give praise & reverence (Jesus) 7/1/99 Vol. 16
Real Presence give reverence (Jesus) 7/18/01 Vol. 24
Real Presence hard for some to believe (Jesus) 4/16/05 Vol. 39
Real Presence hard to believe (Jesus) 8/27/06 Vol. 44
Real Presence hold on to gift of (Jesus) 10/12/02 Vol. 29
Real Presence Holy Communion,church (Jesus) 8/22/99 Vol. 16
Real Presence honored by God (Jesus) 12/15/05 Vol. 41
Real Presence honored long as possible (Jesus) 3/7/99 Vol. 14
Real Presence in all tabernacles (Jesus) 12/25/97 Vol. 9
Real Presence in Blessed Sacrament (Jesus) 5/22/04 Vol. 35
Real Presence in breaking of bread (Jesus) 4/28/05 Vol. 39
Real Presence in consecrated Host (Jesus) 4/18/99 Vol. 15
Real Presence in Consecrated Host (Jesus) 3/12/99 Vol. 14
Real Presence in consecrated Hosts (Jesus) 5/25/06 Vol. 43
Real Presence in Eucharist (Jesus) 8/20/06 Vol. 44
Real Presence in glorified body (Jesus) 4/19/01 Vol. 23
Real Presence in Holy Communion (Jesus) 1/10/08 Vol. 50
Real Presence in Holy Eucharist (Jesus) 5/8/05 Vol. 39
real presence jealous God (Jesus) 10/6/95 Vol. 3
Real Presence Jesus' holiness present (Jesus) 5/28/05 Vol. 39
Real Presence Jesus in consecrated Host (Jesus) 7/30/00 Vol. 20
Real Presence Jesus truly in Host (Jesus) 6/18/06 Vol. 43
Real Presence keep up fervor for (Jesus) 12/23/97 Vol. 9
Real Presence kneel or bow in reverence (Jesus) 4/26/04 Vol. 35
Real Presence love & adoration (Jesus) 8/20/01 Vol. 24
real presence love,personal messages (Jesus) 3/17/96 Vol. 3
Real Presence makes chuch holy (Jesus) 1/25/03 Vol. 30
Real Presence makes churches holy (Jesus) 7/8/04 Vol. 36
Real Presence makes churches holy (Jesus) 6/11/04 Vol. 35
Real Presence many do not believe in (Jesus) 11/17/01 Vol. 25
real presence Mass (Jesus) 1/4/94 Vol. 1
real presence Mass (Jesus) 10/31/93 Vol. 1
Real Presence miracle of love (Jesus) 10/16/04 Vol. 37
Real Presence miracles for non-believers (Jesus) 12/11/06 Vol. 45
real presence miracles of the Eucharist (Jesus) 11/19/97 Vol. 9
real presence monstrance (Jesus) 2/7/96 Vol. 3
Real Presence most sacred treasure (Jesus) 10/11/03 Vol. 33
Real Presence needs reverence,respect (Jesus) 4/15/97 Vol. 7
Real Presence needs reverence,visits (Jesus) 6/25/00 Vol. 19
Real Presence new ark of Covenant (Jesus) 8/13/99 Vol. 16
Real Presence not being taught (Jesus) 7/27/98 Vol. 12
Real Presence not being taught (Jesus) 1/29/00 Vol. 18
Real Presence not taught in pulpits (Jesus) 5/19/04 Vol. 35
Real Presence our prize of heaven (Jesus) 3/29/98 Vol. 10
Real Presence priority of life (Jesus) 7/13/06 Vol. 44
Real Presence radiance of power (Jesus) 5/23/97 Vol. 7

Real Presence red light in chapel (Jesus) 5/20/00 Vol. 19
real presence reverence (Jesus) 3/16/97 Vol. 6
Real Presence sense of sacred lost (Jesus) 11/23/05 Vol. 41
Real Presence sense of the sacred (Jesus) 3/16/99 Vol. 14
Real Presence should have reverence for (Jesus) 4/27/07 Vol. 47
Real Presence spiritual oasis (Jesus) 7/8/02 Vol. 28
Real Presence survey of unbelief (Jesus) 5/7/97 Vol. 7
Real Presence tested by attacks of Satan (Jesus) 7/16/00 Vol. 20
Real Presence thirty per cent believe in (Jesus) 10/25/02 Vol. 29
Real Presence to end of age (Jesus) 2/19/99 Vol. 14
Real Presence to end of time (Jesus) 6/2/02 Vol. 27
Real Presence traditions being lost (Jesus) 11/5/07 Vol. 49
Real Presence doctrine hard to believe (Jesus) 4/28/07 Vol. 47
Real Presence in Host gift of Jesus to us (Jesus) 2/6/06 Vol. 42
Real Presence of Jesus hard to believe for some (Jesus) 3/29/07 Vol. 46
Real Presence reverence kneeling, on tongue (Jesus) 6/6/99 Vol. 15
reality check sports and war (Jesus) 11/22/95 Vol. 3
reality shows in each soul (Jesus) 5/29/04 Vol. 35
rebirth new earth 8/20/93 Vol. 1
recession and finances (Jesus) 6/6/02 Vol. 27
recession travel modes tested (Jesus) 9/5/02 Vol. 28
reconcile with those offended (Jesus) 2/15/08 Vol. 50
Reconciliation cleanse souls in (Jesus) 7/13/99 Vol. 16
reconciliation cleansing of sins (Jesus) 7/28/97 Vol. 8
Reconciliation forgiveness always available (Jesus) 6/15/07 Vol. 47
Reconciliation grace and obedience (Jesus) 5/4/97 Vol. 7
Reconciliation graces for salvation (Jesus) 3/1/98 Vol. 10
reconciliation One Body (Jesus) 6/25/95 Vol. 2
Reconciliation prodigal son, lukewarm (Jesus) 6/5/96 Vol. 3
Reconciliation renew Baptismal beauty (Jesus) 5/24/00 Vol. 19
reconciliation seek good confession (Jesus) 9/21/97 Vol. 8
reconciliation wipers for rain (Jesus) 8/5/97 Vol. 8
record storms weather patterns changing (Jesus) 2/16/06 Vol. 42
re-created earth marvelous to behold (Jesus) 6/15/98 Vol. 11
recyclable fuels to cut oil dependence (Jesus) 7/2/07 Vol. 48
red carpet three kings (Jesus) 1/8/95 Vol. 2
Red China seeking Taiwan and others (Jesus) 10/19/98 Vol. 13
red horse of Revelation (Jesus) 7/12/06 Vol. 44
red lit sky famine and pestilence (Jesus) 3/21/95 Vol. 2
Redeemer foretold in Scripture (Jesus) 12/4/01 Vol. 25
Redeemer fulfill promise of scripture (Jesus) 12/24/97 Vol. 9
Redeemer purpose of Jesus' coming (Jesus) 12/18/04 Vol. 37
Redeemer reason for coming as man (Jesus) 12/2/02 Vol. 29
Redeemer & Savior worthy souls allowed in heaven (Jesus) 12/5/04 Vol. 37
Redeemer promise fulfilled in Jesus (Jesus) 12/13/02 Vol. 29
Redeemer promised Jesus fulfills promise (God the Father) 4/17/99 Vol. 15
Redeemer sent to free mankind of sin (Jesus) 11/29/03 Vol. 33

Redemption gates of heaven opened (Jesus)   4/21/98 Vol. 11
redemption joy (Jesus)   5/8/95 Vol. 2
Redemption Mary suffered in (Mary)   4/7/98 Vol. 11
redemption our most precious gift (Jesus)   2/10/99 Vol. 14
Redemption scripture fulfilled (Jesus)   4/5/98 Vol. 11
redemption through forgiveness (Jesus)   4/8/03 Vol. 31
redemption through Jesus' blood (Jesus)   6/2/05 Vol. 39
redemption of man light to the world (Jesus)   4/15/99 Vol. 15
redemption of mankind through suffering of Jesus (Jesus) 7/26/01 Vol. 24
redemptive healing by calling on your Savior (Jesus)   11/10/99 Vol. 17
redemptive merit in offering our pains (Jesus)   5/17/07 Vol. 47
redemptive suffering atonement for sin (Jesus)   3/5/01 Vol. 22
redemptive suffering do not waste pain (Jesus)   2/23/04 Vol. 34
redemptive suffering for self or others (Jesus)   10/26/03 Vol. 33
redemptive suffering offer up pain for self or others (Jesus) 2/15/02 Vol. 26
redemptive suffering offer up your pain (Jesus)   8/14/05 Vol. 40
redemptive suffering suffer quietly in daily crosses (Jesus) 10/18/03 Vol. 33
Red's funeral thanked all adorers (Jesus)   12/17/07 Vol. 49
refineries restricting gas supplies (Jesus)   5/26/04 Vol. 35
refineries target of terrorists (Jesus)   9/26/01 Vol. 24
refinery sabotage could cause gas shortages (Jesus)   10/18/07 Vol. 49
reflection Confession (Jesus)   3/3/95 Vol. 2
reform lives with love & warnings (Jesus)   1/13/03 Vol. 30
refuge at House of Prayer (Jesus)   8/18/06 Vol. 44
refuge Carmelite Monastery (Jesus)   7/1/94 Vol. 2
refuge everyone to share skills (Jesus)   9/14/08 Vol. 48
refuge hard life but no fear (Jesus)   8/14/98 Vol. 12
refuge hard living conditions (Jesus)   11/26/06 Vol. 45
refuge in Croatia (Jesus)   7/12/02 Vol. 28
refuge in wilderness away from cities (Jesus)   12/16/04 Vol. 37
refuge leave at night,back roads (Jesus)   8/25/07 Vol. 48
refuge living in the woods (Jesus)   7/30/07 Vol. 48
refuge living independently (Jesus)   1/11/07 Vol. 46
refuge manna as in Exodus (Jesus)   8/21/97 Vol. 8
refuge pond for bathing & washing (Jesus)   8/2/07 Vol. 48
refuge stripped of comforts,money (Jesus)   3/27/07 Vol. 46
refuge trust in Jesus (Jesus)   6/23/07 Vol. 47
refuge angels to make us invisible (Jesus)   3/29/07 Vol. 46
refuge builders suffer, but will be rewarded (Jesus)   10/6/04 Vol. 37
refuge building use model in construction (Jesus)   8/2/07 Vol. 48
refuge calling be able to give up everything (Jesus)   9/27/04 Vol. 36
refuge dwellings to be multiplied (Jesus)   10/25/07 Vol. 49
refuge escape will need bicycles (Jesus)   2/3/05 Vol. 38
refuge food & fuel for severe winter (Jesus)   9/22/07 Vol. 48
refuge food, plain be thankful for (Jesus)   12/14/06 Vol. 45
refuge healings from springs, luminous cross (Jesus)   10/18/07 Vol. 49
refuge in desert miracle water wells (Jesus)   5/21/07 Vol. 47

refuge in tribulation test of faith,rid comforts (Jesus)   3/22/01 Vol. 22
refuge jobs shared by all (Jesus)   6/29/07 Vol. 47
refuge leaders blessing to prepare (Jesus)   11/4/06 Vol. 45
refuge life crude with only basics (Jesus)   5/9/00 Vol. 19
refuge living to have inconveniences (Jesus)   9/24/99 Vol. 16
refuge maker after prayer, discernment (Jesus)   2/16/06 Vol. 42
refuge needs shovel,tent, etc. (Jesus)   8/20/02 Vol. 28
refuge of protection Mom's house (Jesus)   9/24/98 Vol. 12
Refuge of Sinners people led to refuges (Mary)   5/23/05 Vol. 39
refuge place Corpus Christi Adoration (Jesus)   8/9/05 Vol. 40
refuge place in Marmora, Canada (Jesus)   10/6/06 Vol. 45
refuge places apparition sites (Jesus)   12/28/06 Vol. 45
refuge places to avoid chips in body (Jesus)   5/30/07 Vol. 47
refuge preparation daily prayer (Jesus)   6/22/07 Vol. 47
refuge protection from dogs,infra-red,etc. (Jesus)   11/1/02 Vol. 29
refuge sites places of protection (Jesus)   8/25/05 Vol. 40
refuge time famine,division,chips in body (Jesus)   11/28/03 Vol. 33
refuge time famine,division,chips in body (Jesus)   12/27/04 Vol. 37
refuge time famine,division,chips in body (Jesus)   3/22/07 Vol. 46
refuge time famine,schism,chips,flu (Jesus)   1/24/08 Vol. 50
refuge time sooner than you think (Jesus)   3/6/06 Vol. 42
refuge time to go famine,schism,chips in body (Jesus)   8/29/04 Vol. 36
refuge types apparition sites,holy ground (Jesus)   10/22/05 Vol. 41
refuge vs. detention center both being setup (Jesus)   5/24/07 Vol. 47
refuge warning like tornado warning (Jesus)   3/29/07 Vol. 46
refuge work mostly by hand (Jesus)   6/29/07 Vol. 47
refuge, Chicago cemetery at cross (Jesus)   11/10/02 Vol. 29
refuge, Eva's statue seen coming to life (Mary)   7/30/04 Vol. 36
refuge, invisible floors added on to houses (Jesus)   5/15/07 Vol. 47
refuge, North Hills, Ca. shelter for many people (Jesus)   2/8/05 Vol. 38
refuge, time to go famine, schism,chips in body (Jesus)   2/25/08 Vol. 50
refugees in war give aid & donations (Jesus)   8/3/06 Vol. 44
refugees all to use skills (Jesus)   1/11/08 Vol. 50
refuges angels bring manna (Jesus)   10/12/02 Vol. 29
refuges angels lead to (Jesus)   10/20/06 Vol. 45
refuges angels protect from demons (Jesus)   7/31/04 Vol. 36
refuges angels provided (Jesus)   10/2/03 Vol. 33
refuges angels to bring Hosts (Jesus)   7/14/05 Vol. 40
refuges angels to lead us to protection (Jesus)   2/28/04 Vol. 34
refuges angels,healing at cross (Jesus)   5/5/00 Vol. 19
refuges apparition sites, holy ground (Jesus)   6/8/04 Vol. 35
refuges apparition sites, holy ground (Jesus)   5/21/05 Vol. 39
refuges apparition sites,holy ground (Jesus)   1/8/04 Vol. 34
refuges apparition sites,holy ground,cave (Jesus)   10/18/04 Vol. 37
refuges as caves (Jesus)   10/27/06 Vol. 45
refuges assigned tasks for all (Jesus)   7/31/05 Vol. 40
refuges at monasteries (Jesus)   5/11/02 Vol. 27

refuges at monasteries (Jesus)	1/17/08 Vol. 50	refuges for protection (Jesus)	2/1/07 Vol. 46
refuges at Our Lady's shrines (Jesus)	4/8/99 Vol. 15	refuges for protection (Jesus)	3/1/07 Vol. 46
refuges at shrines of Our Lady (Mary)	7/14/02 Vol. 28	refuges for survival (Jesus)	1/26/04 Vol. 34
refuges at true apparition sites (Jesus)	8/15/03 Vol. 32	refuges for those who love God (Jesus)	8/21/06 Vol. 44
refuges be able to handle cold (Jesus)	2/6/07 Vol. 46	refuges get them prepared (Jesus)	4/28/05 Vol. 39
refuges be prepared to go (Jesus)	1/3/08 Vol. 50	refuges getting closer each day (Jesus)	8/29/03 Vol. 32
refuges be prepared to leave quickly (Jesus)	6/30/06 Vol. 43	refuges go to soon after Warning (Jesus)	3/2/07 Vol. 46
refuges before authorities come (Jesus)	9/20/06 Vol. 44	refuges go when chips are forced (Jesus)	1/5/04 Vol. 34
refuges better than detention centers (Mark)	10/2/01 Vol. 25	refuges go with little planning (Jesus)	11/8/05 Vol. 41
refuges bikes in working order (Jesus)	12/13/04 Vol. 37	refuges God to do the impossible (Jesus)	7/11/07 Vol. 48
refuges blessed for acting on Word (Jesus)	1/15/01 Vol. 22	refuges grottoes of water, protection (Jesus)	7/24/01 Vol. 24
refuges bring tools of your trade (Jesus)	9/12/06 Vol. 44	refuges grow in prayer (Jesus)	10/13/02 Vol. 29
refuges building multiplied (Jesus)	5/15/07 Vol. 47	refuges have faith in protection (Jesus)	1/9/08 Vol. 50
refuges call for simple life (Jesus)	6/13/03 Vol. 31	refuges have greenhouses (Jesus)	1/14/08 Vol. 50
refuges cannot be destroyed (Jesus)	9/28/00 Vol. 20	refuges have healing water (Jesus)	4/28/05 Vol. 39
refuges caves like catacombs (Jesus)	3/13/03 Vol. 30	refuges have healing water (Mary)	2/11/99 Vol. 14
refuges conditions are rustic (Jesus)	11/15/06 Vol. 45	refuges have miracles of protection (Jesus)	3/2/05 Vol. 38
refuges crude bed of hay (Jesus)	10/15/03 Vol. 33	refuges have miraculous protection (Jesus)	11/8/05 Vol. 41
refuges deer meat provided (Jesus)	3/7/05 Vol. 38	refuges have no fear (Jesus)	1/24/08 Vol. 50
refuges deer meat staple (Jesus)	1/11/08 Vol. 50	refuges have total protection (Jesus)	9/6/03 Vol. 32
refuges do not wait too long to go (Jesus)	10/10/02 Vol. 29	refuges healed by cross and springs (Jesus)	2/25/03 Vol. 30
refuges dwellings multiplied (Jesus)	2/22/07 Vol. 46	refuges healed of diseases (Jesus)	2/18/08 Vol. 50
refuges faithful protected at (Jesus)	11/17/05 Vol. 41	refuges healing of viruses (Jesus)	3/2/08 Vol. 50
refuges faithful remnant protected (Jesus)	6/2/06 Vol. 43	refuges healing place for plagues (Jesus)	2/22/01 Vol. 22
refuges families to be together (Jesus)	6/6/05 Vol. 39	refuges healing springs & protection (Jesus)	8/13/04 Vol. 36
refuges fish for food (Jesus)	11/29/06 Vol. 45	refuges healing water, luminous crosses (Jesus)	12/5/03 Vol. 33
refuges flee for protection (Jesus)	10/17/06 Vol. 45	refuges healing waters (Jesus)	10/3/02 Vol. 29
refuges flee in haste to (Jesus)	8/17/06 Vol. 44	refuges heavenly manna provided (Jesus)	11/30/03 Vol. 33
refuges flee in martial law (Jesus)	2/7/08 Vol. 50	refuges holy ground,apparition places (Jesus)	3/24/03 Vol. 30
refuges flee to in tribulation (Jesus)	10/19/05 Vol. 41	refuges in caves (Jesus)	6/10/05 Vol. 39
refuges flee to, do not fight (Jesus)	8/6/01 Vol. 24	refuges in caves (Jesus)	1/6/08 Vol. 50
refuges follow guardian angel (Jesus)	6/8/02 Vol. 27	refuges interim (Jesus)	8/11/01 Vol. 24
refuges follow your angels, grace (Jesus)	4/18/97 Vol. 7	refuges interim and final (Jesus)	4/21/05 Vol. 39
refuges food & meat multiplied (Jesus)	11/9/03 Vol. 33	refuges interim and final (Jesus)	5/31/97 Vol. 7
refuges food & protection (Jesus)	6/13/02 Vol. 27	refuges interim ones to hide (Jesus)	9/19/06 Vol. 44
refuges food & protection (Jesus)	9/12/96 Vol. 4	refuges invisible shield (Jesus)	5/3/07 Vol. 47
refuges food & water multiplied (Jesus)	4/24/01 Vol. 23	refuges invisible shield from angels (Jesus)	7/5/07 Vol. 48
refuges food multiplied (Jesus)	6/21/05 Vol. 39	refuges invisible to evil ones (Jesus)	12/27/04 Vol. 37
refuges food multiplied (Jesus)	10/6/07 Vol. 49	refuges invisible to evil ones (Jesus)	12/9/05 Vol. 41
refuges food multiplied (Jesus)	4/11/01 Vol. 23	refuges items needed to take along (Jesus)	11/16/05 Vol. 41
refuges food, physical healings (Jesus)	3/6/04 Vol. 34	refuges items provided by God (Jesus)	11/16/05 Vol. 41
refuges food,shelter,protection (Jesus)	1/21/00 Vol. 18	refuges items to take,protection (Jesus)	6/8/06 Vol. 43
refuges food,water, shelter (Jesus)	4/4/06 Vol. 43	refuges Jesus provides protection (Jesus)	10/27/03 Vol. 33
refuges for help (Jesus)	1/1/03 Vol. 30	refuges lead to by angels (Mark)	10/2/07 Vol. 49
refuges for miraculous protection (Jesus)	6/3/04 Vol. 35	refuges leave cities (Jesus)	1/12/01 Vol. 22
refuges for protection (Jesus)	4/2/03 Vol. 31	refuges leave possessions behind (Jesus)	1/7/05 Vol. 38
refuges for protection (Jesus)	5/13/03 Vol. 31	refuges leave quickly at right time (Jesus)	10/9/06 Vol. 45

refuges luminous cross healings (Jesus)	2/25/07 Vol. 46	refuges protected by angels (Jesus)	1/10/01 Vol. 22
refuges luminous cross over them (Jesus)	11/21/05 Vol. 41	refuges protected by angels (Jesus)	7/27/99 Vol. 16
refuges many on farms (Jesus)	11/29/05 Vol. 41	refuges protected by angels (Jesus)	9/20/00 Vol. 20
refuges many places to hide (Jesus)	2/16/07 Vol. 46	refuges protected from Antichrist (Jesus)	7/18/03 Vol. 32
refuges many prepared in wilderness (Jesus)	7/21/05 Vol. 40	refuges protected from demons (Jesus)	5/17/06 Vol. 43
refuges Marian sites, holy ground, caves (Jesus)	5/13/04 Vol. 35	refuges protected from evil ones (Jesus)	6/16/06 Vol. 43
refuges miracles of protection (Jesus)	10/26/06 Vol. 45	refuges protected in miraculous ways (Jesus)	6/19/02 Vol. 27
refuges miracles of protection (Jesus)	1/8/01 Vol. 22	refuges protection during tribulation (Jesus)	3/30/07 Vol. 46
refuges miraculous healing springs (Jesus)	7/17/03 Vol. 32	refuges protection from Antichrist (Jesus)	1/5/02 Vol. 26
refuges miraculous protection (Jesus)	6/6/05 Vol. 39	refuges protection from Antichrist (Jesus)	10/31/05 Vol. 41
refuges miraculous protection (Jesus)	2/15/06 Vol. 42	refuges protection from Antichrist (Jesus)	1/2/01 Vol. 22
refuges miraculous protection (Jesus)	1/18/01 Vol. 22	refuges protection from evil men (Jesus)	9/12/98 Vol. 12
refuges miraculous springs of healing (Jesus)	8/17/02 Vol. 28	refuges protection from evil ones (Jesus)	1/20/06 Vol. 42
refuges modern day Exodus (Jesus)	2/27/05 Vol. 38	refuges protection from evil ones (Jesus)	4/23/06 Vol. 43
refuges modern day Exodus (Jesus)	7/23/04 Vol. 36	refuges protection from killing (Jesus)	5/10/06 Vol. 43
refuges more prayer, angel help (Jesus)	3/13/08 Vol. 50	refuges protection from persecution (Jesus)	1/3/02 Vol. 26
refuges need fresh water (Jesus)	9/19/05 Vol. 40	refuges protection from the Antichrist (Jesus)	12/16/00 Vol. 21
refuges on blessed, consecrated ground (Jesus)	7/21/02 Vol. 28	refuges protection of angels (Jesus)	8/12/06 Vol. 44
refuges only places of help (Jesus)	10/26/02 Vol. 29	refuges provide food, protection (Jesus)	6/1/05 Vol. 39
refuges or martyred, enslaved (Jesus)	4/19/01 Vol. 23	refuges provide food, water, healing (Jesus)	4/20/05 Vol. 39
refuges our relatives protected (Jesus)	7/21/05 Vol. 40	refuges provide for our needs (Jesus)	4/12/05 Vol. 39
refuges people invisible by angels (Jesus)	7/11/07 Vol. 48	refuges provided manna, water, shelter (Jesus)	10/9/03 Vol. 33
refuges place of protection (Jesus)	5/2/02 Vol. 27	refuges ready to leave all behind (Jesus)	11/4/06 Vol. 45
refuges place of protection (Jesus)	3/10/05 Vol. 38	refuges reward in Era of Peace (Jesus)	2/18/07 Vol. 46
refuges place of protection (Jesus)	7/26/06 Vol. 44	refuges rustic setting in wilderness (Jesus)	2/7/05 Vol. 38
refuges place of protection (Jesus)	1/19/07 Vol. 46	refuges safe places (Jesus)	5/25/02 Vol. 27
refuges place to avoid prisons (Jesus)	5/16/07 Vol. 47	refuges safety against evil ones (Jesus)	11/20/07 Vol. 49
refuges places of angel protection (Jesus)	9/5/06 Vol. 44	refuges safety,hiding places (Jesus)	12/30/96 Vol. 5
refuges places of apparition (Jesus)	6/4/05 Vol. 39	refuges save food & water for (Jesus)	8/15/05 Vol. 40
refuges places of apparitions of Mary (Jesus)	2/4/08 Vol. 50	refuges set up for Mass (Jesus)	6/25/98 Vol. 11
refuges places of protection (Jesus)	7/6/01 Vol. 24	refuges shelters multiplied upwards (Jesus)	2/3/05 Vol. 38
refuges places of protection (Jesus)	9/15/03 Vol. 32	refuges shelters to be multiplied (Jesus)	2/3/05 Vol. 38
refuges places of protection (Jesus)	4/21/03 Vol. 31	refuges signs to go (Jesus)	5/1/02 Vol. 27
refuges places of protection (Jesus)	9/10/05 Vol. 40	refuges signs to go (Jesus)	4/14/05 Vol. 39
refuges places of protection (Jesus)	11/3/05 Vol. 41	refuges signs to go (Jesus)	8/7/06 Vol. 44
refuges places of protection (Jesus)	10/3/07 Vol. 49	refuges signs to go to (Jesus)	3/14/05 Vol. 38
refuges pray and discern (Jesus)	6/3/99 Vol. 15	refuges signs to go to (Jesus)	11/4/05 Vol. 41
refuges prayer, trust, at rest (Jesus)	6/6/07 Vol. 47	refuges signs to go to (Jesus)	10/22/05 Vol. 41
refuges prepare for the tribulation (Jesus)	7/24/97 Vol. 8	refuges signs to leave for (Jesus)	10/4/03 Vol. 33
refuges prepare to go to (Jesus)	10/4/06 Vol. 45	refuges signs to leave for (Jesus)	6/27/04 Vol. 35
refuges prepare to leave for (Jesus)	9/10/02 Vol. 28	refuges simple life (Jesus)	1/6/03 Vol. 30
refuges protect from evil (Jesus)	1/1/08 Vol. 50	refuges simple, crude life (Jesus)	10/6/03 Vol. 33
refuges protected as in Exodus (Jesus)	9/7/00 Vol. 20	refuges soon to need protection (Jesus)	5/17/03 Vol. 31
refuges protected at holy ground (Jesus)	1/14/99 Vol. 14	refuges spiritual & physical protection (Jesus)	6/1/02 Vol. 27
refuges protected by angels (Jesus)	5/31/01 Vol. 23	refuges springs, multiplied food (Jesus)	2/15/06 Vol. 42
refuges protected by angels (Jesus)	10/20/01 Vol. 25	refuges stripped of possessions (Jesus)	1/26/06 Vol. 42
refuges protected by angels (Jesus)	6/2/04 Vol. 35	refuges suffer a simple life (Jesus)	4/3/03 Vol. 31

refuges supplies to have (Jesus) — 6/10/05 Vol. 39

refuges take preparations (Jesus) — 11/8/01 Vol. 25

refuges tents for protection (Jesus) — 8/17/00 Vol. 20

refuges thank leaders for (Jesus) — 4/1/03 Vol. 31

refuges thank the builders of (Jesus) — 10/4/07 Vol. 49

refuges things needed (Jesus) — 5/21/05 Vol. 39

refuges three signs of going to (Jesus) — 5/8/05 Vol. 39

refuges three signs to leave (Jesus) — 10/10/02 Vol. 29

refuges three signs to leave for (Jesus) — 6/9/05 Vol. 39

refuges time to go is close (Jesus) — 12/25/07 Vol. 49

refuges to avoid the Antichrist (Jesus) — 4/29/05 Vol. 39

refuges to be places of healing (Jesus) — 3/4/08 Vol. 50

refuges to be protected (Jesus) — 7/12/05 Vol. 40

refuges to have food & water (Jesus) — 5/16/07 Vol. 47

refuges to have your own room (Jesus) — 1/10/08 Vol. 50

refuges to protect from detention centers (Jesus) — 1/13/04 Vol. 34

refuges to provide necessities (Jesus) — 11/22/06 Vol. 45

refuges trust in food, shelter provided (Jesus) — 8/12/98 Vol. 12

refuges trust in God only (Jesus) — 7/1/03 Vol. 32

refuges underground Masses (Jesus) — 8/3/97 Vol. 8

refuges warn people when to come (Jesus) — 9/3/07 Vol. 48

refuges warned when to leave for (Jesus) — 12/25/04 Vol. 37

refuges water provided (Jesus) — 8/26/06 Vol. 44

refuges water, shelter, food (Jesus) — 5/3/07 Vol. 47

refuges water,bread,meat provided (Jesus) — 10/29/04 Vol. 37

refuges water,food,shelter provided (Jesus) — 10/15/03 Vol. 33

refuges when chips forced on you (Jesus) — 6/22/04 Vol. 35

refuges white luminous crosses (Jesus) — 5/10/01 Vol. 23

refuges why do you need them? (Jesus) — 3/28/03 Vol. 30

refuges with signs, call on Jesus,angels (Jesus) — 7/10/04 Vol. 36

refuges with springs of healing water (Jesus) — 11/18/05 Vol. 41

refuges & caves angels lead,protect (Jesus) — 7/26/00 Vol. 20

refuges and caves for hiding in protection (Jesus) — 11/27/98 Vol. 13

refuges away from cities justice coming soon (Jesus) — 10/15/98 Vol. 13

refuges give protection from disasters & diseases (Jesus) — 2/12/05 Vol. 38

refuges have hope God will protect our souls (Jesus) — 8/20/05 Vol. 40

refuges in tribulation stripped of possessions (Jesus) — 3/19/01 Vol. 22

refuges in winter have plenty of fuel (Jesus) — 1/16/07 Vol. 46

refuges needed time close at hand (Jesus) — 6/10/03 Vol. 31

refuges needed to protect souls in tribulation (Jesus) — 5/27/04 Vol. 35

refuges of protection all is possible with God (Jesus) — 4/3/01 Vol. 23

refuges of protection refuse mark of the beast (Jesus) — 6/19/06 Vol. 43

refuges or martyrs avoid worshiping beast (Jesus) — 6/16/00 Vol. 19

refuges protected angels,food provided (Jesus) — 10/20/98 Vol. 13

refuges, evil prepared by evil ones (Jesus) — 4/29/04 Vol. 35

refuges, interim and caves (Jesus) — 7/7/01 Vol. 24

refuges, interim for gradual migration (Jesus) — 6/21/07 Vol. 47

refuges, miracles at will make believers (Jesus) — 6/6/07 Vol. 47

refuges, signs for famine,division,chips (Jesus) — 2/1/06 Vol. 42

refuges, talents making clothes at (Jesus) — 9/12/06 Vol. 44

refuges, travel to bikes, food, backpack (Jesus) — 11/24/04 Vol. 37

refuges,apparition sites angels to provide protection (Mary) — 11/20/98 Vol. 13

refusing temptations goal of the soul (Jesus) — 9/17/99 Vol. 16

register to read chips with biometrics, scanner (Jesus) — 8/8/05 Vol. 40

Reign of Peace joy (Jesus) — 12/3/95 Vol. 3

Reilich, Mary funeral Mass (Jesus) — 4/18/06 Vol. 43

reincarnation not true,from evil one (Jesus) — 8/13/96 Vol. 4

Reinholtz, Joseph message to prayer group (Joe Reinholtz) — 8/28/05 Vol. 40

reins of money favored over freedoms (Jesus) — 9/2/99 Vol. 16

rejoice heaven (Jesus) — 5/4/95 Vol. 2

rejoice always at Christmas (Jesus) — 12/17/06 Vol. 45

Rejoice Sunday Light of Jesus in Eucharist (Jesus) — 12/13/03 Vol. 33

relationships, broken difficult to heal (Jesus) — 2/28/07 Vol. 46

relatives in purgatory need prayers (Jesus) — 2/16/05 Vol. 38

relatives, deceased need prayers in purgatory (Jesus) — 7/9/00 Vol. 20

relic honored grateful to prayer group (St. Theresa) — 10/4/01 Vol. 25

relic of St. Therese keep focus on Jesus (St. Therese) — 10/15/98 Vol. 13

relics display in public at Mass (Jesus) — 6/23/05 Vol. 39

relics treasure and revere (Jesus) — 2/24/99 Vol. 14

relics of the saints display on feasts (Jesus) — 1/7/04 Vol. 34

relics, crosses protection from demons (Jesus) — 12/14/06 Vol. 45

relics,crucifixes needed against demons (Jesus) — 12/30/99 Vol. 17

religions based on love, not hate (Jesus) — 9/21/06 Vol. 44

religions respect others,example (Jesus) — 5/8/97 Vol. 7

religions persecution, US from Islamic terrorists (Jesus) — 9/28/06 Vol. 44

religions teaching war devil is winning (Jesus) — 3/18/04 Vol. 34

religions, other true faith in Jesus only (Jesus) — 11/9/98 Vol. 13

religious & patriots on list to be killed (Jesus) — 1/7/06 Vol. 42

religious & patriots targets after martial law (Jesus) — 10/10/06 Vol. 45

religious beliefs avoid those not following God (Jesus) — 7/8/04 Vol. 36

religious books libraries (Jesus) — 10/5/94 Vol. 2

religious education better than secular ed (Jesus) — 6/11/03 Vol. 31

religious education example (Jesus) — 9/10/95 Vol. 3

religious education for children (Jesus) — 8/15/06 Vol. 44

religious education keep pace with secular ed (Jesus) — 12/27/01 Vol. 25

religious education parental vocation (Mary) — 7/26/94 Vol. 2

religious education pass on faith to children (Jesus) — 11/15/97 Vol. 9

religious education teach children (Jesus) — 3/8/98 Vol. 10

religious fanatics foolish in eyes of world (Jesus) — 7/7/01 Vol. 24

religious freedom appreciate it (Jesus) — 10/17/01 Vol. 25

religious freedom attacks on, taken away (Jesus) — 8/8/06 Vol. 44

religious freedom being persecuted (Jesus) — 11/20/07 Vol. 49

religious freedom challenge to remove 'God' (Jesus) — 6/27/02 Vol. 27

religious freedom stand up for or lose (God the Father) — 8/20/03 Vol. 32

religious freedom at risk new world religion attack (Jesus)　8/3/00 Vol. 20

religious freedoms being threatened in America (Jesus)　11/9/03 Vol. 33

religious freedoms stand up for (Jesus)　11/13/05 Vol. 41

religious freedoms threatened in America (Jesus)　1/3/06 Vol. 42

religious freedoms to be taken away (Jesus)　10/5/00 Vol. 21

religious instruction children (Jesus)　4/12/94 Vol. 1

religious leaders of Jews threatened by Jesus' fame (Jesus)　4/8/01 Vol. 23

religious objects buy & store to take (Jesus)　12/9/96 Vol. 5

religious objects removed from public places (Jesus)　8/16/04 Vol. 36

religious objects sent to prison for having (Jesus)　4/11/97 Vol. 7

religious orders grateful to founders (Jesus)　7/31/96 Vol. 4

religious orders influenced by world (Jesus)　2/16/99 Vol. 14

religious orders suffering for souls, help (Jesus)　8/14/03 Vol. 32

religious persecution able to die for Jesus? (Jesus)　6/22/02 Vol. 27

religious persecution angels will protect you (Jesus)　7/17/97 Vol. 8

religious persecution can happen in America (Jesus)　9/9/99 Vol. 16

religious persecution Churches destroyed,abused (Jesus)　12/15/98 Vol. 13

religious persecution handcuffs on faithful (Jesus)　4/11/97 Vol. 7

religious persecution harassment (Jesus)　3/15/95 Vol. 2

religious persecution Jesus to protect us (Jesus)　3/25/99 Vol. 14

religious persecution lose rights & freedoms (Jesus)　12/9/99 Vol. 17

religious persecution need deep prayer life (Jesus)　12/28/99 Vol. 17

religious persecution on U.S. soil (Jesus)　6/3/97 Vol. 7

religious persecution pray and help needy (Jesus)　1/3/02 Vol. 26

religious persecution set up secret lists (Jesus)　4/23/98 Vol. 11

religious persecution some martyred (Jesus)　6/28/98 Vol. 11

religious persecution start of tribulation (Jesus)　3/28/08 Vol. 50

religious persecution stripped Churches (Jesus)　4/15/99 Vol. 15

religious persecution suffer for Jesus' Name (Jesus)　11/11/99 Vol. 17

religious persecution to cause lost possessions (Jesus)　4/18/00 Vol. 19

religious persecution to get worse (Jesus)　7/26/06 Vol. 44

religious persecution worship to go underground (Jesus)　8/20/99 Vol. 16

religious pictures adds spiritual depth to life (Jesus)　9/7/06 Vol. 44

religious teachers need to teach prayer devotions (Jesus)　5/17/05 Vol. 39

religious traditions keep reverence for Host (Jesus)　11/3/07 Vol. 49

religious training better than secular training (Jesus)　8/25/05 Vol. 40

religious training know what is taught (Jesus)　1/28/99 Vol. 14

religious, patriotic people targets to be removed (Jesus)　9/22/04 Vol. 36

religious, patriots on list for extermination (Jesus)　10/15/07 Vol. 49

remnant constant prayer (Jesus)　11/8/93 Vol. 1

remnant faithful no matter what (Jesus)　4/15/98 Vol. 11

remnant faithful to be saved (Jesus)　7/30/03 Vol. 32

remnant hold back wrath (Jesus)　1/12/97 Vol. 6

remnant in underground Masses (Jesus)　3/23/98 Vol. 10

remnant joy to His heart (Jesus)　7/20/97 Vol. 8

remnant led by John Paul II (Jesus)　2/8/98 Vol. 10

remnant live lives of faith (Jesus)　4/2/04 Vol. 35

remnant many called, few chosen (Jesus)　11/6/97 Vol. 9

remnant persecuted by evil ones (Jesus)　11/22/98 Vol. 13

remnant preserve Church,articles (Jesus)　7/4/97 Vol. 8

remnant preserve traditions (Jesus)　1/12/99 Vol. 14

remnant protected,real presence (Jesus)　1/11/98 Vol. 10

remnant share in triumph (Jesus)　8/8/97 Vol. 8

remnant Church be in hiding (Jesus)　1/4/97 Vol. 6

Remnant Church Blessed Sacrament (Mary)　5/25/97 Vol. 7

remnant Church goes underground (Jesus)　6/16/99 Vol. 15

remnant church going underground (Jesus)　7/15/03 Vol. 32

remnant Church lead by Pope John Paul II (Jesus)　12/31/97 Vol. 9

Remnant Church Pope John Paul II (Jesus)　8/21/96 Vol. 4

remnant Church prepare to hide (Holy Spirit)　5/1/97 Vol. 7

remnant Church preserve, Mass in secret (Jesus)　12/12/96 Vol. 5

Remnant Church secret Masses in homes (Jesus)　12/3/98 Vol. 13

remnant Church to survive tribulation (Jesus)　4/17/00 Vol. 19

Remnant Church will flee to refuges (Jesus)　2/28/06 Vol. 42

remnant faith pass on to children (Jesus)　10/16/98 Vol. 13

remnant faithful pray and fast (Jesus)　10/30/02 Vol. 29

remnant, faithful cannot be complacent (Jesus)　5/7/02 Vol. 27

remnant, faithful preserves faith (Jesus)　4/7/04 Vol. 35

remove bad habits to grow in faith (Jesus)　9/18/99 Vol. 16

renew earth by comet (Jesus)　7/25/06 Vol. 44

renew Lenten intentions before Passion Week (Jesus)　4/11/00 Vol. 19

renew spiritual life as spring renews life (Jesus)　3/30/00 Vol. 18

renewal of earth God's intervention (Jesus)　9/9/03 Vol. 32

renewal of earth restore order (Jesus)　1/27/98 Vol. 10

renewed earth Blessed Sacrament (Jesus)　2/6/95 Vol. 2

renewed earth dead will return (Jesus)　8/19/94 Vol. 2

renewed earth devil chained (Jesus)　10/4/97 Vol. 9

renewed earth faithful will see (Jesus)　1/2/98 Vol. 10

renewed earth from man's mischief (Jesus)　11/17/05 Vol. 41

renewed earth Garden of Eden (Jesus)　4/16/96 Vol. 3

renewed earth hope (Jesus)　1/26/96 Vol. 3

renewed earth resurrected bodies (Jesus)　4/7/96 Vol. 3

renewed earth rising in the sky (Jesus)　11/15/94 Vol. 2

renewed earth shooting star (Jesus)　11/26/94 Vol. 2

renewed earth some taken up (Jesus)　9/12/96 Vol. 4

renewed earth taken to a safe place (Jesus)　4/20/96 Vol. 3

renewed earth that man despoiled (Jesus)　11/12/05 Vol. 41

renounce devil,world or fall into hell (Jesus)　3/27/00 Vol. 18

renovations of hearts, not altars (Jesus)　7/14/98 Vol. 12

repairing souls from sin in Confession (Jesus)　6/19/03 Vol. 31

reparation for sins in suffering (Jesus)　7/21/03 Vol. 32

reparation in prayer & good deeds (Jesus)　1/22/01 Vol. 22

reparation judging (Jesus)　3/6/94 Vol. 1

reparation vocations (Jesus)　11/23/93 Vol. 1

reparation for sin offer up pain for (Jesus) 3/17/07 Vol. 46

reparation for sins in suffering diseases (Jesus) 10/25/04 Vol. 37

reparation, make for your own sins (Jesus) 11/2/04 Vol. 37

reparation, make for your own sins before death (Jesus) 10/30/04 Vol. 37

repent and go to Confession (Jesus) 2/12/07 Vol. 46

repent believe in Good News (Jesus) 7/23/07 Vol. 48

repent for sins of abortion and flesh (Jesus) 9/27/98 Vol. 12

repent Jonah (Jesus) 1/23/94 Vol. 1

repent messengers (Jesus) 10/25/95 Vol. 3

repent second coming (Jesus) 10/10/95 Vol. 3

repent to let grace into soul (Jesus) 12/6/01 Vol. 25

repent and convert to save souls (Jesus) 6/28/07 Vol. 47

repent and save souls shout from the rooftops (Jesus) 10/9/98 Vol. 13

repent for sins America's call to action (Jesus) 9/30/05 Vol. 40

repent now change your lives for Me (Jesus) 11/2/99 Vol. 17

repent now keep focus on eternal life (Jesus) 12/26/07 Vol. 49

repent now or worse destruction to come (Jesus) 10/12/05 Vol. 41

repent now swallow your pride (Jesus) 1/25/00 Vol. 18

repent now while you still have time (Father) 6/16/05 Vol. 39

repent of sin or little to be left standing (Jesus) 9/23/04 Vol. 36

repent of sin or worse disasters follow (Jesus) 8/3/00 Vol. 20

repent of sin reach full potential (Jesus) 3/18/07 Vol. 46

repent of sins better than store gifts (Jesus) 12/17/98 Vol. 13

repent of sins conform to Commandments (Jesus) 1/23/03 Vol. 30

repent of sins purpose to change (Jesus) 10/23/04 Vol. 37

repent of sins to avoid fires of hell (Jesus) 1/12/00 Vol. 18

repent of sins to reconcile with God (Jesus) 2/26/05 Vol. 38

repent of sins Warning a preparation (Jesus) 11/25/05 Vol. 41

repent,pleas refused more disasters as wake-up calls (Jesus) 3/26/02 Vol. 26

repentance call for America (Jesus) 11/25/01 Vol. 25

repentance of America (Jesus) 12/9/01 Vol. 25

repentance or worse destruction to fall (Jesus) 6/21/05 Vol. 39

repentance seek forgiveness (Jesus) 5/7/98 Vol. 11

repentance seeking forgiveness (Jesus) 6/19/03 Vol. 31

rep. & forgiveness needed in frequent Confession (Jesus) 2/23/02 Vol. 26

repentance from prophets listen in all ages (Jesus) 12/15/07 Vol. 49

repentance of Nineveh sign of Jonah (Jesus) 10/8/07 Vol. 49

repentence confession,frequent sins (Jesus) 12/16/96 Vol. 5

repentence tribulation (Jesus) 1/2/96 Vol. 3

repetitive sin grace needed to renew (Jesus) 4/10/01 Vol. 23

requirements for heaven love God,accept as Savior (Jesus) 3/25/00 Vol. 18

resisting mark seen foolish by world (Jesus) 2/2/00 Vol. 18

resolution choice (Jesus) 12/31/95 Vol. 3

resolutions to repent improve spiritual lives (Jesus) 12/30/98 Vol. 13

resources on earth finite & limited (Jesus) 9/24/02 Vol. 28

resources, limited preserve, protect environment (Jesus) 9/9/04 Vol. 36

resources, natural do not abuse (Jesus) 8/26/03 Vol. 32

resources, natural preserve (Jesus) 9/18/03 Vol. 32

respect for life plan for each life (Jesus) 12/14/97 Vol. 9

respect for neighbor peace, not anger (Jesus) 3/12/00 Vol. 18

respect life a gift from God (Jesus) 1/4/01 Vol. 22

response to Jesus yes to call (Jesus) 3/11/00 Vol. 18

responsibility grace to evangelize (Jesus) 8/30/99 Vol. 16

responsibility of faith show love, evangelize (Jesus) 2/16/06 Vol. 42

rest & peace only found in God (Jesus) 4/26/05 Vol. 39

rest of Jesus call on his help in trials (Jesus) 9/2/04 Vol. 36

rest on earth only found in Jesus (Jesus) 7/15/04 Vol. 36

Resurrected bodies new life of love (Jesus) 7/22/96 Vol. 4

resurrected body promised by Jesus (Jesus) 9/6/05 Vol. 40

resurrected body promised to believers (Jesus) 8/6/02 Vol. 28

resurrected Body proof in appearances (Jesus) 3/27/08 Vol. 50

Resurrected Jesus real physical man (Jesus) 4/12/07 Vol. 47

resurrected life focus after death (Jesus) 10/6/00 Vol. 21

resurrected souls perfected in suffering (Jesus) 2/8/01 Vol. 22

Resurrection a foreshadowing for us (Jesus) 3/13/05 Vol. 38

Resurrection a witness for us (Jesus) 1/11/98 Vol. 10

Resurrection act of glory (God the Father) 4/30/98 Vol. 11

Resurrection and the Life to come (Jesus) 7/29/06 Vol. 44

Resurrection apostles doubted it (Jesus) 4/14/07 Vol. 47

Resurrection appearacnes after (Jesus) 4/3/02 Vol. 27

resurrection awaits us in Heaven (Jesus) 5/1/99 Vol. 15

Resurrection belief disputed (Jesus) 4/12/07 Vol. 47

Resurrection choose life in the Spirit (Jesus) 10/5/99 Vol. 17

Resurrection Communion of saints (Jesus) 4/18/95 Vol. 2

Resurrection Confession (Jesus) 3/10/95 Vol. 2

Resurrection conquered sin and death (Jesus) 4/18/98 Vol. 11

Resurrection conversions (Jesus) 4/11/96 Vol. 3

Resurrection core of faith (Jesus) 4/2/04 Vol. 35

Resurrection core of our faith (Jesus) 5/4/03 Vol. 31

Resurrection cornerstone & Eucharist (Jesus) 4/10/96 Vol. 3

Resurrection covenant with Jesus (Jesus) 2/6/06 Vol. 42

Resurrection covered up by Jews (Jesus) 7/3/06 Vol. 44

Resurrection Divine Mercy Chaplet many 3/30/94 Vol. 1

Resurrection dry bones in desert (Jesus) 2/19/08 Vol. 50

Resurrection Easter (Jesus) 4/16/95 Vol. 2

Resurrection Easter people (Jesus) 11/5/96 Vol. 5

Resurrection ecstasy in heaven (Jesus) 4/27/00 Vol. 19

Resurrection faith (Jesus) 1/23/94 Vol. 1

Resurrection faithful in glorified bodies (Jesus) 5/1/00 Vol. 19

Resurrection foretold in Transfiguration (Jesus) 8/6/98 Vol. 12

Resurrection fruits (Jesus) 4/20/95 Vol. 2

Resurrection gains chance of heaven (Jesus) 4/16/98 Vol. 11

Resurrection gives life,dispels darkness (Jesus) 4/15/01 Vol. 23

Resurrection glorified bodies,evil over (Jesus) 10/29/96 Vol. 5

Resurrection God of living, not the dead (Jesus) 2/26/04 Vol. 34

Resurrection great love for us (Jesus) 4/1/97 Vol. 7

Resurrection greatest miracle (Jesus) 4/20/03 Vol. 31

Resurrection greatest miracle (God the Father) 5/8/98 Vol. 11

Resurrection hard to believe (Jesus) 3/22/08 Vol. 50

Resurrection heaven on earth (Jesus) 6/17/95 Vol. 2

Resurrection heaven opened (Jesus) 3/29/97 Vol. 6

Resurrection hope for all sinners (Jesus) 4/15/06 Vol. 43

Resurrection hope for all souls (Jesus) 12/23/05 Vol. 41

Resurrection hope for eternal life (Jesus) 1/9/07 Vol. 46

Resurrection hope for us too (Jesus) 3/17/05 Vol. 38

Resurrection hope in eternal life (Jesus) 4/12/04 Vol. 35

Resurrection hope in Jesus (Jesus) 7/22/04 Vol. 36

Resurrection hope in life's trials (Jesus) 4/11/04 Vol. 35

Resurrection in early morning (Jesus) 4/10/04 Vol. 35

Resurrection is hope for us too (Jesus) 3/20/05 Vol. 38

Resurrection Jesus appeared after (Jesus) 5/29/03 Vol. 31

Resurrection Jesus rose on own power (Jesus) 4/16/01 Vol. 23

Resurrection Jesus' victory over death (Jesus) 5/21/00 Vol. 19

Resurrection Jesus, light of world (Jesus) 4/8/96 Vol. 3

resurrection joining of body & soul (Jesus) 11/25/02 Vol. 29

Resurrection light of the world (Jesus) 4/25/96 Vol. 3

Resurrection man never intended to die (Jesus) 4/4/97 Vol. 7

Resurrection means to salvation (Jesus) 4/29/04 Vol. 35

Resurrection new bodies to come (Jesus) 3/30/97 Vol. 6

Resurrection new hope and new creation (Jesus) 4/7/98 Vol. 11

resurrection of faithful at last judgment (Jesus) 3/9/08 Vol. 50

Resurrection of Jesus (Jesus) 6/2/05 Vol. 39

Resurrection of Jesus & ourselves (Jesus) 5/23/01 Vol. 23

resurrection of Jesus & us (Jesus) 5/6/01 Vol. 23

Resurrection of our bodies and souls (Jesus) 3/15/98 Vol. 10

Resurrection opened heaven after Adam's fall (Jesus) 4/19/03 Vol. 31

resurrection our redemption (Jesus) 7/22/97 Vol. 8

Resurrection prepare during Lent (Jesus) 2/11/99 Vol. 14

Resurrection prepare for your own death (Jesus) 4/23/98 Vol. 11

resurrection preview in Transfiguration (Jesus) 9/21/03 Vol. 32

Resurrection promise of eternal life (Jesus) 4/10/04 Vol. 35

Resurrection promise of eternal life (Jesus) 2/21/07 Vol. 46

Resurrection promise of our resurrection (Jesus) 3/26/05 Vol. 38

Resurrection promise to faithful (Jesus) 3/28/99 Vol. 14

Resurrection proof in witnesses (Jesus) 3/23/08 Vol. 50

Resurrection proof of Divinity (Jesus) 4/16/06 Vol. 43

resurrection reward in glorified bodies (Jesus) 10/25/00 Vol. 21

Resurrection sacraments (Jesus) 4/2/95 Vol. 2

Resurrection showed glory & power (Jesus) 6/28/05 Vol. 39

Resurrection soldiers paid to lie (Jesus) 6/2/06 Vol. 43

resurrection soul yearns for its (Jesus) 7/2/04 Vol. 36

Resurrection spread the Good News (Jesus) 3/27/08 Vol. 50

Resurrection sword of fire,justice (Jesus) 4/4/99 Vol. 15

Resurrection the Light & Life (Jesus) 1/29/04 Vol. 34

Resurrection this planet is graced (Jesus) 4/13/98 Vol. 11

Resurrection way to follow Jesus (Jesus) 12/18/04 Vol. 37

Resurrection without it, faith in vain (Jesus) 9/19/98 Vol. 12

Resurrection & Life gift of Jesus (Jesus) 11/13/06 Vol. 45

Resurrection & Life Jesus is (Jesus) 4/7/07 Vol. 47

Resurrection & Life Jesus needed for heaven (Jesus) 11/11/07 Vol. 49

Resurrection & Life promise to all souls (Jesus) 12/15/05 Vol. 41

Resurrection & the Life Jesus is the (Jesus) 2/5/08 Vol. 50

Resurrection (Easter) victory over sin and evil (Jesus) 4/11/98 Vol. 11

Resurrection and Life core belief in Jesus (Jesus) 4/15/06 Vol. 43

Resurrection angel He is risen,angel (Mark) 4/14/99 Vol. 15

Resurrection believed after appeances to apostles (Jesus) 4/26/00 Vol. 19

Resurrection evidence Scripture,Shroud,popes (Jesus) 4/17/06 Vol. 43

Resurrection gives hope victory over sin & death (Jesus) 10/22/98 Vol. 13

Resurrection like spring new life without sin (Jesus) 4/5/01 Vol. 23

Resurrection meaning road to Emmaus (Jesus) 4/7/99 Vol. 15

Resurrection message of Jesus & ourselves (Jesus) 4/17/02 Vol. 27

Resurrection of Jesus model for faithful (Jesus) 9/28/07 Vol. 48

Resurrection of Jesus more focus than earthly (Jesus) 3/14/08 Vol. 50

Resurrection of Jesus promise to all followers (Jesus) 3/16/06 Vol. 42

resurrection of people promise by Jesus (Jesus) 8/6/05 Vol. 40

resurrection of soul as you leave confessional (Jesus) 3/17/02 Vol. 26

resurrection of souls for faithful to God (Jesus) 11/19/04 Vol. 37

resurrection on faith Jesus has power over death (Jesus) 5/11/00 Vol. 19

Resurrection people be joyous (Jesus) 10/28/06 Vol. 45

retaining sins refusal of absolution (Jesus) 4/14/07 Vol. 47

retaliation in war may cause an escalation (Jesus) 8/20/98 Vol. 12

retirement more time to pray (Jesus) 6/28/98 Vol. 11

retirement plan Jesus has best plan,trust (Jesus) 10/30/97 Vol. 9

retreat cruises have better intentions (Jesus) 1/25/01 Vol. 22

retreat,spiritual needed as vacations (Jesus) 6/12/03 Vol. 31

retreats help direct priorities to God (Jesus) 6/1/07 Vol. 47

retreats renew spiritual energy (Jesus) 8/28/97 Vol. 8

retreats & missions to reflect & renew (Jesus) 3/15/07 Vol. 46

retreats & prayer to prepare for trials (Jesus) 4/3/03 Vol. 31

Revelation four horses described (Jesus) 12/19/00 Vol. 21

Revelation four lamp stands & trumpets (Jesus) 4/15/04 Vol. 35

Revelation rejoice in visions (Jesus) 5/20/01 Vol. 23

Revelation the four horses of (Jesus) 10/7/06 Vol. 45

Revelation punishments worshipers of Antichrist (Jesus) 8/15/99 Vol. 16

Revelation,book of being fulfilled (Jesus) 4/30/98 Vol. 11

revenge by man causes many wars (Jesus) 7/27/07 Vol. 48

reverence at Mass (Jesus) 6/17/99 Vol. 15

reverence being minimized (Jesus) 6/14/04 Vol. 35

reverence being removed from churches (Jesus) 2/21/02 Vol. 26

reverence bow & genuflect (Jesus) 7/27/03 Vol. 32

reverence bow,genuflect to praise God (Jesus) 9/17/98 Vol. 12

reverence Confession (Jesus) 8/3/95 Vol. 3

reverence consecration 10/3/93 Vol. 1

reverence display pictures & statues (Jesus) 7/14/98 Vol. 12

reverence dress respectfully (Jesus) 5/27/99 Vol. 15

reverence for traditions of Church (Jesus) 12/29/98 Vol. 13

reverence genuflecting, on tongue (Jesus) 10/27/98 Vol. 13

reverence hearts 10/13/93 Vol. 1

reverence in Holy Communion (St. Michael) 9/29/03 Vol. 32

reverence of Blessed Sacrament (Jesus) 4/26/04 Vol. 35

reverence proper Church behavior (Jesus) 7/10/98 Vol. 12

reverence & respect for Blessed Sacrament (Jesus) 11/23/05 Vol. 41

reverence for Eucharist receive without mortal sin (Jesus) 3/23/99 Vol. 14

reverence for Host give praise,glory to God (Jesus) 4/5/01 Vol. 23

reverence for Host give thanks after Communion (Jesus) 2/27/00 Vol. 18

reverence needed for Host in tabernacle (Jesus) 12/11/06 Vol. 45

reverences at Mass (Jesus) 3/15/07 Vol. 46

review at night to remember sins (Jesus) 8/28/99 Vol. 16

revolt needed to stop US wars (Jesus) 9/28/06 Vol. 44

revolution in America patriots vs. UN,foreign cops (Jesus) 9/22/98 Vol. 12

reward for faithful found in heaven (Jesus) 11/29/04 Vol. 37

reward in heaven beatific vision at banquet (Jesus) 1/27/00 Vol. 18

RFID chips replace bar codes (Jesus) 8/9/07 Vol. 48

rich abuse of power (Jesus) 2/13/02 Vol. 26

rich humbled in losses (Jesus) 9/7/05 Vol. 40

rich money (Jesus) 11/10/93 Vol. 1

rich must share with others (Jesus) 11/28/02 Vol. 29

rich poor (Jesus) 7/5/95 Vol. 3

rich will loose wealth (Jesus) 10/7/99 Vol. 17

rich and famous hard to enter heaven (Jesus) 1/18/00 Vol. 18

rich and famous pray for souls (Jesus) 12/30/97 Vol. 9

rich countries need share or suffer land lose as Israel (Jesus) 10/15/98 Vol. 13

rich leaders made pact with the devil (Jesus) 9/19/98 Vol. 12

rich man hard to accept God's Will (Jesus) 3/18/00 Vol. 18

rich men hard to gain heaven (Jesus) 8/1/03 Vol. 32

rich people plundering jobs,middle class (Jesus) 2/17/05 Vol. 38

rich people profit from wars (Jesus) 12/25/01 Vol. 25

rich people to help poor (Jesus) 8/18/03 Vol. 32

rich people wealth to be destroyed (Jesus) 5/17/02 Vol. 27

rich people will lose their possessions (Jesus) 8/13/98 Vol. 12

rich profit again from losses of the poor (Jesus) 9/18/07 Vol. 48

rich profit most from latest recovery (Jesus) 3/26/04 Vol. 34

rich vs. poor unemployment, mergers (Jesus) 4/29/99 Vol. 15

rich, hard to gain heaven cling to wealth, things (Jesus) 12/21/99 Vol. 17

rich, stockholders lowering standard of living (Jesus) 11/8/07 Vol. 49

riches Heaven (Jesus) 4/13/95 Vol. 2

riches heaven's better than earth's (Jesus) 12/12/98 Vol. 13

riches spiritual over physical (Jesus) 7/10/03 Vol. 32

riches & fame roots evil in 1 world order (Jesus) 4/24/97 Vol. 7

riches & power becoming idols (Jesus) 2/11/05 Vol. 38

riches & power reject for heavenly treasures (Jesus) 6/13/02 Vol. 27

riches & wealth could lead to hell (Jesus) 11/20/01 Vol. 25

riches are fleeting will never satisfy the soul (Jesus) 10/20/98 Vol. 13

riches of the world do not search for (Jesus) 7/14/99 Vol. 16

riches of world do not bring happiness (Jesus) 9/23/97 Vol. 8

riches, fame, beauty all pass away (Jesus) 2/17/04 Vol. 34

right conscience know right from wrong (Jesus) 3/13/99 Vol. 14

righteous & just are always persecuted (Jesus) 3/7/08 Vol. 50

rights & freedoms lost to coming martial law (Jesus) 3/22/00 Vol. 18

ring of flowers symbol of Mystical Body (Jesus) 8/28/99 Vol. 16

rioting & chaos as recession worsens (Jesus) 2/7/08 Vol. 50

riots over jobs & recession (Jesus) 5/1/01 Vol. 23

riots shortages of food & fuel (Jesus) 12/19/96 Vol. 5

riots & fighting a sign of hiding (Jesus) 8/12/99 Vol. 16

riots in France,Australia over unemployment, race (Jesus) 12/13/05 Vol. 41

riots,schism,chips call for nearest refuge (Jesus) 6/9/03 Vol. 31

rising from dead understood after Resurrection (Jesus) 3/26/02 Vol. 26

rising from the dead meaning explained (Jesus) 3/28/05 Vol. 38

rising from the dead our resurrection is goal (Jesus) 6/24/99 Vol. 15

risks physical and spiritual (Jesus) 6/8/06 Vol. 43

Rita vigil of prayer, protection (Jesus) 9/22/05 Vol. 40

rites have same true God (Jesus) 2/27/98 Vol. 10

rivers of grace from sacraments (Jesus) 1/19/07 Vol. 46

road map to heaven by prayer & suffering (Jesus) 2/27/01 Vol. 22

road to heaven perform good deeds (Jesus) 9/2/99 Vol. 16

road to heaven spiritual preparations (Jesus) 9/3/03 Vol. 32

roadside bombs jam or detonate (Jesus) 6/14/07 Vol. 47

Robert Noll Valerie's son, funeral (Jesus) 4/13/07 Vol. 47

robots in industry loss of jobs (Jesus) 9/24/03 Vol. 32

Robstown, Texas Guadeloupe and weeping images (Jesus) 8/4/04 Vol. 36

Robstown, Texas miracle on plywood of Mary (Jesus) 8/15/04 Vol. 36

Rochester chemical accidents (Jesus) 4/29/03 Vol. 31

Rochester Conference rosaries and fasting (Mary) 7/23/94 Vol. 2

Rochester, N.Y. Jesus' face on tree (Jesus) 10/27/05 Vol. 41

rock church (Jesus) 4/28/95 Vol. 2

rock of St. Peter foundation of Church in pope (Jesus) 10/17/00 Vol. 21

Rock of the Church build faith on (Jesus) 12/7/06 Vol. 45

Roger's message of love to family on death (Roger Sotile) 5/21/01 Vol. 23

role models Scripture (Jesus) 2/3/94 Vol. 1

role models words and example (Jesus) 1/30/97 Vol. 6

role of women in Church priests (Jesus) 9/23/95 Vol. 3

Rolfe, George funeral message (Jesus) 12/10/04 Vol. 37

Roman Empire destroyed from within (Jesus) 10/10/02 Vol. 29
Roman Empire signs of likeness to America (Jesus) 1/30/02 Vol. 26
Roman persecution to return to Christians (Jesus) 1/19/07 Vol. 46
Romans registered the Israelites (Jesus) 12/23/07 Vol. 49
root cellar place to store food (Jesus) 5/24/07 Vol. 47
Rosa Mystica Shrine holy ground place (Jesus) 10/28/05 Vol. 41
Rosa Mystica devotion to save souls (Mary) 2/13/97 Vol. 6
rosaries abortion,conversion,peace (Mary) 2/24/97 Vol. 6
rosaries best weapon against evil (Jesus) 3/5/02 Vol. 26
rosaries best weapons against war (Jesus) 11/5/01 Vol. 25
rosaries evangelize souls (Mary) 10/17/97 Vol. 9
rosaries good deeds & example (Mary) 10/24/96 Vol. 5
rosaries heavenly song of praise (Jesus) 7/3/03 Vol. 32
rosaries needed for world peace (Jesus) 11/1/99 Vol. 17
rosaries peace,convert sinners (Mary) 7/17/96 Vol. 4
rosaries pray daily (Jesus) 5/13/02 Vol. 27
rosaries pray three daily (Jesus) 1/10/02 Vol. 26
rosaries spiritual support (Mary) 10/23/97 Vol. 9
rosaries spiritual weapons (Mary) 9/6/97 Vol. 8
rosaries touched with blessings (Mary) 7/10/97 Vol. 8
rosaries weapons against sin (Jesus) 12/28/06 Vol. 45
rosaries well prayed better than fast (Jesus) 2/14/02 Vol. 26
rosaries & scapulars power over Antichrist (Mary) 9/25/97 Vol. 8
rosaries & scapulars protect children (Jesus) 7/17/97 Vol. 8
rosaries needed for Mary's intentions (Jesus) 5/9/04 Vol. 35
rosaries of prayer best weapons against evil (Jesus) 8/4/05 Vol. 40
rosaries requested to stop nuclear destruction (Jesus) 12/25/99 Vol. 17
rosaries, crucifixes weapons against demons (Jesus) 9/8/06 Vol. 44
rosaries,spiritual Communion at tribulation time (Jesus) 12/15/04 Vol. 37
rosary 15 decades for peace (Jesus) 7/12/01 Vol. 24
rosary 15 decades for peace (Mary) 2/19/98 Vol. 10
rosary best weapon (Jesus) 3/14/07 Vol. 46
rosary best weapon against evil (Jesus) 3/10/03 Vol. 30
rosary best weapon against evil (Jesus) 9/26/02 Vol. 28
rosary communication of love (Jesus) 10/7/02 Vol. 29
rosary consolation (Mary) 5/8/96 Vol. 3
rosary defeated Turks (Jesus) 4/4/02 Vol. 27
rosary demons (Mary) 5/11/94 Vol. 1
rosary encourage childen to pray (Jesus) 6/18/04 Vol. 35
rosary family prayer of peace (Mary) 10/7/96 Vol. 5
rosary fasting and confession (Mary) 6/25/96 Vol. 3
rosary graces & conversion (Mary) 5/1/96 Vol. 3
rosary in absence of Mass (Jesus) 1/23/97 Vol. 6
rosary is powerful weapon (Jesus) 8/18/06 Vol. 44
rosary life of Jesus & Mary (Jesus) 10/7/03 Vol. 33
rosary love & peace in family (Mary) 8/28/96 Vol. 4
rosary Marian Psalter, weapon (Jesus) 8/8/06 Vol. 44

rosary Mass 10/7/93 Vol. 1
rosary Mysteries of Light (Jesus) 10/16/02 Vol. 29
rosary peace & conversions (Mary) 9/4/96 Vol. 4
rosary Pope drawing attention to (Jesus) 11/19/02 Vol. 29
rosary powerful weapon (Jesus) 10/5/06 Vol. 45
rosary pray 15 decades (Mary) 10/7/99 Vol. 17
rosary pray daily (Jesus) 10/8/05 Vol. 41
rosary pray daily for strength (Mary) 6/4/05 Vol. 39
rosary pray every day (Jesus) 8/8/07 Vol. 48
rosary pray for Mary's intention (Mary) 7/24/97 Vol. 8
rosary Samuels (Mary) 3/18/95 Vol. 2
rosary tested in life (Mary) 5/15/96 Vol. 3
rosary triumph (Mary) 6/4/94 Vol. 1
rosary unites hearts,Immaculate Heart (Jesus) 9/8/05 Vol. 40
rosary war (Mary) 2/11/94 Vol. 1
rosary weapon (Jesus) 10/7/95 Vol. 3
rosary weapon (Jesus) 10/7/95 Vol. 3
rosary weapon against evil (Jesus) 9/6/07 Vol. 48
rosary weapon against evil (Mary) 8/14/96 Vol. 4
rosary weapon against evil (Mary) 11/14/96 Vol. 5
rosary weapon against Satan (Mary) 11/20/97 Vol. 9
rosary weapon to stop war (Jesus) 9/14/06 Vol. 44
rosary & Eucharist protection in tribulation (Jesus) 4/27/99 Vol. 15
rosary & scapular Blessed Mother intercedes (Jesus) 3/17/05 Vol. 38
rosary & scapular close to Our Lady (Jesus) 3/1/07 Vol. 46
rosary & scapular Mary's protection (Jesus) 5/18/06 Vol. 43
rosary & scapular weapons against Satan (Jesus) 7/16/04 Vol. 36
rosary & scapular weapons to fight evil (Jesus) 6/6/06 Vol. 43
rosary daily defend the families (Mary) 10/7/98 Vol. 13
rosary faithful special place in heaven (Jesus) 4/2/02 Vol. 27
rosary for peace is best weapon (Jesus) 7/2/06 Vol. 44
rosary needed in daily prayer life (Jesus) 7/2/05 Vol. 40
rosary needed to atone for sins (Jesus) 3/4/00 Vol. 18
rosary&spiritual communion when no Mass is available (Jesus)
6/17/02 Vol. 27
Rosary, Holy origins & Mysteries (Mary) 10/7/04 Vol. 37
rosary, personal special blessing (Jesus) 1/13/07 Vol. 46
rose of life be as little children (Jesus) 2/23/07 Vol. 46
rose petals blessed by Maria (Jesus) 2/23/07 Vol. 46
rose, sign of love give glory in creation (Jesus) 11/16/98 Vol. 13
roses smelled at Mass (St. Therese) 10/1/07 Vol. 49
Rosse, Ethel funeral message (Jesus) 11/30/01 Vol. 25
rudderless prayer and fasting (Father) 10/19/93 Vol. 1
rulers Jesus is only one (Jesus) 6/16/05 Vol. 39
rulers to be replaced by Antichrist domination (Jesus) 11/26/98 Vol. 13
rumors of war in Iraq America vulnerable (Jesus) 11/14/97 Vol. 9
rushing to heaven or hell? (Jesus) 5/19/03 Vol. 31

Russia children killed before election (Jesus)	9/2/04 Vol. 36	Russia & China plan after US withdrawal (Jesus)	2/8/07 Vol. 46
Russia communism in power (Jesus)	5/30/97 Vol. 7	Russia & China world war (Jesus)	1/18/94 Vol. 1
Russia communism will return (Jesus)	9/3/98 Vol. 12	Russia spreading errors still a threat to war (Mary)	10/10/98 Vol. 13
Russia controlled by atheism (Jesus)	8/28/98 Vol. 12	Russian planes downed killings before election (Jesus)	8/25/04 Vol. 36
Russia help mission church (Jesus)	10/17/01 Vol. 25	Russian submarine radiation dangers (Jesus)	8/31/00 Vol. 20
Russia nuclear threat (Jesus)	1/28/97 Vol. 6	Russian War Communism (Jesus)	1/14/94 Vol. 1
Russia pray for conversion (Jesus)	7/10/96 Vol. 3	Sabbath made a mockery of (Jesus)	10/25/99 Vol. 17
Russia ripe for unrest in government (Jesus)	12/10/98 Vol. 13	Sabbatine Privilege 1st Saturday after death (Jesus)	7/16/07 Vol. 48

sacramental fight evil (Jesus)	9/18/97 Vol. 8	sacraments fountain of grace (Jesus)	7/9/98 Vol. 12
sacramental Church headed by St. Peter (Jesus)	6/7/00 Vol. 19	sacraments free from sin (Jesus)	1/15/98 Vol. 10
sacramentals to fight evil (Jesus)	10/4/07 Vol. 49	sacraments give grace to the soul (Jesus)	3/24/08 Vol. 50
sacramentals best protection vs evil (Jesus)	6/28/01 Vol. 23	sacraments give life to spirit (Jesus)	8/17/03 Vol. 32
sacramentals for protection (Jesus)	6/2/01 Vol. 23	sacraments give rush of grace (Jesus)	4/14/02 Vol. 27
sacramentals for protection (Jesus)	5/13/03 Vol. 31	sacraments gives spiritual enlightenment (Jesus)	3/30/03 Vol. 30
sacramentals for protection (Jesus)	7/12/01 Vol. 24	sacraments heal & feed souls (Jesus)	6/8/06 Vol. 43
sacramentals for protection (Jesus)	1/1/08 Vol. 50	sacraments invite sinners to (Jesus)	1/13/00 Vol. 18
sacramentals for protection (Jesus)	5/14/98 Vol. 11	sacraments life blood of Church (Jesus)	6/13/04 Vol. 35
sacramentals for protection from evil (Jesus)	7/10/03 Vol. 32	sacraments lifeblood of the soul (Jesus)	8/13/00 Vol. 20
sacramentals for protection of evil (Jesus)	1/23/03 Vol. 30	sacraments lifeblood of the soul (Jesus)	7/7/00 Vol. 20
sacramentals get prepared (Jesus)	11/24/01 Vol. 25	sacraments needed for spiritual health (Jesus)	10/15/04 Vol. 37
sacramentals grace for soul (Jesus)	2/27/03 Vol. 30	sacraments our life blood (Jesus)	10/11/03 Vol. 33
sacramentals guard for protection (Jesus)	5/5/98 Vol. 11	sacraments prepare for hiding (Jesus)	9/15/97 Vol. 8
sacramentals have in each room (Jesus)	4/28/98 Vol. 11	sacraments source of grace by priest (Jesus)	2/10/01 Vol. 22
sacramentals holy water, blessed salt (Jesus)	9/2/03 Vol. 32	sacraments spiritual food (Jesus)	11/24/07 Vol. 49
sacramentals keep on you for protection (Jesus)	10/15/97 Vol. 9	sacraments strength through grace (Jesus)	5/20/00 Vol. 19
sacramentals of rosaries & scapulars (Jesus)	4/21/05 Vol. 39	sacraments strength to do Divine Will (Jesus)	9/25/98 Vol. 12
sacramentals on person for protection (Jesus)	6/8/02 Vol. 27	sacraments strengthen against evil (Jesus)	8/23/98 Vol. 12
sacramentals prepare (Jesus)	6/1/99 Vol. 15	sacraments the Trinity is present in (Jesus)	5/1/05 Vol. 39
sacramentals prepare for hiding (Jesus)	10/7/99 Vol. 17	sacraments throughout life at church (Jesus)	7/25/04 Vol. 36
sacramentals prepare for protection (Jesus)	1/20/02 Vol. 26	sacraments to seek love & peace (Jesus)	2/25/99 Vol. 14
sacramentals preserve books & objects (Jesus)	3/23/97 Vol. 6	sacraments vehicle of grace (Jesus)	6/17/03 Vol. 31
sacramentals protect from evil spirits (Jesus)	5/12/98 Vol. 11	sacraments & angels protection from evil ones (Jesus)	6/20/02 Vol. 27
sacramentals protection from Antichrist (Jesus)	4/2/98 Vol. 11	sacraments,seven tools for spiritual life (Jesus)	3/3/01 Vol. 22
sacramentals protection from demons (Jesus)	7/20/01 Vol. 24	Sacred missing in churches (Jesus)	11/9/99 Vol. 17
sacramentals protection from evil (Jesus)	7/23/98 Vol. 12	sacred missing in modern churches (Jesus)	2/21/02 Vol. 26
sacramentals protection from storms (Jesus)	2/22/07 Vol. 46	Sacred & traditions honor Blessed Sacrament (Jesus)	6/28/07 Vol. 47
sacramentals protects from storms (Jesus)	2/6/08 Vol. 50	Sacred Heart appreciate love (Jesus)	10/16/97 Vol. 9
sacramentals shield from evil ones (Jesus)	5/6/03 Vol. 31	Sacred Heart cross (St. Margaret)	10/16/93 Vol. 1
sacramentals spiritual weapons (Jesus)	9/29/03 Vol. 32	Sacred Heart crown of thorns on (Jesus)	4/12/07 Vol. 47
sacramentals spiritual weapons (Jesus)	12/21/97 Vol. 9	Sacred Heart empty church (Jesus)	2/9/95 Vol. 2
sacramentals take into hiding (Jesus)	8/21/97 Vol. 8	Sacred Heart evangelize souls (Jesus)	6/7/02 Vol. 27
sacramentals to fight evil (Jesus)	6/25/98 Vol. 11	Sacred Heart exposition (Jesus)	10/16/95 Vol. 3
sacramentals to fight the battle (Mark)	3/12/98 Vol. 10	Sacred Heart free will (Jesus)	12/2/93 Vol. 1
sacramentals weapons against evil (Jesus)	9/6/03 Vol. 32	Sacred Heart grow in faith by trials (Jesus)	11/20/97 Vol. 9
sacramentals weapons against Satan (Jesus)	11/9/97 Vol. 9	Sacred Heart heating of hearts,flame (Jesus)	10/14/00 Vol. 21
sacramentals wear for protection (Jesus)	4/17/05 Vol. 39	Sacred Heart Jesus' love for us (Jesus)	6/4/04 Vol. 35
sacramentals worn for protection (Jesus)	10/13/06 Vol. 45	Sacred Heart love (Jesus)	6/10/94 Vol. 1
sacramentals & faith needed in spiritual battle (Jesus)	2/3/00 Vol. 18	Sacred Heart love (Jesus)	1/31/96 Vol. 3
sacramentals & food to travel into hiding (Jesus)	3/16/99 Vol. 14	Sacred Heart love given & received (Jesus)	6/18/04 Vol. 35
sacramentals needed protect from demons (Jesus)	12/25/99 Vol. 17	Sacred Heart Margaret Mary (Jesus)	8/22/94 Vol. 2
sacramentals needed rosaries, Benedictine crosses (Jesus)	10/28/03 Vol. 33	Sacred Heart one with Immaculate Heart (Jesus)	6/27/03 Vol. 31
sacramentals, blessed scapular, cross, rosary (Jesus)	12/18/02 Vol. 29	Sacred Heart rainbow around sun (Jesus)	6/15/07 Vol. 47
sacramentals, blessed share with children (Jesus)	8/25/05 Vol. 40	Sacred Heart share (Jesus/Mary)	6/28/95 Vol. 2
sacramentals, blessed weapons against demons (Jesus)	5/31/07 Vol. 47	Sacred Heart St. Margaret Mary (Jesus)	10/16/07 Vol. 49
sacramentals,blessed protect us from evil (Jesus)	11/30/00 Vol. 21	Sacred Heart strength in trials (Jesus)	9/6/99 Vol. 16

Sacred Heart two hearts united (Mary) — 6/1/97 Vol. 7

Sacred Heart unconditional love (Jesus) — 6/14/96 Vol. 3

Sacred Heart will (Jesus) — 1/10/94 Vol. 1

Sacred Heart Enthronement protects homes (Jesus) — 11/30/06 Vol. 45

Sacred Heart Feast open arms to His love (Jesus) — 6/19/98 Vol. 11

Sacred Heart love died for all our sins (Jesus) — 10/16/04 Vol. 37

Sacred Heart of Jesus focus on love (Jesus) — 6/22/01 Vol. 23

Sacred Heart of Jesus focus on love (Jesus) — 6/11/99 Vol. 15

Sacred Heart of Jesus love for mankind (Jesus) — 6/3/05 Vol. 39

sacred removed causing closed churches (Jesus) — 1/24/08 Vol. 50

sacred removed modernism destroying (Jesus) — 9/26/99 Vol. 16

Sacred Scripture in proper teachings (Jesus) — 9/17/96 Vol. 4

Sacred Traditions preserved by prophets,saints (Jesus) — 6/27/07 Vol. 47

sacred vessels abused in invalid Masses,black masses (Jesus) — 3/21/02 Vol. 26

Sacred,Immaculate heart sign of love for all (Jesus) — 6/29/00 Vol. 19

Sacred,Immaculate Hearts united in love (Jesus) — 6/1/06 Vol. 43

Sacret Heart of Jesus eternal flame of love (Jesus) — 6/22/00 Vol. 19

sacrifice bodily comforts (Jesus) — 6/14/01 Vol. 23

sacrifice harvest of wheat/Will (Jesus) — 6/10/96 Vol. 3

sacrifice heavenly treasures (Jesus) — 12/21/96 Vol. 5

sacrifice & Word mission of Jesus on earth (Jesus) — 12/28/03 Vol. 33

sacrifice in time Jesus redeemed us (Jesus) — 12/24/98 Vol. 13

sacrifice of Mass remember Good Friday (Jesus) — 4/13/01 Vol. 23

sacrifice of Mass renewal of Jesus' death (Jesus) — 1/18/05 Vol. 38

Sacrifice of Mass suffering for sins (Jesus) — 7/10/03 Vol. 32

sacrifice of Mass unbloody re-enactment (Jesus) — 7/30/98 Vol. 12

Sacrifice of the Mass crucifixion through all time (Jesus) — 1/20/08 Vol. 50

Sacrifice of the Mass daily bread (Jesus) — 8/17/97 Vol. 8

sacrifice of the Mass daily bread in Mass (Jesus) — 6/10/97 Vol. 7

sacrifice of the Mass do not hold back your love (Jesus) — 10/8/98 Vol. 13

Sacrifice of the Mass fortunate to have a priest (Jesus) — 1/31/08 Vol. 50

sacrifice of the Mass reenactment of death (Jesus) — 6/27/99 Vol. 15

Sacrifice of the Mass reverence to Blessed Sacrament (Jesus) — 2/24/08 Vol. 50

sacrifice on the cross accepted our sins (Jesus) — 6/3/99 Vol. 15

sacrifice, perfect Jesus' death on the cross (Jesus) — 3/27/01 Vol. 22

sacrifices desire mercy instead (Jesus) — 2/2/04 Vol. 34

sacrilege Communion in mortal sin (Jesus) — 10/4/97 Vol. 9

sacrilege Communion in mortal sin (Jesus) — 2/26/99 Vol. 14

sacrilege do not commit sin of (Jesus) — 6/13/04 Vol. 35

sacrilege do not commit sins of (Jesus) — 4/28/01 Vol. 23

sacrilege Eucharist with mortal sin (Jesus) — 2/15/08 Vol. 50

sacrilege no Communion in mortal sin (Jesus) — 9/21/02 Vol. 28

sacrilege no Communion in mortal sin (Jesus) — 10/12/02 Vol. 29

sacrilege no mortal sin for Host (Jesus) — 1/30/99 Vol. 14

sacrilege receive Communion in sin (Jesus) — 7/30/03 Vol. 32

sacrilege receive Communion unworthily (Jesus) — 8/17/03 Vol. 32

sacrilege receive Communion worthily (Jesus) — 7/17/05 Vol. 40

sacrilege receive worthily (Jesus) — 9/8/03 Vol. 32

sacrilege receiving Communinon unworthily (Jesus) — 9/14/04 Vol. 36

sacrilege receiving Eucharist in mortal sin (Jesus) — 3/24/05 Vol. 38

sacrilege receiving Eucharist unworthily (Jesus) — 5/5/03 Vol. 31

sacrilege receiving Host in mortal sin (Jesus) — 4/10/06 Vol. 43

sacrilege serious sin (Jesus) — 3/16/97 Vol. 6

sacrilege, avoid no Communion in mortal sin (Jesus) — 2/27/00 Vol. 18

sacrilege, sins of do not commit (Jesus) — 1/23/01 Vol. 22

sacrilege,sins of Confession (Jesus) — 7/1/01 Vol. 24

sacrileges, communions mortal sin (Jesus) — 9/16/96 Vol. 4

sacrilegious Communion do not violate gifts (Jesus) — 6/14/98 Vol. 11

sacrilegious communions downplaying Confession (Jesus) — 1/12/99 Vol. 14

sacrilegous Communions abomination in God's sight (Jesus) — 7/27/02 Vol. 28

Saddam Hussein hiding weapons (Jesus) — 1/29/03 Vol. 30

Saddam Hussein live & die by the sword (Jesus) — 8/1/02 Vol. 28

Saddam Hussein reign erroding (Jesus) — 3/20/03 Vol. 30

Saddam Hussein removal, evil replacement? (Jesus) — 9/25/02 Vol. 28

Saddam Hussein saved for another day (Jesus) — 2/21/03 Vol. 30

Saddam Hussein weapons hidden (Jesus) — 3/6/03 Vol. 30

Saddam Hussein found end of chapter of evil (Jesus) — 12/15/03 Vol. 33

safe haven Cabrini Shrine (Mother Cabrini) — 7/16/95 Vol. 3

safe haven end times (Jesus) — 5/27/94 Vol. 1

safe haven in trust of Jesus (Jesus) — 12/17/02 Vol. 29

safe haven interim refuge (Jesus) — 8/21/97 Vol. 8

safe haven travel (Jesus) — 5/18/94 Vol. 1

safe haven and caves protected from diseases (Jesus) — 9/1/98 Vol. 12

safe havens Antichrist (Jesus) — 5/29/94 Vol. 1

safe havens mantle of protection (Mary) — 8/6/98 Vol. 12

safe havens rural areas (Mary) — 8/4/97 Vol. 8

safe place tribulation (Jesus) — 9/5/95 Vol. 3

safe refuge during trial stairway to Heaven (Jesus) — 1/17/95 Vol. 2

safety angels and sacramentals (Mary) — 3/19/98 Vol. 10

safety in workplace alert to accidents (Jesus) — 1/5/06 Vol. 42

sainthood daily struggle (Jesus) — 2/21/08 Vol. 50

sainthood die to self (Jesus) — 1/12/08 Vol. 50

sainthood goal for perfection (Jesus) — 2/21/06 Vol. 42

sainthood goal of all faithful (Jesus) — 11/1/06 Vol. 45

sainthood improve spiritual life daily (Jesus) — 11/5/05 Vol. 41

sainthood is possible (Jesus) — 4/30/99 Vol. 15

sainthood possible through Jesus (Jesus) — 11/1/02 Vol. 29

sainthood possible with Jesus (Jesus) — 10/8/02 Vol. 29

sainthood say 'yes' to Jesus (Jesus) — 10/28/05 Vol. 41

sainthood strive for perfection (Jesus) — 1/4/02 Vol. 26

sainthood struggle to Calvary (Jesus) — 5/25/06 Vol. 43

sainthood crown awaits faithful believers (Jesus) — 11/21/99 Vol. 17

sainthood needed to enter heaven (Jesus) — 8/20/07 Vol. 48

sainthood vs. hell consequences of choices (Jesus) — 5/22/06 Vol. 43

saintly lives focus on Jesus in love (Jesus) — 6/24/04 Vol. 35

saints all are able to be one (Jesus) — 7/2/98 Vol. 12

saints all called to be models (Jesus) — 6/21/02 Vol. 27

saints are real heroes (Jesus) — 11/1/07 Vol. 49

saints as beacons to follow (Jesus) — 1/7/04 Vol. 34

saints as intercessors, patrons (Jesus) — 11/1/07 Vol. 49

saints as our models (Jesus) — 5/1/03 Vol. 31

saints call by name for help (St. Therese) — 2/7/98 Vol. 10

saints call on for help (Jesus) — 6/11/98 Vol. 11

saints call on for help (Jesus) — 1/23/01 Vol. 22

saints crucifix (Jesus) — 8/7/95 Vol. 3

saints defended the Church (Jesus) — 6/30/98 Vol. 11

saints difficulties of life (St. Therese) — 5/29/96 Vol. 3

saints disposed of wealth (Jesus) — 2/17/04 Vol. 34

saints do not need special lives (Jesus) — 11/1/99 Vol. 17

saints examples in life (Jesus) — 5/26/98 Vol. 11

saints flowers (St. Therese) — 11/1/93 Vol. 1

saints focus on simplicity (Jesus) — 11/16/01 Vol. 25

saints gate of Heaven (Jesus) — 11/1/94 Vol. 2

saints gave up the world (Jesus) — 4/15/04 Vol. 35

saints give us an example (Jesus) — 8/5/99 Vol. 16

saints great prayer intercessors (Jesus) — 2/21/06 Vol. 42

Saints heaven (Jesus) — 11/1/95 Vol. 3

saints honor relics on feast day (Jesus) — 6/23/05 Vol. 39

saints imitate lives, not externals (Jesus) — 3/18/04 Vol. 34

Saints imitate lives,thanks (St. Therese) — 7/10/97 Vol. 8

saints imitate qualities of their lives (Jesus) — 10/15/05 Vol. 41

saints imitate spiritual heroes (Jesus) — 11/22/03 Vol. 33

saints imitate their lives (Jesus) — 5/13/03 Vol. 31

saints inspiration for heaven (Jesus) — 11/1/04 Vol. 37

saints intercessors for petitions (Jesus) — 2/24/99 Vol. 14

saints keep statues to remember (Jesus) — 2/26/98 Vol. 10

saints keep statues visible (Jesus) — 2/26/99 Vol. 14

saints lessons in life (Jesus) — 8/7/96 Vol. 4

saints live on Eucharist (Jesus) — 9/30/96 Vol. 4

saints lives as role models (Jesus) — 6/13/01 Vol. 23

saints model for life (Jesus) — 7/6/96 Vol. 3

saints models for conversion (Jesus) — 6/29/98 Vol. 11

saints models of life (Jesus) — 1/6/05 Vol. 38

saints models to follow in life (Jesus) — 1/20/05 Vol. 38

saints not all known (Jesus) — 7/3/07 Vol. 48

saints pray for help, guidance (Jesus) — 10/24/98 Vol. 13

Saints Purgatory (St. Therese) — 11/1/95 Vol. 3

saints purified on earth,purgatory (Jesus) — 11/1/03 Vol. 33

saints read & imitate lives (Jesus) — 9/1/03 Vol. 32

saints real heroes (Jesus) — 8/23/07 Vol. 48

saints real heroes of heaven (Jesus) — 10/15/03 Vol. 33

saints removed from Churches (Jesus) — 1/12/98 Vol. 10

saints sacraments — 11/1/93 Vol. 1

saints shunned earthly things (Jesus) — 9/16/02 Vol. 28

saints souls like diamonds (Jesus) — 3/6/03 Vol. 30

saints spiritual heroes (Jesus) — 11/11/04 Vol. 37

saints spiritual heroes & models (Jesus) — 1/28/04 Vol. 34

saints spiritual lives (Jesus) — 8/11/95 Vol. 3

saints St. Clare,all can be saints (Jesus) — 8/11/98 Vol. 12

saints suffered for Jesus (Jesus) — 4/2/06 Vol. 43

saints we are all called to be (Jesus) — 7/28/99 Vol. 16

saints & angels adore God constantly (Jesus) — 1/31/03 Vol. 30

saints & angels call on for help (Jesus) — 1/22/99 Vol. 14

saints & martyrs remembered (Jesus) — 8/25/06 Vol. 44

saints & relatives call on intercessory prayer (Jesus) — 7/9/00 Vol. 20

saints are heroes models for spiritual life (Jesus) — 11/6/03 Vol. 33

saints' crown better than fleeting fame (Jesus) — 2/20/02 Vol. 26

saints' example learn from holier people (Jesus) — 8/3/00 Vol. 20

saint's feast day granted more miracles (Jesus) — 1/1/07 Vol. 46

saints holding crucifixes consecrated lives to God (Jesus) — 12/14/06 Vol. 45

saints in martyrs heaven is their reward (Jesus) — 8/20/05 Vol. 40

saints in white robes call souls to wash sins (Jesus) — 11/10/99 Vol. 17

saints need to renounce worldly things (Jesus) — 11/7/03 Vol. 33

saints' poverty source of strength,models (Jesus) — 6/15/00 Vol. 19

saints' relics little of presence & grace (Jesus) — 1/7/04 Vol. 34

saints used suffering to gain heaven (Jesus) — 5/22/00 Vol. 19

saints with crosses suffering with Jesus (Jesus) — 8/8/05 Vol. 40

saints, incorrupt witness God's glory (Jesus) — 1/25/01 Vol. 22

saints, prophets examples, battle over evil (Jesus) — 11/10/98 Vol. 13

saints, to be cleanse soul from world (Jesus) — 1/9/08 Vol. 50

saints, unknown celebration entering heaven (Jesus) — 11/1/00 Vol. 21

salaries, high in sports, corporations (Jesus) — 9/19/02 Vol. 28

salt of the earth can lose flavor (Jesus) — 6/19/04 Vol. 35

salvation accept Jesus,forgiveness of sins (Jesus) — 6/18/02 Vol. 27

salvation accept personal Savior (Jesus) — 12/14/97 Vol. 9

salvation actions (Jesus) — 6/16/95 Vol. 2

salvation Blessed Mother's role in (Jesus) — 12/4/04 Vol. 37

salvation blessings of (Jesus) — 12/21/01 Vol. 25

salvation consecrate (Mary) — 1/1/94 Vol. 1

salvation death (Jesus) — 3/19/94 Vol. 1

salvation evaluation of life (Jesus) — 2/20/96 Vol. 3

salvation follow Will of God (Jesus) — 3/4/04 Vol. 34

salvation foretold by angels (Jesus) — 12/19/05 Vol. 41

salvation gates of heaven open (Jesus) — 1/1/08 Vol. 50

salvation gates of heaven opened (Jesus) — 12/29/97 Vol. 9

salvation give praise at Christmas for (Jesus) — 11/29/01 Vol. 25

salvation have enthusiasm (Jesus) — 11/20/00 Vol. 21

salvation history of mankind (Jesus) — 12/17/96 Vol. 5

salvation Jesus died for love of all (Jesus)	1/4/05 Vol. 38	Satan attacks by lies & deceptions (Jesus)	5/3/05 Vol. 39
salvation Jesus is personal savior (Jesus)	4/21/98 Vol. 11	Satan attacks priests, Eucharist (Jesus)	8/8/03 Vol. 32
Salvation light (Jesus)	4/29/94 Vol. 1	Satan avoid his enticements (Jesus)	11/18/06 Vol. 45
Salvation light in the darkness (Jesus)	12/5/96 Vol. 5	Satan be on guard he never sleeps (Jesus)	1/26/98 Vol. 10
salvation light of faith and love (Jesus)	5/20/97 Vol. 7	Satan darkness (Jesus)	10/1/94 Vol. 2
salvation many called, few chosen (Jesus)	8/19/04 Vol. 36	Satan do not sell soul to (Jesus)	2/8/01 Vol. 22
salvation many called, few chosen (Jesus)	10/9/05 Vol. 41	Satan encourages evil deeds (Jesus)	7/5/99 Vol. 16
salvation many called, few chosen (Jesus)	10/9/05 Vol. 41	Satan encourages killing (Jesus)	2/10/08 Vol. 50
salvation Mass unbloody sacrifice (Jesus)	10/21/97 Vol. 9	Satan hate for mankind (Jesus)	5/19/98 Vol. 11
salvation now is acceptable time (Jesus)	6/17/99 Vol. 15	Satan hates man, wants death (Jesus)	4/17/98 Vol. 11
salvation now is the time (Jesus)	6/23/04 Vol. 35	Satan knows time is short (Jesus)	1/3/01 Vol. 22
salvation of Jews & Gentiles (Jesus)	4/22/02 Vol. 27	Satan knows time is short (Jesus)	9/22/00 Vol. 20
salvation opportunity (Jesus)	4/16/94 Vol. 1	Satan little time left (Jesus)	1/9/98 Vol. 10
salvation passion and death (Jesus)	3/18/97 Vol. 6	Satan lurking for souls (Jesus)	8/22/97 Vol. 8
salvation prayer & Divine Will (Jesus)	1/10/97 Vol. 6	Satan misleads by lies (Jesus)	8/9/01 Vol. 24
salvation preach the Good News (Jesus)	12/24/96 Vol. 5	Satan never sleeps (Jesus)	3/14/07 Vol. 46
salvation recognize we are sinners (Jesus)	2/1/98 Vol. 10	Satan never sleeps (Jesus)	3/22/98 Vol. 10
salvation redemption (Jesus)	4/16/94 Vol. 1	Satan only a created angel (Jesus)	7/9/99 Vol. 16
salvation repent of sins (Jesus)	2/12/97 Vol. 6	Satan only allowed so far (Jesus)	1/26/01 Vol. 22
salvation Resurrection (Jesus)	5/12/95 Vol. 2	Satan only gives hate & hell (Jesus)	1/5/99 Vol. 14
salvation revealed in Scripture (Jesus)	2/9/99 Vol. 14	Satan sell souls to (Jesus)	6/15/01 Vol. 23
salvation stable (Jesus)	12/24/93 Vol. 1	Satan stirring up war (Jesus)	2/5/98 Vol. 10
salvation suffer for sins (Jesus)	2/11/96 Vol. 3	Satan temptations of new apple (Jesus)	2/20/99 Vol. 14
salvation suffering (Jesus)	12/6/95 Vol. 3	Satan tested Jesus 3 times (Jesus)	7/10/03 Vol. 32
salvation talents (Jesus)	7/18/95 Vol. 3	Satan tries to ruch & irritate us (Jesus)	4/20/04 Vol. 35
salvation through Jesus' death (Jesus)	9/14/02 Vol. 28	Satan wants to kill Christians (Jesus)	7/25/02 Vol. 28
salvation through Jesus' death (Jesus)	2/19/04 Vol. 34	Satan war of destruction (Jesus)	2/12/98 Vol. 10
salvation through the cross (Jesus)	9/9/03 Vol. 32	Satan why created by God (Jesus)	8/21/02 Vol. 28
salvation history controlled by Jesus (Jesus)	5/7/00 Vol. 19	Satan & Antichrist defeated by Jesus (Jesus)	5/2/03 Vol. 31
Salvation history plan of God (Jesus)	3/25/00 Vol. 18	Satan & Antichrist have a brief reign (Jesus)	10/5/02 Vol. 29
salvation history planned since Adam's sin (Jesus)	4/13/07 Vol. 47	Satan & Antichrist rule briefly,then God's victory (Jesus)	11/2/00 Vol. 21
salvation in Gospels by love of God & neighbor (Jesus)	8/19/99 Vol. 16	Satan & demons chained in hell (Jesus)	7/30/03 Vol. 32
salvation,1st step in birth of Mary (Jesus)	9/8/01 Vol. 24	Satan & demons loosed from hell,tribulation (Jesus)	4/29/97 Vol. 7
same sex marriage defying Matrimony (Jesus)	10/15/04 Vol. 37	Satan & masons removing Blessed Sacrament (Jesus)	11/9/04 Vol. 37
same sex marriage overturned in many states (Jesus)	11/3/04 Vol. 37	Satan chained daily offering (St. Michael)	9/29/95 Vol. 3
same sex marriages Church position (Jesus)	3/4/04 Vol. 34	Satan crushed stop abortions (Mary)	11/25/97 Vol. 9
San Francisco earthquake, falls in ocean (Jesus)	1/23/08 Vol. 50	Satan loses the final battle (Jesus)	1/10/04 Vol. 34
San Francisco earthquake bridge affected (Jesus)	5/23/07 Vol. 47	Satan will lose have no fear of evil (Jesus)	9/10/98 Vol. 12
San Francisco quake geography change (Jesus)	9/10/07 Vol. 48	Satan worship witch doctor (Jesus)	2/1/95 Vol. 2
San Francisco quake wrath of God for sin (Jesus)	7/26/05 Vol. 40	Satan, Antichrist Jesus will triumph over (Jesus)	12/11/98 Vol. 13
San Vittorino refuges worldwide (Mary)	6/15/97 Vol. 7	Satanic attacks witness (Jesus)	2/21/95 Vol. 2
sanctifying grace leaves soul in sin (Jesus)	9/23/02 Vol. 28	Satanic companies trouble for Christians in jobs (Jesus)	10/31/03 Vol. 33
Santa Fe Cathedral Franciscan missionaries (Jesus)	8/16/97 Vol. 8	Satanic mass devil worship (Jesus)	3/10/95 Vol. 2
SARS man-made (Jesus)	5/1/03 Vol. 31	Satanic power Exodus (Jesus)	8/9/95 Vol. 3
SARS & diseases man-made (Jesus)	5/7/03 Vol. 31	Satanic power to gain riches (Jesus)	5/7/98 Vol. 11
Satan a real fallen angel (Jesus)	5/13/99 Vol. 15	Satanic worship living dead (Jesus)	7/8/95 Vol. 3
Satan attacking families (Jesus)	2/27/03 Vol. 30	Satan's attacks on priests & Eucharist (Jesus)	4/16/05 Vol. 39

Satan's control can cause suicide (Jesus)   4/12/06 Vol. 43
Satan's deception avoid mark of the beast (Jesus)   6/27/97 Vol. 7
Satan's desires death & destruction (Jesus)   9/26/02 Vol. 28
Satan's head crushed triumph of Mary (Mary)   6/8/97 Vol. 7
Satan's influence need Jesus to help (Jesus)   1/24/00 Vol. 18
Satan's reign about to be vanquished (Jesus)   1/31/01 Vol. 22
Satan's traps appear as good (Jesus)   1/16/02 Vol. 26
Satan's web of sin sexual sins,greed for money (Jesus)   3/13/02 Vol. 26
Satan's webs internet,masons,sin,killing (Jesus)   7/27/02 Vol. 28
satellites Antichrist (Jesus)   8/26/95 Vol. 3
satellite nuclear accident,prayer (Jesus)   9/19/97 Vol. 8
satellite to see universe (Jesus)   9/12/02 Vol. 28
satellite communications coordinates terrorists (Jesus)   8/27/07 Vol. 48
satellite communications precursor to Antichrist (Jesus)   1/13/00 Vol. 18
satellite killer devices warfare extended to space (Jesus)   9/29/04 Vol. 36
satellite laser for killing satellites (Jesus)   2/21/06 Vol. 42
satellite reference direction to Jesus needed (Jesus)   12/20/99 Vol. 17
satellite systems to control mark of beast (Jesus)   11/24/99 Vol. 17
satellite weapon can attack cities (Jesus)   3/24/06 Vol. 42
satellites Antichrist (Jesus)   7/28/95 Vol. 3
satellites chips and banks (Jesus)   6/19/97 Vol. 7
satellites connect smart chips (Jesus)   1/31/00 Vol. 18
satellites controlled by (Jesus)   4/30/98 Vol. 11
satellites coordinated for global use (Jesus)   5/29/02 Vol. 27
satellites for spying (Jesus)   6/1/04 Vol. 35
satellites for surveillance (Jesus)   9/26/96 Vol. 4
satellites have all land mapped for use (Jesus)   8/29/01 Vol. 24
satellites low orbit surveillance (Jesus)   10/24/96 Vol. 5
satellites low orbits (Jesus)   5/1/97 Vol. 7
satellites monitor your calls (Jesus)   7/24/97 Vol. 8
satellites natural disruptions (Jesus)   5/26/98 Vol. 11
satellites nuclear contamination (Jesus)   6/19/97 Vol. 7
satellites part of one world control (Jesus)   6/13/00 Vol. 19
satellites scanning people (Jesus)   6/20/97 Vol. 7
satellites signs and wonders,Antichrist (Jesus)   7/27/98 Vol. 12
satellites tracking of cars,chips (Jesus)   5/12/97 Vol. 7
satellites,banks to control buying & selling (Jesus)   6/25/99 Vol. 15
satellites,low orbitting new communications,chip (Jesus)   4/23/97 Vol. 7
satisfaction of soul found in presence of Jesus (Jesus)   4/24/00 Vol. 19
save souls by prayers, encouragement (Jesus)   5/23/07 Vol. 47
save souls encouraged by Maria, heaven (Mary)   12/12/07 Vol. 49
save spiritual life by losing earthly life (Jesus)   8/29/99 Vol. 16
saving requirements Jesus Savior, forgive sins (Jesus)   11/9/98 Vol. 13
saving souls a lasting benefit (Jesus)   5/16/02 Vol. 27
saving souls better than saving lives (Jesus)   2/15/01 Vol. 22
saving souls eternal reward for (Jesus)   10/20/06 Vol. 45
saving souls fame and fortune (Jesus)   6/30/96 Vol. 33

saving souls heaven rejoices over (Jesus)   9/16/99 Vol. 16
saving souls most important duty (Jesus)   2/6/05 Vol. 38
saving souls most rewarding work (Jesus)   1/22/07 Vol. 46
saving souls top priority (St. Therese)   10/1/97 Vol. 9
saving,praying for soul most spiritual satisfaction (Jesus) 12/30/06 Vol. 45
Savior accept to be saved (Jesus)   2/13/99 Vol. 14
Savior & forgiveness needed to be saved (Jesus)   9/3/01 Vol. 24
Savior & forgiveness needed to gain heaven (Jesus)   3/3/02 Vol. 26
Savior & Redeemer Jesus as a man (Jesus)   12/26/05 Vol. 41
Savior, accept as sets us free from sin (Jesus)   4/1/01 Vol. 23
scales of justice on side of evil (Jesus)   1/29/98 Vol. 10
scales of justice weighing against America (Jesus)   10/23/98 Vol. 13
scandal in Church priest's bad example (Jesus)   7/17/07 Vol. 48
scandal in Church protect souls from being violated (Jesus) 9/3/04 Vol. 36
scandal in Church Satan's attack (Jesus)   4/10/02 Vol. 27
scandal in the Church homosexual problem (Jesus)   7/30/05 Vol. 40
scandal of Church exploited by media (Jesus)   4/21/02 Vol. 27
scanning intrusion of privacy (Jesus)   2/27/04 Vol. 34
scapular and mantle of protection (Jesus)   10/14/97 Vol. 9
scapular asked to wear (Jesus)   10/7/03 Vol. 33
scapular promise of salvation (Mary)   5/22/97 Vol. 7
scapular & rosary devotions (Mary)   7/21/01 Vol. 24
scapular, brown flames of hell avoided by (Mary)   7/17/96 Vol. 4
scapulars for protection (Mary)   9/6/97 Vol. 8
Scarantino Wedding sacrament of marriage (Jesus)   9/5/98 Vol. 12
Schaefer, Bob Queenship Publisher,funeral (Jesus)   12/22/04 Vol. 37
Schiavo, Terry euthanasia,quality of life (Jesus)   3/31/05 Vol. 38
schism above & below ground church (Jesus)   9/22/03 Vol. 32
schism angels guide,proper Mass (Jesus)   11/9/97 Vol. 9
schism as John Paul II leaves (Jesus)   1/26/99 Vol. 14
schism authority in Church (Jesus)   9/10/97 Vol. 8
schism battle of good and evil (Jesus)   6/22/98 Vol. 11
schism break from John Paul II (Jesus)   11/7/97 Vol. 9
schism caused by divisions in Church (Jesus)   5/4/00 Vol. 19
schism church   10/6/93 Vol. 1
schism churches (Jesus)   5/6/94 Vol. 1
schism coming soon in Church (Jesus)   9/28/98 Vol. 12
schism decision of priests, laity (Jesus)   6/15/98 Vol. 11
schism desolation in Church (Jesus)   1/3/03 Vol. 30
schism faithful underground (Jesus)   8/25/97 Vol. 8
schism go to underground Masses (Jesus)   9/3/98 Vol. 12
schism hide from persecution (Jesus)   3/23/98 Vol. 10
schism hold traditional teachings (Jesus)   2/25/99 Vol. 14
schism is already present (Jesus)   2/3/99 Vol. 14
schism know old Bibles & catechism (Jesus)   8/25/98 Vol. 12
schism laity,priests choose sides (Jesus)   11/4/98 Vol. 13
schism masonic elements (Jesus)   10/13/97 Vol. 9

schism masons stripping reverence (Jesus) 7/15/02 Vol. 28
schism Mass underground (Jesus) 6/7/99 Vol. 15
schism miracles to protect faithful (Jesus) 4/28/99 Vol. 15
schism modernism vs remnant (Jesus) 10/5/96 Vol. 5
schism money & social events (Jesus) 1/12/98 Vol. 10
schism New Age & sexual sins (Jesus) 10/31/02 Vol. 29
schism Pope John Paul II (Jesus) 9/3/96 Vol. 4
schism pope removed (Jesus) 9/26/96 Vol. 4
schism pray for clergy (Mary) 9/8/98 Vol. 12
schism priests (Jesus) 2/19/96 Vol. 3
schism remain faithful (Jesus) 7/20/02 Vol. 28
schism remnant, save books (Jesus) 5/30/96 Vol. 3
schism save your souls (Jesus) 6/29/96 Vol. 3
schism sign of end times (Jesus) 7/13/03 Vol. 32
Schism trust in protection, angels (Jesus) 9/27/97 Vol. 8
schism underground church (Jesus) 9/17/03 Vol. 32
schism underground Church (Jesus) 3/20/97 Vol. 6
schism underground church (Jesus) 10/24/97 Vol. 9
schism underground Church (Jesus) 5/22/98 Vol. 11
schism underground Mass (Jesus) 4/16/98 Vol. 11
schism underground Masses (Jesus) 2/8/98 Vol. 10
schism underground Masses (Jesus) 1/11/98 Vol. 10
schism underground Masses (Jesus) 4/7/98 Vol. 11
schism when sexual sins denied (Jesus) 7/4/02 Vol. 28
schism will take over Churches (Jesus) 11/3/97 Vol. 9
schism with home Masses (Jesus) 2/2/99 Vol. 14
schism with New Age in churches (Jesus) 7/6/04 Vol. 36
schism woman ordained in Rochester (Jesus) 11/17/01 Vol. 25
schism & scandals test of faith (Jesus) 6/17/02 Vol. 27
schism in Church exile of faithful remnant (Jesus) 6/27/02 Vol. 27
schism in Church New Age vs. faithful remnant (Jesus) 8/7/06 Vol. 44
schism in Church sign of tribulation (Jesus) 11/22/99 Vol. 17
schismatic church agenda of one world people (Jesus) 4/27/03 Vol. 31
schismatic church attacks on messages (Jesus) 3/31/08 Vol. 50
schismatic church denial of sexual sins (Jesus) 4/21/07 Vol. 47
schismatic church division in Church (Jesus) 11/18/05 Vol. 41
schismatic church New Age teachings (Jesus) 6/22/06 Vol. 43
schismatic church New Age,no sexual sins (Jesus) 5/18/07 Vol. 47
schismatic church New Age,no sins,Real Presence (Jesus) 8/20/04 Vol. 36
schismatic Church not following teachings (Jesus) 5/8/02 Vol. 27
schismatic church persecution in (Jesus) 7/15/03 Vol. 32
schismatic Church sexual sins accepted as ok (Jesus) 6/27/02 Vol. 27
schismatic church to worship idols, beast (Jesus) 12/29/05 Vol. 41
schismatic church traitor present (Jesus) 5/24/07 Vol. 47
schismatic church vs. faithful remnant (Jesus) 7/20/03 Vol. 32
schismatic church vs. faithful remnant (Jesus) 12/14/05 Vol. 41
schismatic church vs. faithful remnant (Jesus) 5/9/07 Vol. 47

schismatic church vs. faithful remnant (Jesus) 11/6/07 Vol. 49
schismatic church with New Age mentality (Jesus) 7/7/02 Vol. 28
schismatic churches avoid, go to homes,refuges (Jesus) 11/10/04 Vol. 37
schismatic churches cause to go to homes, refuges (Jesus) 9/25/04 Vol. 36
Schoen, Betty funeral message (Jesus) 12/5/06 Vol. 45
school killings lack of love, no example (Jesus) 5/13/99 Vol. 15
school problems pray for teachers (Jesus) 5/11/06 Vol. 43
school sexual abuse by peers, teachers (Jesus) 5/11/06 Vol. 43
school shooting caused by evil or chips (Jesus) 10/3/06 Vol. 45
school shootings death culture put in kids (Jesus) 3/9/01 Vol. 22
school terrorism smart card security (Jesus) 9/7/99 Vol. 16
school violence sign of poor parents,TV (Jesus) 3/8/01 Vol. 22
schools do not take God out (Jesus) 2/25/98 Vol. 10
schools New Eve 11/10/93 Vol. 1
schools,churches closing low attendance,few priests (Jesus) 1/24/08 Vol. 50
science complicates choices (Jesus) 6/17/02 Vol. 27
science genes & chromosomes (Jesus) 8/2/01 Vol. 24
science knowledge as god (Jesus) 4/24/96 Vol. 3
science worshipped as a god (Jesus) 9/20/96 Vol. 4
science advances humility (Jesus) 7/13/94 Vol. 2
science as a god by inventions, knowledge (Jesus) 4/4/01 Vol. 23
science, use of driven by financial gain (Jesus) 3/12/01 Vol. 22
scientific advances praised more than God (Jesus) 7/19/07 Vol. 48
scientist analyzes the Shroud (Jesus) 3/24/98 Vol. 10
scientists believe their own theories (Jesus) 1/26/04 Vol. 34
Scripture promise proof of Jesus' rising (Mark) 4/14/99 Vol. 15
scoffers to pay as Great Flood victims (Jesus) 3/15/00 Vol. 18
scorching heat,fires cause of much damage (Jesus) 5/26/00 Vol. 19
scorpions come out of love or fear (Jesus) 8/18/96 Vol. 4
scorpions as horses plagues (Jesus) 1/2/96 Vol. 3
scribing messages mission of love accepted (Jesus) 9/30/99 Vol. 16
Scripture accounts after Jesus' death (Jesus) 2/26/04 Vol. 34
Scripture center of life (Jesus) 5/15/02 Vol. 27
scripture daily (Jesus) 7/29/95 Vol. 3
scripture decision (Jesus) 5/5/94 Vol. 1
Scripture do not distort His Word (Jesus) 2/28/04 Vol. 34
Scripture eager for Good News (Jesus) 6/9/02 Vol. 27
Scripture foretells of end times (Jesus) 9/22/03 Vol. 32
Scripture fulfilled (Jesus) 12/26/96 Vol. 5
Scripture fulfilled promise of coming (Jesus) 12/16/01 Vol. 25
scripture fulfilled to last detail (Jesus) 12/7/97 Vol. 9
Scripture fulfills Jesus' coming (Jesus) 12/22/00 Vol. 21
scripture God's Will 10/27/93 Vol. 1
Scripture has answers of life (Jesus) 4/23/01 Vol. 23
Scripture has to be fulfilled (Jesus) 7/10/99 Vol. 16
Scripture His truth to follow (Jesus) 6/23/04 Vol. 35
Scripture inspired by the Holy Spirit (Jesus) 7/15/98 Vol. 12

Scripture interpreted by the Church (Jesus) — 7/15/98 Vol. 12
Scripture is word of truth (Jesus) — 10/6/06 Vol. 45
Scripture judge those misleading (Jesus) — 3/30/01 Vol. 22
Scripture liberties taken, translation (Jesus) — 2/9/99 Vol. 14
Scripture live out Word (Jesus) — 8/26/00 Vol. 20
Scripture live the Word by example (Jesus) — 6/27/04 Vol. 35
Scripture means of salvation (Jesus) — 4/4/02 Vol. 27
Scripture must be fulfilled (St. Joseph) — 3/19/98 Vol. 10
Scripture not myths (Jesus) — 10/4/97 Vol. 9
scripture popes (Jesus) — 9/30/95 Vol. 3
Scripture prophecies fulfilled in Jesus (Jesus) — 5/6/03 Vol. 31
Scripture prophecies fulfilled now (Jesus) — 6/29/04 Vol. 35
Scripture read daily (Jesus) — 10/14/99 Vol. 17
Scripture read each day (Jesus) — 11/14/96 Vol. 5
Scripture read to benefit soul (Jesus) — 2/15/99 Vol. 14
Scripture read, study,live (Jesus) — 2/20/99 Vol. 14
Scripture revelation of how to gain heaven (Jesus) — 2/24/02 Vol. 26
Scripture saints (Jesus) — 10/12/95 Vol. 3
Scripture saints (Jesus) — 5/7/95 Vol. 2
Scripture second coming (Jesus) — 3/29/95 Vol. 2
Scripture suffer (Jesus) — 4/6/94 Vol. 1
Scripture to be fulfilled in Jesus' coming (Jesus) — 4/14/04 Vol. 35
Scripture to help lead life (Jesus) — 4/28/02 Vol. 27
Scripture to live by (Jesus) — 11/16/01 Vol. 25
scripture will (God the Father) — 3/18/94 Vol. 1
Scripture Word is true (Jesus) — 12/29/96 Vol. 5
Scripture words being changed (Jesus) — 3/22/03 Vol. 30
scripture fulfilled 1st & 2nd Covenants (Jesus) — 4/16/96 Vol. 3
Scripture fulfilled Antichrist's brief rule (Jesus) — 1/27/99 Vol. 14
Scripture prophecies fulfilled in end times (Jesus) — 11/28/07 Vol. 49
Scripture reading need to live your faith (Jesus) — 7/28/00 Vol. 20
Scripture reading read daily (Jesus) — 7/2/04 Vol. 36
Scripture,Word of live out belief in (Jesus) — 3/14/00 Vol. 18
Scriptures fulfilled by Jesus (Jesus) — 1/8/98 Vol. 10
Scriptures knowledge of Word (Jesus) — 6/22/96 Vol. 3
Scriptures Light of His Word (Jesus) — 3/26/98 Vol. 10
Scriptures must be fulfilled (Jesus) — 3/3/97 Vol. 6
Scriptures promised a redeemer (Jesus) — 11/27/00 Vol. 21
scriptures read daily (Jesus) — 1/4/97 Vol. 6
Scriptures needed to know God better (Jesus) — 2/26/00 Vol. 18
Scriptures reveal all necessary for salvation (Jesus) — 11/25/00 Vol. 21
sea of life calmed by Jesus (Jesus) — 6/7/07 Vol. 47
Seal of Living God protection from Antichrist (Jesus) — 4/2/03 Vol. 31
seals of Revelation opened (Jesus) — 10/7/06 Vol. 45
search for life dangers of exploration (Jesus) — 6/16/03 Vol. 31
seashore living high financial risk (Jesus) — 3/23/06 Vol. 42
seasons reminder of cycle of life (Jesus) — 6/13/07 Vol. 47

seasons changes nature's way of remodeling (Jesus) — 3/8/01 Vol. 22
seats,kneelers skewed hearts far from Jesus (Jesus) — 5/25/00 Vol. 19
second coming angels announce purify (Jesus) — 4/4/96 Vol. 3
second coming Annunciation (Mary) — 3/25/96 Vol. 3
second coming Antichrist,warning,book (Jesus) — 4/15/96 Vol. 3
Second Coming be always ready (Jesus) — 11/29/98 Vol. 13
Second coming be prepared (Jesus) — 12/7/97 Vol. 9
Second Coming be prepared (Mary) — 6/21/97 Vol. 7
second coming be watchmen,do not know time (Jesus) — 5/11/02 Vol. 27
second coming Calvaries (Jesus) — 10/24/93 Vol. 1
second coming conversion of sinners (Jesus) — 4/1/96 Vol. 3
Second Coming convert, prepare (Jesus) — 11/9/96 Vol. 5
Second Coming earthquake, sign of (Jesus) — 12/31/96 Vol. 5
second coming end times (Jesus) — 11/26/94 Vol. 2
second coming evangelize (Mary) — 4/3/96 Vol. 3
second coming evil age (Jesus) — 5/13/96 Vol. 3
second coming judgment — 10/27/93 Vol. 1
Second Coming Mary is preparing for (Mary) — 4/23/98 Vol. 11
Second Coming messages stopping (Mary) — 1/30/97 Vol. 6
Second Coming more people sense (Jesus) — 9/19/02 Vol. 28
Second Coming on clouds of glory (Jesus) — 1/30/98 Vol. 10
second coming parallels first coming (Jesus) — 11/18/99 Vol. 17
second coming peace on earth (Jesus) — 8/24/95 Vol. 3
second coming persecution (Jesus) — 10/9/94 Vol. 2
second coming prayer (Jesus) — 11/28/93 Vol. 1
second coming prepare (Jesus) — 9/25/95 Vol. 3
Second Coming prepare for (Mary) — 9/6/98 Vol. 12
Second coming prepare for by confession (Jesus) — 12/29/97 Vol. 9
Second Coming prepare souls for (Jesus) — 12/1/02 Vol. 29
Second Coming prepare souls now (Jesus) — 7/22/98 Vol. 12
Second coming prepare with confession (Mary) — 11/13/97 Vol. 9
second coming purification (Mary) — 2/11/94 Vol. 1
second coming remnant (Jesus) — 11/21/93 Vol. 1
second coming repent — 10/7/93 Vol. 1
Second Coming role of Mary & Holy Spirit in (Jesus) — 4/12/98 Vol. 11
Second Coming seeing many signs of (Jesus) — 12/2/01 Vol. 25
Second Coming sign in apparitions (Jesus) — 8/15/00 Vol. 20
second coming signs (Mary) — 11/5/95 Vol. 3
Second Coming signs of the end times (Jesus) — 11/26/96 Vol. 5
Second Coming special presence (Jesus) — 12/19/96 Vol. 5
second coming statues (Mary) — 10/20/93 Vol. 1
Second Coming triumph over the earth (Jesus) — 7/12/98 Vol. 12
Second coming trumpets,scroll unleashed (Jesus) — 12/10/97 Vol. 9
Second Coming unrepentant hurled to hell (Jesus) — 11/14/97 Vol. 9
second coming warning (Jesus) — 11/13/94 Vol. 2
Second Coming weather as a sign (Jesus) — 1/10/97 Vol. 6
second coming signs proud to be humbled (Mary) — 11/23/99 Vol. 17

secrecy of rich men who controls finances (Jesus) 5/11/00 Vol. 19

secret discoveries for weapons & control (Jesus) 6/24/00 Vol. 19

secret meetings battle of good and evil (Jesus) 2/20/95 Vol. 2

secret one world people agenda to control money (Jesus) 6/24/00 Vol. 19

secret sins seen by God (Jesus) 5/26/05 Vol. 39

secret societies follow Satan (Jesus) 10/10/06 Vol. 45

secrets Confession (Jesus) 9/26/94 Vol. 2

secrets of good and evil (Jesus) 7/7/02 Vol. 28

secrets reparation (Mary) 7/20/95 Vol. 3

secrets revealed soon (Mary) 6/19/97 Vol. 7

secular things leave you empty,cold (Jesus) 11/7/98 Vol. 13

security control by smart cards (Jesus) 3/28/06 Vol. 42

security in God and not gold (Jesus) 12/20/02 Vol. 29

security not found in earthly things (Jesus) 2/19/00 Vol. 18

security at airports still lax (Jesus) 9/14/04 Vol. 36

security lull then more terrorist attacks (Jesus) 3/25/02 Vol. 26

security requirements to need mandatory smart cards (Jesus) 9/28/04 Vol. 36

security vs. privacy freedom vs. captives (Jesus) 1/13/06 Vol. 42

Seder Supper Passover-Mass preview (Jesus) 7/20/07 Vol. 48

seed as Word of God choked by fame,riches (Jesus) 8/1/00 Vol. 20

seed as Word of God which seed are you? (Jesus) 8/10/04 Vol. 36

seed dies to grow soul needs to die to self (Jesus) 5/25/06 Vol. 43

seed of faith allow growth in Jesus (Jesus) 6/3/03 Vol. 31

seed of faith needed for conversion (Jesus) 5/6/04 Vol. 35

Seed of God's 'Word planted in our hearts. (Jesus) 6/30/00 Vol. 19

seed of life should not be abused (Jesus) 9/18/04 Vol. 36

Seed of Life violated in abortions (Jesus) 6/30/00 Vol. 19

seeds use non-hybrid (Jesus) 1/14/08 Vol. 50

seeds of faith gamble souls will love God (Jesus) 6/27/02 Vol. 27

seeds, non-hybrid needed for future seed (Jesus) 2/29/08 Vol. 50

seek peace (Jesus) 2/10/94 Vol. 1

seek and find through power of God (Jesus) 3/10/01 Vol. 22

seek heaven first earthly things less important (Jesus) 9/10/01 Vol. 24

seek heavenly honors not worldly prestige (Jesus) 3/22/00 Vol. 18

seek kingdom of God let earthly things be last (Jesus) 2/15/01 Vol. 22

Segrue, Shirley funeral message (Shirley Segrue) 12/14/06 Vol. 45

self denial TV,abortions (Jesus) 3/22/95 Vol. 2

self emptied rid pride, selfishness (Jesus) 12/21/99 Vol. 17

self image,new rid old habits (Jesus) 3/30/00 Vol. 18

self-centered God-centered (Jesus) 1/1/95 Vol. 2

self-centered,prideful need to give will to God (Jesus) 5/26/00 Vol. 19

self-control bodily habits, excesses (Jesus) 8/7/97 Vol. 8

self-control needed to overcome sins (Jesus) 9/12/07 Vol. 48

self-denial in Lenten penances (Jesus) 3/25/07 Vol. 46

selfish die to self (Jesus) 4/8/96 Vol. 3

selfish spirit give over to God's Will (Jesus) 11/24/00 Vol. 21

selfish wealth help needy (Jesus) 9/23/99 Vol. 16

selfishness cares of the world (Jesus) 8/28/96 Vol. 4

selfishness change by love and mercy (Jesus) 6/12/01 Vol. 23

selfishness cleanse from life (Jesus) 4/25/01 Vol. 23

selfishness cure by good deeds (Jesus) 1/24/01 Vol. 22

selfishness do not refuse to help poor (Jesus) 1/10/02 Vol. 26

selfishness freedom (Jesus) 3/20/94 Vol. 1

selfishness give to the poor (Jesus) 2/27/04 Vol. 34

selfishness help those in need (Jesus) 1/29/98 Vol. 10

selfishness hours wasted (Jesus) 4/16/04 Vol. 35

selfishness love God & neighbor (Jesus) 12/11/97 Vol. 9

selfishness love God and neighbor (Jesus) 10/9/97 Vol. 9

selfishness love is unrestrained (Jesus) 10/29/97 Vol. 9

selfishness needs rooting out (Jesus) 3/10/00 Vol. 18

selfishness no room for God (Jesus) 3/11/98 Vol. 10

selfishness & greed do not be controlled by (Jesus) 4/9/03 Vol. 31

selfishness vs. love take 'I' out of picture (Jesus) 3/14/01 Vol. 22

selfless love widow's mite,give last meal (Jesus) 11/11/00 Vol. 21

self-love,pride change to love of neighbor (Jesus) 5/29/00 Vol. 19

seminaries cleansed of wrong teaching (Jesus) 5/2/02 Vol. 27

seminaries closed because of liberalism (Jesus) 5/1/02 Vol. 27

seminaries undermined (Jesus) 6/14/02 Vol. 27

seminaries with false teachings (Jesus) 4/10/02 Vol. 27

seminary teachers need prayers not praise (Jesus) 5/25/00 Vol. 19

sense of sin lost because of no morals (Jesus) 5/29/04 Vol. 35

separation church & state concocted notion (God the Father) 8/20/03 Vol. 32

separation church & state court's rulings (Mary) 8/28/03 Vol. 32

separation church & state promotes atheism (Jesus) 8/21/03 Vol. 32

separation Church,State loss of freedoms (Jesus) 5/10/97 Vol. 7

separation,church&state ruled by madness (Jesus) 8/28/98 Vol. 12

September 11th attack why allowed? (Jesus) 1/29/02 Vol. 26

September 11th peace then sudden destruction (Jesus) 12/14/01 Vol. 25

September 11th gaps & questions (Jesus) 7/25/03 Vol. 32

September 11th thousands dead (Jesus) 2/24/03 Vol. 30

September 11th mood another coming to church (Jesus) 3/10/04 Vol. 34

serious sin reverence (Jesus) 6/13/95 Vol. 2

serpent forgiveness (Jesus) 8/4/94 Vol. 2

serpent makes evil look good (Jesus) 2/12/99 Vol. 14

serpent head,metal Satan attacking messengers (Jesus) 9/17/01 Vol. 24

serpentine road broad road to hell (Jesus) 7/26/05 Vol. 40

servant evangelize (Jesus) 9/20/94 Vol. 2

serve know, love Me (Jesus) 4/12/01 Vol. 23

serve with humble,contrite hearts (Jesus) 8/29/98 Vol. 12

serve God or self Jesus as Master,consecration (Jesus) 3/25/02 Vol. 26

serve the rest to gain banquet in heaven (Jesus) 11/3/02 Vol. 29

serve your neighbor service witnessed by Jesus (Jesus) 12/29/98 Vol. 13

service call of disciples (Jesus) 7/10/99 Vol. 16

service duty (Jesus) 11/14/95 Vol. 3

service family love (Carm Y.) — 12/23/95 Vol. 3

service in world, not of it (Jesus) — 9/24/98 Vol. 12

service sharing time and gifts (Jesus) — 7/23/96 Vol. 4

service to prepare Easter meals (Jesus) — 4/2/04 Vol. 35

service to God example in Mary (Jesus) — 8/22/05 Vol. 40

service to God in everyday actions (Jesus) — 8/24/05 Vol. 40

servicemen avoid working with UN (Jesus) — 8/13/98 Vol. 12

serving God choice of heaven or hell (Jesus) — 3/9/04 Vol. 34

serving God lifelong commitment (Jesus) — 3/23/08 Vol. 50

serving God real decision (Jesus) — 11/1/01 Vol. 25

serving in faith call of every disciple (Jesus) — 5/6/00 Vol. 19

serving Jesus will care for our needs (Jesus) — 2/18/03 Vol. 30

sewage with storms causes disease,epidemics (Jesus) — 9/29/98 Vol. 12

sex before and during marriage (Jesus) — 1/7/01 Vol. 22

sex outside of marriage mortal sin,need Confession (Jesus) — 2/10/01 Vol. 22

sex, drugs, TV sins getting worse (Jesus) — 5/29/02 Vol. 27

sexual abuse by priests, pray for (Jesus) — 5/2/02 Vol. 27

sexual acts only proper in marriage (Jesus) — 10/22/00 Vol. 21

sexual perversions an abomination (Jesus) — 5/6/98 Vol. 11

sexual sins adultery, fornication (Jesus) — 6/10/01 Vol. 23

sexual sins adultery,fornication (Jesus) — 3/9/97 Vol. 6

sexual sins affect families (Jesus) — 2/8/07 Vol. 46

sexual sins are grave sins (Jesus) — 8/18/06 Vol. 44

sexual sins are mortal sins (Jesus) — 10/18/02 Vol. 29

sexual sins avoid places of (Jesus) — 5/8/06 Vol. 43

sexual sins bring us to knees with disasters (Jesus) — 7/23/05 Vol. 40

sexual sins death to the soul (Jesus) — 4/28/05 Vol. 39

sexual sins defy Commandments (Jesus) — 1/18/03 Vol. 30

sexual sins denied in schism (Jesus) — 7/15/02 Vol. 28

sexual sins kill soul (Jesus) — 5/22/02 Vol. 27

sexual sins mistaught as not mortal sins (Jesus) — 5/28/00 Vol. 19

sexual sins mortal,abuse seed of life (Jesus) — 9/18/04 Vol. 36

sexual sins most dangerous sins for soul (Jesus) — 5/15/04 Vol. 35

sexual sins need Confession (Jesus) — 8/1/06 Vol. 44

sexual sins need forgiveness in Confession (Jesus) — 5/19/04 Vol. 35

sexual sins need to be confessed (Jesus) — 4/12/06 Vol. 43

sexual sins not recognized as sin (Jesus) — 8/1/02 Vol. 28

sexual sins obey 6th Commandment (Jesus) — 12/22/05 Vol. 41

sexual sins reason for chastisements (Jesus) — 6/8/03 Vol. 31

sexual sins require life change to God (Jesus) — 1/26/05 Vol. 38

sexual sins send more souls to hell (Jesus) — 9/23/03 Vol. 32

sexual sins sign of division (Jesus) — 2/14/03 Vol. 30

sexual sins speak out against (Jesus) — 5/26/05 Vol. 39

sexual sins threat to family (Jesus) — 8/8/99 Vol. 16

sexual sins why most are in hell (Jesus) — 1/5/07 Vol. 46

sexual sins worsened (Jesus) — 8/2/01 Vol. 24

sexual sins denied avoid such teachers (Jesus) — 7/6/04 Vol. 36

shackles bury sins, love Me (Jesus) — 3/13/97 Vol. 6

shackles in train cars (Jesus) — 8/30/06 Vol. 44

shackles freed by Jesus' death (Jesus) — 12/25/98 Vol. 13

shame for sin do not forget (Jesus) — 2/3/05 Vol. 38

shame, no sense of for sins of the flesh (Jesus) — 7/29/98 Vol. 12

Shamon, Fr.,funeral tribute and words (Fr. Shamon) — 11/25/03 Vol. 33

share faith & wealth generously (Jesus) — 10/11/05 Vol. 41

share excess, want with neighbor (Jesus) — 5/29/00 Vol. 19

share from heart sincere charity (Jesus) — 6/19/07 Vol. 47

share gifts fabric of life (Jesus) — 10/26/02 Vol. 29

share love,wealth test at judgment (Jesus) — 9/7/01 Vol. 24

share money with others in hard times (Jesus) — 5/24/04 Vol. 35

share things with neighbor out of love (Jesus) — 12/9/03 Vol. 33

share treasures riches in heaven (Jesus) — 8/1/03 Vol. 32

share with others time & donations (Jesus) — 5/7/04 Vol. 35

share with poor in time and money (Jesus) — 12/23/02 Vol. 29

share your wealth help the poor,avoid avarice (Jesus) — 6/5/00 Vol. 19

shared love marriage similar to God's love (Jesus) — 9/4/04 Vol. 36

sharing change selfish hearts (Jesus) — 7/22/01 Vol. 24

sharing good deeds (Jesus) — 3/30/95 Vol. 2

sharing life & needs with others (Jesus) — 5/25/05 Vol. 39

sharing possessions (Jesus) — 6/21/95 Vol. 2

sharing share possessions (Jesus) — 8/2/98 Vol. 12

sharing time, money, & faith (Jesus) — 10/19/03 Vol. 33

sharing & donations time and money (Jesus) — 6/5/99 Vol. 15

sharing faith responsibility to teach neighbor (Jesus) — 2/22/02 Vol. 26

sharing gifts store heavenly treasures (Jesus) — 11/25/99 Vol. 17

sharing love brings God's kingdom (Jesus) — 11/11/99 Vol. 17

sharing wealth money less control over you (Jesus) — 12/21/04 Vol. 37

sharing, consecration help others in need (Jesus) — 11/24/05 Vol. 41

sharing, donations at Thanksgiving (Jesus) — 11/14/02 Vol. 29

Shea, Jack's rosary grateful to faithful (Jesus) — 6/11/99 Vol. 15

sheep folds listen to His voice (Jesus) — 4/22/02 Vol. 27

Sheepgate Jesus path to eternal life (Jesus) — 4/25/99 Vol. 15

shelter shared open heart to Jesus (Jesus) — 12/20/99 Vol. 17

shelter, spiritual call on Jesus' help for trials (Jesus) — 2/28/02 Vol. 26

shelters help house the poor (Jesus) — 7/28/05 Vol. 40

shelters in the hills flee the cities for survival (Jesus) — 10/20/98 Vol. 13

shelters like pagodas at refuges (Jesus) — 2/3/05 Vol. 38

shelters multiplied at refuges (Jesus) — 2/3/05 Vol. 38

Sheol Jesus went to save souls (Jesus) — 4/9/06 Vol. 43

shepherd protection from wolves (Jesus) — 12/26/96 Vol. 5

Shepherd in Jesus will lead us to heaven (Jesus) — 12/26/01 Vol. 25

shepherds faithful to save souls (Jesus) — 6/8/06 Vol. 43

shepherds moral issues (Jesus) — 1/17/94 Vol. 1

Sherlock Holmes' hat British Intelligence alert (Jesus) — 8/27/07 Vol. 48

shield of Jesus rely on His help to win (Jesus) — 7/3/00 Vol. 20

Shine baptism young people need faith (Jesus) 12/8/02 Vol. 29

ships as spiritual lessons (Jesus) 12/8/99 Vol. 17

Shirley Segrue funeral message (Shirley Segrue) 12/14/06 Vol. 45

shoes contribute to help the poor (Jesus) 7/28/05 Vol. 40

shooting star sign of coming disasters (Jesus) 3/5/08 Vol. 50

shopkeepers think money, not Christmas (Jesus) 12/22/07 Vol. 49

shortages food and water (Jesus) 8/28/96 Vol. 4

shortages,necessities get prepared (Jesus) 3/10/99 Vol. 14

shovel take into hiding, dig caves (Jesus) 6/16/98 Vol. 11

Shrine of Miracles of Christ Austin, Texas (Jesus) 8/19/06 Vol. 44

Shrine of Two Hearts Hinckley,Ohio,pool vision (Jesus) 9/8/01 Vol. 24

shrines blessings & signs (Mary) 1/16/97 Vol. 6

shrines graces (Mary) 1/24/96 Vol. 3

shrines Pope / fires (Mary) 12/13/95 Vol. 3

shrines triumph of two hearts (Mary) 6/27/96 Vol. 3

shrines of Our Lady vs shrines of evil (Mary) 7/14/02 Vol. 28

shroud suffering servant (Jesus) 2/23/97 Vol. 6

Shroud of Turin burst of energy (Jesus) 4/7/07 Vol. 47

Shroud of Turin caused by Resurrection (Jesus) 3/13/05 Vol. 38

Shroud of Turin formed by burst of energy (Jesus) 4/11/98 Vol. 11

Shroud of Turin formed by Light of Resurrection (Jesus) 4/10/04 Vol. 35

Shroud of Turin His true image and love (Jesus) 3/24/98 Vol. 10

Shroud of Turin pray 9/4/93 Vol. 1

Shroud of Turin proof of Resurrection (Jesus) 12/27/06 Vol. 45

Shroud of Turin proof of resurrection (Jesus) 7/3/98 Vol. 12

Shroud of Turin Resurrection (Jesus) 11/6/95 Vol. 3

Shroud of Turin Scriptures (Jesus) 4/5/95 Vol. 2

Shroud of Turin speaks words of faith (Jesus) 5/14/98 Vol. 11

Shroud of Turin swaddling clothes compared (Jesus) 12/21/00 Vol. 21

sick pray & remember (Jesus) 3/18/99 Vol. 14

sick & bereaved give comfort to (Jesus) 2/27/07 Vol. 46

sick & care-givers corporal works of mercy (Jesus) 4/3/97 Vol. 7

sick & disabled need your help (Jesus) 3/11/05 Vol. 38

sick & mourners need to be comforted (Jesus) 4/9/01 Vol. 23

sick people visit and help (Jesus) 6/14/01 Vol. 23

sick people visit with flowers,prayers (Jesus) 2/10/07 Vol. 46

sick,help the corporal work of mercy (Jesus) 3/30/00 Vol. 18

sick,sinners need doctor, priest (Jesus) 9/21/99 Vol. 16

sickness Armageddon (Jesus) 1/15/95 Vol. 2

sickness healings (Jesus) 9/6/95 Vol. 3

sickness & death sharing in Jesus' cross (Jesus) 4/8/05 Vol. 39

sickness in elderly desire to live is tested (Jesus) 4/14/04 Vol. 35

sicknesses & diseases pray for people, man's frailty (Jesus) 9/9/04 Vol. 36

sign in moon color big event coming (Jesus) 2/17/95 Vol. 2

sign in skies for war pray for peace (Jesus) 10/8/98 Vol. 13

sign of end times in weather disasters (Jesus) 1/15/04 Vol. 34

sign of Jonah call nations to repent (Jesus) 8/14/99 Vol. 16

sign of Jonah only sign for unbelievers (Jesus) 7/23/07 Vol. 48

Sign of the Cross at birth and at death (Jesus) 1/3/06 Vol. 42

sign of the cross express mail love letter (Jesus) 5/8/03 Vol. 31

Sign of the Cross in Blessed Trinity (Jesus) 1/13/08 Vol. 50

Sign of the Cross reminder of Baptism (Jesus) 3/2/04 Vol. 34

signature of God in creation (Jesus) 1/20/00 Vol. 18

signs asked for, yet not believed (Jesus) 7/20/98 Vol. 12

signs confirmation of faith (Our Lady) 8/15/07 Vol. 48

signs disasters (Jesus) 5/24/95 Vol. 2

signs Herm (Jesus) 8/13/94 Vol. 2

signs in the sky (Jesus) 4/17/96 Vol. 3

signs messages (Jesus) 5/28/95 Vol. 2

signs miraculous water (Mary) 8/26/97 Vol. 8

signs no dates, confession (Jesus) 7/31/97 Vol. 8

signs severe changes this year (Jesus) 4/1/97 Vol. 7

signs warnings (Jesus) 10/21/93 Vol. 1

signs weeping statues (Jesus) 6/19/97 Vol. 7

signs & wonders stop looking only for (Jesus) 10/10/05 Vol. 41

signs and omens red skies and fires (Jesus) 3/18/96 Vol. 3

signs for refuge famine,schism,chips in body (Jesus) 8/7/06 Vol. 44

signs in conversions rejoicing over saved souls (Jesus) 4/29/99 Vol. 15

signs in miracles healings through faith (Jesus) 4/29/99 Vol. 15

signs in sky for coming events (Jesus) 3/12/03 Vol. 30

signs in the sky and events of weather (Jesus) 2/3/04 Vol. 34

signs in the sky be attentive to (Jesus) 1/14/99 Vol. 14

signs in the sky cross (Father) 1/9/94 Vol. 1

signs in the sky for tribulation (Jesus) 6/21/01 Vol. 23

signs in the sky light before WWII (Jesus) 2/23/03 Vol. 30

signs in the sky of evil to come (Jesus) 6/20/05 Vol. 39

signs in the sky omen of things to come (Jesus) 5/14/98 Vol. 11

signs in the sky on day of the Warning (Jesus) 6/22/05 Vol. 39

signs in the sky people still will not believe (Jesus) 3/19/98 Vol. 10

signs in the sky signs of end times (Jesus) 1/27/00 Vol. 18

signs in the sky spinning sun (Jesus) 1/30/98 Vol. 10

signs in the sky Venus,Saturn aligned (Jesus) 2/25/99 Vol. 14

signs in the sky wars and tribulation (Jesus) 10/23/97 Vol. 9

signs in the sky witness end times (Jesus) 5/16/98 Vol. 11

signs of end times are all around us (Jesus) 9/11/06 Vol. 44

signs of end times coming about (Jesus) 12/1/03 Vol. 33

signs of end times floods,fires,earthquakes (Jesus) 7/9/98 Vol. 12

signs of end times increase in disasters (Jesus) 10/22/05 Vol. 41

signs of end times miracles of sun, weeping statues (Jesus) 10/21/04 Vol. 37

signs of end times more evident (Jesus) 8/5/99 Vol. 16

signs of end times open eyes to events (Jesus) 11/26/02 Vol. 29

signs of end times protection in Jesus (Jesus) 1/20/00 Vol. 18

signs of last days found in daily events (Jesus) 3/4/00 Vol. 18

signs of the time events speeded up (Jesus) 3/5/95 Vol. 2

signs of the times caused by man's own hands (Jesus)   6/15/98 Vol. 11

signs of the times in disasters (Jesus)   9/9/05 Vol. 40

signs of the times renew the earth (Jesus)   9/18/97 Vol. 8

signs of the times science & inventions (Jesus)   8/30/03 Vol. 32

signs of this age witness My coming is soon (Jesus)   11/12/98 Vol. 13

signs of times evil time will be brief (Jesus)   11/7/02 Vol. 29

signs of times read them (Jesus)   10/16/06 Vol. 45

signs of times time running out (Jesus)   10/13/05 Vol. 41

signs of times violence reflected in weather (Jesus)   8/26/98 Vol. 12

signs of tribulation famine,schism,forced chips (Jesus)   7/10/04 Vol. 36

signs of tribulation weather,earthquakes (Jesus)   6/17/99 Vol. 15

silence to help spiritual life (Jesus)   1/2/08 Vol. 50

silence in monastery helps focus on Jesus (Jesus)   6/2/07 Vol. 47

silver purified suffering,persecution needed (Jesus)   2/20/01 Vol. 22

Simeon prophecy of (Jesus)   2/2/04 Vol. 34

Simeon's prophesy Our Lady's sorrows (Mary)   2/2/98 Vol. 10

Simon image to help others (Jesus)   10/25/05 Vol. 41

simple life brings you closer to God (Jesus)   11/24/06 Vol. 45

simple life daily trust (Jesus)   2/8/03 Vol. 30

simple life faith of a child (Jesus)   3/20/06 Vol. 42

simple life goal of Jesus (Jesus)   5/5/06 Vol. 43

simple life imitate Jesus (Jesus)   12/7/00 Vol. 21

simple life less distractions (Jesus)   12/5/02 Vol. 29

simple life more pleasing to God (Jesus)   12/26/02 Vol. 29

simple life more time to pray (Jesus)   4/30/98 Vol. 11

simple life way to heaven (Jesus)   12/31/05 Vol. 41

simple life without materialism (Jesus)   6/26/05 Vol. 39

simple life needed to avoid desire of wealth (Jesus)   1/18/05 Vol. 38

simple life needed to gain heaven (Jesus)   8/11/07 Vol. 48

simple lifestyle fits lower wages (Jesus)   5/12/06 Vol. 43

simple lives, lead avoid riches & comforts (Jesus)   8/11/04 Vol. 36

simpler life needed stop rushing (Jesus)   2/14/05 Vol. 38

simpler lives seek heavenly riches (Jesus)   5/6/99 Vol. 15

sin abuse of spiritual body (Jesus)   12/22/97 Vol. 9

sin accept responsibility (Jesus)   9/25/98 Vol. 12

sin adds to Jesus' suffering (Jesus)   4/4/07 Vol. 47

sin admit pride,submit to Will (Jesus)   12/19/97 Vol. 9

sin against the Holy Spirit (Jesus)   7/9/99 Vol. 16

sin avoid occasions of (Jesus)   9/19/03 Vol. 32

sin avoid, and change life (Jesus)   12/11/04 Vol. 37

sin begets more sin (Jesus)   1/30/04 Vol. 34

sin bringing God's justice (Jesus)   10/11/07 Vol. 49

sin confession (Jesus)   6/30/94 Vol. 1

sin confession,forgiveness (Jesus)   11/20/96 Vol. 5

sin consequences & guilt (Jesus)   3/3/03 Vol. 30

sin control occasions of (Jesus)   10/23/02 Vol. 29

sin death (Jesus)   4/2/94 Vol. 1

sin defiles the soul (Jesus)   7/1/04 Vol. 36

sin effect on soul (Jesus)   9/23/02 Vol. 28

sin free will to choose (Jesus)   6/12/98 Vol. 11

sin hell (Jesus)   11/20/93 Vol. 1

sin individual and national (Jesus)   6/11/05 Vol. 39

sin is ignored & rationalized (Jesus)   6/27/05 Vol. 39

sin is way of life (Jesus)   4/12/02 Vol. 27

sin Jesus died for our sin (Jesus)   5/7/98 Vol. 11

sin keep it from getting worse (Jesus)   6/30/05 Vol. 39

sin keep track of (Jesus)   3/13/03 Vol. 30

sin lost sense of shame for (Jesus)   10/26/05 Vol. 41

sin no presence in love (Jesus)   2/21/99 Vol. 14

sin not recognized in lives (Jesus)   5/29/04 Vol. 35

sin prayer (Jesus)   5/16/95 Vol. 2

sin preach conversion (Jesus)   1/22/97 Vol. 6

sin remove control over your life (Jesus)   4/25/07 Vol. 47

sin repentance (Jesus)   12/16/93 Vol. 1

sin responsible for actions (Jesus)   3/6/98 Vol. 10

sin seduction of evil one (Jesus)   2/8/99 Vol. 14

sin snares of the devil (Jesus)   7/5/03 Vol. 32

sin spiritual laziness (Jesus)   8/23/97 Vol. 8

sin stages of temptation (Jesus)   2/24/04 Vol. 34

sin take up the cross (Jesus)   3/26/96 Vol. 3

sin that is habitual (Jesus)   12/11/01 Vol. 25

sin the wages are death (Jesus)   9/1/03 Vol. 32

sin the wages is death (Jesus)   3/26/03 Vol. 30

sin Trinity feels pain (Jesus)   4/5/04 Vol. 35

sin TV (Father)   9/27/93 Vol. 1

sin weakness to humble us (Jesus)   5/2/02 Vol. 27

sin will (Jesus)   5/23/94 Vol. 1

sin worst spiritual contamination (Jesus)   12/2/03 Vol. 33

sin & death Resurrection, victory over (Jesus)   3/22/08 Vol. 50

sin & punishment understand relationship (Jesus)   9/8/05 Vol. 40

sin addictive in dulled consciences (Jesus)   9/18/06 Vol. 44

sin against Holy Spirit unforgiving heart (Jesus)   9/15/02 Vol. 28

sin against Holy Spirit unforgiving heart (Jesus)   4/8/03 Vol. 31

sin as oil in water each nation held on abortions (Jesus)   7/20/00 Vol. 20

sin dressed up devil's tactic to disguise sin (Jesus)   3/1/02 Vol. 26

sin forgiven, more the more greatful the sinner (Jesus)   9/16/04 Vol. 36

sin like snow needs constant removal (Jesus)   2/19/00 Vol. 18

sin limited by avoiding evil movies (Jesus)   6/17/03 Vol. 31

sin rampant weather (Jesus)   8/17/94 Vol. 2

sin, addiction healed in Confession,forgiveness (Jesus)   5/17/04 Vol. 35

sin, areas of justice will fall (Jesus)   5/23/07 Vol. 47

sin, consequences of death to the soul (Jesus)   10/25/07 Vol. 49

sin, effects of Confession needed (Jesus)   1/14/06 Vol. 42

sin, everyone's Jesus took on (Jesus)   3/27/05 Vol. 38

sin, falling into see filth of sin, cleanse (Jesus)   1/17/07 Vol. 46

sin, filth of needs cleansing by Confession (Jesus)   12/16/03 Vol. 33

sin, habitual ways to correct (Jesus)   4/8/02 Vol. 27

sin, less less suffering for Jesus (Jesus)   3/19/08 Vol. 50

sin, mortal is the living dead (Jesus)   2/17/04 Vol. 34

sin, mortal needs Confession (Jesus)   4/12/02 Vol. 27

sin,disease of soul sinful lifestyle,habitual sin (Jesus)   11/2/00 Vol. 21

sin,man's weakness to repeated sins (Jesus)   4/10/01 Vol. 23

sinful behaviors never right before God (Jesus)   7/15/04 Vol. 36

sinful desires control by love of Jesus (Jesus)   4/24/07 Vol. 47

sinful habits avoid occasions of sin (Jesus)   1/3/05 Vol. 38

sinful habits be open to change (Jesus)   3/1/04 Vol. 34

sinful habits can make you prisoners of sin (Jesus)   10/21/03 Vol. 33

sinful habits how to improve life (Jesus)   9/2/05 Vol. 40

sinful habits turn life around to God (Jesus)   2/15/02 Vol. 26

sinful lifestyle please God instead of self (Jesus)   1/26/05 Vol. 38

sinful lifestyles need to change (Jesus)   1/5/07 Vol. 46

sinful souls remove clutter of sin (Jesus)   12/15/05 Vol. 41

singing praises, joy & love (Jesus)   10/10/96 Vol. 5

singing rejoice in song (Jesus)   11/15/01 Vol. 25

singing at Mass practice for heaven (Jesus)   10/5/98 Vol. 13

singing God's praises prepares you for heaven (Holy Spirit) 7/23/07 Vol. 48

singing in heaven witness to Jesus' glory (Jesus)   10/5/98 Vol. 13

singing to God only to please God (Jesus)   3/5/00 Vol. 18

singing with baton songs join your hearts (Mary)   6/5/97 Vol. 7

Sinj, Our Lady of physical & spiritual healings (Jesus)   7/15/02 Vol. 28

sinless mediatrix (Mary)   12/8/94 Vol. 2

sinlessness of Jesus & Mary (Jesus)   12/24/04 Vol. 37

sinner admit imperfections in sins (Jesus)   11/30/00 Vol. 21

sinner too comfortable to avoid sinful pleasures (Jesus)   5/18/00 Vol. 19

sinner,admit being be contrite,seek forgiveness (Jesus)   6/23/00 Vol. 19

sinner,forgiveness acceptance,conversion (Jesus)   9/21/99 Vol. 16

sinners addicts to sin (Jesus)   11/19/03 Vol. 33

sinners all called to forgiveness (Jesus)   1/14/06 Vol. 42

sinners all sin, or else they are liars (Jesus)   9/11/04 Vol. 36

sinners convert life (Jesus)   6/5/05 Vol. 39

sinners forgiveness (Jesus)   11/18/94 Vol. 2

sinners heavy price of souls (Jesus)   1/11/97 Vol. 6

sinners humbled by destruction (Jesus)   9/7/05 Vol. 40

sinners need conversion,save souls (Jesus)   12/7/04 Vol. 37

sinners need prayer, conversion (Jesus)   7/25/07 Vol. 48

sinners need repentance & prayer (Jesus)   11/29/07 Vol. 49

sinners need to admit their faults (Jesus)   10/21/00 Vol. 21

sinners need to carry own cross (Jesus)   5/9/06 Vol. 43

sinners need to repent, forgiveness (Jesus)   9/25/05 Vol. 40

sinners not abandoned by God (Jesus)   3/30/06 Vol. 42

sinners one last chance to be saved (Jesus)   6/7/07 Vol. 47

sinners salvation (Jesus)   5/6/94 Vol. 1

sinners seek forgiveness (Jesus)   3/10/05 Vol. 38

sinners seek forgiveness than despair (Jesus)   4/11/06 Vol. 43

sinners trouble admitting to be one (Jesus)   6/9/00 Vol. 19

sinners warned of their sins (Jesus)   9/4/05 Vol. 40

sinner's conversion heaven rejoices over (Jesus)   11/4/04 Vol. 37

sinner's habits Jesus forgives all sin (Jesus)   7/1/00 Vol. 20

sinners in denial wake to truth of actions (Jesus)   5/6/99 Vol. 15

sinners, poor pray for salvation (Jesus)   5/16/06 Vol. 43

sinners, pray for connection of storms to sins (Jesus)   9/15/04 Vol. 36

sins a slap in the face to Jesus (Jesus)   7/12/97 Vol. 8

sins admit them & confess (Jesus)   11/29/00 Vol. 21

sins and bad habits (Jesus)   2/9/03 Vol. 30

sins bring about war (Jesus)   7/11/05 Vol. 40

sins bring on disasters (Jesus)   10/5/05 Vol. 41

sins cannot hide from God (Jesus)   2/12/07 Vol. 46

sins confess,do not cover up (Jesus)   7/9/98 Vol. 12

sins confession (Jesus)   3/23/94 Vol. 1

sins confession,die to self (Jesus)   5/9/96 Vol. 3

sins death to the soul (Jesus)   6/8/99 Vol. 15

sins detach by prayer & fasting (Jesus)   10/30/05 Vol. 41

sins do not follow crowd (Jesus)   1/9/04 Vol. 34

sins forgiveness (Jesus)   1/27/96 Vol. 3

sins heal habitual ones (Jesus)   3/6/07 Vol. 46

sins Jesus continues to suffer (Jesus)   1/12/98 Vol. 10

sins Jesus still suffers (Jesus)   7/19/97 Vol. 8

sins nations held accountable for (Jesus)   7/18/06 Vol. 44

sins of omission (Jesus)   9/23/06 Vol. 44

sins of omission,be gracious (Jesus)   2/27/97 Vol. 6

sins offend you as garbage (Jesus)   11/12/99 Vol. 17

sins reparation for now or later (Jesus)   4/7/03 Vol. 31

sins reparation needed (Jesus)   7/29/02 Vol. 28

sins reparation on earth, purgatory (Jesus)   10/24/03 Vol. 33

sins scorching the earth (Jesus)   10/24/96 Vol. 5

sins strike Jesus (Jesus)   3/22/05 Vol. 38

sins stripped of possessions (Jesus)   6/10/99 Vol. 15

sins suffering/cross/purgatory (Jesus)   5/3/96 Vol. 3

sins USA (Mary)   12/8/93 Vol. 1

sins & actions each soul responsible for (Jesus)   5/29/04 Vol. 35

sins & bad habits bury in Jesus' tomb (Jesus)   3/29/07 Vol. 46

sins & bad habits root out as junk in house (Jesus)   3/17/00 Vol. 18

sins & bad habits weed out (Jesus)   5/15/03 Vol. 31

sins & Confession spiritual shower (Jesus)   3/7/03 Vol. 30

sins are not secret cannot deny being sinners (Jesus)   7/17/00 Vol. 20

sins cause lost blessings (Jesus)   9/24/06 Vol. 44

sins cleaned out as refrigerators need cleaning (Jesus)   8/10/00 Vol. 20

sins condemned not the sinner (Jesus)   7/17/00 Vol. 20

David John Leary's Intercessions
(Our baptized son died after four days)

In 1983, when I was forty years old, our only son, David, was born and only lived four days. He had a blockage in the development of his urinary tract and one kidney obliterated. The other kidney formed a huge cyst so that his lungs failed to develop properly and he suffocated. It was after this that John took up the computer for ten years. This addiction is what he was healed from at Medjugorje in April of 1993. After twenty years he told John that the reason the Lord took him was that he would have been too young for us to leave him for doing this mission. (January 11, 2004 - volume 34)

David comes every year on the anniversary of his death near January 11. He has interceded for us in many ways.

In January, 1995 we were in Utica, N.Y. and Virginia Southworth asked for prayers to become pregnant. She was forty-six years old and had four miscarriages, but no children that lived. John said that since it was the anniversary of David's death that week, that we should for ask his intercession. She became pregnant two weeks later and delivered James on October 11, 2005, exactly nine months to the day of David's death. He confirmed that Jesus listens to His little ones. (January 12, 2006 - volume 42)

David has intervened for three of our grandchildren's lives. Once he came in March and asked us to pray for the grandchildren. They were all fine but we took his advice. That week three of them nearly died. Christina nearly choked to death on a pretzel. Amanda pulled a dresser over on top of her. Jeanette's daughter, Katrina, had her lung collapse as soon as they arrived in Charleston, S.C. They were all under five years old. (April 10, 1996 - volume 3)

On the following Sunday our daughter, Donna, who had two of the children, came back from Communion at Mass and there were various colored glitter all over her pew where she was sitting. David said that this was a sign of his protection for them.

(May 6, 1996 - volume 3)

This is a reminder to all of you to pray to your friends and relatives who are in heaven. They can intercede for us as the saints do. When we ask them by name, they have more power.

Jan. 12, 2006 Vol. 42
The birth of James Southworth to Jim and Virginia.

sins flaunted have war & disasters (Jesus)	1/9/05 Vol. 38	sins of the flesh downfall of many nations (Jesus)	1/20/00 Vol. 18
sins from the day write down for Confession (Jesus)	8/2/04 Vol. 36	sins of the flesh forgiven in confession (Jesus)	7/4/97 Vol. 8
sins in life cause break in God's love (Jesus)	11/8/98 Vol. 13	sins of the flesh know what they are (Jesus)	9/21/97 Vol. 8
sins in lifestyles to cause loss of homes (Jesus)	1/8/00 Vol. 18	sins of the flesh lost our shame (Jesus)	7/11/01 Vol. 24
sins in secret cannot be hidden from God (Jesus)	3/11/02 Vol. 26	sins of the flesh morals lost (Jesus)	7/6/94 Vol. 2
sins in secret known by God (Jesus)	7/19/07 Vol. 48	sins of the flesh more go to hell for (Jesus)	4/23/03 Vol. 31
sins legalized invites destruction (Jesus)	2/1/07 Vol. 46	sins of the flesh mortal sins (Jesus)	10/3/01 Vol. 25
sins of America calling down God's wrath (Jesus)	1/12/05 Vol. 38	sins of the flesh mortal sins, need forgiveness (Jesus)	7/6/04 Vol. 36
sins of life cleansed with Blood of Jesus (Jesus)	3/29/02 Vol. 26	sins of the flesh need to be confessed (Jesus)	5/4/05 Vol. 39
sins of man break relationship to God (Jesus)	3/31/06 Vol. 42	sins of the flesh reckoned at the judgment (Jesus)	7/31/97 Vol. 8
sins of omission acts of mercy (Jesus)	2/13/97 Vol. 6	sins of the flesh serious sins (Jesus)	7/1/98 Vol. 12
sins of omission corporal acts of mercy (Jesus)	5/8/96 Vol. 3	sins of the flesh speak out against (Jesus)	8/8/03 Vol. 32
sins of omission in refusing to help (Jesus)	10/3/05 Vol. 41	sin's snare trapped by Satan (Jesus)	12/25/98 Vol. 13
sins of omission in selfishness (Jesus)	10/25/06 Vol. 45	sins vs. good deeds weighing evil against good (Jesus)	9/19/05 Vol. 40
sins of omission passed choices in helping (Jesus)	2/20/06 Vol. 42	sins, drowning in need inner strength,faith (Jesus)	10/25/04 Vol. 37
sins of omission refuse God's call (Jesus)	7/13/06 Vol. 44	sins, hidden all are seen by Jesus (Jesus)	8/25/03 Vol. 32
sins of omission we are held responsible (Jesus)	4/19/98 Vol. 11	sins, unrepentant God's justice to fall (Jesus)	3/10/04 Vol. 34
sins of omission,commission revealed at death (Jesus)	3/22/02 Vol. 26	sins, your own make reparation (Jesus)	11/2/04 Vol. 37
sins of passion serious sins (Jesus)	7/30/03 Vol. 32	skilled workers finances & competition test (Jesus)	2/2/01 Vol. 22
sins of people Confession with priest (Jesus)	12/2/04 Vol. 37	skin,satellites at risk from sun (Jesus)	5/26/00 Vol. 19
sins of sacrilege Confession (Jesus)	7/1/01 Vol. 24	skull & bones people behind wars (Jesus)	7/21/06 Vol. 44
sins of the flesh abortion,sterilization (Jesus)	5/18/96 Vol. 3	skull & crossbones battle of good and evil (Jesus)	8/13/98 Vol. 12
sins of the flesh adultery, fornication (Jesus)	4/30/98 Vol. 11	sky omens signs of the end times (Jesus)	11/8/03 Vol. 33
sins of the flesh are mortal sins (Jesus)	11/28/01 Vol. 25	skyscrapers and pyramids (Jesus)	4/25/02 Vol. 27
sins of the flesh avoid sexual sins (Jesus)	12/22/05 Vol. 41	skyscrapers another attack planned (Jesus)	5/12/03 Vol. 31

skyscrapers cities will be in rubble (Jesus)   9/1/01 Vol. 24
skyscrapers to be knocked down (Jesus)   12/4/97 Vol. 9
slain in the Spirit permanent vision (Mary)   10/23/94 Vol. 2
slow down and follow Jesus' agenda (Jesus)   1/27/03 Vol. 30
slow down lead simple lives (Jesus)   7/14/03 Vol. 32
small children encourage,give attention (Jesus)   2/23/00 Vol. 18
small farmers bankrupt from competition (Jesus)   3/15/06 Vol. 42
smart card and chips in hand (Jesus)   4/25/01 Vol. 23
smart card detention centers (Jesus)   4/27/96 Vol. 3
smart card mark of beast forerunner (Jesus)   6/26/96 Vol. 3
smart card National ID from terrorists (Jesus)   9/18/01 Vol. 24
smart card needed at borders,planes (Jesus)   4/27/00 Vol. 19
smart card Olympics, terrorism (Jesus)   8/14/96 Vol. 4
smart card control could lose electronic money (Jesus)   4/21/05 Vol. 39
smart card forms shopper card,cellphones (Jesus)   6/14/00 Vol. 19
smart card monitoring satellites (Mary)   1/3/96 Vol. 3
smart card required linked to health coverage (Jesus)   6/13/00 Vol. 19
smart cards and national ID (Jesus)   12/20/01 Vol. 25
smart cards and terrorism (Jesus)   4/7/05 Vol. 39
smart cards as ids (Jesus)   8/29/06 Vol. 44
smart cards as ids (Jesus)   9/20/06 Vol. 44
smart cards becoming mandatory (Jesus)   2/10/05 Vol. 38
smart cards better not to carry (Jesus)   9/21/06 Vol. 44
smart cards buying and selling (Jesus)   9/26/96 Vol. 4
smart cards buying and selling (Jesus)   2/13/97 Vol. 6
smart cards chip in the hand coming (Jesus)   6/3/97 Vol. 7
smart cards chips in hand (Jesus)   10/1/02 Vol. 29
smart cards coming in driver's licenses (Jesus)   5/9/05 Vol. 39
smart cards control buying & selling (Jesus)   5/1/01 Vol. 23
smart cards do not accept (Jesus)   6/28/01 Vol. 23
smart cards do not take (Jesus)   8/22/01 Vol. 24
smart cards fear,security,national ID (Jesus)   9/12/01 Vol. 24
smart cards for buying and selling (Jesus)   5/7/03 Vol. 31
smart cards for security (Jesus)   11/19/01 Vol. 25
smart cards forced in licenses,passports (Jesus)   12/23/05 Vol. 41
smart cards forced on people (Jesus)   3/30/97 Vol. 6
smart cards forced on the military (Jesus)   7/15/04 Vol. 36
smart cards forerunner to chips in hand (Jesus)   5/1/02 Vol. 27
smart cards identities compromised (Jesus)   4/28/05 Vol. 39
smart cards in licenses & passports (Jesus)   8/10/06 Vol. 44
smart cards jobs (Jesus)   6/20/97 Vol. 7
smart cards lead to chip in hand (Jesus)   11/16/00 Vol. 21
smart cards lead to chips in hand (Jesus)   5/23/02 Vol. 27
smart cards lead to chips in the body (Jesus)   5/3/04 Vol. 35
smart cards lead to chips in the hand (Jesus)   3/17/01 Vol. 22
smart cards manipulated & controlled (Jesus)   4/14/05 Vol. 39
smart cards mark of the beast (Jesus)   4/21/96 Vol. 3

smart cards mark of the beast (Jesus)   3/21/97 Vol. 6
smart cards mark of the beast, food (Jesus)   11/10/97 Vol. 9
smart cards massive campaign for (Jesus)   6/9/98 Vol. 11
smart cards media, Pope exiled (Jesus)   5/15/97 Vol. 7
smart cards not condemned,avoid taking (Jesus)   5/25/02 Vol. 27
smart cards precursors to chip, for travel (Jesus)   9/28/00 Vol. 20
smart cards preparation for Antichrist (Jesus)   9/17/01 Vol. 24
smart cards preparation for chips in hand (Jesus)   7/2/98 Vol. 12
smart cards privacy abused (Jesus)   10/17/06 Vol. 45
smart cards refuse chip of Antichrist (Jesus)   11/20/97 Vol. 9
smart cards refuse chips in body (Jesus)   10/27/04 Vol. 37
smart cards refuse to take (Jesus)   8/4/99 Vol. 16
smart cards reject control of your life (Jesus)   9/28/04 Vol. 36
smart cards result of attack (Jesus)   9/20/01 Vol. 24
smart cards to control money (Jesus)   5/21/05 Vol. 39
smart cards to get on airplanes (Jesus)   2/14/06 Vol. 42
Smart cards to travel, buy & sell (Jesus)   4/23/99 Vol. 15
smart cards tracked by microwaves (Jesus)   9/2/00 Vol. 20
smart cards used as debit, ATM cards (Jesus)   3/23/01 Vol. 22
smart cards will replace money (Jesus)   5/28/99 Vol. 15
smart cards & biometrics in our future (Jesus)   1/16/02 Vol. 26
smart cards & chips control of people (Jesus)   6/22/02 Vol. 27
smart cards & chips control travel (Jesus)   10/7/99 Vol. 17
smart cards & chips mandatory ID (Jesus)   1/3/02 Vol. 26
smart cards & chips to control us (Jesus)   1/6/01 Vol. 22
smart cards mandatory control buying & selling (Jesus)   8/8/05 Vol. 40
smart cards, chips for all transactions (Jesus)   6/27/04 Vol. 35
smart cards, chips from security fears (Jesus)   12/26/06 Vol. 45
smart cards, mandatory control buying & selling (Jesus)   7/8/05 Vol. 40
smart cards, mandatory in martial law takeover (Jesus)   9/21/04 Vol. 36
smart cards, mandatory lead to chips in body (Jesus)   7/3/05 Vol. 40
smart cards, mandatory leads to chips in the body (Jesus) 10/18/04 Vol. 37
smart cards, mandatory threatens loss of your money (Jesus) 7/28/04 Vol. 36
smart cards,chips avoid Antichrist influence (Jesus)   9/30/99 Vol. 16
smart cards,chips promotion of chips in hand (Jesus)   10/12/00 Vol. 21
smart cards,watches for Antichrist control (Jesus)   5/5/01 Vol. 23
smile,friendship wakes up cold hearts (Jesus)   12/12/02 Vol. 29
Smith, Barb encourages mission continued (Barb Smith)   10/29/03 Vol. 33
smokers irritate people (Jesus)   3/8/03 Vol. 30
snake second Eve (Mary)   8/22/94 Vol. 2
snake bites cross (Jesus)   7/30/94 Vol. 2
snakes as demons threaten to darken Light (Jesus)   4/29/00 Vol. 19
sniper sick evil mind (Jesus)   10/10/02 Vol. 29
sniper killings pray he makes a mistake (Jesus)   10/23/02 Vol. 29
snow to return in bands (Jesus)   1/16/06 Vol. 42
snow uniqueness of flakes like us (Jesus)   1/7/05 Vol. 38
snow & ice more of same (Jesus)   9/11/03 Vol. 32

snow and ice testing this winter (Jesus) — 9/24/99 Vol. 16
snow and rain major problems in West (Jesus) — 12/13/06 Vol. 45
snow blizzards have fuel & food (Jesus) — 1/15/08 Vol. 50
snow scenes purity (Jesus) — 2/27/95 Vol. 2
snowstorm in D.C. sign against war (Jesus) — 2/16/03 Vol. 30
sobbing purification (Mary) — 7/13/95 Vol. 3
Social Security running out of money (Jesus) — 2/5/04 Vol. 34
Social Security strained to meet obligations (Jesus) — 2/24/04 Vol. 34
society bring order or collapse (Jesus) — 2/12/98 Vol. 10
society cesspool of evil (Jesus) — 1/11/97 Vol. 6
society depends on all talents (Jesus) — 11/12/02 Vol. 29
society effected by family life (Jesus) — 5/13/99 Vol. 15
society follow God or decay (Jesus) — 5/7/98 Vol. 11
society full of hate & apathy (Jesus) — 8/28/04 Vol. 36
society in moral decadence (Jesus) — 7/14/03 Vol. 32
society instant gratification (Jesus) — 5/24/02 Vol. 27
society is Godless in sins (Jesus) — 7/15/05 Vol. 40
society is too fast paced (Jesus) — 11/23/05 Vol. 41
society lost sense of sin (Jesus) — 1/9/05 Vol. 38
society mentality of killing (Jesus) — 3/26/98 Vol. 10
society morality at low ebb (Jesus) — 5/6/98 Vol. 11
society on brink of ruin (Jesus) — 3/26/98 Vol. 10
society ruin if God's laws ignored (Jesus) — 6/26/04 Vol. 35
society seeks instant gratification (Jesus) — 1/29/98 Vol. 10
society too permissive (Jesus) — 12/29/96 Vol. 5
society needs to speak against sins of the flesh (Jesus) — 11/5/99 Vol. 17
Sodom & Gomorrah America worse than (Jesus) — 4/24/05 Vol. 39
Sodom & Gomorrah as America is going (Jesus) — 5/15/01 Vol. 23
Sodom & Gomorrah as in Noah's day (Jesus) — 5/29/02 Vol. 27
Sodom & Gomorrah as people of today (Jesus) — 5/13/02 Vol. 27
Sodom & Gomorrah destroyed, Lot & family saved (Jesus) — 6/27/05 Vol. 39
Sodom & Gomorrah fire for less than our evil (Jesus) — 8/18/96 Vol. 4
Sodom & Gomorrah in America today (Jesus) — 1/18/01 Vol. 22
Sodom & Gomorrah justice & mercy of God (Jesus) — 6/30/03 Vol. 31
Sodom & Gomorrah like United States (Jesus) — 3/12/05 Vol. 38
Sodom & Gomorrah not even 10 just men (Jesus) — 6/30/07 Vol. 47
Sodom & Gomorrah our sins are worse than (Jesus) — 9/3/04 Vol. 36
Sodom & Gomorrah US on same path (Jesus) — 12/28/00 Vol. 21
Sodom & Gomorrah we are more guilty than (Father) — 1/24/97 Vol. 6
Sodom and Gomorrah apostasy (Jesus) — 7/30/95 Vol. 3
Sodom and Gomorrah destroyed for less (Jesus) — 5/6/98 Vol. 11
sodomy laws repealed attack on marriage (Jesus) — 7/24/03 Vol. 32
solar energy devices to heat homes (Jesus) — 11/7/06 Vol. 45
solar flares affect atmosphere,phones (Jesus) — 3/31/01 Vol. 22
solar flares damage to satellites (Jesus) — 11/4/03 Vol. 33
solar flares strong Northern Lights, sign (Jesus) — 10/30/03 Vol. 33
solar flares threaten man's technology (Jesus) — 11/18/03 Vol. 33

soldier of Christ proclaim His Word (Jesus) — 3/29/99 Vol. 14
'Soldier of Christ' at Confirmation (Jesus) — 1/15/08 Vol. 50
soldiers poor (St. Martin) — 11/11/93 Vol. 1
soldiers for Christ must be willing to suffer (Jesus) — 9/9/01 Vol. 24
soldier's funerals deserve respect (Jesus) — 3/15/07 Vol. 46
Soldiers of Christ battle of good & evil (Jesus) — 1/14/97 Vol. 6
Solemnity of Mary as Mother of God (Jesus) — 1/1/04 Vol. 34
Solomon feel into idol worship (Jesus) — 2/12/04 Vol. 34
Somalia incursion Congressional authority (Jesus) — 1/11/07 Vol. 46
son evil times (Father) — 10/8/93 Vol. 1
Son of David meaning for stump (Mary) — 12/8/07 Vol. 49
songs of adoration most desired by God (Jesus) — 3/5/00 Vol. 18
Songs of praise Jesus opens arms (Jesus) — 1/12/03 Vol. 30
sorrow change into rejoicing (Jesus) — 5/30/00 Vol. 19
sorrow crucified (Mary) — 9/15/94 Vol. 2
sorrow Savior (Jesus) — 10/17/94 Vol. 2
sorrow for sin seen in Jesus' death (Jesus) — 3/21/08 Vol. 50
sorrowful need to be comforted (Jesus) — 5/30/00 Vol. 19
sorrowful Mother prayer warriors (Mary) — 5/16/95 Vol. 2
Sorrowful Mother support for jobless (Mary) — 12/2/97 Vol. 9
soul beauty in eyes,forgive (Jesus) — 11/10/96 Vol. 5
soul gives us life (Jesus) — 2/16/03 Vol. 30
soul is immortal (Jesus) — 6/4/01 Vol. 23
soul keep pure for judgment (Jesus) — 1/10/07 Vol. 46
soul keep sin from leaking in (Jesus) — 9/13/06 Vol. 44
soul lives on forever (Jesus) — 6/14/07 Vol. 47
soul needs spiritual food, Host (Jesus) — 1/21/08 Vol. 50
soul nothing worth giving up (Jesus) — 11/27/98 Vol. 13
soul only taken past grave (Jesus) — 11/2/01 Vol. 25
soul priority of soul (Jesus) — 2/9/96 Vol. 3
soul purified for heaven (Jesus) — 11/1/06 Vol. 45
soul receives heavenly gifts (Jesus) — 4/15/07 Vol. 47
soul traveling in the air (Jesus) — 12/18/94 Vol. 2
soul & body need exercise and care (Jesus) — 12/19/03 Vol. 33
soul & guardian angel provided at conception (Jesus) — 5/13/06 Vol. 43
soul & heaven two doors of importance (Jesus) — 5/13/04 Vol. 35
soul around dead body during transition to spirit (Jesus) — 5/17/06 Vol. 43
soul as flower only never fades away (Jesus) — 5/10/07 Vol. 47
soul at death time on earth before judgment (Jesus) — 11/5/04 Vol. 37
soul body always in thirties (Jesus) — 4/7/06 Vol. 43
soul conversations after death (Jesus) — 6/5/07 Vol. 47
soul healed greater healing in conversion (Jesus) — 10/25/04 Vol. 37
soul holy, keep by not wasting time (Jesus) — 3/23/07 Vol. 46
soul in heaven worth more than anything (Jesus) — 7/10/00 Vol. 20
soul in sin as dirty clothes (Jesus) — 10/28/04 Vol. 37
soul in sin like unkept house (Jesus) — 9/25/03 Vol. 32
soul in sin real embarrassment (Jesus) — 4/25/02 Vol. 27

soul is immortal plan eternal destination (Jesus) — 2/8/01 Vol. 22

soul is prized possession interior castle,St. Teresa (Jesus) 10/15/98 Vol. 13

soul is spirit enables body to function (Jesus) — 4/12/00 Vol. 19

soul is spirit made for heaven (Jesus) — 7/25/00 Vol. 20

soul is spiritual seeks heavenly satisfaction (Jesus) — 11/7/98 Vol. 13

soul lives forever glorified body of resurrection (Jesus) — 4/22/00 Vol. 19

soul maintenance Confession to cleanse sin (Jesus) — 1/11/07 Vol. 46

soul needs saving before comforts (Jesus) — 11/2/06 Vol. 45

soul of baby at Baptism (Jesus) — 7/15/06 Vol. 44

soul of man reflection of God's love (Jesus) — 11/4/01 Vol. 25

soul purified from selfish,earthly desires (Jesus) — 2/20/01 Vol. 22

soul seeks God as total love, perfection (Jesus) — 4/6/01 Vol. 23

soul vs. body desires of soul vs. body (Jesus) — 6/1/03 Vol. 31

soul vs. bodily calling conform to God's plan (Jesus) — 6/19/06 Vol. 43

soul vs. body battle for control (Jesus) — 4/26/06 Vol. 43

soul vs. body determines eternal life (Jesus) — 6/17/06 Vol. 43

soul vs. body spiritual vs. worldly (Jesus) — 3/5/02 Vol. 26

soul vs. body struggle of good & evil (Jesus) — 2/27/01 Vol. 22

soul worth more than possessions (Jesus) — 3/10/00 Vol. 18

soul, eternal worth more than fame, riches (Jesus) — 7/9/04 Vol. 36

soul, healthy when free of sin (Jesus) — 12/1/07 Vol. 49

soul, immortal satisfied only in God (Jesus) — 9/13/98 Vol. 12

soul, inside of cleanse as the outside (Jesus) — 10/30/04 Vol. 37

soul, own best gift to God (Jesus) — 12/21/04 Vol. 37

soul, protect with prayers,sacraments,crosses (Jesus) — 10/19/04 Vol. 37

soul, saving better than gaining whole world (Jesus) — 9/1/07 Vol. 48

soul, saving your more important than pleasures (Jesus) — 5/15/04 Vol. 35

soul, sin on hard to see, need forgiveness (Jesus) — 12/16/03 Vol. 33

soul, value of not worth whole world (Jesus) — 8/5/05 Vol. 40

soul,body of man unique creation (Jesus) — 4/6/99 Vol. 15

soul,spirit of life most precious of gifts (Jesus) — 2/2/00 Vol. 18

soul/ashes USA (Jesus) — 2/16/94 Vol. 1

souls analogy to a house (Jesus) — 9/19/00 Vol. 20

souls Antichrist (Jesus) — 6/12/94 Vol. 1

souls Augustine (St. Ambrose) — 12/7/93 Vol. 1

souls bring to Confession (Jesus) — 1/30/99 Vol. 14

souls care for as body (Jesus) — 4/2/07 Vol. 47

souls each has a price (Jesus) — 5/27/02 Vol. 27

souls given at conception (Jesus) — 6/20/01 Vol. 23

souls God's love for (Jesus) — 9/7/04 Vol. 36

souls have a price (St. Anne) — 7/26/97 Vol. 8

souls image of creator (Jesus) — 5/27/98 Vol. 11

souls immortal, seeks God (Jesus) — 2/16/99 Vol. 14

souls on battle lines (Jesus) — 5/6/05 Vol. 39

souls parched,heal soul first (Jesus) — 11/21/96 Vol. 5

souls Purgatory (Jesus) — 11/2/94 Vol. 2

souls Purgatory — 11/2/93 Vol. 1

souls responsibility to save (Jesus) — 1/17/05 Vol. 38

souls seek to be with God (Jesus) — 2/1/99 Vol. 14

souls some have a high price (Jesus) — 3/26/98 Vol. 10

souls some sell to devil for money (Jesus) — 9/28/06 Vol. 44

souls the eyes of (Jesus) — 6/18/96 Vol. 3

souls varying love of God (Jesus) — 12/6/05 Vol. 41

soul's appearance always looks young (Jesus) — 12/3/05 Vol. 41

soul's appearance how God is pleased,more value (Jesus) 3/12/02 Vol. 26

soul's appearance less care than body (Jesus) — 6/19/07 Vol. 47

soul's appearance more important than body (Jesus) — 6/20/00 Vol. 19

soul's appearance more important than physical (Jesus) — 8/25/03 Vol. 32

souls are traveling to & from earth every day (Jesus) — 8/18/05 Vol. 40

souls at risk remove risk by Confession (Jesus) — 3/18/01 Vol. 22

souls cleansed by Confession (Jesus) — 8/26/99 Vol. 16

soul's cravings satisfied only with Jesus (Jesus) — 12/9/03 Vol. 33

soul's destination body dies, soul lives (Jesus) — 11/19/98 Vol. 13

soul's destination determined by faith (Jesus) — 9/19/98 Vol. 12

soul's destination heaven,purgatory,hell (Jesus) — 6/5/03 Vol. 31

soul's destination most important (Jesus) — 11/12/05 Vol. 41

soul's destination to be in heaven (Jesus) — 11/5/98 Vol. 13

souls drifting from God to worldly things (Jesus) — 1/16/05 Vol. 38

souls endangered protect souls from harm (Jesus) — 5/7/06 Vol. 43

souls ever ready by Confession,daily prayer (Jesus) — 3/31/00 Vol. 18

souls headed to hell need influence of faithful (Jesus) — 8/30/02 Vol. 28

souls in hell a hideous appearance (Jesus) — 9/7/06 Vol. 44

souls in purgatory are saved, need prayers (Jesus) — 11/2/03 Vol. 33

souls in purgatory come to heaven on feast days (Jesus) 12/17/07 Vol. 49

souls in Purgatory need more rosaries,Masses (Mary) — 9/10/98 Vol. 12

souls in purgatory pray for (Jesus) — 11/2/06 Vol. 45

souls in sin need sins forgiven (Jesus) — 1/12/07 Vol. 46

soul's loss worst disaster (Jesus) — 9/8/05 Vol. 40

souls lost refuse to believe in Word (Jesus) — 11/15/98 Vol. 13

soul's meaning immortal, life spirit (Jesus) — 2/2/00 Vol. 18

souls need saving be persistent in pursuing (Jesus) — 1/28/05 Vol. 38

souls of Light in spiritual realm (Jesus) — 12/24/06 Vol. 45

souls of people most important to save (Jesus) — 9/21/04 Vol. 36

souls on earth acts of love lessen time (Jesus) — 11/2/99 Vol. 17

soul's protection more important than comforts (Jesus) — 8/7/05 Vol. 40

soul's satisfaction found in Jesus (Jesus) — 2/16/00 Vol. 18

souls satisfied in God's peace & love (Jesus) — 12/15/02 Vol. 29

souls saved important to spiritual life (Jesus) — 2/20/08 Vol. 50

souls saved more important than food (Jesus) — 8/31/01 Vol. 24

souls saved through Gospel for all nations (Jesus) — 5/20/04 Vol. 35

soul's separation eternal destination (Jesus) — 7/11/96 Vol. 4

souls to be saved family our responsibility (Jesus) — 5/22/01 Vol. 23

soul's transition change to spirit world (Jesus) — 4/27/00 Vol. 19

souls traveling to earth, then to heaven (Jesus) — 8/30/02 Vol. 28

soul's value not worth selling for riches (Jesus) 2/8/01 Vol. 22

souls, clean keep pure in Confession (Jesus) 6/30/05 Vol. 39

souls, doors of Jesus knocking, Confession (Jesus) 6/28/07 Vol. 47

souls, freed help us on earth, purgatory (Jesus) 5/29/07 Vol. 47

souls, heaven no room for hate (Jesus) 12/24/06 Vol. 45

souls, life precious at all ages (Jesus) 12/28/06 Vol. 45

souls, pure by Baptism, Confession (Jesus) 9/7/06 Vol. 44

souls, pure confess sins, contrite hearts (Jesus) 10/21/03 Vol. 33

souls, saving everyone's mission (Jesus) 11/19/07 Vol. 49

souls, saving most important job (Jesus) 10/7/07 Vol. 49

souls, saving most important task (Jesus) 11/6/06 Vol. 45

souls, vigilant need Confession (Jesus) 5/4/06 Vol. 43

souls,keep pure like new fallen snow (Jesus) 3/2/00 Vol. 18

sound from Heaven angels (Jesus) 8/20/95 Vol. 3

South Korea blessed with faith,Pusan (Jesus) 10/19/01 Vol. 25

sower,parable of Word of God in seed (Jesus) 1/23/05 Vol. 38

sowing & reaping at the harvest (Jesus) 10/20/99 Vol. 17

space & defense money better spent on poor (Jesus) 5/16/02 Vol. 27

space exploration costs high, help others (Jesus) 1/19/04 Vol. 34

space failures man's imperfections in sin also (Jesus) 9/9/04 Vol. 36

space program tested because of man's pride (Jesus) 8/25/07 Vol. 48

space station passes away like body (Jesus) 3/22/01 Vol. 22

space station used for moon trips (Jesus) 1/10/07 Vol. 46

space station used to destroy comet (Jesus) 2/20/01 Vol. 22

space station,satellites subject to radiation (Jesus) 4/26/01 Vol. 23

space station,satellites to be abused by Antichrist (Jesus) 12/10/98 Vol. 13

space stations have secret plans for (Jesus) 9/22/00 Vol. 20

space travel humbled for pride (Jesus) 1/22/04 Vol. 34

space travel to moon & Mars too costly (Jesus) 1/15/04 Vol. 34

space travel cost better spent on poor (Jesus) 11/10/05 Vol. 41

spaceship time (Jesus) 12/6/94 Vol. 2

spacestation to destroy comets (Jesus) 6/14/02 Vol. 27

Spanish contractors to avoid American backlash (Jesus) 5/25/07 Vol. 47

Spanish influence bringing more into churches (Jesus) 8/26/04 Vol. 36

Span.speaking people great love for Jesus and Mary (Jesus) 8/4/04 Vol. 36

speak out not stifled by evil men (Jesus) 4/29/00 Vol. 19

speak out on evils of society (Jesus) 4/7/05 Vol. 39

speaking out on moral issues (Jesus) 11/11/06 Vol. 45

spectator vs. participant concern to help poor (Jesus) 3/15/01 Vol. 22

speech stop arguing & criticism in (Jesus) 5/16/04 Vol. 35

speech, comforting comfort sick,dying,prisoners (Jesus) 2/18/02 Vol. 26

speech, malicious swearing,gossip,abuse (Jesus) 2/18/02 Vol. 26

speed & knowledge human nature not changed (Jesus) 1/5/00 Vol. 18

speed in devices trains,cars,computers (Jesus) 9/17/99 Vol. 16

speed up of events fire (Jesus) 11/9/93 Vol. 1

Spicer, Karl funeral (Jesus) 9/25/03 Vol. 32

spies for Russia traitor for money as Judas (Jesus) 3/1/01 Vol. 22

spiral staircase miracles help faith (Jesus) 3/25/04 Vol. 34

Spirit abortion (Jesus) 1/23/95 Vol. 2

spirit always young, never ages (Jesus) 4/30/07 Vol. 47

spirit emanates light of holiness (Jesus) 8/15/06 Vol. 44

Spirit of Jesus in eyes of faithful (Jesus) 12/22/02 Vol. 29

spirit of law Jesus fulfills the law (Jesus) 1/21/08 Vol. 50

Spirit of Love is in everyone, share (Holy Spirit) 4/13/97 Vol. 7

spirit of the law love in heart sets you free (Jesus) 10/14/98 Vol. 13

spirit of the law over letter of the law (Jesus) 5/19/99 Vol. 15

spirit vs. flesh constant battle (Jesus) 12/26/07 Vol. 49

spirit vs. flesh struggle for perfection (Jesus) 1/24/06 Vol. 42

spirit world life prepares for (Jesus) 1/17/06 Vol. 42

spirits discerning (Jesus) 2/28/96 Vol. 3

spiritual house cleaning (Jesus) 1/16/03 Vol. 30

spiritual ladder (Jesus) 12/9/95 Vol. 3

spiritual & physical gifts give thanks to God (Jesus) 11/2/02 Vol. 29

spiritual appearance more important than earthly (Jesus) 5/6/04 Vol. 35

spiritual armor faith & prayer (Jesus) 4/1/03 Vol. 31

spiritual armor needed in battle against evil (Jesus) 3/21/02 Vol. 26

spiritual bankruptcy spreading in America (Jesus) 5/15/00 Vol. 19

spiritual bar raised with teachings of Jesus' love (Jesus) 3/24/02 Vol. 26

spiritual battle armor of faith (Jesus) 12/18/02 Vol. 29

spiritual battle armor of faith and trust (Jesus) 10/15/98 Vol. 13

spiritual battle constantly going on (Jesus) 3/14/07 Vol. 46

spiritual battle for souls (Jesus) 9/29/00 Vol. 20

spiritual battle going on for each soul (Jesus) 10/20/03 Vol. 33

spiritual battle need Lenten penances (Jesus) 1/24/08 Vol. 50

spiritual battle on the front lines (Jesus) 8/5/06 Vol. 44

spiritual battle requires rosaries,fasting (Jesus) 12/27/99 Vol. 17

spiritual battle rosary best weapon (Jesus) 8/18/06 Vol. 44

spiritual beacons to navigate life (Jesus) 8/26/04 Vol. 36

spiritual beauty better than physical beauty (Jesus) 3/7/01 Vol. 22

spiritual blackout underground (Jesus) 11/7/95 Vol. 3

spiritual blessings better than gifts (Jesus) 11/30/03 Vol. 33

spiritual blinders need complete vision of Jesus (Jesus) 10/29/00 Vol. 21

spiritual blinders off to see entire life (Jesus) 3/29/99 Vol. 14

spiritual blindness darkness of evil (Jesus) 2/8/06 Vol. 42

spiritual blindness how people cheat (Jesus) 2/15/06 Vol. 42

spiritual blindness need eyes of faith (Jesus) 10/26/03 Vol. 33

spiritual body needs exercise to be fit (Jesus) 5/30/04 Vol. 35

spiritual books higher plane satisfies soul (Jesus) 11/3/99 Vol. 17

spiritual books read saints, Hours (Jesus) 2/1/08 Vol. 50

spiritual bouquet prayers for Mary's intentions (Mary) 5/14/00 Vol. 19

Spiritual Bread needed for eternal life (Jesus) 3/16/00 Vol. 18

spiritual celebration of sacraments (Jesus) 8/23/05 Vol. 40

spiritual cleansing imitate the saints (Jesus) 4/8/99 Vol. 15

spiritual communication by prayer lines (Jesus) 12/22/05 Vol. 41

Spiritual Communion angels help at refuges (Jesus)   8/20/99 Vol. 16
spiritual communion angels provide Host (Jesus)   7/31/01 Vol. 24
spiritual Communion angels to deliver Hosts (Jesus)   2/12/00 Vol. 18
spiritual communion angels to deliver manna (Jesus)   3/4/01 Vol. 22
Spiritual Communion available from Jesus (Jesus)   12/30/99 Vol. 17
spiritual communion brings Jesus into your heart (Jesus) 10/11/03 Vol. 33
Spiritual Communion brought by angels (Jesus)   9/24/99 Vol. 16
Spiritual Communion Exodus manna (Jesus)   7/12/96 Vol. 4
Spiritual Communion for the asking (Jesus)   6/15/98 Vol. 11
spiritual communion Host for nourishment (Jesus)   5/5/00 Vol. 19
spiritual communion if no Mass (Jesus)   11/27/07 Vol. 49
Spiritual Communion manna from angels (Jesus)   12/23/97 Vol. 9
spiritual communion needed when no Mass (Jesus)   11/30/03 Vol. 33
Spiritual Communion real presence in manna (Jesus)   11/19/97 Vol. 9
Spiritual Communion tribulation (Jesus)   6/26/96 Vol. 3
spiritual communion when Mass is not allowed (Jesus)   7/7/00 Vol. 20
spiritual communion when no Eucharist (Jesus)   10/10/00 Vol. 21
Spiritual Communion when no Mass (Jesus)   4/20/06 Vol. 43
spiritual communion when no Masses (Jesus)   10/12/02 Vol. 29
spiritual communion without daily Mass (Jesus)   10/27/00 Vol. 21
spiritual compass prayer, fasting,Scripture (Jesus)   5/21/00 Vol. 19
spiritual conversions better than physical healing (Jesus) 3/4/08 Vol. 50
spiritual darkness Light of Jesus dispels (Jesus)   1/19/06 Vol. 42
spiritual decline church & prayer groups (Jesus)   10/29/02 Vol. 29
spiritual defense heavenly riches over earthly (Jesus)   1/17/04 Vol. 34
spiritual discipline be submissive & obedient (Jesus)   3/1/02 Vol. 26
Spiritual doctor to remove mortal sin (Jesus)   1/19/00 Vol. 18
spiritual drowning offer invitation to Jesus (Jesus)   11/28/98 Vol. 13
spiritual education for children on prayers (Jesus)   6/27/02 Vol. 27
spiritual education important as secular (Jesus)   8/21/04 Vol. 36
spiritual enthusiasm needed for Mass (Jesus)   11/13/07 Vol. 49
spiritual exercises Mass,rosary,Confession (Jesus)   9/4/99 Vol. 16
spiritual filters to clean out sin (Jesus)   12/3/03 Vol. 33
spiritual filth sins need purifying (Jesus)   9/20/05 Vol. 40
spiritual filth wash, Baptism, Confession (Jesus)   12/16/06 Vol. 45
spiritual fork in road serve God or the world (Jesus)   6/29/02 Vol. 27
spiritual fortress build around soul (Jesus)   11/29/03 Vol. 33
spiritual freedom found only in Jesus' help (Jesus)   7/2/00 Vol. 20
spiritual freedom free from sin's control (Jesus)   7/4/05 Vol. 40
spiritual freedom glorifying God than self (Jesus)   1/13/05 Vol. 38
spiritual garbage bad movies & books (Jesus)   2/28/07 Vol. 46
spiritual garden weed out sin, habits (Jesus)   7/26/07 Vol. 48
spiritual gifts better than Christmas gifts (Jesus)   12/8/04 Vol. 37
spiritual gifts for Christmas (Jesus)   11/2/05 Vol. 41
spiritual gifts more important (Jesus)   12/14/06 Vol. 45
spiritual gifts need sharing (Jesus)   9/17/04 Vol. 36
spiritual gifts share to help others (Jesus)   7/12/07 Vol. 48

spiritual goal please & love God (Jesus)   8/27/01 Vol. 24
spiritual growth evaluate progress (Jesus)   2/25/99 Vol. 14
spiritual growth surpass status quo (Jesus)   3/6/03 Vol. 30
spiritual healing before physical healing (Jesus)   9/11/06 Vol. 44
spiritual healing better than physical (Jesus)   12/4/06 Vol. 45
spiritual healing more important than physical (Jesus)   1/12/06 Vol. 42
spiritual healing the most important (Jesus)   10/31/07 Vol. 49
spiritual hurricane of evil prepare for evil coming (Jesus) 9/18/95 Vol. 3
spiritual improvement always room for (Jesus)   1/11/06 Vol. 42
spiritual improvement take stock of past year (Jesus)   12/31/01 Vol. 25
spiritual journey grace (Jesus)   12/11/95 Vol. 3
spiritual laziness affecting Church (Jesus)   8/9/02 Vol. 28
spiritual laziness blessings removed (Jesus)   3/9/05 Vol. 38
spiritual laziness can lead to hell (Jesus)   4/25/07 Vol. 47
spiritual laziness wastes good intentions (Jesus)   9/27/01 Vol. 24
spiritual laziness, avoid to reach out to poor souls (Jesus) 3/26/04 Vol. 34
spiritual lessons to grow in holiness (Jesus)   9/4/02 Vol. 28
spiritual life before human traditions (Jesus)   7/22/07 Vol. 48
spiritual life decisions of faith (Jesus)   4/22/01 Vol. 23
spiritual life discernment and grace (Jesus)   3/27/03 Vol. 30
spiritual life eternal & immortal (Jesus)   3/31/01 Vol. 22
spiritual life focus on heaven (Jesus)   10/31/02 Vol. 29
spiritual life focus on priorities (Jesus)   2/25/99 Vol. 14
spiritual life follow God's plan (Jesus)   11/8/02 Vol. 29
spiritual life giving over our wills (Jesus)   6/10/99 Vol. 15
spiritual life improve daily (Jesus)   5/12/99 Vol. 15
spiritual life improve with Scripture,reading (Jesus)   9/27/01 Vol. 24
spiritual life in God's Will (Jesus)   3/6/03 Vol. 30
spiritual life increasing or decreasing (Jesus)   1/23/99 Vol. 14
spiritual life is highest priority (Jesus)   2/18/99 Vol. 14
spiritual life Jesus as crutches (Jesus)   12/2/03 Vol. 33
spiritual life know, love & serve God (Jesus)   3/19/03 Vol. 30
spiritual life lasts forever (Jesus)   7/15/06 Vol. 44
spiritual life let no earthly thing control you (Jesus) 2/16/08 Vol. 50
spiritual life mirror to expose sins (Jesus)   1/11/07 Vol. 46
spiritual life need healing in conversion (Jesus)   2/13/05 Vol. 38
spiritual life needs rebuilding (Jesus)   1/25/08 Vol. 50
spiritual life new perspective for improving (Jesus)   10/21/04 Vol. 37
spiritual life over idols, New Age (Jesus)   11/2/98 Vol. 13
spiritual life permanent relationship (Jesus)   1/16/97 Vol. 6
spiritual life practice like pianist (Jesus)   5/27/99 Vol. 15
spiritual life prayer time & charity (Jesus)   4/16/04 Vol. 35
spiritual life prayer, harmony with God (Jesus)   3/4/04 Vol. 34
spiritual life recharge batteries (Jesus)   4/3/05 Vol. 39
spiritual life suggestions to help (Jesus)   10/17/01 Vol. 25
spiritual life take retreats (Jesus)   8/3/06 Vol. 44
spiritual life training for temptations (Jesus)   3/1/03 Vol. 30

spiritual life transcends that of the body (Jesus) 5/16/00 Vol. 19

spiritual life saver God on duty all the time (Jesus) 9/30/01 Vol. 24

spiritual life status improving,declining,stagnant? (Jesus) 8/23/02 Vol. 28

spiritual life,better no greed, no lust, prayer (Jesus) 9/5/01 Vol. 24

spiritual Light needed as plants need light (Jesus) 7/22/00 Vol. 20

spiritual lives share (Jesus) 4/11/94 Vol. 1

spiritual love needs to be shared (Jesus) 6/10/97 Vol. 7

spiritual mission save souls (Jesus) 9/28/05 Vol. 40

spiritual mistakes clean souls as well (Jesus) 9/22/05 Vol. 40

spiritual nature rule over physical (Jesus) 7/11/06 Vol. 44

spiritual needs calls for conversions (Jesus) 3/22/06 Vol. 42

spiritual needs compared to a tree (Jesus) 6/25/98 Vol. 11

spiritual needs prayer,fasting,sacraments (Jesus) 11/4/04 Vol. 37

spiritual needs quick attention (Jesus) 6/21/07 Vol. 47

spiritual needs support parish (Jesus) 5/18/06 Vol. 43

spiritual opportunities struggles in life (Jesus) 10/2/04 Vol. 37

spiritual opportunities to save those around us (Jesus) 3/26/04 Vol. 34

spiritual peace comes only from God (Jesus) 1/12/08 Vol. 50

spiritual peace guard from distractions (Jesus) 2/23/06 Vol. 42

spiritual peace in Real Presence (Jesus) 9/1/07 Vol. 48

spiritual peace need frequent Confession (Jesus) 1/27/06 Vol. 42

spiritual peace needed in all souls (Jesus) 5/24/04 Vol. 35

spiritual perfection conform to God's Will (Jesus) 5/18/01 Vol. 23

spiritual perfection varies in souls (Jesus) 12/20/05 Vol. 41

spiritual pit grace, intercessor needed (Jesus) 3/19/07 Vol. 46

spiritual planning important for family souls (Jesus) 12/3/04 Vol. 37

spiritual pollution pornography,violence,drugs (Jesus) 1/19/00 Vol. 18

spiritual poor need evangelization (Jesus) 11/7/06 Vol. 45

spiritual poor need love & prayers (Jesus) 3/19/06 Vol. 42

spiritual potential by prayer & fasting (Jesus) 1/26/03 Vol. 30

spiritual potential need grace to realize (Jesus) 2/22/00 Vol. 18

spiritual poverty loss of morals (Jesus) 7/7/06 Vol. 44

spiritual preparation Confession (Jesus) 3/11/95 Vol. 2

spiritual preparation most important (Jesus) 9/10/99 Vol. 16

spiritual preparation needed for Christmas (Jesus) 12/16/02 Vol. 29

spiritual preparation needed to endure Warning (Jesus) 11/29/05 Vol. 41

spiritual preparations instead of material gifts (Jesus) 11/30/99 Vol. 17

spiritual preparations love, faith, Confession (Jesus) 9/3/03 Vol. 32

spiritual pride be nothing before God (Jesus) 3/13/06 Vol. 42

spiritual priorities better than earthly ones (Jesus) 7/9/06 Vol. 44

spiritual priorities do what Jesus wants (Jesus) 5/27/06 Vol. 43

spiritual priorities needed to save soul (Jesus) 10/24/03 Vol. 33

spiritual prisoners in sins (Jesus) 3/29/03 Vol. 30

spiritual problems call on Jesus,saints,angels (Jesus) 6/1/06 Vol. 43

spiritual progress learn from mistakes (Jesus) 6/11/98 Vol. 11

spiritual progress needs checking often (Jesus) 6/17/00 Vol. 19

spiritual progress needs improving to perfection (Jesus) 10/15/00 Vol. 21

spiritual progress check new resolutions to keep (Jesus) 1/4/07 Vol. 46

spiritual protection in stripping possessions (Jesus) 12/27/04 Vol. 37

spiritual reading gives food for thought (Jesus) 3/4/99 Vol. 14

spiritual reading Gospel,Liturgy of Hours (Jesus) 11/11/03 Vol. 33

spiritual reading help toward perfection (Jesus) 2/8/05 Vol. 38

spiritual reading Lenten penance (Jesus) 2/8/08 Vol. 50

spiritual reading priority (Jesus) 4/1/04 Vol. 35

spiritual reflection supercedes physical goals (Jesus) 7/13/00 Vol. 20

spiritual relief in Confession (Jesus) 3/23/07 Vol. 46

spiritual resolution help soul the most (Jesus) 12/29/05 Vol. 41

spiritual resolutions not forgotten in new year (Jesus) 12/27/01 Vol. 25

spiritual restraint fasting, almsgiving (Jesus) 5/26/05 Vol. 39

spiritual retreat better than vacation (Jesus) 9/23/99 Vol. 16

spiritual road harder road to suffer in life (Jesus) 11/16/03 Vol. 33

spiritual safety net in Jesus (Jesus) 3/10/06 Vol. 42

spiritual satisfaction found only in God (Jesus) 6/22/06 Vol. 43

spiritual sharing share love of God (Jesus) 5/6/99 Vol. 15

spiritual shield strong faith, prayer (Jesus) 3/6/06 Vol. 42

spiritual sickness healing needed for heaven (Jesus) 3/14/08 Vol. 50

spiritual spring cleaning of faults (Jesus) 3/29/99 Vol. 14

spiritual stamina to stand up to persecutors (Jesus) 8/14/00 Vol. 20

spiritual strength by prayer and fasting (Jesus) 7/19/04 Vol. 36

spiritual strength found in God, not arms (Jesus) 7/27/00 Vol. 20

spiritual strength keep up for battle (Jesus) 4/22/05 Vol. 39

spiritual strength needed to fight evil one (Jesus) 11/10/99 Vol. 17

spiritual survival avoid deadly mortal sin (Jesus) 1/21/05 Vol. 38

spiritual talents share love of God (Jesus) 11/14/99 Vol. 17

spiritual things are forever (Jesus) 8/28/07 Vol. 48

spiritual trash forgiven in Confession (Jesus) 9/6/06 Vol. 44

spiritual trash can empty ugly sins to priest (Jesus) 11/12/99 Vol. 17

spiritual treasures are timeless (Jesus) 2/19/02 Vol. 26

spiritual umbrella in sacraments (Jesus) 2/22/05 Vol. 38

spir. vs worldly goals love demands in persecution (Jesus) 8/11/00 Vol. 20

spiritual warfare discernment (Jesus) 3/25/95 Vol. 2

spiritual wealth share faith in evangelizing (Jesus) 7/6/05 Vol. 40

spiritual weapons holy water,relics,blessed salt (Jesus) 6/15/06 Vol. 43

spiritual weapons rosary,holy water,crosses (Jesus) 9/13/05 Vol. 40

spiritual weapons stronger than physical weapons (Jesus) 3/23/04 Vol. 34

spiritual weapons too valuable to lose (Jesus) 3/16/08 Vol. 50

spiritual wings pruning (Jesus) 11/24/94 Vol. 2

spiritually blinded worldly cares,pleasures (Jesus) 5/4/99 Vol. 15

spiritually dead without grace of forgiveness (Jesus) 2/22/00 Vol. 18

spiritually lazy need to come to Confession (Jesus) 7/26/04 Vol. 36

Spitzer, Gov. compared to King David (Jesus) 3/13/08 Vol. 50

spoiled child America defying laws (Jesus) 8/19/02 Vol. 28

sponsors are blessed in this work (Jesus) 3/15/98 Vol. 10

sports an idol in excess (Jesus) 1/31/02 Vol. 26

sports are idols for some (Jesus) — 9/22/05 Vol. 40

sports avoid obsession (Jesus) — 1/25/01 Vol. 22

sports can become an idol (Jesus) — 11/29/01 Vol. 25

sports develop skills and bodies (Jesus) — 8/19/04 Vol. 36

sports do not honor Sunday (Jesus) — 5/13/98 Vol. 11

sports do not make idol of (Jesus) — 9/9/02 Vol. 28

sports earthly idols (Jesus) — 9/9/97 Vol. 8

sports exercise,but limit time on (Jesus) — 5/3/01 Vol. 23

sports faith (Jesus) — 7/14/95 Vol. 3

sports heroes instead of saints (Jesus) — 6/18/98 Vol. 11

sports idols brought low (Mary) — 3/20/98 Vol. 10

sports keep spiritual priorities (Jesus) — 1/29/04 Vol. 34

sports made a god (Jesus) — 2/22/99 Vol. 14

sports practice spiritually (Jesus) — 11/20/00 Vol. 21

sports priorities (Jesus) — 8/27/95 Vol. 3

sports society (Jesus) — 10/14/95 Vol. 3

sports Sunday worship first (Jesus) — 12/20/01 Vol. 25

sports treated like a god (Jesus) — 9/22/96 Vol. 4

sports waste of time (Jesus) — 8/23/01 Vol. 24

sports & money addicts to TV & stock market (Jesus) — 10/25/00 Vol. 21

sports & money do not make gods of (Jesus) — 7/25/02 Vol. 28

sports as a god seek God first (Jesus) — 6/27/97 Vol. 7

sports events obsession with idols (Jesus) — 5/9/03 Vol. 31

sports obsession can take away faith (Jesus) — 11/17/03 Vol. 33

sports obsession takes time from prayer (Jesus) — 9/9/99 Vol. 16

sports stars not gods (Jesus) — 7/12/01 Vol. 24

sports stars salaries too high, worship (Jesus) — 8/23/01 Vol. 24

sports watching avoid too much, and control (Jesus) — 9/6/04 Vol. 36

spotlights protected — 8/16/93 Vol. 1

spouse & children better than earthly things (Jesus) — 5/31/06 Vol. 43

spread love than anger & complaints (Jesus) — 2/18/00 Vol. 18

spring beauty in flowers, new life (Jesus) — 5/26/05 Vol. 39

spring slow starting,more floods (Jesus) — 4/12/97 Vol. 7

spring cleaning good look for your soul (Jesus) — 3/29/06 Vol. 42

spring cleaning physically & spiritually (Jesus) — 4/16/02 Vol. 27

spring cleaning,spiritual by frequent confession (Jesus) — 4/24/97 Vol. 7

spring healing water Denver, Mother Cabrini's (Jesus) — 3/9/04 Vol. 34

spring water present at refuges (Jesus) — 11/9/03 Vol. 33

springs of water found at refuges, healings (Jesus) — 10/29/04 Vol. 37

springs, cross healings at refuges (Jesus) — 10/18/07 Vol. 49

springs, healing at refuges (Jesus) — 7/17/03 Vol. 32

spying to find Christians (Jesus) — 5/29/97 Vol. 7

spying with electronic devices (Jesus) — 2/7/07 Vol. 46

spying by listening government intrusion in US (Jesus) — 1/7/06 Vol. 42

St. Agnes a young martyr as babies (Jesus) — 1/21/99 Vol. 14

St. Anne, Joachim models for grandparents (Jesus) — 7/26/07 Vol. 48

St. Anne & Joachim grandparents' day (Jesus) — 7/26/02 Vol. 28

St. Anthony answers many prayers (Jesus) — 6/13/06 Vol. 43

St. Anthony Fr. Charlie (St. Anthony) — 6/16/03 Vol. 31

St. Anthony of the desert feast (Jesus) — 1/17/08 Vol. 50

St. Anthony pray to find faith (Jesus) — 6/13/01 Vol. 23

St. Anthony of Padua seek spiritual gifts (St. Anthony) — 6/14/99 Vol. 15

St. Anthony of the Desert inspiration for monastic life (Jesus) — 1/17/04 Vol. 34

St. Benedict's Cross sacramentals, angels (Jesus) — 5/27/97 Vol. 7

St. Bernadette imitate her life (Mary) — 2/11/08 Vol. 50

St. Bernadette message for Jocelyn (St. Bernadette) — 2/2/08 Vol. 50

St. Catherine another antipope to come (Jesus) — 4/29/99 Vol. 15

St. Catherine of Sienna dealth with schism (Jesus) — 4/29/03 Vol. 31

St. Dominic rosary, heresy defense (Jesus) — 8/8/07 Vol. 48

St. Elizabeth Ann Seton help physically,spiritually (Elizabeth A Seton) — 1/7/99 Vol. 14

St. Frances Cabrini give cheerfully (Jesus) — 8/29/00 Vol. 20

St. Francis of Assisi call to peace & love (Jesus) — 10/4/03 Vol. 33

St. Grimwald saints (Jesus) — 9/16/95 Vol. 3

St. James strengthened him (Mary) — 10/5/97 Vol. 9

St. John took care of Blessed Mother (Jesus) — 6/8/02 Vol. 27

St. John Fisher a saint to imitate (Jesus) — 6/22/05 Vol. 39

St. John Fisher executed for the faith (Jesus) — 6/22/04 Vol. 35

St. John Lateran angels protect Churches (Jesus) — 11/9/97 Vol. 9

St. John the Baptist a good role model (Jesus) — 6/24/98 Vol. 11

St. John the Baptist announced first coming (Jesus) — 6/24/99 Vol. 15

St. John the Baptist call to repent (Jesus) — 12/7/03 Vol. 33

St. John the Baptist call to repentance (Jesus) — 6/24/97 Vol. 7

St. John the Baptist calling in desert (Jesus) — 12/4/05 Vol. 41

St. John the Baptist change spiritual life (Jesus) — 12/9/01 Vol. 25

St. John the Baptist conversion (Jesus) — 9/27/96 Vol. 4

St. John the Baptist courage against Herod (Jesus) — 12/21/06 Vol. 45

St. John the Baptist courage to speak out (Jesus) — 12/13/04 Vol. 37

St. John the Baptist criticized Herod (Jesus) — 7/8/03 Vol. 32

St. John the Baptist herald of Jesus (Jesus) — 12/17/06 Vol. 45

St. John the Baptist message of repentance (Jesus) — 8/29/02 Vol. 28

St. John the Baptist prepared first coming (Jesus) — 6/24/05 Vol. 39

St. John the Baptist prepared the way in the desert (Jesus) — 12/15/07 Vol. 49

St. John the Baptist prepares first coming (Jesus) — 12/23/00 Vol. 21

St. John the Baptist repent to start new life (Jesus) — 12/1/98 Vol. 13

St. John the Baptist speak out as he did (Jesus) — 8/29/03 Vol. 32

St. John the Baptist speaks out fearlessly to Herod (Jesus) — 7/31/04 Vol. 36

St. John the Baptist stirred in womb (Jesus) — 5/31/01 Vol. 23

St. John the Baptist support truth (Jesus) — 8/29/00 Vol. 20

St. John the Evangelist spread word of Revelation (Jesus) — 12/3/00 Vol. 21

St. John, apostle gifts in Gospel,letters,Revelation (Jesus) — 12/27/03 Vol. 33

St. John, apostle Revelation in 2nd coming (Jesus) — 12/4/05 Vol. 41

St. John, Ephesus place of writing gospel (St. John) — 11/1/98 Vol. 13

St. Joseph evangelize (St. Joseph) — 3/20/95 Vol. 2

St. Joseph fled to Egypt (Jesus) — 1/9/97 Vol. 6
St. Joseph grace of work, intercessor (St. Joseph) — 5/1/97 Vol. 7
St. Joseph happy death & model (Mary) — 3/19/96 Vol. 3
St. Joseph led into Egypt (Jesus) — 1/27/01 Vol. 22
St. Joseph lineage of David (St. Joseph) — 3/19/98 Vol. 10
St. Joseph protector of Catholic Church (Jesus) — 3/19/02 Vol. 26
St. Joseph protector of Holy Family (Jesus) — 3/19/02 Vol. 26
St. Joseph struggle for family support (St. Joseph) — 3/18/99 Vol. 14
St. Joseph teacher of Jesus (Jesus) — 3/15/08 Vol. 50
St. Joseph travel from home,storm (St. Therese) — 12/6/95 Vol. 3
St. Joseph work is a blessing (St. Joseph) — 3/13/97 Vol. 6
St. Joseph the worker fair wages (St. Joseph) — 5/1/98 Vol. 11
St. Joseph,Blessed Mother united wills (Jesus) — 3/19/05 Vol. 38
St. Joseph,St. Patrick great models (Jesus) — 3/15/01 Vol. 22
St. Joseph's Oratory Real Presence makes holy (Jesus) — 7/4/01 Vol. 24
St. Lazarus healed by Jesus (Jesus) — 12/4/99 Vol. 17
St. Louis Church demons (Jesus) — 11/18/95 Vol. 3
St. Maria Goretti example of faith (Jesus) — 7/6/06 Vol. 44
St. Martha role model for women (Jesus) — 7/29/98 Vol. 12
St. Mary Magdalene more forgiven,more thanks (Jesus) — 7/22/00 Vol. 20
St. Matthew follow call to evangelize (Jesus) — 9/21/06 Vol. 44
St. Michael angels make one choice (St. Michael) — 9/29/05 Vol. 40
St. Michael at side when help needed (St. Michael) — 9/29/03 Vol. 32
St. Michael Communion in apparitions (Jesus) — 9/30/96 Vol. 4
St. Michael devil and hell do exist (St. Michael) — 9/29/98 Vol. 12
St. Michael guardian of U.S. (St. Michael) — 2/26/98 Vol. 10
St. Michael leads angels,Armageddon (St. Michael) — 9/29/07 Vol. 48
St. Michael man dependent on God for all (St. Michael) — 9/29/04 Vol. 36
St. Michael more powerful than Satan (St. Michael) — 7/20/97 Vol. 8
St. Michael power of prayer & angels (Jesus) — 10/27/01 Vol. 25
St. Michael powerful prayer to (Jesus) — 3/14/07 Vol. 46
St. Michael Satan (Jesus) — 1/31/96 Vol. 3
St. Michael to separate evil from elect (Jesus) — 10/25/98 Vol. 13
St. Michael underground (Jesus) — 10/28/95 Vol. 3
St. Michael Prayer demons seek ruin of souls (Jesus) — 10/9/03 Vol. 33
St. Michael prayer fights demons (Jesus) — 2/10/08 Vol. 50
St. Michael prayer with cross (Jesus) — 3/8/03 Vol. 30
St. Nicholas give without repayment (Jesus) — 12/6/03 Vol. 33
St. Patrick awaits our visit (Jesus) — 7/1/99 Vol. 16
St. Patrick evangelize (St. Patrick) — 3/17/95 Vol. 2
St. Patrick follow the Trinity (St. Patrick) — 3/18/99 Vol. 14
St. Patrick personal mission (St. Patrick) — 3/17/97 Vol. 6
St. Patrick pray for his intercession (Jesus) — 3/17/05 Vol. 38
St. Patrick Trinity in shamrock (Jesus) — 3/15/07 Vol. 46
St. Patrick intercessor Irish rosary lauded (St. Patrick) — 1/13/07 Vol. 46
St. Patrick's shamrock teaching on Trinity (Jesus) — 3/17/04 Vol. 34
St. Paul conversion (Jesus) — 1/29/01 Vol. 22

St. Paul exemplary in conversion (Jesus) — 1/25/02 Vol. 26
St. Paul fight the good fight (Jesus) — 4/27/05 Vol. 39
St. Paul finish the race (Jesus) — 11/20/00 Vol. 21
St. Paul fought the good fight (Jesus) — 9/27/06 Vol. 44
St. Paul learned by gifts (Jesus) — 2/8/04 Vol. 34
St. Paul saw the Light (Jesus) — 5/18/03 Vol. 31
St. Paul, missionary suffered persecution (Jesus) — 5/22/07 Vol. 47
St. Peter 1st pope with Holy Spirit (Jesus) — 7/7/98 Vol. 12
St. Peter as the rock (Jesus) — 1/17/01 Vol. 22
St. Peter built Church on rock of (Jesus) — 7/11/01 Vol. 24
St. Peter fisher of souls (Jesus) — 9/4/03 Vol. 32
St. Peter Get behind me, Satan (Jesus) — 3/4/04 Vol. 34
St. Peter given keys to heaven (Jesus) — 11/9/97 Vol. 9
St. Peter Jesus is the Christ (Jesus) — 2/19/04 Vol. 34
St. Peter live & die by the sword (Jesus) — 5/20/03 Vol. 31
St. Peter live or die by the sword (Jesus) — 4/20/98 Vol. 11
St. Peter put back the sword (Jesus) — 3/27/98 Vol. 10
St. Peter represents first pope (Jesus) — 4/1/05 Vol. 39
St. Peter tested & died on cross (Jesus) — 4/25/04 Vol. 35
St. Peter the rock of Church (Jesus) — 6/28/01 Vol. 23
St. Peter uphold the keys of (Jesus) — 4/26/98 Vol. 11
St. Peter & Judas different denials (Jesus) — 4/11/06 Vol. 43
St. Peter & Judas reaction to denial differs (Jesus) — 3/15/08 Vol. 50
St. Peter & Judas reaction to denials (Jesus) — 4/3/07 Vol. 47
St. Peter & St. Paul go out to preach as they did (Jesus) — 6/29/05 Vol. 39
St. Peter & successors head of Church of Jesus (Jesus) — 7/21/04 Vol. 36
St. Peter, popes progression from Jesus (Jesus) — 2/22/08 Vol. 50
St. Peter's rock Satan will not prevail (Jesus) — 4/17/06 Vol. 43
St. Philip Neri Church historical roots (Jesus) — 5/29/98 Vol. 11
St. Pio Barto, Pa. Shrine on life (Jesus) — 9/18/04 Vol. 36
St. Pius X lowered age for Communion (Jesus) — 8/21/07 Vol. 48
St. Raphael pray for marriages (Jesus) — 6/4/99 Vol. 15
St. Rose Ferron victim soul (Jesus) — 5/17/06 Vol. 43
St. Stephen bold & courageous to death (Jesus) — 4/27/04 Vol. 35
St. Stephen religious persecution (Jesus) — 4/11/05 Vol. 39
St. Stephen witnessed his life (Jesus) — 4/30/01 Vol. 23
St. Teresa love of Jesus (Jesus) — 10/15/03 Vol. 33
St. Teresa of Avila focus on Jesus in prayer (St. Teresa) — 10/15/99 Vol. 17
St. Theresa Divine Will (St. Theresa) — 8/26/93 Vol. 1
St. Theresa's Little Way (Jesus) — 8/11/03 Vol. 32
St. Therese 100th Anniversary (St. Therese) — 10/19/97 Vol. 9
St. Therese call on her for help (St. Therese) — 10/1/96 Vol. 5
St. Therese follow her Little Way (Jesus) — 10/1/03 Vol. 33
St. Therese helps in mission (Jesus) — 10/1/02 Vol. 29
St. Therese Lenten preparation (St. Therese) — 3/13/97 Vol. 6
St. Therese message on taping (St. Therese) — 9/7/02 Vol. 28
St. Therese National Basilica (St. Therese) — 10/1/07 Vol. 49

St. Therese our response to God's love (St. Therese)   10/1/05 Vol. 41
St. Therese our response to God's love (St. Therese)   10/1/05 Vol. 41
St. Therese prepare for the battle (St. Therese)   5/1/97 Vol. 7
St. Therese roses and cross (St. Therese)   9/29/07 Vol. 48
St. Therese saint for little way (St. Therese)   12/10/04 Vol. 37
St. Therese simple,faithful life (Jesus)   7/31/99 Vol. 16
St. Thomas doubted resurrection (Jesus)   7/3/98 Vol. 12
St. Thomas doubts and faith (Jesus)   7/3/99 Vol. 16
St. Thomas felt wounds to believe (Jesus)   4/18/98 Vol. 11
St. Thomas My Lord & My God (Jesus)   7/3/04 Vol. 36
St. Thomas My Lord & My God (Jesus)   7/3/06 Vol. 44
St. Thomas saw and believed (Jesus)   7/3/01 Vol. 24
St. Thomas saw and believed (Jesus)   4/16/01 Vol. 23
St. John the Baptist evangelize, personal (Jesus)   12/7/97 Vol. 9
St. John, apostle model of faith and hope (Mary)   12/27/97 Vol. 9
St. Patrick's Purgatory retreat in Ireland (Jesus)   7/12/99 Vol. 16
St. Peter as rock Pope is authority (Jesus)   8/19/97 Vol. 8
stadium persecution (Jesus)   10/14/94 Vol. 2
stage actors (Jesus)   10/25/94 Vol. 2
stage of life accountable for one's actions (Jesus)   10/27/04 Vol. 37
stage of life good works (Jesus)   8/1/94 Vol. 2
stage of life nothing is secret,all seen (Jesus)   11/19/98 Vol. 13
stage of life watched by heaven (Jesus)   1/21/00 Vol. 18
stages in life ask Jesus' help for (Jesus)   6/17/05 Vol. 39
stages of life metamorphosis of butterfly (Jesus)   6/13/98 Vol. 11
stages of life to save souls (Jesus)   2/10/02 Vol. 26
stairway to heaven by daily struggles (Jesus)   12/13/01 Vol. 25
stairway to heaven carry daily crosses (Jesus)   7/3/97 Vol. 8
stairway to heaven daily consecration (Jesus)   12/20/04 Vol. 37
stairway to heaven focus of life (Jesus)   5/20/96 Vol. 3
stairway to heaven graces given for (Jesus)   7/13/06 Vol. 44
stairway to heaven keep clear by forgiving soul (Jesus)   5/18/00 Vol. 19
stairway to Heaven life long path (Jesus)   4/12/99 Vol. 15
stalactite stalagmite meet,one with God (Jesus)   1/12/08 Vol. 50
Stan Gutowski helped against abortion (Jesus)   2/5/01 Vol. 22
stand up for faith even if persecuted (Jesus)   6/29/05 Vol. 39
standard of living being lowered in US (Jesus)   5/21/03 Vol. 31
standard of living decreasing (Jesus)   9/11/03 Vol. 32
standard of living decreasing by job losses (Jesus)   8/11/05 Vol. 40
standard of living down by wars,terrorism,disease (Jesus)   8/23/02 Vol. 28
standard of living going down because of sins (Jesus)   7/27/04 Vol. 36
standard of living is decreasing (Jesus)   5/10/02 Vol. 27
standard of living is going down (Jesus)   6/30/04 Vol. 35
standard of living is in decline in America (Jesus)   5/24/04 Vol. 35
standard of living lifestyle lowered (Jesus)   6/4/02 Vol. 27
standard of living lowered to rural life (Jesus)   4/27/00 Vol. 19
standard of living materialism (Jesus)   10/27/95 Vol. 3

standard of living to continue in decline (Jesus)   11/11/03 Vol. 33
standard of living will be declining (Jesus)   9/14/06 Vol. 44
standard of living lower because of exported jobs (Jesus)   1/27/05 Vol. 38
standard of living lower less manufacturing (Jesus)   11/23/00 Vol. 21
standard of living lowered need more trust in Jesus (Jesus)   8/7/96 Vol. 4
standards of judgment man's vs. God's (Jesus)   8/18/99 Vol. 16
star light (Jesus)   12/19/95 Vol. 3
star tribulation start (Jesus)   6/14/95 Vol. 2
star in sky sign of Antichrist coming (Jesus)   1/5/95 Vol. 2
Star of Bethlehem disperses darkness of sin (Jesus)   12/10/07 Vol. 49
Star of Bethlehem foretold coming (Jesus)   12/16/96 Vol. 5
Star of Bethlehem light (Jesus)   12/25/93 Vol. 1
star of Bethlehem means to announce events (Jesus)   12/5/02 Vol. 29
Star of Bethlehem miracle of God (Jesus)   12/24/05 Vol. 41
Star of Bethlehem miracle of God (Jesus)   12/22/04 Vol. 37
Star of Bethlehem more proof of God in babe (Jesus)   12/21/98 Vol. 13
star of Christmas burning flame of love (Jesus)   12/17/02 Vol. 29
Star of light reveals Jesus' Word (Jesus)   10/30/98 Vol. 13
Stations of Cross model to carry our cross (Jesus)   8/8/05 Vol. 40
Stations of Cross on Fridays of Lent (Jesus)   2/17/05 Vol. 38
Stations of the Cross crucifix on altar (Jesus)   6/28/07 Vol. 47
Stations of the Cross follow Jesus' footsteps (Jesus)   2/10/05 Vol. 38
Stations of the Cross Lenten devotion (Jesus)   3/29/07 Vol. 46
Stations of the Cross model for our lives (Jesus)   12/9/07 Vol. 49
Stations of the Cross pray on Fridays (Jesus)   3/6/08 Vol. 50
Stations of the Cross pray on Fridays of Lent (Jesus)   2/14/02 Vol. 26
Stations of the Cross say more in Lent (Jesus)   3/2/00 Vol. 18
Stations of the Cross sufferings of Jesus (Jesus)   3/9/06 Vol. 42
Stations of the Cross we will be stripped (Jesus)   7/20/01 Vol. 24
Statue of Liberty America to lose freedoms (Jesus)   5/22/98 Vol. 11
Statue of Liberty symbol of freedom (Jesus)   4/7/98 Vol. 11
Statue of Liberty will fall in ruin (Jesus)   11/19/00 Vol. 21
statue,Corpus Christi,Tex miracle in hearts (Jesus)   8/28/98 Vol. 12
statues inspire us to pray (Jesus)   7/12/01 Vol. 24
statues removed from churches (Jesus)   12/6/01 Vol. 25
statues & crucifixes removed from Churches (Jesus)   9/18/97 Vol. 8
statues & crucifixes stripped from churches (Jesus)   2/5/99 Vol. 14
statues & icons remembrance of God,saints (Jesus)   2/17/00 Vol. 18
statues & icons reminds us of saints (Jesus)   6/15/00 Vol. 19
statues & icons to think of saints (Jesus)   5/5/00 Vol. 19
statues & icons weeping (Jesus)   8/7/97 Vol. 8
statues & pictures are inspiration to Christians (Jesus)   8/21/06 Vol. 44
statues & pictures display in homes (Jesus)   7/13/02 Vol. 28
statues & pictures inspiration and model (Jesus)   8/25/06 Vol. 44
statues & pictures needed at church as at home (Jesus)   3/8/02 Vol. 26
statues & pictures reminder of heroes,models (Mary)   6/18/98 Vol. 11
statues and icons desecration in persecution (Jesus)   7/23/98 Vol. 12

statues and icons inspire the faithful (Jesus) — 8/5/99 Vol. 16

statues and icons weeping over our sins (Jesus) — 8/15/04 Vol. 36

statues and pictures in homes and churches (Jesus) — 9/1/98 Vol. 12

statues and pictures on walls of Church,home (Jesus) — 7/4/97 Vol. 8

statues crying over abortions (Jesus) — 8/22/06 Vol. 44

statues crying signs to save souls (Mary) — 3/10/97 Vol. 6

statues not worshiped models to imitate (Jesus) — 3/30/01 Vol. 22

statues weeping effects of sin (Mary) — 1/23/97 Vol. 6

statues, icons removing the Sacred (Jesus) — 11/18/99 Vol. 17

statues, icons stripped from Churches (Jesus) — 10/2/97 Vol. 9

statues, paintings inspires sainthood (Jesus) — 12/28/06 Vol. 45

statues, rosaries shared with prayer group (Jesus) — 2/17/05 Vol. 38

stealth airplane, new with masonic symbols (Jesus) — 7/5/05 Vol. 40

stealth planes outrun missiles (Jesus) — 11/9/05 Vol. 41

stealth weapons Antichrist's,will not work (Jesus) — 8/13/98 Vol. 12

steel factories new security threat (Jesus) — 5/25/07 Vol. 47

steering wheel course of life's decisions (Jesus) — 6/5/97 Vol. 7

Steger, Fr. good life, but weaknesses (Jesus) — 3/6/08 Vol. 50

stem cell research acting like God (Jesus) — 7/18/02 Vol. 28

stem cell research against plan of creation (Jesus) — 8/2/01 Vol. 24

stem cell research cannot use embryos (Jesus) — 8/9/01 Vol. 24

stem cell research defying God's creation (Jesus) — 7/7/05 Vol. 40

stem cell research organ replacement to fail (Jesus) — 7/15/04 Vol. 36

stem cell research playing God (Jesus) — 8/23/01 Vol. 24

stem cells abuse of nature (Jesus) — 8/10/01 Vol. 24

stem cells and aborted babies (Jesus) — 7/11/01 Vol. 24

stem cells from aborted fetuses (Jesus) — 3/4/04 Vol. 34

stem cells from body parts of babies (Jesus) — 1/22/03 Vol. 30

stem cells use aborted babies (Jesus) — 9/20/02 Vol. 28

stem cells violation of God's laws (Jesus) — 11/8/01 Vol. 25

stem cells & DNA abuse of nature (Jesus) — 4/20/04 Vol. 35

stem cells & DNA abuses of science (Jesus) — 9/26/02 Vol. 28

stem cells & DNA upset God's plan (Jesus) — 7/2/06 Vol. 44

stem cells in elderly failure of man (Jesus) — 3/8/01 Vol. 22

stem cells, cloning admonished (Jesus) — 1/2/02 Vol. 26

stem cells,cloning violate God's plan (Jesus) — 11/20/05 Vol. 41

stench of sin as in time of Noah (Jesus) — 9/16/99 Vol. 16

stench of sin to God souls need purification (Jesus) — 2/26/01 Vol. 22

Steubenville love (Jesus) — 12/17/95 Vol. 3

stewards people are not owners (Jesus) — 11/1/03 Vol. 33

stewards, not owners relation to possessions (Jesus) — 10/22/07 Vol. 49

stewardship man's life & talents to manage (Jesus) — 3/10/02 Vol. 26

stewardship use gifts properly (Jesus) — 11/4/05 Vol. 41

stiff-necked people America like Israel (Jesus) — 6/22/02 Vol. 27

stigmata Padre Pio suffered (Padre Pio) — 4/6/98 Vol. 11

stirring wheel choice of God's vs man's way (Jesus) — 11/10/00 Vol. 21

stock crash caused,one world people (Jesus) — 11/30/97 Vol. 9

stock market bubble broke (Jesus) — 5/22/03 Vol. 31

stock market collapse (Jesus) — 10/3/07 Vol. 49

stock market collapse with greed (Jesus) — 7/16/98 Vol. 12

stock market concerned only with profits (Jesus) — 6/20/02 Vol. 27

stock market crash to strip things (Jesus) — 1/26/99 Vol. 14

stock market economy deteriorates (Jesus) — 4/27/01 Vol. 23

stock market major depression (Jesus) — 6/20/02 Vol. 27

stock market manipulated (Jesus) — 9/26/02 Vol. 28

stock market manipulated (Jesus) — 6/2/02 Vol. 27

stock market manipulated and controlled (Jesus) — 4/13/98 Vol. 11

stock market manipulated by the rich (Jesus) — 10/27/97 Vol. 9

stock market obsession for money (Jesus) — 12/17/99 Vol. 17

stock market speculation bubble breaking (Jesus) — 8/2/02 Vol. 28

stock market war could collapse (Jesus) — 1/30/03 Vol. 30

stock market crash One World Government (Jesus) — 11/19/96 Vol. 5

stock market fraud cheating stockholders (Jesus) — 3/4/04 Vol. 34

stock market greed causing stress in workplace (Jesus) — 1/7/00 Vol. 18

stock market losses focus on heavenly treasures (Jesus) — 4/18/02 Vol. 27

stock market,freedoms will be ruined & lost (Jesus) — 10/12/00 Vol. 21

stock prices volatile caused by speculation (Jesus) — 3/8/00 Vol. 18

stockbrokers, corporations collusion for profit (Jesus) — 11/30/07 Vol. 49

stocks & money let go and give to charity (Jesus) — 11/26/01 Vol. 25

stocks to lose money in change to new economy (Jesus) — 11/23/00 Vol. 21

stocks,commodities one world people control (Jesus) — 11/2/00 Vol. 21

Stonehenge sign of special events (Jesus) — 4/20/05 Vol. 39

stones can be raised to life (Jesus) — 1/23/99 Vol. 14

stony cold hearts need to open to Jesus (Jesus) — 1/31/99 Vol. 14

stop Iraq war peace is best gift (Jesus) — 12/17/98 Vol. 13

stoppage of messages sign testing time is done (Mary) — 4/17/97 Vol. 7

store food famine coming (Jesus) — 6/25/98 Vol. 11

storm of boat calmed by Jesus (Jesus) — 5/12/05 Vol. 39

storm victims need help with necessities (Jesus) — 9/23/04 Vol. 36

storm victims need prayers, food, water (Jesus) — 9/13/04 Vol. 36

storm water dictating its own course (Jesus) — 9/16/04 Vol. 36

storms abortions & sins of the flesh (Jesus) — 1/29/98 Vol. 10

storms chastisement for abortion (Jesus) — 12/29/00 Vol. 21

storms chastisement for sins (Jesus) — 3/5/98 Vol. 10

storms chastisements/weather (Jesus) — 6/8/96 Vol. 3

storms continue to bring us to knees (Jesus) — 8/25/98 Vol. 12

storms financial losses,get attention (Jesus) — 9/22/98 Vol. 12

storms loss of possessions, jobs (Jesus) — 9/8/96 Vol. 4

storms pray to mitigate (Jesus) — 8/27/98 Vol. 12

storms punishment for not repenting (Jesus) — 9/10/98 Vol. 12

storms rebellion of nature (Jesus) — 6/15/98 Vol. 11

storms sin (Jesus) — 8/25/95 Vol. 3

storms sins need cleansing (Jesus) — 2/19/98 Vol. 10

storms spiritual weapons (Jesus) — 8/16/95 Vol. 3

storms strip possessions (Jesus)   1/20/98 Vol. 10
storms test of end days (Jesus)   10/10/97 Vol. 9
storms tested by (Jesus)   8/30/06 Vol. 44
storms wealthy humbled,disasters (Jesus)   9/17/98 Vol. 12
storms will continue (Jesus)   12/7/97 Vol. 9
storms will take toll of lives (Jesus)   8/26/99 Vol. 16
storms & flooding enhanced by HAARP (Jesus)   7/6/06 Vol. 44
storms & terrorism hurricanes, election threat (Jesus)   8/10/04 Vol. 36
storms and fires chastisements for sins (Jesus)   8/23/98 Vol. 12
storms and fires last wake up call (Jesus)   5/6/98 Vol. 11
storms and fires stripped of our possessions (Jesus)   6/13/98 Vol. 11
storms and fires to get our attention (Jesus)   6/30/98 Vol. 11
storms and hurricanes reflect violence in society (Jesus)   8/29/97 Vol. 8
storms and poor finances require trust in God (Jesus)   10/8/98 Vol. 13
storms as chastisements one after the other (Jesus)   8/20/99 Vol. 16
storms in life calmed by Jesus (Jesus)   5/27/00 Vol. 19
storms of life Jesus is our anchor (Jesus)   3/2/97 Vol. 6
storms to get worse link of sins to lost blessings (Jesus)   8/6/98 Vol. 12
storms to increase above average flooding (Jesus)   12/4/97 Vol. 9
storms, parade of coming to test endurance (Jesus)   8/12/04 Vol. 36
storms,war damage help destitute neighbors (Jesus)   11/7/98 Vol. 13
straight road avoid spiritual detours (Jesus)   12/26/98 Vol. 13
strange light in the sky sign as at Fatima (Jesus)   10/4/01 Vol. 25
strangers & neighbors need your help (Jesus)   7/11/04 Vol. 36
strength trust in trial (Jesus)   2/7/96 Vol. 3
strength & endurance needed for faith in God (Jesus)   10/8/04 Vol. 37
strength of Church depends on bishop's leadership (Jesus) 12/29/01 Vol. 25
stress in life from daily problems (Jesus)   2/19/06 Vol. 42
stresses of life Jesus there for us (Jesus)   9/6/05 Vol. 40
strip unnecessary concentrate on spiritual (Jesus)   11/16/99 Vol. 17
stripped people see control of worldly things (Jesus)   9/16/04 Vol. 36
stripping churches removes reverence,traditions (Jesus)   2/3/05 Vol. 38
struggles of life (Jesus)   11/16/00 Vol. 21
struggles of life consecrate everything (Jesus)   1/9/02 Vol. 26
struggles of life serve God,love neighbor (Jesus)   3/29/00 Vol. 18
Sts. Martha & Mary follow God's Will (Jesus)   7/29/99 Vol. 16
Sts. Paul & Barnabas saved souls (Jesus)   6/11/02 Vol. 27
Sts. Peter & Paul inspired to evangelize (Jesus)   6/29/04 Vol. 35
Sts. Peter & Paul persecuted (Jesus)   9/28/00 Vol. 20
Sts. Peter & Paul persecuted for evangelizing (Jesus)   6/2/06 Vol. 43
stubbornness in Adam, children (Jesus)   12/26/98 Vol. 13
students of life learn from mistakes (Jesus)   7/22/99 Vol. 16
Stump of Jesse in mother & child stump (Mary)   12/8/07 Vol. 49
submarine,Russian nuclear weapons on board (Jesus)   6/13/01 Vol. 23
submissive to others for submission to Jesus (Jesus)   6/24/99 Vol. 15
substance abuse pray for problems (Jesus)   7/31/97 Vol. 8
substance abusers reach out for help (Jesus)   6/29/98 Vol. 11

subways hiding places (Jesus)   2/2/00 Vol. 18
success worldly vs. heavenly (Jesus)   7/3/07 Vol. 48
success in life God is reason for gifts (Jesus)   1/5/04 Vol. 34
success in life use God's measure (Jesus)   4/7/04 Vol. 35
success to God not found in possessions (Jesus)   1/9/00 Vol. 18
suffer cross (Mary)   3/7/94 Vol. 1
suffer double portion (Jesus)   2/10/94 Vol. 1
suffer sins (Jesus)   5/23/95 Vol. 2
suffering a grace to be stronger (Jesus)   1/10/98 Vol. 10
suffering a secret blessing (Jesus)   3/1/97 Vol. 6
suffering accept the cup of (Jesus)   5/24/99 Vol. 15
suffering be examples & deny self (Jesus)   4/11/05 Vol. 39
suffering be prepared for disasters (Jesus)   12/10/03 Vol. 33
suffering call on Jesus' help (Jesus)   3/16/06 Vol. 42
suffering carry cross as Jesus did (Jesus)   1/17/03 Vol. 30
suffering carry cross daily (Jesus)   8/9/97 Vol. 8
suffering carry daily crosses (Jesus)   5/18/98 Vol. 11
suffering daily crosses (Jesus)   9/17/97 Vol. 8
suffering daily crosses (Mary)   2/2/98 Vol. 10
suffering do not waste pain (Jesus)   7/31/98 Vol. 12
suffering expected in life (Jesus)   2/28/08 Vol. 50
suffering famine and torture (Jesus)   2/23/96 Vol. 3
suffering Fonda (Kateri T.)   5/7/95 Vol. 2
suffering for belief in Jesus (Jesus)   2/27/03 Vol. 30
suffering for self or others (Jesus)   6/25/01 Vol. 23
suffering grace in daily trials (Jesus)   6/6/98 Vol. 11
suffering helps our salvation (Jesus)   8/1/01 Vol. 24
suffering hidden blessings (Jesus)   12/15/00 Vol. 21
suffering in hospitals (Jesus)   6/17/04 Vol. 35
suffering Jesus is with us (Jesus)   10/15/01 Vol. 25
suffering love (Jesus)   5/15/95 Vol. 2
suffering means of salvation (Jesus)   8/14/97 Vol. 8
suffering necessary for faith in Jesus (Jesus)   4/15/00 Vol. 19
suffering of Jesus for us (Jesus)   7/21/03 Vol. 32
suffering offer all up (Jesus)   8/20/00 Vol. 20
suffering offer for sinners (St. Theresa)   4/10/96 Vol. 3
suffering offer it up (Holy Spirit)   5/3/01 Vol. 23
suffering offer up daily crosses (Jesus)   2/23/04 Vol. 34
suffering offer up each day (Jesus)   11/25/96 Vol. 5
suffering offer up, self-denial (Jesus)   2/13/97 Vol. 6
suffering part of life on earth (Jesus)   12/26/05 Vol. 41
suffering price for souls (Jesus)   12/4/96 Vol. 5
suffering ready to accept (Jesus)   2/16/01 Vol. 22
suffering refines rough edges (Jesus)   6/11/01 Vol. 23
suffering Resurrection (Jesus)   4/12/95 Vol. 2
suffering share with Jesus (Jesus)   3/8/03 Vol. 30
suffering spiritual glasses (Jesus)   8/23/97 Vol. 8

suffering strengthen for battle (Jesus) — 3/31/97 Vol. 6

suffering struggles of life (Jesus) — 7/29/96 Vol. 4

suffering suffering servants (Jesus) — 2/16/96 Vol. 3

suffering sufficient grace to endure (Jesus) — 8/18/03 Vol. 32

suffering test of endurance (Jesus) — 11/16/96 Vol. 5

suffering the price for souls (Jesus) — 3/5/98 Vol. 10

suffering to gain crown in heaven (Jesus) — 12/16/97 Vol. 9

suffering to save souls (Jesus) — 8/13/99 Vol. 16

suffering torture & martyrdom (Jesus) — 12/19/96 Vol. 5

suffering tries & purifies the soul (Jesus) — 10/18/98 Vol. 13

suffering understanding of suffering (Jesus) — 12/3/96 Vol. 5

suffering violation of God's law (Jesus) — 10/13/97 Vol. 9

suffering & afflictions purify for heaven (Jesus) — 11/11/05 Vol. 41

suffering & crosses accept for reward (Jesus) — 3/9/07 Vol. 46

suffering & fasting vs. desires & pleasures (Jesus) — 9/19/07 Vol. 48

suffering & penances ways to atone for sins (Jesus) — 1/31/05 Vol. 38

suffering & sorrows is life on earth (Jesus) — 3/7/99 Vol. 14

suffering & trials lessen purgatory (Jesus) — 9/30/03 Vol. 32

suffering at refuges purgatory here (Jesus) — 7/18/03 Vol. 32

suffering criticism price of souls (Jesus) — 5/8/99 Vol. 15

suffering for heaven on earth and in purgatory (Jesus) — 12/28/01 Vol. 25

suffering for others gains heavenly treasures (Jesus) — 2/16/00 Vol. 18

suffering in Jesus shared in daily cross (Jesus) — 12/23/04 Vol. 37

suffering in life seek God's help (Jesus) — 5/27/99 Vol. 15

suffering in tribulation call on Jesus' help (Jesus) — 3/23/06 Vol. 42

suffering Jesus from killing in abortion,wars (Jesus) — 11/15/04 Vol. 37

suffering on earth all are called to be like Jesus (Jesus) — 5/11/00 Vol. 19

suffering pain use pain as prayer offering (Jesus) — 11/15/97 Vol. 9

suffering people help them bear pain (Jesus) — 8/14/05 Vol. 40

suffering refused causes heavier cross (Jesus) — 8/30/99 Vol. 16

suffering servant atonement for sin (Jesus) — 2/21/08 Vol. 50

suffering servant come as child in humility (Jesus) — 2/26/04 Vol. 34

suffering servant family & consolation (Chelsea) — 2/8/96 Vol. 3

suffering servants consecrate everything up (Jesus) — 9/12/03 Vol. 32

suffering servants for world's sins (Jesus) — 2/14/08 Vol. 50

suffering servants pain, redemptive value (Jesus) — 12/2/06 Vol. 45

suffering trials steps closer to heaven (Jesus) — 8/27/99 Vol. 16

suffering, criticism faithful must accept (Jesus) — 11/5/03 Vol. 33

suffering, death cannot be avoided (Jesus) — 12/16/98 Vol. 13

suffering, personal share with Jesus' cross (Jesus) — 3/14/08 Vol. 50

suffering, redemptive offer up to Jesus for sins (Jesus) — 4/5/01 Vol. 23

suffering, window of do not question God (Jesus) — 10/4/96 Vol. 5

sufferings Blessed Sacrament (St.John Cross) — 12/14/93 Vol. 1

sufferings offer them up for sins (Jesus) — 4/8/05 Vol. 39

sufferings offer up (Jesus) — 10/22/01 Vol. 25

sufferings offer up (Jesus) — 2/11/99 Vol. 14

sufferings Purgatory — 11/2/93 Vol. 1

sufferings rest in Jesus' help (Jesus) — 4/15/99 Vol. 15

sufferings share with people, Jesus (Jesus) — 10/13/07 Vol. 49

sufferings united with Jesus (Jesus) — 4/23/06 Vol. 43

sufferings in life confidence in God's help (Jesus) — 3/11/99 Vol. 14

sufferings in life picking up cross (Jesus) — 5/22/00 Vol. 19

sufferings in life shared with Jesus' suffering (Jesus) — 10/25/04 Vol. 37

sufferings offered up intentions for activities (St. Therese) — 10/1/98 Vol. 13

sufferings offered up preparation for Christmas (Jesus) — 12/14/00 Vol. 21

Sugar Bush refuge of protection (Jesus) — 6/21/03 Vol. 31

suicide Jesus' mercy (Jesus) — 8/11/06 Vol. 44

suicide teaching on (Jesus) — 5/10/03 Vol. 31

suicide & despair ask for help (Jesus) — 1/9/02 Vol. 26

suicide bombers discourage peace (Jesus) — 7/18/02 Vol. 28

suicide bombers not love of God (Jesus) — 5/23/02 Vol. 27

suicide bombers not martyrs at all (Jesus) — 12/7/01 Vol. 25

suicide bombers pray for peace (Jesus) — 4/25/02 Vol. 27

suicide bombers see no future in lives (Jesus) — 10/24/02 Vol. 29

summer & fall more heat,droughts,fires (Jesus) — 7/29/02 Vol. 28

summer heat more droughts, storms (Jesus) — 6/20/07 Vol. 47

summer heat scorching heat,drougts (Jesus) — 4/27/00 Vol. 19

summer vacation no vacation from God (Jesus) — 6/26/97 Vol. 7

summer,scorching droughts cause of fires (Jesus) — 6/15/00 Vol. 19

sun darkened at triumph (Jesus) — 8/24/00 Vol. 20

sun light and man's light (Jesus) — 12/2/04 Vol. 37

sun pulsating sign of love (Jesus) — 7/21/99 Vol. 16

Sunday as day of worship (Jesus) — 7/25/99 Vol. 16

Sunday pray and do not work (Mary) — 9/29/96 Vol. 4

Sunday sports instead of Mass (Jesus) — 6/18/98 Vol. 11

Sunday Mass absence of people (Jesus) — 5/6/07 Vol. 47

Sunday Mass encourage attendance (Jesus) — 12/19/06 Vol. 45

Sunday Mass keep holy Lord's Day (Jesus) — 1/23/01 Vol. 22

Sunday Mass more than just Easter (Jesus) — 4/12/07 Vol. 47

Sunday Mass sin to miss (Jesus) — 3/4/07 Vol. 46

Sunday Mass worship God once a week (Jesus) — 9/2/07 Vol. 48

Sunday Mass young not attending (Jesus) — 8/27/05 Vol. 40

Sunday Mass effort remember God in prayer (Jesus) — 10/10/00 Vol. 21

Sunday Mass missed divorce, unmarried (Jesus) — 11/13/07 Vol. 49

Sunday Mass needed bring your heart to Mass (Jesus) — 10/8/98 Vol. 13

Sun. Mass,few people spiritual life most important (Jesus) — 11/23/98 Vol. 13

Sunday reverence rest on seventh day (Jesus) — 7/27/01 Vol. 24

Sunday worship need souls to praise God (Jesus) — 3/1/01 Vol. 22

Sunday worship needed to show love of God (Jesus) — 2/11/01 Vol. 22

Sundays a day of rest (Jesus) — 7/15/05 Vol. 40

Sundays do not work for gain on (Jesus) — 12/21/00 Vol. 21

Sundays respect for,fall of USA (Jesus) — 12/29/96 Vol. 5

Sundays, no work obey Commandments (Jesus) — 3/26/00 Vol. 18

sun's energy can be better harnessed (Jesus) — 11/7/06 Vol. 45

sunspot peak and computer problems (Jesus)   6/17/99 Vol. 15
superhighway in US NAFTA Treaty (Jesus)   8/31/06 Vol. 44
supernatural intervention for Era of Peace (Jesus)   3/24/08 Vol. 50
superstitions replace faith (Jesus)   10/31/01 Vol. 25
support of Jesus strength for endurance (Jesus)   11/12/03 Vol. 33
Supreme Court abortion to be decided (Jesus)   9/29/05 Vol. 40
Supreme Court and abortion decision (Jesus)   11/3/05 Vol. 41
Supreme Court pray for leaders (Jesus)   1/11/01 Vol. 22
Supreme Court pray for new justices (Jesus)   7/14/05 Vol. 40
Supreme Court changes possible abortion law change (Jesus) 1/12/06 Vol. 42
Supreme Court judges pray to be prolife (Jesus)   7/19/05 Vol. 40
Supreme Court rock judgment sign against US (Jesus)   12/1/05 Vol. 41
surplus to famine America wastes food (Jesus)   8/26/02 Vol. 28
surprise takeover by martial law (Jesus)   12/8/98 Vol. 13
surprises, serious could affect elections (Jesus)   3/5/04 Vol. 34
surrender love (Jesus)   9/19/95 Vol. 3
surrender all to God road to perfection (Jesus)   3/13/01 Vol. 22
surrender, total through God's help (Jesus)   11/6/04 Vol. 37
surrender,complete to follow Jesus (Jesus)   4/29/00 Vol. 19
surveillance in cameras & phones (Jesus)   8/10/06 Vol. 44
surveillance cameras banks,traffic,borders (Jesus)   6/22/99 Vol. 15
survival faith (Jesus)   12/5/95 Vol. 3
survival pilot (Jesus)   6/9/95 Vol. 2
survival trust (Jesus)   9/4/95 Vol. 3
survival trust & faith in Jesus (Jesus)   7/27/99 Vol. 16
survival in weakness test of faith (Jesus)   2/6/00 Vol. 18
survivors pray for them (Jesus)   4/5/06 Vol. 43
swearing & gossip filth from mouth (Jesus)   3/13/03 Vol. 30
swearing to be avoided Christian living examples (Jesus) 10/21/98 Vol. 13
sword live by it, die by it (Jesus)   8/9/01 Vol. 24
sword preserve life (Jesus)   3/13/99 Vol. 14
sword sheepgate (Jesus)   8/6/94 Vol. 2
swords into plowshares to stop wars (Jesus)   12/4/07 Vol. 49
tabernacle do not put in back rooms (Jesus)   1/19/03 Vol. 30
tabernacle genuflect in presence (Jesus)   2/19/99 Vol. 14
tabernacle gone from churches (Jesus)   9/4/94 Vol. 2
tabernacle Jesus makes church holy (Jesus)   9/27/02 Vol. 28
tabernacle lost sense of sacred (Jesus)   2/13/97 Vol. 6
tabernacle prisoner (Jesus)   12/5/94 Vol. 2
tabernacle real presence (Jesus)   12/17/94 Vol. 2
tabernacle sanctuary of love (Jesus)   10/14/06 Vol. 45
tabernacle thanksgiving (Jesus)   7/6/94 Vol. 2
tabernacle damaged in attempt to remove Hosts (Jesus)   11/15/07 Vol. 49
tabernacle position should be in prominent location (Jesus) 2/21/02 Vol. 26
tabernacle position suffering (Jesus)   6/24/95 Vol. 2
tabernacle, sinless in Mary for Jesus (Jesus)   12/20/07 Vol. 49
tabernacles angels preserve (Jesus)   7/12/02 Vol. 28

tabernacles as center of attention (Jesus)   1/15/02 Vol. 26
tabernacles do not move from main church (Jesus)   1/24/02 Vol. 26
tabernacles give place,honor in Church (Jesus)   2/19/99 Vol. 14
tabernacles guarded by angels (Jesus)   6/14/02 Vol. 27
tabernacles hidden away (Jesus)   6/8/98 Vol. 11
tabernacles in back rooms (Jesus)   9/18/02 Vol. 28
tabernacles in prominent places (Jesus)   6/14/04 Vol. 35
tabernacles Jesus in center as in life (Jesus)   6/28/05 Vol. 39
tabernacles keep in main church (Jesus)   7/8/04 Vol. 36
tabernacles keep visible (Jesus)   4/22/01 Vol. 23
tabernacles new Holy of Holies (Jesus)   10/3/99 Vol. 17
tabernacles placed in back rooms (Jesus)   2/5/99 Vol. 14
tabernacles protection of Eucharist (Jesus)   8/2/07 Vol. 48
tabernacles safety from evil ones (Jesus)   7/29/04 Vol. 36
tabernacles to be removed (Jesus)   10/11/03 Vol. 33
tabernacles to places of disrespect (Jesus)   1/12/98 Vol. 10
tabernacles visible in main church (Jesus)   8/2/99 Vol. 16
tabernacles attacked sign of coming tribulation (Jesus)   9/1/04 Vol. 36
tabernacles destroyed by evil ones stealing Hosts (Jesus) 9/24/04 Vol. 36
tabernacles of God need visits, and protection (Jesus)   12/27/07 Vol. 49
tabernacles stripped to preserve Hosts (Jesus)   9/24/04 Vol. 36
tabernacles,adoration reverence Real Presence (Jesus)   11/5/99 Vol. 17
take over plan by one world people (Jesus)   2/17/06 Vol. 42
takeover all in place (Jesus)   7/19/01 Vol. 24
takeover blueprint by chips,price controls (Jesus)   3/3/01 Vol. 22
takeover of America vulnerable, troops at war (Jesus)   11/14/97 Vol. 9
takeover, Antichrist created chaos,diseases (Jesus)   3/16/01 Vol. 22
takeover, emergency by intense storms (Jesus)   9/27/05 Vol. 40
takeover, surprise by tunnels (Jesus)   12/7/05 Vol. 41
taking mark road to hell (Jesus)   3/8/00 Vol. 18
talent do not waste in despair (Jesus)   11/17/02 Vol. 29
talents equal value of souls (Jesus)   2/12/04 Vol. 34
talents for God's glory (Jesus)   7/8/02 Vol. 28
talents fulfill God's plan (Jesus)   8/31/96 Vol. 4
talents gifts (Jesus)   4/24/94 Vol. 1
talents more given, more expected (Jesus)   9/13/03 Vol. 32
talents need to be used (Jesus)   2/2/01 Vol. 22
talents share your fruits (Jesus)   12/6/98 Vol. 13
talents to fulfill life's plan (Jesus)   11/19/00 Vol. 21
talents unique to each person (Jesus)   8/5/01 Vol. 24
talents use best to serve God (Jesus)   12/19/05 Vol. 41
talents use for God and neighbor (Jesus)   2/16/98 Vol. 10
talents use for God's glory (Jesus)   2/7/07 Vol. 46
talents use for God's purpose (Jesus)   3/11/07 Vol. 46
talents use for God's Will (Jesus)   6/23/04 Vol. 35
talents use to best ability (Jesus)   7/16/05 Vol. 40
talents use to best of our ability (Jesus)   7/13/04 Vol. 36

talents use to help others (Jesus)	9/26/05 Vol. 40	talents & gifts thank God for (Jesus)	2/20/03 Vol. 30
talents use to the fullest (Jesus)	4/27/02 Vol. 27	talents & gifts use to best ability (Jesus)	1/8/04 Vol. 34
talents use to the fullest (Jesus)	6/16/04 Vol. 35	talents & make up God's plan for each (Jesus)	1/26/03 Vol. 30
talents use, do not waste (Jesus)	11/17/04 Vol. 37	talents & resources use for good purpose (Jesus)	10/17/03 Vol. 33
talents witness of glory to God (Jesus)	7/27/97 Vol. 8	talents & skills unique to each person (Jesus)	2/7/07 Vol. 46
talents & gifts share with each other (Jesus)	6/15/05 Vol. 39	talents & skills use for the glory of God (Jesus)	1/31/02 Vol. 26

talents and love share with others (Jesus) 10/6/02 Vol. 29
talents from God used for good or evil (Jesus) 7/13/00 Vol. 20
talents from God used for our mission (Jesus) 5/27/07 Vol. 47
talents fulfilled give God glory (Jesus) 6/27/00 Vol. 19
talents of each person need work to discover (Jesus) 6/27/00 Vol. 19
talents of faith share for conversion (Jesus) 9/1/07 Vol. 48
talents used do not bury, or waste (Jesus) 2/14/06 Vol. 42
talents, natural use in following Jesus (Jesus) 6/19/06 Vol. 43
talents, unique as spokes of bicycle wheel (Jesus) 11/12/02 Vol. 29
talents, use do not bury them (Jesus) 8/31/05 Vol. 40
talk schedule to increase for updates (Jesus) 9/13/07 Vol. 48
talking praying (Jesus) 10/15/93 Vol. 1
tanks Europe (Jesus) 11/27/94 Vol. 2
tanks one world government (Jesus) 2/14/95 Vol. 2
tasks & trials easy with God's help (Jesus) 6/8/06 Vol. 43
tax protection to be lost by fighting abortion,homosexuals (Jesus)
11/1/05 Vol. 41
tax supported benefits to be compromised (Jesus) 1/17/08 Vol. 50
taxes causing burdens (Jesus) 3/10/05 Vol. 38
teach all nations requires Holy Spirit (Jesus) 1/23/00 Vol. 18
teacher of faith best in Jesus (Jesus) 8/17/99 Vol. 16
Teacher,greatest shows lessons in Gospels (Jesus) 6/27/99 Vol. 15
teachers faith (Jesus) 5/29/95 Vol. 2
teachers thank, pray for them (Jesus) 6/17/04 Vol. 35
teachers & priests needed to teach (Jesus) 7/20/06 Vol. 44
teachers of religion teach prayer, avoid occult (Jesus) 9/30/06 Vol. 44
teaching errors stand up for Church laws (Jesus) 8/20/98 Vol. 12
teaching faith to youth important task (Jesus) 9/9/06 Vol. 44
teaching materials for tsunami victims (Jesus) 1/20/05 Vol. 38
teaching others avoid being a hypocrite (Jesus) 3/14/02 Vol. 26
tears of Blessed Virgin Mary symbolized by rain (Jesus) 6/2/02 Vol. 27
tears of love precious to Jesus (Jesus) 7/26/07 Vol. 48
tears on statues sadness for sins (Jesus) 9/24/04 Vol. 36
technology abused by evil (Jesus) 5/28/98 Vol. 11
technology abused by one world people (Jesus) 4/20/04 Vol. 35
technology avoid turning against nature (Jesus) 8/19/04 Vol. 36
technology becomes an idol (Jesus) 6/1/98 Vol. 11
technology breakdown in society (Jesus) 6/1/99 Vol. 15
technology buy & sell,Antichrist (Jesus) 6/18/97 Vol. 7
technology chips fail from radiation (Jesus) 5/7/02 Vol. 27
technology controlling our lives (Jesus) 5/3/04 Vol. 35
technology creation being abused (Jesus) 3/8/98 Vol. 10
technology do not be distracted by (Jesus) 9/14/00 Vol. 20
technology do not be distracted by (Jesus) 12/9/99 Vol. 17
technology electronic control (Jesus) 6/18/98 Vol. 11
technology exploited for control (Jesus) 9/14/00 Vol. 20
technology fail because it is Godless (Jesus) 12/25/97 Vol. 9

technology failures keep us humble (Jesus) 12/4/99 Vol. 17
technology for power over others (Jesus) 7/1/03 Vol. 32
technology good, but can be abused (Jesus) 6/10/04 Vol. 35
technology keen competition (Jesus) 6/17/02 Vol. 27
technology knowledge just surface (Jesus) 7/10/97 Vol. 8
technology made for failure (Jesus) 5/26/98 Vol. 11
technology our undoing, leisure (Jesus) 5/22/97 Vol. 7
technology Satan's organization (Jesus) 8/12/97 Vol. 8
technology to bring America's demise (Jesus) 7/31/02 Vol. 28
technology to control us (Jesus) 8/17/00 Vol. 20
technology to spread Word of God (Jesus) 10/14/02 Vol. 29
technology to strip our comforts (Jesus) 5/12/99 Vol. 15
technology trust more in God's power (Jesus) 7/30/98 Vol. 12
technology used by evil ones (Jesus) 5/10/03 Vol. 31
technology will be America's downfall (Jesus) 11/23/00 Vol. 21
technology will be brought to our knees (Jesus) 5/14/98 Vol. 11
technology will be downfall (Jesus) 2/11/99 Vol. 14
technology will be our downfall (Jesus) 9/26/02 Vol. 28
technology will be our downfall (Jesus) 2/27/99 Vol. 14
technology will be your downfall (Jesus) 11/29/98 Vol. 13
technology in ruin imperfect from beginning (Jesus) 10/1/98 Vol. 13
technology,our downfall science has become a god (Jesus) 10/4/00 Vol. 21
technology's downfall stripped of possessions (Jesus) 4/10/01 Vol. 23
teckle,peres,mene hand writing on the wall (Jesus) 8/14/99 Vol. 16
Tehachapi place of refuge (Jesus) 2/14/97 Vol. 6
telephone lines free calls to Jesus (Jesus) 6/19/02 Vol. 27
telephones monitored,evangelize (Jesus) 5/8/97 Vol. 7
telephones & electricity targets of terrorists (Jesus) 10/7/04 Vol. 37
telephones & TV fiber optic,2-way listening (Jesus) 8/30/01 Vol. 24
Television avoid evil influence (Jesus) 12/11/98 Vol. 13
television cn control time, 1hr only (Jesus) 8/1/03 Vol. 32
television disconnect from,radio,etc. (Jesus) 11/10/97 Vol. 9
television do not watch so much (Jesus) 7/2/01 Vol. 24
television occasion of sin,waste of time (Jesus) 6/10/02 Vol. 27
television stops family interaction (Jesus) 12/4/06 Vol. 45
television to control minds (Jesus) 1/25/01 Vol. 22
television & monitors get rid of after Warning (Jesus) 6/10/02 Vol. 27
television,high definition do not use (Jesus) 4/19/02 Vol. 27
TV, high definition two-way communication (Jesus) 4/11/02 Vol. 27
television,refuse better to pray,help others (Jesus) 6/13/00 Vol. 19
Televisions remove after Warning (Jesus) 5/28/03 Vol. 31
televisions remove after Warning (Jesus) 11/4/05 Vol. 41
televisions removed avoid watching Antichrist (Mary) 5/15/00 Vol. 19
temperature record highest ever in January (Jesus) 2/9/06 Vol. 42
temperatures, record changing weather patterns (Jesus) 1/25/06 Vol. 42
Temple of Solomon St. John the Baptist's birth (Jesus) 6/24/02 Vol. 27
Temples of Holy Spirit each soul has Presence (Jesus) 4/19/98 Vol. 11

temples of Holy Spirit power in all (Holy Spirit) 5/14/98 Vol. 11

temporal news lost in the wind (Jesus) 11/8/03 Vol. 33

temporal punishment due to sin (Jesus) 1/31/98 Vol. 10

temptation call on for help (Jesus) 2/21/99 Vol. 14

temptations a daily battle (Jesus) 2/24/04 Vol. 34

temptations at every turn (Jesus) 9/19/02 Vol. 28

temptations avoid occasions of sin (Jesus) 5/22/02 Vol. 27

temptations be grounded in faith (Jesus) 12/24/97 Vol. 9

temptations be prepared to fight (Jesus) 5/14/04 Vol. 35

temptations be prepared to withstand (Jesus) 3/31/01 Vol. 22

temptations call on grace of Jesus (Jesus) 12/7/01 Vol. 25

temptations call on Jesus' help (Jesus) 8/24/04 Vol. 36

temptations call upon Jesus in (Jesus) 2/2/04 Vol. 34

temptations constant battle with (Jesus) 4/23/05 Vol. 39

temptations devil taunts you (Jesus) 8/17/01 Vol. 24

temptations do not dwell on (Jesus) 2/9/08 Vol. 50

temptations evil one always there (Jesus) 5/16/02 Vol. 27

temptations evil one, guard soul (Jesus) 5/22/97 Vol. 7

temptations gluttony, greed, pride (Jesus) 4/9/05 Vol. 39

temptations how to fight them (Jesus) 7/23/02 Vol. 28

temptations keep prayerful life (St. Michael) 7/20/97 Vol. 8

temptations of Jesus by Satan (Jesus) 3/4/04 Vol. 34

temptations of world to sin (Jesus) 10/15/02 Vol. 29

temptations weakness to sin (Jesus) 6/14/04 Vol. 35

temptations with pleasures & comforts (Jesus) 4/24/07 Vol. 47

temptations & distractions Satan's attacks (Jesus) 6/28/07 Vol. 47

temptations of Satan in rationalizations (Jesus) 5/4/05 Vol. 39

temptations of Satan will not stop (Jesus) 5/27/04 Vol. 35

temptations of sin avoid by prayerful lives (Jesus) 10/26/00 Vol. 21

temptations of sin avoid occasions of sin (Jesus) 7/9/05 Vol. 40

temptations,many from terrorist acts (Jesus) 9/16/01 Vol. 24

Ten Commandments a way of life (God the Father) 7/23/99 Vol. 16

Ten Commandments and natural law (Jesus) 6/12/98 Vol. 11

Ten Commandments being mocked (Jesus) 9/16/03 Vol. 32

Ten Commandments broken on golden calf (Jesus) 6/20/98 Vol. 11

Ten Commandments cannot deny (Jesus) 7/4/02 Vol. 28

Ten Commandments covenant with Moses (Jesus) 8/13/99 Vol. 16

Ten Commandments display everywhere (Jesus) 5/21/02 Vol. 27

Ten Commandments distorted judges (Jesus) 8/25/03 Vol. 32

Ten Commandments division with Moses & today (Jesus) 8/21/03 Vol. 32

ten commandments Eucharist (Jesus) 8/1/94 Vol. 2

Ten Commandments follow to be free (Jesus) 6/18/05 Vol. 39

Ten Commandments given in love (Jesus) 7/28/03 Vol. 32

Ten Commandments history repeated (God the Father) 6/2/99 Vol. 15

Ten Commandments interventions in history (Jesus) 3/13/97 Vol. 6

Ten Commandments laws abused (Jesus) 7/24/03 Vol. 32

Ten Commandments live by His Will (Jesus) 8/2/01 Vol. 24

Ten Commandments love God & neighbor (God the Father) 8/20/03 Vol. 32

Ten Commandments love God & neighbor (Jesus) 3/13/07 Vol. 46

Ten Commandments love God and neighbor (Jesus) 6/4/98 Vol. 11

Ten Commandments love of God & neighbor (Jesus) 8/31/03 Vol. 32

Ten Commandments plan for life (Jesus) 5/18/01 Vol. 23

ten commandments sinners (Jesus) 11/19/94 Vol. 2

Ten Commandments spirit & letter of law (Jesus) 1/4/03 Vol. 30

ten commandments support traditional values (Jesus) 3/9/99 Vol. 14

Ten Commandments test of faith (Jesus) 8/29/97 Vol. 8

Ten Commandments the greatest is love (Jesus) 6/8/06 Vol. 43

ten flags regions of world control (Jesus) 1/27/99 Vol. 14

ten regions world wide,nation wide (Jesus) 3/9/01 Vol. 22

tents & beds for earthquakes,floods (Jesus) 8/25/99 Vol. 16

Terelya, Olena message at funeral (Olena Terelya) 11/20/04 Vol. 37

terminal illnesses last chance to be saved (Jesus) 3/13/06 Vol. 42

terminal life mortality of man's life (Jesus) 10/6/00 Vol. 21

terminal lives prepare for judgment (Jesus) 7/21/06 Vol. 44

terminally ill care for them (Jesus) 7/16/99 Vol. 16

termites apostasy (Jesus) 3/7/95 Vol. 2

terror vehicle of choice for takeover (Jesus) 5/21/02 Vol. 27

terror incident mandatory smart cards (Jesus) 10/27/04 Vol. 37

terrorism affect economy,freedoms (Jesus) 10/24/02 Vol. 29

terrorism against US interests (Jesus) 11/10/05 Vol. 41

terrorism Antichrist (Jesus) 7/10/96 Vol. 3

terrorism backlash on America (Jesus) 10/3/02 Vol. 29

terrorism because of hate of America (Jesus) 1/19/05 Vol. 38

terrorism biological weapons (Jesus) 7/20/05 Vol. 40

terrorism by fires (Jesus) 12/5/06 Vol. 45

terrorism causes fear in travellers (Jesus) 7/7/05 Vol. 40

terrorism could lead to World War III (Jesus) 1/1/02 Vol. 26

terrorism criticizing cause of 9-11 (Jesus) 5/16/02 Vol. 27

terrorism destruction in many forms (Jesus) 1/30/03 Vol. 30

terrorism divide Muslims & Christians (Jesus) 4/29/04 Vol. 35

terrorism do not expand the war (Jesus) 10/4/01 Vol. 25

terrorism do not spread to world war (Jesus) 11/29/01 Vol. 25

terrorism do not spread war on terrorism (Jesus) 2/14/02 Vol. 26

terrorism exploited freedoms (Jesus) 6/6/02 Vol. 27

terrorism explosives on trucks (Jesus) 9/10/02 Vol. 28

terrorism fear and chaos allowed (Jesus) 1/6/04 Vol. 34

terrorism fear to destroy economy (Jesus) 5/22/03 Vol. 31

terrorism freedoms compromised (Jesus) 1/3/02 Vol. 26

terrorism impossible to stop completely (Jesus) 3/29/04 Vol. 34

terrorism Iraq & elsewhere (Jesus) 1/27/04 Vol. 34

terrorism keeps changing methods (Jesus) 9/19/02 Vol. 28

terrorism leading to war (Jesus) 4/4/02 Vol. 27

terrorism leading to war (Jesus) 4/1/02 Vol. 27

terrorism means of global control (Jesus) 12/12/03 Vol. 33

terrorism more attacks planned (Jesus) 10/24/02 Vol. 29

terrorism never justified (Jesus) 8/27/98 Vol. 12

terrorism new threat to fuel supplies (Jesus) 9/24/05 Vol. 40

terrorism not stopped by war (Jesus) 5/27/04 Vol. 35

terrorism on larger scale, control (Jesus) 3/6/03 Vol. 30

terrorism on oil & fuel supplies (Jesus) 1/2/03 Vol. 30

terrorism paid by one world people (Jesus) 5/29/03 Vol. 31

terrorism possible tunnels under D.C. (Jesus) 8/11/04 Vol. 36

terrorism power outages threatened (Jesus) 11/7/05 Vol. 41

terrorism pray for compromise (Jesus) 4/25/02 Vol. 27

terrorism pray for peace (Jesus) 6/15/06 Vol. 43

terrorism prearranged (Jesus) 5/7/03 Vol. 31

terrorism retaliation worse (Jesus) 6/1/04 Vol. 35

terrorism rivalry of Jews & Arabs (Jesus) 7/27/96 Vol. 4

terrorism technology of chips (Jesus) 4/26/95 Vol. 2

terrorism to cause war of retaliation (Jesus) 3/3/04 Vol. 34

terrorism to continue until we leave Iraq (Jesus) 10/27/05 Vol. 41

terrorism tool of one world people (Jesus) 4/15/04 Vol. 35

terrorism tool to giving up freedoms (Jesus) 11/21/02 Vol. 29

terrorism TWA 800 flight/Olympics (Jesus) 10/11/96 Vol. 5

terrorism used to take freedoms away (Jesus) 12/20/01 Vol. 25

terrorism way of life for Arab militants (Jesus) 3/11/02 Vol. 26

terrorism will attack us again (Jesus) 2/9/04 Vol. 34

terrorism with crop dusters (Jesus) 2/25/03 Vol. 30

terrorism & disasters fires in cities (Jesus) 1/28/02 Vol. 26

terrorism & disasters result of sin (Jesus) 3/26/06 Vol. 42

terrorism & security used by one world people (Jesus) 10/27/05 Vol. 41

terrorism & war never the answer (Jesus) 2/13/03 Vol. 30

terrorism in America on going struggle (Jesus) 8/20/04 Vol. 36

terrorism increasing innocent lives in abortion (Jesus) 7/19/96 Vol. 4

terrorism of oil not all revealed by governments (Jesus) 9/2/04 Vol. 36

terrorism on increase stirring America to war footing (Jesus) 9/12/01 Vol. 24

terrorism on planes not always revealed (Jesus) 8/17/05 Vol. 40

terrorism staged to control people (Jesus) 2/14/06 Vol. 42

terrorism to increase to destroy economy (Jesus) 7/23/05 Vol. 40

terrorism, false for control of people (Jesus) 9/28/06 Vol. 44

terrorism, false forced on America (Jesus) 1/6/07 Vol. 46

terrorism, natural disasters to bring US to its knees (Jesus) 6/22/02 Vol. 27

terrorism, war on will not be effective (Jesus) 6/20/02 Vol. 27

terrorism, world threatens economy,lives (Jesus) 9/11/01 Vol. 24

terrorism,wars,diseases being manipulated (Jesus) 4/6/03 Vol. 31

terrorist pray hate turns to love (Jesus) 9/19/02 Vol. 28

terrorist acts precipitate smart cards (Jesus) 5/10/02 Vol. 27

terrorist attack planned for martial law (Jesus) 9/5/07 Vol. 48

terrorist attacks in Muslim countries (Jesus) 11/20/03 Vol. 33

terrorist attacks more loss of freedom (Jesus) 5/21/02 Vol. 27

terrorist attacks on coastal cities (Jesus) 6/23/05 Vol. 39

terrorist attacks to continue in future (Jesus) 9/26/01 Vol. 24

terrorist bombing prepare food (Jesus) 12/22/98 Vol. 13

terrorist bombings on scale yet to see (Jesus) 6/8/04 Vol. 35

terrorist bombs African bombing foretold (Jesus) 8/6/98 Vol. 12

terrorist countries facing destruction (Jesus) 4/18/02 Vol. 27

terrorist incident loss of American lives (Jesus) 7/25/03 Vol. 32

terrorist killings used for political gain (Jesus) 3/18/04 Vol. 34

terrorist threats new tapes (Jesus) 8/23/07 Vol. 48

terrorist threats trust in God,not security (Jesus) 11/21/02 Vol. 29

terrorist war could spread to world war (Jesus) 9/27/01 Vol. 24

terrorists abusing religion (Jesus) 9/11/02 Vol. 28

terrorists bombs in cities (Jesus) 8/7/04 Vol. 36

terrorists cannot destroy with bombs (Jesus) 10/30/01 Vol. 25

terrorists could return to Washington (Jesus) 12/25/03 Vol. 33

terrorists do not go to war, pray (Jesus) 9/12/02 Vol. 28

terrorists driven by Satan (Jesus) 10/1/01 Vol. 25

terrorists exploited by masons (Jesus) 12/17/01 Vol. 25

terrorists financed by one world people (Jesus) 6/15/06 Vol. 43

terrorists hard to eliminate (Jesus) 10/16/02 Vol. 29

terrorists in assassination attempts (Jesus) 4/27/05 Vol. 39

terrorists in schools & abortion clinics (Jesus) 1/16/02 Vol. 26

terrorists keep crop dusters from (Jesus) 6/13/02 Vol. 27

terrorists misled in thinking (Jesus) 7/21/05 Vol. 40

terrorists no religious meaning (Jesus) 11/8/01 Vol. 25

terrorists no religious reason (Jesus) 10/22/02 Vol. 29

terrorists not following Commandments (Jesus) 12/3/03 Vol. 33

terrorists paid by one world people (Jesus) 3/24/03 Vol. 30

terrorists paid by one world people (Jesus) 5/2/03 Vol. 31

terrorists pay at judgment (Jesus) 1/29/02 Vol. 26

terrorists planning skyscraper attack (Jesus) 5/12/03 Vol. 31

terrorists pray for them (Jesus) 11/29/01 Vol. 25

terrorists risk lives (Jesus) 1/8/98 Vol. 10

terrorists target financial buildings (Jesus) 8/11/04 Vol. 36

terrorists to control people (Jesus) 2/4/03 Vol. 30

terrorists use weapons and missiles (Jesus) 6/21/04 Vol. 35

terrorists want to remove Jews (Jesus) 7/20/06 Vol. 44

terrorists wars of retaliation (Jesus) 1/29/04 Vol. 34

terrorist's activity fear is not worth martial law (Jesus) 8/20/98 Vol. 12

terrorists attacks on infrastructure (Jesus) 8/28/03 Vol. 32

terrorists attacks still possible (Jesus) 10/22/04 Vol. 37

terrorists vs. America killing not the answer (Jesus) 9/13/01 Vol. 24

terrorists, Islamic hate and revenge not satisfied (Jesus) 8/20/04 Vol. 36

terrorists, killers spiritual disaster in hell (Jesus) 12/12/03 Vol. 33

terrorists, spiritual snuf out faith (Jesus) 10/11/02 Vol. 29

Tesla standing wave patterns (Jesus) 9/28/96 Vol. 4

test of evil days requires God's help (Jesus) 12/7/98 Vol. 13

test of hardships small and large (Jesus) 1/5/00 Vol. 18

test spirits in accord with Scripture (Jesus)	6/5/98 Vol. 11	Thanksgiving needed to thank God for gifts (Jesus)	10/10/04 Vol. 37
test the spirits traditions,commandments (Jesus)	12/19/97 Vol. 9	Thanksgiving of family (Jesus)	11/16/00 Vol. 21
tested by sin call on Jesus Name (Jesus)	9/29/03 Vol. 32	thanksgiving responsibility of gifts (Jesus)	11/25/99 Vol. 17
testing fire, water and killings (Jesus)	3/15/96 Vol. 3	Thanksgiving thank God for everything (Jesus)	1/28/06 Vol. 42
testing of rude people and jobs (Jesus)	8/16/98 Vol. 12	Thanksgiving to God for gifts (Jesus)	11/24/05 Vol. 41
testing & hardships snow removal,spiritual life (Jesus)	11/27/96 Vol. 5	Thanksgiving we are blessed with gifts (Jesus)	11/28/96 Vol. 5
testing by demons need God's protection (Jesus)	2/7/01 Vol. 22	Thanksgiving Day be grateful for live & faith (Jesus)	11/22/01 Vol. 25
testing by idols of money, fame, sports (Jesus)	11/14/05 Vol. 41	Thanksgiving Dinner help provide for the poor (Jesus)	11/15/07 Vol. 49
testing by the elements warning (Jesus)	2/22/95 Vol. 2	Thanksgiving for gifts after Communion (Jesus)	4/29/07 Vol. 47
testing ground in life on earth (Jesus)	7/22/99 Vol. 16	Thanksgiving help gracious in food & money (Jesus)	11/17/97 Vol. 9
testing in life make best of life's chances (Jesus)	3/28/01 Vol. 22	Thanksgiving model in one leper's thanks (Jesus)	11/22/07 Vol. 49
testing needed to appreciate blessings (Jesus)	2/16/01 Vol. 22	thanksgiving to God for all of His gifts (Jesus)	11/10/04 Vol. 37
testing of faith die for Him (St. Therese)	5/18/98 Vol. 11	Thanksgiving to God for spiritual,physical gifts (Jesus)	12/4/04 Vol. 37
testing required to purify your sins (Jesus)	4/19/00 Vol. 19	Thanksgiving tradition remember to thank God (Jesus)	11/27/03 Vol. 33
testing time protection and manna (Jesus)	4/19/96 Vol. 3	thanksgiving, quick for favors received (Jesus)	6/28/07 Vol. 47
testing time troubles of life (Jesus)	4/18/96 Vol. 3	The Father gratitude for Jesus' birth (God the Father)	12/18/97 Vol. 9
testing time of life handling misfortunes (Jesus)	7/15/96 Vol. 4	The Holy Family unite families in love (Jesus)	1/15/98 Vol. 10
testings & temptations of Satan on us (Jesus)	7/10/03 Vol. 32	theologians liberal interpretations (Jesus)	10/4/97 Vol. 9
testings in life not beyond endurance (Jesus)	2/14/08 Vol. 50	theologians should not distort the truth (Jesus)	2/28/04 Vol. 34
tests of life graduate to heaven (Jesus)	3/4/99 Vol. 14	theologians & priests twist words (Jesus)	10/20/97 Vol. 9
Texas fires from man's pollution (Jesus)	1/12/06 Vol. 42	thick cross The Church	8/21/93 Vol. 1
thank God for all He gives us (Jesus)	11/28/02 Vol. 29	think before acting test if against God's law (Jesus)	8/5/00 Vol. 20
thankful for blessings not complaints of troubles (Jesus)	11/11/99 Vol. 17	think of God while working at job (Jesus)	2/20/00 Vol. 18
thankfulness for creation,death on cross (Jesus)	8/20/00 Vol. 20	think slowly then act properly (Jesus)	10/20/03 Vol. 33
thankfulness to God for all of our gifts (Jesus)	11/12/03 Vol. 33	thoughts & actions guard from sin (Jesus)	9/1/02 Vol. 28
thanks prayer (Adelaide)	8/30/95 Vol. 3	thread of life very fragile and thin (Jesus)	1/19/00 Vol. 18
thanks for messages witness to the truth (Jesus)	6/12/97 Vol. 7	threats of sin to soul's eternal life (Jesus)	3/17/99 Vol. 14
thanks needed when prayers are answered (Jesus)	10/20/07 Vol. 49	threats to freedom do not bear arms (Jesus)	2/2/97 Vol. 6
Thanks to God for all creation (Jesus)	11/23/06 Vol. 45	threats to life call for spiritual preparation (Jesus)	9/13/01 Vol. 24
thanks to God for all He does for us (Jesus)	10/6/04 Vol. 37	three & 1/2 years time shortened (Jesus)	10/3/01 Vol. 25
thanks to God for gifts, on Sunday (Jesus)	9/2/07 Vol. 48	three daily rosaries for Mary's intentions (Mary)	10/29/98 Vol. 13
thanks to God for spouses, faith, possessions (Jesus)	12/26/03 Vol. 33	three days of darkness caves (Jesus)	10/8/95 Vol. 3
thanks to God for work (Jesus)	9/5/05 Vol. 40	three days of darkness triumph over evil (Jesus)	7/20/99 Vol. 16
thanksgiving banquet (Jesus)	11/23/94 Vol. 2	three sources of evil peers, devil, self (Jesus)	3/6/06 Vol. 42
Thanksgiving comfort lonely,bad feeling (Jesus)	11/20/97 Vol. 9	three wisemen star over tabernacles (Jesus)	1/4/03 Vol. 30
thanksgiving count your blessings (Jesus)	11/15/00 Vol. 21	thrones in heaven for those worthy,perfected (Jesus)	8/31/02 Vol. 28
Thanksgiving family roots (Jesus)	11/18/04 Vol. 37	tidal wave abortion (Jesus)	1/22/95 Vol. 2
thanksgiving foodshelves,make amend (Jesus)	11/14/96 Vol. 5	tidal wave, massive to East US coast (Jesus)	5/3/04 Vol. 35
thanksgiving for faith & creation (Jesus)	10/30/01 Vol. 25	tidal waves earthquake or asteroid (Jesus)	4/16/02 Vol. 27
thanksgiving for family & safe travel (Jesus)	11/15/01 Vol. 25	tidal waves record devastation & deaths (Jesus)	12/29/04 Vol. 37
Thanksgiving for life and grace (Jesus)	11/17/05 Vol. 41	time Antichrist (Jesus)	4/11/94 Vol. 1
thanksgiving for spiritual & physical gifts (Jesus)	11/2/02 Vol. 29	time battle (Jesus)	6/14/94 Vol. 1
thanksgiving gifts (Jesus)	12/22/95 Vol. 3	time do not waste (Jesus)	3/27/03 Vol. 30
Thanksgiving gifts of life in family (Jesus)	11/21/02 Vol. 29	time do not waste (Jesus)	10/23/02 Vol. 29
Thanksgiving give thanks for blessings (Jesus)	11/26/98 Vol. 13	time do not waste (Jesus)	9/9/02 Vol. 28
Thanksgiving home roots to share family (Jesus)	11/25/03 Vol. 33	time do not waste (Jesus)	4/23/05 Vol. 39
Thanksgiving love, denial of pride (Jesus)	11/12/97 Vol. 9	time do not waste (Jesus)	6/17/04 Vol. 35

time do not waste (Jesus) — 9/27/06 Vol. 44
time do not waste (Jesus) — 6/19/96 Vol. 3
time do not waste on entertainment (Jesus) — 11/17/03 Vol. 33
time do not waste on TV (Jesus) — 7/20/06 Vol. 44
time do not waste on worldly things (Jesus) — 11/4/04 Vol. 37
time events speeding up (Jesus) — 10/25/96 Vol. 5
time fleeting, life is short (Jesus) — 1/24/01 Vol. 22
time God's Will (Jesus) — 2/12/96 Vol. 3
time law (Jesus) — 4/23/94 Vol. 1
time laws (Jesus) — 6/20/94 Vol. 1
time love (Uncle Jim) — 4/20/94 Vol. 1
time not much left (Mary) — 7/21/01 Vol. 24
time on earth very short (Jesus) — 7/24/02 Vol. 28
time people go at different speeds (Jesus) — 9/13/03 Vol. 32
time personal mission (Jesus) — 5/17/96 Vol. 3
time prayer (Jesus) — 1/31/95 Vol. 2
time presence (Jesus) — 12/31/95 Vol. 3
time prioritize, do not waste (Jesus) — 4/26/01 Vol. 23
time purification (Jesus) — 1/11/94 Vol. 1
time set priorities for God & neighbor (Jesus) — 1/23/02 Vol. 26
time speeded up (Jesus) — 5/2/01 Vol. 23
time speeding up (Jesus) — 10/10/03 Vol. 33
time universe (Jesus) — 12/10/95 Vol. 3
time use wisely for God (Jesus) — 7/24/03 Vol. 32
time use wisely for love of God (Jesus) — 9/9/07 Vol. 48
time warning (Jesus) — 5/30/94 Vol. 1
time wasted on TV,sports (St. Therese) — 10/2/97 Vol. 9
time wasting & abusing (Jesus) — 9/23/02 Vol. 28
time will be speeded up (Jesus) — 9/9/95 Vol. 3
time will speed up (Jesus) — 11/21/96 Vol. 5
time & evil battle to save souls (Jesus) — 11/27/02 Vol. 29
time & money need to be shared (Jesus) — 2/27/06 Vol. 42
time & money spend generously on others (Jesus) — 3/4/02 Vol. 26
time & talents share generously (Jesus) — 10/7/05 Vol. 41
time & talents share with others (Jesus) — 1/3/05 Vol. 38
time & talents use for God (Jesus) — 7/20/06 Vol. 44
time & talents use wisely (Jesus) — 7/29/03 Vol. 32
time & temptations endurance of faithful (Jesus) — 12/23/02 Vol. 29
time accounting good deeds vs selfishness (Jesus) — 3/8/02 Vol. 26
time available use wisely (Jesus) — 3/1/04 Vol. 34
time being wasted on sports,personal agenda (Jesus) — 7/5/00 Vol. 20
time best spent in adoring Jesus of Host (Jesus) — 12/18/99 Vol. 17
time continuum warning & life review (Jesus) — 11/6/95 Vol. 3
time distractions tested by affluence (Jesus) — 8/16/99 Vol. 16
time for God or too occupied with world (Jesus) — 11/8/04 Vol. 37
time for Jesus spent on selfish pursuits (Jesus) — 10/25/00 Vol. 21
time for prayer tithing 10% of your time (Jesus) — 1/30/05 Vol. 38

time frame anxious (Jesus) — 10/25/95 Vol. 3
time is an opportunity prepare for the tribulation (Jesus) — 10/8/98 Vol. 13
time is fast compare time of your life (Jesus) — 10/24/00 Vol. 21
time is precious not wasted frivolously (Jesus) — 10/31/00 Vol. 21
time is short end times near (Jesus) — 8/25/06 Vol. 44
time is short in this life (Jesus) — 12/17/04 Vol. 37
time line to point of death (Jesus) — 6/11/07 Vol. 47
time of conversion race and abortion (Jesus) — 11/1/95 Vol. 3
time of day shifting faster in tribulation (Jesus) — 12/31/05 Vol. 41
time of grace for prayer,fasting,Confession (Jesus) — 4/2/98 Vol. 11
time of life short on earth (Jesus) — 9/24/05 Vol. 40
time of mercy do not despair (Jesus) — 1/3/00 Vol. 18
time on earth short use time wisely (Jesus) — 7/30/02 Vol. 28
time passes quickly plan for death early (Jesus) — 2/25/01 Vol. 22
time priorities take away busy distractions (Jesus) — 9/30/04 Vol. 36
time priority to get closer to Jesus (Jesus) — 11/11/03 Vol. 33
time restraints remove for more prayer time (Jesus) — 10/21/04 Vol. 37
time running out to prepare for heaven (Jesus) — 3/23/00 Vol. 18
time saving devices less dependence on God (Jesus) — 1/28/00 Vol. 18
time short to work toward salvation (Jesus) — 11/3/03 Vol. 33
time shortened by unrestrained evil (Jesus) — 10/2/06 Vol. 45
time shortened for sake of elect (Jesus) — 8/12/06 Vol. 44
time shortened for sake of elect (Jesus) — 8/30/06 Vol. 44
time speeded up in all universe (Jesus) — 9/2/06 Vol. 44
time spent accounting at judgment (Jesus) — 6/11/07 Vol. 47
time suspended power and pride (Jesus) — 6/2/95 Vol. 2
time used best for spiritual life (Jesus) — 4/4/06 Vol. 43
time used held accountable for (Mark) — 10/2/04 Vol. 37
time wasted analyzed by Jesus (Jesus) — 3/6/00 Vol. 18
time wasted on news & new things (Jesus) — 12/18/03 Vol. 33
time wasting keep focus on Jesus (Jesus) — 5/10/01 Vol. 23
time wisely spent on charities,not pleasures (Jesus) — 2/10/00 Vol. 18
time, faith share with others (Jesus) — 2/23/05 Vol. 38
time, free how best to spend it (Jesus) — 3/12/02 Vol. 26
time, make set aside for Jesus (Jesus) — 1/6/06 Vol. 42
time, priority spiritual reading (Jesus) — 4/1/04 Vol. 35
time, talent, treasure to be shared (Jesus) — 10/2/06 Vol. 45
time, wasted on worldly distractions (Jesus) — 10/25/03 Vol. 33
time, wasting avoid worldly distractions (Jesus) — 2/8/05 Vol. 38
time,cannot waste prepare for day of reckoning (Jesus) — 3/25/01 Vol. 22
time,sands of cross is a lifetime work (Jesus) — 4/24/99 Vol. 15
time,talent,treasure sacrifice convenience (Jesus) — 9/18/06 Vol. 44
time,talent,treasure use properly (Jesus) — 11/4/05 Vol. 41
time,talent,wealth do not waste, accountable (Jesus) — 11/5/05 Vol. 41
timeless God pray to infant, adult Jesus (Jesus) — 12/25/05 Vol. 41
times and dates cannot be determined (Jesus) — 8/26/99 Vol. 16
timing of events chosen by God, not man (Jesus) — 10/5/04 Vol. 37

timing of events happens in God's time (Jesus) 3/7/00 Vol. 18
tingling feeling at Communion (Jesus) 8/17/03 Vol. 32
Titanic failure of man,God's success (Jesus) 7/30/98 Vol. 12
tithe or share with poor of the world (Jesus) 8/16/05 Vol. 40
tithing 10% to charity (Jesus) 11/9/05 Vol. 41
tithing a lesson in almsgiving (Jesus) 6/5/99 Vol. 15
tithing be generous to poor (Jesus) 10/6/03 Vol. 33
tithing builds up heavenly treasures (Jesus) 6/9/01 Vol. 23
tithing give to poor (Jesus) 1/17/03 Vol. 30
tithing hearts on right road (Jesus) 10/23/06 Vol. 45
tithing rewarded in heaven (Jesus) 10/15/06 Vol. 45
tithing stores treasure in heaven (Jesus) 5/6/04 Vol. 35
tithing to charities (Jesus) 1/17/04 Vol. 34
tithing to help poor (Jesus) 1/3/02 Vol. 26
tithing to help poor, Church (Jesus) 2/28/08 Vol. 50
tithing to help the needy (Jesus) 6/6/06 Vol. 43
tithing treasures in heaven (Jesus) 1/5/03 Vol. 30
tithing 10% to charity, support Church (Jesus) 8/9/04 Vol. 36
tithing 10% to church & charities (Jesus) 10/16/05 Vol. 41
tithing for the poor share faith, money (Jesus) 12/14/06 Vol. 45
tithing generously to charity (Jesus) 3/1/04 Vol. 34
tithing income almsgiving to be substantial (Jesus) 11/10/04 Vol. 37
tithing needed to Church and charities (Jesus) 7/27/04 Vol. 36
tithing to Church held accountable (Jesus) 1/28/99 Vol. 14
Tobago message for people (Jesus) 1/11/03 Vol. 30
Tobiah marriages (St. Raphael) 6/8/95 Vol. 2
Tobias & Sarah pray to rid demon (Jesus) 6/1/05 Vol. 39
Tobias and Sarah pray on wedding night (Jesus) 6/4/99 Vol. 15
today, focus on instead of future or past (Jesus) 5/7/04 Vol. 35
tolerance for other Christians (Jesus) 10/1/06 Vol. 45
toll passes patterns by entrances,exits (Jesus) 9/21/98 Vol. 12
tomb, focus on remember our resurrection (Jesus) 3/24/01 Vol. 22
Tomball, Texas confirmed refuge (Mary) 7/30/04 Vol. 36
tombstone epitaph how you are remembered (Jesus) 3/22/01 Vol. 22
tombstones & money soul only taken past grave (Jesus) 11/2/01 Vol. 25
tongue keep it under control (Jesus) 2/18/02 Vol. 26
Tony Fenwalt visionaries (Mary) 12/17/95 Vol. 3
Torah New Covenant (Jesus) 12/6/93 Vol. 1
tornadoes era of peace (Jesus) 4/28/95 Vol. 2
tornadoes,disasters signs of coming tribulation (Jesus) 3/31/00 Vol. 18
torture with electrical devices (Jesus) 5/21/98 Vol. 11
total commitment die to self (Jesus) 11/3/99 Vol. 17
total commitment life long love of God (Jesus) 5/28/04 Vol. 35
Tower of Babel dream of large buildings (Jesus) 5/21/02 Vol. 27
tower of Babel in computer failures (Jesus) 8/26/99 Vol. 16
Tower of Babel language of leaders (Jesus) 2/16/07 Vol. 46
Tower of Babel man made into god (Jesus) 5/14/98 Vol. 11

Tower of Babel pride & science (Jesus) 7/29/03 Vol. 32
Tower of Babel pride and humility (Jesus) 3/19/97 Vol. 6
Tower of Babel pride in technology (Jesus) 2/19/97 Vol. 6
Tower of Babel purification of world (Jesus) 3/10/96 Vol. 3
toxic gases angel protection at refuges (Jesus) 6/19/02 Vol. 27
toxic weapons put poisons in the air (Jesus) 2/19/98 Vol. 10
tracking devices avoid electronic chips (Jesus) 11/26/02 Vol. 29
trade agreements by president only, dangerous (Jesus) 2/1/07 Vol. 46
trade agreements remove duties (Jesus) 4/26/01 Vol. 23
trade agreements to remove middle class (Jesus) 2/15/07 Vol. 46
trade center and other disasters (Jesus) 11/25/01 Vol. 25
trade center promote peace (Jesus) 10/3/02 Vol. 29
trade controls and wars for takeover (Jesus) 5/16/03 Vol. 31
trade deficit as jobs are exported (Jesus) 5/22/03 Vol. 31
trade, free ruin home industries (Jesus) 2/9/03 Vol. 30
Tradition & Scripture foundation of faith (Jesus) 7/6/06 Vol. 44
tradition in faith passed to next generation (Jesus) 12/29/98 Vol. 13
tradition taught Mary and Jesus (Mary) 11/21/98 Vol. 13
traditional church priest vocations abundant (Jesus) 5/18/06 Vol. 43
traditions being stripped (Jesus) 3/22/03 Vol. 30
traditions follow authority of Church (Jesus) 12/6/96 Vol. 5
traditions for future generations (Jesus) 8/22/01 Vol. 24
traditions from the heart (Jesus) 8/18/97 Vol. 8
traditions keep for good faith (Jesus) 7/10/07 Vol. 48
traditions keep in churches (Jesus) 8/7/01 Vol. 24
traditions keep souls near Jesus (Jesus) 9/6/07 Vol. 48
traditions pass on the faith (Jesus) 12/9/99 Vol. 17
traditions preserve for children (Jesus) 10/2/02 Vol. 29
traditions restore & preserve (Jesus) 1/13/98 Vol. 10
traditions restored in churches (Jesus) 7/19/06 Vol. 44
traditions stripped away (Jesus) 6/21/01 Vol. 23
traditions stripped from churches (Jesus) 10/5/07 Vol. 49
traditions teach children (Jesus) 4/2/04 Vol. 35
traditions & old laws held society together (Jesus) 1/31/02 Vol. 26
Traditions & Sacred birthright of faithful (Jesus) 7/7/07 Vol. 48
traditions in Church being attacked by worldly souls (Jesus) 3/27/04 Vol. 34
traditions of faith being watered down (Jesus) 6/19/06 Vol. 43
traditions of faith kept and shared (Jesus) 8/31/99 Vol. 16
traditions stripped children have not seen (Jesus) 8/31/04 Vol. 36
trailer trucks carrying to detention centers (Jesus) 4/1/00 Vol. 19
train new air propulsion (Jesus) 2/20/07 Vol. 46
train as judgment life is short lived (Jesus) 1/6/00 Vol. 18
train of chemicals possible terrorist attack (Jesus) 10/1/01 Vol. 25
train station places of terrorist attacks (Jesus) 4/29/06 Vol. 43
trains to detention center enemies of Antichrist (Jesus) 10/3/96 Vol. 5
traitors in our own country (Jesus) 4/30/03 Vol. 31
traitors military & financial (Jesus) 3/15/03 Vol. 30

traitors of money in government (Jesus) — 7/4/99 Vol. 16

Transfiguration and glory of return (Jesus) — 8/6/99 Vol. 16

transfiguration blessings (Jesus) — 3/22/94 Vol. 1

Transfiguration Communion (Mary) — 2/17/96 Vol. 3

Transfiguration foreshowing of Resurrection (Jesus) — 3/7/04 Vol. 34

Transfiguration foretelling of Jesus' death (Jesus) — 8/6/00 Vol. 20

Transfiguration gives hope and faith (Jesus) — 2/18/99 Vol. 14

Transfiguration glorified body (Jesus) — 6/6/02 Vol. 27

Transfiguration glorified body (Jesus) — 8/6/03 Vol. 32

Transfiguration glorified body (Jesus) — 3/13/05 Vol. 38

Transfiguration glorified Body of Jesus (Jesus) — 5/1/00 Vol. 19

transfiguration glory (Jesus) — 6/2/95 Vol. 2

Transfiguration Jesus' Body glorified (Jesus) — 8/6/05 Vol. 40

Transfiguration Moses/Elijah messages (Jesus) — 8/4/96 Vol. 4

Transfiguration Mystery of Trinity (Jesus) — 1/31/98 Vol. 10

Transfiguration presence of Trinity (Jesus) — 8/6/97 Vol. 8

Transfiguration preview of glorified bodies (Jesus) — 2/17/08 Vol. 50

Transfiguration preview of glorified body (Jesus) — 8/6/04 Vol. 36

Transfiguration preview of our resurrection (Jesus) — 2/24/02 Vol. 26

Transfiguration preview to resurrection (Jesus) — 8/6/01 Vol. 24

Transfiguration request for picture (God the Father) — 4/2/98 Vol. 11

transition death (Jesus) — 1/14/95 Vol. 2

transition life stages (Jesus) — 8/8/95 Vol. 3

transition to heaven live consecration (Jesus) — 12/16/02 Vol. 29

Transubstantiation miracle of Real Presence (Jesus) — 1/18/99 Vol. 14

transubstantiation miraculous gift (Jesus) — 5/22/97 Vol. 7

transubstantiation real Body and Blood (Jesus) — 4/5/98 Vol. 11

Transubstantiation sacrifice of the Mass (Jesus) — 8/3/97 Vol. 8

travel affected by war & terrorism (Jesus) — 4/24/03 Vol. 31

travel as part of life (Jesus) — 12/18/05 Vol. 41

travel control by one worlders (Jesus) — 10/20/06 Vol. 45

travel crossing state lines (Jesus) — 6/20/97 Vol. 7

travel electrical devices (Jesus) — 6/1/95 Vol. 2

travel final trip to heaven (Jesus) — 8/10/97 Vol. 8

travel gasoline shortages (Jesus) — 2/13/97 Vol. 6

travel passing delights (Jesus) — 8/28/97 Vol. 8

travel safer at night (Jesus) — 6/27/04 Vol. 35

travel seek spiritual goals (Jesus) — 8/12/97 Vol. 8

travel to be limited by chips (Jesus) — 4/21/05 Vol. 39

travel to be more controlled (Jesus) — 5/23/02 Vol. 27

travel to be restricted on borders (Jesus) — 8/21/03 Vol. 32

travel will be restricted (Jesus) — 12/17/97 Vol. 9

travel difficulties have holy water,blessed salt (Jesus) — 1/15/08 Vol. 50

travel for talks need protection (Jesus) — 1/4/08 Vol. 50

travel for talks to be more difficult (Jesus) — 10/15/07 Vol. 49

travel hazards control of highways (Jesus) — 12/15/99 Vol. 17

travel limited without smart cards,chips (Jesus) — 10/7/99 Vol. 17

travel times in Jesus' day (Jesus) — 12/21/06 Vol. 45

travels limited by increasing persecution (Jesus) — 5/8/99 Vol. 15

treasure where your heart is (Jesus) — 2/23/05 Vol. 38

treasure box good deeds,intimate times (Jesus) — 6/12/00 Vol. 19

treasure in heaven for gifts without pay back (Jesus) — 12/27/07 Vol. 49

treasure in heaven more than earthly treasure (Jesus) — 6/2/03 Vol. 31

treasure in heaven reward for generosity (Jesus) — 5/8/07 Vol. 47

treasure lies where heart lies (Jesus) — 3/2/06 Vol. 42

treasure location where the heart is (Jesus) — 8/28/05 Vol. 40

treasure, earthly sought in lotto,casinos,stocks (Jesus) — 12/23/03 Vol. 33

treasures seek heavenly, not earthly (Jesus) — 6/7/04 Vol. 35

treasures seek those of heaven (Jesus) — 8/27/98 Vol. 12

treasures in heaven best to have at death (Jesus) — 2/10/05 Vol. 38

treasure's place where heart is found (Jesus) — 2/11/06 Vol. 42

treaties step to global control (Jesus) — 9/4/01 Vol. 24

Tree of Life all humanity a part of (Jesus) — 9/24/06 Vol. 44

Tree of Life as Jesus died on cross (Jesus) — 9/17/06 Vol. 44

Tree of Life Garden, now in Jesus (Jesus) — 1/23/07 Vol. 46

Tree of Life grace in Holy Communion (Jesus) — 2/22/07 Vol. 46

Tree of life Jesus source of all things (Jesus) — 12/3/01 Vol. 25

Tree of Life vine & branches (Jesus) — 3/30/03 Vol. 30

Tree of Life, new Jesus source of Life (Jesus) — 8/26/05 Vol. 40

trees protected to preserve environment (Jesus) — 7/28/05 Vol. 40

trial seduction of demons (Jesus) — 3/3/96 Vol. 3

trial shortened for sake of the elect (Jesus) — 5/14/99 Vol. 15

trials bear for Jesus (Jesus) — 6/15/01 Vol. 23

trials comfort of God and others (Jesus) — 1/2/97 Vol. 6

trials endured by His graces (Jesus) — 3/24/98 Vol. 10

trials joy (Jesus) — 12/23/95 Vol. 3

trials new life (Jesus) — 9/11/94 Vol. 2

trials on the sea of life (Jesus) — 6/17/05 Vol. 39

trials opportunities for grace (Jesus) — 4/2/06 Vol. 43

trials perfection of life (Jesus) — 2/23/96 Vol. 3

trials persevere in love (Jesus) — 9/18/96 Vol. 4

trials take up cross daily (Jesus) — 1/16/01 Vol. 22

trials test (Jesus) — 8/1/95 Vol. 3

trials test (Jesus) — 7/24/95 Vol. 3

trials tested in suffering (Jesus) — 3/11/97 Vol. 6

trials trust in God, fasting (Jesus) — 8/29/97 Vol. 8

trials unknown life (Jesus) — 6/6/95 Vol. 2

trials & stress grace given is sufficient (Jesus) — 6/1/06 Vol. 43

trials & suffering prepare us for heaven (Jesus) — 1/16/02 Vol. 26

trials & suffering test of faith (Jesus) — 2/23/04 Vol. 34

trials and tests prepare with prayer (Jesus) — 7/17/97 Vol. 8

trials each day pray for strength (Jesus) — 10/19/06 Vol. 45

trials in life give over to Jesus (Jesus) — 11/4/02 Vol. 29

trials in life let the Lord lead (Jesus) — 4/5/03 Vol. 31

trials in life need God's help, opportunities (Jesus) 10/2/04 Vol. 37

trials of life ask God for help (Jesus) 7/13/06 Vol. 44

trials of life be positive with Jesus (Jesus) 12/13/00 Vol. 21

trials of life faith and rest (Jesus) 5/8/96 Vol. 3

trials of life from original sin (Jesus) 10/5/06 Vol. 45

trials of life Jesus is our strength (Jesus) 4/2/98 Vol. 11

trials of life necessary to test faith (Jesus) 1/8/04 Vol. 34

trials of life seek God's help (Jesus) 5/2/05 Vol. 39

trials of life stairway to Heaven (Jesus) 10/2/97 Vol. 9

trials of life stripped of our goods (Jesus) 5/8/97 Vol. 7

trials of life tests of faith (Jesus) 8/16/01 Vol. 24

trials of life trust in God (Jesus) 2/7/03 Vol. 30

trials of life trust more (St. Theresa) 10/1/01 Vol. 25

trials, accept don't let storms upset your faith (Jesus) 9/13/04 Vol. 36

trials, difficulties from greed of money,things (Jesus) 12/11/02 Vol. 29

tribulation a living purgatory (Jesus) 7/31/01 Vol. 24

tribulation about to begin (Jesus) 6/21/01 Vol. 23

tribulation adoration will give strength (Jesus) 7/1/99 Vol. 16

tribulation all demons released (Jesus) 7/31/04 Vol. 36

tribulation all demons released from hell (Jesus) 11/19/01 Vol. 25

tribulation all hell unleashed (Jesus) 6/8/05 Vol. 39

tribulation angels will help (Mark) 3/12/98 Vol. 10

tribulation Antichrist (Jesus) 12/1/94 Vol. 2

tribulation as 3 days in the tomb (Jesus) 4/30/00 Vol. 19

tribulation austere life, no comforts (Jesus) 4/25/97 Vol. 7

tribulation barrier of God's love as shield (Jesus) 7/15/00 Vol. 20

tribulation begins soon (Mary) 6/19/97 Vol. 7

tribulation can start any time (Mark) 3/12/98 Vol. 10

tribulation caves (Jesus) 10/5/95 Vol. 3

tribulation caves,high ground inland (Jesus) 12/14/99 Vol. 17

tribulation chaos, looting & fires (Jesus) 12/30/96 Vol. 5

tribulation choice of God or worldly comforts (Jesus) 10/7/04 Vol. 37

tribulation choose god or world (Jesus) 8/27/00 Vol. 20

tribulation churches destroyed (Jesus) 2/12/04 Vol. 34

tribulation churches taken away (Jesus) 10/19/94 Vol. 2

tribulation could begin if war expands (Jesus) 11/23/01 Vol. 25

tribulation could begin world war (Jesus) 2/6/03 Vol. 30

tribulation darkness of evil very great (Jesus) 7/20/05 Vol. 40

tribulation demons and angels (Jesus) 6/16/94 Vol. 1

tribulation demons out of volcano (Jesus) 10/22/95 Vol. 3

tribulation demons roam the earth (Jesus) 2/17/98 Vol. 10

tribulation demons unleashed (God the Father) 8/7/99 Vol. 16

tribulation demons unleashed from hell (Jesus) 3/17/04 Vol. 34

tribulation diseases,famine,manna (Jesus) 8/17/96 Vol. 4

tribulation do not be fearful (Jesus) 6/10/99 Vol. 15

tribulation earthly purgatory (Jesus) 12/16/99 Vol. 17

tribulation ends in triumph (Jesus) 6/2/04 Vol. 35

tribulation Eucharist (Jesus) 8/8/94 Vol. 2

tribulation evangelize, save souls (Jesus) 5/30/06 Vol. 43

tribulation events will quicken (Jesus) 10/20/94 Vol. 2

tribulation evil has a short reign (Jesus) 6/11/06 Vol. 43

tribulation evil worse than seen (Jesus) 11/18/05 Vol. 41

tribulation face of earth changed (Jesus) 9/7/97 Vol. 8

tribulation faith will be tried (Jesus) 3/15/05 Vol. 38

tribulation famine,possessions stripped (Jesus) 11/7/98 Vol. 13

tribulation fear (Jesus) 9/4/94 Vol. 2

tribulation focus on Light of Jesus (Jesus) 9/25/01 Vol. 24

tribulation foreign to our life (Jesus) 12/3/99 Vol. 17

tribulation government taken over (Jesus) 10/10/96 Vol. 5

tribulation grateful to postpone (Jesus) 6/18/98 Vol. 11

tribulation have food,water,fuel (Jesus) 9/27/01 Vol. 24

tribulation have hope and trust (Jesus) 10/13/02 Vol. 29

tribulation home Masses (Jesus) 12/3/00 Vol. 21

tribulation hour of darkness (Jesus) 4/13/03 Vol. 31

tribulation increased earthquakes,volcanoes (Jesus) 7/29/04 Vol. 36

tribulation is at hand (Jesus) 4/28/05 Vol. 39

tribulation is near at hand (Jesus) 12/6/01 Vol. 25

tribulation Israel & America compared (Jesus) 12/17/00 Vol. 21

tribulation know meaning of Word (Jesus) 11/3/96 Vol. 5

tribulation leave home for refuge (Jesus) 6/1/00 Vol. 19

tribulation like a train in a tunnel (Jesus) 1/6/98 Vol. 10

tribulation living purgatory on earth (Jesus) 6/12/07 Vol. 47

tribulation living purgatory on earth (Jesus) 8/30/07 Vol. 48

tribulation lukewarm (Jesus) 1/20/94 Vol. 1

tribulation martyrdom & refuges (Jesus) 3/28/06 Vol. 42

tribulation martyrs (Jesus) 6/4/02 Vol. 27

tribulation meet again in secret (Jesus) 8/24/04 Vol. 36

tribulation money & possessions stripped (Jesus) 8/11/04 Vol. 36

tribulation must happen (Jesus) 11/27/00 Vol. 21

tribulation my mission to prepare for (Jesus) 12/1/07 Vol. 49

tribulation need rosaries and hosts (Jesus) 1/10/95 Vol. 2

tribulation need spiritual strength (Jesus) 3/2/05 Vol. 38

tribulation not beyond endurance (Jesus) 7/18/99 Vol. 16

tribulation not tested beyond endurance (Jesus) 7/19/01 Vol. 24

tribulation not tested beyond endure (Jesus) 10/28/99 Vol. 17

tribulation peace (Jesus) 1/27/95 Vol. 2

tribulation persecuted for beliefs (Jesus) 9/14/02 Vol. 28

tribulation persecution (Jesus) 6/2/94 Vol. 1

Tribulation physical,spiritual prep (Jesus) 5/14/99 Vol. 15

tribulation place of holy ground (Jesus) 10/2/07 Vol. 49

tribulation plagues healed at refuges (Jesus) 4/14/98 Vol. 11

tribulation pray for conversions before (Jesus) 4/20/00 Vol. 19

tribulation pray for strength (Jesus) 3/2/07 Vol. 46

tribulation pray for strength (Jesus) 9/5/00 Vol. 20

tribulation preparation & new era (Jesus) — 3/4/96 Vol. 3
tribulation prepare and pray (Jesus) — 1/8/02 Vol. 26
tribulation prepare for testing (Jesus) — 8/16/98 Vol. 12
tribulation prepare physically,spiritually (Jesus) — 10/7/05 Vol. 41
tribulation prepare sacramentals (Jesus) — 12/9/99 Vol. 17
tribulation prepare with sacramentals (Jesus) — 10/7/99 Vol. 17
tribulation protection as in Exodus (Jesus) — 6/11/96 Vol. 3
tribulation protection from Antichrist (Jesus) — 3/17/96 Vol. 3
tribulation punishment and a test (God the Father) — 6/2/99 Vol. 15
tribulation purgatory on earth (Jesus) — 5/16/03 Vol. 31
tribulation purgatory on earth (Jesus) — 7/9/01 Vol. 24
tribulation purgatory on earth (Jesus) — 1/23/03 Vol. 30
tribulation purgatory on earth (Jesus) — 9/13/05 Vol. 40
tribulation purgatory on earth (Jesus) — 1/24/08 Vol. 50
tribulation purgatory or hell on earth (Jesus) — 12/31/00 Vol. 21
tribulation purge imperfections (Jesus) — 6/21/02 Vol. 27
tribulation refuges for hiding (Jesus) — 12/27/04 Vol. 37
tribulation religious persecution (Jesus) — 5/10/96 Vol. 3
tribulation reparation (Jesus) — 12/23/94 Vol. 2
tribulation safe haven (Jesus) — 8/11/94 Vol. 2
tribulation saved only by Jesus (Jesus) — 2/27/05 Vol. 38
tribulation schism & destruction (Jesus) — 6/22/02 Vol. 27
tribulation shortened for elect (Jesus) — 2/6/07 Vol. 46
tribulation signs of end times (Jesus) — 8/17/06 Vol. 44
tribulation signs of it to begin (Jesus) — 2/10/98 Vol. 10
tribulation simpler life;depend God (Jesus) — 4/17/97 Vol. 7
tribulation spiritual, physical prep (Jesus) — 6/10/99 Vol. 15
tribulation spiritual,earthly life threatened (Jesus) — 2/22/02 Vol. 26
tribulation standing at the door (Jesus) — 9/24/03 Vol. 32
tribulation strength in trials (Jesus) — 10/26/02 Vol. 29
tribulation stripped of possessions (Jesus) — 7/27/99 Vol. 16
tribulation suffer for Jesus (Jesus) — 5/21/98 Vol. 11
tribulation suffering Good Friday, Easter (Jesus) — 3/26/02 Vol. 26
tribulation test (Jesus) — 12/26/94 Vol. 2
tribulation test faith to the limit (Jesus) — 9/20/00 Vol. 20
tribulation test of faith (Jesus) — 5/13/04 Vol. 35
tribulation test of faith (Jesus) — 5/7/99 Vol. 15
tribulation test of faith (Jesus) — 9/9/00 Vol. 20
tribulation test of our faith (Jesus) — 2/18/99 Vol. 14
tribulation time for refuges (Jesus) — 2/24/06 Vol. 42
tribulation time is moving fast (Jesus) — 10/9/06 Vol. 45
tribulation time is short, prepare for (Jesus) — 5/16/98 Vol. 11
tribulation time moving closer (Jesus) — 7/24/01 Vol. 24
tribulation time of fasting,ministering (Jesus) — 2/26/00 Vol. 18
tribulation time of great persecution (Jesus) — 11/29/06 Vol. 45
tribulation time of persecution (Jesus) — 7/16/03 Vol. 32
tribulation time of testing (Jesus) — 4/29/98 Vol. 11

tribulation time of testing (Jesus) — 9/26/98 Vol. 12
tribulation time shortened (Jesus) — 8/12/06 Vol. 44
tribulation to begin soon (Jesus) — 12/5/99 Vol. 17
tribulation to occur in our lifetime (Jesus) — 2/12/02 Vol. 26
tribulation triumph (Mary) — 7/24/94 Vol. 2
tribulation trust (Jesus) — 8/7/95 Vol. 3
tribulation trust in miraculous protection (Jesus) — 5/4/98 Vol. 11
tribulation underground (Jesus) — 4/30/94 Vol. 1
tribulation underground Masses (Jesus) — 11/24/01 Vol. 25
tribulation underground Masses (Jesus) — 10/25/99 Vol. 17
tribulation use only spiritual weapons (Jesus) — 7/23/04 Vol. 36
tribulation will demand God's help (Jesus) — 1/7/00 Vol. 18
tribulation beginning if 3rd world war starts (Jesus) — 9/18/01 Vol. 24
tribulation begins Antichrist declares himself (Jesus) — 4/2/03 Vol. 31
tribulation close wars, chips coming together (Jesus) — 12/19/02 Vol. 29
tribulation coming purgatory on earth (Jesus) — 6/8/00 Vol. 19
tribulation coming trial of Antichrist (Jesus) — 12/17/02 Vol. 29
tribulation martyrs as early Christian martyrs (Jesus) — 3/16/00 Vol. 18
tribulation martyrs before getting to refuges (Jesus) — 12/22/06 Vol. 45
tribulation martyrs vindicated in Christ's coming (Jesus) — 12/1/04 Vol. 37
tribulation persecution loss of comforts (Jesus) — 7/29/01 Vol. 24
tribulation protection have confidence in God (Jesus) — 11/27/97 Vol. 9
tribulation sequence warning,pope leaves,mark (Jesus) — 12/13/98 Vol. 13
tribulation sign in the sky need frequent Confession (Jesus) — 3/28/04 Vol. 34
tribulation signs earthquakes,famine,chaos (Jesus) — 11/8/98 Vol. 13
tribulation signs many disasters (Jesus) — 9/2/05 Vol. 40
tribulation signs with increasing earthquakes (Jesus) — 3/29/05 Vol. 38
tribulation time leave everything behind (Jesus) — 12/28/07 Vol. 49
tribulation time messages prepared remnant (Jesus) — 4/21/05 Vol. 39
Tribulation time need preparation (Jesus) — 4/24/99 Vol. 15
tribulation time persecution of Christians (Jesus) — 1/2/06 Vol. 42
tribulation time saints,angels to help you (Jesus) — 10/16/98 Vol. 13
Tribulation, Great prepare for end times (Jesus) — 11/21/04 Vol. 37
tribulation, signs of famine,schism,forced chips (Jesus) — 7/10/04 Vol. 36
Trinidad deep spirit of people (Jesus) — 1/12/03 Vol. 30
Trinidad love of people (Jesus) — 1/10/03 Vol. 30
Trinidad & St. Vincent message for people (Jesus) — 1/9/03 Vol. 30
Trinity ball of fire — 9/4/93 Vol. 1
Trinity baptism (Jesus) — 1/13/94 Vol. 1
Trinity Baptism in Jordan (Jesus) — 7/23/97 Vol. 8
Trinity baptismal vows (Jesus) — 1/11/03 Vol. 30
Trinity blessing of each person (God the Father) — 5/25/97 Vol. 7
Trinity call on all 3 persons (Jesus) — 3/30/99 Vol. 14
Trinity creation (Father) — 5/29/94 Vol. 1
Trinity Father,Holy Spirit feel pain (Jesus) — 4/5/04 Vol. 35
Trinity follow their Will (Jesus) — 1/31/01 Vol. 22
Trinity force of all life (Jesus) — 5/4/01 Vol. 23

Trinity in consecrated host (Holy Spirit)	1/14/98 Vol. 10
Trinity infinitely perfect (Jesus)	10/1/99 Vol. 17
Trinity linked to their being (Jesus)	12/11/97 Vol. 9
Trinity love (Jesus)	5/16/94 Vol. 1
Trinity meaning of (Jesus)	5/26/02 Vol. 27
Trinity mystery of faith (Jesus)	2/7/98 Vol. 10
Trinity perfection (Jesus)	6/11/95 Vol. 2
Trinity pray to all three Persons (Jesus)	2/4/04 Vol. 34
Trinity present in Host (Jesus)	7/18/01 Vol. 24
Trinity protection (Jesus)	5/14/97 Vol. 7
Trinity receive one, receive all (Jesus)	4/26/99 Vol. 15
Trinity Redeemer (God the Father)	12/15/94 Vol. 2
Trinity relation of Divine Persons (Jesus)	6/2/96 Vol. 3
Trinity repent (Jesus)	2/15/95 Vol. 2
Trinity shown at Jesus' Baptism (Jesus)	1/9/05 Vol. 38
Trinity three persons in one (Jesus)	1/4/99 Vol. 14
Trinity understanding of (Jesus)	5/30/99 Vol. 15
Trinity visit Ireland (St. Patrick)	3/17/94 Vol. 1
Trinity in Host gift in Holy Communion (Jesus)	12/18/99 Vol. 17
Trinity mystery Father continuing creation (Jesus)	6/18/00 Vol. 19
trinity of evil Satan, two beasts of Revelation (Jesus)	10/11/04 Vol. 37
Trinity, Blessed in Sign of the Cross (Jesus)	1/13/08 Vol. 50
Trinity, Blessed infinite God, 3 persons (Jesus)	6/15/03 Vol. 31
Trinity, Blessed mystery of three Persons (Jesus)	5/22/05 Vol. 39
Trinity, Blessed operates as One (Jesus)	9/13/00 Vol. 20
Trinity, Blessed role of each Person (Jesus)	6/6/04 Vol. 35
Trinity, Blessed role of each Person (Jesus)	12/26/00 Vol. 21
Trinity, Holy 3 person always present (Jesus)	6/10/01 Vol. 23
Trinity, Holy received in Holy Communion (Jesus)	8/12/03 Vol. 32
trinity,false Satan,Antichrist,false witness (Jesus)	11/30/00 Vol. 21
triumph after tribulation (Mary)	6/12/99 Vol. 15
triumph all evil will be cast into hell (Jesus)	5/23/98 Vol. 11
Triumph at end of tribulation (Jesus)	6/4/05 Vol. 39
triumph before man destroys self (Jesus)	2/12/98 Vol. 10
Triumph bridge to Era of Peace (Mary)	5/31/96 Vol. 3
Triumph brings paradise on earth (Mary)	2/13/99 Vol. 14
Triumph calm war,eternal peace (Jesus)	11/12/98 Vol. 13
triumph come to save souls (Jesus)	6/20/97 Vol. 7
triumph comes with comet (Jesus)	8/4/01 Vol. 24
triumph conquer evil (Jesus)	10/11/96 Vol. 5
Triumph crushes Satan's head (Jesus)	8/22/03 Vol. 32
triumph demise of all evil (Jesus)	9/24/96 Vol. 4
triumph earth cleansed (Jesus)	1/30/97 Vol. 6
triumph evil chained (Jesus)	6/24/97 Vol. 7
Triumph evil cleansed from earth (Jesus)	2/6/99 Vol. 14
Triumph evil ones chained in hell (Jesus)	1/20/99 Vol. 14
triumph glorified body (Jesus)	11/13/94 Vol. 2

Triumph harmony in nature (Mary)	1/25/96 Vol. 3
triumph harmony,great spirituality (Jesus)	12/18/97 Vol. 9
triumph hearts (Mary)	5/31/94 Vol. 1
Triumph heaven on earth (Jesus)	5/21/96 Vol. 3
triumph hope in new earth (Jesus)	4/9/95 Vol. 2
Triumph Jesus returns on clouds (Jesus)	6/26/99 Vol. 15
triumph justice on earth (Jesus)	9/26/97 Vol. 8
triumph of good over evil (Jesus)	7/21/97 Vol. 8
triumph of good over evil (Jesus)	10/31/99 Vol. 17
Triumph of Jesus and Mary (Mary)	2/11/99 Vol. 14
triumph of two hearts (Mary)	8/21/97 Vol. 8
triumph over evil (Jesus)	8/15/03 Vol. 32
triumph over evil (Jesus)	8/24/00 Vol. 20
Triumph over evil (Jesus)	8/10/99 Vol. 16
Triumph over evil when all seems lost (Jesus)	9/6/03 Vol. 32
triumph over Satan, Antichrist (God the Father)	6/2/99 Vol. 15
triumph prayer warriors (Jesus)	7/25/94 Vol. 2
Triumph preach the Gospel (Jesus)	4/24/96 Vol. 3
Triumph road to heaven (Jesus)	4/17/96 Vol. 3
triumph Satan crushed (Mary)	1/25/95 Vol. 2
triumph scripture fulfilled (Jesus)	1/17/97 Vol. 6
Triumph sooner than asteroid (Mark)	3/12/98 Vol. 10
triumph the Lord is coming soon (Mary)	5/25/97 Vol. 7
triumph tribulation (Jesus)	7/16/94 Vol. 2
triumph two hearts (Mary)	9/13/97 Vol. 8
triumph ushers in renewed earth (Jesus)	5/14/98 Vol. 11
Triumph will be at crucial moment (Jesus)	2/18/99 Vol. 14
triumph will bring true peace (Jesus)	7/22/99 Vol. 16
triumph message preview before tribulation (Jesus)	9/23/99 Vol. 16
triumph of 2 Hearts all completed (Mary)	7/29/99 Vol. 16
Triumph of Cross Jesus came to deliver man (Jesus)	9/14/98 Vol. 12
Triumph of Cross over sin and death (Jesus)	9/14/04 Vol. 36
Triumph of Cross to gain our sainthood (Jesus)	9/14/00 Vol. 20
triumph of Jesus coming grows closer (Mary)	7/17/00 Vol. 20
Triumph of Jesus,Mary at end of tribulation (Mary)	5/23/05 Vol. 39
triumph of Mary in crushing Satan's head (Mary)	7/17/00 Vol. 20
Triumph of the Cross did not resurrect from cross (Jesus)	9/14/03 Vol. 32
Triumph of the Cross evil became greater good (Jesus)	4/9/04 Vol. 35
Triumph of the Cross offers resurrection to heaven (Jesus)	9/14/06 Vol. 44
Triumph of the Cross over evil & diseases (Jesus)	2/25/08 Vol. 50
Triumph to come when all appears lost (Jesus)	6/9/05 Vol. 39
triumphs over evil (Jesus)	8/18/00 Vol. 20
troops spread thin (Jesus)	5/25/98 Vol. 11
troubles all possible by prayer (Jesus)	10/1/95 Vol. 3
troubles seek God instead of drink (Jesus)	4/27/97 Vol. 7
troubles calmed by Jesus' actions at sea (Jesus)	8/7/05 Vol. 40
troubles,earthly should not disturb your peace (Jesus)	2/15/00 Vol. 18

troups, foreign in our country (Jesus) 6/21/01 Vol. 23
trucks prisoners to detention (Jesus) 12/4/97 Vol. 9
true Christian imitate Jesus' suffering (Jesus) 1/15/00 Vol. 18
trumpets sound birth & end times (Jesus) 12/10/02 Vol. 29
trumpets & drums announce 2nd coming (Jesus) 6/17/00 Vol. 19
trumpets of Revelation chaos of nature for sins (Jesus) 1/27/01 Vol. 22
trust angels (Jesus) 7/10/95 Vol. 3
trust child-like (Jesus) 8/16/03 Vol. 32
trust eyes of faith (Jesus) 5/27/96 Vol. 3
trust heavenly food (Jesus) 2/1/96 Vol. 3
trust in daily trials (Jesus) 9/11/97 Vol. 8
trust in God instead of self (Jesus) 7/6/02 Vol. 28
trust in God, not man (Jesus) 4/26/03 Vol. 31
trust in Jesus, not our devices (Jesus) 1/12/99 Vol. 14
trust in the tribulation (Jesus) 10/31/97 Vol. 9
trust only in Jesus (Jesus) 4/25/01 Vol. 23
trust only trust in Jesus (Jesus) 5/23/01 Vol. 23
trust road map & Divine Will (Jesus) 5/17/97 Vol. 7
trust seek first the Kingdom of God (Jesus) 6/18/05 Vol. 39
trust training in life (Jesus) 2/17/96 Vol. 3
trust trials as preparation (Jesus) 7/7/96 Vol. 3
trust will (Jesus) 3/14/94 Vol. 1
trust & depend on God for everything (Jesus) 3/31/04 Vol. 34
trust & faith God will provide (Jesus) 6/7/05 Vol. 39
trust & love God to satisfy soul (Jesus) 11/6/06 Vol. 45
trust and faith help in mission (St. Joseph) 3/19/98 Vol. 10
trust in God always loves us (Jesus) 10/24/04 Vol. 37
trust in God and not in money (Jesus) 11/2/06 Vol. 45
trust in God as God cares for birds (Jesus) 7/29/04 Vol. 36
Trust in God despite earthly trials (Jesus) 1/5/06 Vol. 42
trust in God even in difficult moments (Jesus) 3/19/04 Vol. 34
trust in God for all our needs (Jesus) 11/1/03 Vol. 33
trust in God for everything (Jesus) 8/21/01 Vol. 24
trust in God for help in everything (Jesus) 10/29/07 Vol. 49
trust in God for necessities of life (Jesus) 12/10/04 Vol. 37
trust in God for needs, not your money (Jesus) 5/27/04 Vol. 35
trust in God grace will be given (Jesus) 2/7/03 Vol. 30
trust in God have no fear or worries (Jesus) 12/6/06 Vol. 45
trust in God instead of gold, money (Jesus) 2/28/08 Vol. 50
trust in God not left as orphans (Jesus) 1/28/04 Vol. 34
trust in God overcomes fear (Jesus) 1/5/05 Vol. 38
trust in God poor trust, rich very little (Jesus) 2/13/08 Vol. 50
trust in God to calm storms of life (Jesus) 8/3/00 Vol. 20
trust in God to carry on after trials (Jesus) 11/11/99 Vol. 17
Trust in God to do impossible (Jesus) 3/10/06 Vol. 42
Trust in God to provide for our needs (Jesus) 2/8/06 Vol. 42
trust in God to support Church (Jesus) 3/21/07 Vol. 46

trust in God to take care of us (Jesus) 8/4/01 Vol. 24
trust in God,full needed in tribulation (Jesus) 3/20/00 Vol. 18
trust in Jesus now as in past (Jesus) 3/26/06 Vol. 42
trust in Jesus to gain eternal life (Jesus) 7/7/05 Vol. 40
trust in Jesus to get through life (Jesus) 3/23/06 Vol. 42
trust vs. doubt faith in Jesus (Jesus) 6/23/07 Vol. 47
trust, faith in Jesus' protection (Jesus) 3/31/07 Vol. 46
trust, faith in God takes away all fears (Jesus) 1/19/06 Vol. 42
truth easier to deny than live (Jesus) 12/14/98 Vol. 13
truth gives perfect understanding (Jesus) 4/25/04 Vol. 35
truth properly formed conscience (Jesus) 6/9/03 Vol. 31
truth suppressed in history (Jesus) 4/22/03 Vol. 31
Truth to free you of anxieties (Jesus) 6/1/00 Vol. 19
truth unchangeable, sets you free (Jesus) 7/18/04 Vol. 36
truth & authority of Jesus (Jesus) 9/15/06 Vol. 44
truth held from wise revealed to little ones (Jesus) 8/4/00 Vol. 20
truth of faith needs telling when unpopular (Jesus) 10/17/00 Vol. 21
truth of Jesus will set you free (Jesus) 4/11/07 Vol. 47
tsunami diseases from (Jesus) 2/8/08 Vol. 50
tsunami on East coast (Jesus) 2/18/08 Vol. 50
tsunami warning systems needed (Jesus) 7/20/06 Vol. 44
tsunami & disaster show power of nature (Jesus) 1/4/05 Vol. 38
tsunami areas prostitution,porn & children (Jesus) 1/10/05 Vol. 38
tsunami could occur from microwave devices (Jesus) 2/27/06 Vol. 42
tsunami disaster give help to them (Jesus) 1/6/05 Vol. 38
tsunami victims help generously (Jesus) 1/8/05 Vol. 38
tsunamis more common than thought (Jesus) 11/29/07 Vol. 49
tsunamis ongoing Indonesia earthquake (Jesus) 8/30/07 Vol. 48
Tummler, Peter funeral (Mary,Peter) 5/31/05 Vol. 39
tunnel of light warning (Jesus) 2/27/95 Vol. 2
tunnel vision no peripheral vision (Jesus) 5/28/06 Vol. 43
tunnels places of protection (Jesus) 12/14/99 Vol. 17
tunnels for hiding protection from evil ones (Jesus) 5/4/00 Vol. 19
tunnels, secret for military, VIPs (Jesus) 12/7/05 Vol. 41
turkeys & chickens take care to feed (Jesus) 11/9/06 Vol. 45
TV do not waste time on (Jesus) 7/20/06 Vol. 44
TV events, help neighbor (Jesus) 1/16/97 Vol. 6
TV limit time for (Jesus) 8/11/06 Vol. 44
TV movies (Jesus) 11/4/93 Vol. 1
TV remove after Warning (Jesus) 2/3/03 Vol. 30
TV used by Antichrist (Jesus) 6/9/99 Vol. 15
TV & computers two-way communication (Jesus) 7/29/97 Vol. 8
TV & movie violence corrupts (Jesus) 4/3/07 Vol. 47
TV & movies bad example (Jesus) 10/17/02 Vol. 29
TV & movies can influence morals (Jesus) 5/19/05 Vol. 39
TV and monitors remove after the Warning (Jesus) 5/30/02 Vol. 27
TV and movies avoid violent & indecent movies (Jesus) 3/20/02 Vol. 26

TV distractions brainwashes children (Jesus) 8/9/98 Vol. 12
TV entertainment too time consuming (Jesus) 6/17/00 Vol. 19
TV paralysis can warp mind,wastes time (Jesus) 6/13/00 Vol. 19
TV programming bad for children, adults (Jesus) 12/18/04 Vol. 37
TV programming corrupting children & adults (Jesus) 11/18/04 Vol. 37
TV programs evil babysitter (Jesus) 7/11/98 Vol. 12
TV violence on news & programming (Jesus) 11/13/03 Vol. 33
TV vs. prayer time too much time wasted (Jesus) 9/16/99 Vol. 16
TV, less more time for prayer,deeds (Jesus) 12/4/06 Vol. 45
TV, movies avoid, do not support (Jesus) 9/29/01 Vol. 24
TV, movies keep bad content from kids (Jesus) 1/26/07 Vol. 46
TVs & computers removed after Warning (Jesus) 8/30/04 Vol. 36
TVs & monitors remove to avoid Antichrist (Jesus) 8/13/02 Vol. 28
TVs & monitors rid to avoid seeing Antichrist (Jesus) 9/8/06 Vol. 44
TVs, computers distractions to waste time (Jesus) 1/28/00 Vol. 18
twin tower related American cities in flames (Jesus) 7/27/01 Vol. 24
twin tower related deep feeling of dread (Jesus) 7/24/01 Vol. 24
twin tower related modern city in flames (Jesus) 7/28/01 Vol. 24
twin towers & pyramids man's pride (Jesus) 1/30/03 Vol. 30
twin towers destruction feeling revealed,no killing (Jesus) 9/11/01 Vol. 24
twin towers destruction wake up call for America (Jesus) 9/18/01 Vol. 24
twin towers related world depression (Jesus) 9/1/01 Vol. 24
Two Commandments love God, love neighbor (Jesus) 10/31/98 Vol. 13
Two Hearts be united in love (Jesus) 9/15/06 Vol. 44
Two Hearts focus on love (Jesus) 7/20/02 Vol. 28
Two Hearts gift of love (Jesus) 8/5/06 Vol. 44
Two Hearts inseparable, Mary & Jesus (Jesus) 9/28/02 Vol. 28
Two Hearts intertwined as one (Jesus) 1/8/03 Vol. 30
Two Hearts Jesus & Mary (Jesus) 6/15/07 Vol. 47
Two Hearts Jesus & Mary are as one (Mary) 7/30/04 Vol. 36
Two Hearts joined as one (Jesus) 3/25/03 Vol. 30
Two Hearts last week in June (Jesus) 6/28/03 Vol. 31
Two Hearts love and peace (Mary) 6/5/96 Vol. 3
Two Hearts Mary & Jesus (Jesus) 8/15/02 Vol. 28
Two hearts Mother, Kingship (Jesus) 12/14/96 Vol. 5
Two Hearts one in Divine Will (Jesus) 8/5/04 Vol. 36
two hearts seek God's Presence (Mary) 9/12/97 Vol. 8
Two Hearts shared pain in death (Jesus) 9/15/98 Vol. 12
Two Hearts united (Mary) 7/21/01 Vol. 24
Two Hearts devotion helps at judgment (Jesus) 7/20/06 Vol. 44
Two Hearts, The open to all (Mary) 6/11/98 Vol. 11
Two hearts/Jesus & Mary Mary,mother of all children (Jesus) 4/19/97 Vol. 7
U. S. government controlled by 1 world people (Jesus) 11/4/98 Vol. 13
U.S. evil men to martyr Christians (Jesus) 11/4/98 Vol. 13
U.S. morals almost non-existent (Jesus) 6/27/00 Vol. 19
U.S. takeover by Antichrist (Jesus) 3/11/06 Vol. 42
U.S.A. time is running out (Jesus) 9/1/97 Vol. 8

ultimate power in Jesus over evil ones (Jesus) 2/17/00 Vol. 18
UN assists in one world wars (Jesus) 11/11/02 Vol. 29
UN has Chinese soldiers in US (Jesus) 4/26/01 Vol. 23
UN armies of Antichrist protection by Jesus' victory (Jesus) 4/9/01 Vol. 23
UN army supplies transferred over U.S. (Jesus) 3/22/00 Vol. 18
UN foreign troops to take over U.S. (Jesus) 1/20/00 Vol. 18
UN governance for Antichrist's takeover (Jesus) 4/5/01 Vol. 23
UN inspectors Iraq War (Jesus) 1/29/03 Vol. 30
UN police state Antichrist (Jesus) 10/10/94 Vol. 2
UN powerless in Sudan without troops (Jesus) 9/23/04 Vol. 36
UN resolutions are useless (Jesus) 8/4/06 Vol. 44
UN troops in our country (Jesus) 7/17/97 Vol. 8
UN troops moving in USA (Jesus) 1/30/97 Vol. 6
UN troops raiding houses in vision (Jesus) 2/7/08 Vol. 50
UN troops seeking removal of guns (Jesus) 9/22/98 Vol. 12
UN troops to enforce martial law (Jesus) 2/12/00 Vol. 18
UN world control through central bankers (Jesus) 4/5/01 Vol. 23
Unamann funeral as at Baptism (Jesus) 3/30/04 Vol. 34
unborn children in St. John & Jesus,Visitation (Jesus) 12/22/03 Vol. 33
unborn children second class citizens (Jesus) 6/28/02 Vol. 27
unborn heroes Jesus, St. John, Baptist (Jesus) 3/4/97 Vol. 6
unborn mission abortion denies God's plan (Jesus) 12/22/03 Vol. 33
unclean sinners restored to health by Jesus (Jesus) 2/13/00 Vol. 18
unconditional love (Jesus) 6/23/95 Vol. 2
unconditional love always available to us (Jesus) 7/23/01 Vol. 24
unconditional love come in child-like faith (Jesus) 1/29/99 Vol. 14
unconditional love follow the Divine Will (Jesus) 8/31/97 Vol. 8
unconditional love forgiveness and mercy (Jesus) 8/23/00 Vol. 20
unconditional love God calls man to share in (Jesus) 6/30/00 Vol. 19
unconditional love God seeks every soul (Jesus) 12/29/05 Vol. 41
unconditional love Jesus waits for us (Jesus) 2/1/00 Vol. 18
unconditional love will (Jesus) 7/23/95 Vol. 3
underground abortions (Jesus) 1/24/94 Vol. 1
underground angels bring manna (Jesus) 7/19/95 Vol. 3
underground churches 11/8/93 Vol. 1
underground faith (Jesus) 11/27/95 Vol. 3
underground prayer 10/11/93 Vol. 1
underground Church during tribulation (Jesus) 3/19/07 Vol. 46
underground Church for not taking chips (Jesus) 5/8/02 Vol. 27
underground church for real Mass (Jesus) 5/29/01 Vol. 23
underground Church given strength to survive (Jesus) 3/8/99 Vol. 14
underground Church hard to find Mass (Jesus) 4/17/07 Vol. 47
underground church in future persecution (Jesus) 1/31/05 Vol. 38
underground Church Mass kit needed (Jesus) 11/27/07 Vol. 49
underground Church needed for protection (Jesus) 3/28/08 Vol. 50
underground Church to carry on Real Presence (Jesus) 1/26/99 Vol. 14
underground church USA (Jesus) 1/7/94 Vol. 1

The Foot of Jesus on the TV

Each year when we go to Texas, we have been at My Father's House in Corpus Christi. Alberto Huerta, a prominent lawyer, began this House after the miraculous healing of his son. His son landed on a tree stump while skiing. The stump went into his head and there was little chance of his survival. Alberto took his check book into the hospital chapel and he said to the Lord that he was prepared to write out a check for one million dollars if God would heal his son. He just needed to know to whom the check should be written out to. Obviously, there was no answer. The next day, he returned to the chapel and this time he promised to spend the rest of his life working for God. The doctor came in and his son was healed. The Texas Sky Stadium in Corpus Christi had many rock concerts where kids wore "I love Satan" T-shirts. Alberto took it over and made it into My Father's House where they have weekly healing Masses. It is now converted into a beautiful shrine. He has been given frequent TV time after the station manager had a healing there. John's presentation was aired and as John said: "Now that Jesus is with us," the foot like the Divine Mercy appeared on the TV.

We know through Jesus' Great Mercy that he truly is always with us and sometimes gives us physical proof.

underground churches because of persecution (Jesus)	1/3/08 Vol. 50	United Nations control of finances (Jesus)	6/1/01 Vol. 23
underground churches when consecration changed (Jesus)	5/25/01 Vol. 23	United Nations control of government (Jesus)	12/22/96 Vol. 5
underground cities secret for dignitaries (Jesus)	2/15/05 Vol. 38	United Nations control trade and laws (Jesus)	6/28/01 Vol. 23
underground Mass prepare supplies (Jesus)	5/12/98 Vol. 11	United Nations controlled by Antichrist (Jesus)	5/28/98 Vol. 11
underground Mass threat of martyrdom (Jesus)	6/29/99 Vol. 15	United Nations controlled by the rich (Jesus)	12/29/01 Vol. 25
underground Masses for faithful (Jesus)	9/5/97 Vol. 8	United Nations controlling troops (Jesus)	6/5/01 Vol. 23
underground Masses if no valid Masses (Jesus)	12/23/97 Vol. 9	United Nations detention centers in US parks (Jesus)	7/18/02 Vol. 28
underground Masses in tribulation (Jesus)	3/6/99 Vol. 14	United Nations detention centers,US park (Jesus)	7/10/97 Vol. 8
underground Masses need good priests (Jesus)	5/11/05 Vol. 39	United Nations faces ruin, in defiance of God (Jesus)	3/9/01 Vol. 22
underground Masses no more public worship (Jesus)	8/4/98 Vol. 12	United Nations forces to claim power (Jesus)	5/29/97 Vol. 7
underground Masses prepare Mass supplies (Jesus)	11/3/97 Vol. 9	United Nations grab for global control (Jesus)	1/3/02 Vol. 26
underground Masses preserve My Presence (Jesus)	5/30/97 Vol. 7	United Nations in turmoil over Iraq (Jesus)	11/4/02 Vol. 29
underground Masses preserve statues (Jesus)	6/8/98 Vol. 11	United Nations joined with one world government (Jesus)	6/9/05 Vol. 39
underground Masses remnant Church (Jesus)	6/28/97 Vol. 7	United Nations one world government (Jesus)	8/11/96 Vol. 4
underground Masses when churches are taken over (Jesus)	1/20/04 Vol. 34	United Nations one world government (Jesus)	3/28/96 Vol. 3
underground shuttles connect secret cities (Jesus)	2/15/05 Vol. 38	United Nations police state of foreign troops (Jesus)	4/12/98 Vol. 11
underground tunnels in and out of cities (Jesus)	9/21/04 Vol. 36	United Nations power & money (Jesus)	4/4/07 Vol. 47
unemployed,poor need your time & money (Jesus)	10/22/98 Vol. 13	United Nations rule over all (Jesus)	8/24/00 Vol. 20
unemployment refuge (Mother Cabrini)	9/20/95 Vol. 3	United Nations servicemen's decision (Jesus)	5/16/97 Vol. 7
unfaithful suffer hell here and later (Jesus)	1/14/99 Vol. 14	United Nations spiritual arm in New Age (Jesus)	7/7/02 Vol. 28
United Nations abused Christianity (Jesus)	9/20/00 Vol. 20	United Nations storm troopers in black (Jesus)	1/27/01 Vol. 22
United Nations and one world government (Jesus)	6/19/05 Vol. 39	United Nations supports 1 world religion (Jesus)	5/14/99 Vol. 15
United Nations control by martial law (Jesus)	4/6/99 Vol. 15	United Nations to control the world (Jesus)	4/23/98 Vol. 11
United Nations control money & troops (Jesus)	5/6/97 Vol. 7	United Nations to take us over (Jesus)	3/14/03 Vol. 30

The foot of Jesus next to John that came
out on the television in Corpus Christi, Texas

United Nations to take us over (Jesus)	5/23/98 Vol. 11
United Nations to take us over (Jesus)	2/6/98 Vol. 10
United Nations troops abused, Antichrist (Jesus)	8/8/97 Vol. 8
United Nations troops for takeover (Jesus)	8/31/00 Vol. 20
United Nations troops here to control (Jesus)	10/16/97 Vol. 9
United Nations troops in position (Jesus)	1/3/01 Vol. 22
United Nations trrops to take us over (Jesus)	11/30/01 Vol. 25
United Nations vehicle for global control (Jesus)	10/27/03 Vol. 33
United Nations vehicle to control nations (Jesus)	9/11/03 Vol. 32
United Nations work with one world people (Jesus)	8/24/98 Vol. 12
United Nations workforce decimated (Jesus)	5/7/01 Vol. 23
United Nations armies to takeover nation (Jesus)	9/21/00 Vol. 20
United Nation's flags new kingdoms over nations (Jesus)	12/10/98 Vol. 13
United Nations troops material power of Antichrist (Jesus)	7/5/00 Vol. 20
United Nations troops separate people (Jesus)	7/31/01 Vol. 24
United Nations troops to control armies (Jesus)	9/7/00 Vol. 20
United Nations' troops on our soil (Jesus)	3/15/03 Vol. 30
UN, WHO trying to control herbs,vitamins (Jesus)	4/21/05 Vol. 39

United States armed camps (Jesus) — 9/18/97 Vol. 8
United States black in its sins (Jesus) — 2/11/99 Vol. 14
United States book of God thrown at us (Jesus) — 6/20/98 Vol. 11
United States decaying from within (Jesus) — 5/22/98 Vol. 11
United States founded on God (Jesus) — 2/12/98 Vol. 10
United States freedoms usurped (Jesus) — 2/9/97 Vol. 6
United States hand out,greed for power (Jesus) — 10/19/96 Vol. 5
United States judged for killings (Jesus) — 4/16/98 Vol. 11
United States lost faith,world control (Jesus) — 1/9/97 Vol. 6
United States not world peacekeeper (Jesus) — 12/28/98 Vol. 13
United States rejects blessings, perish (Jesus) — 10/24/96 Vol. 5
United States separation church & state (Jesus) — 8/7/96 Vol. 4
United States will fall from within (Jesus) — 7/17/97 Vol. 8
unity division (Jesus) — 10/31/95 Vol. 3
unity in loving everyone (Jesus) — 5/18/02 Vol. 27
unity lost sense of the sacred (Jesus) — 6/26/95 Vol. 2
universe creation (Jesus) — 3/7/95 Vol. 2
universe give glory to God (Jesus) — 9/12/02 Vol. 28
universe order of God, obey laws (Jesus) — 9/3/03 Vol. 32
universe we are very small (Jesus) — 4/17/01 Vol. 23
universe has order not created out of chaos (Jesus) — 8/19/05 Vol. 40
universe of creation order of stars & galaxies (Jesus) — 3/24/04 Vol. 34
universe's vastness power of God over evil (Jesus) — 10/8/98 Vol. 13
unknown causes fear & anxiety (Jesus) — 5/10/00 Vol. 19
unknown prayer (Jesus) — 12/7/93 Vol. 1
unrepentant sins calling for destruction (Jesus) — 9/14/05 Vol. 40
unseen sins revealed at judgment (Jesus) — 12/16/99 Vol. 17
unwanted pregnancy not part of the mother (Jesus) — 11/25/99 Vol. 17
unwise vs wise virgins hell vs heaven (Jesus) — 8/5/02 Vol. 28
US bankruptcy possible from wars (Jesus) — 5/11/06 Vol. 43
US government hiding — 10/24/93 Vol. 1
US government to register people with chips (Jesus) — 12/23/07 Vol. 49
US manufacturing being destroyed (Jesus) — 5/11/06 Vol. 43
US to leave Iraq impatience of people (Jesus) — 5/10/07 Vol. 47
USA abortion (Jesus) — 11/23/93 Vol. 1
USA Babylon (Jesus) — 11/28/95 Vol. 3
USA chastisements (Jesus) — 7/4/95 Vol. 3
USA demons (Jesus) — 2/3/95 Vol. 2
USA destroyed & taken over (Jesus) — 1/23/97 Vol. 6
USA destruction — 8/28/93 Vol. 1
USA disunity — 8/21/93 Vol. 1
USA freedoms taken away (Jesus) — 10/5/94 Vol. 2
USA immorality (Jesus) — 5/21/94 Vol. 1
USA judgment (Father) — 1/29/94 Vol. 1
USA leaders (Jesus) — 12/9/94 Vol. 2
USA morality (Jesus) — 5/9/94 Vol. 1
USA police state (Jesus) — 1/16/97 Vol. 6

USA separation,church&state (Jesus) — 3/28/96 Vol. 3
USA stock market (Jesus) — 1/6/94 Vol. 1
USA tidal wave — 8/25/93 Vol. 1
USA Titanic (Jesus) — 12/4/94 Vol. 2
USA weather (Jesus) — 1/16/94 Vol. 1
USA coup one world government (Jesus) — 3/19/95 Vol. 2
USA government falling into ruin (Jesus) — 4/3/97 Vol. 7
utilities to house electricity,gas,water,telephone (Jesus) — 12/2/04 Vol. 37
vacant chair daily Eucharist (Jesus) — 2/28/95 Vol. 2
vacation travel practice for refuges (Jesus) — 3/6/06 Vol. 42
vacations rest for body & soul (Jesus) — 8/21/03 Vol. 32
vaccines manipulated for control (Jesus) — 4/16/98 Vol. 11
vaccines means to spread viruses (Jesus) — 8/13/98 Vol. 13
valley of darkness fear of death for some (Jesus) — 12/28/01 Vol. 25
vanity pleasing God,not looks (Jesus) — 3/4/99 Vol. 14
Vatican Carol (wife) lost (Jesus) — 12/9/00 Vol. 21
Vatican immorality attacking (Jesus) — 5/26/05 Vol. 39
Vatican announcement on organizational change (Jesus) — 4/21/07 Vol. 47
Vatican II, spirit of Trojan horse of evil (Jesus) — 11/3/98 Vol. 13
Venezuela pray for suffering people (Jesus) — 8/13/07 Vol. 48
Venezuela riots over oil (Jesus) — 1/2/03 Vol. 30
Venezuela spiritual threat of one worlders (Jesus) — 10/26/06 Vol. 45
Venezuela aid need food & shelter (Jesus) — 2/10/00 Vol. 18
Venezuela people share love with (Mary) — 12/7/07 Vol. 49
venial sins need forgiveness for sinners (Jesus) — 6/12/03 Vol. 31
Verichip, FDA approval control of buying & selling (Jesus) — 10/20/04 Vol. 37
Veronica's veil gift of suffering for us (Jesus) — 12/21/00 Vol. 21
Veterans Day honoring of war dead (Jesus) — 11/11/98 Vol. 13
vices of the flesh do not let them control you (Jesus) — 3/25/04 Vol. 34
victim soul beauty of life (Jesus) — 1/9/96 Vol. 3
victim souls atonement for sin (Jesus) — 2/21/08 Vol. 50
victim souls bring conversion (Jesus) — 8/30/07 Vol. 48
victim souls caregivers (Jesus) — 1/24/96 Vol. 3
victim souls fire of Purgatory and hell (Jesus) — 5/7/96 Vol. 3
victim souls suffer to save souls (Jesus) — 5/3/06 Vol. 43
victim souls to protect faithful (Jesus) — 9/27/01 Vol. 24
Victimhood offer up personal sufferings (Jesus) — 5/17/06 Vol. 43
Victimhood of Jesus suffered all human trials (Jesus) — 5/3/06 Vol. 43
victory defeat of evil (Jesus) — 10/28/02 Vol. 29
victory of Jesus over death & evil (Jesus) — 11/12/05 Vol. 41
victory of Jesus over Satan (Jesus) — 10/9/03 Vol. 33
victory over evil (Jesus) — 10/26/02 Vol. 29
victory over sin and death (Jesus) — 6/27/01 Vol. 23
victory of Jesus over the demons (Jesus) — 3/30/07 Vol. 46
victory, Iraq hard to measure (Jesus) — 9/15/07 Vol. 48
video taping (St. Therese) — 9/7/02 Vol. 28
view of life needs change to convert (Jesus) — 4/16/99 Vol. 15

Vigil of Prayer for conversion (Jesus) 9/25/97 Vol. 8

vigil of prayer for heaven's intentions (Jesus) 5/13/02 Vol. 27

Vigil of prayer for sins of the world (Jesus) 8/4/05 Vol. 40

vigilance trials (Jesus) 9/21/95 Vol. 3

vigils of prayer for abortion, poor sinners,etc. (Jesus) 8/23/07 Vol. 48

vine love 10/17/93 Vol. 1

Vine & Branches can do nothing without God (Jesus) 9/17/06 Vol. 44

vine & branches good & bad fruit (Jesus) 5/16/01 Vol. 23

vine & branches Jesus and us (Jesus) 2/22/07 Vol. 46

vine & branches Jesus provides for all (Jesus) 10/21/99 Vol. 17

vine & branches keep focused (Jesus) 1/3/99 Vol. 14

vine & branches need Holy Spirit to breathe (Jesus) 11/12/00 Vol. 21

vine and branches cannot survive without Jesus (Jesus) 12/19/98 Vol. 13

vine and branches need for life (Jesus) 9/30/97 Vol. 8

vine and branches nothing without God (Jesus) 5/20/00 Vol. 19

vine is Jesus we are branches (Jesus) 3/9/00 Vol. 18

vine of Jesus apart, can do nothing (Jesus) 8/10/00 Vol. 20

violence do not show to children (Jesus) 5/27/99 Vol. 15

violence in killing, wars, abortions (Jesus) 8/28/04 Vol. 36

violence movies,TV,society (Mary) 12/30/97 Vol. 9

violence never an option (Jesus) 7/5/99 Vol. 16

violence on TV and killings (Jesus) 8/29/98 Vol. 12

violence in man mirrored in violent weather (Jesus) 3/2/02 Vol. 26

violence in sports need good works,not lazy (Jesus) 10/15/98 Vol. 13

violence in weather mirrors violence in society (Jesus) 4/12/97 Vol. 7

violent children from TV and movies (Jesus) 5/4/99 Vol. 15

violent movies encourage violence in youths (Jesus) 9/14/06 Vol. 44

violent movies,TV influencing children (Jesus) 4/22/99 Vol. 15

Virgin birth belief hard for Jews (Jesus) 3/25/06 Vol. 42

Virgin birth foretold in Scriptures (Jesus) 12/19/07 Vol. 49

Virginia Tech massacre deranged student killer (Jesus) 4/19/07 Vol. 47

virgins, wise prepare for wars, Y2K (Jesus) 4/9/99 Vol. 15

virtual reality danger of mind control (Jesus) 10/22/04 Vol. 37

virtual reality do not use (Jesus) 10/14/99 Vol. 17

virtual reality mind control (Jesus) 8/17/94 Vol. 2

virtual reality mind control (Jesus) 1/2/01 Vol. 22

virtual reality opening for demon attacks (Jesus) 5/29/07 Vol. 47

virtuous life based on love (Jesus) 7/7/01 Vol. 24

virus carried by new bug (Jesus) 2/8/08 Vol. 50

virus attack by one world people (Jesus) 11/17/06 Vol. 45

virus vaccine cost-chip in body (Jesus) 11/17/06 Vol. 45

virus, pandemic healed at refuges (Jesus) 3/2/08 Vol. 50

viruses deliberately created (Jesus) 4/9/02 Vol. 27

viruses, man-made threats to control people (Jesus) 12/12/05 Vol. 41

viruses, new from satellite,chem trails (Jesus) 12/12/05 Vol. 41

viruses,designed for biological warfare (Jesus) 4/28/99 Vol. 15

viruses,man-made to cause epidemics,AIDS (Jesus) 4/4/01 Vol. 23

visionaries call to conversion (Jesus) 9/29/97 Vol. 8

visionaries coming to an end (Mary) 4/17/96 Vol. 3

visionaries prepare (Mary) 12/19/93 Vol. 1

visions second coming (St. Theresa) 10/15/93 Vol. 1

visions of hell have converted souls (Jesus) 12/26/03 Vol. 33

visions stopping second herald (Mary) 8/26/94 Vol. 2

visit Shrine (Mother Cabrini) 6/14/95 Vol. 2

visit prisoners need conversion (Jesus) 2/24/00 Vol. 18

Visit sick & disabled joyful spirit to give time (Jesus) 4/17/97 Vol. 7

visit the sick before & after death (Jesus) 3/13/06 Vol. 42

Visitation announcing of Messiah (Jesus) 12/21/06 Vol. 45

Visitation Blessed Mother prepared for (Jesus) 5/31/03 Vol. 31

Visitation chores of Blessed Mother (Jesus) 5/31/07 Vol. 47

Visitation Mary reached out (Jesus) 5/31/01 Vol. 23

Visitation of Elizabeth by Mary (Jesus) 5/31/07 Vol. 47

Visitation reach out, help others (Mary) 5/31/99 Vol. 15

visitation repent (St.Elizabeth) 12/21/93 Vol. 1

visitations reach out in love (Mary) 3/10/97 Vol. 6

visiting the sick treasure for acts of love (Jesus) 12/11/03 Vol. 33

visitors show peace and love (Mary) 7/3/97 Vol. 8

vitamins & herbs to fight disease (Jesus) 2/21/03 Vol. 30

vitamins & herbs to strengthen immunity (Jesus) 5/15/03 Vol. 31

vitamins, herbs UN, WHO trying to control (Jesus) 4/21/05 Vol. 39

vocation be faithful (Jesus) 5/25/05 Vol. 39

vocation prayer & discernment (Jesus) 9/21/02 Vol. 28

vocation to live consecration (Jesus) 10/3/07 Vol. 49

vocation call religious, married, single (Jesus) 11/30/07 Vol. 49

vocation fulfilled by discernment in prayer (Jesus) 3/18/00 Vol. 18

vocation in life keep vows (Jesus) 9/28/05 Vol. 40

vocation strength maintained by prayer,fasting (Jesus) 11/2/01 Vol. 25

vocational call married, religious, single (Jesus) 1/13/07 Vol. 46

vocations accept responsibilities of (Jesus) 7/30/02 Vol. 28

vocations answer the call of God (Jesus) 7/13/06 Vol. 44

vocations blessing of Adoration (Jesus) 2/5/04 Vol. 34

vocations by prayer and example (Jesus) 4/21/02 Vol. 27

vocations commitment to God (Jesus) 12/7/99 Vol. 17

vocations contrived shortages (Jesus) 12/5/96 Vol. 5

vocations encourage & pray for clergy (Jesus) 4/25/98 Vol. 11

vocations encourage and nurture (Jesus) 1/5/99 Vol. 14

vocations encourage children (Jesus) 5/3/98 Vol. 11

vocations from Adoration (Jesus) 8/19/06 Vol. 44

vocations harvest master (Jesus) 10/22/95 Vol. 3

vocations life of commitment (Jesus) 9/7/02 Vol. 28

vocations pray for more holy (Jesus) 6/18/98 Vol. 11

vocations prayer groups (St. Therese) 6/21/95 Vol. 2

vocations priests (Jesus) 11/17/93 Vol. 1

vocations seminaries (Jesus) 6/10/95 Vol. 2

vocations some called, not answering (Jesus)   8/10/06 Vol. 44
vocations teach properly, pray for (Jesus)   5/9/98 Vol. 11
vocations tested in commitments (Jesus)   2/16/99 Vol. 14
vocations total service to God (Jesus)   4/15/04 Vol. 35
vocations & priests need prayers (Jesus)   7/12/07 Vol. 48
vocations lacking more priests,fertile ground (Jesus) 4/20/97 Vol. 7
vocations to priesthood lifeblood of Church (Jesus)   1/9/00 Vol. 18
vocations to priesthood not encouraged,more prayer (Jesus) 2/24/01 Vol. 22
vocations to priesthood pray, to give sacraments (Jesus) 10/30/98 Vol. 13
voice patterns for identification (Jesus)   6/18/98 Vol. 11
volcanic disturbance in Western America (Jesus)   3/20/04 Vol. 34
volcanic eruption affects weather, temperature (Jesus) 2/29/08 Vol. 50
volcanic eruption, huge to cause weather effects (Jesus) 12/26/04 Vol. 37
volcanic eruptions sign of end times (Jesus)   9/9/99 Vol. 16
volcanic explosion loss of life, weather affected (Jesus) 1/25/08 Vol. 50
volcanic pollution could affect weather,crops (Jesus) 4/6/00 Vol. 19
volcano Japan   8/30/93 Vol. 1
volcano sign of coming tribulation (Jesus)   6/29/00 Vol. 19
volcano to affect weather (Jesus)   6/9/06 Vol. 43
volcano to effect our weather (Jesus)   2/4/02 Vol. 26
volcano explosion part of world famine (Jesus)   1/2/06 Vol. 42
volcano in West disaster of demise (Jesus)   10/9/03 Vol. 33
volcano, huge affect weather, quakes (Jesus)   1/2/04 Vol. 34
volcanoes cause 3 days darkness (Jesus)   7/23/96 Vol. 4
volcanoes colors   8/1/93 Vol. 1
volcanoes continue to increase (Jesus)   6/11/01 Vol. 23
volcanoes could affect weather (Jesus)   2/2/06 Vol. 42
volcanoes demons coming on earth (Jesus)   6/15/06 Vol. 43
volcanoes demons released through (Jesus)   7/10/04 Vol. 36
volcanoes demons unleashed through (Jesus)   9/13/03 Vol. 32
volcanoes earthquakes, fires,droughts (Jesus)   6/10/98 Vol. 11
volcanoes effect on atmosphere (Jesus)   1/19/99 Vol. 14
volcanoes increased activity (Jesus)   3/12/98 Vol. 10
volcanoes large ones to affect weather (Jesus)   1/15/04 Vol. 34
volcanoes out West (Jesus)   3/5/07 Vol. 46
volcanoes reduce sun for crops (Jesus)   6/30/06 Vol. 43
volcanoes sign of end times (Jesus)   1/7/99 Vol. 14
volcanoes sign of sin (Jesus)   1/2/03 Vol. 30
volcanoes threat of fire in America (Jesus)   2/28/02 Vol. 26
volcanoes & earthquakes affect weather (Jesus)   4/22/05 Vol. 39
volcanoes & earthquakes on increase (Jesus)   2/12/02 Vol. 26
volcanoes & earthquakes shake earth's core (Jesus)   3/5/05 Vol. 38
volcanoes & earthquakes sign of end times (Jesus)   9/2/04 Vol. 36
volcanoes & earthquakes to increase, intensify (Jesus) 6/9/06 Vol. 43
volcanoes & earthquakes Yellowstone, Cascades (Jesus) 6/27/06 Vol. 43
volcanoes, earthquakes to change geography (Jesus)   1/18/06 Vol. 42
volcanoes,earthquakes signs of end times (Jesus)   12/21/00 Vol. 21

Volume III Pope & messages (Jesus)   5/11/96 Vol. 3
voting is Christian obligation (Jesus)   11/3/05 Vol. 41
vulnerability,man's to forces of nature (Jesus)   11/12/03 Vol. 33
vultures in Israel Battle of Armageddon (Jesus)   7/18/96 Vol. 4
Waco, Texas sign of future persecution (Jesus)   8/26/99 Vol. 16
wages decreasing with loss of good jobs (Jesus)   2/23/06 Vol. 42
wages of sin culture of death (Jesus)   4/4/02 Vol. 27
wages of sin death to soul (Jesus)   7/10/01 Vol. 24
wages, decreasing layoffs, plant closings (Jesus)   5/13/06 Vol. 43
wages, low still problem for workers (Jesus)   11/6/03 Vol. 33
wages, lower as factory jobs decrease (Jesus)   5/12/06 Vol. 43
Wailing Wall and deep traditions (Jesus)   12/9/99 Vol. 17
wake up from spiritual laziness (Jesus)   7/15/06 Vol. 44
wake up call for America's prayer need (Jesus)   9/13/01 Vol. 24
wakeup forgetful (Jesus)   2/8/94 Vol. 1
wakeup US Russian conversion (Jesus)   12/20/95 Vol. 3
walk in shoes imitate Jesus (Jesus)   1/9/04 Vol. 34
walks of life to love God & neighbor (Jesus)   9/19/00 Vol. 20
Wall Street bankruptcy   8/12/93 Vol. 1
Wall Street greed to bring destruction (Jesus)   10/2/03 Vol. 33
Wall Street stealing from workers (Jesus)   10/11/07 Vol. 49
war a major one planned (Jesus)   8/27/03 Vol. 32
war abortion and reparation (Jesus)   5/27/96 Vol. 3
war angels (Jesus)   8/5/95 Vol. 3
war Antichrist (Jesus)   5/26/95 Vol. 2
war as a chess game (Jesus)   3/6/03 Vol. 30
war avoid killing & make peace (Jesus)   5/21/04 Vol. 35
war bankers & oil interests (Jesus)   9/4/96 Vol. 4
war Bread of Life (Jesus)   4/22/94 Vol. 1
war cannot justify deaths (Jesus)   7/31/03 Vol. 32
war causes economic difficulties (Jesus)   7/22/02 Vol. 28
War commemorate Hiroshima (Jesus)   8/6/96 Vol. 4
war communist countries (Mary)   2/20/97 Vol. 6
war consequences of (Jesus)   1/15/03 Vol. 30
war continues to drain U.S. (Jesus)   7/3/03 Vol. 32
war control your responses (Jesus)   8/27/98 Vol. 12
war desired by one world people (Jesus)   5/12/04 Vol. 35
war do not let evil cause killings (Jesus)   9/7/98 Vol. 12
war do not spread to other nations (Jesus)   12/13/01 Vol. 25
war double your prayer efforts (Jesus)   8/3/06 Vol. 44
war escalation in Iraq (Jesus)   9/4/96 Vol. 4
war ethnic & religious causes (Jesus)   8/7/98 Vol. 12
war excuses, consequences of (Jesus)   3/2/04 Vol. 34
war for profit, no winners (Jesus)   5/28/01 Vol. 23
war gunboat (Jesus)   12/21/94 Vol. 2
war has no winners (Jesus)   6/18/98 Vol. 11
war intervene (Jesus)   4/20/94 Vol. 1

war involving other nations (Jesus) 7/20/06 Vol. 44

war is not answer (Jesus) 2/17/03 Vol. 30

war Israel & Arabs (Jesus) 7/27/06 Vol. 44

war Jesus abhors (Jesus) 3/20/03 Vol. 30

war leaders (Jesus) 2/6/94 Vol. 1

war live by sword,die by sword (Jesus) 10/8/01 Vol. 25

war love (Jesus) 4/21/94 Vol. 1

war mid-east area (Jesus) 1/19/98 Vol. 10

war much killing expected (Jesus) 3/9/03 Vol. 30

war never has any winners (Jesus) 3/27/08 Vol. 50

war never solves problems (Jesus) 11/29/01 Vol. 25

war never solves problems (Jesus) 9/20/03 Vol. 32

war no support for risks (Jesus) 3/13/03 Vol. 30

war nobody really wins (Jesus) 10/4/01 Vol. 25

war not a solution (Jesus) 9/4/03 Vol. 32

war not answer for peace (Jesus) 12/8/05 Vol. 41

war of Arabs & Christians possible (Jesus) 10/4/01 Vol. 25

war over oil or money (Jesus) 7/27/97 Vol. 8

war over power and greed (Jesus) 7/22/99 Vol. 16

war peace (Jesus) 6/16/95 Vol. 2

War peace (Jesus) 4/9/94 Vol. 1

war planes 7/28/93 Vol. 1

war pray extra to stop (Jesus) 8/12/06 Vol. 44

war pray for peace (Jesus) 8/10/06 Vol. 44

war pray for peace (Jesus) 10/25/97 Vol. 9

war pray for peace (Jesus) 6/23/98 Vol. 11

war pray for peace (Jesus) 7/9/98 Vol. 12

war pray for peace (Jesus) 2/16/98 Vol. 10

war pray for peace (Jesus) 1/22/99 Vol. 14

war pray, not weapons (Jesus) 12/7/01 Vol. 25

war prayer for peace (Jesus) 5/8/96 Vol. 3

war prayers gave reprieve (Mary) 3/12/98 Vol. 10

war pride of leaders seek (Jesus) 2/26/98 Vol. 10

war pride, greed, arms (Jesus) 5/15/97 Vol. 7

war punishment (Jesus) 12/16/93 Vol. 1

war punishment for sin (Jesus) 3/20/03 Vol. 30

war purification (Jesus) 6/6/94 Vol. 1

war reconcile differences (Jesus) 7/8/06 Vol. 44

war refuse fighting for leaders (Jesus) 12/4/97 Vol. 9

war senseless killing (Jesus) 7/31/97 Vol. 8

war sign of Fatima (Jesus) 2/13/94 Vol. 1

war symptom of hate & sin (Jesus) 5/13/99 Vol. 15

war the result of sin (Jesus) 4/11/02 Vol. 27

war tool of devil to divide (Jesus) 7/27/06 Vol. 44

war use money to help people (Jesus) 10/4/07 Vol. 49

war vote against (Jesus) 7/21/06 Vol. 44

war vultures,pray for peace (Jesus) 12/11/97 Vol. 9

war weapons into plowshares (Jesus) 12/13/01 Vol. 25

war what does Jesus think of (Jesus) 3/22/03 Vol. 30

war will not settle disputes (Jesus) 1/8/98 Vol. 10

war & jobs answers needed (Jesus) 11/13/03 Vol. 33

war & killing senseless, pray for peace (Jesus) 8/21/03 Vol. 32

war & peace choice of (Jesus) 7/13/06 Vol. 44

war & terrorism only love brings peace (Jesus) 11/10/05 Vol. 41

war against terrorism do not expand (Jesus) 10/8/01 Vol. 25

war against terrorists could start 3rd world war (Jesus) 9/20/01 Vol. 24

war and food missile cost could feed poor (Jesus) 11/14/02 Vol. 29

war clouds avoid innocent victims (Jesus) 9/15/01 Vol. 24

war clouds in Middle East (Jesus) 8/13/01 Vol. 24

war clouds gather larger war could come (Jesus) 3/24/99 Vol. 14

war cost recession or depression (Jesus) 11/27/02 Vol. 29

war costs postponing infrastructure fix (Jesus) 10/10/07 Vol. 49

war costs vs. helping poor, homeless (Jesus) 9/29/05 Vol. 40

war drums beaten by media (Jesus) 2/3/07 Vol. 46

war drums for war on Iraq (Jesus) 8/27/02 Vol. 28

war footing no turning back,no escape (Jesus) 9/21/01 Vol. 24

war for profit needs to stop (Jesus) 3/22/07 Vol. 46

war if futile killing does not stop terrorists (Jesus) 12/25/01 Vol. 25

War illogical over just threat of weapons (Jesus) 8/16/02 Vol. 28

war in Bosnia peace (Mary) 8/31/95 Vol. 3

war in Iran grave consequences of (Jesus) 3/27/07 Vol. 46

War in Iran pray to stop (Jesus) 3/9/06 Vol. 42

War in Iran wanted by central bankers (Jesus) 3/9/06 Vol. 42

war in Iraq could cause World War (Jesus) 11/12/98 Vol. 13

war in killing,destruction pray for peace (Jesus) 10/15/98 Vol. 13

War in Kosovo prayer for peace (Jesus) 4/1/99 Vol. 15

war in Middle East pray for peace in this area (Jesus) 10/12/00 Vol. 21

war inevitable when money & weapons on hand (Jesus) 3/23/02 Vol. 26

war machine missiles & torpedoes (Jesus) 7/11/05 Vol. 40

war money better spent on peace uses (Jesus) 7/18/07 Vol. 48

war money competing with relief aid (Jesus) 9/23/05 Vol. 40

war money in America overshadows aid money (Jesus) 2/18/06 Vol. 42

war on terror has not made US safer (Jesus) 9/14/06 Vol. 44

War on terror profit for one worlders (Jesus) 8/20/07 Vol. 48

war on terror shut off funds (Jesus) 2/1/07 Vol. 46

'War on terror' manufactured (Jesus) 2/5/08 Vol. 50

war on terrorism arms makers profit (Jesus) 7/18/02 Vol. 28

war on terrorism do not expand to WWIII (Jesus) 11/27/01 Vol. 25

war on terrorism do not expand war (Jesus) 11/23/01 Vol. 25

war on terrorism endless situation (Jesus) 9/10/02 Vol. 28

war on terrorism killing not the answer (Jesus) 12/12/01 Vol. 25

war on terrorism pray for peace (Jesus) 11/13/01 Vol. 25

war on terrorism pray for peace (Jesus) 1/29/02 Vol. 26

war on terrorism repent & stop killing (Jesus) 12/5/01 Vol. 25

war on terrorism too costly in troops, money (Jesus) 10/31/04 Vol. 37

war on terrorism will not remove terrorism (Jesus) 3/14/04 Vol. 34

war on terrorists impossible to win (Jesus) 9/10/04 Vol. 36

war plan meant to ruin America (Jesus) 11/28/06 Vol. 45

war plans government not truthful (Jesus) 11/30/01 Vol. 25

war potential from revenge,cause famine (Jesus) 9/12/01 Vol. 24

war potential over oil & gasoline (Jesus) 9/1/05 Vol. 40

war preparations spy satellites,troop movements (Jesus) 8/27/02 Vol. 28

war prevention prayer & peace (Jesus) 8/3/07 Vol. 48

war profits keep wars happening (Jesus) 10/4/07 Vol. 49

war promoters answer to God's wrath (Jesus) 4/19/07 Vol. 47

war protests could become more public (Jesus) 1/6/07 Vol. 46

war readiness weapons threaten peace (Jesus) 9/13/01 Vol. 24

war reasons Satan behind (Jesus) 2/17/07 Vol. 46

war threatened Middle East,Afghanistan,Iraq (Jesus) 3/18/02 Vol. 26

war threats affecting commodity prices (Jesus) 4/29/06 Vol. 43

war weapons overkill against insurgents (Jesus) 2/28/08 Vol. 50

war with Iran crossroads for America (Jesus) 3/8/06 Vol. 42

war, avoid started by planned events (Jesus) 5/28/07 Vol. 47

war, cause of media for brainwashing (Jesus) 8/16/05 Vol. 40

war, future Congress should control (Jesus) 10/18/07 Vol. 49

war, Korea & Iraq pray for peaceful solution (Jesus) 1/16/03 Vol. 30

war, St. Peter live by sword, die by sword (Jesus) 9/10/04 Vol. 36

war, stop by stop funding (Jesus) 8/3/07 Vol. 48

war, weapons of spend money to help people (Jesus) 5/2/02 Vol. 27

war, world over energy sources (Jesus) 7/12/06 Vol. 44

warm & comfortable keep some from converts (Jesus) 11/17/99 Vol. 17

warmer temperatures more ice problems (Jesus) 1/2/07 Vol. 46

warming weather droughts,violent storms (Jesus) 4/6/00 Vol. 19

Warning 2nd chance to change lives (Jesus) 11/23/04 Vol. 37

Warning a comet on day of (Jesus) 3/18/05 Vol. 38

warning a detailed experience (Jesus) 5/25/98 Vol. 11

warning a sign given (Jesus) 7/2/97 Vol. 8

Warning a time for conversion (Jesus) 5/28/99 Vol. 15

warning a wake up call soon (Jesus) 1/9/01 Vol. 22

Warning after, work at fever pitch (Jesus) 2/20/03 Vol. 30

Warning after,get rid of TV (Jesus) 5/10/03 Vol. 31

Warning alert to God's existence (Jesus) 3/23/99 Vol. 14

warning all will know who God is (God the Father) 2/22/98 Vol. 10

warning angels (Jesus) 12/7/94 Vol. 2

warning Antichrist (Jesus) 2/9/94 Vol. 1

Warning anxiously awaited (Jesus) 6/3/04 Vol. 35

warning Armageddon (St. Michael) 5/25/95 Vol. 2

Warning as near death experience (Jesus) 7/24/01 Vol. 24

Warning as priest who went to hell (Jesus) 12/20/97 Vol. 9

Warning avoid chip & Antichrist (Jesus) 9/25/07 Vol. 48

Warning avoid chip in body,Antichrist (Jesus) 4/2/03 Vol. 31

Warning awake souls to Jesus (Jesus) 10/26/01 Vol. 25

Warning be prepared to hide (Jesus) 10/1/06 Vol. 45

Warning before Antichrist comes (Jesus) 2/13/03 Vol. 30

Warning blessing, mercy to see judgment (Jesus) 10/17/03 Vol. 33

warning brief darkness over land (Jesus) 4/7/98 Vol. 11

Warning buzzing sound for speed (Jesus) 7/2/99 Vol. 16

Warning call to repent (Jesus) 7/18/01 Vol. 24

Warning Catholic Church is true (Jesus) 5/9/02 Vol. 27

Warning chance to change life (Jesus) 11/18/05 Vol. 41

Warning chance to convert (Jesus) 6/9/05 Vol. 39

warning choice (Jesus) 3/28/95 Vol. 2

warning choices of life (Jesus) 1/22/96 Vol. 3

warning choose God or world (Jesus) 12/21/96 Vol. 5

warning choose life (Jesus) 9/22/94 Vol. 2

warning choosing eternal fate (Jesus) 3/3/96 Vol. 3

Warning circling scenes (Jesus) 11/8/06 Vol. 45

Warning come to appear at (Jesus) 1/1/03 Vol. 30

Warning comes before Satan's hour (Jesus) 4/20/05 Vol. 39

Warning comes first (Jesus) 1/1/08 Vol. 50

Warning comet at that time (Jesus) 1/26/07 Vol. 46

Warning comet of (Jesus) 9/4/00 Vol. 20

Warning comet on day of (Jesus) 9/20/07 Vol. 48

Warning comet on day of (Jesus) 10/16/06 Vol. 45

warning confession (Jesus) 5/19/96 Vol. 3

warning confession (Jesus) 2/21/96 Vol. 3

Warning darkness a sign in sky (Jesus) 3/24/99 Vol. 14

warning day of mercy (Jesus) 4/10/96 Vol. 3

Warning do not take mark of beast (Jesus) 5/5/01 Vol. 23

warning effect on priests (Jesus) 7/2/96 Vol. 3

Warning effect on relatives,friends (Jesus) 6/4/99 Vol. 15

warning enlightenment of soul (Jesus) 3/20/96 Vol. 3

warning evangelize lost souls (Jesus) 9/9/97 Vol. 8

Warning evangelize souls (Jesus) 4/29/01 Vol. 23

Warning examine your lives (Jesus) 4/10/97 Vol. 7

Warning experience described (Jesus) 8/9/06 Vol. 44

Warning extension of mercy (Jesus) 9/12/02 Vol. 28

Warning first event before Antichrist (Jesus) 7/9/03 Vol. 32

warning first event to happen (Jesus) 5/10/98 Vol. 11

Warning first of major events (Jesus) 8/28/01 Vol. 24

Warning first of major signs (Jesus) 6/20/05 Vol. 39

Warning flash in sky suddenly (Jesus) 7/9/03 Vol. 32

Warning followed by takeover (Jesus) 7/24/99 Vol. 16

warning football field, repent (Jesus) 10/25/96 Vol. 5

warning football season (Jesus) 9/1/95 Vol. 3

Warning get rid of TV & monitors (Jesus) 8/11/03 Vol. 32

Warning get rid of TV after (Jesus) 5/30/02 Vol. 27

Warning get rid of TV's after (Jesus) 9/9/99 Vol. 16

Warning gives souls second chance (Jesus) 7/10/02 Vol. 28
Warning glow with light,confession (Jesus) 2/23/97 Vol. 6
Warning God vs. money (Jesus) 5/24/05 Vol. 39
Warning good and bad actions (Jesus) 6/6/01 Vol. 23
Warning guilt laid bare by grace (Jesus) 11/3/01 Vol. 25
warning harvest is ready (Jesus) 3/22/97 Vol. 6
warning hope in new era (Jesus) 6/5/96 Vol. 3
Warning hour of evil after (Jesus) 2/21/08 Vol. 50
Warning informed not to take chips (Jesus) 8/22/01 Vol. 24
Warning it is close (Jesus) 6/4/99 Vol. 15
warning kaleideoscope (Jesus) 7/7/94 Vol. 2
Warning know not to take chip in hand (Jesus) 2/2/02 Vol. 26
Warning know not to take mark (Jesus) 3/12/05 Vol. 38
Warning know salvation through the cross (Jesus) 4/18/05 Vol. 39
Warning know to come through Jesus (Jesus) 5/6/05 Vol. 39
warning last call, confession (Jesus) 1/3/97 Vol. 6
Warning last chance for mercy (Jesus) 12/27/05 Vol. 41
Warning last chance for some (Jesus) 7/2/99 Vol. 16
warning last visitation of mercy (Jesus) 4/14/96 Vol. 3
Warning leave soon after (Jesus) 3/2/07 Vol. 46
warning life review (Jesus) 8/2/94 Vol. 2
Warning life review of every hour (Jesus) 8/5/03 Vol. 32
Warning Light at end of tunnel (Jesus) 11/23/04 Vol. 37
Warning meaning of judgment (Jesus) 1/3/07 Vol. 46
Warning mercy of second chance (Jesus) 6/8/05 Vol. 39
Warning mercy to save souls (Jesus) 6/19/99 Vol. 15
Warning more will go to church (Jesus) 1/11/01 Vol. 22
Warning needed for conversions (Jesus) 11/19/99 Vol. 17
Warning needed to change lives (Jesus) 3/18/03 Vol. 30
Warning no microchip,no worship of beast (Jesus) 1/22/08 Vol. 50
Warning no middle ground (Jesus) 10/6/03 Vol. 33
Warning not far off (Jesus) 10/29/04 Vol. 37
Warning omens in the sky (Jesus) 10/4/02 Vol. 29
Warning only signs given, no dates (Jesus) 2/3/05 Vol. 38
Warning open to God's love (Jesus) 11/7/02 Vol. 29
Warning opportunity to be saved (Jesus) 7/5/07 Vol. 48
Warning out of body experience (Jesus) 1/9/06 Vol. 42
Warning outside of time (Jesus) 10/25/03 Vol. 33
warning persecution (Jesus) 5/18/94 Vol. 1
Warning personal experience (Jesus) 8/25/00 Vol. 20
Warning playback of your life (Jesus) 2/20/06 Vol. 42
Warning pray to save souls (Jesus) 9/26/00 Vol. 20
Warning preparation for tribulation (Jesus) 9/25/01 Vol. 24
Warning prepare for by good works (Jesus) 10/10/01 Vol. 25
Warning prepare souls now (Jesus) 2/2/99 Vol. 14
Warning prepare with Confession (Jesus) 3/17/05 Vol. 38
warning prepare with confession (Jesus) 10/13/96 Vol. 5

Warning protection at refuges told (Jesus) 9/25/07 Vol. 48
warning purification (Jesus) 1/17/97 Vol. 6
Warning remember unforgiven sins (Jesus) 7/4/07 Vol. 48
Warning remove TVs & monitors (Jesus) 5/28/03 Vol. 31
Warning remove TVs after (Jesus) 2/3/03 Vol. 30
Warning remove TVs after (Jesus) 11/4/05 Vol. 41
Warning remove TVs after (Jesus) 8/9/98 Vol. 12
Warning remove TVs,monitors (Jesus) 2/10/00 Vol. 18
warning repent (Jesus) 1/27/94 Vol. 1
warning repent (Jesus) 8/29/96 Vol. 4
warning repent before tribulation (Jesus) 6/28/96 Vol. 3
warning repentence (Jesus) 6/25/94 Vol. 1
warning sacraments (Jesus) 5/9/94 Vol. 1
Warning salvation in Jesus (Jesus) 4/1/05 Vol. 39
warning Satan worship (Jesus) 9/6/95 Vol. 3
Warning second chance in suffering (Jesus) 8/6/07 Vol. 48
Warning second chance to convert (Jesus) 11/9/00 Vol. 21
Warning see each life's contents (Jesus) 4/4/06 Vol. 43
Warning see how others see you (Jesus) 10/14/05 Vol. 41
Warning see life, second chance (Jesus) 4/22/01 Vol. 23
Warning see where we are judged (Jesus) 1/26/01 Vol. 22
Warning see whole life, be prepared (Jesus) 2/20/03 Vol. 30
Warning see your sins&offenses (Jesus) 10/3/99 Vol. 17
Warning seek forgiveness of sins (Jesus) 9/21/03 Vol. 32
Warning seen on stage of life (Jesus) 6/12/02 Vol. 27
Warning short time for conversion (Jesus) 8/18/01 Vol. 24
Warning short time to evangelize (Jesus) 9/9/99 Vol. 16
Warning signal for tribulation (Jesus) 10/3/03 Vol. 33
warning signs (Jesus) 8/6/95 Vol. 3
Warning signs in the sky (Jesus) 6/22/05 Vol. 39
warning signs of end times (Jesus) 11/25/95 Vol. 3
Warning sinners given mercy of God (Jesus) 6/6/07 Vol. 47
Warning sinners more responsible (Jesus) 5/17/00 Vol. 19
warning sins exposed to light (Jesus) 9/25/97 Vol. 8
warning soul's status (Jesus) 8/5/94 Vol. 2
warning spinning saucer (Jesus) 11/30/94 Vol. 2
warning supernatural event (Jesus) 12/23/96 Vol. 5
warning (Terelya) 9/11/93 Vol. 1
warning test of faith (Jesus) 5/11/95 Vol. 2
warning testing (Jesus) 3/30/94 Vol. 1
warning time (Jesus) 4/22/94 Vol. 1
warning time of enlightenment (Jesus) 8/21/96 Vol. 4
Warning time of mercy (Jesus) 11/26/00 Vol. 21
Warning time stopped, conversions (Jesus) 5/31/05 Vol. 39
Warning time to stop in suspension (Jesus) 3/15/02 Vol. 26
Warning to convert lost souls (Jesus) 9/15/00 Vol. 20
Warning to help lost souls (Jesus) 10/19/01 Vol. 25

Warning to help priests hear confessions (Jesus)   8/28/03 Vol. 32
Warning to wake people up (Jesus)   2/8/99 Vol. 14
Warning to wake up sinners (Jesus)   7/14/03 Vol. 32
Warning told to refuse chips (Jesus)   8/29/06 Vol. 44
warning train (Jesus)   3/8/95 Vol. 2
warning triumph many   4/6/94 Vol. 1
Warning truly is coming (Jesus)   9/11/06 Vol. 44
Warning understand truths (Jesus)   9/13/00 Vol. 20
warning visitation (Mary)   5/31/95 Vol. 2
Warning wake up and prepare (Jesus)   10/11/02 Vol. 29
warning wake up from complacency (Jesus)   1/25/98 Vol. 10
warning war (Jesus)   8/18/95 Vol. 3
warning war (Jesus)   3/8/94 Vol. 1
WARNING warning (Jesus)   7/11/95 Vol. 3
Warning will bring Confessions (Jesus)   10/9/01 Vol. 25
Warning will know Jesus saves (Jesus)   2/6/07 Vol. 46
Warning will reveal mark of beast (Jesus)   10/12/99 Vol. 17
Warning will see sins of omission (Jesus)   11/6/06 Vol. 45
Warning with major celestial event (Jesus)   10/8/99 Vol. 17
Warning with major sign in sky (Jesus)   7/20/99 Vol. 16
Warning conversions faithful to bring souls to God (Jesus) 4/6/00 Vol. 19
Warning description eclipse of the sun (Jesus)   1/20/07 Vol. 46
Warning description mercy from God (Jesus)   8/18/01 Vol. 24
Warning description reflection of state of soul (Jesus) 10/28/00 Vol. 21
Warning event brightness in shy on day of (Jesus)   9/3/04 Vol. 36
Warning experience accept Jesus or not (Jesus)   8/21/02 Vol. 28
Warning experience all to see Savior (Jesus)   8/3/00 Vol. 20
Warning experience centers around Jesus, Host (Jesus)   12/9/07 Vol. 49
Warning experience complete knowledge (Jesus)   2/9/06 Vol. 42
Warning experience described (Jesus)   1/6/05 Vol. 38
Warning experience earthquakes,volcanoes on day (Jesus) 1/22/08 Vol. 50
Warning experience first major sign to Antichrist (Jesus) 8/7/06 Vol. 44
Warning experience last chance to be saved (Jesus)   4/13/00 Vol. 19
Warning experience life review in judgment (Jesus)   12/23/99 Vol. 17
Warning experience more back to Mass (Jesus)   2/20/05 Vol. 38
Warning experience more descriptions as it comes (Jesus) 11/24/05 Vol. 41
Warning experience no chips in the body warning (Jesus) 11/13/02 Vol. 29
Warning experience review of life's decisions (Jesus)   8/6/07 Vol. 48
Warning experience see body & soul develop (Jesus)   1/17/06 Vol. 42
Warning experience true judgment, no surprise (Jesus)   8/26/05 Vol. 40
Warning for rulers confound war machines (Jesus)   11/23/99 Vol. 17
Warning life review spread love around (Jesus)   1/5/00 Vol. 18
Warning mercy accept Jesus or forever dead (Jesus)   4/17/00 Vol. 19
Warning mercy last chance for lost souls (Jesus)   4/6/00 Vol. 19
warning messages near completion (Mary)   12/8/99 Vol. 17
Warning messages personal mission (Jesus)   3/31/98 Vol. 10
warning messages preparation for Jesus (Jesus)   5/6/99 Vol. 15

Warning needed to change lives (Jesus)   7/4/03 Vol. 32
warning of end times evil as in Noah's day (Jesus)   2/15/01 Vol. 22
warning of martial law to be given for faithful (Jesus) 9/29/06 Vol. 44
Warning preparation change life now (Jesus)   9/5/05 Vol. 40
Warning preparation sacramentals,prayers (Jesus)   7/4/00 Vol. 20
Warning preparation with acts of love (Jesus)   5/24/05 Vol. 39
Warning sign comet appearance on day of (Jesus)   11/29/05 Vol. 41
Warning sign comet at Warning time (Jesus)   8/8/00 Vol. 20
Warning sign comet from behind the sun (Jesus)   6/8/00 Vol. 19
Warning sign large orange cloud (Jesus)   7/4/00 Vol. 20
Warning time likely in football season (Jesus)   7/2/05 Vol. 40
Warning to Jesus' return Transfiguration to Easter (Jesus) 2/20/05 Vol. 38
Warning, comet of view behind in space (Jesus)   6/7/07 Vol. 47
Warning, coming supernatural revelation (Jesus)   3/22/01 Vol. 22
Warning,Antichrist announced by comets (Jesus)   12/5/02 Vol. 29
Warning,pain more knowledge of sins (Jesus)   4/24/97 Vol. 7
Warning,signs in sky struggle to save souls (Jesus)   10/1/98 Vol. 13
Warning,spinning galaxy everyone to have life review (Jesus)
                                                        10/11/98 Vol. 13
Warning,wake America good life passing away (Jesus)   10/8/98 Vol. 13
warnings avoid dangerous areas (Jesus)   2/14/01 Vol. 22
warnings of tribulation remember spiritual prep (Jesus) 11/11/99 Vol. 17
warnings of tsunami needed quickly (Jesus)   2/27/06 Vol. 42
warriors for God fight to save souls (Jesus)   2/9/00 Vol. 18
wars all have evil causes (Jesus)   2/10/08 Vol. 50
wars always a tragedy (Jesus)   6/20/02 Vol. 27
wars always fruitless (Jesus)   4/11/03 Vol. 31
wars are planned & contrived (Jesus)   12/26/07 Vol. 49
wars bankrupting America (Jesus)   5/20/05 Vol. 39
wars be peacemakers (Jesus)   5/26/97 Vol. 7
wars caused by one worlders (Jesus)   7/30/06 Vol. 44
wars cease with love (Jesus)   12/25/98 Vol. 13
wars choice of people in Congress (Jesus)   9/23/04 Vol. 36
wars compromise, pray for peace (Jesus)   6/14/06 Vol. 43
wars created by one worlders (Jesus)   2/13/03 Vol. 30
wars destroy economy & military (Jesus)   10/14/06 Vol. 45
wars die by the sword (Jesus)   4/5/07 Vol. 47
wars disengage from (Jesus)   10/5/06 Vol. 45
wars do not fight for one worlders (Jesus)   5/2/03 Vol. 31
wars driven by pride (Jesus)   10/10/02 Vol. 29
wars encouraged by masons (Jesus)   7/7/03 Vol. 32
wars evil men profit by (Jesus)   8/9/01 Vol. 24
wars fight with prayer & rosaries (Jesus)   7/4/06 Vol. 44
wars focus on help not killing (Jesus)   6/16/06 Vol. 43
wars for profit and test weapons (Jesus)   7/25/05 Vol. 40
wars gain in intensity (Jesus)   8/21/97 Vol. 8
wars greed (Jesus)   10/10/94 Vol. 2

wars greed and power (Jesus) — 7/3/97 Vol. 8
wars have no winners (Jesus) — 2/12/07 Vol. 46
wars have selfish objectives (Jesus) — 5/27/99 Vol. 15
wars killing (Jesus) — 9/12/94 Vol. 2
wars killing is the worst (Jesus) — 2/23/03 Vol. 30
wars make one worlders rich (Jesus) — 2/27/03 Vol. 30
wars make peace instead (Jesus) — 1/1/05 Vol. 38
wars more being planned (Jesus) — 2/1/07 Vol. 46
wars never better, pray for peace (Jesus) — 9/11/03 Vol. 32
wars next ones being planned (Jesus) — 5/12/03 Vol. 31
wars oil & weapons needed (Jesus) — 3/19/05 Vol. 38
wars oil deposits a source of (Jesus) — 12/6/04 Vol. 37
wars one world people causing (Jesus) — 11/22/02 Vol. 29
wars peace has high cost (Jesus) — 11/11/04 Vol. 37
wars perpetrated by one worlders (Jesus) — 6/5/06 Vol. 43
wars persecution — 1/7/94 Vol. 1
wars power and greed (Jesus) — 6/23/96 Vol. 3
wars pray for peace instead of (Jesus) — 3/10/05 Vol. 38
wars pray not to expand (Jesus) — 5/27/99 Vol. 15
wars pray to end (Jesus) — 7/24/03 Vol. 32
wars pride, greed, anger (Jesus) — 4/5/07 Vol. 47
wars punishment for sin (Jesus) — 3/7/03 Vol. 30
wars rich instigated, profit from (Jesus) — 12/19/03 Vol. 33
wars rich profit from (Jesus) — 8/10/06 Vol. 44
wars Satan's hour (Jesus) — 12/29/05 Vol. 41
wars stop in Middle East (Jesus) — 8/24/06 Vol. 44
wars stop or be consumed by them (Jesus) — 4/18/04 Vol. 35
wars stretching troops thin (Jesus) — 4/14/05 Vol. 39
wars suffering & refugees (Jesus) — 10/7/99 Vol. 17
wars ten commandments (Jesus) — 4/26/95 Vol. 2
wars to begin again (Jesus) — 7/25/05 Vol. 40
wars to strip and ruin America (Jesus) — 3/18/03 Vol. 30
wars waste of money & lives (Jesus) — 12/16/04 Vol. 37
wars weather and rosary (Jesus) — 4/23/96 Vol. 3
wars & abortions crosses of death (Jesus) — 11/13/05 Vol. 41
wars & abortions initiated by evil (Jesus) — 3/15/07 Vol. 46
wars & arms use money for helping (Jesus) — 6/1/06 Vol. 43
wars & bombings pray to stop (Jesus) — 6/1/06 Vol. 43
wars & deficits promoted by the rich (Jesus) — 2/15/05 Vol. 38
wars & deficits to destroy America (Jesus) — 7/26/03 Vol. 32
wars & depression laying takeover for Antichrist (Jesus) — 8/30/01 Vol. 24
wars & destruction reflected in destruction in nature (Jesus) — 7/15/04 Vol. 36
wars & finances bring America to its knees (Jesus) — 9/11/03 Vol. 32
wars & killings avoided by love (Jesus) — 4/8/99 Vol. 15
wars & killings bring only hate (Jesus) — 12/24/06 Vol. 45
wars & killings pray to stop (Mark) — 10/2/06 Vol. 45
wars & money solve by diplomacy (Jesus) — 1/29/04 Vol. 34

wars & terrorism pray for peace (Jesus) — 7/14/05 Vol. 40
wars & weapons devil uses against man (Jesus) — 1/20/04 Vol. 34
wars & weapons madness of Satan (Jesus) — 8/13/01 Vol. 24
wars & weapons waste money,help poor (Jesus) — 2/16/06 Vol. 42
wars & weather chastisements for sins (Jesus) — 5/5/99 Vol. 15
wars abroad need to end (Jesus) — 12/30/06 Vol. 45
wars and rumors of wars love your enemies (Jesus) — 7/14/96 Vol. 4
wars and sin weigh God down (Jesus) — 7/17/06 Vol. 44
war's effects stop repeating history (Jesus) — 11/5/02 Vol. 29
wars for freedom be peacemakers (Jesus) — 2/15/01 Vol. 22
wars for profit by one world people (Jesus) — 11/18/99 Vol. 17
wars need stopping for peace, less deficits (Jesus) — 2/3/05 Vol. 38
wars need to stop tell Congress to stop (Jesus) — 1/29/05 Vol. 38
wars of attrition to bring down America (Jesus) — 8/29/02 Vol. 28
wars on holy days test of resolve of the West (Jesus) — 10/12/00 Vol. 21
wars orchestrated one world influence (Jesus) — 3/27/99 Vol. 14
wars promoted for money (Jesus) — 4/29/04 Vol. 35
wars repeated for greed & control (Jesus) — 7/22/05 Vol. 40
wars stopped by prayers for peace (Jesus) — 11/10/05 Vol. 41
wars to come from anger & hate (Jesus) — 5/3/00 Vol. 19
wars, avoid to have peace (Jesus) — 8/12/05 Vol. 40
wars, constant speak out against war (Jesus) — 1/20/05 Vol. 38
wars, constant to destroy US economy (Jesus) — 6/14/03 Vol. 31
wars, continual to weaken America (Jesus) — 9/20/02 Vol. 28
wars, continuous need stopping for peace (Jesus) — 9/23/04 Vol. 36
wars, justified unprovoked wars - not (Jesus) — 5/25/06 Vol. 43
wars, not answer bring only death,destruction (Jesus) — 3/5/02 Vol. 26
wars, planned to ruin US financially,militarily (Jesus) — 9/5/04 Vol. 36
wars, rumors of wars power struggle with NATO (Jesus) — 10/12/98 Vol. 13
wars, stop by love and prayer (Jesus) — 10/31/04 Vol. 37
wars, stop by removing profit (Jesus) — 12/4/07 Vol. 49
wars, stop make peace (Jesus) — 9/3/07 Vol. 48
wars, stop pray for peace (Jesus) — 11/9/06 Vol. 45
wars, stop to have peace (Jesus) — 5/25/06 Vol. 43
wars, unjust rich profit from (Jesus) — 5/28/07 Vol. 47
wars, unnecessary no gain for Americans (Jesus) — 3/20/04 Vol. 34
wars,controlled nuclear war held back (Jesus) — 10/3/00 Vol. 21
wars,deficits,poor trade America's demise (Jesus) — 5/28/05 Vol. 39
wars,finances controlled,one world people (Jesus) — 10/2/00 Vol. 21
wars,terrorism,disasters cause of deaths (Jesus) — 12/4/02 Vol. 29
washing of feet purifying soul (Jesus) — 3/20/08 Vol. 50
Washington, D. C. disaster or terrorism (Jesus) — 2/7/08 Vol. 50
Washington,D.C. event terrorism & disasters (Jesus) — 3/26/06 Vol. 42
wasted time analyzed by Jesus (Jesus) — 3/6/00 Vol. 18
water can be good or bad (Jesus) — 7/23/99 Vol. 16
water contaminated in war (Jesus) — 2/19/98 Vol. 10
water famines and floods (Jesus) — 3/7/96 Vol. 3

water fresh water threatened (Jesus)   6/25/98 Vol. 11
water growing shortages (Jesus)   5/20/03 Vol. 31
water miraculous springs (Mary)   1/16/98 Vol. 10
water pray for (Jesus)   5/24/05 Vol. 39
water shortages of fresh water (Jesus)   5/29/03 Vol. 31
water store for the trial (Jesus)   10/14/99 Vol. 17
water uses and gift of (Jesus)   5/14/03 Vol. 31
water vital to life of body (Jesus)   5/10/00 Vol. 19
water & air need cleaning,less disease (Jesus)   8/11/05 Vol. 40
water & food store to multiply later (Jesus)   4/14/05 Vol. 39
Water & Light Easter symbols (Jesus)   3/24/08 Vol. 50
water & Light Easter symbols of Baptism (Jesus)   4/10/07 Vol. 47
water & sewage problems with computers (Jesus)   10/28/99 Vol. 17
water a problem from droughts & and floods (Jesus)   6/6/00 Vol. 19
water and fire testing purification (Jesus)   12/27/95 Vol. 3
water chastisements for violating God's laws (Jesus)   1/16/05 Vol. 38
water concerns in West better to live near water (Jesus)   3/18/04 Vol. 34
water distillation needed for fresh water (Jesus)   5/17/07 Vol. 47
water gift not always appreciated (Jesus)   10/25/07 Vol. 49
water mill beautiful images (Jesus)   9/10/03 Vol. 32
water needs need sharing (Jesus)   11/13/03 Vol. 33
water pollution 3% of all water is fresh (Jesus)   1/21/03 Vol. 30
water pollution needs to stop (Jesus)   8/3/02 Vol. 28
water purified as our souls (Jesus)   6/18/04 Vol. 35
water scarce,fresh cause of famine (Jesus)   2/3/00 Vol. 18
water scarce,fresh water to be expensive (Jesus)   3/30/00 Vol. 18
water shortages and famine (Jesus)   6/13/02 Vol. 27
water sources wells, rain, desalinate sea (Jesus)   5/19/05 Vol. 39
water storage lines stopped, poisoned water (Jesus)   12/18/03 Vol. 33
water stored and multiplied (Jesus)   10/24/02 Vol. 29
water to be saved water at risk of control (Jesus)   8/20/98 Vol. 12
water, air pollution destroying environment (Jesus)   12/19/07 Vol. 49
water, fresh becoming scarse (Jesus)   3/26/99 Vol. 14
water, fresh fresh water threatened (Jesus)   4/24/01 Vol. 23
water, fresh in short supply (Jesus)   9/21/06 Vol. 44
water, fresh provided at refuges (Jesus)   8/26/06 Vol. 44
water, fresh shortage of (Jesus)   7/5/03 Vol. 32
water, fresh supply decreasing (Jesus)   6/10/04 Vol. 35
water, fresh symbol of life and grace (Jesus)   6/21/01 Vol. 23
water, fresh treasure, no pollution (Jesus)   12/20/06 Vol. 45
water,fresh one world control (Jesus)   3/14/00 Vol. 18
waterfall by a cave tribulation (Jesus)   1/7/95 Vol. 2
waves,relentless God melts hearts (Jesus)   1/24/99 Vol. 14
way of the cross narrow path (Jesus)   1/23/95 Vol. 2
ways of God discern for every project (Jesus)   12/14/07 Vol. 49
wayward souls prayers for (Jesus)   12/8/03 Vol. 33
weak moment time of devil's temptation (Jesus)   2/17/02 Vol. 26

weakness in sin find strength in Jesus (Jesus)   7/31/00 Vol. 20
weaknesses demons use to tempt us (Jesus)   9/19/03 Vol. 32
weaknesses make us strong (Jesus)   7/9/06 Vol. 44
weaknesses overcome by prayer (Jesus)   8/1/06 Vol. 44
wealth cannot serve 2 masters (Jesus)   3/8/96 Vol. 3
wealth cold without love (Jesus)   6/21/02 Vol. 27
wealth do not strive for (Jesus)   11/16/01 Vol. 25
wealth does not satisfy soul (Jesus)   9/21/00 Vol. 20
wealth handle properly (Jesus)   10/24/06 Vol. 45
wealth rich for themselves (Jesus)   2/7/08 Vol. 50
wealth share with others (Jesus)   3/3/05 Vol. 38
wealth share with others (Jesus)   8/12/99 Vol. 16
wealth share with poor (Jesus)   9/7/00 Vol. 20
wealth should not be an idol (Jesus)   9/2/06 Vol. 44
wealth some sold souls for (Jesus)   8/19/03 Vol. 32
wealth soul (Jesus)   12/13/95 Vol. 3
wealth spiritual better than physical (Jesus)   11/8/01 Vol. 25
wealth store spiritual treasures (Jesus)   1/21/99 Vol. 14
wealth stripped sooner or later (Jesus)   8/15/01 Vol. 24
wealth use to help the poor (Jesus)   2/11/99 Vol. 14
wealth will be lost (Jesus)   8/3/01 Vol. 24
wealth will never make you happy (Jesus)   6/12/01 Vol. 23
wealth will not gain heaven (Jesus)   7/3/07 Vol. 48
wealth will not satisfy your soul (Jesus)   9/23/98 Vol. 12
wealth & faith share with all nations (Jesus)   11/16/04 Vol. 37
wealth & possessions end at grave (Jesus)   8/21/00 Vol. 20
wealth & riches weakens faith (Jesus)   8/19/06 Vol. 44
wealth accumulation obsession in market (Jesus)   9/17/99 Vol. 16
wealth of earth seek heavenly treasure instead (Jesus)   8/16/04 Vol. 36
wealth of earth will dissipate (Jesus)   12/22/01 Vol. 25
wealth shared with poor gains graces (Jesus)   10/15/00 Vol. 21
wealth to be lost for those without mark (Jesus)   3/8/00 Vol. 18
wealth vs poor disparity in necessities (Jesus)   5/7/07 Vol. 47
wealth will be lost confidence in God (Jesus)   6/12/97 Vol. 7
wealth, elusive cannot be a god (Jesus)   2/5/00 Vol. 18
wealth, fame will not gain heaven (Jesus)   9/11/07 Vol. 48
wealth, shared to gain heavenly riches (Jesus)   6/26/03 Vol. 31
wealth, sharing gains merits in heaven (Jesus)   1/24/05 Vol. 38
wealth, spiritual in love of God, neighbor (Jesus)   5/20/04 Vol. 35
wealth, true heavenly treasure (Jesus)   9/23/07 Vol. 48
wealth,comforts are not our goals,God is (Jesus)   6/5/00 Vol. 19
wealth,fam stripped accept God's Will in life/Job (Jesus)   9/27/04 Vol. 36
wealth,give up than be rich in hell (Jesus)   8/4/00 Vol. 20
wealth,quick not mastered by money (Jesus)   2/24/00 Vol. 18
wealthy have no peace (Jesus)   6/25/02 Vol. 27
wealthy men acting as modern day kings (Jesus)   4/18/00 Vol. 19
wealthy people pray for conversions (Jesus)   9/27/00 Vol. 20

weapon spending accountable to God (Jesus) 2/17/00 Vol. 18
weapon spending use money for peace (Jesus) 2/21/01 Vol. 22
weapon technology in wrong hands is harmful (Jesus) 6/21/04 Vol. 35
weapons disarm, work for peace (Jesus) 6/19/97 Vol. 7
weapons do not build war machines (Jesus) 6/18/98 Vol. 11
weapons exploit for money (Jesus) 6/25/98 Vol. 11
weapons focus on peace (Jesus) 8/2/01 Vol. 24
weapons futile to use (Jesus) 8/4/99 Vol. 16
weapons killing (Jesus) 1/24/96 Vol. 3
weapons microwaves transmit diseases (Jesus) 10/31/05 Vol. 41
weapons of mass destruction (Jesus) 10/29/02 Vol. 29
weapons of mass destruction (Jesus) 8/28/00 Vol. 20
weapons of war (Jesus) 9/6/02 Vol. 28
weapons one worlders profit from (Jesus) 6/8/01 Vol. 23
weapons pray for peace (Jesus) 5/14/98 Vol. 11
weapons pray they are not used (Jesus) 4/30/04 Vol. 35
weapons spiritual & physical (Jesus) 8/24/96 Vol. 4
weapons spiritual, not guns (Jesus) 7/24/97 Vol. 8
weapons stop weapon research (Jesus) 10/9/97 Vol. 9
weapons technology and power (Jesus) 6/16/96 Vol. 3
weapons triumph (Jesus) 5/15/95 Vol. 2
weapons use money for poor (Jesus) 1/11/01 Vol. 22
weapons will not protect you (Jesus) 12/28/98 Vol. 13
weapons & arms do not take up (Jesus) 10/4/03 Vol. 33
weap. against demons angels,blessed salt,exorcism (Jesus) 9/13/07 Vol. 48
weap.against faithful stealth weapons inactivated (Jesus) 8/13/98 Vol. 12
weapons are deadly will consume you (Jesus) 10/22/98 Vol. 13
weapons blinded miraculous protection (Jesus) 3/17/00 Vol. 18
weapons business money made in wars (Jesus) 6/18/07 Vol. 47
weapons money better spent on poor (Jesus) 2/19/06 Vol. 42
weapons money spend more on poor (Jesus) 11/12/98 Vol. 13
weapons of destruction pulse energy beam (Jesus) 8/3/05 Vol. 40
weapons of mass destruction how to react to (Jesus) 3/14/03 Vol. 30
weap.of mass destruction pray they are not used (Jesus) 4/25/02 Vol. 27
weapons of mass killing destroy all life (Jesus) 2/12/98 Vol. 10
weapons of war many nations building (Jesus) 10/24/02 Vol. 29
weapons projects no money for poor (Jesus) 1/12/02 Vol. 26
weapons restrictions ironic for North Korea,Iraq (Jesus) 12/12/02 Vol. 29
weapons, new tried out in wars (Jesus) 1/18/07 Vol. 46
weapons,deadly nuclear,biological (Jesus) 10/24/00 Vol. 21
weapons,mass destruct could end man's existence (Jesus) 8/4/98 Vol. 12
weather abortion (Jesus) 1/19/94 Vol. 1
weather abortions (Jesus) 6/19/96 Vol. 3
weather and volcanoes (Jesus) 6/1/02 Vol. 27
weather chastisements for sins (Jesus) 6/12/96 Vol. 3
weather chastisements of (Jesus) 3/10/05 Vol. 38
weather chastisements, pray, fast (Jesus) 5/16/97 Vol. 7

weather choice (Jesus) 2/9/94 Vol. 1
weather destruction to increase (Jesus) 1/8/04 Vol. 34
weather disasters (Jesus) 7/3/02 Vol. 28
weather disasters as signs (Jesus) 7/5/98 Vol. 12
weather disturbances (Jesus) 6/4/02 Vol. 27
weather do not complain about (Jesus) 10/28/06 Vol. 45
weather dramatic shifts in cycles (Jesus) 1/15/04 Vol. 34
weather effect on food supply (Jesus) 6/9/99 Vol. 15
weather effects on crops (Jesus) 6/3/99 Vol. 15
weather events one after another (Jesus) 1/16/06 Vol. 42
weather extremes of hot and cold (Jesus) 6/15/02 Vol. 27
weather extremes of hot and cold (Jesus) 8/28/00 Vol. 20
weather extremes,sign of times (Jesus) 5/22/97 Vol. 7
weather falls on areas of sin (Jesus) 9/15/00 Vol. 20
weather flooding (Jesus) 12/20/95 Vol. 3
weather food production (Jesus) 6/19/96 Vol. 3
weather food shortages & disease (Jesus) 2/26/98 Vol. 10
weather havoc over whole world (Jesus) 1/15/03 Vol. 30
weather heat (Jesus) 7/30/95 Vol. 3
weather increased storms (Jesus) 1/3/97 Vol. 6
weather intensified storms (Jesus) 11/13/97 Vol. 9
weather killings (Jesus) 8/23/95 Vol. 3
weather living water (Jesus) 6/20/95 Vol. 2
weather manipulated (Jesus) 1/15/99 Vol. 14
weather more severe,be prayerful (Jesus) 1/10/97 Vol. 6
weather reacting to abuses and sin (Jesus) 10/28/06 Vol. 45
weather record storms (Jesus) 1/6/97 Vol. 6
weather reflection of violence (Jesus) 1/16/03 Vol. 30
weather reflects hot & cold hearts (Jesus) 4/7/97 Vol. 7
weather sign of displeasure (Jesus) 6/4/98 Vol. 11
weather signs of end times (Jesus) 12/6/01 Vol. 25
weather snow and fires (Jesus) 11/2/96 Vol. 5
weather storms increase, sin (Jesus) 1/8/98 Vol. 10
weather storms reflect violence (Jesus) 12/18/97 Vol. 9
weather Tesla machines (Jesus) 12/22/96 Vol. 5
weather testing (Jesus) 1/10/96 Vol. 3
weather testing time (Jesus) 1/21/94 Vol. 1
weather to be more severe (Jesus) 6/12/06 Vol. 43
weather unusual storms as signs (Jesus) 1/11/05 Vol. 38
weather used to stop wars (Jesus) 12/24/05 Vol. 41
weather weather machines (Jesus) 3/11/97 Vol. 6
weather will affect movie industry (Jesus) 3/2/98 Vol. 10
weather & water problems of pollution (Jesus) 1/28/02 Vol. 26
weather calamities chastisements for sins (Jesus) 6/6/02 Vol. 27
weather changes by pole shift (Jesus) 10/9/03 Vol. 33
weather chaos another one world tactic (Jesus) 5/25/04 Vol. 35
weather chastisement for sins of flesh (Jesus) 7/4/03 Vol. 32

white robes second coming (Jesus) — 1/7/95 Vol. 2

white robes washed prayer warriors (Jesus) — 8/16/99 Vol. 16

white witches worship gods of nature (Jesus) — 6/24/99 Vol. 15

wilderness trust (Jesus) — 12/30/95 Vol. 3

wilderness living to avoid Antichrist (Jesus) — 8/20/02 Vol. 28

wilderness refuge away from cities (Jesus) — 12/30/04 Vol. 37

will cross (Jesus) — 7/23/95 Vol. 3

will handmaid (Mary) — 12/15/93 Vol. 1

Will hearts (Jesus) — 3/11/94 Vol. 1

Will prayer (Mary) — 9/10/95 Vol. 3

Will of God dying to self (Jesus) — 4/29/96 Vol. 3

Will of God follow, forgiveness (Jesus) — 2/10/97 Vol. 6

Will of God needs to replace our will (Jesus) — 6/17/00 Vol. 19

wills honor deceased wishes (Jesus) — 4/5/06 Vol. 43

wind & power outages this winter (Jesus) — 12/3/07 Vol. 49

window of opportunity to always be saved (Jesus) — 1/13/00 Vol. 18

window to soul clean filth of sins (Jesus) — 1/26/00 Vol. 18

windshield wipers constantly cleanse sins (Jesus) — 1/26/00 Vol. 18

wine first miracle,Blood of Jesus (Jesus) — 12/29/98 Vol. 13

wine, consecrated consume properly (Jesus) — 2/21/02 Vol. 26

winter coming unusual events (Jesus) — 11/16/06 Vol. 45

winter cooler in North (Jesus) — 10/31/02 Vol. 29

winter have supplies ready (Jesus) — 10/1/03 Vol. 33

winter like cold hearts (Jesus) — 11/17/00 Vol. 21

winter prepare for power outages (Jesus) — 9/4/04 Vol. 36

winter & disasters testing for sins & cold hearts (Jesus) — 1/19/04 Vol. 34

winter disasters in ice storms (Jesus) — 12/11/02 Vol. 29

winter fires unusual from dryness (Jesus) — 3/30/06 Vol. 42

winter heating affected by war,ID cards (Jesus) — 9/26/01 Vol. 24

winter season '06 to be difficult (Jesus) — 11/2/06 Vol. 45

winter signs compare to tribulation (Jesus) — 11/8/98 Vol. 13

winter solstice Jesus the Light (Jesus) — 12/21/00 Vol. 21

winter weather high winds, accidents (Jesus) — 11/12/07 Vol. 49

winter, hard keep snowblowers ready (Jesus) — 11/16/02 Vol. 29

winter, rugged foretold, coming about (Jesus) — 1/22/00 Vol. 18

winter, violent snow, ice and wind (Jesus) — 12/21/02 Vol. 29

wisdom gift of Holy Spirit (Jesus) — 1/10/00 Vol. 18

wisdom of age should stop fighting (Jesus) — 12/25/98 Vol. 13

wise & foolish virgins judgment (Jesus) — 3/4/03 Vol. 30

wise man depends on God's help (Jesus) — 2/8/00 Vol. 18

wise virgins be watchful of tribulation (Jesus) — 8/31/07 Vol. 48

wise virgins have souls always ready (Jesus) — 11/8/99 Vol. 17

wise virgins oil in lamps (Jesus) — 9/14/00 Vol. 20

wise virgins oil in their lamps (Jesus) — 4/2/98 Vol. 11

wise virgins prepare food (Jesus) — 8/30/96 Vol. 4

wise virgins prepare for His Coming (Jesus) — 10/29/96 Vol. 5

wise virgins prepared with Confession (Jesus) — 7/19/99 Vol. 16

witchcraft martyrdom (Jesus) — 12/23/93 Vol. 1

witchcraft promoted among the young (Jesus) — 2/20/02 Vol. 26

witchcraft & occult holds people in captivity (Jesus) — 9/5/03 Vol. 32

witchcraft & witches should be avoided (Jesus) — 1/5/06 Vol. 42

witchcraft, occult can lead to demon possession (Jesus) — 11/15/02 Vol. 29

witchcraft, occult from Harry Potter books (Jesus) — 7/27/05 Vol. 40

witchcraft,Occult avoid all connections to (Jesus) — 11/2/98 Vol. 13

witches with powers public witness (Jesus) — 11/8/95 Vol. 3

witches,black & white claim right to teach children (Jesus) — 7/11/00 Vol. 20

witches,black masses covens worship Satan (Jesus) — 3/2/01 Vol. 22

witness Conference (Jesus) — 8/5/95 Vol. 3

witness faith (St. Jude) — 10/28/93 Vol. 1

witness Name of Jesus (Jesus) — 6/23/94 Vol. 1

witness publicly to the truth (Jesus) — 8/7/03 Vol. 32

witnessing hypocritical (Jesus) — 9/12/95 Vol. 3

wolves unborn (Jesus) — 12/28/93 Vol. 1

woman's value not measured in money (Jesus) — 9/13/99 Vol. 16

women lead men to church (Jesus) — 7/12/99 Vol. 16

women pray to be faithful to God (Jesus) — 1/21/06 Vol. 42

women role models of faith (Jesus) — 3/5/98 Vol. 10

wood renewable fuel for winter (Jesus) — 12/29/03 Vol. 33

wood safer alternate fuel (Jesus) — 11/20/03 Vol. 33

wood stove to prepare for cold (Jesus) — 8/3/99 Vol. 16

wood stoves need plenty of wood (Jesus) — 9/23/99 Vol. 16

Wood to Jesus manger,carpenter,cross (Jesus) — 12/6/05 Vol. 41

wood uses paper products, make cross (Jesus) — 1/23/07 Vol. 46

wood, kerosene alternative fuels (Jesus) — 9/1/06 Vol. 44

woods trust (Jesus) — 10/23/94 Vol. 2

Word light of truth (Jesus) — 11/30/98 Vol. 13

word messenger (Jesus) — 8/9/94 Vol. 2

word pride (Jesus) — 10/11/94 Vol. 2

word scripture (Jesus) — 10/27/94 Vol. 2

word games on abortion cannot avoid killing (Jesus) — 8/6/02 Vol. 28

Word in four pillars Commandments,prophets (Jesus) — 7/6/00 Vol. 20

Word in hearts needs cultivation to grow (Jesus) — 7/27/00 Vol. 20

Word is truth stable as a rock in pope (Jesus) — 10/18/98 Vol. 13

Word of God about love & peace on earth (Jesus) — 12/31/03 Vol. 33

Word of God authority comes through (Jesus) — 8/31/04 Vol. 36

Word of God gift of revelation to all (Jesus) — 6/28/00 Vol. 19

Word of God has power&spiritual wisdom (Jesus) — 10/18/04 Vol. 37

Word of God hear & keep it (Jesus) — 3/22/07 Vol. 46

Word of God Light of understanding (Jesus) — 10/10/04 Vol. 37

Word of God Light to heaven (Jesus) — 11/12/04 Vol. 37

Word of God listen to understand at Mass (Jesus) — 11/6/03 Vol. 33

Word of God listen with open heart (Jesus) — 9/7/00 Vol. 20

Word of God live faith by (Jesus) — 8/16/01 Vol. 24

Word of God needed for conversion (Jesus) — 11/30/04 Vol. 37

Word of God opens door to Jesus Light (Jesus)   2/1/08 Vol. 50
Word of God plant seed in hearts (Jesus)   5/31/07 Vol. 47
Word of God revealed in Jesus (Jesus)   12/25/01 Vol. 25
Word of God rocky,bushes,good ground (Jesus)   8/10/04 Vol. 36
Word of God sowing of seed (Jesus)   1/29/03 Vol. 30
Word of God spread by faithful (Jesus)   9/22/01 Vol. 24
Word of God-seed what is personal response? (Jesus)   1/24/07 Vol. 46
word of knowledge on unknown death (Jesus)   10/18/07 Vol. 49
Word of Scripture live out belief in (Jesus)   3/14/00 Vol. 18
Word of Truth burn in hearts as Emmaus (Jesus)   4/27/06 Vol. 43
Word vs world lasting vs passing (Jesus)   7/27/00 Vol. 20
Word, hear put it into action (Jesus)   2/28/00 Vol. 18
Word,Real Presence important at refuges (Jesus)   7/25/00 Vol. 20
Words of Bible means to holiness (Jesus)   5/31/07 Vol. 47
work bread (Jesus)   9/5/94 Vol. 2
work means of salvation (Jesus)   10/9/96 Vol. 5
work means to salvation (Jesus)   3/18/99 Vol. 14
work talents (St. Joseph)   5/1/96 Vol. 3
work (Labor Day) do fair share (Jesus)   9/7/98 Vol. 12
work of hands means for salvation (Jesus)   4/15/99 Vol. 15
work of hands skill benefits others (Jesus)   8/30/07 Vol. 48
work on Sunday abusing Lord's day of rest (Jesus)   11/19/99 Vol. 17
work together love each other (Jesus)   9/6/00 Vol. 20
work together to help each other (Jesus)   3/10/00 Vol. 18
workers injustices done to (Jesus)   9/1/03 Vol. 32
workers must bear daily cross (Jesus)   11/5/03 Vol. 33
workplace example (Jesus)   12/14/95 Vol. 3
workplace trials how you react to them (Jesus)   8/31/07 Vol. 48
works of mercy feed,clothe,& visit poor (Jesus)   3/17/07 Vol. 46
works of mercy gain in faith by (Jesus)   11/22/03 Vol. 33
works of mercy needed for the poor (Jesus)   12/27/01 Vol. 25
World Bank electronic money controlled (Jesus)   6/28/01 Vol. 23
world churches united evangelize (Jesus)   8/21/94 Vol. 2
world control central bankers through debts (Jesus)   7/12/07 Vol. 48
World Court persecute Church's teachings (Jesus)   6/29/06 Vol. 43
world depression bankruptcies,spiritual (Jesus)   9/18/98 Vol. 12
world depression economic collapse (Jesus)   8/24/97 Vol. 8
world depression greed of the rich (Jesus)   3/5/98 Vol. 10
world depression layoffs,tax loss,turmoil (Jesus)   9/17/98 Vol. 12
world famine caused by floods,droughts (Jesus)   5/8/00 Vol. 19
world famine coming from disasters (Jesus)   10/12/05 Vol. 41
world famine food supplies low,controlled (Jesus)   8/4/00 Vol. 20
world famine from abused land (Jesus)   9/10/98 Vol. 12
world famine from outbreaks of disease (Jesus)   7/26/01 Vol. 24
world famine pestilence & scarcities (Jesus)   2/1/01 Vol. 22
world famine seen in disasters all over (Jesus)   9/27/04 Vol. 36
world famine sign to go to refuges (Jesus)   3/6/04 Vol. 34

world famine sign to go to refuges (Jesus)   7/28/05 Vol. 40
world famine store food in preparation (Jesus)   12/3/97 Vol. 9
world famine to lead into tribulation (Jesus)   8/26/01 Vol. 24
world famine, disasters coming quickly (Jesus)   11/2/06 Vol. 45
world famine, drought Australia,China,Africa (Jesus)   5/7/07 Vol. 47
world famine,depression chaos by one world people (Jesus) 10/13/98 Vol. 13
world governments to see major upheavals (Jesus)   12/21/07 Vol. 49
world organizations under one world people (Jesus)   3/6/01 Vol. 22
world peace pray for, only answer to war (Jesus)   9/14/04 Vol. 36
world police state caused by terrorism (Jesus)   11/20/97 Vol. 9
world take over excuse in global warming (Jesus)   11/17/07 Vol. 49
world takeover by the Antichrist (Jesus)   10/5/00 Vol. 21
world things, news time consumed by (Jesus)   12/18/03 Vol. 33
World War could begin from Iraq (Jesus)   2/6/03 Vol. 30
World War could bring on Antichrist (Jesus)   9/7/06 Vol. 44
world war possible with more terrorism (Jesus)   2/26/02 Vol. 26
world war potential for (Jesus)   8/7/04 Vol. 36
world war pray not to start (Jesus)   2/5/98 Vol. 10
World War say "no" to it (Jesus)   12/1/01 Vol. 25
World War threatened in Kosovo (Jesus)   3/30/99 Vol. 14
World War II dictators financed (Jesus)   5/20/03 Vol. 31
World War II learn from mistakes (Jesus)   6/7/01 Vol. 23
World War II stop one war after another (Jesus)   6/24/04 Vol. 35
World War II monument fought evil masters of Axis (Jesus) 4/29/04 Vol. 35
World War III beginning of tribulation (Jesus)   11/3/01 Vol. 25
World War III crossroads in time (Jesus)   3/5/96 Vol. 3
World War III evil bringing about (Jesus)   11/17/05 Vol. 41
World War III if war on Moslem states (Jesus)   2/14/02 Vol. 26
World War III peace (Jesus)   5/27/95 Vol. 2
World War III pray for peace (Jesus)   11/8/01 Vol. 25
World War III prayers (Jesus)   12/27/93 Vol. 1
World War III serve (Jesus)   5/10/95 Vol. 2
World War III sign in the sky,Finland (Blessed Mother)   10/14/01 Vol. 25
World War III staged events (Jesus)   10/1/01 Vol. 25
World War III strange light in sky (Jesus)   10/4/01 Vol. 25
World War III three rosaries for peace (Mary)   2/14/97 Vol. 6
World War III triumph (Jesus)   1/23/96 Vol. 3
World War III via Bosnia Antichrist (Jesus)   9/29/95 Vol. 3
World War possible over oil, bombs (Jesus)   6/20/06 Vol. 43
World War threatened three rosaries needed (Mary)   4/8/99 Vol. 15
worldly Blessed Sacrament (Father)   4/18/94 Vol. 1
worldly cares/heaven battle for souls (Jesus)   5/15/04 Vol. 35
worldly desires keep proper priorities (Jesus)   9/18/96 Vol. 4
worldly distractions can detour souls from heaven (Jesus) 3/25/04 Vol. 34
worldly distractions keep from thinking about God (Jesus) 9/8/04 Vol. 36
worldly love compared 2 hearts of spiritual love (Jesus) 2/14/95 Vol. 2
worldly pursuits leave no time for God (Jesus)   7/31/07 Vol. 48

worldly success God's success (Jesus) 1/26/95 Vol. 2
worldly things man running after (Jesus) 9/23/01 Vol. 24
worldly things put away man's ways (Jesus) 3/21/00 Vol. 18
worldly treasures are temporary (Jesus) 4/3/06 Vol. 43
worldly vs. spiritual sins vs. true faith (Jesus) 6/17/06 Vol. 43
worldly wise pride (Jesus) 9/3/94 Vol. 2
worries & anxieties fear not with Jesus (Jesus) 2/29/00 Vol. 18
worries & troubles place God first (Jesus) 7/29/99 Vol. 16
worry & trials trust in Jesus (Jesus) 4/30/03 Vol. 31
worrying accept crosses (Jesus) 7/16/98 Vol. 12
worship God (Jesus) 9/24/95 Vol. 3
worship God only, jealous God (Jesus) 8/19/01 Vol. 24
worship only God, not money (Jesus) 8/12/01 Vol. 24
worship God and not idols (Jesus) 11/8/02 Vol. 29
worship of Antichrist new religious persecution (Jesus) 9/7/99 Vol. 16
worship of Antichrist tests our faith in God (Jesus) 3/9/00 Vol. 18
worship of earthly things as New Age thinking (Jesus) 4/3/01 Vol. 23
worship of God is first priority in life (Jesus) 10/4/05 Vol. 41
worship of Jesus 1st over entertainment (Jesus) 5/22/06 Vol. 43
worthy to receive Holy Communion,clean soul (Jesus) 5/1/00 Vol. 19
Wrath of God Abortion 8/28/93 Vol. 1
wrath of God people refused to repent (Jesus) 3/21/03 Vol. 30
Wrath of God unrepentant sinners 8/29/93 Vol. 1
wreath, circle symbol of endless love (Jesus) 7/14/00 Vol. 20
wrist watches, different speed different in people (Jesus) 9/13/03 Vol. 32
WWII light in sky as sign (Jesus) 2/23/03 Vol. 30
WWW, 666 chips in body control (Jesus) 7/5/07 Vol. 48
Y2K a scheme for takeover (Jesus) 5/29/99 Vol. 15
Y2K deliberately overlooked (Jesus) 6/10/99 Vol. 15
Y2K do not believe media (Jesus) 10/22/99 Vol. 17
Y2K longer to fix (Jesus) 2/4/99 Vol. 14
Y2K loss of power and fuel (Jesus) 3/4/99 Vol. 14
Y2K massive chaos (Jesus) 2/27/99 Vol. 14
Y2K not told the truth (Jesus) 8/3/99 Vol. 16
Y2K planned destruction (Jesus) 6/17/99 Vol. 15
Y2K prepare for (Jesus) 5/11/99 Vol. 15
Y2K problems will be serious (Jesus) 10/7/99 Vol. 17
Y2K store food,water,fuel (Jesus) 3/2/99 Vol. 14
Y2K travel will be difficult (Jesus) 5/8/99 Vol. 15
Y2K used by powers for chaos (Jesus) 3/2/99 Vol. 14
Y2K will be our undoing (Jesus) 1/4/99 Vol. 14
Y2K worldwide problems (Jesus) 2/4/99 Vol. 14
Y2K & military control coming to head soon (Jesus) 8/5/99 Vol. 16
Y2K chaos in governments,finances (Jesus) 4/29/99 Vol. 15
Y2K computer problems domino failures (Jesus) 10/27/99 Vol. 17
Y2K food shortage food will be multiplied (Jesus) 5/7/99 Vol. 15
Y2K lies truth not told (Jesus) 9/22/99 Vol. 16

Y2K problem unfixed by managers (Jesus) 9/22/99 Vol. 16
Y2K problem vulnerable to date code (Jesus) 10/12/98 Vol. 13
Y2K satellite system will control chips in hand (Jesus) 9/29/99 Vol. 16
Y2K shortages manipulation by terrorists (Jesus) 11/16/99 Vol. 17
Y2K,computers,comet preparations for (Jesus) 8/5/99 Vol. 16
Year 2000 one year's food, water (Jesus) 11/11/99 Vol. 17
Year 2000 plans of one world people (Jesus) 11/19/99 Vol. 17
Year 2000 problem will cause power losses (Jesus) 12/26/98 Vol. 13
Year of Eucharist honor for Blessed Sacrament (Jesus) 10/21/04 Vol. 37
years of life pass fast to end of life (Jesus) 10/19/04 Vol. 37
Yellowstone disasterous volcano (Jesus) 3/5/05 Vol. 38
Yellowstone to bring America to our knees (Jesus) 6/27/06 Vol. 43
Yellowstone unsettled because of sins (Jesus) 3/20/04 Vol. 34
Yellowstone volcano ready to erupt (Jesus) 6/27/06 Vol. 43
Yellowstone volcano threat to life on earth (Jesus) 11/7/07 Vol. 49
yes choice trust (Mary) 12/20/94 Vol. 2
Yes, as Mary call to consecrate all to Jesus (Mary) 12/11/07 Vol. 49
yoke is easy daily bread (Jesus) 8/31/94 Vol. 2
young adults keep chaste (Jesus) 8/17/01 Vol. 24
young adults need example from parents (Jesus) 5/22/04 Vol. 35
young people encourage by example (Jesus) 1/24/02 Vol. 26
young people not as strong in faith (Jesus) 6/21/06 Vol. 43
younger generation not coming as much to Mass (Jesus) 4/7/00 Vol. 19
Yugoslavia, Iraq bombing,more resistance (Jesus) 3/24/99 Vol. 14
Yugoslavian war pray for peace (Mary) 10/7/98 Vol. 13
Yugoslavian war threat of widdening war (Mary) 10/10/98 Vol. 13
Zionist Jews persecutors & judgment (Jesus) 4/2/96 Vol. 3